Investment Management

FOURTH EDITION

Harry C. Sauvain

Indiana University

PRENTICE-HALL, INC., *Englewood Cliffs, New Jersey*

Library of Congress Cataloging in Publication Data

SAUVAIN, HARRY CHARLES.
Investment management.

Bibliography: p.
1. Investments. 2. Securities. I. Title.
HG4521.S335 1973 332.6'78 73–1617
ISBN 0–13–503094–3

Printed in the United States of America.

10 9 8 7 6 5 4 3

Prentice-Hall International, Inc., *London*
Prentice-Hall of Australia, Pty. Ltd., *Sydney*
Prentice-Hall of Canada, Ltd., *Toronto*
Prentice-Hall of India Private Limited, *New Delhi*
Prentice-Hall of Japan, Inc., *Tokyo*

Contents

Preface

This book is about the management of investments in securities. It presents a complete and integrated system of thought about investment policy decisions. The system begins with the basic problem of risk-return relationships and moves progressively to practical problems of managing security portfolios. Each concept is related to the next concept, and the series of concepts provides a system of thought. One critic was kind enough to say that I have a philosophy of investment management. I hope he is right.

First, the problem of investment management is stated in fundamental and theoretical terms. But to invest in securities you must have practical understanding of securities and security markets. The first group of three chapters presents the problem and its setting.

The concept of risk-return relationships is developed in the next part of the book. Risk is uncertainty, and there are multiple causes of uncertainty. The principal causes are examined. Expected rates of return are related to levels of risk.

The discussion of risk and return provides the base for a third group of chapters on the analysis of individual security issues. The problem at this point is one of estimating risk and return for particular stock and bond issues. The addition of financial analysis is a major difference between this edition and the previous edition.

Every investor has some limitations on ability to assume risk. Those limits must be established before investment policy decisions can be made. It is not easy to estimate these limitations. Theoreticians discuss at length the concepts of risk aversion and of differences in peoples' utility curves, but to set limits on risk-taking ability you must learn a great deal about individuals' personal financial circumstances. Indeed, it is often necessary to change personal financial arrangements before estimating investment constraints. The fourth group of chapters deals with this part of the problem.

Then we come to investment policies. Investors have their choice of a wide variety of policies and combinations of policies. Part V describes policies in constructing securities portfolios and in managing portfolios. Some kinds of policies are aggressive and some are defensive.

The capstone is the last group of chapters on investment constraints and investment policies of principal types of financial institutions. This is where you see the practical application of the concept of investment constraints and of efforts to maximize returns within constraints. In the facts and figures about institutional investors you see a demonstration of their solutions to the risk-return problem.

The major theoretical concepts of contemporary investment literature are used throughout this discussion, but they are not developed very far. This book is written for undergraduate students and for readers with an undergraduate education. These people generally do not have sufficient ability in mathematics and mathematical logic to grasp readily theories of portfolio construction expressed in mathematical terms and the treatment of a number of other topics as presented in contemporary math-theory literature.

Some elementary statistical methods are used, particularly in the section on financial analysis. My own experience is that these uses of statistics must be explained carefully even to students who have had college courses in mathematics, statistics, accounting, and business finance.

Everyone who studies and teaches over a period of years draws upon many sources for his concepts—the published literature, the unpublished research of graduate students, conversations with colleagues, and even discussions with undergraduate students. I acknowledge my indebtedness to all these sources.

My severest and best critic in the preparation of this manuscript was Dr. Robert H. Trent, Research Administrator, The Institute of Chartered Financial Analysts. He strongly influenced my treatment of several topics. Because I did not do everything he said I should do, he is absolved of my errors. I also appreciate the comments of Professor David A. Rush of the University of Colorado and Professor Travis Pritchett of Virginia Commonwealth University.

Harry C. Sauvain

I

The Problem and Its Setting

1

The Problem Of Investment Management

- I. The problem of risk and return
  - A. The risk-return relationship
  - B. The design of a securities portfolio
  - C. Competition among investors
- II. A portfolio and some questions about it
  - A. What securities to own?
  - B. When to buy and when to sell?
- III. About risk and expected rate of return
  - A. Expected rate of return
  - B. Calculating total expected rate of return
  - C. The concept of risk
  - D. Risk as a probability distribution of rates of return
- IV. A framework of theory
  - A. The objective: to maximize returns
    - 1. It is utilities that count
    - 2. Risk aversion and psychic income
  - B. The means: to maximize risk
  - C. The limitation: ability to assume risk
- V. Plan of study

This book deals with the problem of managing a portfolio of securities. Investment management would be a rather simple task if it were not for some very basic conditions imposed on investment managers by the securities in which they deal, markets for those securities, price fluctuations, alternative investment opportunities, and the competition of other investors. Investment managers do not just manage portfolios, anymore than a football player just plays football. The athlete plays to win and he plays against other players who play to win. One popular author calls the business of investment in securities "the money game."[1] Whether it is a game is open to question, but investment management is a competitive activity in which the success of an individual manager is measured by the results he achieves, much as the score in an athletic contest measures the success of one team against another.

THE PROBLEM OF RISK AND RETURN

An investment manager aims to secure the largest possible rate of return at the highest level of risk an investor is able to assume. Risk means uncertainty about the size of future returns on a principal amount invested. Rate of return is the relationship between returns realized and the principal amount invested, usually expressed as an annual rate.

The first sentence of the preceding paragraph states the two central concepts of the theory of investment management. One is the concept of maximizing returns. This is what you as an investment manager try to do. The rate of return you realize on the portfolio you manage is your score, and it is subject to comparison either publicly or privately with the scores of other investment managers.

The second concept states that the ability of investors to assume risk limits the effort to maximize returns. To assume risk is to take the chance of loss as well as the chance of gain. All investments carry some risk of loss and of gain but the level of risk varies widely among the different kinds of securities. Some investors can afford to risk larger losses than others. It is a governing rule that investors should not assume the risk of greater loss than they can afford to realize without courting financial disaster.

The Risk-Return Relationship

There is a positive relationship between the amount of risk assumed in managing a portfolio of securities and the amount of expected return. In very general terms, the greater the risk the larger the expected return.

The risk-return relationship is usually depicted as in Figure 1–1. Risk as a general concept is measured along the vertical line x to y. The level of risk rises from bottom to top. Expected rate of return is measured on the horizontal line x to x_j, increasing from left to right. The segment of the horizontal line between points x and x_i is the pure interest rate, the theoretical

[1]Adam Smith (George J. W. Goodman), *The Money Game*, New York, 1967, Random House.

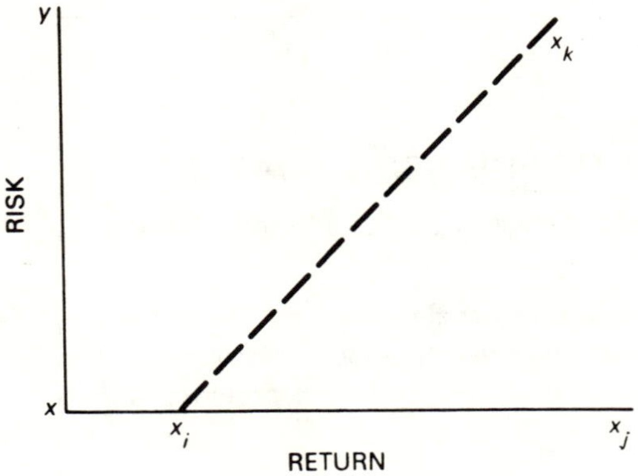

FIGURE 1–1

The Positive Relationship Between Risk and Return

rate of return of riskless investments. The continuation of the horizontal line on to the right from x_i to x_j depicts the concept of increasing rates of return. The diagonal line x_i to x_k illustrates the concept of expected rates of return increasing as levels of risk increase. Although we have drawn the relationship between risk and return as a straight line, it is usually curved in one way or another. At this point, however, all we want to show is that there is a positive relationship between risk and return.

The Design of a Securities Portfolio

One part of the problem of investment management, then, is to estimate the highest level of risk an investor is able to assume. Estimates of ability to take risk are essentially subjective, although quantitative data are used in making estimates. We will in due course consider in some detail how such estimates may be made.

The other part of the problem is to select individual security issues with such risk characteristics that, when they are combined and averaged in a securities portfolio, the risk level of the portfolio will be the highest that the investor can afford to assume. This is no easy task. You must first select from among all security issues at a given level of risk those that you think will provide the better risk-return relationships; that is, those that promise highest returns at that level of risk.

You must also try to select those issues that are least likely to be adversely affected by the same hazards in the economy, or in the industry, or by any other factors that might influence future returns. In statistical terms, you want issues with the least covariance in future returns. By minimizing covariance you can assemble a securities portfolio that represents a lower level of risk than an arithmetic average of the risks of the issues that compose it.

THE PROFESSION OF FINANCIAL ANALYSIS

The Institute of Chartered Financial Analysts defines the profession in part as follows:

The modern profession of financial analysis includes the primary functions of investigation, evaluation, selection and management of all types of investments, particularly in bonds and preferred and common stock.

Professional activities are concentrated in two major categories, (1) financial analysis involving investment research, and (2) portfolio management or supervision of investment funds. Individuals engaged in these activities are designated, in general, as financial analysts. The profession also includes economists, and university professors who teach finance and investments or specialize in academic research. Financial analysts are employed in all segments of the financial industry including commercial banking, brokerage and investment counseling, mutual funds, endowment and pension or profit-sharing funds and financial publishing.

The financial analysts may be engaged in studying securities of specific companies and may be assigned responsibility for one or more industries. This requires a thorough knowledge not only of the companies and industries concerned, but also of their relative competitive positions and the underlying economic conditions that affect their profitability.

The second major category in the profession is that of portfolio management or the supervision of investment funds. Portfolio managers are largely employed by institutions. In some organizations in this field, such as banks or investment counseling firms, the manger supervises funds for his clients; in other organizations such as mutual and endowment funds, insurance companies or other institutions, the manager is responsible for the supervision of substantial investment funds either in a single portfolio or in a group of portfolios assigned to him.

Source: *The Profession of Financial Analysis and the Chartered Financial Analyst*, The Institute of Chartered Financial Analysts, Charlottesville, Virginia, 1971, pp. 1–2.

Competition Among Investors

Investing in securities is a game in that investors compete with one another. Professional investment managers understand this point very well. The returns they achieve are measured by numbers and "scores" are compared; it is not uncommon for the low man to be put out of the game. The professional careers of persons are very much influenced by the rates of return they obtain, and the financial success of the institutions that employ them is also affected.

The professionals, as we have termed them, have increased greatly in number, in financial sophistication, and in influence in the past several decades. A growing percentage of the total value of outstanding securities is being bought or managed by financial institutions who employ professional financial analysts to handle their portfolios. There is a national organization devoted to the training of financial analysts and to the certifying of persons who pass a series of examinations to become chartered financial analysts. This organization has defined the term "financial analyst" broadly so that it means professional investment manager. A description of the profession of financial analysis is presented on page 6.

There are of course millions of individual investors who more or less manage their own securities investments. They are not very competitive among themselves. The rates of return they realize are known usually only to themselves, if they are known at all, and there is no basis for comparing one investor with another. But they do compete. Each individual tries and each is satisfied or dissatisfied with his results.

A PORTFOLIO AND SOME QUESTIONS ABOUT IT

Table 1–1 is a sketch of a securities portfolio. If you imagine yourself the owner of this portfolio and consider it's for you, you will grasp quickly some of the problems of investment management. This sketch specifies only the percentage of the portfolio in the several categories of securities, so you can imagine as many dollars involved as you please.

What Securities to Own?

One of the first questions that comes to mind is whether this portfolio is too risky for you, or not risky enough. To answer that question you have to examine your own ability to assume risk. That could involve a rather lengthy examination of details of your financial circumstances. However you might estimate your own ability to assume risk, you might very well ask whether you should own those high-risk common stocks. They are stocks of companies with little or no earnings and they pay no dividends. Their market

TABLE 1–1
Sketch of a Securities Portfolio

	Percentage of Total Portfolio
A. Common Stocks	
1. High-risk common stocks	15%
2. Low-risk common stocks	15
3. Average-risk common stocks	20
Total common stocks	50
B. Bonds	
1. U.S. Government bonds	15
2. Low-risk municipal bonds	15
3. Average-risk corporate bonds	20
Total bonds	50
Total securities	100%

prices fluctuate widely. You could make a lot of money, or lose a lot of money, with stocks such as these. Are you willing and able to risk a lot of money?

The low-risk common stocks are those of large, well-established companies with broad product lines and a record of relatively stable earnings. They are the kind often described as "blue-chips." You are not likely to get rich owning these stocks, but neither are you likely to take serious losses on the aggregate amount invested if you hold a number of them over a considerable period of time. If you cannot assume the risk associated with this category of stocks, you should not invest in common stocks at all.

Many individual investors would question the desirability of owning all those bonds. Investors generally have been common-stock-minded in recent years and they have also been inflation conscious. Stocks are said to be a good inflation hedge and bonds are not. But maybe you need the stability of income that these bonds provide. The chance of not receiving interest payments as promised is very small. Maybe your circumstances require you to maximize your income with little regard for possible returns in the form of capital gains.

The U.S. government bonds are often thought of as without risk, but this is true only if you mean that there is no uncertainty of future payments of interest and principal as promised. But there is more to risk than that, and in fact there is considerable risk in government securities.

When you consider the municipal bonds you have to take account of the fact that interest from these obligations is exempt from the federal income tax. Do you need tax exemption?

There are many other kinds of questions you might raise as you think about the suitability of this portfolio for you. You would want to know the length of the period to maturity for each of the bonds because length of maturity affects their price stability. It certainly would be desirable to inquire about the number of issues in each of the categories. The larger the number, the broader the average of rates. Information about the marketability of both stocks and bonds also is relevant.

These questions concern policies in the *construction* of the securities portfolio; that is, questions about the categories of securities that should be owned at a particular time. There are also questions of policy involved in *managing* a securities portfolio. You need policies to guide you in buying and selling securities.

When to Buy and When to Sell

Suppose you decide that you should sell the U.S. government bonds and buy more common stocks. However, bond prices are rising and there is a general expectation in financial circles that they will continue to rise for awhile. Should you delay selling the bonds and try to realize a somewhat higher price a few weeks or few months from now? If you do, you take the risk that bond prices will decline and you finally may have to sell at lower prices. There is also the question of how stock prices will change in the future. You want to buy stocks. If you think that the stock market is going up, you would want to buy the stocks now. Or, you may think stock prices will decline and decide to wait awhile and buy them when they are cheaper. One kind of policy is to ignore all these estimates of which way prices will change and make your sales and purchases now.

Your consideration of this simple securities portfolio has raised a few of the questions of policy that are involved in investment management. They serve as a kind of prologue for what follows.

ABOUT RISK AND EXPECTED RATE OF RETURN

We have used the term "risk" in the general sense and have mentioned "returns" on securities. Since the whole problem of investment management centers around those concepts, we must understand clearly what they mean.

Expected Rate of Return

Returns on securities are what you get back from owning them. We mentioned interest on bonds and dividends on stocks. These are the usual forms of income paid to owners of securities. They are usually paid at regular time intervals and are considered a current payment by issuers to investors for use of their money. The other kind of return is the recovery of a principal amount at the end of a period of time. This return may take the form of a payment of principal by the issuer to the security owner at the time an obligation matures, or it may be an amount obtained by sale of a security in the market. The amount of principal paid back or recovered may be more or less than the amount that was invested. If the amount is more, it is a gain—a capital gain—and a return on investment. If it is less, there is a loss. Gains and losses of principal are taken into consideration, along with amounts of income received, in calculating the total rate of return on an investment.

You might, for example, buy a stock at $40 a share. If the annual dividend on the stock is $2, the rate of return represented by the dividend is 5 per cent. But stocks fluctuate in price. If you sell the stock after several years at, say, $50 a share, you would take account of the $10 per share capital gain in calculating the total rate of return on investment in that stock.

Calculating Total Expected Rate of Return

It is easy to divide the annual amount of income from a security by its cost and thus to derive an annual rate of income return. But it takes some more arithmetic to bring the capital gain or loss into the calculation of rate of return.

The total rate of return on an investment is the rate that discounts all the amounts received as income and as repayment or recovery of principal from the date received to present values at date of investment that in total equal the cost of the investment. This is the method used in the tables of bond yields to maturity. If you should buy a $1,000 bond bearing interest at 5 per cent and due in one year at a price of 99, what is the yield to maturity? The easy way to get the answer is to look up the coupon rate and maturity in tables of bond yields. You will find that the yield is 6 per cent. You can check that figure by discounting the first $25 of interest on the bond at 3 per cent, since it will be received in 6 months rather than a year. The second interest payment of $25 at the end of a year and the principal of $1,000 at the end of the year are discounted at 6 per cent. The sum of the present values is $990.40, which is very close to the $990 paid for the bond.

Table 1–2 is a page from a table of bond yields, which is often called a "basis book" because it converts prices of bonds to a yield basis.

You can apply the same method to calculate the expected rate of return on stocks. First, you estimate the amounts of dividend payments likely to be received periodically over a period of time and then estimate the market price at the end of the time period when you assume that you will sell the stock. You will have the same kind of series of expected future returns for the stock as for the bond in the preceding example.

The arithmetic is described by the present-value formula, which is:

$$PV_0 = \sum_{t=1}^{T} \frac{I^t}{(1+k)^t} + \frac{P_t}{(1+k)^t}$$

This equation states that the present value of a series of future amounts

TABLE 1–2

A Page from a Bond Yield Table

COUPON **4**

Years and Months

Yield	19-5	19-6	19-7	19-8	19-9	19-10	19-11	20-0
3.00	114.63	114.68	114.73	114.77	114.82	114.86	114.91	114.96
3.05	113.84	113.89	113.93	113.97	114.01	114.06	114.10	114.15
3.10	113.05	113.10	113.14	113.17	113.22	113.26	113.30	113.34
3.15	112.27	112.31	112.35	112.39	112.42	112.46	112.50	112.54
3.20	111.50	111.54	111.57	111.61	111.64	111.68	111.71	111.75
3.25	110.73	110.77	110.80	110.83	110.86	110.90	110.93	110.97
3.30	109.97	110.01	110.04	110.06	110.09	110.13	110.16	110.19
3.35	109.22	109.25	109.28	109.30	109.33	109.36	109.39	109.42
3.40	108.47	108.50	108.53	108.55	108.58	108.60	108.63	108.66
3.45	107.73	107.76	107.78	107.80	107.83	107.85	107.87	107.90
3.50	107.00	107.02	107.04	107.06	107.08	107.10	107.13	107.15
3.55	106.27	106.29	106.31	106.33	106.35	106.36	106.38	106.41
3.60	105.55	105.57	105.58	105.60	105.61	105.63	105.65	105.67
3.65	104.84	104.85	104.86	104.88	104.89	104.91	104.92	104.94
3.70	104.13	104.14	104.15	104.16	104.17	104.19	104.20	104.21
3.75	103.42	103.44	103.44	103.45	103.46	103.47	103.48	103.50
3.80	102.73	102.74	102.74	102.75	102.76	102.76	102.77	102.78
3.85	102.04	102.04	102.05	102.05	102.06	102.06	102.07	102.08
3.90	101.35	101.36	101.36	101.36	101.36	101.37	101.37	101.38
3.95	100.67	100.68	100.67	100.67	100.68	100.68	100.68	100.69
4.00	100.00	100.00	100.00	100.00	100.00	100.00	100.00	100.00
4.05	99.33	99.33	99.33	99.32	99.32	99.32	99.32	99.32
4.10	98.67	98.67	98.66	98.65	98.65	98.65	98.65	98.64
4.15	98.01	98.01	98.00	97.99	97.99	97.98	97.98	97.98
4.20	97.36	97.36	97.35	97.34	97.33	97.32	97.32	97.31
4.25	96.71	96.71	96.70	96.69	96.68	96.67	96.66	96.65
4.30	96.07	96.07	96.05	96.04	96.03	96.02	96.01	96.00
4.35	95.44	95.43	95.42	95.40	95.39	95.38	95.37	95.36
4.40	94.81	94.80	94.78	94.77	94.75	94.74	94.73	94.72
4.45	94.19	94.17	94.16	94.14	94.12	94.11	94.09	94.08
4.50	93.57	93.55	93.53	93.51	93.50	93.48	93.47	93.45
4.55	92.96	92.94	92.92	92.90	92.88	92.86	92.84	92.83
4.60	92.35	92.33	92.31	92.28	92.26	92.24	92.23	92.21
4.65	91.74	91.73	91.70	91.68	91.65	91.63	91.61	91.60
4.70	91.15	91.13	91.10	91.07	91.05	91.03	91.01	90.99
4.75	90.55	90.53	90.50	90.48	90.45	90.43	90.41	90.39
4.80	89.97	89.94	89.91	89.89	89.86	89.83	89.81	89.79
4.85	89.38	89.36	89.33	89.30	89.27	89.24	89.22	89.20
4.90	88.80	88.78	88.75	88.72	88.69	88.66	88.63	88.61
4.95	88.23	88.20	88.17	88.14	88.11	88.08	88.05	88.03
5.00	87.66	87.63	87.60	87.57	87.53	87.50	87.48	87.45
5.05	87.10	87.07	87.03	87.00	86.97	86.93	86.90	86.88
5.10	86.54	86.51	86.47	86.44	86.40	86.37	86.34	86.31
5.15	85.99	85.95	85.92	85.88	85.84	85.81	85.78	85.75
5.20	85.44	85.40	85.36	85.33	85.29	85.25	85.22	85.19
5.25	84.89	84.86	84.82	84.78	84.74	84.70	84.67	84.64
5.30	84.35	84.32	84.27	84.23	84.19	84.16	84.12	84.09
5.40	83.28	83.25	83.20	83.16	83.12	83.08	83.04	83.01
5.50	82.23	82.19	82.15	82.10	82.06	82.02	81.98	81.94
5.60	81.20	81.16	81.11	81.07	81.02	80.98	80.94	80.90
5.70	80.19	80.14	80.09	80.04	80.00	79.95	79.91	79.87
5.75	79.68	79.64	79.59	79.54	79.49	79.45	79.40	79.36
6.00	77.24	77.19	77.14	77.08	77.03	76.98	76.93	76.89
6.50	72.64	72.59	72.52	72.46	72.40	72.35	72.29	72.24
7.00	68.41	68.35	68.28	68.21	68.15	68.08	68.02	67.97

Source: *Executive Bond Values Tables*, Boston, 1955, Financial Publishing Company.

of dividends (I^t) and of the principal amount recovered at the end of the series of periods (P_t) is the sum of those amounts discounted at a discount rate (k). If present value is a principal amount invested, you solve the equation for k, that is, for the discount rate.

Use of the present-value formula is illustrated in Table 1–3. Assume that you have studied a common stock very carefully and concluded that the annual amount of dividend will increase at 6 per cent per year over the next 5 years, and that the market price of the stock at the end of 5 years will be 25 times its annual dividend in the fifth year. Your study shows that this stock is slightly more risky than the average of a large number of stocks. You think that you should have an expected rate of return of 10 per cent per annum to compensate you adequately for the risk. The expected rate is the rate you will realize if your estimates are exactly right.

The upper part of Table 1–3 shows amounts of dividends beginning with $1.00 per share and increasing at 6 per cent a year. It also shows that the estimated price at the end of 5 years is $33.50 per share. These amounts are discounted at 10 per cent and their present values are in the last column to the right. The sum of the present values is $25.29. However, the current market price of the stock is $25⅞, or $25.875. Since this is a higher price than the

TABLE 1–3

Use of Present Value Formula to Calculate Expected Rate of Return on a Stock.

Years	*Estimated annual dividends*	*Estimated price at end of period*	*Present value factors*	*Present values of estimated returns*
Values at 10 per cent discount rate:				
Time zero	$1.00	–	–	–
Year 1	1.06	–	.909	$ .964
Year 2	1.12	–	.828	.927
Year 3	1.19	–	.752	.895
Year 4	1.26	–	.690	.869
Year 5	1.34	–	.621	.832
End of 5 years		$33.50	.621	20.803
Sum of present values				$25.290
Values at 9 per cent discount rate:				
Time zero	1.00	–	–	–
Year 1	1.06	–	.917	.972
Year 2	1.12	–	.841	.942
Year 3	1.19	–	.772	.919
Year 4	1.26	–	.709	.893
Year 5	1.34	–	.650	.871
End of 5 years		$33.50	.650	21.775
Sum of present values				$26.372

indicated sum of present values, a purchase at this price will provide a slightly lower rate of return than 10 per cent.

The same kind of calculation at a discount rate of 9 per cent is shown in the lower part of Table 1–3. The sum of present values at 9 per cent is $26.37, which is higher than the market price; therefore, the discount rate is more than 9 per cent. The mid-point between the two sums of present values is $25.83, which is about the same as the market price of $25⅞. Thus the discount rate and the expected rate of return on the current market price is about 9½ per cent. If you perform the calculation again at 9½ per cent, you will find that the sum of present values is $25.81.

For simplicity of illustration we have ignored transactions costs and assumed that dividends are paid once a year at end of year instead of quarterly or semi-annually, as is usually the case.[2] Actually, returns from common stocks are so uncertain that no great effort at precision in calculation is justified.

The Concept of Risk

Risk is uncertainty about future rates of return on investments. Since the future is unknown, there is always some risk. We may believe it to be small or large, but it is always there. Sometimes the term "risk" is used to mean only the risk of loss, or of less favorable returns than expected. But this is a too narrow view. Risk means uncertainty concerning both less favorable and more favorable returns than expected.

There are several causes of uncertainty in future returns from securities that can be identified and generalized about. In estimating the riskness of a security, or of a general category of securities, it is necessary to recognize these different causes and to try to estimate how they are likely to affect future returns from security issues. Returns from some securities are more affected by some causes than by others.

The cause of uncertainty that is most familiar and most readily understood is change in the financial ability of issuers to make the payments promised to, or expected by, investors. If a company becomes less profitable and its financial condition deteriorates, its securities become more risky. There is always some chance that this will happen. Conversely, if a company becomes more prosperous, uncertainty about its ability to pay decreases.

Market prices tend to rise and fall as a company prospers or fails to prosper. Investors watch changes in the financial abilities of companies and the prices they are willing to pay for securities change with what they see.

[2]It is not too difficult to make these calculations with an ordinary calculator, or even with pencil and paper. In most libraries there are volumes that give the present-value factors for many rates of discount for long series of years. Some have tables showing the present value of $1.00 to be received at the end of years 1, 2, 3, ... *n*. With a computer you use an iteration program that tests each of a number of rates within a programmed range until it finds the rate that reduces the series of future cash receipts to the specified present value.

Investors also make estimates of future changes in the financial abilities of companies, and the prices they pay for securities vary with their estimates of the direction and magnitude of future change. These market prices are an important element of risk because they are the prices at which principal can be recovered by sale in the market. The size of gain or loss of principal is an important element of the total rate of return on securities.

A second major cause of uncertainty is change in open-market rates of interest. These are the rates, or yields, at which all kinds of securities are bought and sold in the market. An increase in interest rates tends to cause a decline in market prices for securities, and a decline exerts an upward pressure on prices.

When we speak of rates of return usually we mean returns in current dollars, that is, in dollars of whatever purchasing power they may have at the time received. But almost everyone knows that the purchasing power of the dollar changes from one time to another. Investors often think about returns from investments in constant dollars, that is, in current dollars adjusted for change in the purchasing power of the dollars. If you measure returns in constant dollars, then there is a third cause of uncertainty, namely, change in the purchasing power of the currency unit.

There are some other causes of uncertainty about future returns, but they are less important or cannot be readily generalized. We will mention some of them in subsequent discussions of risk.

Risk as a Probability Distribution of Rates of Return

Since risk is uncertainty, no one knows at the time he buys a security what rate of return he will realize. A financial analyst may estimate what he thinks the rate will be, but he knows that his estimate may be off the mark. So he compensates for uncertainty by estimating several rates—the most likely rate and several other rates both higher and lower. He indicates the most likely rate by giving it a greater weight in a distribution of rates than that assigned to other rates. To the highest and lowest rates in his distribution he assigns relatively low weights to indicate that there is little chance that these rates actually will be realized. The first column in Table 1–4 shows an analyst's estimated distribution of rates. The second column shows the weights assigned to these rates, and the third is the rates multiplied by the weights to provide a weighted probability distribution. The rates and numbers are subjectively determined; they represent the analyst's beliefs.

Now you can use these quantitative statements to measure statistically the analyst's estimate of risk by calculating the variance and the standard deviation of the distribution.[3] The deviation of the estimated rates in the distribution from their mean may be squared and multiplied by their weighted value to get the variance shown in column (6). The square root of the variance is the standard deviation. In this example the standard deviation of 1.96

[3]There are other measures of deviation or dispersion, such as quartile deviation, semi-deviation, and mean or average deviation. Statisticians debate the merit of the different methods of measurement, but standard deviation is commonly used.

TABLE 1–4

Measurement of Risk By a Probability Distribution of Estimated Rates of Return on a Common Stock

Estimated Rates X	*Probability Weights*	*Weighted Values of the Estimated Rates*	*Deviation of Rates from Mean* $(X-\bar{X})$	*Deviation Squared* $(X-\bar{X})^2$	*Variance (Probability Times Squared Deviation)* $(X-\bar{X})^2 \cdot \rho$	*Standard Deviation (Square Root of Variance)*
(1)	(2)	(3)	(4)	(5)	(6)	(7)
18%	.1	1.8	+8	64	6.4	
14	.2	2.8	+4	16	3.2	
10	.4	4.0	0	0	0	
6	.2	1.2	−4	16	3.2	
2	.1	0.2	−8	64	6.4	
Σ 50 $\bar{X}$ 10	1.0	10.0			5)19.2 $\sigma^2 = 3.84$	1.96

The notation for calculation of the standard deviation of a series of numbers may be written:

$$s = \sqrt{\frac{\Sigma\,(X-\bar{X})^2}{N}}$$

is rather large, which means that the analyst does not have great confidence in his most likely rate and recognizes that the rate actually realized may vary within a considerable range.[4]

If you estimate the rates of return on this stock in a narrower range such as 12, 11, 10, 9, and 8 per cent, you find a smaller variance and standard deviation. With the same probability weights, the variance would be 1.2 and the standard deviation, 1.10.

A distribution with only 5 estimated rates is of course an oversimplification. Actually there are a great many possible rates that may be realized on an investment and one could have a distribution with many more numbers. For practical purposes distributions such as those we have used for illustration may be sufficient to indicate an analyst's uncertainty about the rate of return that will ultimately be realized from an investment.

A FRAMEWORK OF THEORY

Until fairly recent years there was no clearly defined or generally accepted theory of investment management. Investors had some "rules of thumb" and they knew that certain kinds of strategies seemed to work well under certain conditions, but there was no very coherent way of thinking about problems of investment policy. Frequently fear dominated peoples'

[4]It may be helpful to recall that in a normal distribution 68.27 per cent of the outcomes fall within 1 standard deviation on each side of the mean. In this example a standard deviation of 1.96 means that the analyst would be 95 per cent confident that the actual rate would be between 8.04 and 11.96 per cent. There is no evidence that for a single stock the distribution of outcomes in any given period would be normal.

thinking so that they seemed to be more concerned about avoiding loss than about realizing gain. Or, they were concerned with maintaining liquidity, or with avoiding taxes. These concerns emphasized the negative—they focused on obstacles rather than on objectives.

Even when objectives were recognized, they were sometimes poorly defined and not well generalized. People often talk of determining an investor's "goals," as though there are a number of possible objectives and one must choose among them. In so doing, they lose sight of the total rate of return and focus on "liberal income," "capital gains" or some combination of those forms of investment returns. There is a danger of not seeing through these components to the total rate of return concept. Sometimes people become so committed to the idea of seeking capital gains and to thinking that capital gains are realized by investing in common stock that they are oblivious of the opportunities for realizing a high rate of return from other types of securities. The sophisticated investor doesn't really care what form his returns take, except for tax considerations, or from what kind of securities they are derived. He just wants to maximize returns at his risk level.

In more recent years, however, both theoreticians and practitioners have evolved a logical framework of thought about the problem of investment management. On the academic side the theoreticians and mathematicians have more sharply defined basic concepts and improved the logic of reasoning about them. On the practical side, new generations of investment managers have been receptive to new ways of thinking and innovative in developing them.

It would be too much to say that a full and definitive theory has been formulated, but a set of general propositions has emerged that provides a basis for thinking about investment problems. These propositions have already appeared in our discussion, but they require some further development.

The Objective: To Maximize Returns

There are good theoretical grounds for the proposition that generally investors try to obtain the largest returns they can get from their security investments, subject to whatever limitations that restrain their effort. And there is good reason to believe that usually they behave in this way.

The idea that investors try to maximize investment returns goes back to the classical economists and their concept of "economic man" who was concerned solely with increasing his wealth and was always rational in his effort to do so. In the course of time both economists and behavioral psychologists recognized that man has other concerns than that of increasing his wealth and he is not always rational in his economic behavior.

It Is Utilities That Count. A major theoretical contribution is that where there is risk and return, it is the utilities of the various possible returns that govern investors' behavior rather than the dollar amounts. Utility means the satisfaction of receiving, or of owning. One person may derive a certain amount of satisfaction from receiving $1,000, and another may obtain twice as much from the same amount of money, or half as much. More important for our purpose, an investor may obtain a certain utility from the first $1,000 he receives and less utility from the next $1,000.

For a great many people equal increments of wealth bring diminishing increments of satisfaction; they are said to have diminishing utility of wealth. This concept is illustrated in Figure 1–2, in which units of utility (an abstract concept) are measured on the vertical axis and increments of wealth are depicted by the horizontal axis. Notice that the curve representing the utility of additional returns rises at first, moving from left to right, but that the rate of increase diminishes and if the curve were extended far enough, it would practically level off.

Brealey has illustrated how the diminishing utility of returns might affect investment decisions. He described a hypothetical investment that had a 50 per cent chance of a 15 per cent gain and a 50 per cent chance of a 5 per cent loss and postulated that these were the only possible outcomes. The utility curve of the hypothetical investor provided an additional 13½ units of satisfaction for the 15 per cent gain and a minus 6½ units of satisfaction for the wealth represented by the 5 per cent loss. The value of this distribution in units of utility is 3½ units. The 13½ units times the 50 per cent probability equals 6.75. The minus 6½ units times the 50 per cent probability is −3.25, and the sum of the plus and minus numbers is 3.5 units of utility. This investor would derive more utility from an investment opportunity at a lower level of risk where there would be very little chance of appreciable loss and a large chance of a smaller gain. He would prefer an investment opportunity offering a 10 per cent chance of loss of 1 unit of utility and a 90 per cent chance of a gain equal to 5 units of utility; the sum of the two is 4.4 units of utility.[5]

[5]Richard A. Brealey, *An Introduction to Risk and Return from Common Stocks*, Cambridge, Mass., 1969, The MIT Press, p. 135.

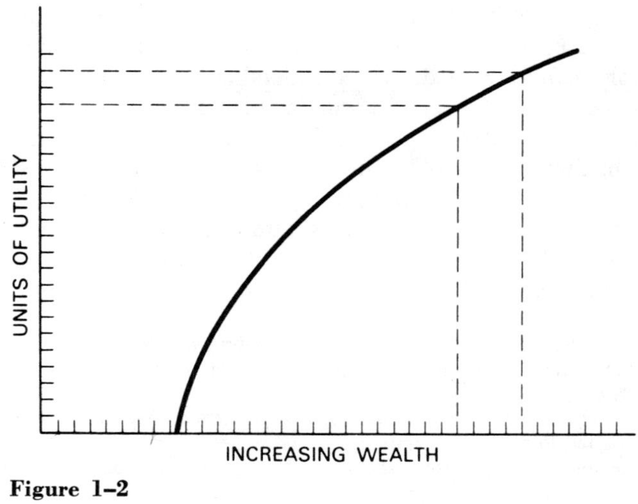

Figure 1–2

The Diminishing Utility of Increments of Wealth

However, the utility curves of different persons take quite different shapes. For some the curve rises steeply with the first few increments of wealth but soon begins to rise more slowly and then tends to level off.[6] Another kind of curve rises at a moderate rate but continues to rise with additional wealth and only after many increments begins to level off. It appears that for some people the utility curve rises at a diminishing rate, tends to level off as wealth increases further, and then rises again more steeply for still more increments of wealth. This is sometimes called an *S*-type curve. A man might try very hard for his first million dollars, work less hard for his second million, but redouble his efforts to make his third million. As measured by his effort, the third million had greater utility than the second million.

Risk Aversion and Psychic Income. The diminishing utility of wealth is explained chiefly by peoples' aversion to risk. Generally people like to avoid risk; it worries them; there is a kind of pain involved. This aversion cancels the satisfactions to be derived from the larger returns that might be derived by taking risks. At some point the former outweighs the latter, and an investor says, "I won't take that much risk even if it does provide a good chance for a large return." One scholar writes that, " . . . diminishing utility of income is no more than an analytical expression of the concept of risk aversion."[7]

Some investors, of course, are much more risk averse than others, and there is a graduation from the most to the least risk averse. But that is not the end of the spectrum. Some people like to take risk; they enjoy it; they think it is fun. In fact they deliberately create uncertainty so that they can bet on the results. Often they enjoy the risk so much that they pay more for an uncertain outcome than its actuarial worth. In gambling games, where "the house takes a cut" of amounts wagered, the odds are against the gamblers. In aggregate all gamblers lose because the amount that can be won is less than the amount bet. People like this will often pay much more for a very speculative stock than it is worth by any system of rational estimation.

Completing the sketch of attitudes toward risk and returns is the idea that some part of the returns from investments consists of non-pecuniary satisfactions. For example, a man may derive considerable satisfaction from going into a broker's office and being received as an important customer. It may flatter his ego to talk with others about his investments and even to brag about the stock he bought that soon doubled in price. Another kind of satisfaction may be a sense of security derived from owning some gilt-edged bonds.[8]

These are but general descriptions of investors' attitudes toward assumption of risk. As we go on with the problems of portfolio management they will be further developed and applied.

[6]A man with a heavy suitcase offered a boy who was loafing nearby a dollar to carry his suitcase to his hotel. The boy declined saying, "I've got a dollar." His utility curve had leveled off at $1.

[7]William J. Baumol, *Portfolio Theory: The Selection of Asset Combinations*, New York, 1970, The McCaleb-Seiler Publishing Company, p. 17.

[8]For a more complete and more precise discussion of utility theory see Baumol, *op. cit.*, pp. 15–18.

The Means: To Maximize Risk

Both theorists in investment and practical investment managers believe that in the entire universe of security investments and over relatively long time periods realized rates of return are positively related to levels of risk. Thus the way to maximize returns is to maximize the level of risk assumed. But this proposition requires careful examination.

First, the terms of the proposition must be clearly understood. The statement covers all securities and their owners, securities of all kinds and descriptions that come within the definition of marketable securities. It is about total rates of return on the aggregate of large numbers of issues differentiated by level of risk. It is not about any one security or any one investor's return on a portfolio of securities. The statement describes the relative size of net returns to all investors. Losses suffered by large numbers of investors in many issues of the various grades of securities are deducted from gains and the aggregate amount of net returns is related to the aggregate amount of investment. The phrase "over relatively long time periods" is important. Even aggregate net returns may vary widely over short time periods as business expands or recedes, as investors' confidence in future investment experience waxes and wanes, and as interest rates fluctuate. A long time period is one long enough to average out cyclical and erratic variations in investment returns.

Second, this general proposition does not depend on foresight in buying when prices are relatively low and selling when they are high. Rather, it assumes that for large numbers of investors and many transactions the effect of cyclical and erratic price fluctuations on rates of return is neutral. Insofar as individual investors are able to estimate future changes in security prices and to time their purchases and sales accordingly, they enhance their individual rates of return.

Some of the theoretical reasoning that supports the concept of a positive relationship between risk and return has already been suggested. If most investors experience decreasing marginal utility of wealth because most of them are risk averse, then there must be larger expected returns on the more risky securities relative to rates on the less risky to provide sufficiently greater utility to overcome aversion to risk. More simply, investors would not assume the greater risks if expected returns were not large enough in utility to compensate them for risk. Some investors do in fact assume the greater risks. Therefore, they must expect to obtain returns commensurate with the higher levels of risk.

This proposition assumes that investors in the aggregate are sufficiently good judges of risk to differentiate the more risky from the less risky securities, and that their estimates of the size of expected returns are sufficiently accurate that generally they associate the higher expected rates of return with the higher levels of risk. If they do not judge risks and returns accurately enough, they will pay too much or too little for securities at the several risk levels and distort risk-return relationships.

Some investors at some times are poor judges of risk. Some simply lack the ability to estimate risk and some do not even try. Sometimes their judgments, as evidenced by changes in market prices for particular security issues, prove to be wrong. And there have been times when large numbers of investors have been caught up in a speculative fervor to such an extent that the consensus about risk and size of probable returns for the more risky securities has been wrong.

Nevertheless, there is reason to think that most investors make good appraisals of risk most of the time. In the first place, the risk appraisals of security issues made by acknowledged experts are well known to investors. Thus, several investment information services publish widely used "ratings" that differentiate securities according to risk. Professional investment managers make their own appraisals, and their judgments influence investment decisions for a large amount of security investments. The whole investment process involves constant appraisal and reappraisal of thousands of security issues by a great many financially sophisticated people, and in this process there is a consensus of risk judgments.

The Limitation: Ability to Assume Risk

The objective of investors, we have said, is to obtain the highest possible total rate of return at the highest acceptable level of risk. Thus, the third principal proposition in this system of thought is that there must be a careful determination of the ability of investors to assume risk. The conditions that limit risk-taking are called constraints.

Analysis of limitations requires negative thinking. When we think of risk as a weighted probability distribution of expected rates of return, we look at the entire distribution. We see a mean of the distribution and the possible variation of rates above and below the mean. Now, in this phase of our thinking we focus sharply on those rates in the distribution below the mean. They may include negative rates, that is, rates of loss. How far below the mean do they extend? Can a particular investor in his unique circumstances suffer the lower rates without financial or emotional disaster?

The problem of ability to assume risk is not a simple one. It is not one that can be solved adequately by taking a quick look at a man and saying, "He can take a businessman's risk." Neither is it a matter of putting some investors in the "widows and orphans" category and concluding that these people can tolerate little risk.

The problem of estimating risk constraints can be solved adequately only by examining all the principal conditions that affect the ability of people and institutions to absorb the impact of low rates of return, and even of high rates of loss, without catastrophe. Just what constitutes catastrophe is a subjective judgment, but it is sufficient for our purpose to say that whatever an investor thinks is catastrophe is catastrophe.

The problem of ability to assume risk is complex because adverse outcomes may take several forms. Most frequently they take the form of market price depreciation and loss of principal, but there also may be a decrease in amounts of income payments or complete loss of income. Adverse outcomes may be measured in current dollars or in constant dollars. For some kinds of investors one form of adverse outcome may be more important than another form. Adverse investment outcomes have not only financial consequences, but also emotional impacts. Sometimes it appears that an investor who can well afford a given risk as far as his pocketbook is concerned cannot take it as far as his psyche is concerned.

Any very careful study of conditions limiting risk-taking ability leads almost always to consideration of an investor's assets other than securities and his sources of income other than income from investments. Usually securities constitute one kind of asset in a diverse set of assets and sources of income. One can take these other assets as given and try to design a securities portfolio that fits in well with them, but a better course is to consider all the assets of an investor as one set of assets, and to think about the risk-return problem in terms of the entire set. This broad view may very well bring into question the desirability of owning kinds of assets other than securities.

PLAN OF STUDY

The plan of study of this book develops the framework of thought we have just described. The problem is one of risk and return, so we must first learn about risks—about the principal causes of uncertainty of future returns, about how securities are graded in terms of the principal causes of uncertainty, and about the size of expected returns usually associated with the different levels of risk. We can generalize about risk and return in securities, but at some point someone must select specific security issues to be bought, held, or sold. Appraisal of risk and expected rate of return for specific securities is usually termed financial analysis. There is a set of chapters on this subject.

Study of investment constraints follows logically. The principal purpose in discussing this topic is to develop a system of analysis that will bring into view all the conditions affecting ability to assume risk. Any very thorough study of investment constraints of individuals leads into the area of personal financial and estate planning and we will deal briefly with this subject.

When all this is done we will be in a position to think intelligently about assembling a portfolio and what policies to follow in managing portfolios. An investor can do a great deal to minimize risk by carefully selecting risks in individual security issues and to maximize returns at any given level of portfolio risk.

The last several chapters describe principal types of investing institutions, the constraints that affect them generally, and the kinds of investment policies they usually follow. This description shows how the risk-return problem is solved in real life by professional investment managers, and the survey of their investment constraints and policies shows the practical application of concepts previously presented in general terms.

QUESTIONS FOR DISCUSSION

1. Your broker advises you to buy five "growth stocks." These are stocks of relatively small companies with specialized product lines that have had an unusually high rate of increase in earnings in the past several years. You object that stocks of this kind are very risky. He agrees, but points to the graph of risk-return relationships (Figure 1–1) to prove that if you assume a high level of risk you get a high rate of return. Do you believe him?

2. You own the portfolio of securities shown in Table 1–1. You have decided to sell the U. S. government bonds and to buy some low-risk common stocks. The time is now. Will you make the sale now and buy the stocks now, or will you wait a while for lower stock prices or higher bond prices? Whatever your decision, justify it.

3. One of the stocks recommended to you is now selling at $26 to $26½ per share, but your broker says that it will sell at no less than $40 per share within three years. This stock pays no dividends and is not expected to do so within the three years. If you buy the stock at the current price and sell it at $40 per share after three years, what rate of return will you realize on your investment? Disregard transaction costs.

4. You have bought a $1,000 bond of the kind described as high-grade (very little risk of the issuer not paying as promised). You will hold it for 5 years, receive $60 in interest each year, and receive the par amount at the end of the period. If the general price level as measured by the Consumer Price Index increases at an annual rate of exactly 3 per cent during the period of this investment, exactly what will be the amount of interest and principal payments in constant dollars?

5. The most likely total rate of return on a common stock of a financially strong electric utility company is estimated at 9 per cent, and the analyst's probability distribution is 7, 8, 9, 10, and 11 per cent, with probabilities of 0.1, 0.2, 0.4, 0.2, and 0.1, respectively. What is the standard deviation of this distribution and what does it mean?

6. Some of your friends have organized a small-scale lottery. One lottery ticket will be sold to each of 100 persons for $1 per ticket. The tickets and ticket stubs are numbered from 1 to 100. The stubs will be put in a bowl and thoroughly mixed. Then a blindfolded child will draw one stub from the bowl. The lucky owner of the ticket with the same number as that on the stub will receive a prize of $80. Should you buy a ticket?

7. Can you afford to take the risk that you would assume by buying 100 shares of each of the thirty stocks included in the Dow-Jones Industrial Average? Look at a chart of fluctuations in the average price of these stocks. If this question is not realistic for you, think of someone else for whom it would be realistic.

2

The Kinds of Securities You Can Buy in the Market

I. Classification of corporate securities by their legal nature
   A. The basic distinction between bonds and stocks
   B. Varieties of bonds and stocks

II. Stocks of business corporations
   A. Common stock
   B. Preferred stock
   C. Par value and no-par value stock

III. The terms of corporate bonds
   A. The corporate trustee
   B. Security for bonds
   C. Debenture bonds
   D. Amortization, redemption and conversion provisions

IV. Classification of corporate securities by type of issuer

V. United States Government securities
   A. Kinds of government securities
   B. Securities of federally sponsored agencies

VI. Securities of political subdivisions
   A. General characteristics of municipals
   B. General obligation municipals
   C. Revenue bonds
   D. Local housing authority obligations

VII. Foreign government securities

If you look at the advertisements on the financial pages of newspapers and magazines, you often see the caption "Investment Securities" in large type, with the name of an investment banking firm underneath. The investment banker wants you to know that he deals in the kinds of stocks and bonds that may be bought and sold in the securities markets. Investors, of course, have to understand the nature of these investment securities and be able to differentiate one kind of security from another.

There are securities issued by different kinds of issuers, securities that represent many variations of contractual relationships between issuer and investor, and securities of widely diverse investment risk. But the principal legal and economic features of securities can be classified in an orderly fashion. If you understand the general pattern of classification, you can readily recognize these features and place them in their proper categories.

The most fundamental distinction is between securities of *private business enterprises* and those of *public bodies*, that is, governments and agencies of governments. Almost all business enterprises that issue securities are organized as corporations; thus we have the broad category of corporate securities.

CLASSIFICATION OF CORPORATE SECURITIES BY LEGAL NATURE

A fundamental basis for classifying corporate securities is the kind of contract or legal relationship existing between the issuer and the security holders. The two main categories of securities on this basis are stocks and bonds. Stocks and bonds in turn can be subclassified according to the different provisions in corporate charters that determine the rights and limitations of stockholders and according to the provisions of bond indentures that establish the contractual rights of bondholders.

Basic Distinction Between Bonds and Stocks

Bonds are evidence of debt; stock is evidence of ownership—that is the basic distinction. If you buy a bond, you become a creditor of the business corporation or government that issued the bond. If you buy shares of stock, you become a part-owner of a business enterprise. Whenever there is any doubt about the nature of a security, it is necessary only to determine whether the provisions of the issue establish a creditor relationship by a promise to pay interest or repay principal at some future date. If there is a such a promise, it is a bond; if not, it is a stock.

Thus, bonds have a specified maturity date on which the issuer is legally obligated to pay the principal amount (the amount written on the face of a bond) to the bondholder. If the issuer fails to do so, the contract is violated and the bondholder may take steps legally to compel payment. In contrast, the provisions of stock issues never include a promise to repay the principal amount invested. The stockholder is an owner and he has no right to repayment unless the enterprise is liquidated. Of course, he can always sell his stock to someone else. In a broad sense the right to sell is an alternative to the right to repayment of principal.

Bonds contain a promise to pay stipulated amounts of interest periodically (usually semi-annually) to bondholders. Ordinarily, failure to make an interest payment in full is a default, or breach of contract. There are variations, however. Sometimes very short-term obligations (generally called notes or bills rather than bonds) contain no promise to pay interest, but only a promise to pay principal. Investors buy them at a discount and their yield is simply the amount of discount earned to maturity. Another variation is the "income" bond, which is usually issued in the reorganization of a company that has failed. These bonds contain a promise to pay a stipulated rate of interest, but payment is contingent on earnings being sufficient for the purpose.

The provisions of stock issues never include an outright promise to make dividend payments to stockholders. Stockholders of a corporation receive dividends when, and in whatever amounts, the directors see fit to declare them. Sometimes one class of a stock of a company has a preference as to dividends over another class of stock, but this is only a preference and not a right. In very rare instances, however, the courts of equity have required corporations to pay dividends to stockholders when failure to do so was clearly inequitable.

Still another distinction that may be made between bonds and stocks is that bonds do not ordinarily give their holders a voice in the management of the company that issued them, whereas ownership of stock usually does. The general idea is that bondholders are creditors, and that as long as they receive the payments promised them, management is strictly a function of the owners. For stockholders, on the other hand, the right to vote for directors and on certain major questions of corporate policy is an inherent right of ownership. Under the laws of some states, that right may be denied to certain classes of stock of a company, and it is often denied to preferred stock, but there must always be one class of voting stock.

Varieties of Bonds and Stocks

We have stressed the basic differences between bonds and stocks because the number of variations in the legal provisions of both of these categories is limited only by the ingenuity of issuers and their investment bankers and lawyers in devising special provisions to make securities attractive to investors and, sometimes, to limit the promises of issuers. But these variations fit into a general pattern, and when that pattern is familiar, the significance of special rights and limitations is easy to understand.

By far the most important legal distinction among stocks is that between common stock and preferred stock. Common stock represents ownership pure and simple. The ownership rights of common stock are basically the same as those of the proprietor of a business, but they have been modified in various ways by the state and federal laws under which corporations are organized.

Thus, common stockholders have no right as stockholders to engage in the management of companies whose stocks they own. Neither do they have the personal liability for debts of the business that attaches to owners of unincorporated businesses.

Preferred stock represents ownership, but owners of this kind of stock have special rights in some respects and special limitations in others. In general, preferred stockholders as a class stand before common stockholders in the distribution of dividends and in the distribution of funds from the liquidation of a corporate enterprise. They are limited, however, in the amounts of such distributions, and frequently, in other respects.

STOCKS OF BUSINESS CORPORATIONS

It is easy to describe common and preferred stocks in general terms, but an investor who goes about scrutinizing particular stock issues runs into many different statements concerning rights, limitations, and special promises by issuers to their stockholders. These legal provisions affect the attractiveness of securities to investors; therefore, we must understand their significance.

Common Stock

The articles of incorporation promise common stockholders nothing but the basic rights of owners. They say nothing about an amount or rate of dividends to be paid and there is nothing about repaying the principal invested in common stock. The right to vote for directors and to vote on certain questions of corporate policy is regarded by most investors as of little or no importance. And, yet, common stocks are very popular with investors.

Dividend Rights. What makes common stock attractive is that there is no limit on the amount of dividends stockholders may receive, if their company prospers, and no limit on appreciation in market value. Common stockholders own the residue of earnings after taxes, interest, and preferred dividends (if any) have been paid. It can be paid to them as dividends or retained in the business, as corporate directors may decide. The size of potential returns to investors are greater for this kind of security than for any other.

The greatest risk of loss also attaches to common stock. There is nothing to protect this kind of security from the ill fortunes of business enterprise. Bondholders may be paid their interest even when earnings are small, and preferred stockholders may receive dividends in poor years, but common stockholders are seldom spared from reduction or omission of dividends when the final figures in profit-and-loss statements are written in red ink. Often common stockholders of a company go for years without dividends while holders of other classes of securities receive interest or dividends regularly.

Sometimes dividend payments on common stocks fluctuate with the business cycle, since corporate earnings tend to vary with the general level of business activity. However, the relationship of dividends to earnings also varies with other conditions. A relatively new and rapidly growing company may pay no dividends on its common stock for a period of years, even though earnings increase, because the directors consider it a good policy to "plough back" the earnings. Established companies in manufacturing and merchandising generally pay out about 50 to 60 per cent of earnings applicable to common stock and keep the remainder in the business. Some companies try to stabilize dividend payments by disbursing a smaller portion of earnings in good years and a larger portion in poor years. Others try to maintain a "regular" dividend rate and in time of unusual prosperity pay "extra" dividends. Most companies whose stock is widely distributed pay dividends quarterly; others pay semi-annually or annually.

Voting Rights. Usually stockholders have one vote for each share of stock they own; they may vote their stock at stockholders' meetings for the election of directors and on such questions of policy as are submitted to stockholders. Common stockholders generally have to give their approval to proposals for mortgaging the corporate property, merging or selling the business, or increasing the amount of stock authorized to be issued.

Sometimes it is provided that, in the election of directors, shareholders vote *cumulatively*. This means that each stockholder has as many votes as the number of shares he owns times the total number of directors to be elected. He may cast the full number of votes for only one or a few directors instead of dividing them among a full slate of directors to be elected. This voting arrangement is designed to permit owners of a substantial minority of the total voting stock of a company to obtain representation on the board of directors by voting all of their stock for one or for only a few directors.

Most investors, however, do not take their voting rights very seriously. It is the usual practice for common stockholders to sign "proxies" mailed to them by the management of their company. By signing and returning proxies they legally transfer to persons associated with the management the right to vote their stock, so that at the typical stockholders' meeting most of the votes are controlled by the management group. There have been instances, however, in which dissatisfied stockholders have gotten together to bring about a change in management or in policies of management. There is much to be said for the idea that common stock investors ought to use their right to vote much more intelligently and effectively.

Preemptive Rights. As a general rule of common law, common stockholders have *preemptive rights* to any new issue of common stock. That is, they have the right to subscribe to any additional common stock issued by their company in proportion to their present stock holdings before such stock is offered to persons not presently shareholders. The general rule of common law, however, has been superseded by statute law in most states. Some state laws provide unequivocally that stockholders will have the preemptive right. Others say that they will have the right unless otherwise provided by articles of incorporation. This kind of provision permits incorporators to write into the articles a denial of the preemptive right. And still other state laws declare that stockholders will not have the preemptive right unless the articles of incorporation affirmatively confer the right.

The reasoning behind the common-law rule is that stockholders are part-owners in incorporated business enterprises and, as part-owners, have an interest in earnings and assets proportionate to the fraction of voting shares they own. Having such a proportionate interest, the laws reason, stockholders may be harmed if they are not permitted to maintain that interest when the number of shares of common stock is increased.

An investor may be interested in subscribing to additional stock simply because the terms are advantageous. When new stock is offered to present stockholders the offering price is usually less than the current market price. Stockholders who do not want to exercise their rights to subscribe can sell them in the market and realize their cash value.

Preferred Stock

Preferred stock, we have said, has special rights in some respects and special limitations in others. These rights and limitations represent a sort of bargain between the common stockholders and the preferred stockholders of a company. In effect the preferred stockholders say to the common stockholders, "Let us have dividends before you receive dividends and regardless of whether you receive them; we will agree that our dividends may be limited to so much a share—you can have whatever more there may be." This is the main point of the bargain, but there are other provisions that may be important to investors.

Dividend Rights. The title of preferred stock issues usually includes a dollar amount or percentage figure to indicate the extent of its preference to dividends. A $5 preferred stock has the privilege of receiving an annual dividend at the rate of $5 per share before any dividend is paid to common stockholders (or to holders of a junior class of preferred). If the dividend preference is expressed as a percentage, the annual amount of dividend is the stipulated percentage of the par value of stock. Usually it is provided that preferred dividends are to be paid on specified quarterly dates.

The dividend on preferred stock is not "promised." A corporation does not have to pay dividends on preferred stock, and if the directors decide to pay none at all, or to pay only a part of the stipulated rate or amount, the preferred stockholders must accept the decision. The right of preferred stockholders is only a right to be paid *before* the common stockholders are paid. The dividend preference is, nevertheless, a valuable one. Sometimes business corporations are able to achieve only small or moderate earnings, and the dividend preference may make the difference between no dividends and some dividends.

The preference of preferred stock in the matter of dividends is worth a great deal more to investors when the preferred dividends are *cumulative.* A preferred stock is cumulative when the issuer contracts that any dividend not paid on schedule, or any unpaid part of the dividend, must be paid in the future before any dividend is paid on common stock of the company. If a stock is preferred to the extent of a $5 annual dividend and no dividend is paid during a year, the $5 per share accumulates and the preferred stock is said to be in arrears of dividends. Dividends in arrears on preferred stock do not constitute a liability of the issuer; stockholders still retain only the right to be paid the dividend arrears before any dividend is paid on common stock. Even so, the cumulative provision is a strong influence for the full payment of preferred dividends because the accumulation of dividend arrears prevents payment of common dividends and generally makes the further sale of either preferred or common stock difficult.

Most preferred stock is cumulative but some is not. *Noncumulative* preferred stock is often issued when a company is reorganized and its financial future is particularly uncertain. This is a weak kind of preferred stock from the investment viewpoint because management has less incentive to pay the dividend regularly. If noncumulative preferred dividends are not paid on the scheduled dates, they are just forgotten. Of course, no dividend can be paid on the common stock in any dividend period when the preferred dividend is not paid in full.

The typical preferred stock issue is *nonparticipating*, which means that it may not receive a dividend greater than the stipulated rate or amount per share per annum. In that case all the remaining profits—no matter how large—belong to the common stockholders. Thus, the nonparticipating preferred stockholder has no opportunity to share in the prosperity of a successful company beyond a stipulated rate of dividend on his money.

Occasionally, one finds *participating* preferred stocks in the security markets, but they are rather unusual. This kind of preferred stock is permitted to participate in some manner with the common stock in the distribution of profits beyond its regular rate or amount.

Voting Rights. The people who devise the terms of corporate security issues often reason that as long as the preferred stockholders get their full dividends regularly they have no vital interest in the election of directors or the determination of business policies. Therefore, preferred stock is often nonvoting. Nonvoting preferred, however, sometimes has voting rights in certain circumstances. A frequent provision in preferred stock is that the holders will be entitled to vote if they have not received their full dividends for some stipulated period of time.

Redemption Provisions. In modern financial practice the provisions of preferred stocks almost always include a provision for redemption of the entire issue at a specified price. Redemption is at the option of the issuer. When preferred stocks have par value, the redemption price is usually a slightly higher figure than the par value. Thus, a $100 par value preferred stock might be redeemable (another term is callable) at $104 or $105 per share. A provision for redemption limits the market price of a preferred stock; investors will not pay more than approximately the redemption price for a stock that the issuer may redeem at any time on short notice at the redemption price.

Sometimes there are sinking funds for preferred stocks. That is, the issuer promises to apply an amount periodically that may be defined as a percentage of the par amount of stock originally issued, or presently outstanding, to redemption or repurchase of preferred stock.

Conversion Rights. Sometimes preferred stock issues contain a provision for conversion of preferred into common stock at the option of the preferred stockholders. A conversion rate is specified in the provisions setting forth the rights and limitations of preferred stockholders. For example, a $100 par value preferred stock might be made convertible into common stock of the issuer at a price of $25 per share for the common with the preferred taken at par. This means that preferred stockholders, whenever they wish to do so, may "trade in" one share of preferred for four shares of common. At the time a convertible preferred stock is issued the conversion price for the common is usually fixed at a larger amount than the current market price. A conversion price of $25 might be specified when the market price for the common is in the neighborhood of $20 per share. The idea is to make conversion of preferred into common profitable for the preferred shareholders only if and when the market price of the common rises substantially.

Par Value and No-par Value

Stock may also be classified as "par value" and "no-par value" stock. Both common and preferred stocks may have par value or be of no-par value.

Par value is a value in dollars arbitrarily assigned to shares of stock by the corporate charter or articles of incorporation. In the early development of the corporation as a form of business organization, the drafters of state corporation laws seemed to think it necessary to require that stock have some specified value for accounting and financial purposes, so that anyone could see how much capital a company had by looking at its balance sheet.

As time passed corporate promoters found various ways to get around the proposition that a share of stock having a specified par value represents that amount of capital actually paid in to a corporation. Stock was often issued in exchange for property, or for services, at whatever valuation the directors chose to place on the services. Thus it often came about that the par value of stock issued by a company was far greater than the amount of money or the reasonable market value of the property received by the company as capital. It finally came to be recognized that the par value requirement does not serve its purpose very well and today most states permit corporations to issue stock without par value.

No-par stock is simply stock that has no par value assigned to it. Usually it may be sold by the issuing corporation at any price fixed by the board of directors, although in some states a minimum initial sale price per share is fixed by law. A variation of the no-par idea is stock without par value but with a "stated value." The stated value is the minimum amount per share at which stock may be sold initially and the minimum amount at which issued stock may be credited to the capital-stock account. The stated value is usually a nominal amount, such as $1, and is well below the price at which the stock is issued.

As a practical matter the classification of stock as par or no-par does not have any great significance to investors because it does not affect risk and return, but we must be familiar with the distinction in order to understand the vocabulary and technical usages of finance.

THE TERMS OF CORPORATE BONDS

Bonds differ from stocks mainly in their terms concerning interest payments, security pledged, provisions for repayment of principal, and in various other technical features.

When you buy a bond in the market, you receive an engraved piece of paper that evidences the debt of the issuer to you. Corporate bonds are usually issued in denominations of $1,000 and multiples thereof. In common usage "a bond" means one of $1,000 denomination. Each bond is one of a number of bonds all issued under the same contract, or trust indenture. All bonds issued under the same indenture have the same rights and are protected by the same promises on the part of the issuer. However, bonds under the same indenture may be divided into different series, designated as Series A, Series B, etc. The different series may be issued at different times, bear different interest rates, and mature at different dates. All bonds of one series, however, have the same terms.

Interest is usually paid semi-annually. Some bonds have a series of coupons attached to them, each representing a semi-annual interest payment due on a specified date. The bondholder collects his interest by clipping each coupon just before its due date and depositing it with a bank for collection. Such bonds are called *coupon bonds*. Other bonds are *registered*, meaning that the name of the owner is registered with a registrar. These fully registered bonds have no coupons, and interest is paid to holders by check.

The Corporate Trustee

The contract under which corporate bonds are issued is not made directly with bondholders, but with the corporate trustee, who acts on behalf of the bondholders. The trustee for the issue is a third party in the relationship, one who performs very important functions from the viewpoint of investors. Legally the promises to pay interest and principal and to do various other things that are contained in the trust indenture are made to the trustee, who holds them for the benefit of the bondholders.

The trustee is normally a bank or trust company with a department organized to perform the functions of trustee under bond issues. One simple function of a corporate trustee is to authenticate the bonds issued, that is, to certify that they are valid obligations issued in accordance with the provisions of the indenture. Another is to examine from time to time the manner in which the company is keeping its promises to preserve the value of property pledged as security, to maintain its working-capital position, and to issue additional bonds only in accordance with the restrictions of the indenture. Perhaps most important, the trustee has the duty to take whatever legal action is appropriate to enforce the rights of bondholders if the issuer fails to pay interest or principal.

Federal law requires that trust indentures for all corporate issues in the amount of more than $1 million sold to the public in interstate commerce must be "qualified" with the Securities and Exchange Commission. In order to qualify, the trustee named must be a financially responsible institution, the instrument must impose adequate requirements for performance of the trustee's duties on behalf of bondholders, there must be no conflict between the trustee's interest as trustee and any other interest it may have, and there must be provision for reports to bondholders by the trustee.

Security for Bonds

The most significant classification of corporate bonds is according to the pledge of security to protect investors in case the issuer is unable to keep its promise to pay. The two major classes of bonds on this basis are *secured* and *unsecured*.

A secured bond is one issued under an indenture providing that bondholders will have a lien on certain designated property of the issuer. A lien is a right given to the bondholders to seek enforcement of their claims as creditors by sale of the pledged property if interest or principal is not paid in full. The purpose of the pledge of security is to strengthen the bonds and thus to make them more attractive to investors. In practice, it is very seldom that property pledged to secure a corporate bond issue is actually sold when default occurs. The usual course is financial reorganization and the issuance of new securities of the reorganized company for the defaulted bonds. However, the nature of the lien and the value of the property on which it lies have considerable influence on the treatment bondholders receive during reorganization.

The most obvious way to classify secured bonds is according to the type of asset pledged. On this basis we can differentiate between real estate mortgage bonds, collateral trust bonds, and equipment trust obligations.

Mortgage Bonds. A substantial portion of the assets of the typical business corporation consists of land, buildings, and equipment. Such property has traditionally been regarded as good security for loans, and it is naturally the first thing most corporate officials think of when they come to the question of providing security for bonds. Consequently, the most common type of corporate bond issue is the mortgage bond.

A corporate mortgage bond issue is usually secured by a lien on all the fixed, immovable property of a company, such as land and buildings, and also on machinery, equipment, and other assets not coming within the legal definition of real property. Such a pledge is sometimes called a "blanket" mortgage. On the other hand, companies that own several plants or other separate items of real estate may mortgage only one plant or one part of its property for a bond issue. One of the first things you find out about a mortgage bond is exactly what the mortgage covers.

Another thing to find out at the beginning is the priority of the mortgage lien. The mortgage first placed on property has the first lien; the holders of that lien come first in the distribution of proceeds from sale of the property if it ever has to be sold to satisfy the claims of creditors. After the first mortgage there may be second, third, and other mortgages; holders of such mortgages share in the proceeds of sale in the order of their priority. Obviously, the value of a lien decreases as its priority decreases.

If a mortgage is to be effective in providing protection to bondholders, the value of the property pledged must be greater than the amount of debt. Usually bonds are issued to the extent of no more than 50 to 60 per cent of the estimated value of pledged property. In some instances the indenture expressly prohibits the issue of any bonds after the initial issue and so ensures that the debt/property ratio will not be reduced by further borrowing. On the other hand, many business corporations find it disadvantageous to close a mortgage in this manner. They like to keep the mortgage open, so that they can sell additional bonds under the same indenture and secured by the same lien as their financial requirements develop. In practice they accomplish this by putting in the trust indenture an *after-acquired clause*, combined with an open-end provision.

The after-acquired clause provides that whatever property the company may acquire in the future shall also be subject to the mortgage. If a company is prosperous and adds to its plant and equipment, the after-acquired clause brings about an increase in the value of property subject to the mortgage. This increased property value is then a basis for an increase in amount of the debt it secures.

There are usually a number of conditions that must be satisfied before additional series of bonds may be issued under an existing mortgage. A common requirement is that bonds may be issued only to the extent of some stipulated percentage of the value of additional property acquired and subject to the mortgage. A second condition affecting the issuance of additional bonds, usually, is that earnings in the last fiscal period will have been equal to some given number of times the amount required to pay interest on the bonds outstanding plus those proposed to be issued.

Collateral Trust Bonds. There are companies whose assets consist entirely, or in large part, of securities of other companies. They often find it expedient to pledge the securities they own as security for the bonds they issue. These bonds are called *collateral trust bonds.*

The lien on pledged collateral in favor of bondholders is usually created by the simple device of transferring its ownership to the corporate trustee, subject to the provisions of the trust indenture. The effect is that the trustee holds legal title, but the company may recover title by paying off the bonds. It is commonly stipulated in the trust indenture that, while the bonds are outstanding and being paid according to their terms, the income from the pledged collateral goes to the company and that company has the right to vote any voting stock included in the collateral. This provision permits the holding company to carry on its relations with its subsidiary companies as usual. However, it may be provided that in case of default on interest or principal, the right to receive income from pledged collateral and to exercise voting rights reverts to the corporate trustee. In that situation the trustee would also have the right to sell the collateral and apply the proceeds to the payment of bonds, although this right may be restrained by receivership or trusteeship of the holding company.

It is a common practice to provide that the issuing company will maintain the value of collateral at some stipulated minimum ratio to the amount of bonds outstanding, such as 150 per cent. If the value of the collateral, as measured by market prices or as appraised by the trustee, falls below the required ratio, the company is obligated to supply more collateral.

Equipment Trust Certificates. A major category of assets for companies in the transportation industries is equipment used to move freight and passengers, such as railway cars, airplanes, trucks, and even ships. To finance acquisition of this kind of property a particular kind of instrument has been developed called equipment trust certificates.

Railway companies usually finance the purchase of new cars and locomotives by selling equipment trust certificates secured by pledge of the new equipment. The most common arrangement involves vesting legal title to railway rolling stock in a trustee, who then leases the equipment to the railroad that wishes to acquire it.

The railroad makes an initial rental payment equal to about 15 to 25 per cent of the cost of the equipment leased and agrees to make periodic rental payments for the period of lease. The trustee then sells certificates of participation in the trust property (the railway rolling stock) to investors. He uses the funds so obtained, plus the initial rental payment, to pay the manufacturer for the rolling stock. Then the periodic rental payments are used to retire the certificates, which are arranged to mature at intervals over a period of 10 to 20 years, as well as to pay interest on those outstanding. Usually the railway company guarantees payment of principal and interest. When the certificates are all paid off, legal title to the equipment is transferred to the railway company for a nominal consideration and the trust is dissolved.

This method of pledging transportation equipment does not give security holders a lien on property. It does better than that by placing full legal title in the trustee for their benefit. Thus, if a railroad fails to make the rental payments due under the lease, there is no need for awkward legal proceedings. The lessor of the equipment has simply broken his lease by not paying the rent due and the owner can take his property back. Because railway rolling stock is highly essential to the operation of a railroad, and because it may readily be sold or leased to another company, it makes excellent security.

This kind of arrangement is also used to finance other kinds of transportation equipment.

Debenture Bonds

Unsecured bonds, usually called debenture bonds or merely debentures, are obligations issued under indentures that grant no special lien on property of the issuer. This does not mean that bondholders have no claim on the assets of the issuer in case of default but rather that they have only the claim of general creditors. The position of general creditors can best be understood by considering what happens when a company is adjudged bankrupt and its assets are liquidated to pay its creditors. In liquidation the proceeds from sale of any assets specifically pledged to secure debts are applied first to payment of the secured creditors and prior claims (after payment of taxes and expenses). Then any balance left over is available for the general creditors.

Debenture bonds are issued for the most part by relatively strong companies; financially weak companies seldom are able to sell unsecured issues. But even the stronger companies include in their indentures various provisions for the protection of debenture holders. Frequently the total principal amount of debentures that may be issued is limited to the amount of the present issue, or it is provided that additional debentures may be issued in the future only if earnings for the past several years have been equal to not less than two or three times the amounts required for payment of debenture interest.

The trust indentures for debenture bonds commonly include a number of restrictions called covenants for the protection of bondholders. One kind of covenant provides that if in the future the issuer pledges assets as specific security for another bond issue, the present issue will be secured equally with the subsequent issue. Another covenant requires that the working capital of the issuer be maintained at some minimum ratio to the principal amount of debentures outstanding. The effect is to require that there be current assets sufficient to pay not only current liabilities but also some part of the principal amount of debentures. Cash dividends are usually restricted to an amount of earned surplus at date of issuance of bonds plus earnings subsequent to that date.

In recent years there has been considerable use of a kind of bond known as a *subordinated debenture*. The distinctive characteristic of this kind of obligation is that it is not only unsecured, but in its claim on assets it is expressly made subordinate to other defined general creditors. The relatively weak legal claim of subordinated debentures is often compensated in some part by a provision making them convertible into common stock of the issuer on specified terms.

Amortization, Redemption, and Conversion Provisions

Bond issues often contain provisions for payment of principal before maturity, for amortization of principal during the period to maturity, and for conversion into other securities of the issuers. These provisions are similar to those we have described for preferred stocks, but in some ways they have more influence on the attractiveness of bonds to investors than they do in the case of preferred stocks.

Amortization of Principal. Most corporate bond issues contained some provision for periodic repayment of principal, commonly called amortization of principal, during the period from date of issuance to the final due date. Corporate financial managers like the idea of gradual reduction of debt so that they are not finally confronted with a large amount of principal to be paid at the end of the term for which bonds were issued. Investors also like arrangements for debt reduction because it tends to reduce the risk that issuers will be unable to pay their debts at some time in the future. The sinking fund arrangements is by far the most common device for periodic amortization of principal, but the serial maturity arrangement is used for some special types of issues.

There are a great many variations in sinking fund provisions, but a common arrangement is one that requires a stipulated dollar amount, or a stipulated percentage of the initial principal amount, to be applied periodically to retirement of bonds. These amounts are usually calculated so that the payments will retire most of the initial principal amount by the due date of the issue. However, the proportion to be retired by maturity varies considerably.

Sinking fund payments may be applied to reduction of debt in any of several ways. One method is to call bonds by lot for repayment. Bonds are given serial numbers at time of issue and are called by selecting at random enough numbers to use up the amount of a sinking fund payment. The other principal method of retiring bonds by the sinking fund is to purchase them in the market at market prices. This method is used, of course, when market prices are lower than redemption prices.

The other method of amortization of principal, used chiefly for equipment trust certificates, is to divide an issue into a number of parts and specify a different maturity date for each part. This is the serial maturity arrangement. In effect, the issuer sells a series of obligations all under one legal instrument with the first part maturing in a year or so and other parts maturing at intervals of about a year over a considerable period of time. Sometimes there are different coupon rates for different maturities, with the shorter maturities bearing lower rates than the longer maturities. The serial maturity arrangement has the advantage to investors of permitting them to pick their maturities. If they want an obligation due in, say, 5 years, they can buy bonds of that maturity; if they want an obligation due in 15 years, they can buy that arrangement.

Redemption of Issue Before Maturity. It is not unusual for a company that has sold bonds to want to retire the entire issue before maturity. So issuers commonly include in bond indentures a provision permitting them to call, or redeem, all outstanding bonds at some time after they have been issued. Ordinarily the right to call an issue is limited by a provision that it may not be redeemed until some number of years have elapsed from date of issue, such as 5 or 10 years. Thus an issue is non-callable during that period and callable thereafter. In some instances the prohibition against call during the initial period of years applies only to call for the purpose of refunding with another security issue. When bonds are callable before maturity the issuer must pay a premium over par to bondholders. The call price may range from 101 to 110 per cent of par. The premium is to compensate investors for having their bonds taken away from them and becoming obliged to find another investment.

The right of redemption, or call, before maturity generally operates to the disadvantage of bondholders and to the benefit of issuers. It enables issuers to terminate their bond contracts whenever it is in their interest to do so. Usually it is to their advantage when interest rates have declined from the level prevailing when their bonds were issued; then they can sell new bond issues at lower rates of interest. Proceeds of new issues are used to call and pay off outstanding issues in what is termed a refunding operation. The effect of refunding is to give investors new bonds bearing lower coupon rates and providing lower yields.

The Conversion Privilege. The conversion privilege in bond issues is the same in purpose, in operation, and in significance to investors as it is in preferred stock issues. Its purpose is to make a bond issue more attractive to investors by giving them both the safety of a bond and the opportunity for speculative gain from appreciation of common stock. But investors should have no illusion about getting this speculative opportunity for nothing. The conversion privilege is an option to buy stock at a predetermined price; as an option it has a price. The price is the difference between the yield on a convertible bond at time of purchase and the yield at the same time on a nonconvertible bond with the same investment risk. This difference may be several percentage points; that is, a bond that would sell on an 8 per cent yield basis as a straight bond might sell on a 4 to 5 per cent yield basis as a convertible bond. The price of the conversion privilege in any particular instance would depend of course on the terms of conversion and investors' estimates of the likelihood that the common stock obtainable by conversion will in the future significantly exceed its conversion price.

Usually convertible bonds are callable, and the call provision has particular significance to owners of convertible bonds. It enables issuers to call convertible bonds whenever the market value of stock obtainable by conversion is greater than the call price of the bonds, and thus to "force" conversion of the bonds. The call of an issue forces conversion in that bondholders have to choose between accepting cash at the call price, or of converting to stock with a greater market value.

There are many variations of conversion terms. Sometimes the conversion right may not be exercised until a specified date after the issue date, and sometimes after it becomes effective it expires before maturity of the bonds. Usually the conversion price of the stock increases with the passage of time; for example, it might be 100 during the first time period, 110 in a second time period, 121 in a third time period, and so forth. There is always a provision that the conversion rights not be "diluted" by stock splits, stock dividends, and other procedures that increase the number of shares of stock outstanding without a proportionate increase in amount of assets. Convertible bond indentures contain elaborate provisions for adjusting established conversion prices for stock to compensate for any such dilution.

CLASSIFICATION OF CORPORATE SECURITIES BY TYPE OF ISSUER

If you listen to conversations among financial analysts and other professionals in the securities business, you will hear such terms as "industrial stock," "municipal bonds," and "utility preferred." Notice that these terms not only indicate the main legal classifications of securities but also identify the types of issuers. The types of issuers is the second important thing to learn about securities.

In this type of classification the basic distinction is between business concerns and government bodies. Business concerns, usually corporations, are further classified according to the nature of the business in which they engage, and governmental bodies are grouped according to their level in the system of governmental organization.

Some years ago practically all corporate issues were classified as "rails," "utilities," and "industrials." But as the business system developed and companies from a greater variety of industries sold securities in the capital markets, a somewhat more elaborate system of industry classification came into use. Four main industry categories are generally recognized: utilities, transportation companies, industrial companies, and financial institutions. Each of these groups is further subdivided by industry. The utilities group includes principally the electric power industry, the gas industry, the telephone industry, and the water industry. The transportation group consists of railway companies, airlines, bus companies, and truck companies. Industrials, the broadest group, may be divided into manufacturing industries, mining or extractive industries, and merchandising companies. Then each of these divisions may be further subdivided.

Perhaps it should be mentioned here that securities may also be classified as domestic and foreign. Most of us limit our thinking about securities to those issued by governments and business concerns in the United States. There are, however, a considerable number of bond issues of foreign governments and their political subdivisions outstanding in the securities markets of this country. Some foreign corporations have also sold bonds in the United States, and the stocks of a number of foreign companies are traded on American exchanges.

UNITED STATES GOVERNMENT SECURITIES

Treasury obligations are generally conceded to be safer than any other kind of bond in the sense that there is virtually no risk that the United States government will fail to pay principal and interest to bondholders in dollars. Since the federal government has unlimited power to tax in order to obtain money to pay its debts, its bonds are in effect secured by a first-tax lien on the entire wealth and income of the nation. Moreover, it has the power to borrow and sufficient control over our banking system to assure that there will be lenders. The fear is sometimes expressed that our huge volume of federal spending and our frequent budget deficits will bankrupt the nation, but for a sovereign government there can be no such thing as bankruptcy in the sense of inability to pay debts in current monetary units.

This is not, however, to say that government obligations are without investment risk. Market prices of Treasury issues rise and fall as interest rates decline or rise; an investor may realize a gain or a loss by selling a government bond for more or less than he paid for it. Amounts of income from these issues also change as principal is repaid or recouped in the market and the proceeds are reinvested in other issues at higher or lower interest rates.

There is also uncertainty about the future purchasing power of the dollar amounts received as interest and recovery of principal. Even if you were sure that amounts received in current dollars would be exactly the amounts promised, there would still be uncertainty about how much the dollars would buy.

Kinds of Government Securities

If you look at a statement of the public debt you find that about two-thirds of the total amount consists of marketable securities, about one-sixth is represented by nonmarketable securities, and the remainder is special issues sold by the Treasury to various government agencies and trust funds.[1]

Marketable Issues. The marketable portion of the public debt consists of securities that have been offered initially for sale to the public and subsequently traded in the security markets like other publicly distributed issues. New issues of these securities are usually offered for sale by the Federal Reserve Banks as fiscal agents for the Treasury and are not underwritten by investment bankers.

Although Treasury bonds are listed on the New York Stock Exchange, virtually all trading in government securities is over the counter. Several wholesale firms specialize in government securities and several large banks are important dealers in these securities. Most of the important government bond dealers publish daily offering sheets giving their bid and asked prices for all marketable Treasury issues as well as for issues of governmental agencies. Governments are quoted in 32nds of 1 per cent of par, with the fraction written as though it were a decimal; thus, 99.12 means 99 and 12/32 per cent of par. When quoted prices are converted to yields, the asked price is used. For issues callable before maturity, yield is figured to the earliest call date when price is more than par and to maturity when price is less than par.

[1]A full statement of the public debt may be found in the *Treasury Bulletin,* published monthly by the U.S. Treasury Department.

Marketable issues are divided into three general categories, differentiated chiefly by length of period to maturity. They are: *bills, notes*, and *bonds*.

Treasury bills are of the shortest term; they mature in 13 weeks, 26 weeks, or 52 weeks from date of issue. It has been the Treasury's practice in recent years to make an offering of 13- and 26-week bills on Monday of each week and to offer an issue of 52-week bills monthly. The amounts offered vary from time to time according to the cash requirements of the Treasury. A distinctive feature of Treasury bills is that they do not bear interest, but are sold on a discount basis. The yield is the discount earned from date of investment to maturity. Bills are sold at auction. Dealers and institutional investors submit bids expressed as a percentage of par for specified amounts. The Treasury accepts bids beginning with the highest price and moving downward until the amount of bills offered is sold, except that subscriptions for relatively small amounts are filled at the average of the prices of the bids accepted. The average yield on new issues of bills as reported in the financial press is computed on the average price of bids accepted. After bills are issued they are traded actively in the market. Ordinarily you can buy bills maturing in from 1 day to 1 year.

From time to time the Treasury has issued certificates of indebtedness with a maturity of 1 year, but this type of issue has not been offered in recent years.

Treasury notes are an intermediate-maturity type of obligation at time of issue, with maturities varying from 1 to 5 years. They bear interest at rates that vary from time to time with fluctuations in rates of yield in the market. Notes are issued at par and are subsequently traded in the market. In recent years the Treasury has relied heavily on notes in its financing, and the total of these obligations has come to represent almost one-half of all its marketable issues.

The largest fraction of the marketable debt, however, continues to be Treasury bonds. The main difference between bonds and notes is in length of maturity—bonds are issued with maturities of 10 to 30 years. Some Treasury bonds are callable beginning on a date 5 years before the date of maturity at the option of the Treasury, and on any interest payment date thereafter. They are identified in market price quotation lists by both the maturity date and the earliest call date. Certain designated Treasury bonds, when owned by a decedent and part of his estate, are accepted by the Treasury at par and accrued interest in payment of federal estate taxes. This is advantageous to some investors when prices for such issues are below par.

Frequently the Treasury offers new securities in exchange for maturing issues on a par-for-par basis and usually these refunding offers give bondholders a choice of two or three issues with different maturity dates and sometimes different interest rates. Holders of matured bonds may of course elect to receive payment in cash. From time to time the Treasury has also offered "advance refunding" of issues not yet due, with choice of several relatively long maturities. These refunding offerings are advantageous to investors who want to continue their commitment in government securities, for they usually provide new obligations on a slightly better yield basis than obligations of the same maturity could be purchased in the market at the time. They are advantageous to the Treasury in extending the maturity of the debt.

Nonmarketable Issues and Special Issues. Another portion of the public debt consists of security issues that are nonmarketable. Among the nonmarketable issues are the U.S. Savings Bonds that have been widely distributed to individuals. It is worth noting that the Savings Bonds involve no uncertainty about future market prices because there are no market prices. They are not traded in the markets and the only values for them are the redemption prices fixed by the Treasury. The special issues that make up the remainder of the public debt are obligations issued by the Treasury directly to certain government agencies and trust funds. They are not available to investors.

Securities of Federally Sponsored Agencies

Bond dealers group under the general heading of "agency issues" the obligations of a half-dozen agencies or institutions created by the government of the United States. These securities are not obligations of the federal government and they are not guaranteed by the government. They sell in the market on a slightly higher yield basis than government obligations of corresponding maturity. However, agency issues are generally regarded as almost certain to pay interest and principal because they are strongly supported by the income and assets of the institutions that issue them and because it seems extremely unlikely that the federal government would permit institutions it has created for quasi-public functions to default on their debt.

The principal federally sponsored issuers are: the Federal Home Loan Banks, the Federal National Mortgage Association, the Bank for Cooperatives, the Federal Intermediate Credit Banks, and the Federal Land Banks. These institutions have outstanding notes and bonds in the total amount of more than $40 billion.

Bonds of the International Bank for Reconstruction and Development, frequently called the World Bank, are often grouped with the agency issues. However, the World Bank is not an agency of the United States; it is the creation of a large number of member nations that have subscribed to its stock.

SECURITIES OF POLITICAL SUBDIVISIONS

Municipals is the simple term applied in investment circles to securities issued by all governmental units in the United States other than the federal government and its agencies. But municipals are by no means a simple category of securities. In fact, this classification includes more varieties of securities than does any other general category.

General Characteristics of Municipals

Bonds of the state governments are called municipals by security dealers; so are bonds of counties, parishes, townships, boroughs, and villages, as well as those of cities and towns. In addition there are obligations of special tax districts, which are municipal corporations set up for special and limited governmental purposes. There are also securities of various agencies and instrumentalities of state and local governments, such as public authorities, toll road commissions, and state colleges and universities. Moreover, these many different kinds of issuers have devised a great many kinds of contracts to be offered to investors. Some make a simple promise to pay from all resources available to them; others limit their obligations in various ways. Some pledge as security specific taxes, tolls, fees, or property; others offer no security, and there is one category of municipals secured by contractual payments from the federal government.

One important characteristic of municipal securities of all kinds is that the income from them is exempt from the federal corporate and personal income tax. This exemption stems from the historic case of M'Culloch *v.* Maryland, in which the Supreme Court ruled that the states do not have the power to tax an instrumentality of the federal government. This rule has been applied in reverse fashion to read that the federal government does not have the power to tax securities of the state and local governments and their instrumentalities. The Sixteenth Amendment to the Constitution, which authorizes the federal income tax, says nothing about exemption of income from municipal bonds. Efforts have been made from time to time in Congress to apply the income tax to state and municipal obligations, but they have always been defeated. It is entirely possible that at some time in the future interest from municipals will be made subject to the federal income tax.

Another characteristic of municipals is that they are generally high-grade, that is, there is little uncertainty about payment of interest and principal in current dollars. There are exceptions, of course. Some local governments have become so heavily burdened with debt that they do not enjoy a high credit rating; some communities are so poor or so unstable economically that their bonds cannot be highly regarded by investors; some local government units have such limited taxing power that their securities are not in the high-grade category; and some obligations supported by a limited pledge of revenues have speculative elements. But by far the greater part of the debt of the state and local governments consists of the kind of securities sought by conservative investors.

The amount of new municipal issues of all kinds publicly offered for sale in the securities markets has in recent years equaled one-half or more of the amount of new corporate bonds and stocks publicly issued. Municipal bonds are therefore a very important part of the business of investment bankers both in the primary and secondary markets. Most broker-dealer firms participate to some extent in the markets for municipals and a few are specialists in this area. Some commercial banks have municipal bond departments and do business both as primary distributors and as dealers.

The tax-exemption feature makes municipals particularly popular with individual investors in the higher income tax brackets. About two-fifths of all outstanding issues are owned by individuals, partnerships, and personal trusts. Financial institutions that pay the full corporate income tax rates—commercial banks and fire and casualty insurance companies—own about one-half. The balance is in the hands of life insurance companies, mutual savings banks, business corporations, and other institutional investors.

General Obligation Municipals

The largest category of municipals, classified by type of issue, is called *general obligations.* In the usual sense of the term, municipals are obligations of state and local governments for which their "full faith and credit" is pledged. The traditional meaning of this phrase is that issuers promise to pay interest and principal from all funds and resources at their disposal. The word "general" is used in apposition to "limited" or "special." There is no pledge of property, revenues, or specific tax revenues for general obligations. In effect, the issuer of general obligations promises to levy and collect taxes to whatever extent may be necessary for servicing its debt.

However, some units of local government have only limited power to levy property taxes (which is the principal source of tax revenues in most instances). Cities are limited by state law in some states in the rate of their levy on real property, and some cities have real property tax limitations in their charters. A local government subject to such tax limitation may pledge its full faith and credit, but its pledge is subject to the limitation of taxing power. If there are no specific limitations on the *sources of funds* for payment (as distinguished from *rate of tax*), obligations of municipalities with limited taxing power are usually regarded as general obligations but further identified as "limited tax" general obligations.

Tax notes is a term applied to a particular kind of general obligation. These are short-term securities issued to tide over the borrower while taxes are being collected. Although it is expected that they will be paid from taxes soon to be collected, they are not limited to payment from this source and are in fact payable from any resources available to the issuer. Tax notes are different from *tax-anticipation warrants*, which are payable from taxes levied and still to be collected and thus fall in the class of limited obligations.

Revenue Bonds

The great innovation in municipal financing in the past several decades is a category of obligations generally termed revenue bonds. Briefly, revenue bonds are obligations secured by pledge of specified revenues such as rents, fees, and special taxes, and *payable only from the pledged revenues.* Thus they differ sharply from general obligations in that full faith and credit of issuers is not pledged—only the specified revenues. If pledged revenues are not sufficient to pay interest and principal on bonds, bondholders may not legally require issuers to provide funds from other sources. Usually the pledged revenues are charges in one form or another for use of facilities that have been financed by the sale of the revenue bonds.

Although the use of revenue bonds can be traced back to the nineteenth century, they have come into widespread use only since the mid-1930's, when the federal government encouraged local governments to enact laws authorizing their use to finance public works. In recent years the volume of new revenue bonds has substantially increased as states and cities have used them to finance a wide variety of public facilities ranging from toll roads to college dormitories. At the same time the financial and legal innovators in this field have evolved new ways of creating and pledging revenues to secure revenue bonds.

Municipal Utility Revenue Bonds. The earliest and still among the most common types of revenue bonds are utility revenue obligations. Their distinctive feature is that they are secured by pledge of revenues from municipally owned utilities such as water-supply systems, sewage-disposal systems, and electric and gas utility operations. Usually the *net revenue* of such utilities, after operating expenses and provision for depreciation, is pledged to secure bonds. Enabling legislation normally includes a covenant that rates will be charged for utility services sufficient to pay debt service. Occasionally utility revenue bonds are secured by a mortgage on the utility plant.

Quasi-Utility Revenue Bonds. After the concept of financing governmentally owned utilities with revenue bonds became well established, it was applied to financing a number of other kinds of municipal facilities that are not exactly public utilities in the traditional sense of the term, but are used to render service to the public. They are generally called quasi-utilities. Airports, swimming pools, and bowling alleys come under this heading. But the most important types of quasi-utilities are roads, tunnels, and bridges for movement of automobile traffic.

Quasi-utility revenue bonds are frequently issued by public authorities or commissions created for the specific purpose of owning and operating facilities for public service. These commissions are usually created by state laws and their powers are limited to those necessary to accomplish their specific purposes. Their revenues are limited to tolls, fees, fares, and rents charged for use of the facilities they provide; ordinarily they have no taxing power.

The first of the public authorities to engage in revenue bond financing on a large scale was the Port of New York Authority, created by the states of New York and New Jersey to construct and operate bridges, tunnels, airports, and other transportation facilities in the New York metropolitan area. The "Port Authority," as it is often called, pioneered in the financing of these quasi-utilities, improved its techniques of pledging its revenues to better secure its bonds, and has been a model for other public authorities or similar instrumentalities of state government.

Special-tax Revenue Bonds. A variation of the revenue bond concept is a kind of municipal obligation generally termed special-tax revenue bonds. These bonds, usually issued by states, are payable from specified tax revenues of the issuers and only from such revenues. They differ from other categories of revenue bonds in that the revenues pledged are not the particular charges made for the particular facilities financed by sale of the bonds. The taxes pledged are usually excise taxes and they are paid by all buyers of the products on which the excise taxes are imposed. However, there is usually a relationship between the excise taxes and the purpose for which bonds are issued. The kind of tax revenue most frequently pledged is a state excise tax on gasoline; the purpose usually is construction and maintenance of roads.

Rental Revenue Bonds. Still another kind of revenue bond that has come into general use only in recent years is the rental revenue type of obligation, which is payable solely from rents received by a public body for the use of physical facilities financed by issue of the bonds. This kind of revenue bond has been used particularly to finance construction of public schools for local governments that are unwilling, or unable because of limitations imposed by state laws, to finance school construction through general obligation bonds.

Financing by revenue rental bonds sometimes requires the existence or creation of a special public body to own property to be rented, to issue bonds to finance construction or acquisition of property, to collect rents, and to apply the funds to servicing its bonds. Sometimes special legislation is necessary to authorize creation of such public bodies and to govern their operations. Thus the State of Indiana has a law authorizing the creation of school building holding companies, which are public corporations. Such a holding company sells its revenue bonds, uses the proceeds to construct a school building, leases the school building to the unit of local government that operates local schools, uses the rent to pay interest and principal on its bonds, and, when the bonds are paid off, transfers title to the school building to the local school authorities for a nominal consideration. The rents paid to school building holding companies by local governments come mainly from local tax revenues. Such bonds, therefore, rest on the same local government revenue base as general obligations.

Another kind of rental revenue bond that has appeared in the capital markets in relatively large amounts is college and university dormitory revenue bonds. The purpose, of course, is to finance construction of dormitories or other living facilities for students in institutions of higher education. The revenues pledged are the net incomes derived from rents paid by students for their rooms and charges for meals. The issuers are usually the boards of trustees, or other similar governing bodies, of the colleges and universities. Their legal liability usually is limited to the application of pledged revenues to servicing revenue bonds. Some states have created state authorities to finance construction of buildings for an entire state system of colleges and universities. Such a state authority then stands in place of the board of trustees of a particular institution, the proceeds of its bond issues may be applied to construction at several state schools, and the revenues pledged may be the net incomes of student residence facilities at several institutions.

Industrial Revenue Bonds. A kind of rental revenue bond that has come to be widely used in many states in recent years is termed an industrial revenue bond. The issuer is a city or other unit of local government; thus the bonds are municipals. Their purpose is to finance construction of a plant or other industrial facility. The plant is leased to a privately owned company and the rent paid by the company to the local government is used to pay interest on the bonds and to amortize the principal. Only the lease rentals are pledged for payment of the bonds.

The purpose of industrial revenue bonds is to attract industry to a community by offering a plant made to order for a company at a comparatively low rental. The low rental is possible because the rate of interest a local government has to pay on its industrial revenue bonds is lower than a company would have to pay if it financed a plant by sale of its own bonds. The difference is chiefly that interest on the industrial revenue bonds is exempt from the federal income tax. There has, however, been considerable criticism of the use of the tax-exempt status of municipal issues to attract industry in this manner and the Internal Revenue Code has been amended to eliminate the tax exemption for industrial revenue bond issues of relatively large size.

Local Housing Authority Obligations

The efforts of the federal government to assist local communities in redeveloping blighted areas and improving housing have given rise to a kind of municipal bond generally described as local housing authority obligations. Federal legislation provides for local governments to build and operate low-rent housing facilities with financial aid from the federal treasury through the Department of Housing and Urban Development. Local governments may themselves act as public-housing agencies, or may create special authorities for the purpose.

The basic arrangement is that the local housing agencies issue their bonds to finance housing construction. These bonds are secured by a first pledge of annual contributions unconditionally payable by HUD to the local public agencies according to a contract between the two. The annual contributions are provided by contract in an amount that, together with other funds of the Local Public Agency will be sufficient to pay the principal and interest on the bonds when due. Federal law pledges the faith of the United States to assure payment of the annual contributions by the HUD.

Local housing authority bonds may be general obligations of cities or of other units of local government having general taxing power. When issued by special public authorities, however, they are usually payable only from the HUD's annual contributions and net revenues of housing facilities. In either case the pledge of HUD's annual contributions is heavily relied on to provide the funds required for debt servicing.

FOREIGN GOVERNMENT SECURITIES

Investors are by no means limited to obligations of the government of the United States and of its political subdivisions. Foreign national or federal governments and their political subdivisions also issue bonds, and these securities are traded in their own capital markets. An American investor can buy Treasury bills of the government of Great Britain or notes of the Republic of France through a New York broker-dealer firm almost as easily as he can buy U.S. Treasury bills. However, these securities have the disadvantage of being payable in the currency of the country in which they are issued. Few investors have use for funds in foreign currencies, and the interest and principal received must eventually be converted into U.S. dollars. The hazard here is the possible depreciation of foreign currencies relative to the dollar. There is also an opportunity for gain in dollar amounts by possible depreciation of the dollar relative to the foreign currency.

To make their securities more attractive to American investors, many foreign governments and political subdivisions have created bond issues payable in dollars and have publicly distributed them in the United States through the investment banking system. From the viewpoint of their issuers, these are "external" issues; from the viewpoint of American investors they are "foreign dollar bonds."

QUESTIONS FOR DISCUSSION

1. You have invested $1,000,000 for your company in Treasury bills. Now you receive the instrument evidencing the Treasury's indebtedness, but there are no interest coupons attached and the instrument itself says nothing about payment of interest. How do you get a return on your investment?

2. You can buy U.S. Treasury notes due in 6 months to yield, say, 4.50 per cent. At the same time obligations of the Federal Home Loan Bank due in 6 months may be purchased to yield 4.83 per cent. Would you be willing to take the risk involved in the Federal Home Loan Bank obligations for the difference in yield between the two kinds of issues?

3. In your study of a particular issue of municipal bonds you find an expert legal opinion to the effect that these bonds are valid and legally binding on the city that issued them and that the city is required by law to levy on all the property taxable by the city, within the limits prescribed by the laws of the state, such property taxes as are necessary to pay the bonds and the interest on them. Are these general obligation bonds?

4. The state university you attend needs a new student union building (or an addition to the present building). You know that the legislature is not at all inclined to appropriate taxpayers' money for this purpose. Present a plan for financing such a building with details of the pledge you would have the university make to bondholders.

5. The 6 per cent preferred stock of a large electric utility company is described to you as a sort of hybrid between a bond and a stock. Your informant explains that the company's earnings are equal to several times the amounts required for the annual dividend payments and that these earnings are stable. He says that the dividend is as safe as interest on a bond, but you can never get more than the 6 per cent dividend because this preferred stock is nonparticipating. In that respect, too, it is like a bond. So what is it —a stock or a bond?

6. You own 100 shares of Electron-Electronics, Inc., and the company has informed you that you have a preemptive right to subscribe to an additional 10 shares at a price of $50 per share. The market price of this stock is $55 to $56. What will you do?
7. The Public Service Company of your state has just sold to the public a new issue of first mortgage bonds. The prospectus states that they are issued under a general mortgage dated January 31, 1945. The balance sheet shows that the company has a lot of other first mortgage bonds. How can you explain the issuance of these new bonds under that old mortgage, and the existence of a lot of other bonds that are also described as first mortgage bonds?
8. A security salesman comes in and tries to sell you a new issue of railway equipment trust certificates. The promised rate of return is good, but the railway company that is buying the new equipment is not doing very well financially. Is there anything about this kind of financing that would cause you to look with favor on the certificates?
9. Now that security salesman is back and wants to sell you some convertible debenture bonds. These bonds pay interest at 4½ per cent and the bonds are convertible into stock of the issuer at $50 per share. The bonds are described as medium-grade, which means a fairly high level of risk for bonds, and the yields on similar nonconvertible bonds in the market at present is 8½ per cent. The current market price of the stock into which the bonds are convertible is $40 a share. Will you buy some of those convertible bonds? How can you justify your purchase?
10. The next security issue offered to you is a first mortgage bond issue of a financially strong company. It looks good, but as you read the prospectus you find that the entire issue is callable at any time after 1 year from date of issue at a price of 105 per cent of par. Is this satisfactory?

3

The Markets for Securities

I. . The main elements of the market system
  A. The issuers of securities
  B. The investors in securities
  C. The middlemen in the market

II. The primary market for securities
  A. The federal Securities Act of 1933
    1. Registration of new issues
    2. The prospectus for new issues
  B. Direct placement of securities
  C. Negotiated purchase and public offering
  D. Standby underwriting of additional stock offerings
  E. Competitive bidding for new issues

III. The secondary markets for securities
  A. The Securities Exchange Act
  B. The stock exchanges
    1. Government of the exchanges
    2. Listing of securities
    3. Trading in securities
    4. The specialists
    5. Odd-lots and large blocks
    6. The automation of settlements
  C. The over-the-counter markets

In the United States and in many other countries there is a well-developed system of markets for securities. This system makes possible investment in publicly distributed security issues by enabling investors to buy or to sell according to their needs and their estimates of the future. The securities markets are wonderfully complex in all the details of their organization and procedures, and a person may spend a lifetime learning about only one aspect. But our main concern here is to see the system in perspective from the viewpoint of investors, and for this purpose it is important, first, to outline its main elements.

THE MAIN ELEMENTS OF THE MARKET SYSTEM

In the broad structure of the securities markets there are issuers of securities, investors in securities, and the middlemen in securities. To see how the system works you have to look at all three parts.

The Issuers of Securities

The federal government is the largest single issuer of securities in the securities markets. There are also the federal agency issues, which bring the total amount up to between $300 and $400 billion. So important are these issues that some broker-dealer firms specialize in making markets for them and the business of buying and selling government issues is a significant part of the business of most broker-dealer firms.

A second major category of issuers is the state and local governments. This segment has grown rapidly in size in recent years and most broker-dealer firms do a sizable business in municipals.

Corporate and foreign bonds (mostly domestic corporate) are outstanding in larger amounts than municipals and the rate of increase in recent years has been higher. Indeed, the volume of new corporate bond issues reached unprecedented levels in the late 1960s and early 1970s.

Corporate shares (mostly common stocks) taken at market value is the largest category of all. The increase in recent years is partly a result of change in market prices, but also of a marked increase in new common stocks publicly sold.

In Table 3–1 you can see the total amount of outstanding securities of each of these categories of issuers.

The Investors in Securities

Investors are sometimes divided into only two categories—individuals and institutions. But institutional investors are further differentiated by principal types of institutions. Table 3–2 shows these principal categories of securities owners.

Although there has been considerable institutionalization of investment in recent years, individuals remain by far the most important owners of secu-

TABLE 3–1

The Issuers of Securities
(Outstanding amounts in billions of dollars)

Category	End of Year 1965	1971	Percentage Increase
Federal government			
Securities included in the public debt	$ 257.7	$ 316.9	23%
Sponsored agency and other budget issues	16.4	51.7	215
Total federal government	$ 274.2	$ 368.6	35
State and local governments, short-term and long-term	100.3	166.5	66
Corporate and foreign bonds	125.7	231.6	84
Corporate shares (market value)[a]	778.0	1,085.5	40
Total amounts	$1,278.2	$1,852.2	45%

[a]Includes shares of open-end investment companies. These shares largely duplicate shares of business corporations in their portfolios.

Source: *Federal Reserve Bulletin*, June, 1972, Board of Governors of the Federal Reserve System, pp. A 73.13 and A 73.14.

rities as measured by amount of their holdings. The first line in Table 3–2, "Households, personal trusts and non-profit organizations," means essentially people. It includes securities owned directly by individuals, those held in trust for them by fiduciaries, and the holdings of non-profit organizations, which generally exist to serve people. Thus people own about 57 per cent of the outstanding securities. If the British are a nation of shopkeepers, as has been said, Americans are a nation of investors. People and institutions for their direct benefit own more than 80 per cent of all corporate shares outstanding.

This nation has by no means achieved such affluence or such uniformity in the distribution of wealth that everyone is a stockholder, but the census of shareownership conducted by the New York Stock Exchange shows that we have gone some distance in that direction. The latest figures (for 1970) show that about 31 million people owned stock in some 10,000 companies whose securities have been distributed to the public. In the decade of the 1960's the number of shareowners increased more than 50 per cent while the total population of the country increased only 6 per cent. Shareownership is by no means the sole province of the rich, as evidenced by the fact that the median household income of shareowners in 1970 was $13,500.[1]

The other five categories of investors shown in Table 3–2 are kinds of financial institutions. Commercial banks invest heavily in government and municipal bonds, but not in common stocks. Life insurance companies have the greater part of their security investments in corporate bonds, but they have been increasing the relative size of their holdings of common stocks. Pension funds, both those of private and public employers, are large investors

[1]*The 1971 Fact Book*, New York, 1971, New York Stock Exchange, p. 47.

TABLE 3–2

The Investors in Securities, end of 1971 (Amounts in billions of dollars)

Categories of Investors	*Kinds of Securities*				
	Government Obligations (including agency issues)	*State and Local Obligations*	*Corporate and Foreign Bonds*	*Corporate Shares*	*Total Securities*
A. Households, personal trusts and non-profit organizations	$ 77.1	$ 52.3	$ 47.5	$878.7	$1,055.6
B. Commercial banks and affiliates	83.5	82.9	4.0	0.5	170.9
C. Life insurance companies	4.0	3.5	79.3	20.5	107.3
D. Private pension funds	2.7	—[a]	29.0	86.6	118.3
E. State and local government retirement funds	6.0	1.9	36.2	11.2	55.3
F. Open-end investment companies	0.6	—[a]	4.9	47.1	52.6
Totals for these categories	$173.9	$140.6	$200.9	$1,044.6	$1,560.0

[a]Not reported

Source: *Federal Reserve Bulletin,* June, 1972. Board of Governors of the Federal Reserve System. pp. 73.15–73.21.

in stocks as well as in corporate bonds. The open-end investment companies (mutual funds) have the greater part of their investments in common stocks.

The Middlemen in the Market

In between the issuers of securities and the investors are the vital middlemen and their market organizations. The most general term for firms that perform the middleman function is broker-dealer. This term conveys the idea that they do business as brokers for their customers' accounts and also engage in buying and selling for their own account as dealers. Broker-dealer firms are also sometimes referred to as investment bankers, particularly when an important part of their business involves underwriting and distributing new issues of securities.

There are basically two kinds of markets for securities. One is the market for new issues, or primary market, where stocks and bonds are first offered to investors. The other kind of market, the secondary market, is the one in which securities are traded after they have been publicly distributed.

Anyone who invests in securities should know his way around in the securities markets. It may make considerable difference to him whether a security in which he is interested is listed on the New York Stock Exchange or is traded over the counter. It may make some difference to him whether the investment banking firm that handles his order is acting as broker or as dealer. If he wants to buy or sell more than a small lot, knowledge of the markets will affect his market strategy.

THE PRIMARY MARKET FOR SECURITIES

There are several ways by which new securities issues of corporate and municipal issuers may be distributed to investors. One is direct sale by an issuer to one or more institutional investors. The buyer or buyers take an entire issue directly from the issuer; there is no public offering and no public distribution. This arrangement is generally known as direct placement.

The traditional method of selling new security issues to the public, and the one still commonly used by unregulated companies, is termed negotiated purchase. Investment bankers negotiate both terms and price with a prospective issuer and when agreement is reached they purchase securities and publicly offer them to investors.

A variation of the traditional method is one in which companies determine for themselves the terms and provisions of their new issues and offer them for sale to investment bankers by competitive bids. The group of investment bankers that submits the most favorable bid buys the issue and then publicly offers the securities to investors. This method is called competitive bidding.

Obligations of the United States Treasury are sold without the aid of investment bankers. The several Federal Reserve Banks act as agent for the Treasury in offering new issues and in accepting subscriptions.

Figure 3–1 shows how the primary market for securities is organized.

The Federal Securities Act of 1933

One of the important facts of life in the securities markets is that this business is regulated rather strictly by the federal government. There were

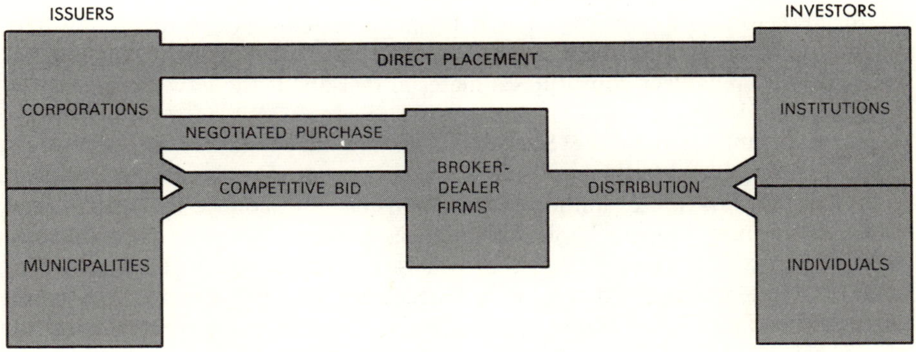

FIGURE 3–1

The Primary Market for Securities

several federal statutes enacted in the 1930's following the stock market crash and a series of revelations of practices by brokers and financial institutions that were considered contrary to the public interest. All of these statutes are administered by the Securities and Exchange Commission. The public offering of securities in interstate commerce is subject to the Securities Act, and you have to know the main outlines of this statute to understand the methods used in distributing new security issues to the public.

The Securities Act reverses the old legal principle, "let the buyer beware," and in effect substitutes the principle, "let the seller beware." There is good reason for doing so. When you buy tangible property it is reasonable to assume that you have an opportunity to examine it and, further, that you ought to do so. The principle of *caveat emptor* is not a good rule, however, when it comes to buying securities, because a bond or stock is a legal right and not tangible property that can be examined to observe its qualities. A bond is a right to receive interest, but you can tell nothing about the ability of the issuer to pay interest by looking at the piece of paper that is called a bond. You can examine the issuer's financial statements, but you have to take somebody's word for it that the statements fairly present the condition and the earnings of the business. You can personally verify little of the information used in security analysis.

The Securities Act recognizes the difference between securities and some other kinds of property by placing expressly on the seller of new issues of securities the legal responsibility to provide the buyers with truthful and reasonably complete information about them. With good reason this act has been called, "The truth in securities law."

Registration of New Issues. The heart of the Securities Act is the requirement that securities issues offered for public sale in interstate commerce, unless exempted, must be registered with the Securities and Exchange Commission. The registration statement must contain all the information about the issuing company and its business that the SEC considers necessary in the interest of investors. Although the requirements vary for different types of issuers, they generally include a full description of the kind of business conducted, the services or products sold, the physical assets owned, the identity of the directors and officers, audited financial statements for the past three years, the terms of the issuer's contract with investment bankers, and many other details. Whatever constitutes a material fact about the issuer or the issue must be included.

Important teeth in the Securities Act are the penalties for failure to comply properly with the registration requirement. The issuer and almost everyone in a position of authority or responsibility in connection with a registered issue may be held liable for damages suffered by investors as a consequence of a false statement in the registration statement, an omission of a material fact, or failure to state a fact necessary to keep a stated fact from being misleading. This liability applies to the issuer as a corporate entity, to the directors and officers personally, to the investment bankers underwriting the issue, and to the accounting and engineering experts with respect to data provided by them for the registration statement. There are also criminal penalties for fraud.

The staff of the SEC checks all registration statements for compliance with the law and the regulations. When apparent omissions or errors are found, they are pointed out to the registrant and additions or corrections are requested. If the SEC is not satisfied that a registration statement meets requirements, it may issue an order preventing the statement from becoming effective. Unless such action is taken, a statement becomes effective 20 days after it is filed. Statements for some kinds of issues may become effective after a shorter period of time by action of the Commission.

In spite of its careful scrutiny of registration statements, the SEC takes no responsibility for their accuracy or completeness and makes no finding concerning the investment merit of a registered issue. This fact should be emphasized. Some people think that, because a new security issue has been registered with the SEC, it is a good one. The most highly speculative security imaginable can be registered with the SEC, and there is always the possibility of some misrepresentation that the SEC has not detected. The SEC tries to make these things clear to the investing public by requiring on the front of each prospectus a statement in large print to the effect that it has made no finding concerning the accuracy or completeness of the statements therein. If the issue described in the prospectus is speculative by ordinary standards, there must also be a statement to that effect on the front of the prospectus. We may not always read the small print, but we should read what is written in large type.

The Prospectus for New Issues. The prospectus mentioned in the preceding paragraph is a printed document, or pamphlet, which is the principal means of making available to investors information about a new security issue. The registration statement is filed at the office of the SEC. Anyone may look at it, or obtain photocopies, but the drafters of the law realized that few investors would take such pains to examine a lengthy technical document. So they wrote into the act the second major requirement that a prospectus describing a registered issue be delivered to each buyer by the seller at or before the time of delivery of securities sold. The prospectus is an abridged aversion of the registration statement, but it tells a nearly complete story about the issuer and the issue. There are both civil and criminal penalties for failure to comply with the provisions of the law regarding the prospectus.

The Securities Act does not apply to all securities and to all transactions in securities; it has loopholes that were made deliberately. Certain types of securities are exempted from the registration requirement—mainly issues of governments, municipals, and some closely regulated business organizations such as railroads and banks. Issues in amounts of $300,000 or less need not be registered, but the SEC must be notified of their issuance and grant an exemption. Certain types of transactions are also exempted. A very important exemption involves transactions not in the process of primary distribution—in other words, regular trading on the stock exchanges and the over-the-counter markets. Registration is not required for issues distributed solely in intrastate commerce nor for those that are sold privately, that is, not publicly offered.

There is one important section of the law, however, that applies to all securities without exception. It is a general anti-fraud statute, which makes it unlawful for anyone to sell securities by means of an untrue statement of a material fact or failure to state a material fact necessary to make a statement not misleading. It is just as much a violation of the law to make a false statement to induce the purchase of a government bond as it is to misstate the facts about a gold-mining stock.

The Securities Act has provided great protection to investors generally. Its enactment inaugurated a new era for the investment banking business—an era of higher ethical standards, with more scrupulous regard for the interests of investors, and much more complete dissemination of investment information about new security issues. Complaints about the severity of the act have largely died out. Although modifications are proposed from time to time, very few people even in the financial community would like the law repealed.

Direct Placement of Securities

The direct placement of securities became a common practice after passage of the Securities Act of 1933; since that time it has sometimes increased and sometimes decreased in relative importance for corporate securities. In some years the amount of corporate bonds sold by this method has exceeded the amount distributed by public offerings. In other years it has represented a relatively small percentage of public offerings. Almost all issues sold by private placement are debt instruments.

The method itself is very simple. A company that wants to sell new securities communicates its interest to one or more investing institutions. Life insurance companies are the principal buyers of securities by this method, but pension funds and other kinds of institutional investors sometimes participate. Frequently broker-dealer firms aid in getting prospective buyer and seller together. If both sides are interested, officers of the business corporation meet with representatives of the investing institution and negotiate terms. This makes the process sound much easier than it is. In fact, negotiations are often difficult and prolonged; there are many details of the terms to be worked out and agreed on by top management people representing both the borrower and the lender.

There are several important advantages for corporate issuers in this arrangement. First, a direct placement is a private transaction, not a public offering. Thus it need not be registered under the Securities Act. Registration is not difficult, but it takes time and money. The saving in time by direct placement may be important. Second, the terms negotiated with a few sophisticated officers of financial institutions may be better suited to the issuer than the terms that would be necessary for a public offering. A third important advantage is that the issuer may continue to deal directly with institutional owners after the transaction has been completed. It is not unusual for business developments to prompt the issuer to arrange modifications in covenants, restrictions, and other terms of a security issue after it has been purchased. When such modifications do not have a materially adverse effect on the position of the institutional investor, they can usually be arranged without difficulty. Finally, it is sometimes possible for a company to place securities directly that could not be offered to the public on advantageous terms because the issuer is not well known in the security markets, or the size of the issue is too small, or even because the credit of the issuer is slightly below the quality generally acceptable in the public markets.

From the viewpoint of institutional investors these direct placements afford an opportunity to try to maximize rate of return. Because they are advantageous to issuers, institutions may be able to obtain a higher expected rate of return than they could obtain by purchasing equivalent securities in the open market. In addition, issuers sometimes give lenders an equity participation. The equity participation may take the form of an option to convert debt to common stock of the issuer at a price not far above the current market price of the stock. Or, it may be in the form of warrants, or rights, to buy stock of the issuer at a price likely to be favorable to the lender. If the borrower prospers and the price of its stock rises, the lending institution may realize a good profit on converting or exercise stock options in addition to interest income.

It is often an advantage to both sides when the flow of cash from lender to borrower can be arranged to suit their particular needs. Usually the borrower does not want the money at the time the direct placement is arranged, but prefers to "take it down" a few months or a year later when it is needed. An insurance company has a steady and fairly well predictable inflow of cash and it can arrange a disbursement schedule that matches its cash flow.

Securities placed directly are not marketable securities. They are not traded in the market, but are owned entirely by one or a few institutional lenders. Generally the investors hold these issues until they are paid off. However, it is possible for such an investor to sell part or all of its holdings of a directly placed issue to another large investor by a private transaction. Sometimes broker-dealer firms aid in arranging such transactions.

Negotiated Purchase and Public Offering

A negotiated purchase of securities from an issuer begins when the issuer approaches the investment banker (broker-dealer firm) and expresses interest in selling publicly a new issue of stocks or bonds. Terms are negotiated; the investment banker seeks to arrange those terms that will make the issue most acceptable in the public market and therefore most readily saleable. Ordinarily there is no competition among investment bankers once negotiations have begun, but corporate issuers may shop around in the preliminary stage to find the banker most interested in their proposed offering and most likely to do a good job of distributing it. There is, of course, competition in terms of performance. An investment banker who has a dissatisfied client after the deal has been completed suffers in competition for future underwritings.

When there is a substantial meeting of minds, the prospective issuer registers its issue with the Securities and Exchange Commission as required by the Securities Act for corporate issuers (with a few exceptions). The investment banking firm proceeds to organize a *purchase group*, that is, a group of other investment banking houses that joins with it in purchasing the new issue. The firm that initiated and carried on the negotiations is termed the *originator*. There may be a half-dozen to several dozen firms in the purchase group.

A few days before the registration statement is expected to become effective, the manager of the purchase group organizes a selling group. The selling group consists of a rather large number of firms that agree to participate in retail distribution of the proposed new issue. Firms with good retail sales organizations are especially sought out for membership in the selling group. There may be a dozen to a thousand firms in the group, depending on the size of the new issue and the expected intensity of the sales effort required to sell it quickly.

A day or two before the registration statement becomes effective, the members of the purchase group sign the purchase contract with the issuer. Each firm agrees to buy a stipulated amount of bonds, or shares of stock, at a price that has been negotiated; they agree to pay the issuer on the closing date—usually 2 or 3 weeks after the public offering date. At the same time they enter into an agreement among themselves to sell the securities to the public at the offering price, which is the same for all firms, and to carry on their distribution in accordance with provisions of the agreement. The firm that originated the issue is ordinarily the manager of the group, although sometimes another major firm serves as co-manager.

One of the principal powers conferred on the purchase group manager is that of stabilizing the market during the period of primary distribution. Dealers in securities usually begin trading in a new issue as soon as it is publicly offered. Sometimes investors who have been sold some of the new securities change their minds and resell in the market. Clearly it would be disastrous to the primary distribution if the market price should drop below the public offering price—investors would buy at the lower market price rather than from the investment bankers' salesmen. In order to prevent this from happening, the manager is commonly authorized to buy back in the market any bonds of a new issue offered for sale at the public offering price. In effect, the manager "pegs" the market price. This operation is entirely lawful, provided public notice is given and provided there is no upward manipulation of the market price. It is of course discontinued when the primary distribution is complete or has been abandoned.

Figure 3–2 diagrams the relationship of issuer, purchase group, and selling group.

The big selling effort begins immediately after the registration statement becomes effective. Prospectuses are sent to all members of the purchase and selling groups. The manager of the purchase group offers some part of the new issue to the selling group. He may offer the selling group firms a specified

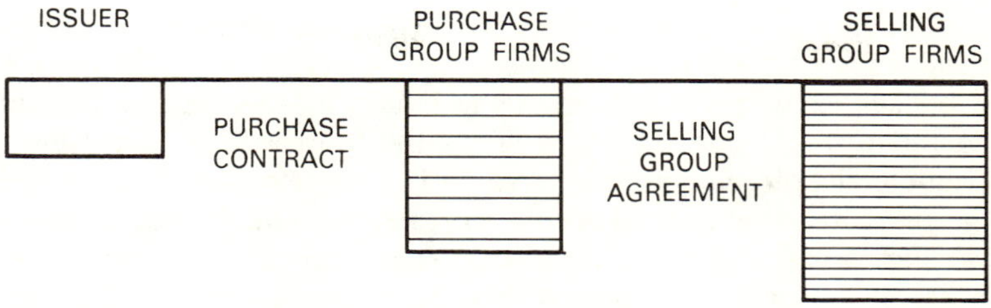

FIGURE 3–2

Organization of Investment Bankers for Purchase and Public Offering

number of bonds or shares, or he may ask them to subscribe for the amount they think they can sell. On the date of offering, a display advertisement announcing the issue appears in financial publications and newspapers, and the members of both the purchase group and the selling group begin retailing the issue.

The members of the purchase group are the *underwriters*, meaning that they have bought the issue and they are the ones that stand to lose if the offering is not successful. Usually each firm in the purchase group reserves a portion of the bonds or shares it has bought for its own retail distribution, and gives up the balance of its portion to the manager. The manager offers the securities given up to the selling group. Sometimes the manager offers a portion of the issue to large institutional investors for the purchase group's account. The movement of securities in the process of distribution is illustrated in Figure 3–3.

Investment bankers make their profit just as other merchants do, by

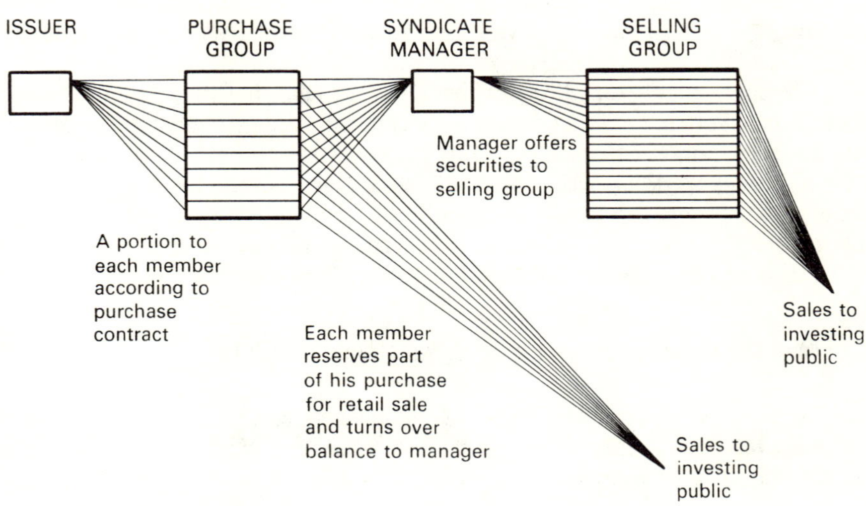

FIGURE 3–3

The Movement of Securities in the Distribution Process

selling at prices higher than the prices they pay. The total mark-up on a large corporate bond issue of good quality is usually less than 1 per cent of par. That is, the bankers may buy bonds from the issuer at, say, 98 per cent of par and offer them to the public at 98⅞. Thus the "spread," as it is usually called, is seven-eighths of one percentage point. The members of the purchase group get the full spread on securities sold for their account by the manager and on those they retail themselves. They must of course pay their shares of purchase group expenses and their own retail selling expenses. But they get only a part of the spread on securities retailed by members of the selling group, because the selling group firms are allowed a discount from the public offering price. If the total spread is seven-eighths of a point, the selling group discount might be one-half of a point. Thus they would buy from the purchase group at 98⅜, sell at the offering price of 98⅞, and make a gross profit of one-half of 1 point. Members of the purchase group would get the difference between the price they paid the issuer (98) and the price at which they sell to the selling group firms (98⅜). This is their compensation for the risk they have assumed as underwriters. Firms that are not members of the selling group may "sell off the list" of a member and receive an allowance of perhaps one-eighth of a point.

The underwriting risk is a very real one. There is always the hazard that the investment bankers may misjudge the market and price an issue too high. Or, more commonly, there is the risk of a general decline in market prices to such an extent as to make the new issue unattractive to investors at the public offering price. Then the underwriters may reduce the offering price by agreement among themselves and complete the distribution. If an unsold portion remains on the closing date, when the bankers have to pay the issuer and when the agreements among themselves expire, the usual practice is for each firm to take its portion of the unsold securities and try to find buyers when it can at whatever prices it can get. There have been instances in which losses realized in this manner have substantially impaired the capital of underwriting firms.[2]

There are many variations in the arrangements that investment bankers make with issuers for a negotiated sale and in the arrangement the investment bankers make among themselves. But they are simply modifications of the basic pattern just described. There are also great differences in the size of spreads on new security issues. Generally, the greater the risk, the more difficult the selling job, and the smaller the size of the issue, the larger is the spread as a percentage of public offering price.

Standby Underwriting of Additional Stock Offerings

New issues of common stock of established companies are sometimes sold to investment bankers by negotiated arrangements in much the same manner that corporate bonds are sold. However, there are two other principal

[2] Wall Streeters have some colorful language to describe their experience in selling new security issues. An issue that sells quickly is said to "go out the window." One that sells poorly is "a turkey"; one that sells very poorly is a "turkey with feathers."

methods of marketing additional issues of stock after an initial public distribution of stock. By one method additional stock is offered to stockholders of a company on a subscription basis; that is, they are allowed to subscribe to one share of additional stock for some specified number of shares presently owned. The subscription price of the additional stock is somewhat below the market price of outstanding stock at the time of offering. Thus there is an inducement to stockholders to subscribe. If some stockholders do not exercise their rights to subscribe, or do not sell their rights to someone else who does, the entire new issue is not sold.

The alternative to that method is to make the offering to stockholders but to have it underwritten by investment bankers. The usual practice is for the issuing corporation to issue to each of its stockholders "rights" to subscribe to as many shares of the new stock as will increase the number of shares he owns in the same proportion that the total number of outstanding shares will be increased by the stock offering. Thus, if the total number of outstanding shares is to be increased by 10 per cent, each stockholder will receive rights to subscribe to the number of shares that will increase his holdings by 10 per cent.

The rights are evidenced by certificates issued to the stockholders. One "right" is the right attached to one share of stock owned on a specified date immediately preceding the date of offering; if you owned 100 shares, you would get 100 rights. If the total number of shares outstanding is to be increased 20 per cent, each of your rights would entitle you to subscribe to one-fifth of a new share.

These stock rights are negotiable. If you are unable or unwilling to subscribe for additional stock, you can sell them in the market and the buyer can exercise your rights to subscribe to the new stock. The rights have value, provided the offering price for the new stock is less than the prevailing market price for the outstanding stock. If, for example, the offering price is $40 a share and the market price is $50, one can get the stock $10 per share cheaper by exercising rights. If five rights are required to subscribe to one share of new stock, each right would be worth $2.00. Actually, a right would have to be priced at a little less than $2.00 in order for a buyer to obtain any advantage from buying rights and subscribing to new stock. Usually the subscription period is about 3 weeks; at the end of the period subscription rights expire.

You might think that whenever new stock is offered to current stockholders at a price well below the market price they would be sure to buy all the stock offered. But this is not so. For one thing, some stockholders do nothing with their rights because they do not understand the meaning of the offer; some are unable or unwilling to subscribe to additional stock and do not realize that they can sell their rights; and some neglect to do anything within the subscription period. A greater hazard to success of a rights offering, however, is the threat of a substantial decline in market price for the stock during the subscription period. If the market price dropped from $50 to $40, and the subscription price is $40, there would be no advantage to stockholders in exercising their rights and the rights would be of no value.

If a large portion of new stock issue offered in this manner remains unsold, the company will fail to obtain the amount of new capital it intended to raise. The danger of failure of a rights offering is the reason why many companies have such new stock issues underwritten by investment bankers. The underwriting agreement, when this arrangement is used, provides that the investment bankers will purchase whatever amount of stock is not subscribed for by the exercise of rights. Thus it is termed a *standby underwriting*. The issuer is assured that all the stock offered will be sold and that it will obtain the full amount of capital to be raised by the issue. The investment bankers, of course, have to resell whatever amount of stock they buy in this manner.

The organization of investment bankers for a standby underwriting is much the same as that for a negotiated purchase and distribution of an entire issue. One firm works out the underwriting agreement with the issuer and then invites a number of other firms to join it in the agreement. Usually each firm in the underwriting group assumes liability for a percentage of the total amount of new stock offered and takes that proportion of whatever amount is not subscribed by the use of rights. The underwriting group may publicly re-offer whatever stock they are obliged to take up at the same offering price, or the members may each take their shares and distribute the stock through their own retail selling facilities at whatever prices they can get.

Standby underwriting is used most frequently in connection with the offering of additional common stock to existing common stockholders. However, it may also be used when preferred stock is offered to common stockholders or even for the offering of bonds to stockholders, particularly convertible bonds. It is used occasionally in corporate reorganizations when stockholders of a company in financial trouble are offered rights to subscribe to securities of a new company created in reorganization.

Competitive Bidding for New Issues

Another way in which investment bankers buy new security issues outright from issuers for distribution to investors is by competitive bidding. A prospective issuer sends out invitations to the investment banking community to bid on a new security issue; the invitation describes the proposed issue and the terms of sale. The bankers submit bids for the issue, stating the price they will pay for it, and the firm that bids the highest price gets the issue. The issuer must work out all the details, register with the Securities and Exchange Commission when that is required, and be able to offer to the investment bankers a finished issue of securities that they can proceed at once to distribute. Thus competitive bidding is quite different from negotiated purchase.

Most state and local governments sell their bond issues by competitive bidding. In fact, the practice orginated in this area as a means of preventing collusion between local government officials and investment bankers in the sale of new issues. Today state laws generally require competitive bidding for municipal issues. The sale of corporate issues by competitive bidding dates from the 1940's when the Securities and Exchange Commission ruled that all public utility holding companies and their subsidiaries subject to its jurisdiction under the Public Utility Holding Company Act must sell their new securities by competitive bidding, unless exempted by the Commission. The Interstate Commerce Commission adopted a similar rule for railroad companies. The securities sold by this method are chiefly bonds.

The investment banking firms organize to bid for new issues in much the same manner that they form purchase groups for negotiated purchases. When it becomes known that an issue is to be offered for sale by bidding, several of the leading firms set about forming groups to submit bids. At first membership is tentative and there are often changes in membership up to the date of bidding. The price to be bid is discussed in group meetings, but frequently the exact figure is not agreed on until the morning of the sale.

The bidding actually takes place at a time and place that have been made known to the bankers well in advance, usually at about noon, at the office of the issuer. Representatives of the groups meet with the appropriate corporate officials and submit sealed bids. At the hour fixed for the sale the bids are opened, usually in the presence of the bidders, and the most favorable bid to the issuer is determined. The most favorable bid on a bond issue is the one that provides the lowest interest cost to the issuer. When a common stock is sold, the highest price per share is the best bid. A sale is completed at once to the best bidder, and that group in turn proceeds promptly to make a public offering of the issue.

THE SECONDARY MARKETS FOR SECURITIES

When the primary distribution of security issues has been completed, further transactions are between investors, with brokers or dealers as middlemen. Investors who bought securities in the primary distribution of an issue often decide for one reason or another to sell them, and investors who were not able or willing to buy when securities were initially offered subsequently become interested in buying them. There is an economic need for markets in publicly distributed issues.

In fact, the secondary markets do more business in dollar value and are much more in the public eye than the primary market. There are about 5,000 issues of stocks and bonds listed on all the stock exchanges and about 14,000 issues are quoted more or less regularly by dealers in over-the-counter securities. The value of all transactions on the stock exchanges runs in excess of $125 billion a year. There is no tabulation of the annual value of trading in the over-the-counter market, but it is believed to exceed that of the exchanges, so we are talking about something like $250 billion in value of transactions per year. Public interest in activities in these secondary markets is widespread. News of changes in prices is disseminated daily by all the principal news media, and any unusual rise or decline in stock prices is front-page news.

The structure of the secondary markets for securities is shown in Figure 3–4.

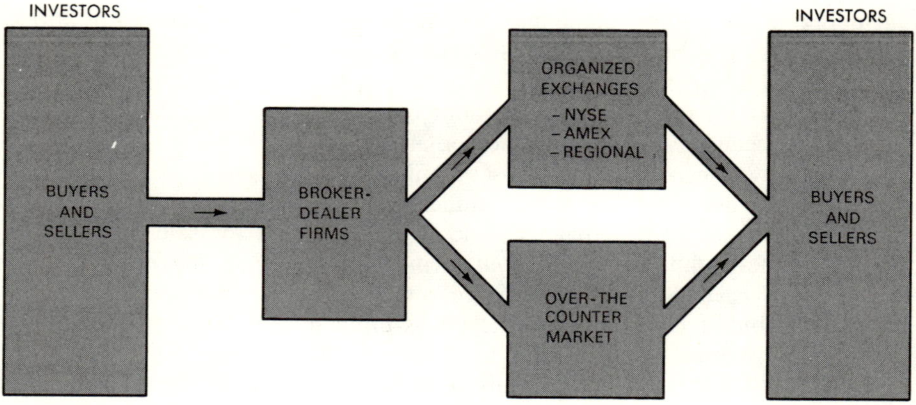

FIGURE 3–4

The Structure of the Secondary Markets

The Securities Exchange Act

During most of their history the securities markets operated without governmental regulation or supervision of any kind. But the stock market crash of 1929 caused a great outcry from a public that had been hurt in its pocketbook. Congress responded by passing the Securities Exchange Act, which established a very strict system of federal supervision of the stock exchanges by the Securities and Exchange Commission.

The Securities Exchange Act requires all stock exchanges operating in interstate commerce to register with the SEC (unless exempted because their operations are too small to be of public interest). The Commission may refuse registration of an exchange on the grounds that its rules are unsatisfactory or that administration is inadequate to enforce them. Registration of an exchange, once granted, may be suspended or withdrawn for violation of the act or the regulations of the Commission, or for failure to enforce compliance on its members. This registration requirement, then, is a powerful lever to bring about strict rules and their effective enforcement.

The SEC may suspend or expel from an exchange any officer or member found guilty of violating the act. It may make rules for registered exchanges or invalidate rules made by the exchanges. It has the right of entry and examination of the records of a registered exchange and may completely suspend trading on an exchange, with the approval of the President of the United States, in a period of emergency.

A second major provision of the act is that all securities listed on registered security exchanges must be registered with the SEC by their issuers. This is very much like registration under the Securities Act, in that a statement must be filed containing detailed information about the issue and the issuer. This provision extended the federal requirement for full disclosure of information to many securities issues not registered under the Securities Act. Registration statements must be kept up to date by filing annual reports with the SEC, and in recent years issuers have been required to file quarterly earnings statements.

These registration requirements of the Securities Act and the Securities Exchange Act have exerted a strong influence in the direction of more complete, more accurate, and more uniform reporting of corporate financial information. Today companies subject to these federal laws must conduct their financial affairs in the proverbial goldfish bowl. The investor has benefited. People still make mistakes in judging securities, but their mistakes are seldom caused by unavailability of pertinent information.

The Securities Exchange Act also contains provisions aimed at correcting various specific abuses in the securities markets. Manipulation of stock prices in any manner is outlawed. Corporate insiders, defined as directors, officers, and principal stockholders, are not permitted to sell short their company's stock and they may be compelled to turn over to their company any profit made on a purchase and sale transaction in stock of their company completed within 6 months.

When the Securities Exchange Act was drafted, its sponsors wanted it to provide for regulation of all the securities markets. But the amorphous, unorganized over-the-counter market presented such a difficult problem of regulation that it was temporarily bypassed. Finally it was concluded that the best way to regulate this market was through an organization of security dealers that would establish and enforce rules of business conduct for its members. The Maloney Amendment to the Securities Exchange Act authorized such an organization, and the National Association of Security Dealers was created in 1939.

Most firms of importance in the investment banking business are now members of the NASD and subject to its rules of fair business practice. The rules are enforced through a system of regional business conduct committees composed of members of the Association. A member found guilty of improper practice may be suspended or expelled from the Association. These penalties are serious, not only because of the damage done to business reputations but also because they mean loss of the discounts and allowances on security sales that members may grant only to members. Disciplinary action by the NASD is subject to review by the SEC.

The SEC was not entirely satisfied with the system of regulation of the over-the-counter markets and further study provided evidence of need for stronger regulatory legislation. Upon recommendation of the Commission, Congress enacted a law, commonly referred to as the Securities Acts Amendments of 1964, which greatly extended federal regulation both of security issues and of broker-dealer firms in the over-the-counter market.

One major portion of the 1964 legislation extended to a large number of over-the-counter issues and their issuers certain rules for the protection of investors such as have long been in effect for exchange-listed issues. The law now requires over-the-counter companies with 500 or more shareholders and more than $1 million in assets to file a registration statement with the SEC containing material information regarding their businesses and to keep such information current by periodic reports. The general effect is to require reporting of information about over-the-counter issues registered with the SEC comparable to the requirement for listed securities.

A second portion of the new law increased the authority of the SEC over broker-dealer firms in the over-the-counter markets. It authorized the Commission to set standards for entrance of firms into the securities business, particularly with respect to amount of capital required, and also to require registered securities associations (the National Association of Securities Dealers is the only such association) to adopt rules establishing standards of training, experience, and competence for their members and for employees of member firms.

The Stock Exchanges

A stock exchange is an organization of individuals and firms established to trade among themselves in securities. Historically they were membership associations and only members were permitted to use their facilities and to be represented in their management. More recently the corporate form has come to be favored. An exchange makes and administers rules that govern member firms in trading and in their relationships with their customers.

In the United States there are less than a dozen securities exchanges registered with the Securities and Exchange Commission. Two are national exchanges—the New York Stock Exchange and the American Stock Exchange, both located in New York City. The others are regional exchanges located in principal cities such as Chicago, Boston, Philadelphia, San Francisco, and Los Angeles. The New York Stock Exchange is by far the largest in number of securities issues listed and in volume of trading. The regional exchanges, however, perform an important function as markets for securities owned by investors in their geographical areas, and many stocks listed on the New York exchanges are also listed on regional exchanges. A considerable part of the volume of trading on these regional exchanges is represented by transactions in dually listed issues.

Since the New York Stock Exchange is the largest and since the other exchanges are organized and operated in much the same manner, a description of "the Big Board" will serve for organized exchanges generally.

Government of the Exchanges. For a long time the New York Stock Exchange was organized and operated like a private club. Members elected a Board of Governors that supervised the activities of the Exchange; members served on standing committees to attend to several principal phases of the association's business. Only members had a voice in the government and operation of the Exchange. That picture has changed drastically. Today the Exchange is organized as a corporation under the Not-For-Profit-Corporation law of the State of New York. There is now a Board of Directors comprised of twenty-one persons. Ten directors are public members, that is, they are not engaged in the securities business. Ten are securities industry directors; they are the principal executive officers of their broker-dealer firms. The twenty-first member is the Chairman of the Board, who is elected by the other twenty. He is the chief excutive officer of the Exchange, devotes full time to its management, and must sever any other business connections, including his connection with any broker-dealer firm. The Chairman appoints other officers of the Exchange.[3]

The membership of the Exchange is limited to 1,366 persons. Members are generally partners or senior officers of member firms, and a member firm, of course, is one that includes one or more members in its senior management personnel. One can become a member by purchasing a membership from a retiring member and by passing the close scrutiny of the Committee on Admissions. A membership usually sells for $200,000 to $300,000; it is valuable because it gives the right to engage in what is usually a profitable business.

The government of the exchanges makes rules that members and member firms must follow in their dealings with each other and with the public. In a recent period of considerable stress there have been some important rule changes that profoundly affect the conduct of the brokerage business and the operations of the exchange.

From the very beginning the New York Stock Exchange has prescribed by rule the minimum schedule of brokerage fees that its member firms could charge their customers for executing transactions. The fee schedule was designed chiefly for transactions in lots of 100 shares or small multiples of that number. But in recent years there has been a great increase in the number and volume of transactions in large lots, or blocks, of stock for the accounts of institutional investors. In one recent period about two-thirds of total public trading (in dollar volume) on the NYSE was for institutions and intermediaries. In the same period about one-sixth of total reported share volume consisted of large blocks of stock (defined as transactions of 10,000 shares or more).[4] Institutional investors protested vigorously that charges for large transactions were excessive because they were based on a fee schedule for 100 shares. The commission on a 10,000 share transaction was simply 100 times the fee for a 100-share lot. The Exchange yielded, after some pressure from the SEC, and adopted a new schedule in which commissions are based chiefly upon value of transactions. It also provides that for transactions with value in excess of $300,000 the commission on value in excess of that amount is subject to negotiation. The latter provision was an important breach in the tradition that there should be a minimum commission. Some members of the financial community think that the minimum commission schedule should be abolished entirely so that brokers could charge whatever fees they can negotiate with their customers.

[3]*Annual Report* 1971, The New York Stock Exchange, Inc., p. 4.

[4]*1971 Public Transaction Study*, New York, 1972, Research Department—New York Stock Exchange, Inc., p. 4.

Some large institutional investors have expressed desire to be permitted to become members of the NYSE so that they can execute their own purchases and sales and so avoid paying brokerage commissions. Certain regional exchanges have accepted institutions as members and the New York markets have accepted institutional membership in principle.

An important rule change in the past several years is one that permits member firms to make public offering of their own securities to investors. This rule change abandons the tradition that member firms must be privately owned. At one time they had to be organized as partnerships; then they were allowed to incorporate but not to sell their securities to the public. The change had to be made because the amount of capital required for large member firms became so great that it could not be provided in the traditional way. Presently several dozen member firms have "gone public" and some have their own securities listed on the NYSE.

Listing of Securities. The members of the New York Stock Exchange may use its facilities to trade only in security issues that have been listed. Many years ago the Exchange began to establish certain requirements that companies had to meet before their securities could be listed, and these requirements have gradually become stricter. One important purpose is to provide adequate and reliable information about securities and their issuers for the benefit of investors. Another is to assure some minimum degree of marketability.

The Exchange has long required, as a condition of listing a company's securities, that the company publish annual (and usually quarterly) reports to its stockholders. Companies must agree to inform the Exchange authorities of any major development in their corporate affairs, to submit to certain requirements concerning the form and content of published financial statements, and not to engage in certain financial practices that might be detrimental to their securities holders. Among other things, the Exchange will not list a common stock issue without voting rights.

For a company seeking an original listing of its stock the Exchange presently requires a minimum of 2,000 round-lot stockholders (owners of 100 share or more), a minimum of 1 million shares in the hands of the public, a market value of at least $16 million for publicly held shares, and for the listing company a minimum amount of net tangible assets of $16 million. Pre-tax income of the company must be at least $2.5 million for the most recent year and $2 million for each of the two preceding years.

Trading in Securities. The members of the Exchange buy and sell securities in the large main trading room and in a smaller room called the annex. The main room is something like the interior of a gymnasium. It has a high ceiling and a hardwood floor. Spaced about on the floor are the trading posts, around the perimeter are telephone booths, and on both side walls are annunciator boards used to call members to their clerks at the telephone booths. Recently a system of radio paging of members has been introduced. At one end of the main room is a visitors' gallery from which people may observe trading on the floor. Bonds and the less actively traded stocks are traded in the annex.

Orders to buy and sell securities converge on this trading floor from all over the country and, indeed, from all over the world. Orders are relayed to the telephone clerks who call members representing their firms by uncovering their numbers on the annunciator boards, or by radio. A member goes to his clerk, or sends a page, to receive orders.

Each listed stock is assigned to a "post," which is a horseshoe-shaped structure. When a member receives a market order, that is, an order to buy or to sell at the best price immediately obtainable, he moves to the post where the stock is traded. Each stock is assigned to a particular position on a post and there is a specialist for each stock. Specialists make the market in their stocks by standing ready to buy or to sell at prices they quote.

A broker with a market order to sell a stock goes to the specialist and asks for a quote. The quote might be, "80 to a half." This means that if you want to sell, he will buy from you at 80; that is the bid price. If you want to buy, he will sell to you at 80½; that is the offer price. A broker with a market order to sell might shout to other brokers nearby an offer to sell at a slightly higher price than the specialist's bid price. If someone accepts his offer at a higher price than the specialist's bid, a transaction is executed. If not, he sells to the specialist at the specialist's bid price.

When a transaction is made, each party makes a note of it. The broker sends his note back to the telephone clerk who relays information that the stock has been sold at the price indicated to his firm's office. The firm then reports the execution to the customer. The specialist hands his note of the transaction to his clerk inside the trading post, and among other things, the clerk reports the transaction to the ticker-tape operator who puts it on the tape.

One of the distinctive features of the New York Stock Exchange (and others) is that all transactions are reported to the public by printing on tape, which is reproduced instantaneously by machines in the offices of all subscribers to the reporting service. The identities of the parties to transactions are not disclosed, but the name of the stock, the number of shares, and the price all appear on the tape. Many newspapers publish stock prices daily.

These trading methods are being changed by automation and modern electronic devices. A pilot program to test a method of executing 100-share orders automatically by a computerized system is now underway. A more revolutionary concept, still in the planning stage, is the "locked in trade." The first step in the locked in trade system is complete automation of the order delivery system. Each order originating in a broker's office will be entered into a computer from a remote terminal and then transmitted from the broker's computer to one at the Exchange. The Exchange computer will add any coding needed to make the written order machine readable and reproduce it on a printer located on the trading floor near the broker to whom it is addressed. The broker will execute the order in the usual way and write the price on the order. The opposite party does the same. Both "tickets" will be handed to an Exchange employee who puts them back into the Exchange computer system. An optical scanner will read the two tickets and if they do not match, they will be returned to the brokers who wrote them. If they do, the transaction is reported to the Exchange's ticker system, to the service for settling transactions, and to the firms represented by the buying and selling brokers. Then all the record keeping is done by automation, including the printing of the order confirmations for the customers. It is said that this system will virtually eliminate error in handling orders and greatly reduce the volume of paper work to be done manually.[5]

Another project in the process of development is a "composite tape." This system would report all transactions in securities on all organized exchanges, and eventually transactions in the over-the-counter market as well, on one tape. The public would then have the opportunity to observe market prices as they are made and wherever they are made. Some imaginative people are talking about a central market that would combine the organized exchanges and the over-the-counter markets into what would be for all practical purposes one market.

One of the "electronic dreams" involves a trading console that would enable a person to sit in his air-conditioned office and communicate with whatever other person in the entire system of securities markets he may want to do business with. This concept includes the use of closed-circuit television so that the people engaged in trading may see one another. If this dream should become reality, it would eliminate the need for a trading floor and the face-to-face communication that characterizes the organized markets.

The Specialists. The function of the specialists is one of the most interesting and controversial in the entire financial community. Specialists have been vigorously criticized throughout the modern history of the Exchange for playing dual roles involving potential conflict of interest, but no one has yet figured out how the Exchange can operate without them.

Many members of the New York Stock Exchange are designated as specialists. Each does business in the one or more stocks assigned to him. Sometimes they merely execute orders for other brokers and receive commissions for their services as agents. At other times they buy and sell stocks for their own account and thus act as dealers. Often they have to decide in a split second whether to assume the role of broker or dealer in a particular transaction.

The use of price-limit orders is the main reason why some members have to serve as specialists. A price-limit order is an order to buy (or to sell) at not more than (or less than) a stipulated price that is "away from" the current market quotation. An investor may be willing to sell 100 shares of stock at, say, 90, when the current bid is 85. He places a price-limit order to sell at 90. The broker cannot execute this order, because the price stipulated is too high, so he turns it over to a specialist in the stock to execute at some time in the future when and if a transaction is executed at 90 or better. Such orders must have a time limit, too, so that they expire if they are not executed within a specified time period. A price-limit order may be good for the remainder of a day, the remainder of a week, or the remainder of a month.

[5]"Wall Street vs. Paper Work," *The Exchange*, September, 1969, pp. 11–34, The New York Stock Exchange.

The specialist who receives a price-limit order enters it in his book along with other price-limit orders for the same stock. Some are orders to sell above the current price and some to buy below the current price. He has a supply-demand schedule for the stock, insofar as supply and demand have been evidenced by price-limit orders.

When a broker comes along with a market order to sell, the specialist has to decide whether to buy the stock for his own account as a dealer, or to buy it as a broker to fill a price-limit order. This is the way possible conflict of interest arises. You might think that the problem could be solved simply by prohibiting specialists from buying and selling for their own account. But that is not a satisfactory solution because transactions by specialists for their own account are sometimes needed to provide reasonable price continuity, a condition in which the price at which a stock is bought and sold changes by no more than fractions of a point from one transaction to another.

The rules of the Exchange have long imposed on specialists the duty of providing price continuity for the stocks in which they specialize. In order to do so they are often obliged to buy for their own account to prevent a sharp downward change of price that would result from matching a sell order with the buy order at the top of the list of price-limit orders, or a sharp upward change of price on execution of the lowest price-limit sell order against a buy order.

The Securities Exchange Act provides that specialists' transactions as dealers must be restricted "so far as practicable to those reasonably necessary to maintain a fair and orderly market." The SEC's interpretation stresses the restrictive tenor of this provision of the statute and holds that specialists' transactions as dealers must be justified on the basis of providing price continuity and stability. The rules prohibit specialists from buying or selling for themselves at the same prices at which they have price-limit orders on their books, and places on them heavy responsibility for stabilizing prices in any period of unusual changes in prices. All specialists' transactions are scrutinized by the staff of the Exchange and anyone who does not perform his function satisfactorily according to the general rules may be penalized by the Exchange to the extent of removal from his assignment as specialist.

Odd-lots and Large Blocks. There are some investors who want to buy and sell in odd-lots, that is, in numbers of shares less than 100 and there are many who buy and sell in lots of several thousand shares or more. The Exchange has special provisions for both the large and the small investors.

Traditionally odd-lot orders were handled by two member firms to whom these orders were transmitted. The procedure is to execute each odd-lot order at the price of the next ensuing round-lot transaction in the stock to be bought or sold. The odd-lot dealers add to that price $0.125 per share when an odd-lot is purchased to compensate them for their service, and they deduct the same fee from market price on orders to sell.

Recently this operation has been largely automated. All odd-lot orders are entered into the Exchange's switching computers and transmitted to the office of one of the odd-lot dealers. There other computers price the orders automatically on the basis of round-lot sales data furnished by the Exchange. Reports of executions are returned instantly to the originating firms through the Exchange's computer system.

The demand by institutional investors for efficient execution of large blocks of stock has led to the development of several special procedures for these orders. A block is an order for 10,000 shares or more in a single transaction. There have been single transactions with a value of as much as $50 million.

The simplest method of executing a block transaction is by a cross. One member firm gets an order to sell a block of a stock; it then finds buyers for that block at an agreed price. The member firm crosses the orders on the floor of the Exchange.

A second method is a specialist block purchase or sale. A firm with an order to sell may negotiate the sale with the specialist in the stock and the transaction takes place outside the regular auction market on the floor. Still a third method is to offer a block of stock for sale to all member firms at a price printed on the ticker tape. Purchases at the offered price are executed on the floor but not as part of the auction market.

There are a number of large broker-dealer firms that specialize in "block positioning." These firms often buy stock offered in large blocks for their own account and then endeavor quickly to resell it to investors at a price higher than the price paid. Sometimes they do not obtain a higher price on some or all of the block and may indeed incur a loss on the transaction. This is called "taking a bath."

The Exchange has also moved in another direction to improve facilities for large-block transactions by establishing its Block Automation System, which is often referred to simply as BAS. This system consists essentially of a computer, terminals in subscribers' offices, and wires linking them together. Member firms and financial institutions may be subscribers. Subscribers may make known their interest in a stock by entering into the computer the stock symbol, whether the interest is in buying or selling; the number of shares; and the name of the member firm authorized to handle any transaction that may ensue. However, the identity of the institution making the entry is not revealed. Other subscribers may view the entry on their display tubes. When a match is made by another subscriber indicating interest in becoming the opposite party, further negotiation is carried on between brokers representing the subscribers. When agreement is reached, the transaction is executed on the floor of the Exchange.

A private organization has established a similar service that goes one step further by enabling subscribers to negotiate directly and to trade with one another without brokers as intermediaries.

The Automation of Settlements. By the rules of the Exchanges securities sold are to be delivered and paid for on the fifth business day following execution. Until quite recent years most of this work was done manually and when volume of trading increased to relatively high levels the system did not work well. Frequently it was not possible for broker-dealer firms to make delivery within the specified period and at one time "fails to deliver" caused a partial breakdown of the whole securities markets system.

However, the problem of automating paper work was recognized years ago and the New York Stock Exchange began development of its Central Certificate Service. This is another application of the computer to the handling of paper work. The CCS, which is now fully operational, is a central depository for stock listed on both the New York Stock Exchange and the American Stock Exchange, and owned by member firms as well as by certain financial institutions. Records of stock ownership are in the computer's memory system and transfers of ownership of stock from one depositor to another can be made by computer instructions. It is expected that this service will be expanded to include securities listed on the regional exchanges, and it seems likely that in time the automated transfer system will make obsolete the use of conventional stock certificates.

The Over-the-Counter Markets

The second major division of the secondary markets is known by the archaic term "over-the-counter markets." In the more remote history of the financial community securities were actually bought, sold, and delivered over the counter of a securities dealer in much the same manner as beaver pelts or Indian blankets. Today's over-the-counter markets are really over-the-telephone markets.

The investing public generally has little familiarity with the O-T-C market. There is no organization comparable to the Exchange, there is no one place where trading is carried on, and there is no listing of securities. The principal firms who make this market generally do not deal directly with individual investors, but they do a large business with institutions.

An over-the-counter market exists wherever a securities firm "makes a market" in a security issue. A firm makes a market when it quotes prices at which it will buy or sell an issue to other members of the financial community or to investors. A local securities firm in Kansas City that makes a market for a few municipal issues operates one of the O-T-C markets, and so does the big dealer in New York City who regularly makes a market in 500 or more stock and bond issues. There are more than 4,000 members of the National Association of Security Dealers, the national organization of firms doing business as security dealers.

The O-T-C market developed historically as a market for bonds and the principal customers were institutional bond investors. However, there has long been a substantial volume of trading in common stocks and in recent years the volume of stock trading has multiplied many times. Considerable impetus to growth in stock trading has been provided by NASDAQ, which is an automated system that enables subscribers to view current price quotations for any of a large list of O-T-C stocks on a display tube. NASDAQ stands for National Association of Security Dealers Automated Quotations service.

The heart of the O-T-C market is the wholesale dealer firms who make markets, that is, who stand ready to buy and sell at quoted prices the securities in which they are registered as market makers by the National Association of Security Dealers. Some firms specialize in bonds, some in stocks, and some deal in a long list of stocks and bonds. The wholesale market is largely an inter-dealer market; market makers deal with one another and with retail firms that in turn serve the public. Most firms, however, deal directly with large institutional investors.

The larger dealer firms are linked together and transact their business by private telephone leased wires and by teletype. In their trading rooms there may be several dozen persons who sit all day at their telephones buying and selling securities.

Individual investors do business with retail firms. If you want to buy an O-T-C stock, you would place your order with the firm that regularly handles your business. The retail firm may buy the stock you want for its own account from a dealer and resell it to you at a mark-up. If it does so, it must disclose to you that it is acting as principal and it may not charge a commission. Most retail firms, however, handle their customers' orders as brokers, buy at the dealer's offering price, and charge you a brokerage commission.

One distinctive feature of the O-T-C market is that transactions are not reported to the public. If you buy 50 bonds, or sell 100 shares of stock, no one knows it but you and the retailer who acted for you. Another feature of the O-T-C market is that it includes trading in Exchange-listed stocks. Member firms of the Exchange may not execute trades off the floor without following a prescribed procedure, but there are important broker-dealer firms that are not members. Many trades in listed stocks are for large blocks; sometimes investors think they can get better negotiated prices in this market than they can get on the Exchange. Trading in listed stocks has been dubbed "the third market." It is not a third market but a component of the O-T-C market.

The O-T-C market shared the tribulations of the exchanges during the crisis period of several years ago and, like the exchanges, it has moved vigorously to improve its system of communications and settlement of transactions. The organization primarily responsible for improvement is the National Association of Security Dealers, and its greatest achievement to date is the automated quotation service. In the course of development is an automated system of reporting transactions in securities in the over-the-counter market that will be comparable to the composite tape of the organized exchanges. There is talk of one central tape that will report transactions both on the exchanges and in the over-the-counter market.

Another project of the NASD is an automated system for settling transactions similar to the Central Certificate Service of the New York exchanges. And of course the concept of a trading console is as readily adaptable to trading over-the-counter as to trading on the exchanges.

QUESTIONS FOR DISCUSSION

1. What makes you think that only rich people own securities?

2. One of your anti-establishment friends says that the big financial institutions make stock prices go up and down according to the way they want them to move. What do you think of that?

3. Some one tries to sell you some stock in a small company. You ask for a prospectus, and he says there is no prospectus. The stock is not required to be registered under the Securities Act, he says, because it is too small and it is being offered for sale only within the state in which you reside. Is that a reasonable explanation?

4. How do the investment bankers make a profit on a new public offering of securities?

5. Should all companies be required to sell their new issues of securities by competitive bidding?

6. Would you say that the organized securities markets are pretty well under the thumb of the Securities and Exchange Commission?

7. The New York Stock Exchange used to be called "a private club." What is it now?

8. Do the requirements for listing stocks on the Big Board provide any protection to investors?

9. Affirm or deny the proposition that specialists on the exchanges should be abolished because they are constantly confronted with conflict of interest.

10. Is the securities business a good place for an ambitious young person?

II

Investment Risk and Return

4

Change in Interest Rates as a Cause of Uncertainty

I. Changes in interest rates and the effect on returns
   A. The uncertainty of rates of return on liquidation
   B. The uncertainty of expected rates of return upon reinvestment
   C. A retrospective view of interest rate fluctuations

II. How securities vary in level of interest rate risk
   A. Interest rate risk—principal
   B. Why price volatility increases as length of maturity increases
   C. Other conditions that affect price volatility
   D. Interest rate risk—income

III. How market rates of yield vary with the level of interest rate risk
   A. Market rates and interest rate risk—principal
   B. Theories of the term structure of interest rates
   C. The changing relationships of supply and demand
   D. Market rates and interest rate risk—income

IV. Interest rate risk affects other categories of securities
   A. Corporate and municipal bonds
   B. Preferred and common stocks

V. The market structure of expected rates of return

Risk, we have said, is uncertainty about the size of investment returns. There are several causes of uncertainty, that is, kinds of change that affect investment returns, and we can generalize that some securities are affected more by one than by another. Indeed, we can estimate the extent to which different categories of securities are affected by the different causes of risk, and this process of risk estimation is essential to the intelligent selection of securities for a portfolio. It is possible to select securities for a portfolio that are likely to be favorably affected by one kind of change and other securities that at the same time may be affected unfavorably by another kind of change. To the extent that favorable and unfavorable developments may be offset, risk in a securities portfolio is minimized.

Expected rates of return from securities are related positively to the size of risk, that is, to the sum of the uncertainties. Generally we can attribute some part of the total rate of return to one cause of uncertainty and another part to another cause. Of course the total expected rate of return is an estimate and so is its apportionment among the several causes of uncertainty. But, again, it is useful in building a portfolio to make some such subjective estimate of the parts of total return that are associated with the several causes of uncertainty. The purpose of portfolio management is to maximize returns relative to risk.

CHANGES IN INTEREST RATES AND THE EFFECT ON RETURNS

A cause of uncertainty that affects all kinds of securities to some extent is changes in market rates of interest. Market rates are the rates of yield at which money is invested in obligations believed to be free of uncertainty regarding payment of promised amounts of interest and principal in dollars of whatever purchasing power they may have at time of payment. Changes in these rates cause changes in the prices at which these default-free obligations may be bought and sold in the market and they influence changes in prices of all kinds of securities. Price changes mean larger or smaller realized rates of return for investors who buy and sell securities at market prices. They also affect the size of income payments that may be obtained by investment and re-investment of funds from time to time.

The uncertainty of the size of investment returns attributable to changes in interest rates is sometimes referred to as *interest rate risk*. This is a shorter way of saying "change in interest rates as a cause of uncertainty." But it should be clearly understood that interest rate risk is but one element of total risk and whatever risk premium is associated with interest rate risk is but part of the total risk premium in the expected rate of return.

The Uncertainty of Rates of Return on Liquidation

When bonds, or notes, are issued they become due on a specified date and bear a rate of interest on the principal amount that is fixed by the contract between issuer and buyer. This interest rate is sometimes called the coupon rate to distinguish it from the rate of yield to maturity. The yield to maturity is usually the expected rate. At the time obligations are issued, the coupon rate is fixed at about the market rate of yield on other obligations of the same kind so that they may be sold in the market at par or a price very near to par.

After obligations have been initially sold to investors, market rates change as supply and demand for funds varies. An investor who bought bonds and now wants to sell them must offer them in the market at a price that provides a buyer the rate of yield prevailing in the market at the time on that kind of bond. If interest rates have increased, he must accept a price that provides a larger yield to maturity than that provided by the coupon rate. You can't change the coupon rate, so you have to change the price. By lowering the price you can afford a buyer a larger yield to maturity.

If an investor bought a government obligation with a coupon rate of 5 per cent and due in 2 years from date of issue at a price of par, he would have an investment that yields him 5 per cent to maturity. But after a year has elapsed he decides to sell the security because he needs the money or wants to invest in some different kind of security. In the year that has passed interest rates have increased and the investor finds that no one will buy his bond unless he offers it at a price to yield the buyer 6 per cent for the 1 year that remains to maturity. You could look in a table of bond yields and find that he would have to sell the bond at approximately 99 per cent of par to yield 6 per cent. Or, you could calculate it yourself, using the present-value formula as follows: $990 = the sum of $25 due at the end of 6 months, $25 due at the end of 1 year, and $1,000 due at the end of 1 year, all discounted at 6 per cent. The amount would be $990.40.

The point is that the investor who bought that Treasury obligation due in only 2 years did not receive the 5 per cent rate of return he expected. He received a return on investment of only 4.04 per cent. The rate that discounts his cash flow to a present value of $1,000 is slightly over 4 per cent.[1]

You could make the opposite assumption, that interest rates have declined, and that the investor sold after 1 year. The prevailing interest rate in the market for this kind of security has decreased to 4 per cent. So he prices his security to yield 4 per cent and receives a price of $1,010, or more precisely by the yield basis book, a price of $1,009.70. This provides a realized rate of return on his investment of 6 per cent. So the investor who started out with just about the "safest" investment in the world might well have ended up with a rate of return of 4, or 5, or 6 per cent, or some other rate, depending on how interest rates in the market changed from the time he bought to the time he sold.

If you are following this line of thought perceptively, you ought to point out here that the investor could have avoided those different rates simply by holding the obligation to maturity and receiving the interest and principal at the dates those sums were due. Yes, but how do you know that he could

[1]
$$\$1{,}000 = \frac{\$25}{102.02\%} + \frac{\$25}{104.04\%} + \frac{\$990}{104.04\%}$$
$$\$1{,}000.09 = \$24.51 + \$24.03 + \$951.55$$

have held to maturity? There is always some chance that an investor who buys a security with the expectation of holding to maturity will be obliged to sell it by the development of conditions he did not expect, or that he will find it desirable to sell. To the extent that there is uncertainty about holding an obligation to maturity, there is uncertainty about the rate of return that will be realized.

The Uncertainty of Expected Rates of Return on Reinvestment

Even if an investor holds a security to maturity, he does not escape the effect of changes in interest rates if he re-invests the proceeds from redemption in another security of about the same kind. When he re-invests, he has to accept the market rate of yield on the new investment. The market rate may be considered the expected rate of return. If the gentleman we have been talking about held his 2-year, 5 per cent coupon Treasury note for 2 years to maturity, got his money back, and bought a new 2-year Treasury note, he might obtain on the new investment a yield of 4 per cent. That would mean a 20 per cent reduction in rate of return. Or, he might get 6 per cent on re-investing, which would be a 20 per cent increase in rate of return. You don't have to invest in common stocks to realize different rates of return from time to time.

This second kind of effect of changes in market rates of interest depends on the assumption that the proceeds of matured obligations are re-invested in similar obligations. The assumption is valid for the most part. Investors who owns bonds usually do not use the principal amounts; they use the income. Commercial banks, life insurance companies, other institutional investors, and well-to-do-persons generally "roll over" their maturities. That is, they replace matured bonds with new bonds of about the same kind. There are exceptions. Sometimes a commercial bank experiences an outflow of funds in the usual course of business and the banker has to sell some securities in the market to obtain the cash to pay off. Sometimes a person who has invested in bonds comes to the point where he needs more than the amount of interest income, and he uses some funds from redemption of bonds for consumption.

We have been thinking about an investor and a bond, but it is more realistic to think about an investor and his bonds. Most bond investors have a portfolio of securities. The market value of the entire portfolio fluctuates as interest rates change. Usually there are obligations with different periods to maturity, so that some mature at one time and some at another, and different rates of yield are obtained on new investments. The rate of return on the entire portfolio changes as money is reinvested.

A Retrospective View of Interest Rate Fluctuations

You may not appreciate the full significance of changes in interest rates for investors until you look back at the magnitude of changes over a period of years past. Figure 4–1 shows the variation in market rates of yield on Treasury bills due in 3 months and in rates for long-term government bonds.[2]

The figure shows clearly the long upward trend of interest rates that began in the 1950's and continued into the 1970's. During this period market rates of yield for long-term governments more than doubled and yields on Treasury bills fluctuated from a low level of less than 1 per cent to more than 7 per cent. The effect of these changes on investors in government and other virtually default-free types of obligations was at least as dramatic as the effects of stock price fluctuations on common stock investors.

HOW SECURITIES VARY IN LEVEL OF INTEREST RATE RISK

The uncertainty of rates of return on default-free obligations caused by changes in interest rates affects some securities more than others. Levels of risk are graduated upward from virtually zero to a relatively high level. This uncertainty is chiefly a function of the length of the period from the present time to date of maturity. Uncertainty about rate of return in event of liquidation in the market increases as the length of maturity increases. It is greater for the longer maturities and lesser for the short maturities. But the contrary

[2]The *Federal Reserve Bulletin* contains monthly data on interest rates and security yields, and the *Federal Reserve Chart Book* presents the same data graphically.

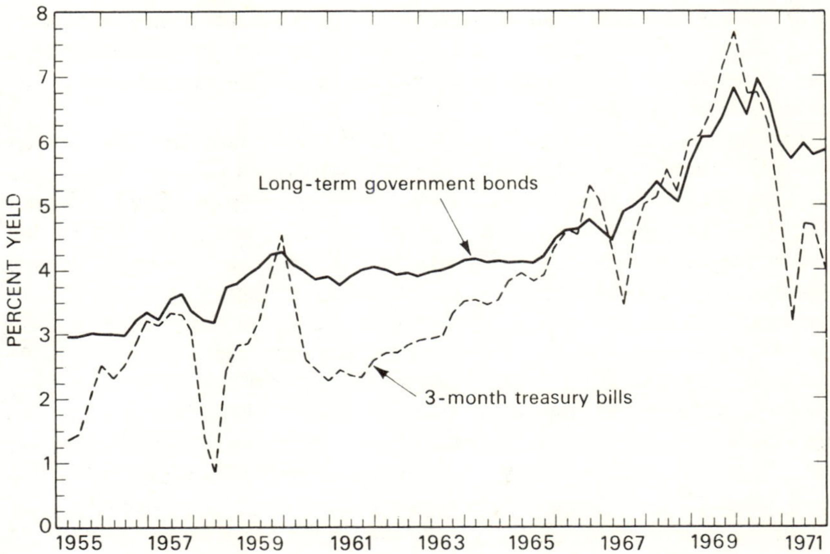

FIGURE 4–1

Fluctuating Yields on Short-term and Long-term Government Obligations

Data are monthly averages for the third month in each calendar quarter.

is true for the uncertainty affecting rate of return on re-investment of the proceeds from sale or maturity in new securities. For that side of interest rate risk, the uncertainty graduates from the shortest maturities with the greatest risk to the long maturities with the least. We will discuss these two facets of interest rate risk separately under the titles, "Interest rate risk—principal" and "Interest rate risk—income."

Interest Rate Risk—Principal

The reason why uncertainty about size of return in event of liquidation increases from shortest to longest maturities is that the size of market price fluctuations accompanying changes in market rates of interest increase as length of maturity increases. Prices of short maturities fluctuate narrowly; prices of long maturities fluctuate widely. If you sell obligations with short maturities in the market, you may realize a gain or loss of principal depending on the direction of change in market rates of interest, but it will be small and your total rate of return will be different from the expected rate of return (yield at time of purchase) by some relatively small difference. But if you sell long maturities, the gain or loss of principal may be large. It may change the initial expected rate of return to a large total rate of return or to a net loss on the transaction.

Figure 4–2 shows in two-dimensional form the operation of this principle of increasing price instability with increasing length of maturity. It depicts market prices for a series of default-free obligations with maturities ranging from 1 to 50 years, all of which have 5 per cent interest coupons, at three levels of interest rates in the market. The idea that all maturities would have the same rate of yield in the market at a given time is unrealistic, but it aids the explanation.

If market rates are at 5 per cent for all of these maturities, the market price for all of them is par. If market rates should rise to 6 per cent for all maturities, market prices would have to decline in order to provide the higher rate to buyers. The lower curved line in the figure shows prices for all the issues when they are priced to yield 6 per cent. There is a very small decline for the shortest maturities, but the size of the decline increases as the length of maturities increases. If market rates should decline to 4 per cent, market prices would rise to the levels indicated by the upper curved line so that purchase at these prices would provide the lower rate to buyers. There is a very small rise for the shortest maturities, but the size of the advance in prices becomes larger as length of maturity increases. Both price curves taper off to small differences in prices for the longer maturities. There isn't much difference in price for a 5 per cent obligation due in 40 years priced to yield 6 per cent, and the price for such an issue due in 50 years on the same yield basis.

You can read from the chart the approximate size of the price declines that would accompany the rise in interest rates. The market price of the 1-year maturity would decline only about 1 percentage point to 99. If you

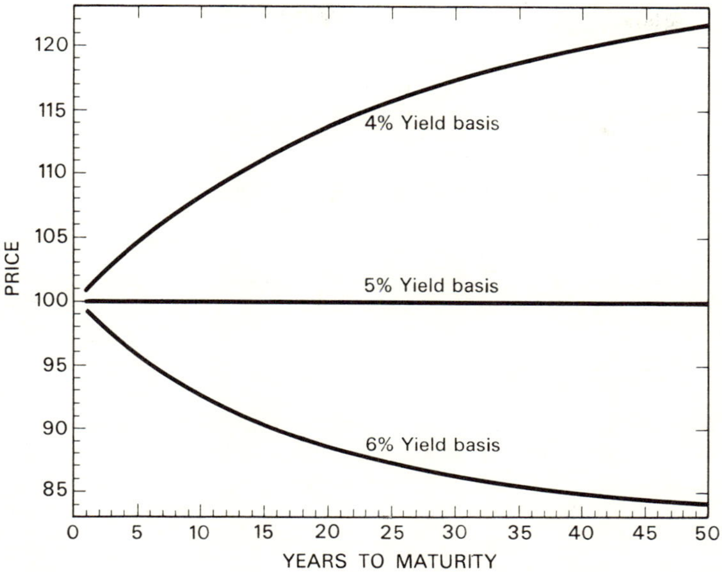

FIGURE 4–2

How Change in Interest Rates Affects Market Prices for Bonds of Varying Lengths of Maturity

Data are for a bond bearing a 5 per cent coupon priced to yield 4 per cent and 6 per cent.

had to sell this 5 per cent obligation after purchasing it at par and holding it for 1 year, your realized rate of return would be 4 per cent. That is not a bad return in view of the substantial increase in the level of market rates of interest.

The long maturities, on the other hand, would have to decline much more drastically to provide the 6 per cent yield required by the market. The 30-year maturity would have to be priced at 86.16 per cent of par. If you had purchased that issue 2 years ago and sold it today, you would have a negative rate of return on investment, because the loss of principal ($138.40) is greater than the interest received ($100).

On the opposite side, the increases in market prices when interest rates decline are small for the short maturities and much greater for the long maturities. The obligation due in 1 year would increase in price by only about 1 percentage point. If you had owned it for a year and sold at 101, you would have a slightly larger realized rate of return (about 6 per cent) than the yield to maturity at the time you purchased. But the 50-year maturity would rise in price to 121½ per cent of par. If you had purchased it 2 years ago and sold at that price, you would have realized a rate of return of about 14½ per cent.

United States government bonds have often been called the safest investments in the world. What does this exposition of the size of potential gains and losses tell you about the validity of that generalization?

Why Price Volatility Increases as Length of Maturity Increases

Prices of the longer-term obligations decline so much more than prices of the shorter-term issues with a given increase in interest rates because the amounts of interest and principal to be received by their owners extend so far into the future that there must be a considerable reduction in their present value to bring about any considerable increase in the rate of return they provide. In opposite terms, this is the reason why prices of long-term issues increase so much more than those of short-term issues when interest rates decline.

Consider, for example, that the $1,000 principal amount to be received at the maturity date 30 years in the future has a present value at 5 per cent of $231. When that amount is discounted at 6 per cent, the present value falls to $174. That is a reduction of $57. Then there are all those interest payments stretching out over 30 years. The more remote in time the dates they are to be received, the more their present values must be reduced to provide a higher discount rate. At 5 per cent the sum of the present values of the interest payments on the bond maturing in 30 years is $769. At 6 per cent it is about $687. You see that the sum of present values has to be reduced from $1,000 to $861 ($174 + $687) in order for that series of interest payments and principal at maturity to provide the 6 per cent rate of return required by the market.

The 1-year maturity, by way of contrast, had to be reduced in price by only 1 percentage point to raise the rate of yield from 5 to 6 per cent. When the two interest payments and the principal amount are discounted at 6 per cent, the sum of their present values is $990.

Other Conditions that Affect Price Volatility

Although length of maturity is the principal cause of differences in the size of price fluctuations of default-free obligations as market rates of interest change, there are two other conditions that affect their price volatility.

One is simply the size of the coupon rate. The lower the coupon rate, the greater the price change for a given maturity and a given change in the market rate of yield. The larger the coupon rate the less is the price change. For example, a bond due in 30 years and bearing an 8 per cent coupon was priced to yield 7.11 per cent to maturity. If the yield was obliged to be increased by one-third to 9.48 per cent, the price would decline 23.09 per cent. By comparison, a bond due in 30 years and bearing a 4 per cent coupon would have to decline in price 25.72 per cent to raise the yield from 7.11 to 9.48 per cent. The explanation for this difference in price change is that a larger proportion of the total cash flow for the high coupon bond consists of interest payments due in the next few years and a smaller portion consists of principal due at the end of 30 years. The present values of the nearer payments do not have to be reduced as much as those of more remote payments to provide a given change in yield to maturity.

Another condition that affects price volatility is the yield level from which a change in yield begins. The higher the starting yield level, the greater is the change in price necessary to bring about a given increase in yield. If a bond bears an 8 per cent coupon, is due in 30 years, and is priced to yield 3 per cent, its price will decline 14.58 per cent to raise the yield to 4 per cent (a one-third increase in yield). But if the initial yield is 5.33 per cent and it is increased to 7.11 per cent (a one-third increase), the decline in price will be 20.57 per cent.[3]

Interest Rate Risk—Income

If you hold a default-free obligation to maturity, receive the principal amount, and re-invest in another such obligation of about the same maturity, the uncertainty of the rate of yield on reinvestment *decreases* as length of maturity increases. The relationship is inverse. This is just the opposite of the preceding generalization about risk affecting rate of return on liquidation. The explanation, however, is easier.

It is redundant to say that obligations with short maturities mature in a short time, but that is an important part of the explanation. If you bought Treasury notes due in 1 year, at the end of the year reinvested in another issue of notes due in 1 year, and continued to do so for 10 years, you would have re-invested 10 times and received 10 different rates of yield. Your investment turned over rapidly and you had to go into the market every year and buy at whatever the market rates of interest might be at the time.

At the opposite extreme, you could buy a bond due in 30 years at the rate of yield prevailing in the market at the time. If you hold it to maturity, you will realize that rate of yield. Your income will be unchanged during all those years and you will get the full principal amount when it is due. If you invested entirely in 30-year maturities, you would turn over your portfolio every 30 years and in a century you would have only 4 different rates of return.

The other part of the explanation for this inverse relationship of risk and length of maturity affecting income is that market rates of yield on short-term issues are much more unstable than rates on long-term issues. You can see this graphically in Figure 4–1. The data for rates on 90-day Treasury bills show a range from less than 1 per cent in 1958 to about 7¾ per cent in 1969. The range for long-term government bonds is from a little less than 3 per cent in 1955 to about 7 per cent in 1970. The significance of the more stable rates on long-term issues is that when you hold them and re-invest, the probability of a greatly different rate on re-investment is less than it is for short-term issues.

[3]Data for these examples were taken from a memorandum entitled, "Inside the Yield Book," by Sidney Homer and Martin Leibowitz, dated January 26, 1971, distributed to customers by Salomon Brothers, New York, N.Y.

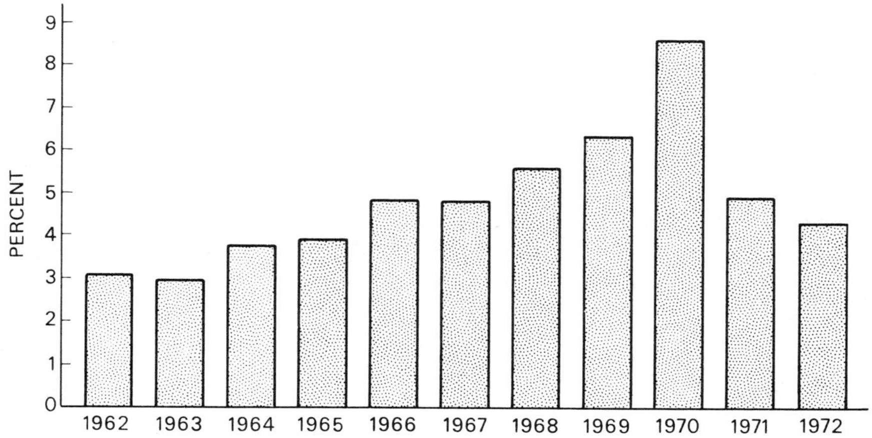

FIGURE 4–3

Yields on One-Year Treasury Obligations

Average yield on Treasury obligations due in 9 to 12 months during first week of each year.

This generalization has to be qualified because there have been some very considerable changes in market rates on long-term issues over very long time periods. In the 1930's this rate fell to only about 2 per cent (on partially tax-exempt issues), and in the period of World War II rates were at about 2¾ per cent (on fully taxable issues). Rates began to rise in the middle 1940's and continued upward with some cyclical declines to a peak in 1970 at about 7 per cent. So the rates you would receive on re-investment would depend very much on where your long maturities fall due in the pattern of fluctuation in rates over a long span of years.

Figure 4–3 shows how rates of return from short-term issues would have fluctuated in a recent 10-year period for an investor who bought obligations due in 1 year in the first week of January of each year and reinvested in the first week of January of each successive year for 10 years. The investor would have benefited from the upward trend of short-term rates in the market until 1970, and realized a sharp decline in the next several years. However, it might have been the other way around. There have been periods in our history in which short-term rates trended downward and brought steep reductions in rates of yield. The conclusion is that over any very long time horizon the policy of investing and reinvesting in short-term issues is likely to result in large variations in rates of yield.

HOW MARKET RATES OF YIELD VARY WITH THE LEVEL OF INTEREST RATE RISK

Our hypothesis is that there is a positive relationship between the size of expected returns and the level of risk. Is this hypothesis valid for uncertainty caused by changes in market rates of interest? The answer must be in two parts: one about interest rate risk as it affects market values of principal, and the other about interest rate risk as it affects the size of income upon reinvestment.

Market Rates and Interest Rate Risk—Principal

We can seek a conclusion only by reviewing the historical data of market rates of yield for default-free obligations of varying lengths of maturity. But the data do not provide the clear, unambiguous answer we would like to have.

Most of the time in the past four or five decades the term structure of yields has been upsloping, as depicted by curve A in Figure 4–4. This means that market rates of yields on default-free obligations (U.S. government securities) have increased as length of maturity increases. In other words, the longer the maturity the higher the yield at which these obligations could be purchased in the market. Taking market rates as expected rates of return, the size of expected rates have graduated upward as length of maturity has increased. To the extent that this generalization is valid, the hypothesis of a positive relationship of risk and returns is valid.

Unfortunately for simplicity of statement, the generalization isn't always valid. You see in Figure 4–4 two other shapes of the yield curve for government obligations. At some times the yield curve has taken the form of a downsloping line, as described by curve *B* in the Figure. This curve depicts an

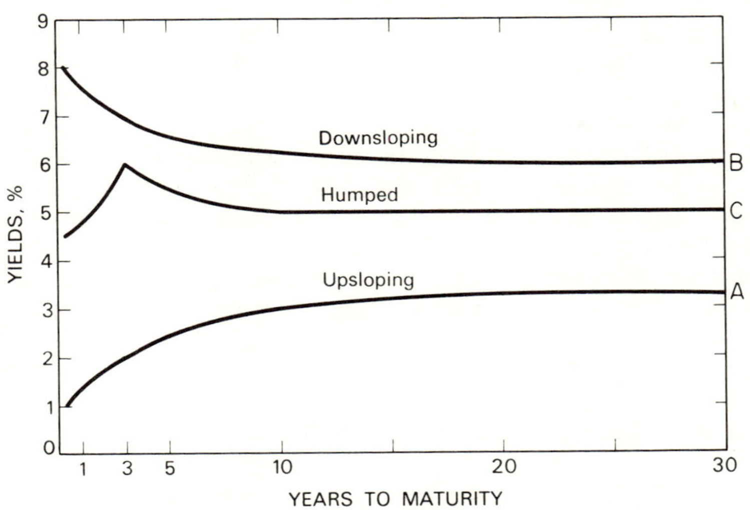

FIGURE 4–4

Yield Curves for Government Obligations

Source: These are conventionalized depictions of curves that have occurred from time to time.

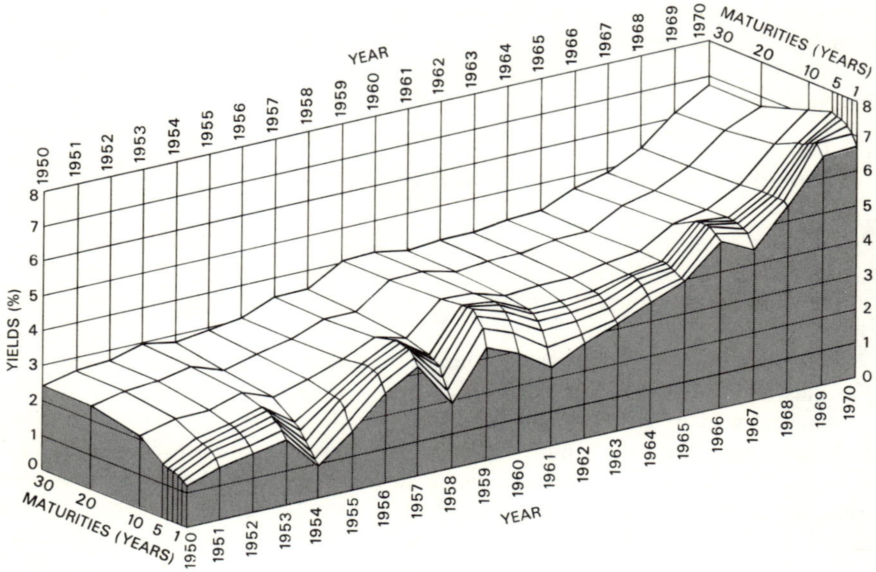

FIGURE 4–5

A Three-Dimensional View of the Term Structure of Interest Rates

Source: Salomon Brothers, *An Analytical Record of Yields and Yield Spreads*, New York, 1972, p. 25.

opposite relationship to that of curve *A* between expected rates and size of risk. It shows that at times investors have obtained higher market rates of return on the short-term issues than on the long-term obligations. Which is to say that they have bought the least risky issues in terms of interest rate risk affecting principal at the highest market rates.

There have been other times when the curve designated *C* has existed in the market. This is a sort of combination of the other two in that it is upsloping from the very shortest maturities to those of about 3 years, and then slopes downward. It is naturally called a humped curve.

Figure 4–5 is a three-dimensional view of the term structure of interest rates and how it has changed from time to time over a period of 2 decades.

Theories of the Term Structure of Interest Rates

Economists have developed several theories to explain the shape of the yield curve and the changes in it from time to time. One is called the liquidity preference theory, because it states simply that investors generally prefer the liquidity of short-term issues and therefore are willing to buy them on a lower yield basis than the longer-term issues. The short-term issues are "liquid" in the sense that they can be sold readily in the market at prices that do not vary greatly from time to time. In other words, investors can get their money back when they want it and with little gain or loss in selling price relative to price paid.

This concept is consistent with the observed behavior of investors, particularly investing institutions. Commercial banks use short-term, default-free obligations as secondary reserves for the express purpose of providing funds by liquidation when funds are needed to meet increasing loan demand or an outflow of deposits. Many business corporations invest in short maturities those funds not immediately required to be employed in the business, but which are expected to be required at some uncertain date in the future.

Then there is the expectations theory, which holds that the term structure of interest rates is explained by the choices of maturities that investors make on the basis of their estimates of future market rates of interest. It is assumed that investors are in general agreement about these estimates and that they are free to select whatever maturities they want with a view solely to maximizing their portfolio rate of return over a period of time. According to this line of thought, when investors expect yields on the longer-term obligations to decline in the future, they shift their funds to these long-term issues. Thus they secure the relatively high current rates on these issues for a long period of investment. And if it should be necessary to liquidate before maturity, they would realize higher prices than those they paid because of the decline in market rates. The widespread sale of obligations of short maturity when this shift is made causes their prices to decline and their yields to rise. Thus the short end of the yield curve moves upward and it may become downsloping.

Still a third influence on the yield curve is emphasized in the institutional hedging theory. It is pointed out that some kinds of financial institutions assume long-term liabilities at fixed or assumed rates of interest. The usual example is life insurance and annuity companies, which issue contracts for insurance and annuities that normally extend for many years into the future. To hedge their long-term commitments at assumed rates of interest, they buy long-term obligations that will provide the yield rate of return for the long periods of their contracts. Thus their preference is for obligations that provide well-assured rates of return for long periods. Their influence on the yield curve is opposite to that of investors who prefer liquidity.[4]

The Changing Relationships of Supply and Demand

The theories of the academicians explain the behavior of some investors in the market for government obligations and for other obligations virtually free of the risk of default. But the story is not complete without considering the effect of the business cycle and of the fiscal and credit policies of the federal government.

The upsloping yield curve is an "easy money" curve. It prevails when

[4]For an excellent discussion of the term structure of interest rates, see Burton G. Malkiel, *The Term Structure of Interest Rates: Theory, Empirical Evidence, and Applications*, New York, 1970, The McCaleb-Seiler Publishing Company.

the supply of funds available for investment in this segment of the securities market is large relative to demand. The relatively large supply causes prices to be bid up and market rates of yield to go down so that interest rates generally are relatively low. The preference of investors for the more liquid kinds of securities, that is, the shorter-term issues, causes a more pronounced demand for securities at that end of the term structure and thus market rates for the shorter maturities are less than rates for the longer maturities.

The condition of easy money commonly occurs in periods of business recession or at times when the economy is expanding at a relatively low rate. At such times the price level usually is stable or rising only slightly. Under these conditions the demand for funds from private enterprise is comparatively low and may be receding. The supply of money, on the other hand, is likely to be increasing under the influence of Federal Reserve credit policy. Generally it is the policy of the Board of Governors of the Federal Reserve System to increase the legal reserves of member banks and to use its influence to expand the money supply.

The downsloping yield curve appears when money is "tight," that is, when demand for funds in the market has strongly increased and growth in supply has been restricted. It is ordinarily associated with a period of business boom, as in the late 1960's, and with a relatively high rate of price inflation, as in the early 1970's. When business is expanding strongly the demand for funds from private enterprise, particularly demand for short-term funds, increases markedly. At the same time the credit policy of the Federal Reserve System becomes more restrictive as the monetary authorities try to check boom and inflation by reducing the rate of expansion in the money supply. Supply and demand equate of course, but at higher levels of market rates of yield. The financial stringency is greatest in the short-term segment of the market because this is where there is the greatest expansion in demand for funds.

The "humped" yield curve evidences a peculiar combination of easy money and tight money. It shows that the supply of money for investment in the very shortest maturities is relatively abundant in that rates for the shortest maturities are low, but the rise in the curve to a hump indicates a relative lack of demand for 2- to 3-year maturities. They are not liquid enough to satisfy investors with a strong preference for liquidity and at the same time are not attractive to institutions that want to commit their funds for relatively long periods. Sometimes there are indications that banks with their strong liquidity preference liquidate securities in this maturity range in order to buy even shorter maturities or to meet an expanding demand for bank loans.

The question that led us into this discussion of the term structure of interest rates is whether there is a positive relationship between the magnitude of risk affecting principal amounts and the size of returns at which these default-free obligations can be purchased in the market from time to time. The answer is a qualified affirmative. There is a positive relationship when the yield curve is upsloping, but it is not always upsloping. The humped yield curve generally provides higher yields for longer maturities, except for the place in the array of maturities where there are unusually high rates for relatively short-term issues. The downsloping curve provides a negative relationship between risk and return; it provides the highest market rates of yield for those maturities that are least affected in price by changes in interest rates. That is why the affirmative answer must be qualified.

We can look back over a period of several decades and observe that the term structure of interest rates has more often than not provided higher expected rates of return for securities with the greater risk affecting principal. But we don't know whether this will be true in the future. A condition of tight money and relatively high short-term rates might become the norm rather than the exception.

Market Rates and Interest Rate Risk—Income

This discussion about the term structure of interest rates also answers the question of the relationship of market rates and uncertainty of the size of returns in the form of income from default-free obligations. The most risky securities in terms of income are the short maturities. Usually market rates are lower for short maturities. Therefore there is a negative relationship between interest rate risk affecting uncertainty of size of income and the usual structure of interest rates. But that generalization has to be qualified, like the one before, by saying that sometimes the opposite is true; that sometimes short-term rates are the highest in the entire structure and do provide higher rates for the greater risk affecting income.

It is a reasonable inference that investors in default-free obligations are generally more concerned with changes in interest rates as a cause of uncertainty of market prices that may be realized on liquidation than they are about the instability of income that is associated with investment and re-investment in obligations of short maturity.

INTEREST RATE RISK AFFECTS OTHER CATEGORIES OF SECURITIES

We have discussed changes in interest rates as a cause of uncertainty in returns from investments in terms of U.S. government obligations, which are generally recognized as free of the risk of default. But there are billions of dollars of other bonds outstanding that are considered virtually free of the default risk and changes in their prices are chiefly a function of changes in interest rates. Market prices for most preferred stocks are strongly affected by changes in market rates of interest, and we must also consider how this kind of risk affects prices for common stocks.

Corporate and Municipal Bonds

Corporate and municipal bonds rated triple A by the bond-rating services have the least default risk among all securities of private and public issuers. Market rates on long-term corporates of this rating grade tend to be about 110 to 120 per cent of yields on long-term governments at the same points in time. That differential is chiefly a compensation in the form of larger expected rate of return for the greater default risk. The somewhat lesser marketability of the corporate issues is also an influence upon the yield differential. There is a further differential in market rates of yield between the triple A issues and those rated triple B, which have a greater default risk. Given these differentials, there is a very high correlation between change in average yields on long-term government bonds and these two categories of corporate issues. You can see the similarity of fluctuations in average yields in Figure 4–6. The coefficient of correlation is high. Using monthly data for a recent 10-year period, the coefficient for triple A corporate bonds relative to government bonds is 0.9786 per cent, and that for Triple B corporate bonds related to governments is 0.9611 per cent.

We could make the same sort of comparison of average yields on municipal bonds with those for long-term governments and there would be much the same correlation of yield changes. However, yields on municipals are affected by the exemption of interest on these issues from the federal income tax and from state income taxes in most states. Thus their yields are generally lower than yields on long-term governments, and the correlation of changes in yields is affected to some extent by changes in the value attributed by investors to the privilege of tax exemption.

The term structure of yields on the better grades of corporate and mu-

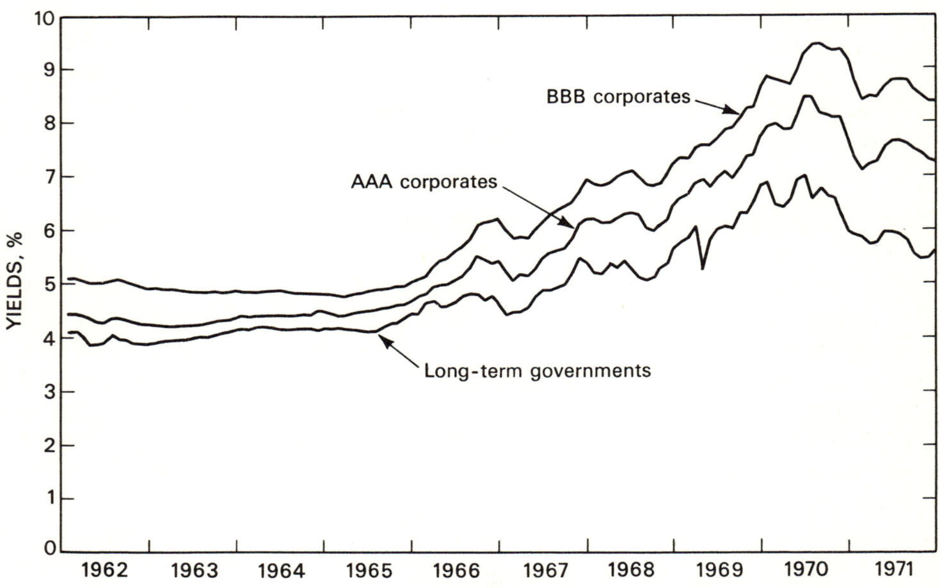

FIGURE 4–6

Yields on Government and Corporate Bonds

Source: *Federal Reserve Bulletin.*

nicipal bonds corresponds approximately to the yield curve for government obligations. When the yield curve is upsloping for governments it is also upsloping for corporates and municipals. The curves are not exactly the same because investors who prefer liquidity prefer governments for their greater liquidity. The yield curves for municipals and for governments are shown in Figure 4–7.

Preferred and Common Stocks

There are many straight preferred stocks that provide fixed amounts of dividend income and but small uncertainty of the payment of future dividends. Yields for these issues change in close correlation with changes in long-term government yields. Figure 4–8 shows average yields on a sample of non-callable preferred stocks. The coefficient of correlation between this series and yields on long-term governments for a 10-year period is 0.9663 per cent.

Prices and expected rates of return on common stocks are also affected to some extent by the rise and decline of market rates of interest. It is more difficult to generalize about returns on common stocks because dividends represent only part of the rate of return expected on most of these issues. The other part is capital gains. There are statistics on rates of dividend yield in the market, but none on expected rates because expectations are peculiar to individual investors.

However, you can see the effect of changes in market rates of interest on dividend yields in those categories of stocks known as "income stocks,"

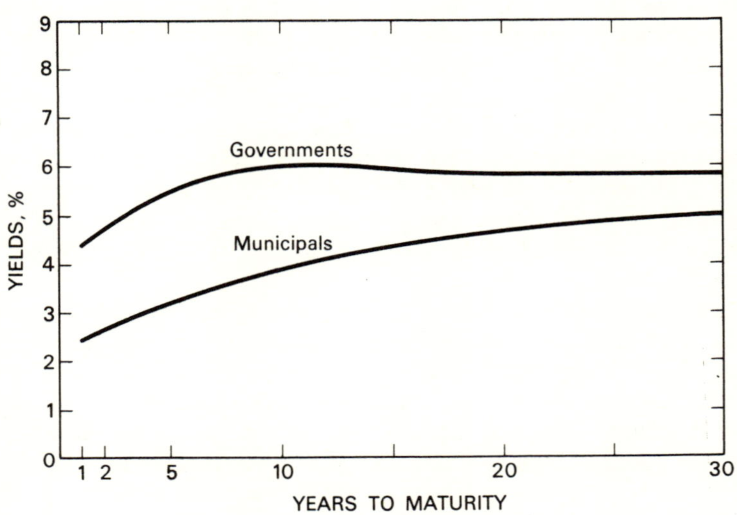

FIGURE 4–7

Yield Curves for Governments and Municipals (as of the end of 1971)

Source: Salomon Brothers, *Bond Market Review*, December 1971.

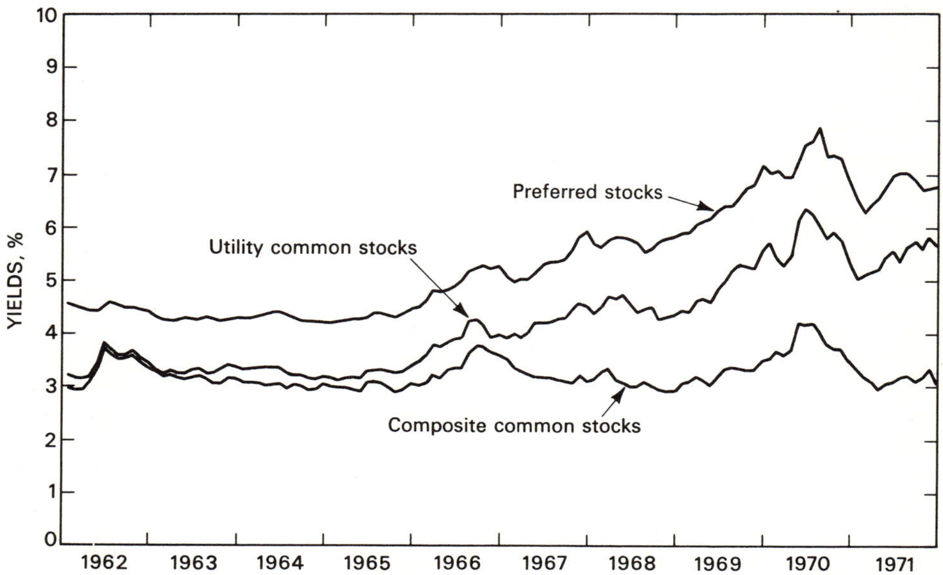

FIGURE 4–8

Yields on Preferred and Common Stocks (Dividends-Price Ratios)

Source: Standard & Poor's, *Trade and Securities Service*, Security Price Index Record.

that is, common stocks that provide relatively high current dividend yields and are bought by investors who expect a relatively large part of their return to be in the form of dividends. Public utility stocks are generally income stocks. They are supported by relatively stable earnings, there is relatively little uncertainty about continuation of dividends at not less than the current amounts, and expected returns in the form of price appreciation are more modest than for common stocks generally. One of the lines in Figure 4–8 shows average dividend yields for a group of public utility common stocks. There is a high positive correlation with yields on long-term governments, with the coefficient at 0.9425 per cent.

Expected rates of return on common stocks generally are subjective estimates in the minds of large numbers of investors and they are not recorded in any statistical series. Frequently, dividends represent the smaller part of expected total rate of return. Even so there is evidence that changes in interest rates affect both dividend yields and expected rates on the average of a large number of common stocks. Figure 4–8 shows that average dividend yields on 500 common stocks did increase as interest rates rose in the latter part of the 10-year period for which data are presented. The coefficient of correlation between that series and the yields on long-term investment rate was a positive but somewhat weak 0.4257 per cent.

THE MARKET STRUCTURE OF EXPECTED RATES OF RETURN

You can begin to see that there is in the market a structure of expected rates of return for different categories of securities according to the manner in which they are affected by different causes of uncertainty. Generally the greater the uncertainty, the higher the expected rate. There is first the usually upsloping yield curve for default-free obligations that provides higher rates for higher levels of interest rate risk affecting principal amounts. Resting on that curve is another component of expected returns that is compensation for the risk of default. In the next chapter we will develop the idea of default risk into a broader concept of changes in the financial abilities of issuers as a cause of uncertainty. The size of this component increases as uncertainty increases. Then there is embedded in this structure some compensation for the uncertainty of the purchasing power of future returns in dollar amounts. It may be included in the expected rates of return for default-free obligations. Finally, there are some differences in expected rates of return among securities that can be attributed to differences among them in certain non-risk qualities that make them more or less desirable to investors. The less desirable securities in terms of these non-risk qualities generally provide higher expected rates than the rates for the more desirable issues.

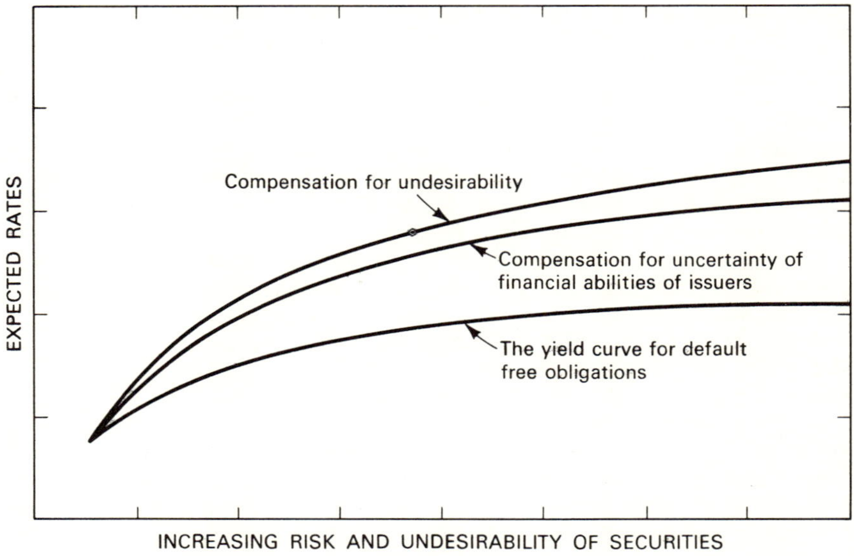

FIGURE 4–9

A Conventionalized Concept of the Market Structure of Expected Rates of Return

The idea of a market structure of expected rates of return is suggested in broad terms by Figure 4–9.

A major principle to be inferred from this concept of a market structure is that when the yield curve for default-free obligations changes, the whole structure of expected rates changes. When that upsloping yield curve shifts upward, the whole structure shifts upward, and when the shape of the yield curve changes, the entire structure is affected.

QUESTIONS FOR DISCUSSION

1. The government of the United States has never failed to pay interest and principal on its bonds and there is no reason to think that it will fail in the future. Why, then, is there any risk in owning a Treasury bond due in 10 years?

2. Is there any risk in ownership of U. S. Government Savings Bonds? How are Savings Bonds different?

3. You and your twin brother (sister) each have $100,000 in cash. You are very conservative and you don't want to lose any of that money. You buy at par a U. S. Treasury bond bearing interest at 4½ per cent and due in 12 years. Your brother (sister) buys U. S. Treasury notes due in 2 years at a price that yields 4.10 per cent. He (she) intends to reinvest the money from these notes when they mature in the same kind of notes.
Which of you has taken the greater risk of loss caused by future changes in interest rates?
Which will receive the higher average rate of return over the next 12 years?

4. Why does the price volatility of default-free obligations increase as the length of maturity increases?

5. Is it normal for the size of market rates of yield to increase as length of maturity increases?

6. You are a professional investment counselor and one of your clients is a nice old lady who worries about how you invest her money. You have put a large part of it in medium-grade bonds, high-grade preferred stocks, and common stocks of companies that are financially strong and stable. Thus you have provided a relatively liberal and stable income for the lady. Business is good, the economy is expanding, and all the companies in which you have invested her money are doing very well. But she comes to your office with a copy of the *Wall Street Journal* and shows you that every one of her bonds and stocks has declined in market price in the past 6 months.
How will you respond to the lady's implicit complaint that you have done a poor job of investing her money?

7. Which of the theoretical explanations for the shape of the yield curve and for changes in its shape seems most reasonable to you?

8. In a period of strong improvement in business and of increase in corporate earnings, would average common stock prices be likely to increase or to decrease? Explain the influences upon average stock prices in such a period.

5

Change in the Financial Abilities of Issuers as a Cause of Uncertainty

I. How this cause of uncertainty operates
   A. The kind of change that happens
   B. The kind of change that is expected to happen
   C. Some related risk concepts

II. Differentiation in levels of risk
   A. Application of the risk formula
   B. The system of security ratings

III. Financial risk and market prices
   A. Prices and published information
   B. Prices and expectations
   C. The stock market as a laboratory
   D. Industries and companies

IV. Risk levels and rates of return
   A. Rates of return for bonds
   B. Rates for bonds compared with stocks
   C. Rates for common stocks by risk levels
   D. The variations from period to period in average returns from common stocks
   E. The variations in returns from millions of stock transactions

In describing change in interest rates as a cause of investment risk, we deliberately limited ourselves to default-free obligations in order to focus on only one cause of uncertainty. But there is a second major cause that must usually be considered at the same time. This is change in the financial ability of issuers to make future payments to owners of their securities. Default-free obligations are by definition securities not affected by this cause of uncertainty, but in practice all securities except U.S. government obligations are affected to some extent. Sometimes this cause of risk is so small as to be negligible and sometimes it is the major cause of uncertainty about future returns. It affects the outcomes of investment in securities at the same time that changes in interest rates affect the size of returns.

This uncertainty about change in financial abilities of issuers is sometimes termed financial risk. The shorter term is more convenient and we will use it in this discussion. However, the concept is not so simple as it might seem at first, and we must be careful to define the term precisely.

HOW THIS CAUSE OF UNCERTAINTY OPERATES

The definition of financial risk reads the same as the definition of interest rate risk up to the point where cause is indicated. The cause is change in the financial abilities of issuers as it affects the amounts actually paid to, or obtained by, investors as they buy, hold, and sell securities. Keep in mind that changes in interest rates affect realized rates of return from securities at the same time that changes in financial ability affect realized rates. Financial risk affects securities in two ways.

The Kind of Change that Happens

It is not difficult to imagine an investor buying a bond, holding it for a number of years, and receiving in due time the interest and principal amounts that were promised. Nothing happened to the issuer's financial ability to make him unable to pay. But something might happen. The issuer's earnings might decline, its condition might become increasingly illiquid, and it might become unable to pay interest due to bondholders. The bondholder would not get his interest and eventually he would probably receive some amount of principal smaller than the amount promised. His rate of return would be reduced by these occurrences.

One who invests in a common stock might have a happier experience. The company whose shares he owns may prosper, realize larger amounts of earnings per share, and pay increasing amounts of dividends. His rate of return in the form of dividends would be increased by these favorable changes in financial ability of the issuer to pay.

If securities could not be bought and sold, we could stop at this point in describing this cause of uncertainty. Without markets each investor would have to hold his securities and accept whatever payments their issuers might be able to make. His rates of return would be determined by what actually happens.

The Kind of Change Expected to Happen

But there are markets for securities and investors do not have to sit still with the securities they have purchased and accept what happens. They can sell in the market at market prices. This is where the kind of change expected to happen affects realized rates of return. Market prices are influenced by investors' estimates of the future. At one time buyers of securities may take a rather pessimistic view of probable future change in the financial ability of an issuer, and at a subsequent time take a more optimistic view. Such a change would be reflected in market prices. When their estimates are optimistic investors will pay higher prices than when they are pessimistic. It isn't necessary that a more optimistic, or more pessimistic, estimate be correct for it to affect market price. In fact, at the point in time when an estimate is made, no one knows whether it will prove correct. It is an estimate of future financial ability.

Changes in market price owing to changes in investor's estimates of the future affect the rate of return realized by investors who liquidate securities in the market. They receive the market price. If it is higher than the price paid it enhances their total rate of return; if it is less, it detracts from the total rate of return and may result in a negative rate. Market prices of common stocks and of securities that have a high level of financial risk fluctuate rather widely as investors' expectations change. And you don't know in advance whether expectations will further change, or in what direction they will change. The uncertainty of how investors' expectations of future change in financial abilities will shift is part of financial risk.

So financial risk has these two sides—actual changes in the financial abilities of issuers that affect rate of return to investors, and expected changes in financial abilities that affect market prices and rate of return to those who sell at market prices.

Some Related Risk Concepts

Some authorities have tried to obtain more precise definitions of this cause of uncertainty by breaking it down into several kinds of risk. They say that one kind of risk is operating risk or business risk. This risk is defined as the uncertainty of future financial abilities as it is affected by changes in the profitability of regular business operations. This version would be measured by what accountants usually term operating income, that is, sales minus operating expenses. If a company's sales decline and there is not a corresponding decline in its operating expenses, operating income declines.

The term "financial risk" is sometimes used in a narrower sense to refer to the uncertainty of amounts of earnings applicable to common stock caused by the use of financial leverage (use of borrowed money) and other financial policies that affect the size of amounts at the bottom line of the income statement. The use of borrowed money increases the instability of earnings per share on common stock relative to the stability there would be if no borrowed money were used. If this element of risk is to be identified separately, it would be better to call it financial policy risk because it is an element of uncertainty of financial abilities attributable to financial policies.

In our concept of financial risk, financial ability means ability to make payments to investors at whatever stage may be appropriate in the accounting determination of income. Thus financial ability to make interest payments to bondholders is often measured by amounts of income available before interest and taxes. However, financial ability to pay dividends on common stock is measured chiefly by amounts of earnings after interest, taxes, and whatever charges rank ahead of dividends. The policy of using borrowed money affects the stability of amounts of earnings available for common dividends, but does not affect stability of income before interest and taxes.

The uncertainty of future market prices is sometimes called market risk, or forecasting risk. The purpose of this terminology is to recognize explicitly that there is uncertainty about the future market prices investors will receive on liquidation, and the chance of large error in attempting to forecast future prices. A similar concept is that of systematic risk. Systematic risk means the uncertainty of broad movements in average stock prices that are usually associated with the business cycle or with other developments that cause marked changes in average stock prices. This implies that some of the fluctuations in prices of individual stocks are a product of the market system of evaluating securities as well as of uncertainties peculiar to individual companies. In statistical terms, that part of the fluctuation in price for a stock that is explained by the correlation of its price and a broad average of prices is systematic risk.

It should be emphasized, though, that the price of each stock is directly linked to estimates of each company's future financial ability. If the price of a stock rises more or less in concert with prices of other stocks, it is because the issuer's future financial ability is appraised more favorably at the same time that the future prospects for other companies are being more favorably appraised. But there are always differences. In a generally rising stock market prices for some stocks rise much more than average prices, and prices for others rise much less. It is not unusual for prices of individual stocks to move counter to the movement of average stock prices.

All of these related concepts are included in our broad definition of financial risk as uncertainty about the future financial abilities of issuers. All of them have to do with financial abilities and investors' estimates of future financial abilities. They are helpful in recognizing that there are several facets to this cause of uncertainty.

DIFFERENTIATION IN LEVELS OF RISK

The level of financial risk in a security is a function of amounts of funds available to the issuer relative to the amount of funds required by contract to be paid, or expected to be paid by its owners, modified by the strength of the owners' claim for payment. That is a highly condensed statement that will be developed in subsequent chapters on security analysis. At this point our purpose is limited to understanding the general idea of differentiating among securities in terms of financial risk.

Application of the Risk Formula

In an analysis of corporate bonds, the most direct measure of funds available to funds required is the "times interest earned" ratio. The amount of earnings for a period of time is taken as the amount available, and the amount of interest on bonds for that period is the amount required. The greater the amount of earnings relative to amount of interest, the greater the ability to pay during that period. When a company's earnings have been many times greater than its bond interest each year for a period of years, the usual inference is that the company is likely to continue in the future to earn many times the amount of bond interest. Moreover, a large excess of earnings beyond what is required for bond interest provides a wide margin for any future shrinkage in earnings without serious impairment in financial ability to make payments to bondholders.

Estimates of the future may of course be somewhat different from the record of the past. An analyst may conclude that future changes in the economy, in the industry, or in the individual company, will cause the times interest earned ratio to increase or decrease in the future. The level of financial risk might be estimated at a little more, or a little less, than that indicated by the past record alone.

For a common stock the usual quantitative measure of sums available is earnings per share, and the amounts "required" are the amounts of dividends generally expected by investors. When a company has paid a stable amount of dividends per share in the past, that amount may be the expected amount. If the trend has been upward, the usual expectation is that it will continue upward. Security analysts examine the record of earnings per share for a series of years past; they study the historical stability and trend of earnings. Then they turn to the future and try to estimate the amounts of earnings that will probably be realized in the next several years. Amounts of dividends per share are usually estimated at some percentage of earnings per share, and these estimated amounts become the amounts required to fulfill the analyst's expectations. The greater the confidence of the analyst that his estimates will be realized in the future, the lower is the risk level of the stock. A high degree of confidence would be evidenced by a probability distribution of estimated amounts of earnings (or dividends) per share with small variance from the mean or projected trend. Professional analysts study continuously the stocks in which they are particularly interested. Sometimes they see developments taking place, or likely to take place, that cause them to raise or lower their expectations.

The other main element is the strength of the requirement to pay. Company managements almost always have some amount of money that could be used for payments to security holders but whether they will use it for that purpose is very much influenced by the importance they attach to making payments relative to using the money for something else. With a given amount of money, management is very likely to make payments to security holders if failure to do so would have seriously adverse consequences for the company. If the penalties are not severe, the decision might be to use the money for something else.

The strength of the requirement to pay is largely determined by the terms of the legal relationships between company and security holders. A company that has issued bonds has a contract with its bondholders to pay specified amounts on particular dates. If it fails to make payments, it violates its contract, and the bondholders have the legal remedies of creditors. Legal remedies, such as receivership or trusteeship for a company, come under the heading of seriously adverse consequences for corporate management. On the other hand, stockholders enjoy no such legal promise to pay dividends and accordingly the consequences of nonpayment of dividends are much less severe. In particular situations there are many different circumstances that affect the strength of the requirement to make payments to security holders, but the contrast between the legal positions of bondholders and stockholders is sufficient to illustrate the concept that financial ability is a product of the availability of money for payments to security holders and of the strength of the requirement to use available money for that purpose.

The System of Security Ratings

The system of bond ratings published by investment information services such as Moody's and Standard & Poor's exemplifies the idea of appraising what we have termed financial risk in securities and assigning individual security issues to risk classifications. In both systems the term "high-grade" is used to mean low financial risk. The highest grade bonds are designated by the letters "Aaa" for Moody's and "AAA" for Standard & Poor's. The next highest grade, which means the next lowest level of financial risk, is indicated by "Aa" for Moody's and "AA" for Standard & Poor's, and the third level is "A" in both systems. There are three B classifications and three C classifications for bonds representing higher levels of risk, differentiated in the same manner as the A classifications. Standard & Poor's has three D classifications for bonds in default.

Moody's says that bonds "rated Aaa are judged to be of the best quality. They carry the smallest degree of investment risk and are generally referred to as 'gilt edge.' Interest payments are protected by a large or by an exceptionally stable margin and principal is secure." A similar statement is used by Standard & Poor's. It reads, "Bonds rated AAA are the highest-grade obligations. They possess the ultimate degree of protection as to principal and interest."

The idea of a much higher level of financial risk appears in the rating services' description of bonds rated double B. Moody's statement is that,

"Bonds which are rated Ba are judged to have speculative elements; their future cannot be considered as well assured. Often the protection of interest and principal payments may be very moderate and thereby not well safeguarded during both good and bad times." Standard & Poor's says, "Bonds given a BB rating are regarded as lower medium-grade. They have only minor investment characteristics. In the case of utilities, interest is earned consistently but by narrow margins. In the case of other types of obligors, charges are earned on average by a fair margin, but in poor periods deficit operations are likely.[1]

There are several systems of rating or ranking for preferred and common stocks. Standard & Poor's ranks stocks in 7 groups, with A+ the highest grade, or lowest risk, and C as the lowest grade, or highest risk. These rankings are derived from statistical measures of historical stability and growth of earnings and dividends.[2] No estimate or judgment of the future is involved. The weight given to trend of earnings and dividends makes the rankings something other than a classification based on uncertainty of future financial abilities of issuers. Growth has no necessary relationship to the uncertainty of future earnings and dividends.

The Value Line Investment Survey includes rankings of stocks on the basis of safety, with grades from 1, which is the safest, down to 5. Rankings are based on historical stability of market price and growth in earnings.[3]

FINANCIAL RISK AND MARKET PRICES

When the financial abilities of companies improve, there is a tendency for market prices of their securities to increase. The higher the level of financial risk in the securities at a time prior to the improvement, the greater is the change in price. And the opposite is true.

Prices and Published Information

If a company has been earning its bond interest by only two or three times and then earnings increase so that they become 4 or 5 times the fixed charges to be paid, it is obvious that the company's financial ability has improved and that the uncertainty of future payments to bondholders has diminished. The rating assigned to this company's bond might very well be raised. An increase in its market price would be a natural consequence of reduction in level of risk.

[1]These statements are taken from 1972 editions of Moody's *Bond Record* and Standard & Poor's *Bond Guide*.

For a discussion of how bond ratings are determined see Thomas F. Pogue and Robert M. Soldofsky, "What's in a Bond Rating," *Journal of Financial and Quantitative Analysis*, Vol. IV, No. 2 (June 1969), pp. 201–228.

[2]Standard & Poor's *Stock Guide*, New York: 1972, Year-end 1971, p. 4.

[3]The Value Line Investment Survey, New York, Arnold Bernhard & Co.

We should keep in mind, though, that changes in bond prices are very much affected by changes in interest rates. It is entirely possible that an upward movement in market rates of interest occurring simultaneously with an improvement in financial ability would cause the market price for such a bond to decline. The effect of change in interest rates could override the effect of change in financial ability. Because there are these dual influences on price, you have to think about interest rate risk along with financial risk.

The information in these last two paragraphs could be put in opposite terms. A decline in the financial ability of an issuer of bonds would tend to bring about a decline in market price so that the higher expected rate of return (yield to maturity) would provide compensation for the higher level of financial risk. But a decline in market rates of interest could influence market price in an upward direction so that the actual change in price would be the net of the two influences.

The relationship of changes in financial abilities and change in market prices is even more obvious for common stocks because the level of risk for common stocks is usually much greater than it is for bonds. When a company reports pronounced increases in amounts of earnings per share for several successive years, dividend payments also increase and market price rises. The improvement in dividends and in price results from the published information about improvement in financial ability.

Prices and Expectations

If reported earnings per share for a stock increase for several successive years and dividends are increased, it is not difficult to project the improvement in financial ability into the future, and investors have a marked tendency to do so. So the price of the stock mentioned above would increase not only because of the publication of information showing that financial ability has improved, but also because investors expect the improvement to continue. Success breeds success. A company that has prospered is expected to continue to prosper. This is a broad generalization that we will qualify in due course, but in general terms market prices reflect expectations and expectations are to a considerable extent projections of past experience.

We described improvement in financial ability; the opposite kind of expectations follow financial adversity. A company that has been doing fairly well financially runs into trouble; earnings decline for several successive years and the dividend is reduced. Obviously the market price of its stock declines, and the decline reflects not only the poor financial reports but some expectation that things will go from bad to worse.

The Stock Market as a Laboratory

You can see the kind of phenomena we have been describing by watching what goes on in the stock market. Watch what happens to prices of stocks of companies that have a record of improved earnings over a period of several years, and to prices of stocks of companies with deteriorating earnings. Compare price and earnings per share by dividing price by current annual earnings per share, thus arriving at the price-earnings ratio. You will find that stocks of the companies with records of steady improvement in earnings sell in the market at much higher price-earnings ratios than those with little improvement. The high P/E ratio (price-earnings ratio) reflects not only the improvement that has occurred but also that which is expected. Conversely, the ratios for stocks of companies with declining earnings are usually quite low.

What is true of individual stocks is also true of large groups of stocks for which data are published as average earnings, dividends, and price per share. You can read the history of the stock market in the data published by Standard & Poor's for a group of 500 stocks and see how both published information and expectations have influenced average stock prices. These data are shown in Figure 5–1.

Look at the three lines in that figure and see how all three have trended upward. Average earnings per share is the independent variable. Average dividends per share have followed the trend of earnings. Average price, however, has increased at a greater average annual rate than the increase in earnings. Why? Because most investors most of the time have expected the upward trends in earnings to continue. There have been exceptions, though, to the generalization about favorable expectations. There have been periods in which average per share earnings have declined for several years in succession. That kind of earnings experience causes a shift in expectations and the shift is reflected in cyclical declines in average stock prices.

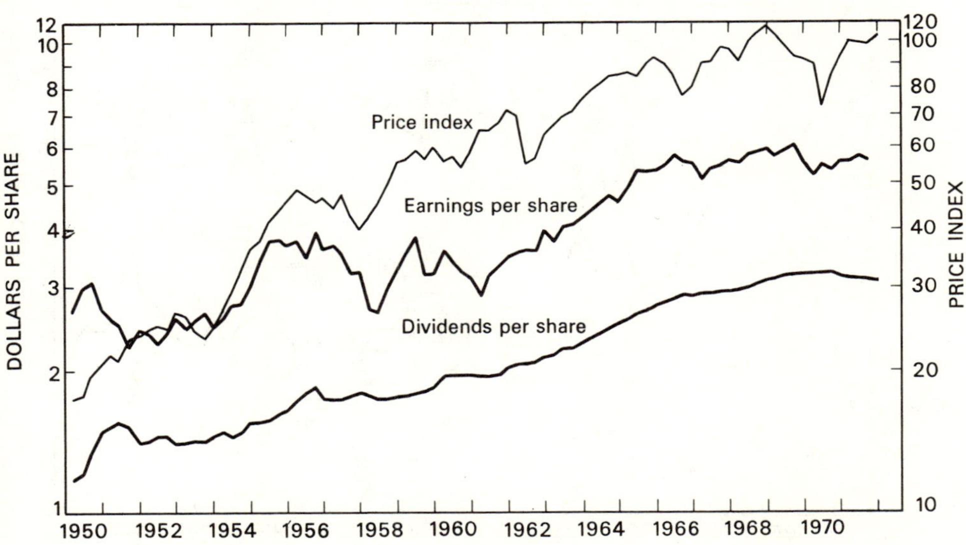

FIGURE 5–1

Average Prices, Earnings, and Dividends per share for Standard & Poor's 500 Common Stocks (Ratio Scale)

An exercise with the regression equation shows that the average annual rate of increase in stock prices as measured by the 500 stock index from 1950 through 1971 was 7.9 per cent, while the average annual increase in per share earnings in the same period was 4.5 per cent. Thus a large part of the increase in prices over this long period resulted from improvement in investor's expectations. Dividends increased at about the same rate as earnings.

Figure 5–2 shows average price-earnings ratios and average rates of dividend yield for the same 500 stocks for the same period of time. The marked increase in the average price-earnings ratio from below 7.5 in 1950 to about three times that figure in 1961 is one of the major events in recent financial history. It contributed greatly to the popularization of common stocks and to important changes in investment policies of individuals and institutions. More recently, that ratio has varied between 15 and 20. The pronounced decline in the average rate of dividend yields indicates that investors have come to rely more on price appreciation than on current income payments to provide a total rate of return on stocks commensurate with the risk of owning these securities.

Industries and Companies

Within this general pattern of influences that affect average stock prices are shifts in investors' estimates of the future that affect prices for stocks of companies in particular industries, and stocks of companies individually.

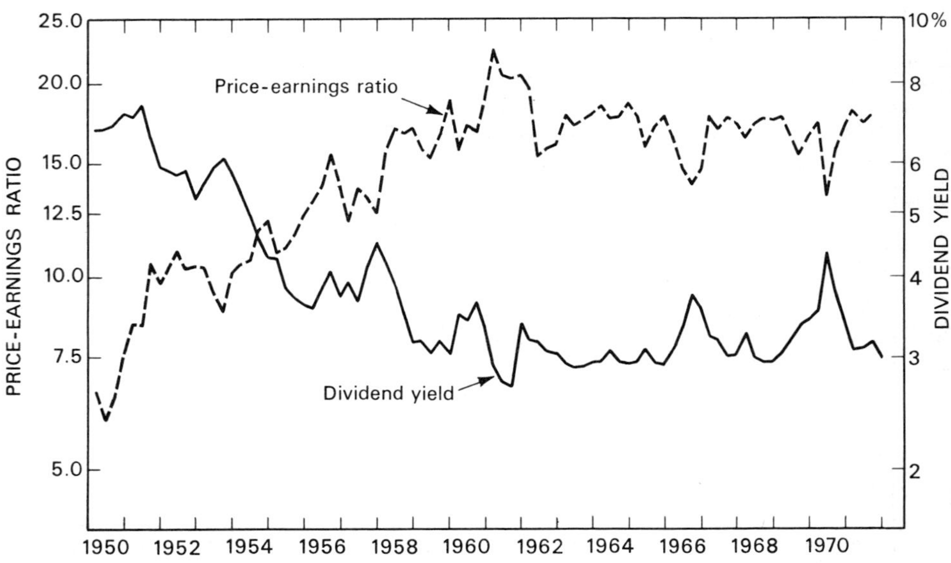

FIGURE 5–2

Price-Earnings Ratios and Dividend Yields for Standard & Poor's 500 Common Stocks (Ratio Scale)

At times industries become popular with investors and prices of stocks in those industry categories rise much more than average stock prices. Popularity is generated by a period of unusual prosperity in an industry. Favored by some shift in demand for their products, or a series of new products, earnings increase to an unusual extent and prices rise. Then the earnings increase is projected into the future and stock prices rise still further in anticipation of continued unusual earnings growth. It has not been uncommon for stocks of companies in such popular industries to sell at 50 times current earnings per share. Then it often happens that expectations prove to be exaggerated and stocks that were the darlings of one period become the dogs of the next. And of course the opposite is often true. An industry falls on hard times, earnings decrease, and prices for their stocks fall. Then the industry gets a bad name and investors turn their backs on those stocks. Often the prejudice continues after the reason for it has disappeared.

The same sort of shift in investors' expectations affects stocks of some individual companies. The shift may be related to a rise or fall in attitudes toward stocks generally, or to stocks of an industry, but there is often a love or hate relationship that is particular to a company. International Business Machines and Xerox have been the sweethearts of millions of investors for a long time. Several of the ethical drug manufacturers were much loved while important new products were coming out of their research and development programs and then were deserted when the stream of new products dried up. The names of several large and financially unsuccessful companies are almost synonyms for investor disappointment.

RISK LEVELS AND RATES OF RETURN

We hypothesized at the very beginning that total rates of return vary positively with levels of risk and we found that, with some qualifications, this concept is valid for securities differentiated by levels of interest rate risk. It also seems to be valid for securities differentiated chiefly on the basis of level of financial risk, but only for average rates of return for long time periods from large numbers of securities classified into risk categories by some measure of the extent to which the uncertainty of future financial abilities contributes to the uncertainty of rates of return. Several studies have shown that when estimated risk is plotted on the vertical axis and realized rate of return on the horizontal axis, average rates of return have a positive relationship to risk. The shape of the curve, however, varies according to the system used for classifying securities by risk level and it may vary from one relatively long time period to another.

Rates of Return for Bonds

You can look at the bond market at any time and see evidence that expected rates of return in the form of yields to maturity at market prices are greater for bonds with larger financial risk than for those with smaller risk.

There is a graduation upward from average yields on triple A rated bonds to double A, to single A, to triple B. When these average market rates of yield are plotted, as in Figure 5–3, they form a moderately rising curve. There is some chance that these rates will not be realized because of defaults, repurchase in the markets at prices less than par, and redemption before maturity at more than par.

A voluminous study of all corporate bonds publicly offered in the United States in initial amounts of $5 million or more during the long period 1900–1943 offered strong empirical evidence that there was a positive relationship between average realized rates of returns and level of risk as measured by bond ratings. In this study life-span yields were calculated from date of issue to date of extinguishment, except that issues outstanding on January 1, 1944, were assumed to have been liquidated at market prices then prevailing. These aggregate data show that average realized yields on bonds in the first three rating grades were about the same, but that there was a marked increase in yields for the lower rated, higher-risk bonds. The curve made by plotting these data on risk-return axes, Figure 5–3, is flat for the higher-grade issues and then rises steeply. The main outline of the curve is convex. The corporate bond study also included data on bonds rated below the B category and showed remarkably high rates realized by C-rated bonds.[4]

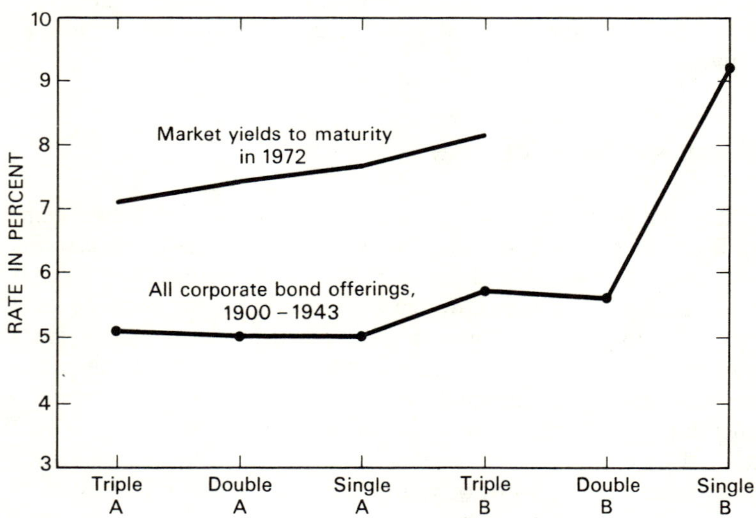

FIGURE 5–3

Rates of Return on Corporate Bonds of Different Risk Grades

[4]W. Braddock Hickman, Statistical Measures of Corporate Bond Financing Since 1900, Princeton, N.J., 1960, National Bureau of Economic Research, pp. 394, 579, and 580.

Rates for Bonds Compared with Stocks

Early researchers concentrated on the differences in rates of return realized from samples of bonds relative to rates from samples of stocks. Their data extend well back into the nineteenth century. The conclusion of most studies was that common stocks provided larger average rates over long time periods than did bonds during the same time periods.[5]

Subsequently, a large-scale study of rates of return actually realized by a sample of large life insurance companies from their total investments in bonds, preferred stocks, and common stocks showed that over a 37-year period from 1929 to 1965, their average annual rate of return on common stocks was 9.39 per cent, on preferred stocks it was 4.72 per cent, and on bonds the rate was 3.49 per cent. Bonds are, of course, regarded as representing the lowest level of financial risk, preferred stocks a somewhat higher level, and common stocks the highest level.[6]

Rates for Common Stocks by Risk Levels

If the thesis that rates of return vary positively with risk is valid, then total rates of return from categories of common stocks graded according to level of risk should rise as risk increases. This thesis was well supported by a study in which all common stocks listed on the New York Stock Exchange were divided into ten deciles according to size of variation in their investment performance relatives[7] computed monthly over periods of several years duration extending from 1926 to 1966. Size of variation was taken as a measure of risk. Average rates of return were calculated for each decile for a series of 1-year holding periods subsequent to periods in which variation was measured. The average annual rates per decile indicated by investment performance relatives are shown in Figure 5–4.

The data show a distinct tendency for average rates to increase from the first decile, the most stable, to the tenth decile, the least stable. There is, however, a marked difference in the shape of the rate of return curve for stocks divided into categories by level of financial risk and the realized rate of return curve for corporate bonds in Figure 5–3. The curve for common stock categories is slightly convex, rather than concave. Rates do not rise so sharply as risk increases from moderate to high. In terms of annual rates, the

[5]A summary of early research is presented in Chelcie C. Bosland, *The Common Stock Theory of Investment*, New York, 1937, The Ronald Press.

[6]James J. O'Leary, 1963 Record of Life Insurance Investments (New York: Life Insurance Association of America, 1964), and subsequent tabulations of LIAA.

[7]An investment performance relative is price at end of a period plus dividend during the period divided by price at beginning of period.

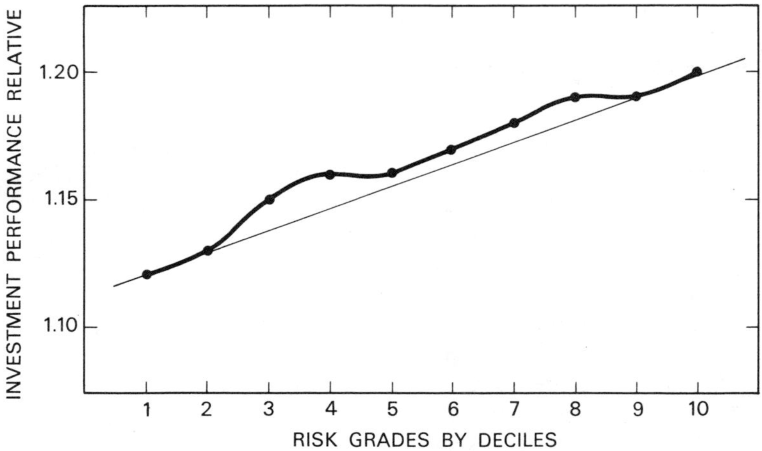

FIGURE 5–4

Investment Performance Relatives for Common Stock Portfolios of Different Risk Grades, 1929–1966.

highest-grade stocks provided an average annual rate of 12 per cent and the lowest grade stocks returned an average rate of 20 per cent.[8]

These data suggest that the steeply rising aversion to higher levels of risk among bond investors, as indicated by the much higher realized rates on bonds of the lower ratings, is not so pronounced in the area of common stocks. Institutional rigidities may explain the strong increase in aversion to bonds of the lower grades and the weaker rise in aversion to risk in the lower grades of stocks. Commercial banks are not permitted by regulatory authorities to buy bonds with ratings lower than triple B and most limit themselves to the three top rating grades. Insurance companies seldom go below the triple B rating in buying publicly offered bonds. Individuals are not large buyers of corporate bonds. In the category of common stocks, however, individual persons own much the larger portion and they are not subject to such regulatory limitations upon their purchases of stocks. Many individual investors appear to be attracted to the more risky stocks by the opportunity for large returns. The most important institutional buyers of common stocks in recent years have been noninsured pension funds that are not subject to governmental regulation of their common stock investments. Thus risk aversion in the market for common stocks seems to rise less steeply than it does in the bond market.

[8]Shannon P. Pratt, "Relationship Between Risk and Return for Common Stocks," unpublished dissertation, Indiana University, Bloomington, Indiana, 1966. The data depicted in Figure 5–4 were developed subsequent to completion of the dissertation and were provided by Prof. Pratt to the author. Prof. Pratt's work is described in Brealey, *An Introduction to Risk and Return from Common Stocks, op. cit.*, pp. 38–50.

The Variations from Period to Period in Average Returns from Common Stocks

There are several studies that tell a great deal about how average rates of return from large numbers of stocks have varied over relatively long time periods. One researcher computed rates of return that would have been realized from investment in all common stocks listed on the New York Stock Exchange during a series of periods. The most significant finding was that there have been relatively long periods in which owners of all NYSE listed common stocks would have realized negative rates of return. If you had bought all of these stocks at the peak of a bull market in September 1929 and sold them at the bottom of a long bear market in June 1932, you would have incurred an annual rate of loss of 48.6 per cent. If you had bought in September 1929 and held for more than a decade, until December 1940, the negative rate would have been 5 per cent. You would have had to hold the September 1929 purchases to December 1950 to obtain an average annual rate of return of 2.2 per cent.

At the opposite extreme, if you had bought all NYSE listed stocks at the low level of prices in June 1932, you would have had a rate of return of 24.4 per cent to December 1940. Holding them from June 1932 to the end of 1950, to 1956, to 1958, or to 1960, would, of course, have provided relatively high rates of return. Data from this study are summarized in Table 5–1.

Table 5–2 summarizes a study of rates of return provided by the Standard & Poor's 500 common stocks for a series of 10-year periods. The rates are the discount rates that reduce the sum of annual average dividends per share for 10 years and market price at the end of ten years to the price at the beginning of the period. The 10-year periods begin with the end of 1942 and move forward 5 years at a time so that there is a series of overlapping 10-year periods. Each of these periods provided a relative high rate of return, but the rate diminishes as the periods move forward in time. The data support the generalization that for some three decades average annual rates of return on a large numbers of common stocks held for relatively long periods were relatively high.

Variations in Returns from Millions of Stock Transactions

Another study that probably had a greater impact on the community of financial analysts and investment managers than any other that has come from academe reported the results of some 56½ million random transactions in all New York Stock Exchange listed stocks over a period from 1926 to 1960. Many professionals were startled by the finding that the median rate of return of the entire distribution of rates of return on transactions was 9.8

TABLE 5–1

Rates of Return on Investment in All New York Stock Exchange Listed Common Stocks. (Per cent per annum compounded annually)

Period	*Rate*
January 1926 to:	
Sept. 1929	19.7%
June 1932	−13.4
Dec. 1940	1.6
Dec. 1950	5.1
Dec. 1960	6.9
September 1929 to:	
June 1932	−48.6
Dec. 1940	− 5.0
Dec. 1950	2.2
Dec. 1960	4.9
June 1932 to:	
Dec. 1940	24.4
Dec. 1950	21.4
Dec. 1960	20.5
December 1950 to:	
Dec. 1956	16.5
Dec. 1958	16.1
Dec. 1960	14.9
December 1955 to:	
Dec. 1960	10.9

Note: This study embraces all common stocks listed on the New York Stock Exchange. It shows the results of investing an equal sum of money in each company having one or more issues of listed common stock at the beginning of a time period and holding to the end of a period. Rate of return is defined as the rate of interest, compounded annually, which an individual would have had to get, on a sum equal to the value of the portfolio at the beginning of a period, in order to equal the value of the portfolio at the end of the period, plus the amount of cash dividends received. The computation is on the basis of cash at beginning of period to cash at end of period with regular round-lot brokerage commissions taken into account. In this table it is not assumed that dividends have been reinvested and no account has been taken of income taxes.

Source: Lawrence Fisher and James H. Lorie, "Rates of Return on Investments in Common Stocks," *The Journal of Business* (January, 1964), pp. 3–7.

per cent a year. It was surprising that such a high median rate would result from transactions effected entirely without expertise either in stock selection or in determining the time of purchase and sale of stocks. The study was at least equally significant in revealing the wide distribution of rates of return from a great many stock transactions.[9]

This study by Professor Fisher used a computer tape with monthly price and dividend data for all NYSE listed stocks for the 1926–1960 period. Each stock was assumed to have been purchased at the market price at the

[9]Lawrence Fisher, "Outcomes for 'Random' Investments in Common Stocks Listed on the New York Stock Exchange," *The Journal of Business* (April 1965), pp. 149–161.

TABLE 5–2

Rates of Return on Standard & Poor's 500 Stock Index for a Series of Ten Year Periods.

Period	*Average annual rate*
1943–52	16.6%
1948–57	16.3
1953–62	13.7
1958–67	13.1
1963–72	9.5*

*Partially estimated.

Source: Standard & Poor's *Trade and Securities Service*. Calculations by the author.

end of the first month of the period and sold at the end of the second month, at the end of the third month, and at the end of each month thereafter until the end of the period. Then each stock was assumed to have been purchased at the end of the second month and sold at the end of each month thereafter. The process of buying was carried on for the end of each successive month, with sale at the end of each month thereafter. The total number of transactions was 56,557,583.

The frequency distribution of the annual rates of loss and gain pre-

TABLE 5–3

Frequency Distribution of Rates of Return for All Combinations of Month-End Purchases and Sales of Each Common Stock on the New York Stock Exchange

	Annual rate of returns (percentage)	*Percentage of total transactions*
Losses:		
	−100% (Total loss)	0.005%
	− 50 to 100	1.4
	− 30 to 50	2.4
	− 20 to 30	2.6
	− 10 to 20	4.8
	− 5 to 10	4.1
	0 to −5	6.5
Gains:		
	0 to +4	8.4
	+ 4 to 8	13.1
	+ 8 to 12	15.1
	+ 12 to 16	13.3
	+ 16 to 20	9.4
	+ 20 to 30	10.7
	+ 30 to 50	5.0
	+ 50 to 100	2.3
	+100 to 1,000	0.9
	Greater than 1,000	0.05
	Total	100.0%

Source: Lawrence Fisher, "Outcomes for 'Random' Investments in Common Stocks listed on the New York Stock Exchange," *The Journal of Business* (April 1965), p. 153.

sented in Table 5–3 is the best set of empirical data presently available on the riskiness of transactions in common stocks. Some transactions resulted in total losses and some provided rates of return in excess of 1,000 per cent. The interquartile range was from 1.8 to 17.3 per cent. The distribution is skewed to the right, with 78 per cent of all transactions yielding a positive rate of return and only 22 a negative rate. The rates on transactions were, of course, very much affected by the upswings and downturns of average market prices, and the entire distribution was affected by the strong rise in stock prices in the 1950's.

At this point you should be deeply impressed with the riskiness of common stocks as well as with the relatively high average rates of return from this category of securities. Whether you win or lose, and how much, depends greatly on changes in the economy associated with the business cycle and the more or less corresponding shifts in investors' estimates of the future. It also depends on which stocks you select. Some have made people rich and others have made them poor.

QUESTIONS FOR DISCUSSION

1. It has been stated that changes in interest rates affect realized rates of return at the same time that changes in financial ability affect rates of return. What does that mean? Think about it in terms of changes in market prices for bonds.
2. How do investors' estimates of future changes in an issuer's financial ability affect the market price for its stock?
3. Is the concept of systematic risk included in the concept of change in financial abilities of an issuer as a cause of uncertainty?
4. Bond ratings are used as a measure of financial risk. Do they also serve as a measure of interest rate risk?
5. What does Figure 5–1 tell you about how change in the financial abilities of issuers have affected average prices for common stocks? Figure 5–2 may be helpful.
6. What does Figure 5–1 tell you about how changes in investors' expectations have affected market prices for common stocks? Figure 5–2 may be helpful.
7. What industries are particularly favored by common-stock investors at the present time? You will have to do some research to arrive at an answer. See investment services or financial periodicals.
8. Select some well-known stock and make a tabulation of its earnings per share for the past several years. Then make a corresponding tabulation of its market price at the end of each of the years. Have the changes in prices been highly correlated with changes in earnings? See investment services and financial periodicals.
9. Is it true that historically average rates of return on large numbers of common stocks held for long time periods have been larger than average rates of return on large numbers of bonds held for long periods?
10. If you buy common stocks of five good companies at a time when you think their prices are low, hold them for some period of time, and sell them when you think prices are high, what are the chances that the total rate of return you realize on the total amount of your investment will be greater than the 9.8 per cent, which was the average rate on a large number of random transactions in common stocks?

6

Changes in the Price Level as a Cause of Uncertainty

I. Price inflation and real returns
   - A. Current dollars converted to constant dollars
   - B. The grades of securities in convertibility
   - C. The Consumer Price Index as a measure of inflation
   - D. Price inflation in other countries

II. The uncertainty of returns in constant dollars
   - A. The uncertainty of constant dollar returns from common stocks
     1. Rates in constant dollars over long time periods
     2. The instability of constant dollar returns
     3. Inflation, deflation, and rates of return
     4. Price inflation and industry stock price averages
     5. The linkage between the price level and returns from common stocks
     6. Earnings rates, earnings retention, and price inflation
   - B. The uncertainty of returns from bonds in constant dollars
     1. Inflation and market rates of interest
     2. Change in portfolio rates of return
   - C. Purchasing-power risk and rates of return

III. Some other contributions to risk
   - A. Moral, legal, and political risks
   - B. The risk of social change

The uncertainties of investment returns caused by changes in interest rates and by changes in the financial abilities of issuers are risks that affect the size of returns in dollars of whatever purchasing power they may have at the time they are received. But there is still another major cause of uncertainty that for most investors is as important as the other two and may be even more important. This is the uncertainty of the size of returns in constant dollars caused by changes in the price level. Constant dollars are dollars that have the same purchasing power in one time period as in another. This cause of uncertainty is often called the purchasing power risk.

You know that when market rates of interest rise or decline, bond prices rise and fall so that the principal amount you may recover through sale of bonds varies. You are familiar with the idea that there are variations in market prices for common stocks that are caused by changes in the financial abilities of companies. And it is evident that amounts of income from principal amounts invested may vary from one time to another. But these amounts of income and market values are in current dollars. The third variable is the price level. How much those dollars of investment returns are worth to you in terms of the quantities of goods and services they will buy in the future is a function of change in the price level.

If rates of return on investments are measured in constant dollars, then realized rates are the algebraic sum of changes attributable to these three causes of uncertainty. The idea that returns in constant dollars are the result of these kinds of uncertainty is depicted in Figure 6–1.

PRICE INFLATION AND REAL RETURNS

Economists and financial analysts often use the term "real" in identifying dollar amounts to mean amounts in constant dollars. Thus real incomes are incomes in current dollars adjusted for change in the price level. Amounts in current dollars received in a series of time periods can be converted to constant dollar amounts by dividing the series of amounts by a price index. In the United States the Consumer Price Index is commonly used for this purpose.

Causes of uncertainty		
Interest rate risk	Returns in current dollars	Returns in constant dollars
Financial risk		
Purchasing power risk		

FIGURE 6–1

Three Causes of Uncertainty Affecting Constant Dollar Returns

Current Dollars Converted to Constant Dollars

Figure 6–2 shows how the rise in the price level in a recent period has affected the real incomes of investors from securities that pay a fixed amount of income and from those that pay variable amounts. The broken line at the top is amounts of interest in current dollars from a principal amount of $100 invested at 6 per cent. The solid line declining across the broken line shows the purchasing power of those amounts of interest income adjusted for change

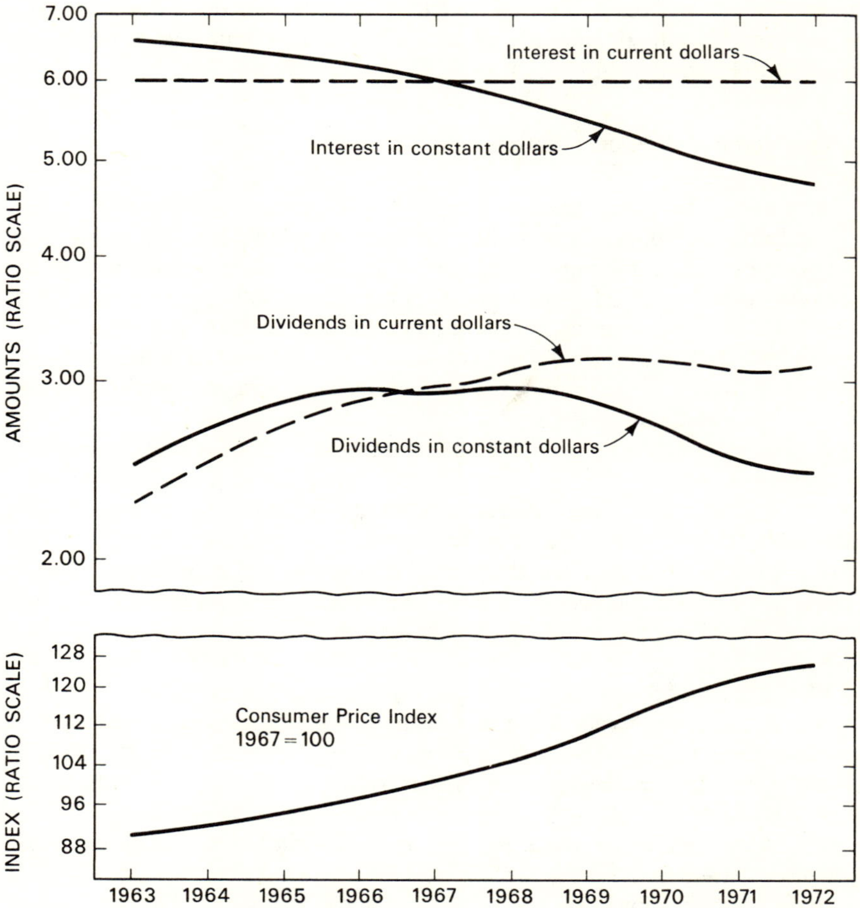

FIGURE 6–2

Investment Returns in Current and Constant Dollars

Interest is at 6 per cent on $100 principal amount; dividends are average annual amounts on Standard & Poor's 500 common stocks; the Consumer Price Index on base 1967 = 100 is the deflator.

in the price level. The rise in the Consumer Price Index in this period of time is shown in the lower part of the graph. In constant dollars the interest received in the last year of the 10-year period was 73 per cent of the amount received in the first year. The broken line identified as dividends in current dollars is the average annual amount of dividends per share for Standard & Poor's 500 common stocks. Here you see that amounts of dividends in current dollars increased in the early part of the period and then leveled off. When these amounts are converted to constant dollars the curve of the solid line rises at first and then declines. In the early part of the period the increase in amounts in current dollars was more than sufficient to compensate for the rise in the price level and amounts in constant dollars increased, but in the latter part of the period it was not and the curve turned downward. In constant dollars the annual amounts of dividends were about the same in the last year of the period as in the first year.

The History of Price Inflation

The history of price inflation is as old as organized society and as universal as human conflict. In primitive societies in which metallic coins were the medium of exchange kings clipped coins to reduce their weight, and prices in debased coins increased. When paper money came into use the method of inflation was that of printing more money. In the modern system of using bank deposits as the principal kind of money, the method of inflation is expansion in amounts of bank deposits and currency (money supply) by action of governments and central banks.

People used to praise an article by saying that it is as sound as a dollar. The analogy is a poor one. In the past 150 years the dollar has lost about 85 per cent of its purchasing power. Most of the inflation in this country has been associated with war. The War between the States in the 1860's caused the price level to double. Then there was a long period of price deflation in the latter part of the nineteenth century, which can be attributed to the fact that we had not become very sophisticated in matters of currency and bank deposits.

World War I brought a new surge of price inflation and again the price level doubled in a relatively few years. But this period was followed by one of relative price stability in the 1920's and of price deflation in the 1930's. The war and inflation phenomenon was repeated in the 1940's with World War II. And again there was a period of relative price stability in the 1950's. The pattern was one of alternate periods of marked inflation and either deflation or price stability.

In the 1960's, however, the pattern seemed to change. Federal budget deficits and monetary policy that permitted a great expansion in money supply caused an acceleration of the rate of increase in the price level. Toward the end of that decade prices were rising at an annual rate of about 5 per cent and inflation came to be regarded as the nation's paramount economic problem.

The significance of this historical sketch is that investors' attitudes toward change in the price level as a cause of uncertainty have changed. They have long been aware of the shrinkage in the purchasing power of investment returns during periods of marked inflation, but they were inclined to view this as an "on again, off again" sort of experience. More recently they have come to regard inflation as a chronic condition and to project into the future a price level rising continuously at two or three times the average annual rate of 1 to 2 per cent that economists have regarded as necessary to the economic growth of the country and to a condition of reasonably full employment. Investment decisions have come to be influenced more and more by the expectation of chronic price inflation.

The Consumer Price Index as a Measure of Inflation

Since the Consumer Price Index is commonly used as a measure of inflation, it is well to recognize that it is not a perfect measure. It is designed to show the cost of a "market basket" of goods and services purchased by families of wage earners and clerical workers living in cities. It is not supposed to measure change in the purchasing power of dollars spent by farmers or by workers in rural areas. Neither does it measure change in cost of living for people in the middle- and upper-income brackets who spend their money in somewhat different proportions for somewhat different things than wage earners and clerical workers.

The content of the market basket of urban wage earners and clerical workers changes from time to time as the kinds of goods and services on which they spend their money change. The index has been revised from time to time to recognize such shifts in spending, but it may not do so perfectly.

An effort has also been made to adjust this price index for changes in the quality of goods and services. There is a more or less continuous process of improvement in quality of goods and services and the tendency is for better quality products to be more expensive. Some statisticians say that this adjustment has not been entirely successful and that to some extent the upward trend in the price index reflects improvement in quality.

Price Inflation in Other Countries

We view with alarm the process of price inflation in the United States, but when we look beyond our borders we see other countries that in the twentieth century have had much worse experiences. The monetary systems of many of the countries of Western Europe were wrecked twice by wars and the consequences of wars. Even in the relatively long period of comparative peace since 1945 the trend of the price level has been upward in most countries of Europe, Asia, and Latin America.

The classic example of inflation to the point of worthless currency is that of Germany after World War I. A weak government beset by grave economic problems resorted to the printing press on a large scale. Finally a new currency was created and exchanged for the old currency at the rate of one new mark for 1 trillion old marks.

France, although on the winning side in both world wars, has repeatedly experienced severe inflation. In the 1920's the franc was devalued to one-fifth of its former value in terms of gold. Again in 1960 the franc was devalued by introducing a new franc, which was exchanged for old francs at a rate of one for ten.

The pound sterling, once the strongest of national currencies, has been battered by the same storms of economics and politics. It was made inconvertible to gold in the 1930's, devalued in the 1960's, and in the 1970's allowed to fluctuate within a moderate range relative to other currencies.

Thus chronic inflation seems to be a characteristic of modern democratic, capitalistic societies. Table 6–1 shows the average annual rates of depreciation in the purchasing power of the currencies of a number of industrialized countries in recent time periods.

THE UNCERTAINTY OF RETURNS IN CONSTANT DOLLARS

Can you differentiate categories of securities according to the uncertainty of their returns in constant dollars? The question is a difficult one be-

TABLE 6–1

The Rates of Depreciation in the Purchasing Power of Currencies of Industrialized Countries.[a]

Country	*1961–1971*	*1966–1971*
United States	3.0%	4.3%
Greece	2.2	2.2
Japan	5.6	5.4
Luxembourg	2.9	3.2
Canada	2.8	3.6
Italy	4.0	3.4
Belgium	3.3	3.4
Germany	2.9	2.8
France	4.2	4.7
Sweden	4.4	4.5
Austria	3.6	3.7
Iceland	10.7	10.6
South Africa	3.1	3.8
Denmark	5.7	6.0
Switzerland	3.7	3.7
Norway	4.7	5.2
Australia	2.7	3.6
United Kingdom	4.4	5.4
Finland	5.1	4.9
New Zealand	4.4	6.0

[a]Data shows average annual rates of depreciation derived from price indexes.

Source: *Monthly Economic Letter,* First National City Bank, September 1972, p. 11.

cause returns in constant dollars are the net result of the two causes of uncertainty of returns in current dollars plus the uncertainty of the price level. Any generalization must take account of all three causes of uncertainty.

First, it should be recognized that price inflation affects all amounts in current dollars. It makes no difference whether a dollar of return is received from bonds or stocks. If a dollar is received at the end of a year as bond interest for that period and the price level has increased 5 per cent in the year, the return in constant dollars is $0.952. The same is true of a dollar received as dividend on stock.

Second, the size of returns in current dollars may change from period to period. An increase in current dollar amounts tends to compensate for (and may more than compensate for) a rise in the price level. If the price level increases 5 per cent in a year and an amount of investment return at the end of the year is $1.05 relative to $1.00 at the end of the immediately preceding year, the return in constant dollars is $1.00. In that example, the effect of uncertainties affecting current dollars exactly compensated for the rise in the price level.

Thus a security would have a low level of purchasing power risk if there was a high probability that the size of returns in current dollars would increase at about the same rate as the increase in the price level. The risk would be higher if there were no significant positive correlation between changes in current dollar amounts and changes in the price level, and it would be highest if the correlation were negative.

This discussion of levels of purchasing power risk associated with different categories of securities is entirely in terms of a rising price level. The likelihood of a decline in prices, or even of a relatively stable price level, seems remote. But the system of analysis would be the same. Under conditions of a declining price level those securities would have the least purchasing power risk that provide returns in current dollars decreasing as the price level decreases.

The Uncertainty of Constant Dollar Returns from Common Stocks

It is sometimes said that common stocks are a good inflation hedge. In more precise language, this means that there has been a strong tendency over relatively long periods in the past for amounts of dividends and market values of stocks in current dollars to increase sufficiently to more or less compensate for the rise in the price level. This proposition refers to average returns from large numbers of common stocks.

Rates in constant dollars over long time periods. If you look at a chart of average stock prices and at average amounts of dividends, such as presented earlier in Figure 5–1, you will see the upward trend in both of these series. In some periods these increases in current dollar amounts were at a higher rate than the rate of price inflation, so that the size of constant dollar amounts increased. At other periods the rise in current dollar returns was less than the rate of price inflation and returns in constant dollars decreased.

Table 6–2 shows average annual rates of return from Standard & Poor's

TABLE 6–2

Average Annual Rates of Return in Current and in Constant Dollars from Standard & Poor's 500 Stocks

Period	*Rates in* *Current Dollars*	*Constant Dollars*
1943–52	16.6%	10.9%
1948–57	16.3	13.5
1953–62	13.7	12.2
1958–67	13.1	11.2
1963–72	9.5[a]	6.1[a]
Average of 10-year period rates	13.8%	10.8%

[a] Partly estimated.

Source: Standard & Poor's *Trade and Securities Service*. Computations by the author.

500 common stocks for a series of overlapping 10-year periods from 1943 to 1972. Rates in constant dollars were calculated by reducing dividends and market prices in current dollars to constant dollars using the Consumer Price Index and then computing rates of return from amounts in constant dollars.

Rates in current dollars were very high during most of this period. They were reduced in each 10-year period by price inflation, but even so the average of the 10-year period rates in constant dollars was 10.8 per cent. In evaluating these data keep in mind that the total time period included the longest and largest bull market in stocks in the history of the country.

The instability of constant dollar returns. The danger in generalizing about common stocks being a good inflation hedge is that the great uncertainty of constant dollar returns over shorter periods will be neglected. The fact is that returns from even such a broad average of stocks as Standard & Poor's 500 have varied widely from year to year. Table 6–3 shows annual total rates of return in constant dollars from that group of 500 stocks.

The annual percentage changes in constant dollar amounts range from − 13.6 to + 52 per cent. The mean of the distribution is +11.9 per cent and the standard deviation is 18.3. On a year-by-year basis constant dollar returns from common stocks have been highly unstable. In these terms they have a high level of uncertainty of constant dollar returns. Changes in constant dollar amounts have not been well correlated with changes in the price level; indeed, the pronounced declines in stock prices in years when the price level was rising indicates negative correlation.

Inflation, deflation, and rates of return. There is considerable evidence that neither inflation nor deflation is good for stocks, but that the larger rates of return are usually realized in periods of relative price stability. In Table 6–3, the larger annual rates of return were realized in years when the price level changed very little. Four of the years in which the highest rates of return in constant dollars were realized were years in which the price level changed less than 1 per cent (1952, 1954, 1955, and 1961). The years of more steeply rising prices later in the period saw negative rates or moderate positive rates.

TABLE 6–3

Distribution of Annual Rates of Return in Constant Dollars for Standard & Poor's 500 Stocks[a]

Year		*Year*	
1954	+52.0%	1956	+10.1%
1961	+45.8	1959	+10.1
1958	+39.9	1968	+ 5.8
1952	+25.0	1960	− 1.2
1955	+24.9	1953	− 1.8
1963	+20.6	1970	− 1.9
1967	+20.1	1962	− 9.9
1951	+16.5	1966	−13.0
1964	+14.9	1957	−13.1
1971	+10.3	1969	−13.6
1965	+10.2		

[a]Computed by converting price and dividend data per share to constant dollars and computing investment performance relatives. The data above are IPR's minus 100.

Source: Standard & Poor's, *Trade and Securities Service*, Computations by the author.

You may also recall that the period of steepest decline in stock prices in recent history, from November 1968 to May 1970, was also a period of relatively high rates of increase in the price level. Stock prices and consumer prices sometimes move in opposite directions.

The only relatively long period of price deflation in recent history occurred during the 1930's. From September 1929 to May 1932, average stock prices declined 86 per cent. During the same period the CPI declined about 22 per cent. The increase in the purchasing power of the dollar by no means compensated for the decline in market values of stocks, and common stockholders suffered heavy losses in purchasing power. The study of rates of return from all New York Stock Exchange listed stocks shows that if they were purchased in September 1929 and held to the end of 1940, they would have provided an annual return of −3 per cent in current dollars. The average annual decline in the price level from the beginning to the end of that period was about 2 per cent. Thus the annual rate of return in constant dollars was slightly on the minus side for more than a decade.[1]

One study addressed directly to the question whether common stocks have been a good inflation hedge concluded that they have not been. The authors examined experience in 5 periods between 1941 and 1968 which were defined as periods of inflation by the relative size of the annual rate of increase in the CPI. Annual rates of return were computed in current dollars to show the "nominal rates of return" and adjusted for the increase in the price level to show "real rates of return." Using Standard & Poor's 500 stocks this study found that in two of the inflation periods the rate of return was negative, in two it was relatively low, and in only one was it high. A part of the data presented in this study are shown in Table 6–4.

[1]Lawrence Fisher and James Lorie, "Rates of Return on Investments in Common Stocks," *The Journal of Business* (January, 1964), pp. 3–71.

TABLE 6–4

Rates of Return During Periods of Inflation from Standard & Poor's 500 Common Stocks

Period	*Length of Periods (Months)*	*Annual rate of change in CPI*	*Nominal rates of return*	*Real rates of return*
3/31/41 to 6/30/43	27	9.8%	16.6%	6.2%
3/31/46 to 9/30/48	30	12.5	−1.5	−12.5
3/31/50 to 12/31/51	21	6.9	28.4	20.2
3/31/56 to 3/31/58	24	3.7	−3.1	−6.5
12/31/65 to 12/31/68	36	3.7	7.1	3.3

Source: Frank K. Reilly, Glenn L. Johnson and Ralph E. Smith, "Inflation, Inflation Hedges, and Common Stocks," *The Financial Analysts Journal*, Vol. 26, No. 1, January–February 1970, pp. 104–110.

Price inflation and industry stock price averages. These studies of common stocks and price inflation have used data that are averages of large numbers of stocks of companies in many different industries. If you look at returns from stocks of companies grouped by industries, you find that returns in constant dollars have varied widely by industry. The data in Table 6–5 show changes in Standard and Poor's price indexes for companies in the several principal industry classifications. Dividend data are not available, so the percentage change in that table is change in average price reduced to constant dollars. You can see that price changes in constant dollars from 1960 to 1971 have varied from an increase of 170 per cent for stocks of electrical equipment companies to a decrease of 59 per cent for stocks of steel companies.

What this means is that changes in financial abilities of companies have been the principal influence on price of stocks in constant dollars. Some industries have prospered and some have not. Conversion of current dollars into constant dollars merely modifies the effect of prosperity or lack of it on market prices.

The linkage between the price level and returns from common stocks. Why should broadly diversified investments in common stock be expected to provide rates of return in current dollars over long time periods that compensate to some extent for increases in the price level? Is there reason to think that the experience of investors with common stocks in the fourth quarter of the twentieth century will be much the same as in the third quarter of the century? If you can explain the experience in the third quarter, you have some basis for estimating the fourth quarter.

The idea is sometimes expressed that there is some sort of automatic linkage between the price level and the size of returns from common stocks. The notion is that when we have price inflation, companies make more money by selling their goods or services at higher prices, and their stocks become more valuable. This is an inaccurate explanation and it leads to over-generalizations about the merits of common stocks as an inflation hedge.

The relatively favorable experience of investors with common stock in the past several decades has stemmed primarily from the ability of companies

TABLE 6–5
Stock Price Indexes for Industry Groups in Constant Dollars

Industry	*Price index at end of 1960 (in current dollars)*	*Price index at end of 1971 (in constant dollars)*	*Percentage of change*
Electrical equipment	82.4	222.8	+170
Office business equipment	368.8	897.6	+143
Drugs	62.0	142.2	+129
Textile products	24.9	43.3	+ 74
Electronics	230.9	397.5	+ 72
Gold mining	16.4	21.8	+ 33
Petroleum	65.5	86.5	+ 32
Machine tools	24.8	29.7	+ 20
Lead and zinc	9.4	9.8	+ 4
Paper	159.3	146.5	− 8
Chemicals	46.9	38.9	− 17
Tire and rubber	226.0	162.8	− 28
Steel	71.0	29.3	− 59

Source: Standard & Poor's, Trade and Securities Service, 1972.

to earn a good rate of return on their equity capital and to retain a substantial part of earnings for reinvestment in the business. Data for the 425 industrial companies in Standard & Poor's stock price index show that in a recent 20-year period the average annual rate of earnings on average book value per share was 12.2 per cent. During the same period the average amount of earnings retained was 44.3 per cent of per share earnings. We have shifted from the 500 stock index to the 425 stock index because book values are published for the industrial companies but not for the entire group of 500 companies. Increase in per share earnings for a period is the rate of return on equity capital multiplied by the percentage of earnings retained. Thus, if these average rates were constant for the 20-year period, the average annual increase in per share earnings would be 5.4 per cent (12.2 times 44.3 per cent).

The relationship between average book value per share and average earnings per share for Standard & Poor's 425 industrial stocks is shown in Figure 6–3. The coefficient of correlation between the two series for the period from 1950 to 1970 is 0.928 per cent. Thus the growth in earnings per share is largely explained by the growth of book value per share.

Changes in book values per share are largely, but not entirely, a result of retaining earnings. They may be affected by conversion of senior securities at values for common stock that are more or less than book value per share at time of conversion, by sale of additional stock at prices greater or less than current book value, and by direct debits or credits to the common equity account because of unusual gains or losses. However, for the average of 425 industrial companies for the period 1950 to 1970 these other effects were approximately offsetting and earnings retention explains 99 per cent of the increase in book value per share for the period.

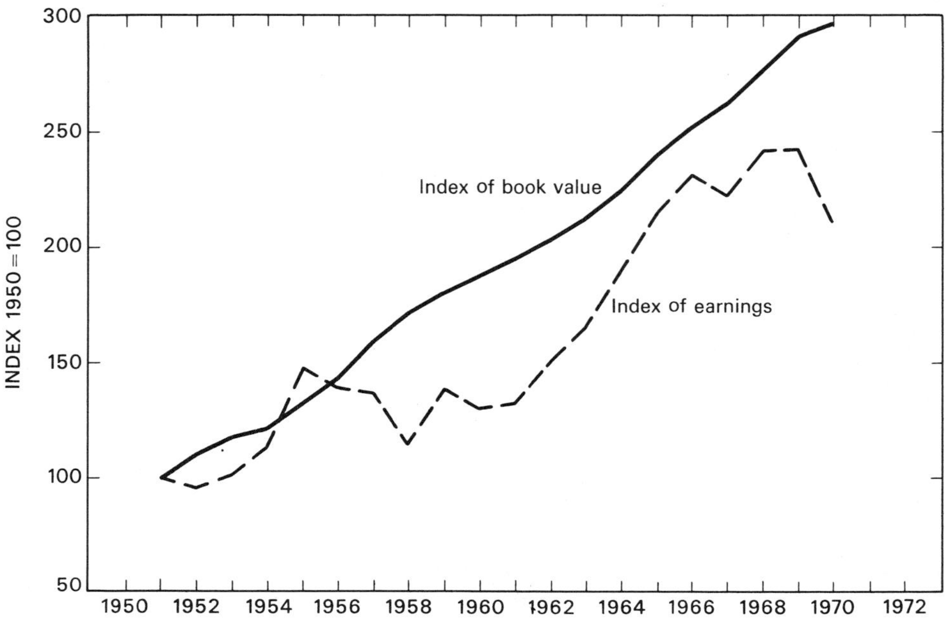

FIGURE 6–3

The Relationship of Book Values per Share and Earnings per Share For Standard & Poor's 425 Industrial Stocks

The ability of these industrial companies to increase earnings per share in a manner almost parallel to the increase in book values per share is not attributable entirely to earnings on the additional equity capital. Many companies use additional equity capital as a base for increasing amounts of senior securities in their capitalization, and favorable leverage provided by senior securities improves rate of earnings on the common equity. Moreover, earnings per share on common stocks may be favorably affected by rates of return earned on new capital raised by the sale of new common shares. One group of researchers found that for a large list of companies the rate of return on additional investment in assets financed by sale of additional securities was greater than the rate earned on additional investment financed by earnings retention.[2]

The steady increase in average amounts of dividends per share and the upward movement of the price-earnings ratio are the other reasons for the relatively high constant dollar rates of return from common stocks over two decades.

Earnings rates, earnings retention, and price inflation. To what extent is this favorable experience with common stocks attributable to price infla-

[2]William J. Baumol, Peggy Heim, Burton G. Malkiel, and Richard E. Quant, "Earnings Retention, New Capital and the Growth of the Firm," *The Review of Economic Statistics*, Vol. LII, No. 4 (November 1970), pp. 345–355.

tion? An immediate response might be: not at all. Inflation has not made companies more profitable if profitability is measured by rate of return on common equity capital. Indeed, the average company has become somewhat less profitable over the past 20 years. The principal explanation is simply the growth of the economy and the existence of economic and political conditions relatively favorable to the private enterprise system. Economic growth and generally favorable conditions for doing business have enabled companies to achieve good average rates of earnings and to reinvest profitably the earnings retained.

Does price inflation have anything to do with economic growth and favorable conditions? Some economists say that it does. They hold that a moderate rate of increase in the price level—an annual rate of 1 to 2 per cent—is necessary to provide a stimulus to the private enterprise system, to achieve low levels of unemployment, and to keep consumers spending their money. However, this thesis is often disputed. Other economists have pointed to past periods of economic growth and prosperity in which the price level was quite stable or even declining.

One lesson from recent experience seems clear. A high rate of inflation is not favorable for common stocks. This has been true in the United States and in other countries that have experienced relatively high inflation rates. The reason is primarily that high inflation disrupts established cost and price relationships. It is hard to do business profitably when you do not know from month to month how much the dollar will be worth in terms of goods and services. The sharpest drop in corporate earnings in recent years occurred during the period of strongly rising consumer prices in 1969 and 1970. Investors' expectations tend to shift downward in times of pronounced inflation. They expect that inflation will not be good for earnings and they worry about governmental action to check inflation, which may also have an adverse effect on corporate earnings.

The Uncertainty of Returns from Bonds in Constant Dollars

Bonds are usually regarded as having a high level of purchasing power risk, because the amounts of interest payments in dollars are fixed for relatively long time periods and a fixed amount of principal is payable at maturity. There is no provision in the usual bond contract for adjusting amounts of payments in current dollars for changes in the price level. Given fixed dollar amounts over periods of years, the size of returns in constant dollars would seem to be a function of changes in the price level. If the price level rises, the purchasing power of fixed amounts received in current dollars declines. However, interest rates change and rates of return on portfolios of bonds increase or decrease as funds are invested and re-invested at different market rates of yield. There is a tendency for interest rates to increase when the rate of inflation rises above some usually acceptable level. Larger portfolio rates in current dollars compensate to some extent for depreciation in the value of the dollar.

Bond investment does not mean merely buying a long-term bond and holding it to maturity. Usually bond investors own a number of issues bought at different times at different rates of yield and maturing at different dates. When bonds mature and principal is repaid, the funds are usually re-invested in new bonds with about the same investment characteristics. Thus bond portfolios turn over gradually with the passage of time. The rate of return that is important to bond investors is the portfolio rate of return earned as portfolios turn over.

Portfolio rates of return vary as interest rates change. At any point in time the rate of yield is a weighted average of the rates at which the various bond issues were purchased with the principal amounts of the individual issues as weights. In a period of rising interest rates portfolio yields tend to rise as the issues purchased earlier at low rates mature and are replaced with issues purchased at new and higher rates. When interest rates decline, the opposite is true. The steepness of the rise or decline in portfolio yield depends on the magnitude of change in market rates of interest and on the rate of turnover of the portfolio.

Inflation and market rates of interest. The statement that there is a tendency for changes in interest rates and changes in the price level to be correlated has to be made in rather weak terms. When the rate of price inflation is low and there is little concern on the part of investors about future inflation, changes in interest rates have little relationship to price-level changes. But when inflation increases and there is fear that it will continue, interest rates rise. In some countries under conditions of severe inflation interest rates have increased to extraordinarily high levels. In the United States the inflation of recent years has been accompanied by a greater rise in market rates of yield for high-grade bonds than in the price level.

Figure 6–4 shows the movement of interest rates and of the CPI over a past period. To facilitate comparison, both series have been converted to indexes with the data for 1960 as 100.

It is sometimes said that when the rate of inflation is high enough to alarm investors about the purchasing power of future returns, they demand and obtain higher rates of interest as compensation for purchasing-power risk. This is an oversimplification of the relationship. Interest rates, like other prices, are determined by levels of supply and demand in the market and factors other than inflation influence the amounts of funds demanded and the amounts investors are willing to supply at various market rates.

The recent period of relatively rapid rising prices in this country was also a period in which both business firms and governments made extraordinarily large demands for borrowed money by offering bonds for sale in the market. The expectation that debt could be repaid in the future in depreciated dollars may have affected their borrowing decisions, but the predominant influence was the need for money to provide additional productive capacity for the private enterprise system and in the public sector to pay for public improvements and to cover budget deficits. Demand by both sectors has been influenced by population growth, expansion of the economy, improvements in living standards, and the expectation that these basic trends would continue. It is very likely that interest rates would have increased considerably during the latter 1960's even if the price level had been highly stable.

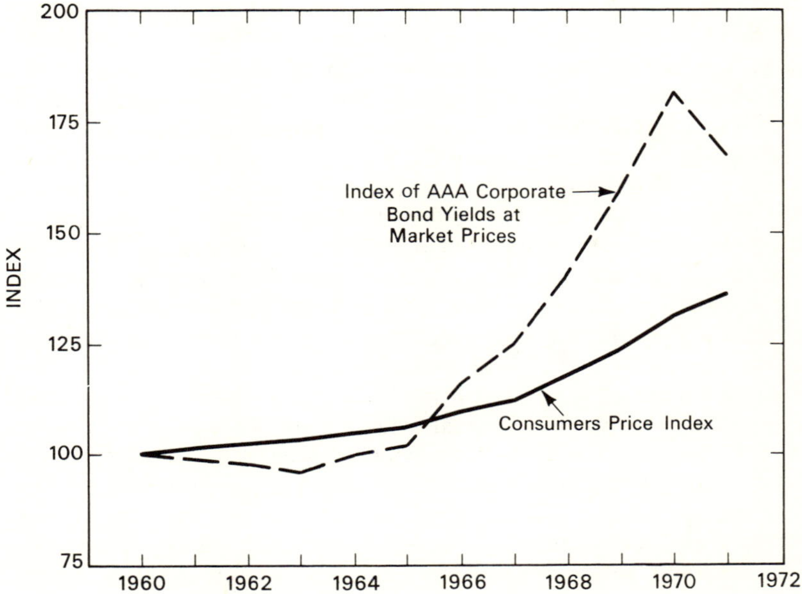

FIGURE 6–4

Price Inflation and the Trend of Interest Rates

You can see from Figure 6–4 how the rise in the CPI gradually accelerated. At first, yields on triple A corporate bonds fluctuated narrowly, but as the annual rate of increase in the price level accelerated, interest rates moved sharply upward. From 1960 to 1970 the rise in market rates was twice as great as the rise in the price index.

Change in portfolio rates of return. If investors could have invested all their money in one year, received repayment in the next year, and continued to invest and re-invest annually, the rise in portfolio rates of return in current dollars would have greatly exceeded the rise in the price index, and investors would have been more than compensated for the decline in purchasing power of their currency. But the rates we have charted are long-term rates and investors cannot invest all their money at long-term rates each year. In practice they invest each year the funds that become available from maturities plus whatever new money becomes available for bond investment. Thus portfolio yields increased gradually during the period of rising interest rates.

The experience of the life insurance companies provides an excellent example of how an upward trend in market rates of interest affects portfolio rates of yield.[3] In the 1960's their annual net rate of return on total assets

[3]Life insurance company assets consist almost entirely of bonds and mortgage loans. Interest rates on mortgage loans change in about the same manner as market rates of yield on bonds.

increased steadily as they made additional investments at higher rates and re-invested money loaned much earlier at lower rates. These current dollar rates may be reduced to constant dollar rates by dividing the series by the CPI with the base shifted to 1960. Figure 6–5 shows rates of return both in current and in constant dollars. For several years the improvement in current dollar rates slightly exceeded the rise in the price level and the constant dollar rate of return moved upward. But as inflation became more severe, the rise in portfolio rate of return was not sufficient to compensate for the loss of purchasing power and rates in constant dollars turned downward. The rates of return of the life insurance companies consist chiefly of income payments on bonds and mortgages, but they may be slightly affected by realized capital gains and losses. They do not take account of changes in market values of securities.

It is remarkable that the rates on life insurance investments in constant dollars have been so stable. The annual rates for the 12 year period varied only from 3.98 to 4.31 per cent. This evidence suggests that there is less uncertainty of rates of return in constant dollars over a relatively long time period from large portfolios of fixed income securities with a low rate of portfolio turnover than there is from a broadly diversified portfolio of common stocks over a similar period, although at a lower average level of return. Some economist generalize that bond investors obtain a basic rate of return at a low rate of inflation and that when the inflation rate increases they receive increased rates of return that more or less compensate for the higher inflation rate.

We must recognize of course that principal amounts invested in bonds depreciate in purchasing power of principal. Indeed, when market rates of interest rise market prices of marketable securities decline and the decline in market prices further reduces the purchasing power of principal at liquidating value. There is no compensation for the depreciation in purchasing

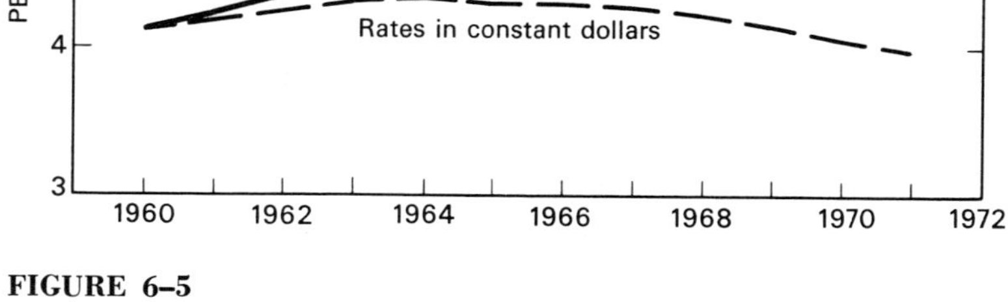

FIGURE 6–5

Net Rates of Return in Current and in Constant Dollars on Total Invested Assets of All Life Insurance Companies

power of principal, but bond investors generally regard income as the form of return that is significant for them.

Purchasing-Power Risk and Rates of Return

How do rates of return in current dollars vary with different levels of uncertainty of the purchasing power of returns? The question is largely moot because empirical data are not conclusive.

To generalize about the variation in current dollar rates with the level of purchasing power risk you have to grade securities into a series of clearly defined classifications in terms of purchasing power risk. Do common stocks represent a low level of purchasing power risk? We found that annual rates of return in constant dollars from large numbers of common stocks have varied widely over short time periods and even over periods as long as 10 years. On this basis common stocks have a high level of purchasing power risk. We also found that constant dollar rates of return from different industry classifications of stocks varied widely during the same time period. It is only on the basis of average annual constant dollar rates for large numbers of stocks over very long time periods that stocks have served well to preserve the purchasing power of returns. If we say that for most practical purposes common stocks have a relatively high level of purchasing power risk, then the relatively high rates of return from stocks in current dollars is positively related both to financial risk and to purchasing power risk.

If bond portfolios represent a low level of purchasing power risk in terms of income returns, then the usually lower rates of return in current dollars is positively related both to purchasing power risk and to financial risk.

A reasonable conclusion is that current dollar rates of return vary chiefly with financial risk and interest rate risk, and that these rates are reduced by whatever the rate of increase in the price level may be. Stocks have usually provided higher current dollar rates than bonds because they represent a higher level of financial risk, and bonds have usually provided lower current dollar rates because their financial risk is less. Then the size of returns in constant dollars from both categories of securities has been the current dollar rate modified by changes in the price level. The extent of modification from time to time has varied greatly as the rate of inflation has been large or small. In any event, we should recognize that experience with both bonds and stocks has varied greatly over long periods of time and that generalizations based on historical experience may not be valid for the future.

SOME OTHER CONTRIBUTIONS TO RISK

Any cause of uncertainty about the size of returns to investors is a risk. We have discussed the three causes of uncertainty that are of most concern to investors generally in managing security investments. But there are other causes of uncertainty that contribute to the total of uncertainties. An imaginative person could draw up a lengthy list, but it would include hazards affecting limited categories of securities, or those of such a general nature that they can hardly be taken into account by investors.

Moral, Legal, and Political Risks

There is, for example, the risk of dishonesty. Managers of companies in which we invest may be swindlers. In a few instances they have proved to be dishonest and have fled to some other country or have been sent to prison. There is little that investors in publicly distributed securities can do about this risk—they have to assume that corporate managements are honest. Generally the assumption is warranted. In order to expose dishonesty when it occurs and to penalize the dishonest, we have an elaborate system of federal and state laws requiring public disclosure of information about companies whose securities have been distributed to the public. We also rely on the general rule that most people are honest. There is no way to grade securities according to the risk of dishonesty of corporate managements.

A special kind of risk involves state and municipal securities. Bonds bought by investors may prove to be legally invalid obligations not binding on issuers. Generally, municipal securities are issued pursuant to state laws expressly authorizing their issuance and also establishing particular conditions and specific procedures that must be followed in their issuance. If the conditions are not met and the procedures not followed, the bonds are not legally authorized and so are not valid obligations.

Still another kind of moral or political risk involves repudiation of debts by sovereign governments. Repudiation sometimes follows political revolution. The historical pattern is for a victorious revolutionary government to declare that the predecessor government was not a legally valid government and, therefore, that its debts are not valid. When the Communists seized the government of Russia they repudiated all debts of the Czarist government. There is little that investors can do about repudiation. Bondholders may organize and try to press their claims, and there are foreign bondholders' protective associations in both the United States and the United Kingdom, but a sovereign government is immune to legal coercion.

Under the heading of foreign investments and in the political area is the risk of confiscation by governments of property belonging to companies of other countries located within their boundaries. Confiscation is generally called nationalization. Governments that confiscate property may refuse payment for the property, or they may promise payment and defer indefinitely fulfillment of the promise, or they may actually pay part or all of the value of confiscated property. This risk is one that can be assessed to some extent on the basis of the political history of countries and the current state of political affairs.

The Risk of Social Change

There is still one major type of risk that we have not yet taken into account, and it is the broadest and most ubiquitous of all. This is the risk that changes will occur in our social system that will deprive investors of their basic rights, or seriously impair those rights. Change is an inherent characteristic of human society, and history is replete with instances in which the evolution of a different order of society has invalidated the rights on which private investment is based.

Investment in securities for private pecuniary gain is based on a political system that we call democracy and on an economic system that we call private capitalism. In this politico-economic system individuals have personal liberty, the privilege of seeking their own economic advantage, and the right to enjoy the fruits of their labor. Government protects the individual in the ownership of property, serves as an agency for the enforcement of contracts, and provides for the maintenance of order and for the national defense. It is a system in which the main economic motivating force is the effort of individuals to improve their material well-being.

The risk of social changes does not mean uncertainty about actions of government within the established and conventional system; it means uncertainty about changes in the system—an uncertainty that is most difficult to assess. Will such a change occur? How soon? How far will it go and in what manner? Obviously the answers to these questions can be nothing more than conjecture.

It is not uncommon, however, to make conjectures about the direction in which our politico-economic system will evolve. One of the most common guesses is that the United States will move farther in the direction of a welfare state with government ownership of a larger portion of the means of production and a higher degree of control over the remaining private sector.

Investors might let their policies be influenced by this kind of thinking and seek to reduce the risk of social change by avoiding securities of those industries or enterprises regarded as most likely to be affected by nationalization. But this is a very dubious basis for investment policy. There is no way to estimate reliably the future course of politico-economic evolution and its possible consequences for investors in securities. And even if there were, there would be no great likelihood of escaping whatever danger the future might bring by choosing some kinds of securities rather than others. Therefore, the risk of social change cannot be taken into account to any appreciable extent in formulating investment policy. Investors must rely largely on the probability that social change in this country will be slowly evolutionary, allowing investment policies to adjust to changing circumstances.

QUESTIONS FOR DISCUSSION

1. Have the United States and other countries with about the same economic and political systems evolved to the point at which an increase in the price level at an average annual rate greater than 2 per cent is a reasonable expectation?
2. Your rich uncle dies and leaves you stocks of six leading industrial companies with a total market value of $100,000. Your dividends amount to $3,500 a year. Does this nice portfolio of common stocks provide a good inflation hedge?

3. It has been said that stocks of companies in extractive industries such as oil and gold mining are more likely to provide stable returns in constant dollars than stocks of companies engaged in general manufacturing. Do you think this is right? Why should they?
4. Is it a pretty sure thing that most companies profit from price inflation?
5. What does the rate of earnings retention have to do with rates of return in current dollars and in constant dollars from common stock investments?
6. Do you think that in the future constant dollar rates of return from bond portfolios will vary only moderately from year to year?
7. What generalization can you offer about the correlation between changes in average prices for common stocks and changes in the Consumer Price Index?
8. Why do interest rates rise when the Consumer Price Index rises?
9. To what extent, if at all, are current dollar rates of return from securities affected by the uncertainty of changes in the price level?
10. If you owned a couple of million dollars in securities, would you be concerned about the likelihood of change in our political and economic system?

7

Desirability of Ownership Qualities

- I. The marketability of securities
  - A. Spreads as a measure of marketability
  - B. Why the sizes of spreads vary
  - C. How expected rates vary with differences in marketability
- II. The taxability of securities
  - A. Differences in taxation of securities
  - B. How expected rates of return vary with taxability
- III. The callability of securities
- IV. The convertibility of securities
  - A. How convertibility makes bonds more desirable
  - B. The grades of securities in convertibility
  - C. Bonds with warrants
- V. Deepness of discount
- VI. Change in the structure of market rates

Expected rates of return from securities are related to risk, and risk is a principal concern of portfolio managers. But rates of return are also affected by several other qualities of securities that make them more or less desirable to own, such as marketability, taxability, callability, convertibility, and deepness of discount. These qualities are not particularly related to risk. Some are the result of laws; some of terms of security issues; and some an effect of the manner in which security markets function. We could call them "non-risk qualities," but the term that best describes them is "desirability of ownership qualities."

Securities can be graded in each of these qualities from low to high grade in the same manner that securities may be graded in terms of risk. A low-grade security is one of low desirability of ownership. Grades move upward to those of high desirability, or high-grade. Expected rates of return are related to grades of securities in the desirability of ownership qualities in the same manner that they are related to risk. Securities offering little desirability afford the higher expected rates of return, other things being equal, and the more highly desirable issues provide the smaller returns. This is just what you would expect. Investors prefer securities of the high grades in desirability of ownership qualities and pay a little more for a series of future payments of a given size and uncertainty. A higher price relative to expected amounts of returns makes a lower expected rate of return. Similarly, investors pay less for securities of the lower grades, which results in market prices that provide somewhat higher expected rates. The differential in rates for the lower grades of securities in these qualities is additional to the compensation in expected rates for the level of risk assumed.

The gradation of securities in desirability of ownership qualities, which we will sometimes reduce to the acronym DOOQ, is important to the problem of maximizing returns on investments. Some investors must select higher-grade securities in DOOQ to meet their particular investment requirements and accept the somewhat lower level of rates they provide. But others can accept lower-grade securities and can make some contribution to maximizing returns by doing so.

THE MARKETABILITY OF SECURITIES

The first distinction to be made is between marketable and unmarketable securities. Marketable securities are those for which there is a regular market within the system of security markets. There is a regular market for a stock or bond when at least one broker-dealer firm continually quotes the issue. To quote is to announce the bid and offered price to other broker-dealer firms that inquire. If there is no quoted market, a security is unmarketable. However, securities for which there is no quoted market are sometimes bought and sold in private transactions between investors and sometimes broker-dealer firms serve as intermediaries in arranging private transactions.

Spreads as a Measure of Marketability

There are great differences in grade of marketability among marketable securities. The basic criterion for grading securities is the size of spread between bid and offered prices quoted by broker-dealer firms, or by specialists on the organized securities exchanges. You can sell a security at the bid price and buy at the offered price. The difference between the two is the dealer's mark-up. In the case of a listed security, it is usually the difference between the highest price at which a specialist has an order to buy and the lowest price at which he has an order to sell. But a specialist has a duty to maintain a reasonable spread (difference) between the bid and offered prices, and he may quote a price at which he will buy or sell for his own account that creates a smaller spread than that provided by the orders on his books.

What is important about the spread at which securities are quoted is that it is an important part of transactions costs and it is the part that varies among securities. The other principal part of transactions costs is the broker's commission. Commissions are based on dollar value of transactions, with certain modifications, but they are the same for all transactions in all listed issues of a given value and number of shares. Generally, if transactions are of the same value and involve the same number of shares, it makes no difference as far as commission is concerned whether you buy Stock *A* or Stock *B*. But it makes considerable difference in size of spread whether stocks are highly marketable or poorly marketable. If highly marketable, there is a small addition (in percentage of value of transaction) to the broker's commission for the dealer's spread. If poorly marketable, the spread is a sizable addition to the commission and the total transactions cost is much larger.

For example, the broker's commission on the sale of 100 shares of a listed stock at $32 per share ($3,200 transaction) is $50.80, which is 1.59 per cent of the value of the transaction. If the dealer's spread is ⅛th, or $12.50 for 100 shares, the total cost of the transaction (ignoring several minor expenses), is $63.30, or 2 per cent of the value. But if the spread is $1 per share, or $100 for 100 shares, the total cost of the transaction is $150.80, or 4.7 per cent of its value. Thus differences in marketability grade make a considerable difference in transaction costs, and this is the reason investors prefer the higher grades of securities in marketability to the lower grades.

There are important differences among spreads for securities, as shown in Table 7–1. To be comparable, spreads in dollars per share must be expressed as a percentage of the offered price (or the bid price). You can see that 4 actively traded issues on the New York Stock Exchange were quoted at spreads of ⅛ of a dollar per share, but when spreads are related to offered prices the spread for American Telephone and Telegraph is almost twice the percentage for General Motors.

There are some inactively traded issues on the Exchange that are quoted with spreads equal to more than 3 per cent of offered price. In the over-the-counter market the size of spreads may range up to 5 per cent. In the bond market the difference between bid and offered prices ranges from about 1 to 3 per cent for corporate and municipal issues, but short-term Treasury issues are usually quoted with a spread of 1 or 2 32nds of 1 per cent and long-term Treasuries at about ½ of 1 per cent.

Why the Sizes of Spreads Vary

You can understand why dealers' markups are different for different securities by considering the way dealers conduct their business in the over-

TABLE 7–1
The Size of Spreads Between Bid and Offered Prices on a Day in 1972

Market	*Quote* Bid	Offered	*Spread* Dollars per share	Percentage of offered price
	(dollars per share)			
New York Stock Exchange				
General Motors	83-3/4	83-7/8	1/8	0.15%
General Electric	64-3/8	64-1/2	1/8	0.19
American Tel & Tel	43	43-1/8	1/8	0.29
U. S. Steel	33-1/4	33-3/8	1/8	0.37
Gulf States Utilities, $4.20 preferred	58	59	1	1.69
Tootsie Roll Industries	14-7/8	15-1/4	3/8	2.46
McKee (Arthur G) & Co.	17-3/8	17-7/8	1/2	2.80
Canadian Southern Ry.	40-1/2	42	1-1/2	3.57
Over-the-counter				
American Express	138-1/8	139	7/8	0.63
Medtronic, Inc.	79-1/2	80-1/2	1	1.24
Auto Train	32-5/8	33-1/8	1/2	1.51
Cannon Mills Co.	96-1/2	99-1/2	3	3.02
Jet Air Freight	23-1/2	24-1/2	1	4.08

the-counter markets. Here price quotations usually are made by dealers to other broker-dealer firms. Broker-dealer firms doing business with the public buy from dealers and sell to dealers.

The factors that influence a security dealer's mark-up are much the same as those that affect mark-ups by dealers in any other kind of business. They must be large enough to cover expenses and the risk of loss and leave sufficient profit to make the business worthwhile. As a general rule the greater the volume of business in a security, the less is a dealer's mark-up. Large volume enables a dealer to spread his expenses over a large value of transactions and thus to take a smaller gross profit. Securities traded actively also tend to have high price continuity, that is, small price changes between transactions or none at all. Active trading and good price continuity reduce the risk that a dealer will have to sell securities in his inventory at a loss, or at less than the usual mark-up. Competition keeps dealers from taking larger mark-ups than required by expense and risk.

People familiar with security markets sometimes say of a stock, or of a bond, that it has a "thin" market. They mean that there is not much stock for sale at the offered price, and not much asked for at the bid price. If you place a market order to buy or to sell a relatively large lot, it may be executed at a price materially different from the price for the last preceding transaction. Poorly marketable securities have thin markets. When a market for a security is characterized by relatively large amounts bid for and offered at prices very near the current quotation, it is said to have "a broad market." When there is a broad market, you can buy or sell several thousand shares at once with little or no effect on the quoted price. Highly marketable securities have broad markets.

The tendency for prices of poorly marketable issues to be strongly affected by large transactions is also a function of dealer's risk and expense. When a dealer is offered a large amount of a poorly marketable issue, he is likely to make a lower bid for it than he would for a smaller amount. He lowers his bid because he needs a larger spread to compensate for the risk of taking the large amount into inventory and for the expense that may be involved in reselling the issue. The same considerations operate when the dealer is asked to offer a large amount of a poorly marketable issue, so that he makes an offer at a higher price than he would if the amount were smaller. He has to assume the risk and expense of acquiring the large amount in the market, or of replenishing his inventory if he has that quantity on hand.

Thus large transactions in poorly marketable securities entail unusually large transactions costs.

How Expected Rates Vary with Differences in Marketability

Highly marketable securities are more advantageous to own than poorly marketable issues. Thus it follows clearly that the more highly marketable issues ought to sell at higher prices relative to expected returns than poorly marketable issues—other things being equal. Or, yields on securities should graduate from lower for the most highly marketable issues to higher for the most poorly marketable. This statement of the proposition parallels the statement that yields on securities ought to increase with increasing levels of risk.

It is difficult, though, to develop good empirical data to measure differences in yields on securities attributable to differences in marketability grade. Differences in yields owing to differences in marketability cannot readily be distinguished from differences in yields owing to differences in risk or in other desirability of investment qualities. If a bond sells to yield 10 or 15 basis points more than another bond, is the difference attributable to a slightly higher level of financial risk, or of interest rate risk, or differences in some of the desirability of ownership qualities we are now considering? However, observation of prices and yields in the market suggests that in the area of relatively high-grade corporate bonds, differences in yield because of differences in marketability may be as much as 5 or 10 basis points between large, well-known actively traded issues and smaller, less actively traded issues. Frequently a relatively small bond issue of an industrial or utility company is underwritten and distributed within a state or in a region. Buyers are chiefly institutions that usually hold bonds to maturity. The over-the-counter market for such issues is usually made by the principal underwriting firm and there is little buying or selling. Frequently the rate of yield on such issues is as much as 100 basis points higher than the yields obtainable at the same time on large, well-known corporate issues of about the same grade for which there is a relatively active national market.

The difficulty of separating differences in expected rates of return among common stocks on the basis of differences in marketability is almost insurmountable. A number of studies have been made of changes in market prices of stocks during a time when they were traded in the over-the-counter market and in a subsequent period when they were listed on the New York Stock Exchange. The hypothesis is that there was an improvement in marketability when stocks were listed. The results have not been conclusive because of the virtual impossibility of filtering out completely other influences on price and isolating the effect of an improvement in marketability.

It is clear, though, that there is a substantial difference between the market value of a marketable stock and that of an unmarketable stock. There have from time to time been private transactions in "letter stock" at discounts of 15 to 30 per cent from the current market price of the same stock registered and listed on an exchange. Letter stock is stock that has not been registered for public distribution with the Securities and Exchange Commission and is not included in the number of shares listed on an exchange. Such stock is not marketable in our definition of marketability because it can only be sold in private transactions to a buyer who states in a letter that he buys it for investment and not with a view to public distribution.

Financial analysts often consider a highly marketable stock to be worth a price-earnings multiple appreciably higher than that they would place on a comparable stock that is poorly marketable.

THE TAXABILITY OF SECURITIES

If all securities were equally taxed to all owners under federal, state, and local tax laws, investors would have no choice so far as taxability is concerned and there would be no differences in the grade of securities on the basis of taxability. But in fact there are marked differences in how the benefits of security ownership are taxed—in tax rates, in kind of benefit taxed, and in the tax liability of different kinds of security owners. Thus we have to recognize differences in taxability as a strong influence on the desirability of owning different kinds of securities by different kinds of investors.

Differences in Taxation of Securities

The federal income tax is by far the heaviest tax on benefits of security ownership for most individuals and business corporations. The income tax is imposed on both income from securities and capital gains realized from the sale of securities. Rates and exemptions of income from taxation differ for individuals and for corporations. The federal income tax on securities is far too complex a topic to be treated adequately here, but we can describe some of the principal differences in the way the benefits of security ownership are taxed and observe the effect of differences on the yields at which securities sell in the market. A taxpayer who has any considerable amount of income from securities and is not himself a tax expert would do well to consult an expert.

The most general rule is that ordinary income from securities in the form of interest and dividends in excess of exemptions, deductions, and exclusions is taxed by the federal government at rates for individuals ranging from 14 to 70 per cent and for corporations at 22 to 48 per cent plus a 2½ per cent surcharge. Rates change from time to time. The most important exception to the general rule is that interest on obligations of states and local governments is fully tax-exempt, both to individuals and to corporations. Thus they often are termed "tax free" bonds. Since 1942 all new federal government issues have been fully taxable.

A second exception is that individuals are permitted to receive a modest amount of dividend income from stocks without paying income tax on it. A single taxpayer may exclude from taxable income up to $100 of dividend income for a year; married taxpayers filing a joint return may exclude up to $200 of dividend income provided both have at least $100 of dividend income. This means that stock is tax-exempt in the manner that municipal bonds are tax-exempt up to a value that provides dividends not greater than the amounts of dividend exclusion. For investors whose dividend income amounts to thousands of dollars, however, the exclusion of $100 or $200 of dividend income provides only slight relief from taxation.

Another exception to the general rule that dividends are fully taxed is the provision that dividends paid by corporations from capital, and not from earnings, are exempt from income tax. The principle is that these dividends represent a return of capital and not income from investment. Some companies have been able in some years to pay dividends either partly or entirely exempt from the income tax under this provision.

Corporations are taxed on their income from securities at their regular tax rates but they may exclude from ordinary income 85 per cent of dividends received from other corporations. The purpose of this exclusion is to minimize the several incidents of taxation of corporate earnings that occur when one company owns stock of another.

Some investors enjoy complete freedom from the federal income tax on returns from securities. They are principally non-profit corporations, such as colleges, hospitals and instrumentalities of the state and local governments; all eleemosynary institutions such as charitable foundations; pension funds for employees that qualify under Treasury regulations; and investment companies that meet certain legal requirements.

The federal income tax applies not only to ordinary income but also to capital gains, that is, profits realized on securities sold. Net capital gains realized on securities held for not more than 6 months are classified as short-term capital gains and are taxed as ordinary income at the regular rates. However, capital gains on securities held for more than 6 months are long-term gains and only one-half of long-term capital gains are subject to the income tax. The one-half that must be reported as income is taxed at regular rates, except that the maximum rate on this kind of income up to $50,000 of net long-term capital gain is 50 per cent, making a maximum effective rate of 25 per cent. Net long-term capital gains in excess of $50,000 are taxed at 35 per cent.

TABLE 7–2

The Taxation of Returns from Securities under the Federal Internal Revenue Code

Category	*What Is Taxed*	*Who Is Taxed*	*Who Is Tax-Exempt*
Government and corporate bonds	Interest Realized Capital Gains —Long-term —Short-term	Individuals and private corporations. —interest and short-term gains at regular rates —long-term gains at reduced rates	Eleemosynary institutions, states, public corporations, qualified pension funds, registered investment companies
Municipal bonds	Realized Capital Gains —Long-term —Short-term (but not interest)	Individuals and private corporations as above	As above
Corporate stocks, common and preferred	Dividends, except dividends paid from capital Realized Capital Gains —Long-term —Short-term	Individuals on dividends over $100 per year (joint $200) Corporations on 15% of cash dividends Capital gains as above	As above

Table 7–2 shows the main outlines of federal taxation of returns from securities.

Securities are also taxed by many state and local governments. Some levy a tax on the value of securities rather than on income. A number of states and some cities have income taxes that apply to the income from some kinds of securities, but not to others. Most states do not tax income from their own bonds or income from bonds of their political subdivisions; for the most part, however, they tax the obligations of other states and their political subdivisions. Obligations of the federal government are exempt from state and local government taxation.

How Expected Rates of Return Vary with Taxability

Theoretically there should be a graduation in expected rates of return from securities on the basis of their desirability of ownership from the standpoint of taxability. The graduation would run from a low rate on securities fully exempt from taxation to a high rate on securities with no tax exemption.

The higher rates would be compensation for taxability. In practice there is no such precise graduation of rates because taxation varies considerably according to who is taxed, the size of tax rates, and the kind of benefit taxed. It is possible, however, to see the effects of general tax advantages and disadvantages in the yields at which some kinds of securities sell in the market.

The clearest distinction, of course, is between corporate bonds with no exemption of income from the federal income tax and municipal obligations that are fully exempt. The highest-grade, long-term corporate bonds of good marketability generally sell to yield about 100 to 200 basis points more than the highest-grade, long-term municipal bonds of good marketability. The difference in yields is attributable almost entirely to the difference in taxability of the income from these two categories of securities under the federal income tax law.

The exclusion from taxable income of 85 per cent of dividends received by corporate owners of preferred stocks has a marked effect on the yields at which this category of securities sells in the market. Although high-grade preferred stocks have at least as much financial and interest rate risk as triple B corporate bonds, their average yield is 150 to 200 basis points less than the yield on medium-grade corporates. This tax advantage also applies to common stocks, but there are so many other investors in common stocks and so much common stock outstanding that the effect on expected rates of return from common stocks is not readily apparent.

It is reasonable to think, though, that expected rates on common stock are affected not only by the 85 per cent dividend exclusion for corporate investors, but also by the $100 (or $200) dividend exclusion for individual investors and by the lower rates on long-term capital gains. The lower rate on long-term capital gains not only reduces the tax rate on these gains relative to the rate on ordinary income, but also provides the opportunity to defer realization of capital gains and thus to postpone payment of the tax until securities are sold.

THE CALLABILITY OF SECURITIES

Securities may be graded in callability by the strength of the protection provided by the terms of the call provision. Call protection is for the most part protection against loss of income because of a decline in interest rates and refunding of bond and preferred stock issues at lower rates of interest or dividend. The highest grade of securities in this respect are those that are non-callable to maturity. Some issues are non-callable for refunding, which protects against refunding, but are callable for redemption with funds from other sources than refunding. The advantage to investors is that they do not have to relinquish securities when their yield is greater than the current market rate of yield. The poorest-grade securities are securities that have no call protection, that are callable at the option of the issuer at any time on short notice.

Between these extremes are different grades of call protection. Most new bond issues in recent years of relatively high interest rates were made non-callable for some defined period from date of issue, such as 5, 10, or even 20 years, but callable on short notice at the expiration of that period. The longer the period of call protection, the higher the grade. Another kind of compromise is to make bonds callable at any time but on condition that the issuer pay a premium over par. Thus a bond might be callable at any time, but at a premium of 110 per cent of par in the first 5 years after date of issue. The premium is designed to compensate investors for whatever disadvantage there may be to them in redeeming an issue early. Usually the call premium declines with the lapse of time. It might be 108 per cent of par in the second 5 years, 106 per cent in the third 5 years, and so forth.

Thus the several grades of securities in terms of callability are determined by length of the call period from the present date, the size of the call premium when bonds are callable, and sometimes by both of these factors in future periods.

Since strong call protection is desirable to investors, there should be differences in the yields at which the more desirable issues sell in the market relative to the less desirable issues, other things being equal. It is of course difficult to keep other things equal and to measure the difference issuing from strong call protection, but there is empirical evidence of such a differential in periods when interest rates are high and may be expected to decline. A comparison of average yields on new issues of high-grade utility bonds containing deferred call provisions with average yields on callable bonds of the same category show that in the early 1960's there was no appreciable difference, but in the later years of that decade when interest rates were relatively high, the differential amounted to about 18 basis points.[1] Investors willing to buy the less desirable issues in terms of call provisions were able to obtain significantly higher yields.

THE CONVERTIBILITY OF SECURITIES

Another kind of contractual provision that affects the desirability of owning securities is the right to convert them into some other kind of security of the issuer at the option of their owners. The conversion right is sometimes provided in bond issues and in preferred stock issues. Ordinarily the right is to convert senior securities into common stock of the issuer on terms specified in the provisions of the senior securities at time of issue. A conversion right is really an option to buy common stock of the issuer at some time in the future at a specified price and to pay for the stock with bonds taken at par.

How Convertibility Makes Bonds More Desirable

The number of shares that may be obtained by conversion is indicated by the conversion price. If the conversion price is $40 per share, for example,

[1]Salomon Brothers, *An Analytical Record of Yields and Yield Spreads,* New York, July 1971.

you would receive twenty-five shares of stock for each $1,000 bond. Such a bond might be initially issued at par when the market price of the stock is, say, $34. There would be no gain by conversion at that time because the value of the stock that could be obtained would be only $850. But if the price of the stock rises a few dollars a share, the bonds would very likely increase in price. The conversion right would become more valuable because the market price of the stock is closer to the conversion price. If the market price of the stock exceeds the conversion price, the price of a convertible bond would exceed par. If, in the example above, the price of the stock becomes $50 a share, the twenty-five shares of stock would be worth $1,250 and the price of the bond would be about 125 per cent of par.

Actually the market price of a convertible bond may be a little higher than the value of the stock into which it is convertible when the price of the stock exceeds the conversion price. The income to be received as interest on the bond may be greater than the dividends that would be obtained from owning equivalent shares of the stock. There is a little less risk in owning the bond, because there is a "floor" under its market price, which is the value of the convertible as a straight bond (one without the conversion right).

The terms of convertible bonds and preferred stocks vary considerably. Sometimes the conversion price increases over time. It might be $40 for the first 5 years from date of issue, $45 in the second 5 years, and $50 in a subsequent time period. The conversion right in some instances becomes effective only after some time has expired from date of issue and sometimes it ceases to be effective after a prescribed period of time has elapsed. Sometimes some part of the price of the stock must be paid in cash when the bonds are converted.

The Grades of Securities in Convertibilty

The conversion right makes bonds and preferred stocks more desirable to own because it provides an opportunity for an investor to realize larger rates of return by capital gains than those that may be obtained by investment in straight bonds and preferred stocks, that is, securities without this right. The value of the conversion right determines the grade of convertible securities in the quality of convertibility.

You can see how convertibility is graded by comparing prices of convertible issues with prices of nonconvertible issues that are approximately equal in risk and in the other desirability of investment qualities. Consider the example of the convertible bond used at the beginning of this discussion. The bond bears interest at 5 per cent, matures in 20 years, and was publicly offered at par to yield 5 per cent to maturity. Market data show that a comparable straight bond with a 5 per cent interest coupon is priced at 62½ to yield 8 per cent to maturity. The difference between $625 (per $1,000 bond) and the public offering price of $1,000 is the value of the conversion right. It is $375 in price and 3 percentage points in yield to maturity.

If the market price of the stock rises to $50, as suggested earlier, the conversion right would become more valuable and the market price of the bond would rise to about 125, or $1,250. If comparable straight bonds are still selling at 62½, or $625, the value of the conversion right has increased to $625 per $1,000 bond. Of course, the market price of the stock could go the other way and so would the price of the convertible bond. At a price of $25 for the stock, the conversion right is worth much less. How much it would be worth would be determined by investors' estimates of the likelihood of a pronounced increase in price of the stock. We might estimate a price of 75 for the bond, and at this price the value of the right is $125 ($750 minus $625.

Market prices for convertible bonds can be converted to the yields to maturity provided by contractual payments of interest and principal. Then the higher the price of a convertible security, the lower its yield. You could use market data to make an array of yields from highest to lowest on outstanding convertible bonds and the array would rank them inversely in order of the desirability of ownership provided by the conversion privilege. The highest yields would be on convertibles selling at prices that attribute no significant value to the conversion right. Those yields would be about the same as yields on comparable straight bonds. Yields would graduate downward in the array as prices for the several issues reflect greater values for the conversion right. At the bottom would be issues selling on a zero-yield basis. A convertible sells on a zero-yield basis when its market price is as high, or higher, than the dollar value of all interest and principal payments to maturity.

Bonds with Warrants

Sometimes bonds are issued with warrants to buy stock. Warrants are rights to buy stock of the issuer of the bonds; they are sometimes called stock rights or simply rights. Each warrant is a right to buy one share of stock at a price fixed at the time the bonds are issued. One bond may have warrants to buy a number of shares of stock. Usually warrants may be detached from bonds and bought and sold separately.

An important difference between convertible securities and bonds with warrants is that the bonds to which warrants are attached are not surrendered when rights to purchase stock are exercised. The warrant holder simply pays cash for the stock at its fixed price. From the viewpoint of the issuer, no debt is extinguished and additional equity capital is raised by exercising the warrants.

From the standpoint of investors, bonds with warrants are similar to convertible securities in that they afford an opportunity to realize a capital gain by purchasing stock at prices less than current market prices. When rights are attached, the grade of bonds with warrants is determined in the same manner as are convertible securities. When rights have been detached from bonds, they sell as straight bonds.

DEEPNESS OF DISCOUNT

In periods of low interest rates corporate issuers of bonds are able to sell their obligations at very low coupon rates. In a subsequent period of higher interest rates, these low coupon bonds have to be priced in the market at a discount from par in order to provide the higher market rate of yield to maturity. When the discount is large, these issues are called deep discount bonds. For example, a company might sell at par an issue of bonds due in 25 years and bearing a 4 per cent coupon. Five years later the market rate of yield might be 7 per cent. To provide that yield, the 4 per cent bonds now with 20 years to maturity would be priced at 68 per cent of par. That is a deep discount.

Deep discount bonds are a result of a rise in interest rates, they provide protection against refunding at lower interest rates, and they afford an opportunity for capital gains in event of a decline in interest rates. Therefore investors like them, and the greater the discount the more desirable they are.

These bonds provide protection against refunding because their coupon rates are low relative to the current level of interest rates. In the example above, interest rates for long-term bonds would have to decline from the level of 7 per cent to less than 4 per cent in order for refunding to be advantageous to the issuer.

If interest rates do decline, market prices for the bonds will rise and provide a capital gain. In the example above, if interest rates in the market should decline from 7 per cent to 5 per cent in a period of 3 years, the bonds would be priced at 88⅝ (with a maturity of 17 years) and the gain would be from the earlier price of 68. It would be $206.25 per $1,000 bond.

There is also a tax advantage in deep discount bonds. Even if interest rates do not decline, only the interest is subject to tax and the periodic amounts are small. If held to maturity, principal will be paid at par and there will be a realized capital gain. It will be taxed at the lower rate for such gains and, of course, payment of the tax will be deferred until it is realized.

Deep discount bonds sell in the market at lower yields than otherwise comparable issues with higher coupon rates and little or no discount from par. And the deeper the discount, the smaller the yield. Or, yields graduate upward from those issues most desirable in this respect to those less desirable.

A compilation of average yields on seasoned high-grade utility bonds classified by size of coupon rates shows these yield differentials. The data in Table 7–3 are annual averages of monthly data for a recent year when interest rates were very high. The differentials tend to be lower when interest rates are at lower levels and the pattern might be less regular.

TABLE 7–3

Yield Differentials by Deepness of Discount.

Size of coupon	*Average yield*	*Differential from high coupon yield*
4-1/4–4-5/8	7.88	0.60%
5-1/4–5-3/4	8.06	0.42
6-5/8–6-7/8	8.17	0.31
7-1/2–7-7/8	8.31	0.17
8 –8-3/8	8.48	0.00

Source: Salomon Brothers, An Analytical Record of Yields and Yield Spreads, New York, 1971. The data are for the year 1970.

CHANGE IN THE STRUCTURE OF MARKET RATES

One of the important phenomena of the securities markets from the point of view of portfolio managers is change in the market structure of yields or expected rates of return. The structure at any point in time recognizes differences in levels of risk and in the grades of securities in desirability of ownership qualities. But these yield differentials change. At one time the differentials may be relatively small and at other times much larger. To investment managers these differences in the structure of yields mean that sometimes there is a relatively large compensation in yield for buying securities of the poorer grades, and sometimes the compensation is small. It follows, then, that the opportunity to obtain larger returns by investing in securities of the poorer grades is best when yields are highest for the poorer grades.

The most general and most useful application of this principle of seeking maximum yield for poorness of grade is in the selection of high-grade bonds according to length of maturity. When the yield curve is steeply upsloping, the yield differential between short-term and long-term issues is large. At this time the compensation for assuming interest rate risk is greatest. For example, when the yield on short-term Treasury issues is 2 per cent and the yield on long-term Treasuries is 6 per cent, there is sizable reward in yield for risk taking. An investor who can afford the risk gets the higher return by investing in the longer maturities. On the other hand, when the yield curve is almost flat, there is little inducement as far as yield differentials are concerned to assume the interest rate risk in long maturities. However, the flat curve usually occurs when interest rates are high, and some investors buy long maturities at high yields in anticipation of a decline in interest rates.

The principle may also be applied to securities graded in terms of other causes of uncertainty. When business is good and investors are optimistic, the difference in yields between the highest grade of corporate bonds and those of medium grade is small. At such times, taking the larger risk in the medium-grade issues provides little more yield. But when a recession in business makes investors nervous, the yield differential between high-grade and medium-grade bonds increases and there is much more compensation for assuming financial risk.

The size of the yield differential between tax-exempt municipals and fully taxable corporate bonds also varies from time to time. It increases when income tax rates have been increased and when the supply of new tax-exempt issues is small. It decreases with a lowering of tax rates and an increase in supply of municipal issues. Sometimes it may be worthwhile for an investor to select taxable bonds relative to tax-exempts and sometimes it may not.

Convertible bonds sell at highest prices and lowest yields to maturity when investors are optimistic about common stocks. The time to buy them at bargains is when stock prices are low and there is pessimism about future changes in common stock prices. Yield differentials for strong call protection are highest when interest rates are high. When they are low, you can buy strong call protection for nothing.

Those who are really expert in portfolio management know about changes in the yield differentials for securities at the several levels of risk and several grades in desirability of investment qualities. They try to manage their funds to assume risk when the compensation for risk is high and to buy DOOQ advantages when the cost is low.

QUESTIONS FOR DISCUSSION

1. You are the treasurer of a big company and the company has $10 million in the bank that it does not need for awhile. But you may need it at almost any time in the next year. So you decide to invest it in securities in such a way as to obtain the highest rate of return at the level of risk you can afford to take. Will you buy long-term governments, short-term governments, short-term municipals, or corporate bonds due in 3 to 5 years? What principal considerations led you to your conclusion?

2. Your friend, Joe, bought some shares of stock of a rather small and obscure company that is traded over-the-counter. The quotation for the stock increased 5 per cent and Joe sold it. But when he figured his rate of return it was zero. How can that be?

3. Your father has accumulated a little money over the years and he invests chiefly in common stocks. His policy is to buy and hold; very seldom does he sell a stock. You notice that he owns General Motors, General Electric, General Mills, General Telephone and Electronics, and General Dynamics. They are all listed on the NYSE and are actively traded. With your newly acquired knowledge of investment, you tell Dad that he is buying and paying for something that he doesn't need. Explain it to him.

4. In the course of the conversation Dad complains that he pays the federal income tax at rates up to 48 per cent. So you give him another argument about not putting all his money in common stocks. What else is there for him to invest in that may be more advantageous?

5. Look at the list of corporate bonds whose prices are quoted in a financial periodical and select several issues of well-known companies. Then look up their call provisions in one of the investment manuals. What differences do you find? Does it appear that their market prices are affected by the call protection provided by these provisions?

6. In that same list of corporate bond price quotations, you will find a number of convertible issues. They are designated by the abbreviation "conv." Observe how many of them are selling at prices well above par. Find the explanation in terms of conversion terms and market prices of stocks.

7. In the price quotations for U. S. Treasury bonds you find one issue with a coupon rate of 3¼ per cent due in 1985 and another due in 1986 with a coupon rate of 6⅛ per cent. Is there any significant difference between these issues from the standpoint of an investor in government bonds?

8. At times in the past the difference between average yields on triple A rated corporate bonds and triple B rated corporate bonds has been as large as 4 per cent, and at other times it has been less than 1 per cent. What makes this differential change so much?

III

Financial Analysis

8

The Problem of Financial Analysis

I. Selecting securities
   A. Selecting for maximum returns
   B. Complexity of the problem

II. Estimating the future
   A. Extrapolating historical data
   B. Subjective estimation of risk and return
   C. The skeptical view

III. The random walk hypothesis
   A. Theory and research
   B. The efficient market premise
   C. The public information premise
   D. The accurate evaluation premise
   E. The quick response premise
   F. Critical comment

IV. A system of financial risk analysis

One of the functions of a financial analyst is to select securities of the kind specified by a statement of investment policy, and to try to pick issues of that kind that are likely to provide higher rates of return over a period of time than other issues of the same kind that might be selected.

That initial statement uses several concepts that must be made more explicit.

SELECTING SECURITIES

First, an analyst starts with a statement of investment policy. The statement describes in terms of risk and desirability of ownership characteristics the kinds of securities to be included in a securities portfolio. It might, for example, state simply that some portion of a total investment fund shall be invested in high-grade, long-term bonds. So the analyst must identify securities that are unmistakably high-grade, long-term bonds. That isn't difficult because the statement of policy is in general terms, but if it is in more particular terms (and it should be) there are some finer distinctions to be made among categories of securities.

The term "high-grade" as it is ordinarily used in investment practice means securities low in uncertainty of financial abilities of issuers. But just how low? The statement of investment policy may mean triple A, or double A, or single A rated bonds, or the equivalent in risk of these rating classifications. If "high-grade" means double A rated bonds, the spectrum of bonds from which selection must be made is considerably narrowed. The analyst must choose issues from this smaller selection and even try to differentiate between the less risky and the more risky within that category.

The statement of investment policy we have used for illustration refers directly to financial risk, but by inference it also prescribes the level of interest rate risk and of purchasing power risk. A high-grade bond of long maturity is a kind of security that is high in interest rate risk affecting market value of principal. At this point an analyst might well ask, "How long may the maturities be?" If the policy statement means maturities of 18 to 20 years, the selection of issues from which the analyst may choose is further restricted. There might even be some specification about the size of the coupon rate desired, so that the analyst would have to limit himself to issues with coupon rates between one number and another.

The decision to invest in high-grade, long-term bonds obviously means that the investor is willing to take the purchasing-power risk usually associated with that category of securities.

If investment policy is defined at all precisely, it would specify the level of advantage required in marketability, taxability, and other desirability of investment qualities. Does the investor want to own corporates or municipals? This is important because there is a great difference in their taxability grade. If the investor wants municipals, the category of securities from which the analyst must choose is entirely different from the corporate bond category. If the investor wants highly marketable municipals, this places an additional limitation on the financial analyst. If the investor wants corporates, the analyst must know whether convertible issues may be included. There is the question of how much call protection is required by the statement of investment policy, and there may be even other limitations specified by the policy maker.

The nub of all this is that an analyst does not just start out and analyze bond issues, or stock issues. He is employed to select the kind, or kinds, of securities that an investor wants to own. The statement of policy may start him in one direction, or in quite a different direction. It may turn him down one road, or cause him to turn to a different road. It may set up a variety of barriers that close off one area, or limit access to it. The analyst has to know rather precisely the divisions and subdivisions of all the securities from which he may select and must identify security issues that are of the right kind.

Selecting for Maximum Returns

When an analyst identifies security issues of the kind prescribed by investment policy, he goes on to the more difficult task of selecting from a number of issues (any of which will do as far as "kind" is concerned) those issues that he expects to provide somewhat larger returns over some future time period than other issues of the same kind. This is to say that he tries to maximize returns at prescribed levels of risk and advantage in desirability of ownership qualities.

This part of the function of security analysis goes back to the basic proposition that the objective of investment management is to realize the highest possible rate of return at the highest acceptable levels of risk. We have hypothesized that there is a positive relationship between risk and return. Now we postulate that in any category of securities defined in terms of risk and desirability of ownership qualities, some issues will provide higher rates of return over a future time period than others. The problem of an analyst is to find those issues.

The postulate and the problem are illustrated in Figure 8–1. The general idea is very simple. You are the analyst and you have determined that three security issues have the same level of risk, say, the level of risk indicated in the figure by R_3 on the vertical axis. You have estimated that each of these three issues will provide a different rate of return. Naturally, you select the issue that provides the highest estimated rate of return at that level of risk, as indicated on the horizontal axis. If investment policy requires securities of risk level R_2, you identify securities at that level of risk, estimate the probable rate of return, and select the issue that provides the highest expected rate of return at that risk level. And so on for other risk levels. All this assumes, of course, that you can estimate risk with sufficient accuracy to say that several issues are at the same level, and that you can estimate future returns with sufficient confidence to put securities at the same level of risk in order by size of expected returns.

Complexity of the Problem

We have, of course, oversimplified the problem of selecting securities to maximize returns. The explanation above is in terms of "risk," and we know that there are several causes of risk. In the figure we have ignored the desirability of ownership qualities that often have a significant influence upon the size of expected returns. Clearly, security issues represent all sorts of

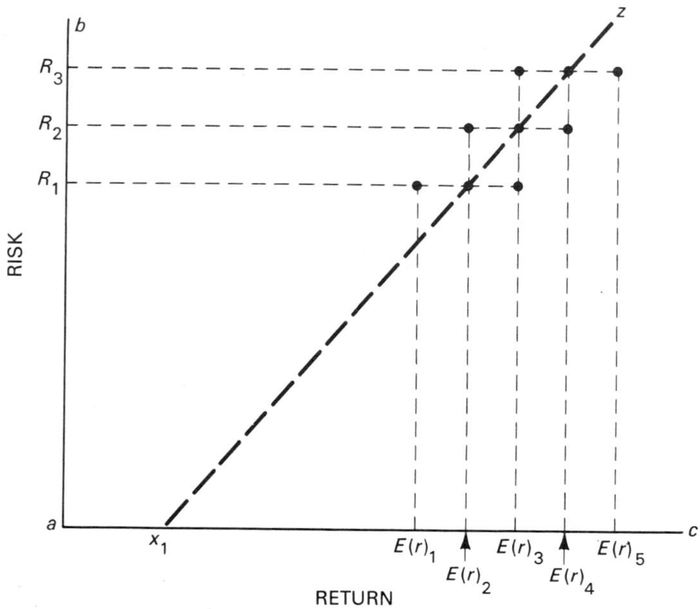

Figure 8–1

The Problem of Selecting Securities With the Best Risk-Return Relationships

combinations of the several causes of risk and of grades in the desirability of ownership qualities. The size of future returns that may reasonably be expected from any security issue is influenced by the combination of all of these influences.

There may be five bonds, for example, each of which is estimated to have a very low level of financial risk. If you are considering only financial risk, you would expect about the same rate of return from each of them. But if the first has a much shorter maturity than the second, it may very well be expected to provide a different rate of return. If the third has the same long maturity as the second but is tax-exempt, its expected rate of return will be smaller than that of the second. A fourth bond issue is about the same as the second (high-grade, long-term, fully taxable), but has much better call protection; its expected rate of return would usually be a few basis points less than that for the second. If there is a fifth high-grade, long-term, taxable bond with good call protection, but with the advantage of very high marketability relative to the other issues, its expected rate of return would be a few basis points less.

When you consider that financial analysts have to select securities from many issues in which individual issues combine infinite variations in levels of several kinds of risk and grades in desirability of ownership qualities, and that all of these levels of risk and desirability affect expected rates of return, you might think the problem is insolvable. But, of course, analysts do solve it routinely with acceptable accuracy.

In practice, the task is not overwhelming because it is taken a step at a time and conclusions at each step contribute to conclusions at subsequent steps. For both bonds and stocks the problem begins with estimating the level of financial risk. When that is done the bond analyst needs to know only the length of maturity and the provisions of the federal income tax law to estimate interest rate risk, purchasing power risk, and tax advantage. A little more information permits grading a bond in terms of the other desirability of ownership qualities. The common-stock analyst is usually concerned chiefly with financial risk. He knows that changes in interest rates in the market influence stock prices and he has some beliefs about common stocks and purchasing-power risk. When marketability is important, it is easy to get data indicative of the general level of marketability.

Traders for broker-dealer firms become remarkably astute in calculating risk-return relationships, particularly in the bond market, and in perceiving very quickly any variation in the market rate of yield, or market price, for an individual issue away from a relationship that they have observed to be normal in the market at the time. Let the yield on a Treasury issue of a given maturity rise a little above the yield curve that prevails in the market and an alert trader will buy that issue until the price rises and the yield declines to normal. The same can be done in the stock market by carefully studying stocks that represent about the same combination of risk and DOOQ's.

The problem of security analysis is made more complex by the fact that the characteristics of the securities change constantly with the passage of time. The passage of time changes the length of the period to maturity of bonds. Events change the level of financial risk and other causes of uncertainty. If you were to estimate the riskiness of a stock, put your conclusion away, go on to another stock and do the same, and so on until after a year you have a fine collection of issues all classified and catalogued, you would find your collection obsolete before you could make much use of it.

Selecting securities is only part of the function of security analysis. The other part involves continuing surveillance of securities initially selected for a portfolio and continuing examination of securities initially rejected. As risk-return relationships change, securities initially rejected may become more desirable than those initially selected.

ESTIMATING THE FUTURE

With these concepts of risk and return, you can easily measure retrospectively the risk that has characterized a security and the rate of return that would have been realized in a past period. Assume that you bought the security at one date at a certain price, held it for a time and received interest or dividends, and then sold it on a subsequent date at the market price. With the present value formula you can calculate the rate of return that would have been obtained. But since prices and dividends vary, the rate would have been different for different past periods. You can make this calculation for a series of time periods in sequence, each of some uniform duration, such as 1 year. Then you will have a series of rates of return. The variation in these rates is an *ex post* measure of the riskiness, that is, the historical uncertainty of rates of return.

But what investors really want to know is how much risk there is in the future and what rate of return they may reasonably expect. Unfortunately there are no numbers for the future. You have to estimate what the numbers will be and make your calculations of risk and return on that basis. An alternative is to take these past measures as the estimate of the future, that is, to extrapolate.

Extrapolating Historical Data

Consider the alternative first. There is something to be said for using historical data as a proxy for future risk and return. Investment services base their financial risk ratings to a large extent on extrapolations, and opinions commonly expressed about the riskiness of securities even among professional investors are strongly influenced by the past record. It is not exaggerating much to say that everybody talks about risk as something in the future but thinks about it as something in the past.

There is some rationale for using extrapolations as estimates. There is frequently a recurring pattern in the financial experience of companies, particularly well-established companies with diversified product lines. Some companies have for years been stable companies with a rising trend of earnings per share and moderate cyclical fluctuations in earnings around the trend line. Some companies have always been cyclical companies with a more or less regular pattern of cyclical fluctuation in earnings. Any estimate of the future must take this historical pattern into account.

The concept of a recurring pattern of change in financial data may be likened to the gyro principle that is applied in navigational aids. A body rotating rapidly on an axis tends to continue to rotate in the same plane and to resist any external force operating to displace it. The earnings of companies seem to be influenced by the gyro principle. A company that has been consistently a highly profitable company is likely to continue to be successful, and one that is marginal financially tends to continue to be marginal.

The trouble with this gyro principle in financial analysis is that it often works poorly. A gyroscope may be forced out of its inertial plane of rotation by external forces, and a company is constantly exposed to forces that make its earnings data different than they were in the past. Products change, markets change, competitive pressures change, management changes, and even the political environment changes. So the pattern of the past is never repeated exactly. The future and past patterns of earnings, dividends, and market prices may differ significantly. Sometimes change is dramatic. There have been many instances of companies that reported a high rate of increase in per share earnings for a series of years, came to be regarded as great growth companies, and then experienced a sudden and drastic decline in earnings with even greater declines in stock prices. The opposite is sometimes true. A company with a record of poor and erratic earnings may turn into a great growth company. If you rely solely on the past record, you may buy historical data that are poorly predictive of the future.

Subjective Estimation of Risk and Return

If extrapolation is inadequate, then you have to make subjective estimates of future financial data. You can do this by examining the historical record, using it as a base for estimating, and trying to judge how the changing forces of competition and the market system will influence the future financial ability of a company to earn money for its security holders. Your estimates are your modification of the historical data.

Are subjective estimates better than extrapolations? If you select securities according to your estimates rather than entirely on the basis of extrapolation, and sell them on the same basis, will you realize a larger rate of return at a level of financial risk over a period of time? If you answer in the affirmative, you assert that your predictive ability is better than extrapolations.

The argument for the affirmative is that experienced analysts with good information can see things happening in a company that are different from what has happened in the past and predict the consequences for the future with some tolerable margin of error. They may see a company's principal product becoming obsolete by reason of improvements in a competitor's product. The happening is historical; the estimate is one of future effect. Or they see changes in the national economy that they believe will operate to increase, or decrease, the demand for a category of goods or services supplied by a company. The changes are evident in statistical data for the economy; the effect on earnings of the company is an estimate. What makes this complex is, first, the difficulty of translating an observed change in the affairs of a company into dollars of future earnings. There is also the fact that companies constantly experience changes that seem likely to have both favorable and unfavorable effects. An estimate of future earnings, then, must be the algebraic sum of a number of plus and minus influences.

This method of estimating the future does not depend on the use of crystal balls. Estimates are based on historical facts and not on some coming event that cannot be prophesied. You use information about past change and draw inferences from it about future change. There is a basis in fact for estimates of the future.

But this is not an exact science. The effect of some observed changes may be underestimated, and the effect of others overestimated. Even the best estimates may be upset by future events that are not predictable. An analyst is not seasoned until he has seen estimates in which he had the greatest confidence prove to be quite wrong. But the requirement is not that each estimate be right. It is that the rate of return from a portfolio of securities managed on the basis of such subjective estimates provide a higher rate of return than a comparable portfolio managed on the basis of extrapolations.

A saving grace for financial analysts, which may contribute significantly to obtaining better than average returns, is the opportunity to revise estimates. You don't make an estimate for a security and stay with it for years. After you make it you watch what happens. If further information coming with the passage of time indicates that an estimate is too high or too low, you change it. If alert, you can correct an error by a market transaction before much damage is done. Indeed, one of the important values of well-considered quantified estimates is that you can constantly compare what is happening in time with very explicit statements of what you thought would happen.

The Skeptical View

There are many theorists and researchers who doubt that financial analysts generally are able to estimate future risks and returns sufficiently well to distinguish within a group of securities of about the same risk category those that eventually provide higher rates of return than the average rate for the category. When two investigators published a study of returns from a very large number of random transactions in New York Stock Exchange stocks over a long period of time and found that the mean annual rate of return was 9.8 per cent,[1] many professional investment managers were embarrassed because their long-term record was no better or not so good.

The skeptics found considerable support in the results of an extensive study of the rates of return realized by the aggregate of a large number of mutual funds representing most of the assets of the industry compared with rates of return on randomly selected portfolios of NYSE stocks during the period January 1960 to June 1968. The researchers concluded that random portfolios of securities performed on the average better over the period than did mutual funds in the same risk class. It was recognized that the funds' performance is net of management fees and transactions costs that are estimated at somewhat more than 1 per cent of assets annually. This would account for a considerable part of the difference in performance between the managed and unmanaged portfolios. Moreover, the comparisons between mutual fund rates of return and those of randomly selected portfolios are not statistically perfect. The random portfolios do not duplicate exactly the risk levels, or the weighting by amount of individual security issues, or the proportions of cash and debt-type obligations. Even so, the conclusion seems justified that in aggregate the professionally managed portfolios provided no better rates of return than could be obtained by randomly selecting stocks of about the same risk class.[2] Of course there were many individual portfolios included in the aggregate with better than average records.

Skepticism about the ability of financial analysts to estimate future returns from securities sufficiently well to select from a risk category of securities those issues that will provide better rates than average for the category

[1]Lorie and Fisher, *op. cit.*

[2]Irwin Friend, Marshall Blume, and Jean Crockett, *Mutual Funds and Other Institutional Investors, 1970*, New York, McGraw-Hill Book Company, pp. 52–59. See also I. Horowitz, "A Rating of Mutual Fund Managements' Investment Ability," *Industrial Management Review*, Vol. 7 (Fall 1965), pp. 65–76.

stems to a considerable extent from studies of academic theorists and researchers. They have attacked some of the Wall Street community's most fervently held beliefs about the ability of experts to select the right securities. The defenders of the faith, however, think that the academicians don't really understand how the investment process is performed and how the security markets work.

The controversy about predictability of future returns centers around the concept known as "the random walk hypothesis." We should take it into consideration at once.

THE RANDOM WALK HYPOTHESIS

The theorists say that changes in market prices of securities are like a random walk. Just as a man may turn first in one direction and then in another while walking about with no particular object in mind, so do stock prices change upward and downward in such manner that the sequence of upturns and downturns cannot be predicted from past price changes. They say that the direction of change from one day to another, or from one month to another, is no more predictable than the direction of change in a series of cumulated random numbers. One author puts it, "Prices have no memory, and yesterday has nothing to do with tomorrow." Every day starts out fifty-fifty. Yesterday's price discounted everything yesterday.[3]

Theory and Research

There have been a number of elaborate studies of stock prices using statistical methods capable of being understood only by those most mathematically sophisticated in an effort to find some system of using past price changes to predict future change. The conclusions are virtually unanimous: there is no system; price changes are not systematic.

Perhaps it should be emphasized, because the matter is often misunderstood, that the statistical tests of the hypothesis have been concerned with the direction of change and not with the magnitude of price changes. A cumulated series of random price changes would follow an upward trend when the size of upward changes is generally greater than the size of downward changes. Thus the upward trend in average stock prices over several decades is not inconsistent with the random walk hypothesis.[4]

More recently the narrow statement of the random walk hypothesis presented above has been broadened. The broadened generalization is that stock prices cannot be predicted on the basis of any historical public infor-

[3]Adam Smith (George J. W. Goodman), *op. cit.*, p. 148. See also Paul H. Cootner (ed.), *The Random Character of Stock Market Prices*, Cambridge, Mass., 1967, The MIT Press.

[4]Richard A. Brealey, *An Introduction to Risk and Return from Common Stocks*, Cambridge, Mass., 1969, The MIT Press, p. 18.

mation. The reasoning is, first, that at any point in time the market price of a security represents the consensus of investors' estimates of its worth on the basis of all information publicly available. At this price there is an equilibrium between supply and demand. When new information appears that affects investors' estimates of a stock's value, the information is quickly disseminated and price moves quickly upward or downward until a new equilibrium price is established. New information is defined as information that has not been deduced from previous information, so it has a new effect on market price.

The validity of the random walk conclusion depends heavily on the validity of several premises about the operation of the security markets and the behavior of investors. First, this thesis asserts that the security markets are highly efficient, that is, prices change quickly in response to change in information and there are no significant impediments to change. Second, it assumes that investors generally have access to the same stream of public information so that what is new information to one is new to everyone. Then it accepts as true that investors evaluate information accurately in terms of its implications for future risk and return. Finally, it is believed that investors act quickly to buy or sell when they have made their evaluations. In a world that is far from perfect, these premises are not perfect.

The Efficient Market Premise

It is quite generally agreed that the security markets are relatively efficient. Anyone with money to buy or securities to sell can put in his order and have it executed in a remarkably short time. No one has a monopoly of anything and there is no oligopoly of sellers or buyers. Large numbers of orders from large numbers of people are executed daily. But there are some qualifying conditions.

One is that there are transactions costs both when you buy and when you sell. The size of costs relative to the value of a transaction varies inversely with the value, but on a majority of transactions it would be in the range of 1 to 3 per cent per transaction and twice that for a round trip in and out of the market. The effect is to deter market action when the size of change in estimate of risk and return is small. You have to earn expenses and something more in order for a purchase and sale to be worthwhile.

A frequent deterrent to selling securities is the income tax liability that would be incurred. Most investors have to pay a tax on capital gains. Especially when realized profit is a substantial part of the total value of a sale, an unwillingness to take a profit and pay the tax may influence how an investor reacts to new information. On the other hand, sometimes people sell securities to realize a loss that can be offset against a realized gain to reduce income tax liability. The tax offset rather than new information may determine the decision. So investors' buy and sell decisions are not solely a product of the evaluation of new information.

Moreover, markets for some securities are not so efficient as for others because trading is less active. Large quantities of the several hundred most actively traded issues usually can be bought and sold with little effect on price. But for thousands of issues, both listed and over-the-counter, the daily volume of trading ranges from zero to a few hundred shares. An investor who buys a few thousand shares of such a poorly marketable stock may cause a considerable change in current price quotations. Once he has exhausted the offers at about the price prevailing when he started buying, he has to bid up the price to a level that attracts new offers of stock. It works the opposite way when a large block is sold. A large buyer or seller may find himself in much the same position as a monopolist in that his bids or offers determine market price until he has completed his purchase or sale. Under such conditions, market price is not entirely a product of the reaction of a great many investors to new information. A further consideration is that many institutional investors do not invest at all in such poorly marketable securities.

The Public Information Premise

The proposition that the investing public receives a series of items of information that represent prompt, accurate, and complete disclosure is essential to the random walk hypothesis. If a few people have more accurate or earlier information than others, then they can buy or sell sooner than others and there will be no completely new price change following publication of new information.

There is no doubt that investors have access to such a stream of public information and that it is available to all at about the same time. Our public information system is excellent because federal laws require companies whose securities are traded in the securities markets to make public promptly information that may affect investors' evaluations of their securities. Those who fail to do so are subject to legal penalties. The organized securities exchanges also use their considerable influence to require prompt and accurate disclosure by listed companies. There is considerable talk in some quarters about "inside information," that is, information that is known only to a few insiders. But the talk is probably greater than the information. The Securities and Exchange Commission has taken the position that profits made by the use of inside information may by legal action be taken away from those who receive them, and the courts have supported this position.[5]

It should be conceded, however, that some people have better knowledge of day-to-day and week-to-week developments in the affairs of a company than does the public by reason of their employment by the company or their business relationships with the company. They may be able to infer that favorable or unfavorable information will soon be released to the public, and sometimes they are the source of rumors that good or bad news will soon appear. It is not uncommon for the market price of a stock to rise shortly before

[5]Alan R. Bromberg, "The Law of Corporate Information," *Financial Analysts Journal*, Vol. 25, No. 2 (March–April 1969), pp. 26–31.

good news is released as people act on such expectations. When good or bad news is discounted in advance, the news release itself may have little further influence on market price.

The Accurate Evaluation Premise

The idea that investors generally evaluate new information accurately in terms of risk and return estimates may be the most doubtful of all the premises. Sometimes they seem completely irrational. At times they sell stock at declining prices on good news and buy stock at rising prices on bad news. Certainly the wide swings in investors' estimates from the peak of a bull market to the trough of a bear market influence strongly the market response to new information about companies.

Then there is the fact that some people buy and sell not on the basis of information about companies but on the basis of charts of past prices and trading volume. The so-called technicians who use such historical data operate on a theory that is exactly opposite to the random walk theory. They believe that they can predict the future from the past statistical record.

There are some investors whose ability to evaluate information is said to be poor or non-existent. Their reaction to any new information is unpredictable. And there are many who simply do not get new information because they are not familiar with the media that publish it.

Finally, there is the undoubted fact that professional analysts, even those of high repute, often disagree on the evaluation of information. Some look at the information and decide to buy; others look at the same information and decide to sell. If you study the published information on purchases and sales of stocks by mutual funds, you will see that in any given calendar quarter some funds buy a stock and some funds sell it. The sum of transactions may be the consensus, but there can be no assurance that the consensus is right.

The Quick Response Premise

The last premise is that investors respond promptly to new information. Some do. There are short-term traders and quick-reaction portfolio managers. Some managers act so quickly that they are called "gunslingers" who shoot from the hip. But generally there is some time lag between news and response to news in the form of market transactions. People have to think about the information, often they have difficulty making up their minds, and sometimes they can't come to a conclusion until they have collected several items of new information all of which point to the same conclusion. The quick response premise, then, is at least dubious. Casual observation of investor behavior suggests that responses are distributed over a considerable period of time following disclosure of new information.

Critical Comment

The sum of this critique is that market prices do not move in a line that represents quick and accurate responses of investors to new information, but rather in a line that wanders below or above the price pattern that would be established by quick and accurate responses. There are variations from the central tendency of this price pattern and they may provide the basis for good security analysts to select issues that provide better than average rates of return (at a level of risk) than other issues.

There is also a tricky question involved in defining new information as information that has not been inferred from past information. Apparently this means not inferred by all the investors who participate in the market. But if a particular analyst makes estimates of future changes in a company's financial ability that are different from the consensus and subsequent news proves his estimates to be about right, then the subsequent news is not new to him. He can be right by drawing the right inferences from news and still not violate the random walk hypothesis as it is usually stated.

The financial community generally accepts the proposition that experts are able to estimate future changes in companies' financial abilities with sufficient accuracy to provide some increment to the rate of return on a securities portfolio beyond that which would be obtained without analysts' contributions. There are other elements in the problem of maximizing investment returns and we will examine them in due course, but analysts' estimates of the future fortunes of companies rank near the beginning of the process of portfolio management.

The evidence that large financial institutions have faith in financial analysts is that they employ so many of them. In large banks financial analysts are organized by squads. Insurance companies and mutual funds seem to have fewer soldiers and more captains, but the financial analysts are the base of their investment management function. Large corporations employ professional investment counsel firms to manage their pension funds, and the counselors employ financial analysts. Many broker-dealer firms base much of their effort to secure the business of institutional investors on the investment research reports their analysts supply to institutions.

A SYSTEM OF FINANCIAL RISK ANALYSIS

The chapters that follow describe a system of financial risk analysis. The system is based on the fundamental concept that the future financial abilities of companies are a function of funds available to them relative to funds required to make promised or expected payments to their security holders modified by the strength of security holders' claims for payment.

In the next chapter that concept is applied to the problem of estimating the financial risk level of corporate bonds. Bond analysis makes a more literal application of this fundamental concept than does stock analysis. It provides a good base for further application to the more complex problem of estimating financial risk in stocks. Usually common stock analysis is more lengthy than bond analysis because the range in size of returns is greater. There is more to be gained by being right and more to be lost by being wrong.

In the development of the system of thought we will move from the general to the more particular. In bond analysis the general relationship is the "times-fixed-charges-earned" ratio, but we must examine the sources of funds available, determine the amounts of fixed charges, observe their past variation, and then try to estimate how amounts will change in the future. In common stock analysis the principal source of funds available is earnings applicable to common stock, and amounts of dividends are funds required.

QUESTIONS FOR DISCUSSION

1. The stocks listed below are all rated A− by Standard & Poor's in a rating system in which A+ is "highest." A is "high," and A− is "above average." The term "highest" means lowest in uncertainty of future financial abilities of issuers. Is there any basis for selecting one rather than another of these issues? Or, is it just as well to select one or two at random?

AMP, Inc.	General Cable Corp.
Anderson, Clayton & Co.	General Tire & Rubber Co.
Armstrong Rubber Co.	Gimbel Brothers, Inc.

2. The earnings and dividends per share for a leading diversified manufacturing company for the last 5 years have been as follows:

Earnings	$3.17	3.42	3.67	4.03	4.35
Dividends	1.80	1.88	2.00	2.10	2.20

What conclusion, if any, can you draw from these data about uncertainty of the future financial ability of this company? The company is American Brands, Inc., and the years are 1967 to 1971.

3. Here is another company that in the same 5 years reported earnings per share as follows:

Earnings	$1.91	2.25	2.72	1.17	d1.20
Dividends	$0.23	0.23	0.24	0.25	0.25

(d means deficit)

How can you estimate the riskiness of that stock? The company is Boise Cascade Corp. and the years are 1967 to 1971.

4. Assume that the random walk hypothesis is entirely valid. Does this mean that no investor can expect better returns from a common stock portfolio than the returns provided by a large list of stocks such as Standard & Poor's 500 common stocks?

5. Several months ago you bought a stock and since then the market price has increased 10 per cent. Today you see in the newspaper that the earnings of the issuer in the last quarter (3 months) were a little less than in the quarter immediately preceding. You consider selling the stock. What considerations, if any, would deter you from selling?

6. A certain professional investment counseling firm was reviewing a client's portfolio with him. The client pointed to one stock on the list and remarked that the issuer's earnings had declined for the past 2 years and that market price had declined 40 per cent in that time period. He asked if the manager intended to sell that stock. The manager replied that he had been concerned about the poor earnings reports but would not do anything until he had made a visit to the company and talked with the management. What does this tell you about how some professional investment managers behave?

7. Your favorite broker has just recommended that you buy a particular stock. He says that he talked with a director of the company and the director has told him that the company's earnings prospects are very favorable. Is this a good reason for buying the stock?

8. In your capacity as an expert financial analyst, you recommended to a client that he buy a stock of a wholesale grocery company. He bought it at 15, the price went down to 10, and has stayed at about that figure for several months. He asks you to justify your recommendation and you give him the per-share-earnings figures, which show that there was a slight decline in quarterly earnings a year ago, but that in each subsequent quarter the earnings figure has slightly improved. Can you offer any explanation for the poor performance of the stock?

9

Analysis of Corporate Bonds

Most students, individual investors, and even some professional investment managers have little enthusiasm for bond analysis. Bonds are not very exciting and the chance of discovering a sensational investment opportunity is poor. You can get a good approximation of the estimated level of financial risk in a bond just by looking up its Moody's and Standard & Poor's ratings. If a bond's rating indicates it is high-grade, you know that changes in its market price will come mainly from changes in interest rates.

Nevertheless, the function of bond analysis is an important one in the total system of securities investment. Financial institutions and some nonfinancial organizations invest largely in bonds. Some are content with the published bond ratings, but many are not. Many want their own appraisals of the riskiness of bonds and often they seek to make finer distinctions in risk than the bond ratings. There are also changes in the financial abilities of bond issuers as time passes that must be considered. Finally, many institutional investors buy bond issues by direct placement, and for these issues they have to perform the entire function of security analysis. Many young people have been lured into the business of investment management by the glamour of common stocks and have found that the more interesting action is in bonds.

It is good to begin the study of security analysis with bond analysis because bonds present the whole problem of appraising financial risk in a clear-cut fashion. The issuer of a bond promises to pay a series of stated amounts of interest and principal. The amounts and the dates are precisely stated. The essential question is whether the issuer will be able to make the payments. The expected rate of return is usually the yield to maturity based on current market price.

A FRAMEWORK FOR DEVELOPMENT

The framework for development takes the form of a series of general propositions. None of them is entirely satisfactory. Each will be subsequently examined, qualified, and supplemented. Keep this in mind as you read.

The Time Horizon

The first proposition is that the time horizon for study of a bond issue is from now to its maturity. The rationale is that bond investors usually buy bonds with the intention of holding them to maturity, or to earlier redemption by the issuer. Thus, the period for which risk is to be estimated may be 20 or 30 years, or even longer. No one in his right mind really thinks he can estimate the uncertainty of a stream of cash flows that far in the future. So as a practical matter you are concerned with the basic elements of strength and weakness that are likely to continue for an indefinite time period. This definition of the time horizon is conventional and it provides a basis for bringing into the discussion all the usual considerations in bond analysis.

However, an alternative proposition is that a shorter time horizon may be used, at least as a supplement to the period to maturity time horizon. As a matter of fact, investors seldom can be sure that they will be able to hold bonds to maturity, and in practice the probability of sale before maturity may be very high. Subsequently, in this discussion, we will consider a quite different method that may be used for estimating the risk in bonds when the time horizon is relatively short.

The Principal Source of Funds

A second proposition is that earnings are the principal source of funds for payments to bondholders. Earnings are funds generated by the operation of a profitable business. At some point in the operation, earnings are cash receipts for goods or services sold in excess of expenses incurred in selling the goods. Funds from earnings are considered by debtor and creditor alike as the normal source of funds for payments to bondholders.

Usually, analysts use the accounting statement of earnings, which is described as "earnings before interest and income taxes" and is frequently reduced to the acronym EBIT. The reason for using earnings before taxes is that the amount of earnings after taxes is affected by the amount of interest paid; interest is a tax-deductible expense. Two companies with the same amount of EBIT would have different amounts of after-tax earnings if they have different amounts of interest. Not everyone uses EBIT. Some say that the amount of earnings actually available for payments to bondholders is the after-tax amount. They hold that the amount of income tax is a cost of doing business and it has a claim on earnings prior to interest claims of bondholders.

The Times-Interest-Earned Ratio

The amounts required for bondholders are the amounts of interest on non-current debt. These amounts are reported in corporate financial statements along with amounts of earnings. Ordinarily, analysts use annual earnings statements.

It follows, then, that the financial ability of a company to make payments to its bondholders is measured to a very large extent by the size and stability of amounts of earnings relative to amounts of interest as reported in income statements of the several most recent years. The relationship is expressed as a ratio—earnings divided by interest—which is commonly called the times-interest-earned ratio. Obviously, the higher the ratio the greater the margin by which interest is earned. If a times-interest-earned ratio for a period is 5 (or 5 to 1), then the issuer had $4 of earnings as a margin above each $1 it had to pay. With such a large margin there could be a substantial reduction in earnings without an impairment in the issuer's ability to pay.

Stability of the ratio over a period of years is important. If a company has been able to earn its interest by a large and stable margin for a series of years past, its financial ability is strong. Instability has the opposite implication. Even a large ratio in one year is not reassuring if in a subsequent year the ratio is small. Often the relative stability of the times-interest-earned ratio can be determined satisfactorily by inspection. If the ratio has varied only between five and six times in the last 5 years, it has been very stable. If the variation has been from two to six, it has been very unstable. For the purpose of making comparisons among a number of bond issuers, however, it may be desirable to compute the mean, the standard deviation, and coefficient of variation of annual ratios for a number of years past. Table 9–1 illustrates the calculation. In this example you can see almost at a glance that Ade Company has a higher average ratio than Cap Company and that it has been

TABLE 9–1

The Stability of Times-Interest-Earned Ratios

	Ade Company			
	Year	*Ratio* X	*Deviation* $(X - \bar{X})$	*Variation* $(X - \bar{X})^2$
	1	5.5	+0.5	0.25
	2	5.3	+0.3	0.09
	3	4.2	−0.8	0.64
	4	5.0	0	0
	5	4.2	−0.8	0.64
	6	5.3	+0.3	0.09
	7	5.5	+0.5	0.25
(1) Sum		35.0	0.0	1.96
(2) Mean		5.0	—	—
(3) Variance		—	—	0.28
(4) Standard deviation		—	—	0.53
(5) Coefficient of variation		—	—	0.106

	Cap Company			
	Year	*Ratio* X	*Deviation* $(X - \bar{X})$	*Variation* $(X - \bar{X})^2$
	1	1.3	−1.7	2.89
	2	3.2	+0.2	0.04
	3	4.5	+1.5	2.25
	4	3.0	0	0
	5	4.5	+1.5	2.25
	6	3.2	+0.2	0.04
	7	1.3	−1.7	2.89
(1) Sum		21.0	0.0	10.36
(2) Mean		3.0	—	—
(3) Variance		—	—	1.22
(4) Standard deviation		—	—	0.38
(5) Coefficient of variation		—	—	0.407

Note: the statistical calculations are as follows:

1. The sum is the total of the annual ratios for 7 years.
2. The mean is the sum divided by 7.
3. The deviation is the difference between each of the annual ratios and the mean, with the deviations above the mean having a + sign and the deviations below having a − sign. The algebraic sum is zero.
4. The variance is the sum of the annual deviations squared and divided by the number of years.
5. The standard deviation is the square root of the variance.
6. The coefficient of variation is the standard deviation divided by the mean.

more stable. But it helps to determine that Ade's mean ratio has been 5 relative to 3 for Cap; Ade has a much larger average margin. Ade's variance in ratios is only 0.28 relative to 1.48 for Cap; Ade has less instability of the earnings ratio. When converted to standard deviation, the figure for Ade is 0.53 compared with 0.38 for Cap; 0.53 is the smaller number because it is the square root of a number less than 1. The coefficient of variation is useful to show the size of variation relative to the mean. In this instance the coefficient for Cap is larger than for Ade.

Strength of Claim

And the last statement is that the greater the strength of bondholders' claim for payment, the less is the uncertainty of payment (other things being equal). The rationale is that corporate managements try harder to provide the money when bondholders are in a strong position and, if default does occur, bondholders with a strong claim are likely to recover most or all of what is due to them.

Among creditors, strength of claim is largely determined by priority of claim on assets and by the value of such assets relative to debts. Holders of obligations secured by a first lien on assets that are capable of being liquidated to realize a value much greater than the amount of debt are in a relatively strong position. Holders of debenture bonds have a general claim on corporate assets along with all other unsecured creditors, and there may be subordinated debentures whose claim ranks below that of specified unsecured debts. On the basis of what has been said about bond analysis up to this point, it seems fairly simple. You compute the times-interest-earned ratios for several years past, measure their mean and variation around the mean, estimate the strength of their claim, and come to a conclusion. A finding of high and stable ratios plus a first mortgage on valuable corporate assets means that there is little uncertainty of ability to make contractual payments to bondholders for some years to come. Reverse these findings and you have a risky bond.

You could do this and be about right most of the time, but you could make some mistakes and your approximations might not be good enough. When you get out of the area of rather obviously high-grade bonds, you would find some situations you would not know how to handle. There is a great deal more to be said, and the remainder of this chapter is devoted to saying it.

SOME OTHER SOURCES OF FUNDS

Earnings are the most obvious source of funds for paying bond interest, but there are other sources and sometimes these other sources are even more important than earnings. Sophisticated investors sometimes buy bond issues of companies that have no earnings and are not likely to have earnings for several years in the future. They rely on cash flow in the form of non-cash expenses, proceeds of liquidation of assets, and possibly other net cash inflows of an unusual nature.

Non-Cash Expenses

Non-cash expenses are those that do not require the disbursement of cash. They are charges against income to record expenses that are very real, but in most instances the cash has previously been spent and the accounting charge is for the purpose of distributing expense to operations in appropriate time periods. The most common and usually the most important non-cash expense is depreciation of fixed assets. Assets were acquired and money was spent at some time in the past. Depreciation is a charge made against income to recover over the estimated life of a fixed asset an amount equal to its cost minus its estimated salvage value at the end of the period of its useful life. Depletion is the same kind of a charge made to recover the cost of an asset that is used up in operating a business. Natural resources such as ore, oil, or timber are depleted. There are several kinds of intangible assets that may be amortized. Goodwill listed as an asset and the accounting value of patents or franchises are usually amortized by periodic charges against income. Sometimes expenditures for research and product development are not charged to income in the period in which they are made, but are capitalized (charged to an asset account) and then amortized over a period of years by charges to income. It is not unusual for the total amount of these non-cash expenses to be large relative to the amount of reported earnings.

Non-cash expenses must, of course, be earned to provide a cash flow. That is, sales (the cash derived from sales) must be sufficient in amount in an accounting period to pay the cash expenses plus the non-cash expenses.

There may, however, be a question whether the non-cash expenses actually represent funds available for payment of fixed charges. Generally, assets that are worn out or depleted have to be replaced in order for a business to continue operations, and in most firms the process of replacement goes on more or less continuously. Corporate managers generally regard the non-cash expenses as the major source of funds for replacing assets and they often complain that the amount of these internally generated cash flows is not sufficient to replace assets under conditions of a rising price level. This suggests that when there is more or less continuous replacement of assets, non-cash expenses may not represent funds available for payment of fixed charges.

In some situations, however, depreciated or depleted assets are not continuously replaced. A new building or plant usually has a useful life of many years and there is no expenditure for replacement during its life. Some depleting assets may not be replaced at all and there is no replacement of intangible assets amortized by non-cash expenses.

Bond analysts may, therefore, find it useful to compute an internal cash flow coverage of interest. This is earnings plus the cash flow from non-cash expenses, or plus whatever part of non-cash expenses may be estimated to be applicable to interest, divided by interest on bonds.

Funds from Liquidation of Assets

Business enterprises more or less continuously liquidate assets and receive some amount of cash inflow from these sales. Net amounts applicable to fixed charges may be too small to be of much significance to a bond analyst. But there are some situations in which they may add materially to the amounts of funds available for payments to bondholders.

Sometimes companies derive funds from sale of fixed assets. Real estate development companies, for example, may devote years to developing a large tract of land, incur considerable debt in the process, and then pay the debt largely or entirely from the proceeds of sales of land. These sales may go on over a considerable period of years. Companies in forest product industries often sell land that has been timbered and is not suitable for reforesting. Many companies obtain significant amounts of revenue from sale of equipment used in the business operation when it reaches the end of its useful life. In some instances companies sell equipment before it has been fully depreciated because it is obsolete.

Current assets, of course, are sold in the ordinary course of business. Usually the cash inflow is matched more or less by the cash outflow to pay for acquiring or producing more goods or services to sell. When this is so, current assets, despite their current nature, are frozen in the business. In periods of business recession, however, many companies experience a net reduction in current assets and generate a cash flow by so doing. When sales decline there is usually a reduction in accounts receivable and in inventories. To some extent this cash flow is used to reduce current liabilities, particularly bank loans, and there may be little or no net accretion to cash or marketable securities. But sometimes there is; experience varies widely. From the point of view of a bond analyst, a history of net cash inflow from current assets during business recession is reassuring.

A relatively large amount of marketable securities among current assets may appear to be a ready source of funds for bondholders if earnings are not adequate. The appearance is likely to be deceptive. Usually, marketable securities represent funds committed or reserved for some specific purpose, such as capital outlays, repayments of short-term liabilities, financing production and marketing of new products, or other specific purpose. There are exceptions, however, and they may be important. When such liquid assets are uncommitted, they represent funds that could be used for payment of bond interest.

In any event, it is well to examine the liquidity of a corporate bond issuer. Sometimes financial failure is caused by a lack of funds for regular operations. Examination of the current position involves more than just the relationship of current assets to current liabilities. It may lead to such questions as the rate of turnover of inventories, the age of accounts receivable, the size of accounts payable relative to cost of goods sold, the terms of bank loans, and the existence of commitments requiring relatively large cash outlays in the relatively near future. The "liquidity crisis" of 1969–1971 caused bond analysts to pay closer attention to corporate balance sheets.

Statements or Sources and Uses of Funds

If you examine a statement of sources and uses of funds for an accounting period, such as usually presented by companies in their annual reports, you will see that there are many different sources of funds and many uses of them. The purpose of such a statement is to show for a fiscal year the sources of funds used by management to finance additions to assets or reductions in liabilities. Although the form varies, the statement usually reports the internal cash flow in the form of earnings and non-cash expenses, and the amounts of funds obtained by external financing. It goes on to show increases (or decreases) in the several principal categories of assets and of liabilities. An increase in an asset is a use of funds and a decrease is a source of funds. An increase in a liability is a source of funds, and conversely. The balance is working capital at the end of the year. Table 9–2 is a typical statement of sources and uses of funds.

A study of statements of sources and uses of funds for a company for the past several years provides the broadest view of its cash inflows and its cash requirements. It puts together in one picture the principal sources of funds we have been discussing and the needs for those funds not only for fixed charges but also for other purposes. It may serve to alert a bond analyst to find inflows and outflows not observed in conventional ratio analysis.

TABLE 9–2

Consolidated Statement of Sources and Uses of Funds
The Proctor & Gamble Company and Subsidiary Companies

Years Ended June 30, 1972 and 1971	*1972*	*1971*
SOURCE OF FUNDS		
Net earnings	$276,310,000	$237,590,000
Depreciation and depletion	64,780,000	57,007,000
Deferred income taxes	17,618,000	7,981,000
Total from operations	358,708,000	302,578,000
New long-term debt	107,208,000	4,804,000
Increase in payables and accruals	59,637,000	23,970,000
Other items, net	9,772,000	10,004,000
	535,325,000	341,356,000
USE OF FUNDS		
Capital expenditures	265,080,000	183,514,000
Dividends to shareholders	122,689,000	114,310,000
Long-term debt repayment	9,174,000	9,153,000
Increase in accounts receivable	11,151,000	19,129,000
Increase in inventories	35,896,000	28,496,000
	443,990,000	354,602,000
INCREASE (DECREASE) IN CASH AND MARKETABLE SECURITIES	$ 91,335,000	$ (13,246,000)

SOME OTHER EXPENDITURES IN THE NATURE OF FIXED CHARGES

In our initial framework of analysis we mentioned only interest on non-current debt as funds required for payments to bondholders. It is time now to say that there may be other financial requirements in the nature of fixed changes that should be considered along with interest.

Some companies have subsidiary companies whose accounts are consolidated with those of the parent company. Interest on non-current debt of these companies is ordinarily included along with interest on parent company bonds in published financial statements. Such charges should be included and the total amount used in calculating the relationship of funds available to funds required. Some companies have guaranteed interest on debt of non-consolidated subsidiaries or affiliated companies. This interest, too, should be included, even though the guarantor is not presently making the payments guaranteed. Another possible item is dividends on outstanding stock of consolidated subsidiary companies owned by other investors than the parent company. Corporate managements sometimes consider these dividends to have such a high priority that they are deducted in the statement of income before arriving at the amount of earnings.

An increasingly important item in the financial statements of corporate issuers is lease rentals, that is, payments made for the use of property under long-term leases. Retail chain-store companies lease space in shopping centers for their stores; transportation companies lease railway cars, trucks, airplanes, shipping containers, barges and terminals. Manufacturing companies sometimes lease entire factory buildings, and financial institutions often lease office buildings. These lease contracts are the equivalent of bonds, because they require the payment of fixed (or minimum) amounts of rent periodically for prescribed time periods. Rental payments are properly included with interest payments as fixed charges. They may even have a stronger claim on funds available than bondholders' claims, because failure to pay rent could result in repossession of leased property by its owner without the usual legal process of receivership and settlement of claims.

There is some disagreement among financial analysts about whether contractual payments for amortization of non-current debt should be considered fixed charges. The argument for including debt amortization in total funds required is that these payments are just as much long-term contractual obligations of issuers as are interest payments. The contrary argument is that a company that is able to earn its interest, lease rentals, and charges on subsidiary company debt by a good margin is not likely to have difficulty with debt amortization. Another view is that non-cash expenses may reasonably be expected to cover debt amortization. This seems to imply that non-cash expenses would not be included in funds available, but left as another cash flow that management may use for debt reduction. The conservative course is to count contractual amortization payments as fixed charges.

In the last several pages we have considerably expanded the concept that financial ability to make payments to bondholders is measured by the times-interest-earned ratio. There are other sources of funds than earnings and they may be significant. There are other payments than interest that are fixed charges.

Recognition of these other sources of funds and of other kinds of charges results in a ratio sometimes called the fixed-charges-covered ratio, or the coverage ratio. The numerator is EBIT plus non-cash expenses earned and whatever other amounts of funds an analyst believes have been available for paying fixed charges, which would be a subjective estimate. The denominator would be interest, whatever charges there may be on securities of subsidiary companies, lease rentals, and contractual debt amortization.

In later pages we will sometimes refer to the times-interest-earned ratio when it is useful to mention that particular relationship, but usually the coverage ratio will be used as the broad measure of financial ability.

TREND OF THE COVERAGE RATIO

The stability of the coverage ratio from year to year is important, but the trend is also important because it may be a basis for estimating future changes in the size of the ratio. If you observe a distinct downward trend, you would certainly try to find out what has caused it and consider whether it is likely to continue in the future. A rising trend would imply future improvement in financial ability.

Trend can be observed just by visual examination of a series of ratios for the past several years. Visual examination is made easier by plotting the ratios on graph paper, with the size of the ratio on the vertical axis and time on the horizontal axis. Then you can draw a trend line by inspection, that is, a straight line drawn in such manner that the differences between values on the trend line and the points representing actual values of the ratios are as small as possible. You measure the distances by eye. When there is a distinct trend upward or downward, this visual trend line may be sufficient. If you find a markedly declining trend for a bond, you may conclude that the risk is too high relative to the expected rate of return and go no further. Or, a rising trend may simply reinforce other evidence of strong financial ability.

However, if you are comparing bond issues and trying to do a good statistical job, you need to measure trends more exactly so that you can compare them in quantitative terms. Trend may be measured by the method of least squares. Table 9–3 illustrates application of this method and there is an explanatory note at the foot of the table.

You can see by inspection of the coverage ratio (column Y in Table 9–3) that the trend of the ratio is downward, and when you plot the ratios on a chart, as in Figure 9–1, you see it more clearly. A precise statistical description is provided by data in the Y_c column in Table 9–3, which shows the trend of the ratio; the trend line is in Figure 9–1.

When there is a significant trend in coverage ratios, the variation from year to year is measured relative to computed trend values rather than relative to the arithmetic mean of the series. Any distinct trend by itself increases

TABLE 9–3
The Trend of Coverage Ratios

Year	X (Time)	Y (Coverage ratio)	X^2	$X \cdot Y$
1	−2	6.2	4	−12.4
2	−1	4.6	1	− 4.6
3	0	5.3	0	0
4	+1	3.2	1	+ 3.2
5	+2	4.0	4	+ 8.0
		23.3	10	− 5.8

$$A = \frac{\Sigma Y}{N} = \frac{23.3}{5} = 4.66$$

$$B = \frac{\Sigma X \cdot Y}{\Sigma X^2} = \frac{-5.8}{10} = -0.58$$

Year	A	+	B_X	=	Y_C (Trend values)
−2	4.66		−1.16		5.82
−1	4.66		+0.58		5.24
0	4.66		0		4.66
+1	4.66		−0.58		4.08
+2	4.66		−1.16		3.50

Note:
The basic formula is $Y_C = A + B_X$. Y_C is the computed trend values of the coverage ratios. *A* is the arithmetic average of *Y*, the actual ratios. *B* is the sum of each *Y* value multiplied by the value of its year in the series, divided by the square of the number of years. B_X for each year is *B* times the value of each year in the series. Additions and multiplications are algebraic. Sometimes this formula is written in lower case instead of capital letters.

This method assumes that there is a positive relationship between the coverage ratios for the series of years and the sequence of time periods. The relationship might be only weakly positive, or even negative, and in such situations the trend values have little or no significance.

instability relative to the mean. The usual statistical method for measuring variation of a series of numbers from trend values is the standard error of the estimate. That term may be misleading by implying that someone made a mistake. The "error" is simply the differences between the computed trend values and the actual values of the ratios. The standard error of the estimate is a measure of how much actual values differ from trend values. The larger the number, the greater the variation. Table 9–4 shows the calculation of the standard error of the estimate for the coverage ratios used in Table 9–3. In this example, the standard error of the estimate is 0.63, which is relatively small. You can see by Figure 9–1, that the annual coverage ratios fluctuate rather narrowly around the computed trend values.

SOME OTHER FINANCIAL RATIOS USED TO ESTIMATE RISK

There are a number of other financial ratios often used by analysts to estimate the financial ability of companies to pay their fixed charges. All of

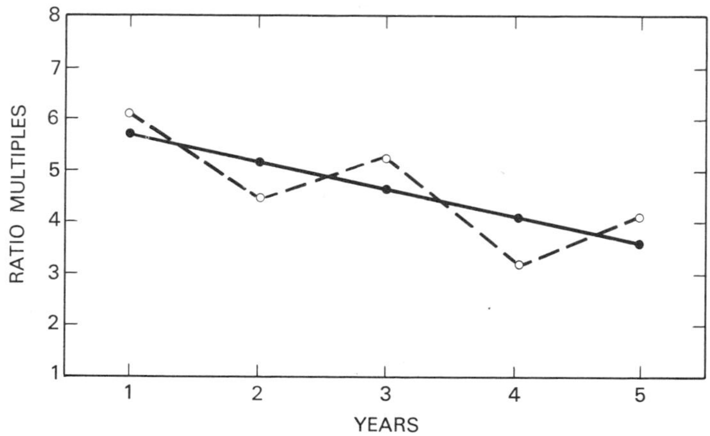

Figure 9–1

The Trend of Coverage Ratios and Variation from the Trend

them influence to some extent the size of the coverage ratios, and thus they may help to explain why that ratio is relatively high or low, or why it has moved upward or downward. Their relationship to the basic question of financial ability to pay fixed charges must be understood in order to interpret them.

One of the most widely used ratios is the total amount of non-current debt as a percentage of total capitalization. Capitalization is the sum of the common equity at book value, preferred stock, and non-current debt. If there is a significant amount of lease rentals, they should be capitalized at about the rate that would have to be paid for long-term debt and the capitalized amount should be added to the debt. Some analysts simply multiply the annual amount of lease rentals by 10 and use that product as the capitalized amount.

This ratio measures the extent of use of non-current debt, and its equivalent in fixed charges to finance the business. The larger the debt ratio, the greater the amount of fixed charges relative to funds available, if everything else is equal. Of course other things are not equal. The amount of annual interest is determined not only by the amount of debt but also by the interest rate at which it was incurred. Amounts of amortization are affected by the amount of debt and the rate of retirement provided by the terms of debt contracts.

Another version of non-current debt to total capitalization uses the common equity at its market value rather than at book value. A high market value for the common stock relative to book value indicates a relatively high rate of earnings on the common equity, year-to-year stability of earnings applicable to the common, or a favorable rate of growth in earnings per share over a period of years, or some combination of these conditions. Any combination that produces a relatively high market value of the common stock is favorable from the viewpoint of bondholders, because it evidences large, or stable, or increasing earnings after taxes and interest payments on debt. A shortcoming of this measure of risk is that market prices fluctuate and a

TABLE 9–4

Standard Error of the Estimate for Coverage Ratios

Year	Y	Y_C	$Y - Y_C$	$(Y - Y_C)^2$
1	6.20	5.82	0.38	.1444
2	4.60	5.24	0.64	.4016
3	5.30	4.66	0.64	.4096
4	3.20	4.08	0.88	.7744
5	4.00	3.50	0.50	.2500
				1.9880

Note:
Y is the annual coverage ratios.
Y_C is trend values of these ratios from Table 9–3.
$Y - Y_C$ is the difference between the columns with those headings.
$(Y - Y_C)^2$ is the square of the numbers in the $Y - Y_C$ column.

The sum of $(Y - Y_C)^2$ is 1.9880. This quantity is divided by the number of Y values, which is 5. This mean is .3976. The square root of the mean is 0.63, which is the standard error of the estimate. The formula may be written:

$$S_Y \cdot X = \sqrt{\frac{\Sigma\,(Y - Y_C)^2}{N}}$$

high market value for the common stock equity at the end of one year may be a low value at the end of the next. Moreover, changes in market value may result partly from changes in market rates of interest, rather than from changes in earnings.

Some analysts think that the rate of earnings on total capitalization is a good measure of financial ability. Earnings may be taken as EBIT and divided by total capitalization at book value. A high rate of earnings means a relatively large amount of funds from earnings for payment of debt. The rate may also be calculated on the basis of earnings after both interest and taxes to total capitalization (EAIT). In this form it measures earnings in excess of amounts required for interest and taxes. Both EBIT and EAIT may be related to total assets to measure rates of profitability for all the funds used in the business.[1]

There is considerable redundancy in most of the ratios used in bond analysis. The relationships they measure are not independent, and you do not add greatly to the basis for estimating financial risk by calculating a variety of ratios. These other ratios are useful chiefly as a means of observing influences on the basic relationship of funds available to funds required.

EVALUATING STRENGTH OF CLAIM

When you sum up what you have learned about financial ability to pay fixed charges, you add on something to represent your estimate of the strength of claim of bondholders. You might think of that "something" as a percentage

[1]Ratios used in bond analysis are discussed in Thomas F. Pogue and Robert M. Soldofsky, "What's in a Bond Rating?" *Journal of Financial and Quantitative Analysis,* Vol. IV, No. 2 (June 1969) pp. 201–228, and Charles Tatham, "A New Perspective on Utility Bonds," *The Institutional Investor*, Vol. 5, No. 6 (June 1971), pp. 52–55.

increase in the coverage ratio. If the average coverage ratio is, say, four times, and bonds are unsecured, you might increase the multiple by, say, 10 per cent to a multiple of 4.4 to give effect to the strength of claim of unsecured creditors relative to stockholders. With the same coverage ratio and a first-mortgage lien on assets believed to be worth much more than the amount of the debt they secure, you might increase the average coverage ratio by 50 per cent to a multiple of 6.0. These numbers merely describe the concept; in practice the value added by presence or absence of strong security would have to be determined subjectively.

There is considerable difference of opinion among bond analysts about the weight that should be given to strength of claim in estimating financial risk. It is said that Moody's bond ratings give considerable weight to first-mortgage security and that Standard & Poor's bond ratings reflect somewhat less weight. This seems to be a principal reason why their ratings for a bond issue sometimes differ.

Difference of opinion on this subject hinges chiefly on interpretation of the experience of bondholders when a company is not able to meet its currently maturing obligations. When this condition appears, creditors may have a choice of putting a company into receivership, or trying to work out some agreement among creditors to waive a default and give the company an opportunity to recover financially. Unsecured creditors like to avoid receivership if possible, because their position in any financial reorganization is relatively weak. Mortgage bondholders, however, often find it advantageous to seek reorganization in receivership because they expect favorable treatment in reorganization. Sometimes a court appointed receiver authorizes continued payment of interest on a particularly well-secured debt.

There is reason for some cynicism about the influence of the pledge of security on the uncertainty of future payments to bondholders. When a company is not able to pay its interest and currently maturing obligations, all of its creditors are in trouble. Owners of particularly well-secured obligations have some advantage over unsecured creditors and less well secured creditors when a company becomes financially distressed, but how it all works out depends very much upon the seriousness of the financial failure and a variety of surrounding circumstances.

ESTIMATING LEVEL OF FINANCIAL RISK

When all the financial analysis has been done and the information about strength of claim has been examined, there is the ultimate problem of making an estimate of the level of financial risk that would be assumed by purchasing a bond issue. Ideally this estimate should be sufficiently well defined to place the issue on a scale of risk varying from very low to very high, and with fine graduations between.

With so much of the information in the form of financial ratios, it would seem that there should be a way of combining them statistically so that the measurement of financial ability would be an exercise in quantitative method.

But no one has yet found a practical way of doing this. Both Moody's and Standard & Poor's bond ratings reflect a judgment of the future and take into account non-statistical factors. One research study found that five explanatory variables that were measured quantitatively accounted for a large part of the difference in the ratings assigned to bond issues by Moody's Investors Service. The unexplained part results from quantitative variables not included in the research study and from the subjectivity of the rating process.[2]

The difficulty of estimating financial risk by quantitative methods stems, first, from the fact that the conditions affecting financial risk vary so greatly from one bond issue to another. In one instance non-cash expenses may be an important source of funds and in another they are not. In one, a strong balance sheet serves to reduce the uncertainty of future payments to bondholders and in another it counts for little. A mortgage on assets may reduce risk significantly for one bond issue and be given little weight in appraising another. There has to be a judgment of the relative weight to be given each condition affecting financial risk.

Even more subjective is the estimate of future developments affecting a company's financial ability. The historical information provides a base for estimation, but the final conclusion about risk depends very much on the analyst's estimate of the future development of the national economy, the prospects for the industry in which the company is principally engaged, and the fortunes of the company itself. Any estimate of the future that would justify estimates of financial ratios different from those extrapolated from the past would require a great deal of study along about the same lines as an estimate of future earnings and dividends for a common stock. This kind of study is described in the next several chapters, so we will omit it here and rely on application of the common-stock method of analysis to bonds whenever it seems desirable to do so.

TWO OTHER METHODS OF MEASURING RISK

There are other ways of measuring risk that are especially useful when the expected period of owning bonds is less than the period to maturity.

One way is to measure risk by the historical record of price instability.[3] If you don't know when you may liquidate, you can estimate the price risk you assume by continuing to hold. The method involves computing price relatives for uniform time periods. A price relative is price at end of period divided by price at beginning of period. Thus, if price at beginning is 100 and price at end of period is 104, the price relative is 1.04. On the other hand, if price declined from 100 to 96, the price relative is 0.96. A series of such relatives for a number of past periods provides a distribution of relatives, and the instability of price can be taken as the standard deviation of the dis-

[2]Pogue and Soldofsky, *op. cit.*, pp. 216–217.

[3]See Robert M. Soldofsky, "*Ex Ante* and *Ex Post* Yields on Bonds: Concepts and Measurements," *Mississippi Valley Journal of Business and Economics*, Vol. V, No. 3 (Spring 1970), pp. 1–10.

tribution. A particular value of this kind of measurement is that it takes account not only of price changes that may be attributable to changes in the issuer's financial ability, but also the effect on price of changes in interest rates and of whatever influence on price may be exerted by investors' reactions to changes in the general price level. Comparisons of standard deviations for a number of bond issues permits the ranking of issues according to the record of price instability. The calculation is illustrated in Table 9–5.

Another kind of statistical measurement of financial risk may be made on an *ex post* basis that shows the difference in price changes between those for a corporate bond and for a Treasury obligation of about the same coupon rate and the same maturity. The theory is that changes in market prices for Treasury issues are entirely a reflection of changes in market rates of interest, since there is no element of financial risk. Prices for corporate issues change under the influence of changes in interest rates and also as a result of changes in investors' estimates of financial risk. We specified comparison with a Treasury issue of about the same coupon rate and maturity, so that the effect of interest-rate changes on price of the Treasury issue would not be distorted by differences in these conditions.

The coefficient of correlation between two such series shows how nearly they moved together. If there is a very high positive correlation, the conclusion is that price changes for the corporate issue were almost entirely a matter of interest-rate risk. The slight effect of financial risk means that the level of this kind of risk is very low. A lower correlation means that considerations of financial risk have had a greater effect. A negative correlation means that financial-risk changes have more than offset the effect of interest-rate changes.

To interpret correlation coefficients you need comparative data. You could compute them for a set of corporate bonds in which you are interested, taking care to compare each with a Treasury issue of about the same maturity and as nearly as possible, the same coupon rate. Then the coefficients arranged by size indicate the rank of the issues in financial risk.

Table 9–6 shows the calculation of the coefficient of correlation between prices for a corporate and a Treasury bond.

TABLE 9–5

Measurement of Risk by Price Relatives

Period	*Price Relative*	*Variation*	*Variation Squared*
1	1.06	+0.06	0.0036
2	1.04	+0.04	0.0016
3	1.00	–	–
4	0.86	–0.04	0.0016
5	0.94	–0.06	0.0036
	Sum		0.0104
	Variation		0.0021
	Standard deviation		0.0458

TABLE 9–6

Coefficient of Correlation Between Prices of a Corporate and a Treasury Bond.

Price at end of month	*Corporate bond* X	*Treasury bond* Y	$X-\bar{X}$ $=x$	$Y-\bar{Y}$ $=y$	x^2	xy	y^2
1	81	83	−3	−2	9	6	4
2	82	83	−2	−2	4	4	4
3	82	84	−2	−1	4	2	1
4	83	85	−1	0	1	0	0
5	83	85	−1	0	1	0	0
6	84	86	0	+1	0	0	1
7	83	85	−1	0	1	0	0
8	84	85	0	0	0	0	0
9	85	86	+1	+1	1	1	1
10	86	87	+2	+2	4	4	4
11	87	86	+3	+1	9	3	1
12	88	85	+4	0	16	0	0
	1,008	1,020			50	20	16
	$\bar{X}=84$	$\bar{Y}=85$					

$$r = \frac{\Sigma\, xy}{\sqrt{(\Sigma\, x^2)\ (\Sigma\, y^2)}} = \frac{20}{\sqrt{50.16}} = \frac{20}{\sqrt{800}} = \frac{20}{28.2} = +0.71$$

Note: The method illustrated is the product-moment formula. Prices have been stated without fractions for simplicity of illustration.

STRAIGHT PREFERRED STOCKS

Although preferred stocks are equity instruments, the problem of estimating the financial risk in this kind of security is much the same as that for bonds. Straight preferred stocks do not participate in earnings above their stipulated rate and are not convertible into common stock. Thus a straight preferred stock is a preference to an annual dividend in a specified amount. The question is the uncertainty of the future dividend payments.

Financial ability is measured very largely by the amounts of internally generated funds available relative to the amounts required for dividend payments. Thus, the first thing for the preferred-stock analyst to do (after reading the legal terms of the issue) is to compute the preferred dividend coverage ratios for the past several years. The most conservative formulation of the coverage ratio for preferred dividends is:

EBIT

The sum of:
Income taxes
Interest and lease rentals
Amortization of non-current debt
Preferred dividend requirement

There exist the same questions we encountered in bond analysis about what items from the income statement shall be taken as representing funds available for payment and what other charges besides preferred dividends shall be taken as funds required. The cash flow from non-cash expenses is more doubtful as a source of funds for preferred dividends than it is for bonds, because the strength of claim of preferred stockholders is weak. If the preferred dividends are not paid according to schedule, usually nothing happens except that the dividend on the preferred falls into arrears. A corporate management hard pressed for funds to replaced depreciated assets, or to repay debt, may very well decide that preferred dividends are a less important application of funds. So, as a general rule, earnings before interest and taxes is taken as the amount of funds available for preferred dividends.

There are, of course, a number of charges against earnings that come before preferred dividends. Income taxes comes first. We did not include income taxes as an amount of funds required in computing coverage ratios for bonds, because the amount of taxes is affected by the amount of interest and lease rentals. This is not true in the case of preferred dividends, because dividends are not deductible as expenses. Clearly, both income taxes, interest on non-current debt, and lease rentals must be paid from funds available before preferred dividends may be paid. Amortization of non-current debt should also be taken as a use of funds that has priority over preferred dividends, because it is a contractual obligation to creditors.

From this point you evaluate the record of preferred dividend coverage using the system of reasoning described earlier for straight bonds. Uncertainty of preferred dividends is chiefly a function of the size and stability of the coverage ratio.

The position of preferred stockholders is obviously weak relative to that of bondholders, but there are some situations in which specific attention may be given to strength of claim. First, an issuer of preferred stock may have no bonds or lease rentals. Then the preferred has the first claim on earnings after income taxes. Second, preferred stockholders sometimes have special voting rights, or vetoing rights when dividends are in arrears, which should give them a strong voice in controlling the issuer. Management would think several times before passing a preferred dividend when the effect would be to jeopardize its control.

Financial risk in preferred stocks may also be measured by price relatives and by the coefficient of correlation between their market prices and prices of long-term Treasury bonds. There are many preferred stocks with such a low level of financial risk that their price fluctuations are well correlated with prices of Treasury obligations.

QUESTIONS FOR DISCUSSION

1. Since two reliable investment information agencies publish ratings for publicly offered bond issues, why should anyone but these agencies be interested in bond analysis?

2. When you estimate the riskiness of bond issues, how far into the future do you try to look?
3. A financial analyst of long experience says that you should not pay much attention to the security pledged for bonds. "If they have the money," he says, "they'll pay. If they don't, they won't." Is this a valid statement?
4. A large and growing manufacturing company has non-cash expenses equal to about the amount of EBIT. To what extent, if at all, would this fact influence your judgment of the risk level of its debenture bonds?
5. What information would you likely find in a company's statement of sources and uses of funds that would aid you in your appraisal of the riskiness of its first-mortgage bonds?
6. If a company's coverage ratios for the past 5 years have fluctuated in a highly erratic manner, would you learn more from the coefficient of variation for the ratios (as in Table 9–1), or from the calculation of trend values (as in Table 9–3)?
7. You are comparing two corporate bond issues and you have computed the trend values of the coverage ratios. The trends for both companies are slightly upward at about the same slope. What can you learn by calculating the standard error of the estimate, as in Table 9–4, that would aid you in estimating the relative riskiness of the two issues?
8. The ratio of non-current debt to total capitalization of ABC Company is 50 per cent when the common equity is taken at book value, but it is only 25 per cent when it is taken at the current market value of the common stock. What, if anything, does this tell you about the ability of the Company to pay its fixed charges? The data are:

Capitalization	*With common equity*	
	at book	*at market*
Non-current debt	$25 mil.	$25 mil.
Common equity	25 "	75 "
Capitalization	$50 mil.	$100 mil.

9. If you find a positive but weak coefficient of correlation between price changes for a corporate bond and price changes for a Treasury bond of about the same maturity in the same series of periods, what inference would you draw about the financial strength of the issuer of the corporate bond?
10. It would be simpler to compute the coverage ratios for dividends on a preferred stock by taking earnings after interest and taxes and dividing by the annual amount required for dividends. What's wrong with that?

10

Selecting Common Stocks

The problem in selecting common stocks is precisely that defined at the beginning of this discussion of financial analysis: it is to estimate the level of risk and the probable rate of return to be realized from ownership of a stock over some period in the future.

You can visualize the problem in a real life setting if you think of yourself as the financial analyst. Somebody who decides policy in the management of a securities portfolio has said to you, "We want to buy several stocks at about such-and-such level of risk. You recommend the stocks to be purchased." You know without being told that the portfolio manager doesn't want just any stocks at that level of risk; he wants the stocks at that level that may be reasonably expected to provide higher rates of return than other stocks at that level. The purpose, as always, is to maximize rates of return at any given level of risk.

THE PROBLEM AND THE THEORY

You have to estimate amounts of dividends to be received by owners of a stock over a period of ownership and the most likely market value at the end of that period. These quantities are the returns to stockholders. The rate of return is the rate that discounts these amounts to the price at which a stock may be bought. In practice you recognize the limitations of your own ability to predict the future by developing a frequency distribution of expected rates of return, with probabilities assigned to each rate in the distribution. The expected rate of return is the value of the distribution, and the variation of the distribution may be taken as a measure of risk. (If you feel a need for review of these concepts, see Chapters 1 and 9.)

The length of the period of the estimates should be defined at least approximately. In theory the rate of return from a stock is the rate that discounts to present value all dividends to infinity. Because stocks have no maturity and corporations may have perpetual life, it is entirely reasonable to think about a stream of dividend payments to infinity. But in fact investors do not buy stocks to hold to infinity; they expect to sell them in some more finite period of time and to recover principal in the form of market value. Market value at time of sale theoretically represents the present value of all future dividends from then to infinity discounted at an appropriate rate.

Investors' time horizons vary widely. Some people buy good common stocks, their experience with them is satisfactory, and they hold the stocks for their lifetimes. But in professionally managed portfolios the time horizon is likely to be a few years. It should be some such period because the financial abilities of issuers change, market prices change, alternative investment opportunities appear, and there is a more or less continuous process of reappraisal and change in the issues that comprise a portfolio. Good management alone creates a probability that security issues will be sold from time to time and replaced by others.

For the purpose of this discussion, the time horizon will be defined as three years. In application, it may be somewhat more or somewhat less, but it should be a sufficiently long period to average, or at least to minimize, the effect of shorter-term fluctuations in financial abilities of companies and in market prices for stocks that are so much a result of random events as to be virtually unpredictable.

When the problem of common stock analysis is defined in these terms, it is called fundamental analysis, which means that the analyst tries to solve the problem by focusing on the fundamental conditions likely to affect the financial abilities of issuers in the future rather than on more transitory changes in earnings and in market prices. This kind of analysis should be sharply differentiated from the effort to estimate how much a company's earnings will be in the next calendar quarter, or whether the price will rise or decline in the next few months. The random walk hypothesis applies rather strongly to such short-term estimates, but when the time horizon is longer the financial analyst has some chance of inferring the direction and rate of change from published information and of making better estimates than those of all investors whose actions determine the path of market prices.

The problem with which we are now concerned is one of estimating the financial abilities of issuers of stocks, but it must be kept in mind that rates of return on stocks are affected to some extent by changes in interest rates and by beliefs of investors about the merit of common stocks as an inflation hedge.

THE RISK FORMULA FOR COMMON STOCKS

The elements of the problem of estimating financial risk in common stocks are essentially the same as for bonds, with some modification in definition of the elements.

Funds Available and Funds Required

The source of funds for payments to common stockholders is earnings after all expenses, interest and other fixed charges, taxes, and preferred dividends. Other possible sources of funds mentioned in the discussion of bond analysis are generally not significant for common stocks. Amounts of expected dividends are "amounts required" as estimated by an analyst. They stand in place of interest payments or fixed charges in the application of the formula to bonds. Dividends are not required in the legal sense; they are required only to fulfill an analyst's subjective expectations. Future market value may also be considered as an amount required in the same sense. The amount of principal that is expected to be recovered by sale of a stock in the market stands in lieu of the principal amount of bonds payable at maturity. It is of course a subjective estimate. With these modifications, we can use the "funds available to funds required" concept in analysis of common stocks.

In this version, earnings are the independent variable while dividends and market price (which determines market value for a number of shares) are the dependent variables. For the average of a large number of stocks over a period of several years there is a positive correlation between changes in amounts of earnings and changes in amounts of dividends. In the same average terms, there is positive correlation between changes in amounts of earnings and changes in market prices. You can see this correlation in Figure 5–1. For a single stock over shorter time periods there are exceptions to this generalization, but it is a valid proposition that an estimate of future changes in earnings per share with a three year time horizon is a good basis for an estimate of future dividends and market prices.

Stockholders' Strength of Claim

The strength of claim of common stockholders is legally very weak. Stockholders are not creditors, and they have no claim for payment of dividends. At best they have a legal right to a pro rata share of assets after all debts are paid when a company is liquidated. But there are differences between companies in the consequences for management of reduction or omission of dividend payments, and to that extent there are differences in the strength of position of owners of different stock issues.

Stockholders can make things unpleasant for management in event a dividend is reduced or omitted, but in varying degrees. Their strength of claim is in direct proportion to their ability to cause developments embarrassing to management. A great deal depends upon circumstances. If a company's earnings have been unstable and dividends have been paid intermittently, the failure of directors to declare a dividend causes stockholders little distress. But if a company has a long record of dividend payments and then suddenly fails to declare a dividend, the shock is great. For this reason many companies have continued regular dividend payments in periods of reduced earnings even to the extent of paying a dividend for a period greater than the amount of EPS.

Another important circumstance is the vulnerability of management to stockholder dissatisfaction. If the members of a board of directors own among themselves a majority of the outstanding voting stock and if they are in agreement, their position is strong and that of stockholders is weak. But if they own collectively only a small percentage of the stock and have to depend for their succession upon obtaining proxies for a majority of the voting stock, their position is weaker and that of stockholders is stronger. There have been more than a few instances in which disgruntled stockholders have organized to solicit proxies in opposition to management, and sometimes they have been successful in electing new directors and causing major changes in the top echelon of operating management.

DEFINITIONS OF EARNINGS

Earnings applicable to common stock is the bottom line of the corporate income statement. The amount of sales after all expenses and deductions belongs to the common stockholders. This amount is usually reduced to an amount of earnings per share for a period, such as a fiscal quarter or year, by dividing it by the average number of shares outstanding during the period. The term earnings per share is commonly reduced to EPS. When EPS are calculated in this manner the amount is called conventionally stated EPS, or reported EPS. However, there are several other versions of earnings per share.

Diluted Earnings Per Share

The conventional statement cf EPS for an accounting period is based on the capitalization of a company as it was during that period. But when a company has outstanding securities convertible into common stock, or warrants (rights) to buy stock, or both, there is potential change in its capital structure at the option of owners of these securities or rights. Conversion of debt and exercise of rights ordinarily result in dilution (reduction) of earnings per share for the common stock.

Suppose, for example, a company has a convertible bond issue. If the market price of its common stock rises well above the conversion price, bondholders may convert bonds to common stock. Or, as often happens, the company calls the bonds for redemption and "forces" conversion. Conversion is forced in that bondholders have the choice of receiving the principal amount plus any call premium in cash, or of receiving a number of shares of stock with a market value greater than the cash redemption amount. The principle of maximization operates almost without exception and bondholders take the stock.

Thus the convertible bonds are eliminated from the balance sheet and interest on them is eliminated from the income statement. The elimination of interest reduces or deletes the amount of fixed charges that precede earnings on common stock. This change increases the amount of the federal income tax, other things being equal, because interest is a tax deductible expense. The net effect ordinarily is to increase the amount of earnings applicable to common stock. But at the same time the number of shares of stock outstanding is increased by the issue of stock in conversion of bonds. The increase in number of shares of stock usually has a greater effect on EPS than the increase in earnings applicable to common stock, and the net effect is to dilute the amount of EPS.

Both financial analysts and public accountants have long been concerned about potential dilution of EPS and the fact that the extent of dilution was not clearly stated in published financial statements. After a great deal of discussion the Accounting Principles Board[1] of the American Institute of Public Accountants published a rule (Opinion No. 15) that requires EPS to be reported on a diluted basis whenever there is potential dilution. It further specifies that EPS and diluted EPS figures are within the scope of audits of CPA firms, which means that a CPA certification of published financial statements includes certification of the earnings per share data. Since the Accounting Principles Board's opinions are rules for member firms of the American Institute of Certified Public Accountants, which includes virtually all firms that audit statements for companies whose securities are publicly traded, and since the Securities and Exchange Commission generally requires that financial statements filed under several federal securities laws must conform to the Board's rules, the requirement of reporting earnings per share on a diluted

[1]Presently known as the Financial Accounting Standards Board.

basis when there is potential dilution applies to most companies whose stocks are traded in the markets.

Diluted earnings per share are calculated by assuming that convertible securities and outstanding warrants have been converted or exercised according to their terms, and that the number of shares of common stock have been increased accordingly. The actual calculation may be complicated, but the general idea should be understood.

One version of diluted EPS is called "primary diluted earnings per share." Outstanding convertible securities, which includes preferred stocks, are considered to have been converted if the cash yield on them at time of issue (annual interest or dividends divided by issue price) was less than two-thirds of banks' prime lending rate at time of issue. By this rule some convertible securities would be considered to have been converted; others would not be.

In computing primary dilution, rights to purchase stock at a fixed price are considered to have been exercised and the stock issued. However, there is deducted from the number of shares that would be issued the number of shares that could be purchased in the market with the amount of cash paid upon exercise of rights. This means that there is dilution only to the extent that the number of shares issued is greater than the number that could be bought in the market.

The other version of diluted EPS is called "fully diluted." This figure results when all convertible securities are considered to have been converted and all stock rights to have been exercised.[2]

In our study of the historical record of earnings per share we will use conventionally stated EPS, that is, without taking account of dilution. This figure shows actual experience according to the accounting statements. If there have been convertible securities and if some have been converted to common stock during an accounting period, the fact is reflected in conventional EPS. To use diluted EPS for past accounting periods would build into the record events that did not actually transpire and would sometimes cause marked variation in diluted EPS not attributable to changes in the earning power of a company.

In estimating future EPS, however, potential dilution must be taken into consideration. Whenever a company has instruments outstanding that may be exercised to obtain stock, there is some probability that conventional EPS will be diluted. Thus, at the end of the entire process of financial analysis amounts of conventionally stated EPS must be converted to a diluted basis.

The Quality of Earnings

There are many technical questions about calculating EPS and accounting practices that affect amounts of earnings applicable to common stock.

[2]See J. T. Ball, *Computing Earnings Per Share: Unofficial Accounting Interpretation of APB Opinion No. 15*, New York, 1970, American Institute of Public Accountants, Inc.

Sometimes accounting practices seem to overstate amounts of earnings and sometimes they may understate them. When financial analysts thinks that a company's accounting practices state earnings conservatively, they say that the quality of earnings is good. If not, they lack confidence in some degree that amounts of reported earnings may be taken at full value.

One troublesome area is the treatment of non-recurring items of income and expense. Suppose, for example, that a company has used a building for many years and has finally sold it at a value much greater than its depreciated value. The difference between depreciated value and the value obtained by sale is a profit. But should it be treated as an addition to earnings for the period in which the sale was made? Accountants generally favor the "clean surplus" principle, which means that the profit must appear in the statement of earnings and not be treated as a direct credit to surplus. But should the financial analyst take the non-recurring profit as an addition to earnings applicable to the common stock? If he does, he permits some distortion in the amount of EPS for the accounting period.

In a period of business recession, management may write down the accounting value of its inventory of raw materials, or write off fixed assets employed in lines of business that have been discontinued. Should such charges be put in the income statement with the effect of reducing the amount of EPS for the accounting period in which they are recorded?

Accountants generally resolve these questions by including non-recurring items in the statement of income, but designating them clearly as non-recurring. Then the financial analyst must decide whether to take them into account in his calculation of EPS. The usual practice of analysts is to omit them on the ground that they distort the period-by-period record of earnings. But if they are relatively large, or if relatively smaller items appear in a series of accounting periods, the analyst can hardly ignore them. A large non-recurring loss has an effect on the balance sheet and it may affect amounts of earnings in future periods. If non-recurring items occur very often, there is the question whether they are actually non-recurring. Perhaps they should be reflected in the record of EPS. The decisions in such situations are subjective judgements of the financial analyst. His primary concern is: What is the implication for future earnings? If there is no significant implication, such non-recurring items may be eliminated from earnings for past periods. If there is some implication that should be taken into account, he may include them or make some adjustment for them. Again, the judgement is subjective.

The Management of Earnings

Financial analysts are well aware that in the field of corporate accounting there is management of earnings. That is, corporate managements are able to make decisions about the amounts of income and expenses recorded on the books for a particular accounting period. It is easy to defer some amount of sales from the latter part of one period to the early part of another, or to record interest earned or lease rental received in one period rather than in another.

The amounts of some expenses during an accounting period may be affected by management decisions. A company may "defer" maintenance of its plant and equipment, that is, not make repairs or follow usual procedures to keep assets in good condition. The effect is to make earnings in the period of deferred maintenance a little larger than they would be otherwise. Or the opposite may be true. A company experiencing unusual improvement in earnings may paint and repair everything in sight in order to dampen the rise in EPS.

The amounts charged against income for depreciation, depletion, amortization of intangible assets and other non-cash expenses is to a considerable extent affected by accounting policies adopted by management. Depreciation expense, for example, may be on an "accelerated" basis, or on a "straight-line" basis. The former causes relatively large depreciation expense in the early years of the accounting life of an asset. A company may use one system of depreciation for some kinds of assets and another for different kinds of assets. It may change from one system in one year to a different system in the next year. The public accountants who audit the financial statements must accept whatever discretion is used by management in these matters in order to provide an unqualified certification, or they must note in their certification whatever change in accounting impairs the comparability of statements from one period to another. Financial analysts read carefully the footnotes to audited financial statements.

There are still other areas in which management has a great deal of latitude. Most companies have pension funds to provide retirement income for their employees, most of these pension funds are not fully funded, and the amounts contributed to them annually is often a matter that management determines in its discretion. If earnings for a period are poor, management can make them look a little better by reducing or even omitting the contribution to the pension fund. Similarly, corporate gifts for charitable purposes may be varied from year to year. The amortization of intangible assets, such as capitalized expenses, can be accomplished on a systematic basis or on the basis of charges now and then according to whether management wants to make earnings for a period a little better or a little worse.

The American Institute of Certified Public Accountants has long debated the question how much latitude management should have in managing earnings and still get an unqualified certification from its auditing firm. Some public accountants argue that management should have considerable discretion, provided that audited statements show how discretion has been used. Others favor strict rules that apply to all firms with little variation. Recently the Securities and Exchange Commission has expressed dissatisfaction with the manner in which the CPA's have handled this problem and one spokesman said that the SEC might try to force the pace at which the profession moves to provide accounting reports that are more comparable and revealing.[3]

It is a function of financial analysts to estimate whether and to what extent earnings have been managed. Sometimes cynical analysts refuse to

[3] *The Wall Street Journal*, October 3, 1972.

consider purchase of a stock because they believe that a company's accounting is too dubious to provide a basis for conclusion.

Adjusting EPS for Stock Dividends and Stock Splits

Many companies split their stock from time to time, or pay stock dividends. A stock split involves dividing common stock into a larger number of shares by issuing for each share outstanding at a time more than one new share, but without any change in the amount of the common stock capital account. A stock dividend is a dividend paid in stock, with the par or stated value of the additional stock charged to surplus and credited to the capital stock account.[4] Neither a stock split or a stock dividend provides additional capital, but serves only to increase the number of shares represented by the amount of capital.

If a company has one or more stock splits or stock dividends in the historical period of your study and if EPS are calculated on the basis of the number of shares outstanding from time to time, the EPS data will be "diluted" by the increase in number of shares. To avoid this distortion, you adjust for such changes in the common stock capitalization by dividing the earnings applicable to common stock in preceding periods by the number of shares outstanding at the end of the last period included in the analysis. The product is EPS adjusted for stock splits and stock dividends.

VARIATION OF EARNINGS PER SHARE

Financial risk is basically a function of variation in EPS. It is true that investors' estimates of the future rise and fall and so affect market prices, but as a general rule the greater the variation in EPS from period to period the greater is the uncertainty of future dividends and of market prices. Thus an important *ex post* measure of risk is the variation in EPS in a series of accounting periods starting back a few years and coming up to the most recent. A common practice is to examine the record of annual EPS for the past 5 years, or the past 7 years. Quarterly earnings data provide a better statistical measurement of earnings variation, provided there is no seasonal variation, but use of such data greatly increases the task of calculation.

Variation of EPS from the Mean

If there has been no particular trend in a series of figures representing EPS, the variation in earnings may be measured by the statistical calculation

[4]Surplus is a common term for the amount of common equity in excess of the amount of the capital stock account. Accountants don't like this term, but prefer to call it the amount of retained earnings, or capital in excess of the stated or par amount of the capital stock.

TABLE 10–1

Measurement of Variation in EPS

	STABLE COMPANY			*GROWTH COMPANY*		
Year	*EPS (X)*	*Deviation* $(X-\bar{X})$	*Deviation squared* $(X-\bar{X})^2$	*EPS*	*Deviation*	*Deviation squared*
1	$ 2.20	+0.20	0.04	$ 1.80	−0.20	0.04
2	1.80	−0.20	0.04	1.60	−0.40	0.16
3	2.00	—	00	2.00	—	00
4	1.80	−0.20	0.04	2.10	+0.10	0.01
5	2.20	+0.20	0.04	2.50	+0.50	0.25
Sum	$10.00		0.16	$10.00		0.46
Mean $(\bar{X})$	2.00			2.00		
Variance (s^2)			0.032			0.092
Standard deviation (s)			.18			0.30

The math notation may be written:

$$s = \sqrt{\frac{\sum_{j=1}^{N} (X_j - \bar{X})^2}{N}}$$

of variation from the arithmetic mean of the series. In Table 10–1, there is no trend in EPS for Stable Company in the 5-year period, but fluctuations in a symmetrical manner result in a variation of 0.032. But if there is a rising trend in EPS, as there is for Growth Company, the variance is greater at 0.092. Both measurements are from the same mean value of EPS. You can see that most of the explanation for the greater instability of Growth's earnings is the upward trend of earnings that cause large variations from the mean in several years.

Variation of EPS from Trend Values

Are Growth Company's earnings that much more unstable? Not if you measure from trend values of EPS rather than from the mean of EPS. When earnings have been growing, as in this example, the instability that is more significant is the variation from the trend values of EPS.[5]

You can compute the trend values of the annual amounts of earnings per share using the least squares equation, as we did with fixed charges coverage ratios in Table 9–3. However, this method produces trend values that change by equal amounts over periods of years. Values that increase at a constant amount per period increase at a decreasing rate. Start with $1.00 and increase it by $.10 each year for 5 years. The rate of increase in the first year is 10 per cent, but the rate from the fourth to the fifth is only a little more than 7 per cent.

Rate of change is more significant for our purpose than amount of

[5]In this discussion of trend and variations from trend it is assumed that there is a linear relationship in annual EPS for a series of years. If there is not, then there is no trend and no measurement of variation from trend.

change. Ordinarily we think of earnings increasing at some average rate per year, and estimates of future amounts of EPS are usually expressed in terms of growth rates. Rates of change (upward or downward) can be calculated by applying the least squares equation to the common logarithms of EPS, calculating trend values in logarithms and converting those values back to dollar values by taking anti-logs of the logarithms. All you need is a table of four-place logarithms and pencil and paper. Table 10–2 illustrates this calculation for Growth Company.

A way to check the accuracy of the trend values calculation is to plot them on graph paper with the vertical axis on a ratio scale.[6] The annual values should form a straight line on the graph, as in Figure 10–1. A graph of trend values plus the actual values of EPS provides a good visual picture of the trend of earnings and of the variation of annual data. Figure 10–1 is a graphic depiction of the data presented in Table 10–2.

You can see from the graph that there has been some variation of reported EPS around the trend values of EPS. It is easy to measure that varia-

[6]A ratio scale expresses a constant amount of increase on an arithmetic scale as a constant percentage of increase in the divisions of space.

TABLE 10–2

Calculating Trend Values of EPS by Rate of Change

Year	*X* (*Time*)	*Y* (*EPS*)	Log *Y*	X^2	$X \cdot \text{Log } Y$
1	−2	$ 1.80	0.2553	4	−0.5106
2	−1	1.60	0.2041	1	−0.2041
3	0	2.00	0.3010	0	0
4	+1	2.10	0.3222	1	+0.3222
5	+2	2.50	0.3979	4	+0.7958
	5	$10.00	1.4805	10	+0.4033

$$\text{Log } A = \frac{\Sigma \text{ Log } Y}{N} = \frac{1.4805}{5} = 0.29610$$

$$\text{Log } B = \frac{\Sigma X \cdot \text{Log } Y}{\Sigma X^2} = \frac{0.4033}{10} = 0.04033$$

X	*Log A*	+	*Log B · X*	=	*Log Y Est.*	=	*Y Est.* (*Anti-Log*)	*Per cent Change*
−2	0.2961		−0.0806		0.2154		$1.63	–
−1	0.2961		−0.0403		0.2558		1.80	110.4%
0	0.2961		0		0.2961		1.98	110.0
+1	0.2961		+0.0403		0.3364		2.19	110.6
+2	0.2961		+0.0807		0.3768		2.39	109.1
							Mean	110.0%

Average annual rate of change in EPS = 10 per cent.

Notes: If the trend of earnings is downward, Log *B* will be a minus number.

If there is a deficit in EPS for 1 or more years, but positive numbers for other years so that the average amount of EPS for the series is positive, add a constant number equal to the largest deficit in EPS to all the numbers in the series. Make the calculation as above and subtract the constant number from the *Y* Est. amounts.

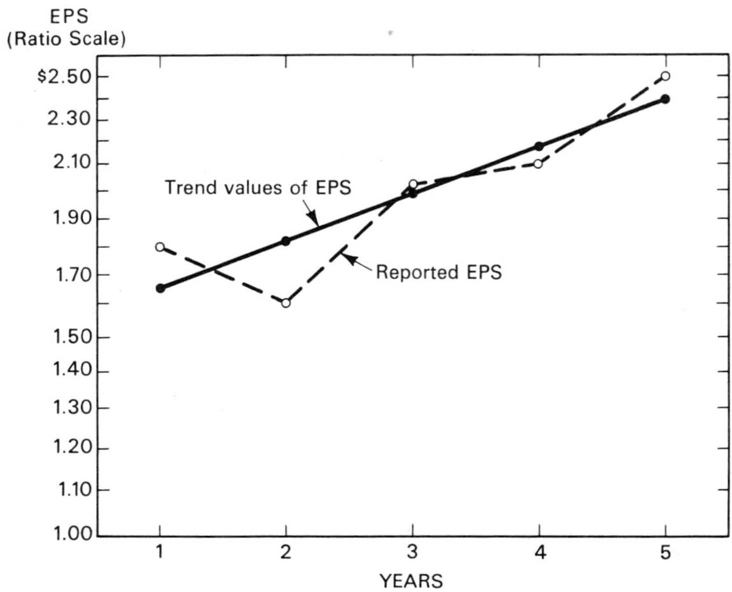

FIGURE 10–1

Reported EPS and Trend Values of EPS for Growth Company

tion statistically and thus to have a number that can be compared with corresponding measures of variation for other stocks.

Coefficient of Determination

The coefficient of determination may be used to arrive at the proportion of the total variation of EPS from the arithmetic mean of the series that is explained statistically by the calculated trend values. The total variation is the sum of the squared differences between the amounts of EPS for each of the several years and their arithmetic mean. The explained variation is the sum of the squared differences between trend values for each of the several years and their mean. The first sum of squared values divided by the second sum of squared values is the coefficient of determination. For Growth Company 79 per cent of the variation from the mean is explained by the trend values. That is a relatively high coefficient and means that variations in EPS around trend values have not been large. You could make this calculation for a number of stocks and have a good comparison of the historical stability of their EPS around their respective trend values.

Table 10–3 shows the calculation of coefficient of determination for Growth Company.

In using time series to make historical measurements it is well to keep

TABLE 10–3

Coefficient of Determination for Growth Company

	Explained Variation $\Sigma (Y\ Est. - \bar{Y})^2$				Total Variation $\Sigma (Y - \bar{Y})^2$			
Year	*Y Est.*	$\bar{Y}$	*Y Est.* $- \bar{Y}$	$(Y\ Est. - \bar{Y})^2$	*Y*	$\bar{Y}$	$(Y - \bar{Y})$	$(Y - \bar{Y})^2$
1	$ 1.63	$2.00	–0.37	0.1369	$ 1.80	$2.00	–0.20	0.0400
2	1.80	2.00	–0.20	0.0400	1.60	2.00	–0.40	0.1600
3	1.98	2.00	–0.02	0.0004	2.00	2.00	–	–
4	2.19	2.00	+0.19	0.0361	2.10	2.00	+0.10	0.0100
5	2.39	2.00	+0.39	0.1521	2.50	2.00	+0.50	0.2500
	$10.00			0.3655	$10.00			0.4600

Coefficient of determination = $\frac{\text{Explained variation}}{\text{Total variation}} = \frac{0.3655}{0.4600} = +0.7946$

Note: The math notation may be written:

$$r^2 = \frac{\Sigma\ (Y\ est. - \bar{Y})^2}{\Sigma\ Y - \bar{Y})^2}$$

in mind that statistical series change as time moves forward. When you add another year to the series and drop off the remotest year, you have a different pattern. In the case of Growth Company, if the next year added to the series should be a relatively poor year, with EPS of, say, $2.00, and the first year of the series is eliminated, the growth rate would decline from 10 per cent to 7.2 per cent, and other measurements in the series would change.

VARIATION IN PRICES AND DIVIDENDS

There is a quite different way to observe financial risk *ex post* by use of historical data. Instead of using EPS as the variable, we can use changes in dividends and in market prices. These are the quantities we have termed dependent variables. Thus, their changes should correspond more or less to changes in EPS, but they also reflect dividend policy and the fluctuations of market prices.

Investment Performance Relatives

Investment performance relatives may be used to measure the instability of short period rates of return in terms of prices and dividends. The period may be a week, a month, a quarter or even a year. The computation is price at end of a period plus dividend for the period, or a pro rata portion of dividend, divided by price at beginning of period. In notation:

$$\text{IPR} = \frac{P_2 + d}{P_1}$$

Thus, if price at end of a quarter was $102, dividend for the quarter was $1, and price at beginning of quarter was $100, the investment performance relative for the period was 103 per cent. Or, the rate of return for the period (disregarding the time value of money) was 3 per cent. Thus, you can construct a series of IPR's for a number of successive periods and the data provide an historical record of variation in rate of return. Table 10–4 illustrates calculation of monthly investment performance relatives for an industrial stock for a 12 month period. This method may be applied to prices only; then the product is price relatives.

You could use the same statistical methods that were applied to the EPS data to measure the variation in a series of investment performance relatives and arrive at a rate of change per period as well as a coefficient of determination. A more common use of IPR's is to measure the instability of the series against a corresponding series for one of the broad stock price averages.

The Beta Coefficient

One of the statistical methods that originated in academe and subsequently was embraced enthusiastically by Wall Street analysts is that of regressing IPR's for a stock against IPR's for a stock price average or index. This method uses the regression equation that we used earlier to compute trend values of earnings per share. The value of B (or β) in this calculation is the slope of the trend line for the IPR's of an individual stock relative to IPR's of the stock price index. It is termed the Beta coefficient, or the Beta factor.

The reason financial analysts adopted the Beta coefficient kind of calculation with so much satisfaction is that it provided a quantitative comparison of the price-plus-dividend behavior of a stock with the same data for "the market." If the IPR's for a stock have been more unstable than those for the average of the stocks comprising a stock price index over a period of time, the Beta coefficient works out at greater than 1.00. If data for the individual stock provide a Beta less than 1.00, the stock has been more stable than the market. It is a more precise method of comparing the "risk record" of stocks with the market and with each other than the descriptive words that have conventionally been used, or the "rankings" published by investment information services.[7]

The statistical method substitutes IPR's of a stock price index for time. Thus the X column, which was in terms of years in Table 10–2, is the IPR series for the stock price index. The Y column is IPR's for the individual stock as they appear in Table 10–4. The method is illustrated in Table 10–5.

You can readily interpret the data if you keep in mind that the Beta coefficient measures the slope of IPR's for a stock relative to the same series for the price index, which means that the series for the price index is equivalent to 1.00. A Beta coefficient of 1.10 for a stock in a rising market in-

[7]Chris Welles, "The Beta Revolution: Learning to Live with Risk," *The Institutional Investor* (September 1971), pp. 21–27, 54–64.

TABLE 10–4

Investment Performance Relatives for a Common Stock (Monthly periods)

Period	*Price at end of month*	*Dividend (One third of quarterly D/S)*	$p_2 + d$	p_1	*IPR*
1971					
June	$66.25	$ –	–	–	–
July	62.50	.08	$62.58	$66.25	94.46%
Aug.	70.75	.08	70.83	62.50	113.33
Sept.	69.75	.09	69.84	70.75	98.71
Oct.	67.50	.08	67.58	69.75	96.89
Nov.	69.00	.08	69.08	67.50	102.34
Dec.	73.00	.09	73.09	69.00	105.93
1972					
Jan.	69.50	.08	69.58	73.00	95.31
Feb.	74.00	.09	74.09	69.50	106.60
Mar.	74.62	.09	74.71	74.00	100.96
Apr.	74.37	.08	74.45	74.62	99.77
May	79.00	.09	79.09	74.37	106.35
June	76.12	.09	76.21	79.00	96.47

Notes: The price at end of month is taken as the price at beginning of next month.
The quarterly dividend in 1971 was $0.25; it was apportioned .08 to each of two months and .09 to the third month. Subsequently it was increased to $0.26 per quarter and was apportioned by months at 8, 9 and 9 cents.

dicates that for the time period of the measurement the relatives for the stock increased 10 per cent more than the relatives for the market increased. The individual stock was more risky, or more unstable, or more volatile than the market. In a declining market you would expect that stock to decline 10 per cent more than the market.

The value of Alpha in the equation is the average rate of return from the individual stock for the period of measurement relative to the rate of return from the stock price index, both as measured by the investment performance relatives. An Alpha of +5 per cent means that the rate of return was 5 percentage points greater than the rate of return on the index; if Alpha is −5 per cent, the rate was 5 percentage points less.

For simplicity of illustration we computed Alpha and Beta in Table 10–5, for time intervals of one month for a period of only 12 months. The time intervals may be too long and the number of time periods may be too few for accurate measurement. Some analysts with computer facilities compute the data for weekly time periods over a period of several years.

The Beta coefficient concept has been hailed as a great boon to portfolio managers. It provided the means to select a stock portfolio according to the size of Betas and thus to shift the portfolio in the direction of higher Beta stocks when the manager anticipated a rise in average stock prices, or in the direction of lower Beta stocks when market prices generally were expected

TABLE 10–5

Calculation of the Beta Coefficient for an Industrial Stock Relative to Standard & Poor's 425 Industrial Stocks

	S&P's 425 Industrials X_i	*Industrial stock* Y_i	$(X_i - \bar{X})$	$(Y_i - \bar{Y})$	$(X_i - \bar{X})\ (Y_i - \bar{Y})$	$(X_i - \bar{X})^2$
Jul. 1971	96.06	94.46	−5.04	− 6.97	35.13	25.40
Aug.	104.26	113.33	+3.16	+11.90	37.60	9.99
Sep.	99.75	98.71	−1.35	− 2.72	3.67	1.82
Oct.	95.80	96.89	−5.30	− 4.54	24.06	28.09
Nov.	100.26	102.34	−0.84	+ 0.91	− 0.76	0.71
Dec.	108.97	105.93	+7.87	+ 4.50	35.41	61.94
Jan. 1972	102.34	95.31	+1.24	− 6.12	− 7.59	1.54
Feb.	103.31	106.60	+2.21	+ 5.17	11.43	4.88
Mar.	100.97	100.96	−0.13	− 0.47	0.06	0.02
Apr.	101.02	99.77	−0.08	− 1.66	0.13	0.01
May	102.26	106.35	+1.16	+ 4.92	5.71	1.35
Jun	98.18	96.47	−2.92	− 4.96	14.48	8.53
Arithmetic sum	1,213.18	1,217.12			159.34	144.28
Mean	$\bar{X}$ 101.10	$\bar{Y}$ 101.43				

$$a = \bar{Y} - \frac{(X_i - \bar{X})\ (Y_i - \bar{Y})}{(X_i - \bar{X})^2} \cdot \bar{X} = 101.43 - \frac{159.34}{144.28} \cdot 101.10 = -10.18$$

$$b = \frac{(X_i - \bar{X})\ (Y_i - \bar{Y})}{(X_i - \bar{X})^2} = \frac{159.34}{144.28} = 1.10$$

to decline. Thus you could get greater than average price appreciation in a rising market and less than average price depreciation in a declining market.

Experience has brought some disillusionment. Alphas and Betas are *ex post* statistical measurements. They are not necessarily good *ex ante* measurements. The pattern of the future may not be the same as the pattern of the past. The probability is that it will be different in some degree, and it may be quite different. A stock that has moved about with the market during a past period of several years (has a Beta of about 1.00) may rise in price in a future period much more than a stock price index. The company (whose stock it is) has reported a conventional pattern of earnings per share in a recent period. Then something happens to result in a marked rise in the company's earnings and in its earnings prospects. Market price might double in a year or so. In this new period of unusual earnings improvement the Beta for the stock would be quite different from its Beta in a past period. The opposite can happen. A company that has been doing about as well as the average company may move into a period of unusually poor earnings, and its Beta may increase due to a decline in price relative to the market. The simple fact is that one can not depend upon periodicity in such time series. Neither the Beta coefficient or any other *ex post* series is a substitute for fundamental analysis.[8]

[8]See: Robert Kinsman, "Why They Call Wells Fargo the Temple of Beta," and Francis A. Mlynarczyk, Jr., "Beta, Alpha or Omega?" both in the *Institutional Investor,* July, 1972, pp. 82–99.

QUESTIONS FOR DISCUSSION

1. How does the equity nature of common stocks make the problem of estimating financial risk for this category of securities different from the problem of risk estimation for bonds?
2. It is said that the greater the variation in *ex post* measures of earnings, dividends, and market prices, the greater the risk. What does this assume about future variation in these quantities?
3. What is the rationale for the conclusion of the Accounting Principles Board (Financial Accounting Standards Board) that public accounting firms should include EPS on a diluted basis in the financial statements they certify?
4. How do corporate managements sometimes "manage" the amounts of reported EPS? Identify specific items of expenses that are particularly capable of being managed.
5. A company has recently paid a 50 per cent stock dividend. How do you adjust amounts of EPS reported in preceding years for change in number of shares of stock outstanding. (There has been no other change in number of shares in the preceding 5-year period.)
6. What is wrong with using the variation from mean of EPS for a series of past periods as a measure of the instability of a company's earnings?
7. What does the coefficient of determination between reported earnings per share and trend values of EPS tell you about the historical stability of earnings?
8. Why use logarithms of EPS to calculate the trend of earnings for a period of past years?
9. Which is the better measure of the historical effect on stockholders of changes in the financial ability of companies, price relatives or investment performance relatives?
10. If you computed the Beta factor for a stock on a weekly basis for 1 year, then did it again for a following year, and still again for a third year, would there likely be much difference among the three numbers? Why?

11

The Historical Record of Change

I. The corporate profile
   A. The products or services
   B. The facilities for production
   C. The characteristics of management

II. The primary financial relationships
   A. The profitability rate
   B. The leverage ratio
   C. The retained earnings ratio

III. The profitability ratios
   A. The total system
   B. Asset turnover and profit margin ratios
   C. Second-level data series
   D. Third-level data series
      1. Sales in units and prices
      2. Principal categories of assets relative to sales
      3. Expenses relative to sales

There are so many possible kinds of changes in the conditions that determine earnings per share for common stocks that we have to develop a method for analyzing the historical record that is both systematic and broad in scope, for it must bring into our field of vision everything that is likely to indicate significant change. It must relate what has happened in one area of a company's operations to what has happened in another. It must reveal the patterns of change that are the basis for numerical estimates of future EPS in dollar amounts and in degree of uncertainty.

The system of analysis to be outlined in the pages following is one that regresses from earnings per share back to all measurable influences on earnings. You may study a company and find that per share earnings have increased in some pattern, or decreased, in the past several years. Why? You study the statistical relationships in historical data that explain the pattern. There are three primary financial relationships that immediately explain changes in per share earnings. You observe how they have changed. Then you go on to financial ratios and statistical series that explain changes in the primary financial relationships. There is an integrated set of relationships called the profitability ratios that bring into the analysis all the accounting series that affect rates of profit.

The explanation for changes in ratios is not to be found in ratios. Indeed, the ratios merely measure changes. You have to try to find out what caused the ratios to change. This requires a great deal of additional information. Some of it is qualitative, that is, descriptive in words. Some information is about the conditions under which a company operates; about external influences on profitability. A financial analyst is like a detective—he looks for explanations in all directions, but in an orderly manner. He finds part of a pattern of continuity in one place and part in another. He fits the parts into a pattern of past change and probable future change.

THE CORPORATE PROFILE

When you talk to an experienced financial analyst about a company he has studied and observed over a period of time, you perceive quickly that he has a clear mental picture of the company. He knows what it makes, or mines, or merchandizes; he places it in its industry, or in several industries; he knows what kinds of physical facilities it owns or leases, and where they are located; he remembers recent changes in the corporate structure by mergers or acquisitions; and when he refers to key people in management he sees them as individuals he has met and talked to. He sees the company as a distinct corporate entity. It has a profile, just as a person has a personality profile in the view of those who know the person well.

You can work out the quantitative data described in the preceding chapter without knowing much more about a company than its name. But to go forward with a study that has as its objective an estimate of future risk and return for its stock, you need to know a great deal about the company. You need information as a background for understanding the quantitative data and the relationships among statistical series. You need to know about changes in the corporate profile in order to understand and evaluate the data series that converge on earnings per share.

The Products or Services

The starting point is what the company makes or mines or sells. Analysts generally classify companies, first, into several broad industry categories such as manufacturing, extractive, transportation, utilities, merchandising, and financial services. Each of these categories, in turn, may be subdivided. There are many kinds of manufacturing industries, a number of extractive industries, several kinds of public utility operations, and several types of financial institutions.

A useful system for classifying industries by kind of product or service is the Standard Industrial Classifications of the U.S. Office of Statistical Standards. This system first divides products into "major groups" designated by two-digit numbers. Then the two-digit groups are divided into three-digit industries, and the three-digit industries are further divided into four-digit industries. This system of industry classification is used by several agencies of the federal government to provide data by industries, such as the wholesale price indexes of the Bureau of Labor Statistics and the indexes of industrial production of the Board of Governors of the Federal Reserve System.

When you have a system of industry classification and know the products of a company, you can fit it into an industry. Some companies' products or services place them into a number of industries even under the broader industry classifications. Some spread their operations over so many industries that they are called conglomerates. At the opposite end are companies with very narrowly specialized product lines. They fit into narrowly defined industry classifications and they may limit themselves to a few products within such an industry classification.

However broad or narrow a company's product line may be, your purpose is to seek evidence of change in the relative importance of the kinds of products sold. Change in products is virtually continuous. Companies add products that are different from those they have been selling, and sometimes they discontinue products. Usually such changes are gradual, but sometimes they are abrupt and large. A major manufacturer of electrical and electronic equipment suddenly announced that it had abandoned the manufacture of main-frame computers. An air transportation company acquired a hotel company. All such changes have an implication for the future profitability of a business enterprise.

Under the rules of the Securities and Exchange Commission, companies with multiple product lines are required to publish a breakdown of sales by product lines. With such data you can observe not only changes in dollar amounts of sales of different product lines over a period of years but also changes in the relative importance of the several lines. Table 11–1 shows sales by principal lines of products for a leading producer of packaged foods. You see at once that sales of consumer non-food products as a proportion of

TABLE 11–1

Distribution of Sales by Principal Product Divisions for a Leading Producer of Packaged Foods (By percentage of total sales)

Years:	*1*	*2*	*3*	*4*	*5*
Foods at home	*66.3%*	*64.5%*	*62.6%*	*60.4%*	*59.7%*
Foods away from home	*18.2*	*16.0*	*15.5*	*14.9*	*14.8*
Total foods	84.5	80.5	78.1	75.3	74.5
Consumer non-foods	10.8	15.3	18.4	21.2	21.9
Specialty chemicals	4.7	4.2	3.5	3.5	3.6
Total sales	100.0%	100.0%	100.0%	100.0%	100.0%

The company is General Mills, Inc., the data are for five fiscal years ended May 28, 1972, and are from a prospectus dated October 3, 1972.

total sales have more than doubled in a five-year period. This is an important indication of the direction of management policy in development of the company's business.

The Facilities for Production

Another part of the profile is the fixed assets of a company. You want to know what kinds of plants it operates and where they are, or how many stores it has in a retail chain and their location, or the principal crude oil producing areas where a petroleum company owns wells, or the routes of a transportation company. Once the pattern has been established, you look for changes in it during the recent past. Where have the new plants been built? Where are the exploratory wells being drilled? What airline routes have been gained or lost? What new stores have been opened by a retail chain store? What size and type of store are they? In what area are they located relative to the areas that have been traditionally the company's market? This kind of information provides a basis for observation of management policy, and it may have important implications for the future development of the business.

Some companies conduct their operations entirely within the geographical limits of the United States, but an increasing number have facilities for production or distribution of goods and services in other countries. A further penetration of the European market may be indicated by construction or acquisition of facilities in that area. Indeed, some companies operate in so many countries that they are called multinational companies. You try to observe which way they are moving in world markets.

The Characteristics of Management

Financial analysts often say that the most important thing to know about a company is the quality of its management. So the profile includes information about the chief executive, the principal operating officers, and persons who are in a position to control or strongly influence operating management. In their research reports analysts frequently mention the ages of principal officers, their formal education, how long they have been with the company, and in what capacities they have served other companies. If a company is controlled by another company, or by individuals not actively engaged in its management, that fact may be important. Those who control often determine the kind of people who are at the top level in management.

The quality of management may be the most important thing to know about a company, but it is also the most difficult to evaluate. Financial analysts like to visit companies and talk to the people who run them. Sometimes this personal interview works well. Analysts appraise top management personnel perceptively and repeated interviews over a period of time bring about a kind of personal-business relationship that enables them to obtain greater insights into individual personality characteristics.

Sometimes, though, visits with management do more harm than good. Officers who are strong personalities and good showmen may make an excellent impression on visiting analysts, and sometimes a company president who has been written up in an analyst's report as a great executive will lead his company into financial trouble and fall from power. In every period of business recession the list of top corporate executives whose "heads have rolled" is shocking. Some analysts say that you should evaluate management by a company's earnings record and not by the show that management puts on for visiting analysts.

A basic concern in this part of the analysis is the personality characteristics of the people at the top echelon of management. You want to know how management is likely to behave in the future, what kinds of decisions they are likely to make, and how aggressively they will implement decisions. Two important qualities are aggressiveness and risk aversion. Generally, the more aggressive individuals have low risk aversion. Aggressive people are innovators; they move vigorously to develop the new product or the new market; they recognize risk and are willing to take it. Managers of this kind represent some hazard to investors, because sometimes innovations fail and earnings suffer. But generally there are rewards for risk-taking in managing a business just as there are in common stock investing. Sometimes, however, management is complacent—they have a good business, earnings are satisfactory from their standpoint, and they have no intention of changing anything very much.

An equally important question is that of succession to top management positions. Who are the people likely to move up from second-level positions to first-level positions? And what are their personality characteristics? Sometimes you see a situation in which one individual is dominant. Sometimes strong men will not permit other strong men in their organization and fail to develop subordinates capable of succeeding them.

Many large companies are managed by a team of professional managers and operating results are a product of a team effort rather than the peculiar ability of any one person. Generally, these professional management groups are self-perpetuating. One man serves as chairman or president and is succeeded by another from the top echelon of officers chosen essentially by the group. The group may slowly evolve different characteristics but the quality of management is not likely to change very much in any very short period of time.

There are many family managements, or family controlled managements, especially among smaller companies. The establishment of a small business by a man with little capital and much ability and the subsequent development of that small company into a large company with publicly distributed stock is an American success story. The management of such a company generally passes to the second and third generation descendants of the founder plus nephews, nieces and sons-in-law. Nepotism sometimes appears, and management deteriorates. It is not uncommon for the controlling family to turn over management largely to professional managers by about the third generation.

In any such management situation as this, the analyst must try to estimate the system of succession. Will the play-boy son succeed his puritan ethic father? Or will the ambitious and able son-in-law be chosen over the son? Will the professional manager who was brought in to head the company succeed in changing the direction in which it has been moving? These are the questions. Sometimes the answers are difficult and sometimes they are obvious.

THE PRIMARY FINANCIAL RELATIONSHIPS

The central value in this system of analysis is earnings per share. Our concern is with future EPS and our approach at this point is historical. We want to find out what has caused past change in EPS and use that knowledge as a basis for estimating future change in EPS.

The starting point is the proposition that change in EPS is a product of change in the profitability rate of a company times its leverage ratio times its retained earnings ratio. It is convenient to develop the data for the ratios on a per share of stock basis.

The profitability rate is the rate of profit on total assets after taxes but before interest. This version of profit is a variation from the more conventional earnings before interest and taxes, or earnings after interest and taxes, but it serves our purpose in this stage of the analysis.

The leverage rate is the rate of earnings on equity capital divided by the profitability rate.

The retained earnings rate is the percentage of EPS that remains for reinvestment in the business after payment of cash dividends.

The profitability rate before interest and after taxes may be expressed by the term $P - T_r$, the leverage ratio is L_r, and the retained earnings rate is RE_r. The rate of return on common equity capital is EC_r.

Table 11–2 shows how the three primary relationships can be multiplied together to produce the rate of increase in EPS from period to period. In the table all three ratios are held constant through three periods in order to

TABLE 11-2

Illustration of Primary Financial Relationships (on a per share of stock basis)

	Period 1	*Period 2*	*Period 3*
Assets at beginning of period	$ 97.00	103.00	109.00
Assets at end of period	103.00	109.00	115.74
Average amount of assets	100.00	106.00	112.37
Profitability rate ($P - T_r$)	10.00%	10.00	10.00
Amount of EPS after taxes and before interest	$ 10.00	10.60	11.24
Equity capital at beginning of period	64.67	68.67	72.91
Equity capital at end of period	68.67	72.91	77.41
Average amount of equity capital	66.67	70.67	74.91
Rate of profit on equity capital	12.00%	12.00	12.00
Leverage ratio	120.00%	120.00	120.00
Amount of EPS	$8.00	8.48	9.00
Dividend paid	$4.00	4.24	4.50
Retained earnings	$4.00	4.24	4.50

Note: Total assets equal 1½ times the amount of equity capital per share, and this relationship is constant. It is assumed that funds are borrowed to maintain this relationship.

The equity capital increases by the amount of retained earnings per share.

The amount of EPS after taxes and before interest is computed on average of assets at beginning and end of year.

The amount of EPS after interest is the rate of profit on equity capital times average amount of equity capital.

facilitate the generalization. $P - T_r$ is .10 per cent, EC_r is .12 per cent, so L_r is 120 per cent. This means that the rate of return on common equity capital has been leveraged upward from .10 to .12 per cent by use of borrowed money. The RE_r is .50 per cent. By multiplication, .10 per cent times 120 per cent is .12 per cent times .50 per cent is .06 per cent. Six per cent is the rate of period to period increase in EPS.

You can change any of the three primary ratios, keep the other two unchanged, and the result is a different rate of change in EPS. If $P - T_r$, is .10 per cent, but L_r rises to 140 per cent, then the EC_r is .14 per cent. With RE_r remaining at .50 per cent, the periodic rate of increase in EPS is 7 per cent. You could reduce RE_r to .40 per cent, with the other relationships as they were, and the rate of change in EPS becomes 4.8 per cent.

In the table above the primary financial relationships have been computed on a per share of stock basis. However, they may be calculated directly from amounts in financial statements.

The Profitability Rate

The first of these profitability ratios, and the one that underlies the others, is the rate of profit on total assets taken as an average amount for a period. Any change in this ratio affects the other primary relationships. Therefore, it is a focus of attention in any study of a common stock, and we will devote a great deal more discussion to it in subsequent chapters. At this point it is important to describe the two versions of the profitability rate and their use in the system of primary financial relationships.

The most familiar form of profitability rate is:

$$P_r \qquad \frac{EBIT}{\frac{TA_1 + TA_2}{2}}$$

This is a kind of shorthand stating that the profitability rate is earnings before interest and taxes divided by the average of total assets at beginning and end of a period.

The trouble with this form of the profitability ratio is that it is not comparable to rate of profit on equity capital because it is before taxes whereas the rate on equity capital is after taxes. We need comparable rates to arrive at the leverage ratio, so we deduct the amount of income taxes from EBIT and it becomes EBIT − T. People accustomed to the accounting derivation of taxable income find this version awkward, because you cannot determine taxable income until you have deducted interest. The answer is that we are not now concerned with deriving either taxable income or amounts of income tax; the accountants have already done that. Our concern is to get data that are useful for our purpose, and we need an after-tax rate of return on total assets. We will, therefore, use an after-tax rate of return and call it the profit minus tax rate. Thus:

$$P - T_r = \frac{EBIT - T}{\frac{TA_1 + TA_2}{2}}$$

This version of the profitability rate is of course affected by the amounts of interest paid and deducted from income to arrive at taxable income. A company with large interest payments relative to EBIT will have smaller amounts of tax and larger amounts of income after tax than a company with relatively small interest payments, all other things being equal. For this reason it is well to compute both P_r and $P - T_r$. Then you can see the effect of tax-deductible interest on $P - T_r$, and take it into account in your analysis of influences on that profitability rate.

The Leverage Ratio

This relationship shows the effect of using borrowed money, lease rentals, and even nonparticipating preferred stock on the rate of return applicable to the common stockholders. To the extent that the cost of capital obtained from such sources is less than the rate of profit on total assets the equity capital rate is increased. Conversely, if the profitability rate is less than the cost of such capital, the equity capital rate is reduced. Thus the use of leverage-type capital instruments increases the instability of earnings applicable to the common stock, which is to say that leverage increases the uncertainty of future earnings for the common stock. But a great many profitable and well-managed companies use leverage to enhance the rate of return to their common stockholders.

In notation:

$$L_r = \frac{EC_r}{P - T_r} \text{ and } EC_r = \frac{EPS}{\frac{EC_1 + EC_2}{2}}$$

The Retained Earnings Ratio

This relationship is simply the amount of EPS after payment of dividends per share divided by EPS. It is the complement of the dividend payout ratio. It may·be indicated by:

$$RE_r = \frac{EPS - DPS}{EPS}$$

The retained earnings ratio has an important influence on change in the amount of earnings per share from one period to another because it is the chief influence on change in amount of book value per share, and that value is the base on which earnings for common stock are calculated. Continued retention of earnings is a process of continuous compounding of equity capital. The greater the rate of increase in book value per share, the greater the rate of increase in EPS when the equity capital ratio is constant. We have previously observed the high positive correlation between average book value per share and average earnings per share for Standard & Poor's 425 industrial stocks (Chapter 6). Retained earnings is not the only cause of change in book values. This amount may be diluted by issue of additional stock, by operation losses and by any direct debits or credits to the surplus account.

THE PROFITABILITY RATIOS

The rate of profit on total assets after taxes is not only the first in order of the three primary ratios, but change in that rate is often first in importance as an influence on change in earnings per share. It is not surprising, then, that financial analysts devote much of their effort to studying past influences on profitability in the hope of seeing a changing pattern that may be expected to continue in the future.

There are any number of possible developments in the business of a company that may affect its rate of profit on total assets. We could list some of them and then look for evidence that they have caused change. But such a search would be in rather general terms, and it might be difficult to see precisely how one cause of change and then another have actually affected the profitability rate. We need a system of analysis that will detect in accounting data whatever causes have been operating, show their interrelationships, and relate them directly to the profitability rate.

The Total System

The profitability ratios provide such a system. Change in the profitability rate after taxes is explained by changes in the asset turnover ratio and the profit margin ratio. Changes in these two first-level ratio series are explained by changes in series of accounting data that may be termed second-level accounting series. Then you can go on to the third-level data, which explain changes in the second-level series.

This set of relationships is described in Table 11–3, in the form of a tree chart. If you have numbers for each of the quantities in the system, you can calculate $P - T_r$ by working from right to left. If you change the num-

TABLE 11–3
The Profitability Ratios

	First level	*Second level*	*Third level*
$P - T_r$	Asset turnover ratio (AT_r)	Dollar amounts of sales	Sales in units —times Price of units
		—divided by	
		Total assets	Sales divided by: Current assets Fixed assets Other assets
	—times		
	Profit margin ratio (PM_r)	Amount of profit (After taxes and all expenses except interest)	Principal items of expense divided by sales: —Wages and salaries —Cost of materials or merchandise —Depreciation —Administrative expense —Other income —Other expense —Income taxes
		—divided by	
		Sales	

bers for any one of the series at the extreme right of the table and all others remain unchanged, you bring about a change in the profitability ratio that expresses that one change. Actually, all the numbers change to some extent from period to period. You use them to try to see a pattern of change, then you try to find the reasons for change, and finally you estimate the effect of whatever continuity of pattern you think will extend into the future.

Look well at the tree chart of profitability ratios. It provides the organization and the rationale for much of our analysis of the past and our effort to anticipate the future. We will develop and examine the asset turnover ratio, the two series that determine this ratio, and then some other data that contribute to understanding of past changes and probable future changes. The profit margin ratio and the influences that affect it represent another broad area for investigation. The particular value of the profitability ratios is that all the relationships affecting profitability are integrated. Each is linked to others so that change in one affects others.

Asset Turnover and Profit Margin Ratios

The $P - T_r$ for any time period is the asset turnover ratio (AT_r) times the profit margin ratio (PM_r). The AT_r in turn is the dollar amount of sales in a period divided by total assets (the average of total assets at beginning and end of year). It shows the productivity of assets in terms of sales. Or, in different terms, it shows how many dollars of sales were obtained for each dollar of assets. The PM_r is the amount of profit remaining after all expenses, including taxes, but not including interest on non-current debt or equivalent charges. It shows the number of cents from each dollar of sales that remains as profit after taxes and before interest.

Suppose that a company has sales of \$200 for a time period and average total assets for that period of \$100. The AT_r is 200 per cent. In the same period the amount of profit was \$10 so the PM_r was 5 per cent (\$10 divided by \$200). Then, $P - T_r$ was 10 per cent (200 × .05 per cent). If you wanted only to compute $P - T_r$ you could do it more easily by dividing the \$10 of profit by the \$100 of assets. It is not our purpose, however, merely to calculate a rate; the purpose now is to measure the two primary relationships that determine $P - T_r$ and to see how they have changed in a series of past periods. When you read AT_r and PM_r for a series of periods, you begin to see what changes have been affecting profitability. Examine Table 11–4.

This is a picture of a company whose sales increased strongly during

TABLE 11–4
The First-Level Profitability Ratios

Year:	*1*	*2*	*3*	*4*	*5*
AT_r	200%	220	250	400	250
PM_r	0.05%	0.04	0.04	0.03	0.03
$P–T_r$	10.0%	8.8	10.0	12.0	7.5

the first 4 years of the 5-year period relative to the amount of assets employed in the business, and then declined in the fifth year. (The amounts of sales and total assets are not shown in the table.) One might infer without further information that changes in AT_r evidence cyclical fluctuation in business conditions. While AT_r was rising, however, PM_r declined. In several years the higher AT_r more than compensated for the lower PM_r and $P - T_r$ increased. In the fifth year the sharp decline in AT_r and the continued low PM_r brought a marked reduction in profitability.

The data in Table 11–4 were deliberately constructed to indicate that profitability is a function of both of the first level ratios and not simply a function of profit margin, as some reporters of change in the financial results of business operations sometimes seem to imply.

Second-Level Data Series

The accounting data at the second level are the series from which the first-level ratios are computed. They are sales, total assets, and the amount of profit after all expenses except interest. Study of these series, how they have changed and what caused them to change, is a further step in the effort to see patterns of change that may continue into the future.

There are some technical questions involved in defining the amounts of these three accounting series. One is whether operating revenues is the same as sales. The answer is affirmative. Some companies that sell chiefly services, such as utilities and transportation companies, use that term to mean receipts from sale of their services.

Sometimes there are income items that report income from sources other than sales or operating revenues. These amounts of non-operating income are sometimes added on to sales in published reports and the sum is termed total income. Some kinds of non-operating income are interest and dividends on securities of non-consolidated subsidiaries or affiliated companies, fees for use of patents owned, and rental of properties not used in the regular operation of the business. Because we are interested in the operating data, these items of non-operating income should not be included along with sales but shifted to a section of the income statement immediately following the operating section.

Similarly, you may find in the earnings statement various items of expense that are not expenses of regular business operations. These other expenses include such things as the interest of minority stockholders in the earnings of consolidated subsidiaries, the cost of owning property not used in regular operations, and share in the loss of a non-consolidated subsidiary. Such expenses, too, should be removed from the itemization of operating expenses and listed in the earnings statement immediately following the items of other income. The balance of non-operating income is added to operating income to arrive at total income (or the balance of non-operating expense is subtracted).

Table 11–5 shows an income statement as published and a rearrangement of it for the purpose of analysis.

TABLE 11-5

Rearrangement of an Income Statement

	(Amounts in hundreds of thousands)
A. *As published*	
Gross income:	
Sales and services	$6,350
Dividends, interest, and other income	428
	$6,777
Deductions:	
Costs and operating expenses	4,192
Selling, general and administrative expenses	628
Dry hole costs	69
Depreciation, depletion, and amortization	370
Interest charges	78
Taxes other than income taxes	211
Provision for income taxes—current and deferred	401
Minority interest in net income	9
	$5,955
Net income	822
B. *Rearranged*	
Operating income:	
Sales and services	6,350
Operating expenses:	
Costs and operating expenses	4,192
Selling, general and administrative expenses	628
Dry hole costs	69
Depreciation, depletion, and amortization	370
Taxes other than income taxes	211
Total operating expenses	5,470
Operating income	880
Non-operating income:	
Dividends, interest, and other income	428
Non-operating expense:	
Minority interest in net income	9
Net non-operating income	419
Operating plus non-operating income	1,300
Interest charges	78
Taxable income	1,222
Provision for income taxes	401
Net income	822

You might think that the amount of total assets is obvious, but often analysts do not accept the statement of total assets in the balance sheet. Instead, they deduct from total assets all intangible assets, such as good will, the value of patents, deferred expenses, and capitalized expenditures, on the ground that they do not represent realizable values and that accounting values are quite arbitrary. This is a desirable practice whenever the amount of intangibles is large enough to be important. When intangibles are deleted from the asset side of the balance sheet, the common equity account should be reduced by a corresponding amount.

Third-Level Data Series

At the third level are the data and ratios that explain statistically changes in the second-level series. You go on to examine them and to find out what lies behind them in order to understand what influences the profitability rate.

Sales in Units and Prices. The dollar amount of sales reported in the income statement is the product of the number of units of goods or services sold multiplied by the prices at which they are sold. In order to analyze influences on dollar amounts of sales, we need data indicating both physical volume of sales and sales prices. Some companies publish these figures, chiefly companies in regulated industries. Other companies give little or no information about volume and prices.

Analysts of electric utility companies, for example, have an abundance of information about the components of total sales in dollars. These companies publish the amount of sales of electric power in kilowatt-hours and the average rate realized per kilowatt-hour. They also break down total kilowatt-hour sales to the amounts and average rates for different segments of their market. Railway companies publish similar information about ton-miles of freight transported in a time period, and airline companies measure their passenger traffic in passenger-miles. Some manufacturing companies provide data on quantities of goods produced per year. The automobile companies disclose production of cars and trucks, the steel companies report figures for tons of steel produced, and oil companies generally report quantities of petroleum products produced.

In other industries, though, companies publish no more than dollar amounts of sales. You may be able to infer the direction and magnitude of change in prices for their products by using the detail of the Wholesale Price Index and the Consumer Price Index. There are fifteen broad categories of products in the Wholesale Price Index, and each of those categories is further divided into product groups. If, for example, you are studying a company in the chemical industry, you can use the monthly index of prices for chemical and allied products, or an annual average of monthly data. If the chemical company published details of sales by product lines, you can use subdivisions of the chemical products price index for the several product lines. You can hardly expect that even a subdivision of the Wholesale Price Index would measure exactly changes in average prices for products sold by a particular company, but an approximation is useful. Given a useful index, or indexes, for a series of years, you can divide a company's sales in dollars by prices and thus deflate the sales figures. The result is an approximation of data for changes in physical volume of sales.

Components of the Consumer Price Index can be used in the same way for companies that sell at retail, such as retail chain stores. This index, too, has a number of components for different kinds of goods and services, and some of them may fit approximately the kinds of goods or services sold by a company.

Table 11–6 shows change in several principal components both of the Consumer Price Index and the Wholesale Price Index during a recent decade. It is clear that the magnitude of price changes has varied widely.

Principal Categories of Assets Relative to Sales. At this level of analysis we become concerned with changes in the relative size of the several principal kinds of assets. Changes in these components of assets relative to sales often aid understanding of change in the total asset turnover ratio.

Sometimes a manufacturing company undertakes a large-scale program of plant expansion. One or more plants are constructed over a period of several years. During this period the amount of fixed assets increases markedly, and there is little or no addition to sales from the new facilities. The effect is a decrease in the fixed asset turnover ratio. Subsequently, the new productive capacity is translated into increased sales, and the fixed asset turnover ratio improves. There may be further improvement as obsolete facilities are scrapped and the fixed asset account is reduced by the value at which they were carried on the books.

Similarly, a retail merchandising company may encourage a shift from cash sales to credit sales with a resulting increase in accounts receivable. Unless this increase is compensated by an increase in sales or reduction in other items of current assets, the current asset ratio would decline. Or there may be changes in relative size of inventories due to change in the production or selling functions that would affect current asset turnover.

Expenses Relative to Sales. Continuing through the third-level data series there is next the principal items of expenses divided by sales. These ratios measure change in the relative size of the several principal kinds of expenses and help to explain changes in the profit margin. In Table 11–7, some of the principal kinds of expenses are listed. However, the breakdown of expenses varies considerably in earnings statements of industrial com-

TABLE 11–6

Changes in Prices Indexes for Categories of Goods and Services (1967–100)

	1961	*1971*	*Percentage increase*
Retail prices			
Food	89.1	118.4	+32.8%
Home ownership	86.9	133.7	+53.7
Fuel oil and coal	91.0	117.5	+29.1
Apparel and upkeep	90.4	119.8	+32.5
Medical care	81.4	128.4	+57.7
Wholesale prices			
Farm products	96.3	112.9	+17.2
Textiles	97.7	108.6	+11.2
Chemicals	100.7	104.2	+ 3.5
Lumber	91.0	127.0	+39.6
Machinery and equipment	91.9	115.5	+25.5

Source: *Federal Reserve Bulletin*, May 1972, A 68.

TABLE 11–7

Analysis of Expenses and Profit Margin for a Manufacturing Company

Years	*1*	*2*	*3*	*4*	*5*
Sales	100.0%	100.0%	100.0%	100.0%	100.0%
Operating expenses					
Employee compensation	40.4	39.6	41.6	43.3	41.2
Materials, supplies and other costs	47.7	48.5	48.8	46.7	47.6
Depreciation	3.6	3.6	4.1	3.8	2.9
Taxes, income and other	5.0	4.7	3.7	3.5	4.4
Less: increase in inventories	−0.5	−0.4	−1.2	−1.1	−0.6
Total operating expenses	96.2	96.0	97.0	96.2	95.5
Profit margin	3.8	4.0	3.0	3.8	4.5

Note: The company is General Electric and data are for the years 1967 to 1971, taken from the Company's annual reports.

panies and you have to use whatever classification of expense is provided. When you set up these items of expense as percentages of sales for a series of years, you can run your eye across and see which kinds have increased and which have decreased relative to sales. Increases reduce profit margin and decreases make it larger. You might, for example, see that a moderate shrinkage in profit margin from one period to another is associated chiefly with an increase in relative amounts of depreciation. Or, it might be that wages or materials costs have increased or decreased with a significant effect on the profit margin. The after-tax version of the profit margin counts income taxes as an expense, and there may be important changes in the income tax ratio over a period of several years.

When you work through the series of quantitative data described in this chapter, you have a good quantitative picture of a company's financial experience. You see what has been going on, and you may see some changes that explain in a statistical sense historical variation in the profitability rates. Changes that have come about recently may be indicative of future change.

QUESTIONS FOR DISCUSSION

1. In the study of a company's historical record as revealed in its financial statements, what is your main objective?
2. Growth companies, that is, companies with an unusually high rate of increase in sales, usually have high retained earnings ratios. Why is this so?
3. A company with a consistently high profitability rate in recent years has called all of its outstanding bonds for redemption. The bonds will be paid off from cash and marketable securities on hand. How will this elimination of debt affect the equity capital ratio, other things being equal?
4. The directors of National General Company have announced an across-the-board increase in prices for its products. Its competitors are making similar price increases. What will be the principal effects on the profitability ratios?

5. A retail chain-store company adopted a vigorous advertising and sales promotion program. It was successful, but it caused the profit margin to decline 10 per cent from one year to the next. What can you infer from this statement about the effect on the company's profitability rate?
6. The latest annual report of a steel company describes in glowing terms plans for scrapping about 40 per cent of its present steel making capacity and replacing it with modern equipment that incorporates the latest technological advances in steel manufacturing. What would be the effect on each of the principal accounting series that enter into the capital turnover and profit margin ratios?
7. In a speech to a society of financial analysts, the president of a computer manufacturing company stated with considerable pride that his company's share of the computer market had increased from 6 per cent 3 years ago to 8 per cent last year. Is it reasonable to think that there has been a similar increase in the company's profitability?
8. A manufacturer of refrigerators has traditionally purchased electric motors and compressors from two other companies. Now it has embarked on a program of vertical integration. Soon it will manufacture the motors and compressors itself. Would you expect this integration program to improve the company's profitability? In terms of the profitability ratios, what will it depend on?
9. A department store that has traditionally sold to its customers for cash has begun to offer charge accounts and to encourage customers to use them. The store charges interest at 1 per cent per month on amounts not paid by the tenth of the month following date of purchase. As the volume of charge account balances increases, what will be the effect on principal items that determine the profitability ratios?
10. How would you calculate the "real" growth in a company's dollar volume of sales over the past 5 years?

12

Interpreting the Record: Asset Turnover

I. Focus on the problem

II. Estimating sales
   - A. Change in the national and world economies
   - B. Change in the structure of the economy
   - C. The development of other industries
   - D. Change within the company
   - E. Changes in selling prices

III. Estimating assets relative to sales
   - A. Sales to current assets
   - B. Sales to fixed assets
   - C. Sales to other assets

IV. Estimating future asset turnover

As you develop the primary financial relationships and the profitability ratios, you can hardly avoid thinking about what caused them to change from one time to another. But it is well to complete the statistical work and look at the whole set of data before you think much about them, because changes in one series affect changes in another and there may be common causes of change in different series.

FOCUS ON THE PROBLEM

In this chapter, then, we will focus on interpreting the record. We are looking for the general pattern of change—for the trends and variations that seem to be typical of the past—but also for recent changes that suggest that the pattern of the future may be different. We want to find explanations for changes. What are the conditions in the company, or in the industry, or in the economy, that caused the general pattern of the past? What evidence is there that these conditions are changing?

The method is simply to go over all the data measuring change and over the corporate profile information in search of explanations. The search for explanation leads beyond the accounting series to information about the economy, the industry, the technology of production, and even to indications of change in the customs and attitudes of people. You have to do it systematically by fitting together manifestations of change in one area with those that appear in another and by trying to see what common cause lies behind them.

Table 12–1 may help to put the problem in perspective and point the way toward the ultimate objective of estimating earnings per share.

Look at the figures for Hypothetical Company and try to see what sort of pattern the analyst has estimated for the 3 future years. He says that during the next 3 years earnings per share will increase at an average annual rate of slightly more than 6 per cent. If he is right, the expected rate of return on this stock will be relatively high. It is currently selling at only about $13 per share, which is about 10 times its EPS in the past several years. He says orally that this stock will be worth $20 to $25 per share within about 3 years,

TABLE 12–1

Estimates of Profitability Rates and Financial Policy Ratios for Hypothetical Company

	PAST YEARS					*FUTURE YEARS*			*Future years*
Rate or ratio	*1*	*2*	*3*	*4*	*5*	*1*	*2*	*3*	*average*
Asset turnover ratio	150%	155	145	140	150	155	158	163	158
Profit margin ratio (After taxes & before interest)	5.2%	5.5	5.0	4.8	5.0	5.1	5.2	5.3	5.2
Rate of profit on total assets (After taxes)	7.8%	8.5	7.2	6.7	7.5	7.9	8.2	8.6	8.2
Leverage Ratio	172%	165	160	150	153	148	152	153	151
Equity Capital Rate	13.4%	14.0	11.5	10.0	11.2	11.7	12.5	13.2	12.4
Earnings per share	$1.34	1.48	1.29	1.19	1.41	–	–	–	–
–Trend values of EPS	$1.37	1.35	1.34	1.32	1.31	1.39	1.48	1.57	–
Dividends per Share	$0.74	0.74	0.74	0.52	0.74	0.69	0.74	0.78	–
Retained Earnings per Share	$0.60	0.74	0.55	0.67	0.67	0.69	0.74	0.78	–
Retained earnings rate	45%	50	43	57	48	50	50	50	–

which would be a nice annual rate of appreciation, and there would also be dividends at 5 to 6 per cent on the current market price. What is the basis for this estimate?

If you start with the first line of the table, you see that the analyst expects a significant upward trend in the asset turnover ratio. In the past this ratio has fluctuated with no distinct trend around 150 per cent, but he expects it to increase in each of the next 3 years, and the annual average for the future period is put at 158 per cent. However, he foresees little improvement in the profit margin ratio. His average for the next 3 years is estimated at 5.2 per cent as compared with an average of 5.1 per cent for the preceding 5 years. But an average asset turnover of 158 multiplied by a profit margin rate of 5.2 per cent indicates an average annual rate of profit on total assets of 8.2 per cent for the next 3 years. That rate is materially better than the average profit rate for the preceding 5 years.

The leverage ratio has been estimated at a lower level than in the past. The record shows a downward trend in this ratio to the fourth of the series of past years, but the analyst foresees a moderate improvement in the 3 future years. Apparently, the improvement will come from an increase in rate of profit on total assets rather than by any change in financial policy. The estimated average leverage ratio of 151 times average rate on total assets (8.2 per cent) results in an average rate on equity capital of 12.4 per cent for the future period. The analyst goes on to estimate that the increase in return on equity capital will result in an average retained earnings rate of approximately 50 per cent. The average equity capital rate times the average retained earnings rate produces an average rate of growth in earnings per share of 6.2 per cent for the next 3 years.

Moving on down to the EPS figures for the past 5 years, the analyst computed the trend values for that period and found a slightly declining trend. He used the trend value of EPS in the last year of the period as a base for extending trend values at an average annual rate of increase of 6.2 per cent. This establishes a quite different trend for the future, with EPS rising to $1.57 in the third year of the future period. Such an increase in EPS ought to be rewarded by a higher price-earnings ratio in the market. At a P/E ratio of 10 to 1, the estimated market price at the end of the next 3 years would be $15 to $16. But if the market should be sufficiently impressed by the rising trend of earnings to put a P/E ratio of 15 to 1 on the stock, the market price would be about $22.50.

You can see that this analyst made his projections of EPS on the basis of annual averages of his per year estimates for the next 3 years. This admits that estimates for individual years in the series may be a little high or a little low and the average permits error in one direction to compensate for error in the opposite direction.

ESTIMATING SALES

The usual place to begin estimating the accounting series from which the profitability ratios are derived is with sales in dollar amounts. Generally, analysts devote more effort to the estimate of future amounts of sales than to any of the other accounting series used in the profitability ratios. The reason is that changes in sales are a major cause of change in all the profitability ratios. A strong increase in sales tends to result in a higher asset turnover ratio and a larger profit margin ratio. The need for additional assets tends to lag behind an increase in sales and the relative rigidity of some expenses permits an improvement in the profit margin. When sales decline the opposite effect occurs. This is a highly generalized statement and there are many exceptions and qualifications to be considered as we move on to other accounting series.

If you ask a veteran financial analyst what is likely to cause a company's sales to increase or decrease, or to change at a different rate than in the past, he is likely to register disbelief that you should ask such a question. There are so many different factors affecting dollar amounts of sales that the question defies a short and simple answer. Anyone can list some causes of change that quickly come to mind, but we need a system of looking for possible influences on dollar volume of sales that will reveal whatever causes may be of importance. Table 12–2 presents a topical outline for developing an estimate of a company's sales.

TABLE 12–2

The Many Factors Affecting the Sales of Companies

DOLLAR AMOUNTS OF SALES	Change in the national and world economies	Components of GNP Components of national income Economies of other countries
	Change in the structure of the national economy	Urbanization of society Age distribution of the population The affluence of society Social institutions
	The development of other industries	Other industries as buyers Other industries as competitors The industry life cycle
	Change within the company	Line of products Parameters of markets Management personnel
	Change in selling prices	Conditions of competition Monopoly, oligopoly, and administered pricing

Change in the National and World Economies

The most general influence on sales of most companies is change in the national economy. We are thinking of United States companies that make their sales chiefly in the domestic market. When the economy is expanding at a relatively high rate of increase in GNP, business conditions are good and companies' sales tend to increase accordingly. In a period of recession, or of relatively slow growth in the economy, companies' sales tend to decline or to increase at a slower rate than usual. The influence of rates of change in the national economy is most pronounced on the sales of durable goods producers and those producing basic materials used in the industrial process. The effect is less for non-durable consumers' goods and for companies with narrow or specialized product lines wherein demand for products is not greatly influenced by cyclical changes in the total economy. Some companies increase their sales at a high rate despite generally unfavorable business conditions, and for others the amplitude of cyclical fluctuations in sales is greater than that of the national economy. We should keep in mind, too, that many companies sell a sizable proportion of their products in other countries, and their sales may be affected significantly by changes in the economies of other countries. For them the total economy is the economies of the principal countries in which they sell their goods.

A good starting point for estimating future sales is the past relationship of a company's sales to the gross national product. The relationship can be observed readily by dividing a company's annual sales in each of the past 5 years by the gross national product for those years, as illustrated in Table 12–3. Usually two digits of the quotient are sufficient, but sometimes three are necessary to show the extent of change. The quotient is termed the GNP

TABLE 12–3

Company Sales Relative to GNP

Years:	*1*	*2*	*3*	*4*	*5*
GNP in current dollars (billions)	$ 749.9	793.9	864.2	929.1	974.1
Diversified manufacturing company					
Sales (millions)	$7,177	7,741	8,382	8,448	8,727
GNP relative	96	97	97	91	91
Office equipment company					
Sales (millions)	$ 528	701	896	1,483	1,719
GNP relative	70	88	104	151	176
Railroad equipment company					
Sales (millions)	$ 777	768	682	751	685
GNP relative	104	96	79	81	70

relative. The table shows the GNP relatives for several companies with quite different records.

The sales of the large diversified manufacturing company relative to GNP were very stable at 96 and 97 for the first 3 years of the 5-year period, but then fell to a lower level in the last 2 years. This suggests some unusually adverse influence on sales in the latter part of the period, and as you proceed with your study of past influences on sales for that company you would look for an explanation of the relative sales decline. If the GNP relative for a company is relatively stable throughout the period, you could make a preliminary estimate that its sales will continue to be closely related to GNP. And if you estimate GNP for the next 3 years, you can compute the dollar amount of the company's sales. However, past relationships do not necessarily continue in the future, so you continue to look for indications that the GNP relative will change.

Sometimes you find that a company's sales have increased much more than GNP has increased during a certain period. The data for the office equipment company in Table 12–3 show at a glance a much greater rate of increase than that of GNP. During the 5 years the average annual rate of increase in GNP in current dollars was 7 per cent and the annual rate of increase in sales of the company was 31 per cent. In this instance the company's sales have increased at 4.45 times the rate of increase in GNP. Any extrapolation of this relationship into the future would be subject to large potential error, but the data do support a first estimate of a much greater rate of sales growth than growth of GNP.

The GNP relative for the railroad equipment manufacturing company tells a sad story of pronounced relative decline in the company's sales, and it also shows some cyclical or erratic changes. Again, extrapolation is hazardous, but at least you see from the beginning the kind of situation you are dealing with.

Sales of many companies are much more closely related to change in some of the components of GNP, or of the national income data, than they are to the total economy. Total personal consumption expenditures for the nation from year to year are indicative of changes in markets for companies making and selling a wide range of consumer products. Total personal consumption expenditures are subdivided into those for durable goods, non-durable goods, and for services. Sales of a company offering convenience-type food products would be related to expenditures in the non-durable goods category, whereas those of an automobile manufacturer would be more closely related to durable goods expenditures. There is another series for personal income, which is a component of GNP, and these data are detailed to show wages and salaries disbursements for several categories of employers, including government, as well as the amount of personal saving.

When you know a company's line of products, or product divisions, it is not difficult to select some of these series for the national economy that ought to relate to a company's sales and to work out relationships as a basis for a tentative estimate of future sales. For the more economically developed countries of the world, there are similar data on national product and income that may be used when their markets are important to a company.

Change in the Structure of the Economy

Change in the structure of the economy means change in the way people earn their money and in what they spend it for. It means shift from demand for one kind of goods or services to another. It may also affect the geographical locations of areas where money is spent. The structure of the economy changes constantly as the way we live changes and as the things we want change. These changes affect the size of demand for some kinds of products and cause some industries to grow and others to decline. Frequently, changes in dollar amounts of a company's sales are much more affected by change in the structure of the economy than in the total size of the economy, especially for smaller companies with specialized products.

If you think about it, you can discern changes in the economy that have occurred in your lifetime. Almost everyone is aware of the *increasing urbanization of society*. Migration from rural areas to cities has affected the whole fabric of society. It has changed peoples' spending patterns and, indeed, changed the spending of government at all levels. Urbanites do not buy the same things as farmers and demand many more governmental services. City dwellers more often rent their living quarters, buy more entertainment, spend more for clothing, and in general spend more for services than for goods. If you can estimate the direction of future change in distribution of population between urban and rural areas, you have a base for estimating future sales of kinds of products and services.

Changes in the *age distribution of the population* affect the structure of the economy. Young people do not buy the same things that old people buy. Thus changes in the proportions of the total population in the several age brackets affect the demand for different kinds of goods and services. In the later 1940's there was a "baby boom" as men in military service returned to civilian life, the marriage rate increased, and the birth rate rose. The babies of the immediate postwar period became the teen-agers of the 1960's; they bought lots of phonograph records, second-hand automobiles, and soft drinks. Their shifting styles of dress brought fortune to some producers of apparel and misfortune to others. Then they became the young married couples of the early 1970's and contributed greatly to the demand for housing, disposable diapers, and new school buildings.

At the opposite end of the life span there has been a relative increase in the proportion of the total population over 65 years of age. This phenomenon, plus changes in some social institutions, increased significantly the demand for things that old people want. Most conspicuous perhaps has been the development of living quarters especially designed for the elderly and to the grouping of such housing into retirement communities where you have to be at least 55 years old to gain admission.

The *increased affluence of society* has often been mentioned as a cause for satisfaction and for dissatisfaction with the uses we have made of it. The fact is that despite inflation, unemployment, and all manner of social ills, the total population has become increasingly able to buy material things. Total personal disposable income in constant dollars more than doubled from 1950 to 1970, while the total population increased at a much lesser rate. A consequence is that a much larger proportion of personal income has become "discretionary income," that is, income in excess of that required for the bare necessities and available to spend for whatever the recipients want to buy.

In the last 2 decades there has also been a decrease in the proportion of the population at the very lowest income levels and an increase in the lower-middle-income category. At the same time there has been an improvement in the stability of incomes at the lower income levels. Labor union leaders are striving for a guaranteed annual wage and political leaders are considering a minimum annual income for everybody, with the money to be provided by government. These changes have increased the market for the things the "blue-collar" workers buy and have created a potential for much greater increase in the future.

Perhaps the greatest cause of change in the structure of the economy is *change in social institutions.* "Social institutions" is a broad term that encompasses all kinds of arrangements for working, receiving income, and distributing income. It includes everything from change in length of the work week in manufacturing to unemployment insurance. Some social institutions are creations of government in response to a perceived public need, such as the social security system; some are developments in the private enterprise system, such as employee pension funds.

There are basic changes from one generation to another in peoples' philosophical values as they affect concepts of how they want to live and their needs for material things. For many years the sons and daughters of poor farmers and factory workers placed great value on education and exerted great effort to escape from life at the poverty level. Some of the sons and daughters of those who escaped and prospered have come to place great value on the simple life in a rural environment and a life style somewhat like that of their grandparents. What will be the important values in the personal philosophies of the children of the late twentieth-century followers of Rousseau and Thoreau?

One of the evolutionary changes in American society in recent years is a great increase in funds available for medical and hospital care. This is to some extent a matter of affluence, but to a greater extent it is a result of the development of private and public medical and hospital insurance systems that cover a large part of the population. The growth in demand for pharmaceuticals, health care products, hospital equipment, and the services of doctors and nurses has been phenomenal.

Entire books have been written about changes in the structure of our economy that have been barely mentioned in these few pages, and we have said nothing about changes in the economies of other countries that are important buyers of the products of our farms and factories. But books are usually obsolete from the viewpoint of financial analysts by the time they appear in print. By the time that changes in our economy have been nicely described and documented, they are known to the sophisticated portion of investors in securities, and they have been discounted in the market. The

TABLE 12–4

Average Annual Rates of Increase in Sales or Revenues for Growth Companies (10 years ended with 1970)

Company	*Percentage*
An air transportation company (Delta)	16.5%
An interstate trucking company (Roadway)	12.5
A manufacturer of forest products (Ga.-Pac.)	11.5
A mobile home manufacturer (Champion)	22.0
A manufacturer of medical care products (Baxter)	15.5
An integrated oil company (Marathon)	11.0
A manufacturer of electronic components (Avnet)	27.0
A producer of precision electronic measuring instruments (Hewlett-Packard)	16.0

Source: *The Value Line Investment Survey*, Arnold Bernhard & Co., New York.

important task for the security analyst is to see changes as they begin to appear, to estimate how they are likely to develop, and to evaluate them sooner and better than others do. The method is simply close, careful, imaginative, and continuous examination of what is going on in our constantly evolving human society.

Table 12–4 shows average annual rates of increase in sales or revenues of a group of companies whose sales have increased at an average annual compound rate greater than 10 per cent during the decade ended with 1970. What developments in the economy do you think have contributed to the high growth rates of sales for these companies?

The Development of Other Industries

For some industries the market for their products is other industries and their sales depend very much on the development of the industries that are their consumers. And for many industries the most severe competition comes from other industries that offer products that are alternatives to theirs.

Dependence on the development of *other industries as buyers* is typical of some of our large and basic industries. If you were asked to name an industry that is dependent on other industries for the demand for its products, probably you would think of the steel industry, because you know that steel is a raw material or semi-finished product for the automobile industry, the construction industry, the railway equipment manufacturing industry, the machinery industry, and a number of others. The chemical industry, too, depends on a number of other industries as consumers of basic chemicals. When the consuming industries comprise virtually the entire industrial complex, an estimate of the trend of sales for a company becomes in considerable part an estimate of the future of the national economy, which is where we started in this discussion of estimating future sales.

In some instances, however, one industry is linked almost entirely to another. The metal fasteners industry depends very heavily on the aerospace and automobile industries. Sales of agricultural machinery obviously depend on the prosperity of farmers, and many companies in the electronics industry sell semi-conductors and other components to manufacturers of electrical and scientific equipment. When the market is principally one or two other industries, you can shift your market analysis to those industries.

In any very long-term study of an industry you would have to consider *other industries as competitors*. In very broad terms all industries compete with all other industries; each tries to increase its share of the national income at the expense of others. But more narrowly, some industries compete very directly with one another and the survival of one may mean the death of another. Investors obviously want to own stocks of companies in industries that not only survive, but prosper at the expense of other industries.

What determines survival and prosperity among industries is their success in developing their products or services so that they are better than those of their competitors, better suited to customers' needs, and can be sold at a price that provides greater utility to the buyers per dollar spent. In the history of American industry there are conspicuous examples of new industries displacing old ones, or greatly reducing the size and profitability of old ones by an improved technology. A hundred years ago the steam railways were the most efficient method of land transportation for both passengers and freight. Automobiles, motor trucks, and airplanes have since taken almost all of their passenger business and much of the freight. The steel industry has had to compete with manufacturers of non-ferrous metals and with plastics; it has not fared well in recent years. In merchandising, the "discount store" type of retailing has provided strong competition to department stores, and mail order merchandising competes with both.

In the literature of investments there has long been a concept of *an industry life cycle*. A new industry comes into being when a new product or service is developed; it grows slowly at first and then more rapidly as the new product becomes more widely accepted. It reaches maturity when its products no longer are distinctly superior to those of other industries, and then it declines when other industries gain a competitive advantage. The idea is that you should invest in companies in an industry that is just beginning its rapid development because this is the phase of unusual growth both in sales and profitability.[1]

Life cycles in industries, however, are not so symmetrical in their sales curves as the concept may seem to suggest. Granted that there is some such pattern of development and decline, the pattern may extend over many decades and the rise and fall in industry sales curves may be quite irregular. The private automobile replaced the electric inter-urban railway industry in about 1 decade; but the dieselized railway industry continues to move a large part of the bulk freight of the nation despite the growth of competitive systems of transportation. Sometimes an industry that seems doomed by products of an advanced technology in another industry improves its own product and not only survives, but prospers. A half-century ago the phonograph industry

[1]Julius Grodinsky, *Investments*, New York, 1953, The Ronald Press, pp. 45–89.

seemed headed for extinction by the competition of radio and motion pictures, but improvements in sound-producing equipment and in the making of records enabled it to grow beyond anything that could have been imagined in the 1920's.

The competition of other industries, nevertheless, remains a problem of vital concern in estimating sales for a company. Products and services do compete; and in an economy characterized by both a high level of technology and rapid advances in technology, the condition of inter-industry competition is ever present and the chance that somebody will build a better mouse-trap is always there.

Industries, meaning groups of products, do develop at different rates, as illustrated by data in Table 12–5.

The import and export of goods is less important to the economy of the United States than it is to most of the industrially developed nations of the world, which is why most of us think of domestic industries as buyers and as competitors of other domestic industries. But the fact is that for some of our domestic industries the most severe *competition has come from other countries* making and selling the same kinds of goods in the United States, and some of our best customers are in other countries.

The great industrial development of Japan in the decade of the 1960's enabled Japanese companies to sell textiles, electronic equipment, and optical instruments in the United States at such prices as to capture a significant portion of the domestic market for those products. European steel companies have been able to deliver steel products in the United States and make a profit at prices our domestic companies have not been able to meet. It is said that imports of small European and Japanese made automobiles have had a

TABLE 12–5

Indexes of Industrial Production by Industry Groupings (Indexes measure physical volume of production as percentages of average production from 1957 to 1959)

	1957–59	*1969*
TOTAL INDEX OF INDUSTRIAL PRODUCTION	100	173%
Larger increases:		
Chemicals and products	100	239
Non-ferrous metals and products	100	181
Electrical machinery	100	197
Instruments and related products	100	194
Rubber and plastic products	100	239
Utilities	100	221
Smaller increases:		
Leather and products	100	102
Tobacco products	100	117
Coal	100	118
Iron and steel	100	141
Lumber and products	100	119
Food manufactures	100	137

Source: *Federal Reserve Bulletin*, Board of Governors of the Federal Reserve System.

traumatic effect on Detroit automobile executives. When you study some of our leading industries, you have to recognize that competition from other countries is a major influence on future sales.

The other side of the coin, however, is that many American companies have made deep penetrations of foreign markets, and some of them report that a substantial portion of their sales are exports to other countries. Obviously their sales prospects in those markets are affected by the competition of domestic producers in those countries and of producers in other countries who compete with them in foreign markets.

The entire business of imports and exports and competition in foreign markets has become even more complex from the viewpoint of a financial analyst by the rise of the multinational companies. Multinational companies are those that, although incorporated in one country, have subsidiaries organized in other countries and do business across national boundaries as one enterprise. It is not uncommon for some components of a product to be manufactured in one country by a subsidiary of a multinational company and assembled in another country by another corporate part of the same business organization. Thus for some companies an estimate of future sales is the sum of estimates for markets in different countries and of competition in the markets of those countries.

Change Within the Company

Early in this discussion we said that one of the first things you learn about a company is its *line of products*. And when analysts estimate sales they soon turn to consideration of particular products or product lines and think about advantages to the company, or disadvantages, relative to other companies in terms of kinds of products. Some companies have prospered in industries not generally prosperous by having unique or specialized products for which the growth of sales has been different from that of the industry. At this point you become interested in markets for specific products, or product lines.

You are looking for products of the company that are different from the products of competitors in the industry and superior to them. Usually the superiority is in technological development, or design, or kinds of materials. Often the uniqueness of a product is protected at least to some extent by patents. One company developed a better office copier using a new system of copying; another developed a new technology in photography that enables photographers to develop their own pictures in a short time. The profitability of these companies attracted strong competitors, but their patent protection was supported by continuing research, new patents, and improved products.

Those are the more dramatic examples of sales growth from unique products. Very often there is little product differentiation. Sometimes only experts can determine that the product of one company is different from that of another, and which is the better may be a matter of opinion. Perhaps the cold rolled sheet steel of one company is a little better finished than that of another. One machine tool manufacturer may make a machine that some customers consider better for certain kinds of operations than those of its competitors. A food manufacturer develops a kind of breakfast cereal that tastes better and is more nutritious than other cereals. These advantages are usually small and they may be transitory. And sometimes there is no real basis for product differentiation; basic raw materials and commodities are much the same.

The big thing that analysts look for when they study a company in an industry in which there is an important potential for technological improvement is the development of new products that will give the company a sales advantage over competitors. A manufacturer of razor blades introduces a new kind of razor blade and increases its share of the market; another introduces a new kind of razor. Chemical and pharmaceutical companies support large research programs and at any time some new product may emerge that will significantly affect a company's competitive position. Most of the larger companies spend millions of dollars annually for research and product development. For some companies the expansion of sales over periods of years has been strongly influenced by the success, or lack of success, of its research and product development.

The old maxim that all that glitters is not gold is peculiarly appropriate in appraising information about new product developments. Most of the forthcoming new products that people talk about with considerable excitement never appear, which is to say that they never get out of the laboratory or, if offered commercially, they flop. Surveys by advertising and marketing firms have shown that only a small percentage of the new products placed on the market succeed; a very large percentage is withdrawn. Some years ago a leading chemical company with an impressive record for product development announced a new material to be used in place of leather that was better than leather. It was widely advertised; many manufacturers of shoes and other leather products used it. It didn't sell very well and after several years the manufacturer ceased to make it. At the very least, an analyst who learns of an important new product about to be introduced should discount heavily the statements of people who are paid to promote its sale and seek an expert opinion both of the merit of the product and its potential market from a competent and unbiased source. There are a number of consulting firms in the business of providing such expert opinions.

There is, on the other hand, such a thing as being too skeptical about new products. The obscure inventor who developed the concept for a dry copying machine tried for years with little success to sell his idea to office equipment companies. The company that finally bought the process and spent a lot of money to further develop it became highly profitable.

As a matter of everyday security analysis, it is the relatively small improvements in products and changes in product lines that provide the main impetus to sales as far as action of management is concerned. Manufacturers of soaps and detergents keep improving their products and adding the word NEW to a brand name that has been widely advertised to indicate that the formula has been changed. Manufacturers of machine tools keep adding more sophisticated numerical controls. Food manufacturers continually improve their cake mixes. Generally it is the company that keeps moving ahead in small steps that keeps up with its competition or gains the advantage.

A very important influence on sales for many companies is simply the acquisition of other companies whose sales are added to those of the acquirer in the consolidated income statement. In these instances it is important to distinguish between increase in sales without acquisitions, which is termed internal growth, and increase with acquisitions. Many companies that have pursued active acquisition programs reveal their rate of internal growth in sales.

The opposite of sales growth by acquisition is sales shrinkage by divestment of products. It is not at all uncommon for a company to sell a subsidiary company manufacturing a part of its product line. This occurs when the company was not profitable, its products did not fit well into the total product line, or management lacked expertise in that kind of business. Sometimes what is sold is just a set of assets and perhaps the right to brand names. Sometimes what appears to be a slump in sales, or a very low rate of increase, for a year or two is explained by this process of divestment. Occasionally a company is required to divest itself of ownership of stock of another company as a result of proceedings under the anti-trust laws.

The next place to look, when you are looking for changes in sales attributable to changes within the company, is at the *parameters of markets.* The boundaries of a company's markets can be defined in different ways. One is in terms of geography. A retail grocery chain may expand its geographical area by establishing new stores in states where it has had none before, and hotel companies operating national chains can expand their market area by building hotels abroad. But markets can be defined in other ways. A company that has been selling merchandise at the low end of a price range may improve or redesign products to enter the medium-price segment of the market. A company that has been very successful in selling clothing designed for young people may capitalize on its success by offering slightly modified styles for somewhat older people who want to look young. There are many different parameters of a company's market. Sometimes company managements publicize some change in one parameter or another, and sometimes an analyst has to be very alert to spot a change.

Changes in Selling Prices

We have been thinking about future sales trends chiefly in terms of quantities of goods and services, but obviously changes in selling prices affect the dollar amount of sales. The historical data previously developed in the study of profitability ratios includes price information for recent years, so you have some idea of how the prices at which a company sells its products have changed. At this point you are concerned with why prices have changed relative to general measures of change in the price level, and you try to reason from this information to an estimate of future price changes.

The explanation for trends in prices for groups of products or services that diverge markedly from the general price level is often to be found in the same kind of developments in the structure of the economy and in the conditions of competition that explain changes in quantity of goods and services demanded. Strong demand usually brings rising prices; weak demand generally goes with lagging prices. Conditions affecting costs also affect selling prices. Sometimes producers are able to increase production of goods in strong demand with little increase in their unit costs, and competition prevents or dampens an increase in selling prices. In some industries rising costs tend to press upward on prices even when demand is weak, and the effect may be some upward movement in prices with little increase in unit volume of sales. You have to examine both change in demand for goods and change in costs.

Table 11–6 in the preceding chapter shows that the price index for medical care has increased more in the past decade than that of any other major component of the Consumer Price Index. The principal reasons are not hard to find. There has been an extraordinary growth in demand for medical services, and the causes of growth are to be found in several kinds of changes in the structure of the economy that we have described. The supply of medical care, on the other hand, could be increased to meet demand only by incurring rising costs. The cost of building hospitals and manufacturing medical equipment rose steadily, and the supply of professionally trained medical personnel could be increased all too slowly. Many people in medical care who had been poorly paid in the past became better paid.

At the opposite extreme, wholesale prices for chemicals and chemical products rose only slightly in the decade of the 1960's even though the output of chemicals more than doubled. The relative stability of prices for these products is explained by the ability of the industry to increase output as demand increased without much change in production costs. The stability of costs, in turn, reflects to a considerable extent technological advances in the production process and realization of increased economies in the construction of new plants. Price competition operated to keep rising demand from pulling prices upward.

These are but two instances. You can study the economics of industries and find the historical explanation for relative changes in prices. But our outlook is to the future. When you have learned the price history, you have to ask how the historical influences on price will operate in the future. Even a rapidly growing market may reach a saturation point and sometimes depressed markets revive as the economy changes. A steep rise in costs may level off, or the intensity of competition may diminish. One industry may be the beneficiary of a revival of another industry. An excess of productive capacity may give way to a shortage of capacity as obsolete equipment is retired and demand increases.

When you bring your perception of probable future changes in prices for a group of products or services to bear on an individual company, you have to examine the company's product line. Some companies are so broadly diversified that average price changes for its entire range of products are likely to follow general trends in the price level. Others are so specialized that you must study markets very narrowly defined.

The extent to which a company's products are differentiated from those of its competitors has a bearing upon changes in selling prices. When they are clearly differentiated by design, brand name, patents or level of technological development, price competition is likely to be less severe than it is for companies whose products are essentially the same as those of other companies. Companies with differentiated products generally try to keep prices stable even under conditions of weak demand because they want to maintain the reputation of their products. Producers of undifferentiated products, on the other hand, often resort to price-cutting when demand weakens in an effort to keep plants operating and possibly to increase their share of the market.

Obviously there is no easy way to estimate future trends in prices for a company's products. There is only the hard way of trying to estimate future demand, the trend of costs, and the intensity of competition. To do this you have to thoroughly understand the industry and know the company. Institutions with a number of analysts often assign an analyst to only one industry, or to a very few. They cannot keep up with very many.

ESTIMATING ASSETS RELATIVE TO SALES

The other component of asset turnover is change in value of assets. Generally, analysts pay a great deal of attention to estimates of future sales, but neglect to estimate changes in assets. It makes a great difference in profitability whether a projected increase in dollar amount of sales is achieved with little further increase in assets or with a large increase in assets. Assets is the denominator of the asset turnover ratio, and change in that amount may be as important as change in the numerator.

You have the historical record of change in total asset turnover as well as turnover ratios for the major categories of assets, and you can see how these ratios have varied. Sometimes changes stand out sharply and you see at once that you must find out what caused the change and try to determine whether it is likely to continue in the future. In other instances it is difficult to discern changes that are not attributable to cyclical changes in business activity. But even then you examine developments in the company that may affect asset turnover ratios.

Sales to Current Assets

Begin with the turnover of current assets. It is more likely than not that you will find a decrease in that ratio in a past 5-year period if you are studying an industrial company. There has been a general tendency for companies, particularly the larger and better financed companies, to provide credit to their customers more generously than in earlier years. Thus accounts receivable grow more than sales. A common explanation for growth in accounts receivable is that more liberal credit terms provide a stimulus to sales. Smaller business firms often have limited access to credit and they welcome credit provided by their larger suppliers. Companies that sell directly to consumers have also found that easy credit terms help to increase sales, and many retailers have made a considerable effort to let their customers know that they can buy on credit. Some larger companies have created finance company subsidiaries to perform the specialized function of holding notes and accounts receivable. When finance companies are consolidated with the parent company in published statements, the growth of receivables relative to sales may be apparent; but if they are not consolidated, you have to look to the separate financial statements of the finance company.

Inventory control is one of the most frequently used terms in the vocabulary of business managers. Everyone tries to reduce inventories or at least to keep them from rising, because each dollar tied up in inventories has a cost. Computerized inventory control systems have become commonplace and product lines are often trimmed of slow-moving items of merchandise. These management efforts, however, are sometimes overridden by broader changes in the operation of a business.

An increase in vertical integration tends to increase the size of inventories relative to sales, because there are inventories at each of several stages of the process of production and distribution. Acquisitions of other companies and divestments of other companies tend to change the product mix of a company and affect the inventory turnover whenever the turnover ratio for the company added or subtracted is greater or less than for the remainder of the business operation. Any major change in the product line may affect inventory turnover. A retail chain store, for example, that has been engaged almost entirely in the sale of "soft goods" (consumers non-durable goods), may add lines of "hard goods" (consumers durable goods) and thus reduce its inventory turnover, because a stock of hard goods must be maintained and these goods "stay on the shelf" longer than soft goods.

At the opposite end of the system there are sometimes changes in the production process that affect inventory turnover. Any development that reduces the size of stockpiles of raw materials operates to improve inventory turnover, and anything that speeds up production reduces the inventory of materials being manufactured. Whatever increases the speed of distribution of finished goods improves inventory turnover. Sometimes there are marked changes in the whole production and distribution process that cause corresponding changes in inventory turnover and thus in the turnover of total current assets.

Other items of current assets are usually much less important than accounts receivable and inventories, but the turnover of current assets may be affected by converting marketable securities into fixed assets or reduction of operating cash balances. Or, change in these kinds of current assets may be in the opposite direction.

Sales to Fixed Assets

The total amount of fixed assets does not usually fluctuate greatly from year to year, except as a result of acquisitions or mergers. There is a more or less continuous process of depreciation and replacement of plant, equipment, buildings, and other assets used in the production of goods and services. For a successful company with an upward trend of sales, the amount of total assets also trends upward as more plant and equipment is required to achieve the increasing amounts of sales. Under conditions of pronounced price inflation there is a tendency for sales in dollars to increase at a somewhat greater rate than sales, because fixed assets go on the books at the time they are acquired at the price paid for them and that value is changed only by depreciation. The prices at which goods are sold are continuously affected by the trend of the general price level, so sales reflect price inflation much more than does the book value of fixed assets.

What you look for in the historical data is divergence from the pattern of relatively constant or slightly rising fixed asset turnover, because change may be indicative of a development in the affairs of a company that will continue into the future.

Sometimes you see fixed assets increasing more than sales. The explanation may be that sales have been lagging because of product obsolescence, stronger competition from other industries, a shift in market demand to different kinds of products, or simply poor merchandising. You have to look for the answer in some of the areas we have been discussing. When you find it, you may have an important clue to the future profitability of the company.

Another kind of explanation may lie in the company's program of fixed asset expansion. In spite of all the attention to capital budgeting and to careful calculations of expected rates of return on new capital outlays, capital budgeting decisions sometimes turn out to be wrong. And when they are wrong on any very large scale there is a discernible effect on the fixed asset turnover ratio. It has often happened that a company has increased its investment in plant and equipment for a period of several years without achieving a corresponding increase in sales because the expected increase in demand did not materialize. Even when new investment is well conceived, there are often time lags of several years between investment and full operation of new plants.

A rising trend in fixed asset turnover, however, may reflect lack of new investment in fixed assets. Plant and equipment on the books is continuously depreciated. If additional investment does not equal depreciation, book value declines even though sales may trend upward. You have to look constantly for the explanation of whatever divergence there may be between the trend of sales and the trend in total amount of fixed assets.

Sales to Other Assets

The third category of assets, which has been termed simply other assets, consists of everything else on the balance sheet than can not be classified as current or fixed. If you examine the assets of a number of companies, you find a wide variety of other assets. Some are fixed assets not used in the regular operation of the business, such as land owned by railroads, securities of non-consolidated subsidiaries, and a wide variety of intangible assets. If intangibles are deleted, as many analysts prefer to do, the size of this class of assets may be materially reduced.

Past changes in amounts of investments in other companies may provide a clue to company strategy in arranging its corporate affiliations and suggest policy likely to be pursued by management in the future. Similarly, you may find evidence of a general program of liquidation of non-operating assets that has an implication for future change in this asset category.

ESTIMATING FUTURE ASSET TURNOVER

The way to arrive at an estimate of the future average annual rate of asset turnover is to assume initially that it will be about the same as the average for the past several years, and then to consider on the basis of your analysis of change in the pattern of sales and total assets what developments are likely to cause it to be different in the future. You may see evidence in the past record of a higher rate of increase in sales than in the past, or of a lower rate. You may see a pattern of unusual growth in total assets that has created productive capacity and current assets sufficient to provide for growth in sales with a lesser rate of asset growth in the future. Such conclusions would be based on patterns of change in any or all components of total sales or total assets that you have observed in the past.

Or, you may find little reason to think that total asset turnover will be very much different in the future and emerge with an estimated asset turnover ratio that is essentially an extrapolation of the past. That kind of conclusion, although something less than sensational, is valuable. It suggests stability in one important relationship affecting future profitability. Stability is the antithesis of uncertainty.

You can hardly expect to pin-point exactly the probable future average asset turnover, so you may do well to express your estimate of the average asset turnover for the next 3 years as a weighted probability distribution and subsequently carry that distribution forward to be combined with estimates of probable future profit margins. Probability distributions may be weighted to show the relative optimism or pessimism of the analyst. The smaller the deviation from the mean and the smaller the probabilities at the extremes, the more confident you are of your estimate. You might, for example, express your conclusion about future asset turnover ratio in this manner:

Size of ratio	*Probability*
220	0.1
210	0.2
200	0.4
190	0.2
180	0.1
	1.0

QUESTIONS FOR DISCUSSION

1. Some years ago a leading chain grocery store decided that the formula for success was to cut prices, accept lower profit margins, and make it up on volume. What do you think of this formula? In what lines of business might it work? In what other lines of business would you be inclined to reverse the formula in order to maximize earnings? (See recent annual reports of The Great Atlantic and Pacific Tea Co.).
2. At a particular time the consensus of business forecasters is that the recession will be over in about 6 months and then there will be a strong increase in Gross National Product. Assume that you believe this forecast. In what industries would you look for stocks that may be underpriced relative to the prospective earnings over the next several years?
3. Population growth in the United States has slowed down. The birth rate is lower and the average longevity of the population has increased. Assuming that these statements are correct, what industries are favored by change in the age distribution?
4. What changes in social institutions can you see occurring today? What industries are likely to experience above average increase in sales as a result?
5. Can you identify an industry that is today threatened by technological developments in another industry?
6. What do you think of the assertion that big companies can control their profit margins because their selling prices are administered? (You might examine change in profit margins of several leading companies in the last few years.)
7. A small and relatively unknown company has recently announced its development of an electronic television tuner, an electronic thermometer that may be thrown away after one use, a small calculator cheaper than anything comparable on the market, and an optical character reader that can interpret textual material and incorporate it into a computer memory bank. Estimate the effect of these new products on the company's sales over the next several years? See the New York Times, July 1, 1972, p. 28, for an account of what actually happened.
8. The largest motel chain in the United States has undertaken a program of expansion in the principal countries of western Europe. Its European motels will be in the American pattern, with modifications to suit the traditions of the countries in which they are located. Will this program increase or decrease the asset turnover of the motel company? (See annual reports of Holiday Inns, Inc.)
9. The largest manufacturer of cameras and photographic equipment in the United States has experienced severe competition in its domestic market from German and Japanese camera manufacturers and from several domestic camera manufacturers. How would you expect this competition to affect this company's sales, asset turnover, and profit margin? You can check your conclusion by looking up Eastman Kodak in one of the investment information services.
10. After studying a company usually identified as a manufacturer of tobacco products, you find that its turnover of current assets has increased markedly in the last several years. Where in the company's financial statements would you look for an explanation? (Look up American Brands, Philip Morris, or Reynolds Industries).

13

Interpreting the Record: The Profit Margin

I. Profit margin as a function of sales
   A. The break-even concept
   B. Selling prices and profit margins

II. Profit margin as a function of operating expenses
   A. Economy of operation
   B. Efficiency of operation
   C. Other applications of concepts of economy and efficiency of operation
   D. Accounting policies as influences on profit margins
   E. The operating ratio

III. Factors influencing the after-tax profit margin
   A. Non-operating income and expense
   B. Non-recurring debits and credits
   C. The income tax ratio

IV. The conclusion: estimates of profitability rate

The profit margin ratio is to the asset turnover ratio as one blade of a scissors is to another. One operates with the other and the effect is the product of the two. So it is in estimating the future profitability of a company. You have to examine the historical accounting data that measure the profit margin ratio, try to estimate how it will change in the future, and use estimates of both of these major relationships to estimate future change in a company's profitability.

Over the longer term there are of course many factors that influence profit margins and frequently several conditions operate at the same time. Therefore, the financial analyst must continue to bring into his field of vision everything that may contribute significantly to change the profit margin ratio.

PROFIT MARGIN AS A FUNCTION OF SALES

Change in the size of the profit margin from time to time is strongly affected by change in the volume of sales. When sales increase, the profit margin tends to increase, and conversely. This simple principle emphasizes again the great importance of sales estimates for reaching a conclusion about the probable future profitability of companies.

One major reason why profit margins vary with sales is that some operating expenses are relatively fixed and some vary more or less with the quantity of production or the volume of sales. These fixed expenses provide what is sometimes termed "operating leverage," which means that they "lever" earnings upward as sales increase and have the opposite effect as sales decline. To the extent that sales fluctuate cyclically and seasonally, there are usually corresponding changes in the profit margin. We are, however, more interested in the longer-term changes brought about by evolutionary changes in the nature of a company's operations.

The Break-Even Concept

Accountants and financial managers of a company are able to calculate the "break-even point" for the company, or for a product division. The break-even point is the amount of sales at which revenues exactly equal costs. As sales rise above that point, the profit margin rises proportionately much more than the increase in sales. With unit costs and prices at the current level, accountants are able to compute the size of the profit margin for any amount of sales above the break-even point.

Financial analysts do not have the internal financial data to compute accurately the break-even point for a business they are observing from the outside, but they can often use published data to see how profit margins have changed as levels of sales have changed in the past. For example, if sales increased from $100 in one period to $110 in the next period, the sales relative is 110. If from the first to the second period the profit margin increased from 5 to 5.5 per cent, the profit margin relative is 110. The ratio of the relatives is 1 to 1. But, if with the 10 per cent increase in sales the profit margin increased from 5 to 6 per cent, the profit margin relative is 120 and the ratio of the relatives is 1.09 to 1 (120 divided by 110). Thus you can measure the relative size of change in sales and profit margin in a series of periods.

Companies that are highly mechanized and automated usually have high operating leverage. They are sometimes described as capital intensive companies because a relatively large part of operating expenses is associated with large investment in plant and equipment. Thus in some companies the expense of depreciation and maintenance of plant and equipment is a substantial portion of operating expenses. These expenses tend to be fixed, subject to some influence by management on depreciation policy and on level of maintenance.

On the other hand, the expenses of some companies include a large proportion of labor cost. These expenses tend to be highly correlated with amounts of sales. They are termed *labor intensive companies* and of course they tend to have low operating leverage. In periods of declining sales they are better able to reduce operating expenses than the capital intensive companies.

The break-even point is closely related to the rate of utilization of productive capacity, and many companies periodically report information on the level of production relative to full productive capacity, particularly in the regulated industries. Electric utility companies, for example, publish data on their average output of electricity per hour relative to their total generating capacity. This ratio is known as the load factor. The higher the load factor, the better the utilization of generating capacity. Air transportation companies report the ratio of total number of seats occupied by passengers on planes in flight to the total number of seats on those planes, and the ratio is known as the seat factor. Some industrial companies report similar data.

Selling Prices and Profit Margins

Changes in selling prices, which are a component of dollar amounts of sales, also affect the size of profit margins. Given a cost of production (or cost of sales) per unit of product at a rate of utilization of productive capacity, the severity of price competition determines the size of the profit margin. There are several kinds of conditions of competition, as we learned in discussing sales trends, and they have sharply different effects on the profit margin during the business cycle and over longer time periods.

When sales are declining, competition presses prices downward most severely for companies that produce *undifferentiated products*. Aluminum ingots are about the same whether made by one company or another. There may be differences in grades of materials, but within grade specifications it makes no difference which company produced them. So it is with a great many of the raw materials, or semi-finished materials, of industry. When demand for such products slackens, there is almost inevitably some price cutting by producers as they endeavor to keep their plants or mills running at a relatively high rate of capacity. Often the price cutting takes the form of discounts, absorption of transportation costs by the seller, or special allowances of one kind or another.

In industries producing these basic undifferentiated products the profit margins of companies at any given time are inverse to their economy and efficiency of operations. The low-cost producers make money while the higher-cost companies break even or lose money. There is a sort of gradation of companies in an industry from those at the margin of profitability, which realize earnings when prices are favorable and losses under unfavorable conditions, to those that are generally well above the margin. With this kind of product, about the only way a company can improve its profit margin over the longer term is to move away from the margin; that is, to improve the economy and efficiency of their operations. That kind of improvement is our next principal topic.

A quite different kind of price and profit margin experience characterizes companies that sell distinctly differentiated products. These companies have more stable profit margins because price competition is not so intense. The strongest kind of differentiation is that provided by patents that protect important differences in products. With such sharp product differentiation, a seller has a legal monopoly of sale of that product. He is not in the position of having to cut prices simply because some other seller of a similar product has cut prices. Such a patent monopoly, however, is far from perfect. Other sellers offer other products that are different, but just as good or better, according to the other sellers. The other products compete, but sales efforts are based more on claims of better products than on lower prices.

There are many industries in which products are differentiated not so much by patents as by differences in materials, ingredients, design, or brand name. The extent of differentiation may not be great, but when producers think their product has an "image" in the minds of their customers they try to preserve it. They compete in sales and advertising more than in price cutting.

The better profit margins on differentiated products often motivate management to try to "upgrade" their product lines by increasing the proportion of differentiated products. What we said in the preceding chapter about change in product lines influencing the trend of sales applies also to change in products influencing profit margin. A company can move in this direction through research and product development directed at entirely new products in the higher profit margin area, or by improving existing products and keeping them in that area. It can "buy" new products to add to its product line by acquiring other companies, and it can eliminate products that have not been profitable.

One way for a bulk producer to upgrade its product line is by moving to more complete fabrication of the bulk product, which is sometimes called forward integration. The more completely manufactured products generally have higher profit margins, because they represent several levels of manufacturing and there is a profit margin at each level.

For example, a chemical company can make salicylic acid and sell it by the ton at a very low profit margin. It could make the salicylic acid into tablets and sell the product as aspirin. There is a much better profit margin on brand-name aspirin tablets than on bulk salicylic acid. Nor is this necessarily the end of that road. The company can add something to aspirin such as caffein or a buffering ingredient and call the product by a name other than aspirin. There is said to be a better margin on aspirin tablets plus another ingredient than there is on straight aspirin tablets.

Vertical integration by a manufacturer may be carried forward to ownership of distribution facilities. Some tire companies and shoe companies, for example, own their own retail stores. The effect on a company's profit margin is to add to the mark-up at the manufacturing level the mark-up at the retailing level.

There are, of course, expenses and capital outlays associated with programs of upgrading products and forward integration, and there is risk that a program will not work out well. Not infrequently, a company expands into a promising new area and the promise is not fulfilled.

PROFIT MARGIN AS A FUNCTION OF OPERATING EXPENSES

When you have a selling price for products and a level of sales in dollars, profit margin is also a function of production expense for manufacturing operations and analogous costs for other kinds of operations. Production expense per unit of output is determined by the economy and efficiency of operations. Economy of operations refers to the characteristics of a set of production facilities that affect the size of costs per unit of output. Efficiency of operation refers to the manner in which a set of assets is managed to affect the cost of production, regardless of what economy they represent.

Economy of Operation

You might study two companies making the same general type of product and conclude that one has the more economical plant. This means that one plant is capable of producing at a lower cost than the other when other conditions affecting costs are about the same. In our era of rapidly improving technology of production, the better plants are those that use the most advanced technology. In the steel industry, for example, a modern mill for producing strip steel would mean one that is highly automated and computer controlled. Precise control results in better product quality and in greater output relative to the designed capacity of a mill. It also means lower labor costs per unit of output. Conversely, an old open-hearth furnace for making steel is uneconomical to operate. As you read the annual reports of companies, you frequently see reports that new plants are being constructed and old plants are being abandoned. Usually this means improvement in economy of operation.

In our innovative society, with its exponential rate of growth in scientific knowledge, there is hardly any method of producing goods or services that has not been affected by important advances in technology. Every schoolboy knows about Eli Whitney and the cotton-gin, about the application of steam power to the movement of people and freight by land and by sea, and about nuclear-powered electric generating plants. But in every industry better equipment is being developed continually and existing equipment is constantly being outmoded. Companies must continually renew their production facilities to bring in the new and scrap the old. For the nation, expenditures for new plant and equipment in the early 1970's aggregated about $80 billion a year.

In studying individual companies, financial analysts look for relative change in the rate of building new technologies into a company's set of assets. Sometimes you can see a company moving out in front of its competitors by building new plants with the most advanced technology, and sometimes you see one company lagging in its industry by failing to modernize. These leads and lags may very well extend over periods of several years and have a pronounced effect on production expenses. It might be pointed out, however, that the construction and start up of new plants often require unusual expenses that for a time tend to impair the profit margin. Plant modernization has to be appraised on a long-term basis.

In some kinds of production the size of production units affects economy of operation. Up to some point there are economies of scale and larger units are more economical than smaller ones. One of the more spectacular developments in the petroleum industry in recent years has been the great increase in size of oil tankers that transport crude oil from distant points to refineries. At one time tankers of 100,000 tons capacity were the usual size. A decade or so later new tankers were put into operation with several times that capacity. The large vessels, of course, transport oil at a lower cost per ton-mile than the smaller ones. In the electric power industry the size of generating plants has steadily increased from those with 100,000 kilowatt-hours capacity to units with more than 1,000,000 kilowatt-hours capacity. Increase in size of units may be another important facet of a company's program of improving economy of operation.

Geographical location of plants often affects economy of operation. Generally, plants using large quantities of bulky raw materials have located close to their supplies of materials to minimize transportation costs. The steel industry at one time was situated chiefly in the Pittsburgh-Youngstown area because that was most economical location in terms of the cost of transporting iron ore, coal, and limestone, and was also close to principal steel-consuming centers. Subsequently, the development of different sources of ore and coal and the further westward movement of steel-consuming industries made other locations more advantageous for some kinds of steel manufacturing.

The spread of population and industry across the United States and improvements in transportation have changed some of the older criteria for geographical location of plants. The attractiveness of a location as a place to live from the standpoint of highly trained and professional-type employees has become important for many companies. Climate has been one reason for the development of industry in California and in the southwestern states.

Proximity to recreation areas for employees has become more important with the shortening of the work-week and the adoption of such employment practices as the 4-day week and the week-on and week-off arrangement. Research facilities of companies have sometimes been located near major universities in order to facilitate consultation with university scientists, and some companies have found that suburban locations close to major cities ensure a high quality labor force. Other companies have moved plants to relatively depressed areas such as Appalachia to take advantage of relatively low labor costs.

For each industry or major category of products you have to learn what are the important location considerations and then examine the relative success of companies in realizing economies of location.

Efficiency of Operation

Efficiency of operation is a matter of management. A set of facilities with whatever characteristics it may have in terms of economy of operation may be managed efficiently or inefficiently. Good management may operate a semi-obsolete plant so efficiently that it is competitive on a cost basis, and poor management may fail to realize the economies expected from modern plants. Appraising efficiency of operation is a very technical problem. The detailed internal cost data necessary to measure efficiency precisely is not generally available to financial analysts, and sometimes they have to rely chiefly on what appears in the earnings statement as evidence of both economy and efficiency. However, those who understand the technology of operation and have observed developments in competing companies can sometimes piece together information sufficiently well to make a judgment.

Financial analysts with long experience can tell a great deal about the efficiency of a plant just by visiting it and seeing what goes on. They observe whether the arrangement of equipment results in orderly flow of work through the production process, whether modern materials handling equipment is used, and whether there are bottlenecks in the operation. An increasingly important consideration is working conditions that affect the productivity of employees. Low levels of noise, good ventilation, and comfortable temperatures contribute to productivity and to stability of the labor force. And you may draw some conclusion by observing the behavior of employees. A certain amount of good-natured conversation may be indicative of good morale; sullen, passive people performing highly repetitive operations have little interest in the quality of their work.

In some industries there is publicly available information that indicates both economy and efficiency of operations. Transportation companies generally make available to the public data on cost of moving passengers or freight per mile. Electric utilities publish data on production costs of power per kilowatt-hour and on the number of British Thermal Units of heat required to produce a quantity of electric power. Some companies make available data on labor costs that can be related to quantities of production.

Other Applications of Concepts of Economy and Efficiency of Operation

These concepts of economy and efficiency of operation can be applied to almost all kinds of business enterprises. Only the applications differ.

In chain store retailing, economy of operation is also a function of size and location of stores. The trend in recent years has been decidedly toward larger units in terms of floor space and location in shopping centers where a number of stores offering different kinds of merchandise draw customers from a radius of many miles. Easy access by main highways and convenient parking add to the economy of location in large shopping centers relative to inner-city stores, where traffic congestion and inadequate parking are diseconomies.

There is also economy in extent and type of services offered to customers. The trend has been toward a lower level of customer services. Supermarkets where customers select merchandise from shelves, pay cash, and carry it away themselves have largely replaced the neighborhood grocery store with clerks behind counters and free delivery. Discount stores that offer little or nothing in the way of delivery, charge accounts, or repair services have made inroads on the business of department stores that offer more services, but at higher prices. Warehouse retailing has come to be used increasingly to further reduce distribution costs.

Efficiency in retail store operation is measured by the behavior of sales personnel, attractiveness of interiors, continuous replenishment of stocks on shelves, allocation of shelf space to high turnover items, and good customer check-out facilities.

In a quite different business such as commercial banking there is economy in location of the central office and in the network of branch offices operated by banks in most states. Drive-in facilities contribute to economy of operation by providing easy access to bank tellers, and convenient parking has become increasingly important for customers who must transact their business inside a bank. In terms of equipment, computers add both to economy and efficiency of operation; such services as night-depositories, lock-boxes and banking-by-mail also are plus factors.

Efficiency of operation in banking is a function of management. Well-trained and courteous personnel are an indication of good management, and so are quick decisions on loan applications. Other indications of efficiency are to be found in the management of both assets and liabilities. A bank operates most efficiently from the standpoint of stockholders by keeping cash and low-yielding secondary reserve assets at a minimum, and loans at a maximum. It buys liquidity when necessary by purchasing federal funds, or Euro-dollars, but generally keeps the cost of the money it uses in the form of deposits at the lowest level consistant with meeting the need for loanable and investable funds.

Accounting Policies as Influences on Profit Margins

Accounting policies may affect the profit margin of a company by changes over periods of years. The public accounting profession has long debated the question of how much latitude business management should have in deciding what accounting policies to use and how they may be changed. Some accountants say that corporate management should determine the accounting policies that they consider appropriate for their companies. Others say that the rules should be more rigid so that published financial statements of different companies will be more nearly comparable. The Financial Accounting Standards Board of the Association of Certified Public Accountants has contributed greatly to uniformity of accounting policies by its series of "Opinions" on specific questions of accounting policy. But there are differences in the way companies keep their books, and companies may change policies from time to time. CPA firms are required by the rules of their profession to point out any change in accounting policies from year to year that materially affect the financial condition of companies whose statements they audit.

One of the more controversial questions about accounting policy is how much depreciation expense should be charged in a given accounting period. There are several facets of this problem. One is the estimate of the useful life of an asset and another is the estimate of salvage value at the time an asset is retired or scrapped. More important in most instances, however, is the rate at which assets will be depreciated per accounting period. There are several different ways that are acceptable to auditors and to the Internal Revenue Service. Some result in much more depreciation expense for an asset in a particular accounting period than others. Any shift in depreciation policy continuing for several years could contribute to an increase or decrease in the profit margin.

Other areas in which accounting practices may vary considerably are capitalization of expenses and subsequent amortization of such capitalized amounts. Some oil companies, for example, charge the cost of exploring for oil to the income account as the cost is incurred; others capitalize the cost on the balance sheet and write it off as an expense from year to year. Expenses for research and product development may also be capitalized and subsequently amortized. Whether a company uses one practice or another may have considerable effect on profit margin for a year, or a series of years.

Pension costs are a variable item, not so much as a matter of accounting policy, but as a matter of management decisions about how much should be contributed to the pension fund per period. With pension funds of most companies invested in part (sometimes in large part) in common stocks, the behavior of stock prices may affect the size of company contributions from time to time. Large rates of return for a period in the form of stock price appreciation sometimes influence management decisions about the amount of additional contributions required.

Financial analysts who study a company in depth scrutinize carefully its accounting policies. If they conclude that a company's policies are conservative (not tending to over-state earnings), they say that the "quality" of earnings is good. Otherwise they may characterize earnings as "liberally stated."

The essential question about how accounting policies influence profit margin over the long run is whether future changes are likely to increase or decrease the statement of expenses relative to sales. You have to rely on observation of past accounting practices to arrive at an answer.

The Operating Ratio

The expenses of regular operations are usually totaled in the income statement and are termed operating expenses. Total operating expense divided by sales, or operating revenues, is termed the operating ratio. Many analysts pay considerable attention to change in the operating ratio as a measure of improvement or deterioration in the over-all economy and efficiency of operation, and in the severity of price competition.

For the purpose of analyzing income statements it is important to differentiate sales, or revenues from regular operations of a business, from income derived from sources other than regular operations. Sales may be termed operating income, and that from other sources is non-operating income. Similarly, operating expenses should be distinguished from expenses not incurred in the regular operation of a business. Separating operating financial data from the non-operating accounting items makes it possible to focus on the profit margin from operations and then on other items of income and expense that affect the final "after everything" profit margin.

You can scan the changes in percentages in each of the items from year to year, as presented in Table 11–7, and see which kinds of expense have absorbed a larger proportion and which have absorbed a smaller proportion of sales. And this is where you may find evidence in quantified data of the effect of some of the patterns of change you have observed in the affairs of a company. Has that plant modernization program really paid off in lower percentages for those expenses most closely associated with economy and efficiency of operations? What was the effect on the operating ratio of more aggressive sales-promotion efforts? The trend of depreciation and other non-cash expenses relative to sales may provide a clue to change in accounting policies.

The categories of expenses you use for this purpose are usually those identified in the published income statement. The items of expense are somewhat different from industry to industry and even from company to company within an industry. In regulated industries, however, the form of income statement is usually prescribed by the regulatory authority and is standard for all companies.

The statements of most electric utility operating companies, for example, are in the form prescribed by the Federal Power Commission, which has also been adopted by many state utility commissions. You can go down through the statements and see an expense item that represents the cost of generating electric power, another for the cost of transmitting power, and a third for distribution costs. Statements of railroads are similarly standardized by rules of the Interstate Commerce Commission, and those of banks by federal bank supervisory authorities.

Companies in non-regulated industries can use any form for published statements acceptable to their auditors. What is acceptable varies from industry to industry. Merchandising companies report as the first and the largest item of expense the cost of goods sold. Then there is some detail on selling and administrative expenses. A diversified manufacturing company may itemize cost of products sold, marketing or selling expense, depreciation, and administrative expenses. Some companies report separately the amounts paid for materials and for labor.

Besides the published statements in corporate annual reports, those companies that have publicly distributed securities are required to file annual statements with the Securities and Exchange Commission, and the Commission prescribes a standard for itemizing operating expenses. Data from these reports to the SEC are to be found in publications of some investment information services. They are particularly useful in comparing companies in the same industry, or those engaged in much the same kind of business operation.

FACTORS INFLUENCING THE AFTER-TAX PROFIT MARGIN

When you have examined the effects of changes in operating expenses relative to sales, you have recognized and interpreted the major influences affecting the operating profit margin. But there are usually some items of other income and other expense that appear in earnings statements below the operating expenses. And there is additional influence of change in effective income tax rates on the after-tax profit margin.

Non-Operating Income and Expense

The terminology used to describe these other kinds of income and expense varies widely, but in general they are more or less regularly recurring, but do not arise from the regular operations of a business. Sometimes they are so small in amount that they have little effect on the final profit margin, but sometimes they are significant and sometimes changes in amounts have a material influence on the profit margin both before and after taxes. At least you have to look at them and consider how they may affect future profit margins.

The obvious questions for the financial analyst are: What are the sources of non-operating income? Is there a trend or pattern of change that may be a basis for estimating future change?

Many items of other income and other expense arise from a company's ownership of securities of other companies that are not included in its consolidated financial statements. This requires some understanding of consolidated financial statements and unconsolidated subsidiary or affiliated companies.

Most of the larger companies in which investors are interested have subsidiary companies that are entirely or largely owned. The company that owns the stock of the other company is the parent and the other is the subsidiary. When all or a majority of the stock of the subsidiary is owned, it is usual for the statements of the subsidary to be consolidated with those of the parent. In effect, they are added together after eliminating accounting items that evidence financial relationships between the parent and subsidiary, and the consolidated statement is for the two or more companies as though they were one.

Many companies also have ownership interests in other companies but do not own a sufficiently large proportion of the stock to justify consolidating statements. The proportion that justifies consolidation varies somewhat according to the judgement of management and its public accounting firm. If there is significant ownership interest, but not enough to justify consolidation, the company that is partially owned is called a non-consolidated subsidiary or an affiliated company.

The company that owns the stock of such a subsidiary or affiliated company shows its ownership of the stock on its balance sheet and the dividends it receives on the stock in its income statement. Dividends appear in the parent company's income statement as "other income," or "dividends from affiliated companies." It has become a fairly common practice for parent companies also to include in their income statements their share in the undistributed earnings of non-consolidated companies, or their share in the loss of such companies. The financial relationship between parent and unconsolidated subsidiary companies often includes loans from parent to subsidiary. Interest on such loans would appear as non-operating income to the parent in its consolidated income statement.

There are many other possible sources of other income in corporate financial statements. There may be other income from patent rights granted to other companies on a royalty basis, and from rental of property owned but leased to another company. Sometimes there is income from sales of services that are not considered part of the regular operation but as incidental to it. Any more or less regularly recurring income of such nature appears in this part of the income statement.

Other expenses of a recurring nature are the same kinds of items in reverse. We mentioned the practice of including a share of the losses of unconsolidated subsidiary companies in the consolidated income statement. The sale of fixed assets retired from operation at values less than depreciated book value would have to be shown as an expense. Royalties paid to other companies may be reported as other expense, or they may be included in operating expense, according to the nature of a royalty agreement and accounting policy decisions.

Non-Recurring Credits and Debits

Non-recurring losses often represent the write-off of a business decision that proved to be wrong. It may be simply a misjudgement in inventory policy that required a write-down in value of inventory. The larger amounts generally represent an effort to expand the business in some direction that did not work out well. Recently, one large electronics firm wrote-off most of its investment in computer manufacturing. A large forest products company wrote-off ventures in real estate development. More often these write-offs are less spectacular. A period of business recession, when operating earnings are not very good anyway, is a time when many corporate managements decide to recognize in their accounting statements some "disappointing" developments in their business. Other non-recurring expenses appear occasionally without particular regard for the business cycle.

Non-recurring income also appears from time to time in the part of the income statement below the operating section. Kinds of accounting items that appear as non-recurring losses may also appear as non-recurring gains. There may be a sizable profit from sale of fixed assets, ranging from real estate no longer used in the business to a complete product division. Sometimes intangible assets are added to the balance sheet with a corresponding gain recorded in the income statement. At times, tangible assets have been revalued upward. A decision to eliminate a large valuation reserve from the balance sheet would require a credit to income. And the peculiarities of the federal corporate income tax sometimes result in extraordinary debits or credits to income.

In practice you find some odd entries toward the bottom of income statements. They should be explained by the public accountants in footnotes to the statements. Reading footnotes to financial statements may be tedious business, but it may be very rewarding to financial analysts.

A problem for analysts that can never be solved to the complete satisfaction of everyone is how to treat these extraordinary items in constructing a record of earnings per share. An easy solution is simply to disregard them on the ground that they serve only to distort the pattern of change in EPS. But if you do so, you may omit from the historical record events that have some implications for the future. Sometimes, extraordinary write-offs serve to eliminate or to reduce operating expenses. Extraordinary gains may provide significant sums of money for re-investment at larger internal rates of return. A common practice is to exclude extraordinary gains or losses in arriving at reported EPS, but to show the net amount of such items on a per share basis along with reported EPS.

When you have subtracted operating expenses from sales to arrive at operating income, and after the net amount of other recurring income and expense has been added or subtracted, you have earnings before interest and taxes. This is the EBIT of the system of ratio analysis. But the final version of the measurement of profitability is earnings before interest and after taxes and this is the numerator of $P - T_r$. So we have to give some attention to amounts of income tax that are the difference between the two rates.

The Income Tax Ratio

The income tax ratio may be taken as the amount of income tax paid or accrued for an accounting period divided by sales, or operating revenues. If the net amount of non-operating income is significant, it may be added to sales and included in the divisor. When this ratio has been prepared for a series of periods, you can see the effect of fluctuations in income tax amounts on EBIT − T, and on the profitability ratio expressed as $P - T_r$. These fluctuations may have some implications for the future profitability of a company, which is what we are interested in.

One influence on the tax ratio is change in the amount of interest and other fixed charges that is deducted in arriving at the amount of taxable income. A sizable decline in such tax-deductible charges from one period to another would increase the tax ratio, other things being equal, because it would increase the amount of taxable income.

Usually the amount of taxable income, and of tax, varies from time to time more than the amount of sales changes. A 10 per cent increase in sales might very well produce a 20 per cent increase in taxable income and in the amount of tax, and thus in the tax ratio.

Changes in the tax rate fixed by law is another element influencing the tax ratio. If the corporate income tax rate is raised or lowered a few percentage points, the amount of tax on a given amount of taxable income would increase or decrease accordingly.

The more difficult kind of change, though, is a result of special provisions of the corporate income tax law. At times in recent years the law has permitted companies to take as a credit against taxable income a percentage of its new investment in plant and equipment. A company might take a relatively large tax credit under this provision in one year and a small credit in another.

The law also provides tax loss carry-forwards. That is, a loss in one year may be carried forward and applied against taxable income in another year. A company with tax losses in several past years might subsequently report taxable income but pay no tax because the past loss offsets the current income. Sometimes companies "buy" tax losses by acquiring a company that has operated at a loss and then apply the loss against the future taxable income of the combined companies. These vagaries of corporate income taxation often have a marked effect on the tax ratio and they may have implications for the future. Using up tax losses would increase taxable income and the tax ratio.

Tax rules concerning acceleration of depreciation permit a company to report a larger amount of depreciation expense in some periods than in previous periods by adopting methods that accelerate, and accordingly reduce, taxable income. The effect of accelerated depreciation on income taxes, however, is complicated by the fact that some companies permit the accelerated depreciation to "flow through" to taxable income as reported in published statements and others do not. Those who do not use the flow-through method show depreciation expense in statements to stockholders as it would be without the acceleration taken on their income tax returns, and then they credit the difference between tax paid and tax reported in published statements as "deferred income taxes," which appears as a liability reserve on the balance sheet. If that seems a bit complicated, it is.

THE CONCLUSION: ESTIMATES OF PROFITABILITY RATE

The conclusion of the study of the profit margin is of course an estimate of the future size and direction of change in profit margin. That conclusion, combined with the previous estimate of future asset turnover, provides the estimate of future rates of profitability.

When you come to an estimate of the probable profit margin for a company for several years in the future, you have the same problem as for other estimates—there are so many possible influences on that margin that you may hesitate to estimate margins very much different from those you have found in the historical record. But you have made a detailed and thoughtful analysis of a company and you must have an impression that its profit margin will change for better or worse. If you conclude that everything will go along about the way it has been going, you should have made an extrapolation and stopped.

Again, a proper regard for the uncertainties of all estimates of the future suggests that there should be a probability distribution of estimated profit margin ratios. The median would be the most likely figure, and other ratios on either side of the median would express the more optimistic and more pessimistic estimates. The range of such an estimated distribution and the weights attached to each ratio in the distribution serve to indicate your level of confidence in the median estimate. The greater the variance, the less your confidence. The distribution may be skewed one way or the other to indicate further your optimism or pessimism about future ratios being better or worse than your median estimate.

We now have estimates of the two relationships that determine profitability rates, that is, the asset turnover ratio and the profit margin ratio. When estimates of asset turnover and profit margin have been expressed as weighted frequency distributions, the profitability ratios can be calculated by multiplying AT_r and $PM - I_r$ horizontally to arrive at $P - T_r$. The average of the probability weights for the first two ratios may be used as weights for the third. Table 13–1 illustrates the method.

Distributions may, of course, be more elaborate. There may be more rates in the distributions to indicate the chances of higher or lower rates at relatively low levels of probability. Weights might be asymmetrical to show that you think the probability of rates higher than your median is greater than the probability of rates lower than the median. Each analyst has to decide for himself how far he wants to go with these distributions, and his

TABLE 13–1

The Weighted Distribution of the Probability Rate

AT_r		$PM - T_r$		$P - T_r$	
Ratio	*Probability*	*Ratio*	*Probability*	*Ratio*	*Probability*
220%	0.10	0.060	0.05	13.20	0.075
210	0.20	0.055	0.15	11.55	0.175
200	0.40	0.050	0.60	10.00	0.500
190	0.20	0.045	0.15	8.55	0.175
180	0.10	0.4000	0.05	7.20	0.075
	1.00		1.00		1.000

decisions may vary according to the kinds of stock with which he is dealing.

You can compute the value of the distribution of estimated after-tax profitability rates by multiplying each rate by its probability weight and summing the products. Thus the value of the $P — T_r$ distribution in Table 13–1 is 10.05. You can also compute the variation or standard deviation of the distribution as a measure of your uncertainty about the future profitability rate.

This process of estimating the asset turnover and profit margin rates brings us to the conclusion of the study of profitability of operations. We have an estimate of future rate of profit. But the rate of return on common equity capital and the rate of change in amounts of EPS from time to time are very much affected by the two financial policies of leverage and earnings retention. Study of these two policies and of the ultimate estimates of earnings, dividends, risk, and expected rate of return are the subject of the next chapter.

QUESTIONS AND PROBLEMS

These questions present the kind of data used in profit margin analysis. Answers may be inferred from whatever you know about the industries and companies. But you will learn more if you get additional information from company annual reports or from investment manuals or reference services. The data below are taken from *The Value Line Investment Service*. They are for the years 1967 through 1971. The first 3 years of this period were the years of strong expansion in the national economy, the fourth was one of recession, and the fifth was one of moderate recovery.

1. What possible explantions are there for the different patterns of change in profit margin for the two mobile home manufacturing companies for which the following data are presented?

Skyline Corp.					
Sales (millions)	\$69.7	107.7	181.2	211.0	252.4
PM_r	9.0%	10.6	11.5	11.6	11.5
Zimmerman Homes					
Sales (millions)	\$13.4	24.5	45.1	29.5	33.4
PM_r	8.4%	9.0	7.4	2.0	3.6

2. Two manufacturers of machine tools suffered during the recession of 1970–71, but one more so than the other. Why?

Cincinnati Milacron					
Sales (millions)	$273.6	281.1	293.1	270.0	242.3
PM_r	13.8%	14.4	12.6	8.7	3.5
Giddings & Lewis					
Sales (millions)	$85.2	100.2	103.4	95.1	48.8
PM_r	14.0%	12.5	9.0	0.4	(d)

3. Here are two companies generally classified as in the same industry. Their sales and profit margin experience has been quite different. You know something about their products. Can you infer possible reasons for differences in these data?

Philip Morris					
Sales (millions)	$904.8	1,109.8	1,142.4	1,509.5	1,852.5
PM_r	11.2%	12.1	13.1	13.1	12.7
General Cigar					
Sales (millions)	$220.6	235.5	246.1	265.3	270.2
PM_r	4.5%	4.7	5.5	6.0	5.2

4. The two companies listed below have similar lines of products; both are relatively large and well financed. But in the same period of years with the same conditions in the economy and in the industry, there has been considerable difference in the size and trends of their profit margins. What are possible explanations?

Burroughs Corp.					
Sales (millions)	$553.9	655.6	759.3	893.4	943.3
PM_r	20.9%	22.6	25.1	28.0	28.3
National Cash Register					
Sales (millions)	$955.5	1,102.2	1,254.6	1,420.6	1,465.7
PM_r	15.8%	14.7	15.2	15.1	14.0

5. Data for two major grocery chain stores are shown below. In the same kind of business under the same general economic conditions, the data are quite different. Why?

The Great A & P Tea Co.					
Sales (millions)	$5,459	5,436	5,574	5,664	5,551
Net income margin[a]	1.0%	0.8	0.9	0.9	0.3
Safeway Stores					
Sales (millions)	$3,361	3,686	4,100	4,860.2	5,359
Net income margin	1.5%	1.5	1.3	1.4	1.5

[a]For the present purpose the net income margin may be taken as the equivalent of the profit margin ratio.

14

Estimating Risk and Return

I. The leverage ratio
  A. Quantitative relationships
  B. The debt ratio
  C. The average cost of debt
  D. The equity capital ratio

II. The retained earnings rate

III. Putting it all together
  A. Projecting uses and sources of funds
  B. Projecting the primary financial relationships
  C. Explicit recognition of the uncertainty of estimates

IV. The expected rate of return
  A. Projections to infinity
  B. Projections for short time periods
  C. Calculation of an expected rate of return
  D. A distribution of expected rates of return

V. How good are these numbers?

When you have arrived at an estimate of the profitability rate for a company for a period of several years in the future, you have to come back to the other two of the three primary financial relationships. These relationships change chiefly as a result of management policy, but policy is, of course, affected by changes in all the financial circumstances of a company. But to carry the analysis to a conclusion about future change in earnings per share, we have to consider probable future change in the leverage ratio and in the retained earnings ratio.

THE LEVERAGE RATIO

The leverage ratio has been described as a measurement of the effect of use of funds from all sources of funds other than equity capital on the rate of return on equity capital. But changes in the leverage ratio are not just a matter of how much borrowed money and its equivalent is used in a business. There are several quantitative relationships that determine the leverage ratio. You can observe historical developments in these measurements, interpret them in the light of developments in the affairs of a company, and they try to estimate how they are likely to change in the future.

Quantitative Relationships

The several quantities that in combination determine the leverage ratio may be depicted by a simple tree chart such as we have used before.

Leverage ratio

1. The profitability rate on an after-tax basis
2. The proportion of total assets represented by non-current debt and its equivalent
3. The rate of interest on debt and its equivalent
4. The proportion of total assets represented by equity capital

FIGURE 14–1

The Relationships that Determine the Leverage Ratio

These relationships may be written in notation and the calculation of leverage ratio expressed as an equation. L_r has previously been used to mean leverage ratio, and $P - T_r$ has been used to mean the profitability rate. The proportion of total assets represented by non-current debt may be D / TA, and the proportion of total assets consisting of equity capital is EC / TA. The rate of interest is I_r. The leverage ratio equation is:

$$L_r = \frac{\dfrac{P - T_r - \left(\dfrac{D}{TA} \cdot I_r\right)}{\dfrac{EC}{TA}}}{P - T_r}$$

The formula is a way of describing a simple arithmetic calculation. Figure 14–2 presents essential data for illustration. Total assets are taken at \$100 so that the principal relationships may be seen easily. The profitability rate is 10 per cent. Current liabilities are shown in the figure because they have a leverage effect. They supply funds for assets at some cost. However, the rate of cost can not be determined from published financial statements and so this kind of leverage cannot be taken into account separately. The leverage effect, however, is reflected in the profitability rate; the calculation is not impaired. Non-current debt represents 36 per cent of total assets and the rate of interest is 3 per cent on an after-tax basis. Thus interest is at the rate of 1.08 per cent on total assets. $P - T_r$ of 10 per cent minus 1.08 per cent is 8.92 per cent on total assets after interest. The 8.92 per cent divided by 54 per cent provides a rate on equity capital of 16.5 per cent. Then EC_r divided by $P - T_r$ indicates a leverage ratio of 165 per cent.

If you substitute these relationships in the leverage equation, you have:

$$L_r = \frac{\dfrac{10\% - (36\% \cdot 3\%) = 8.92\%}{54\%} = 16.5\%}{10\%} = 165\%$$

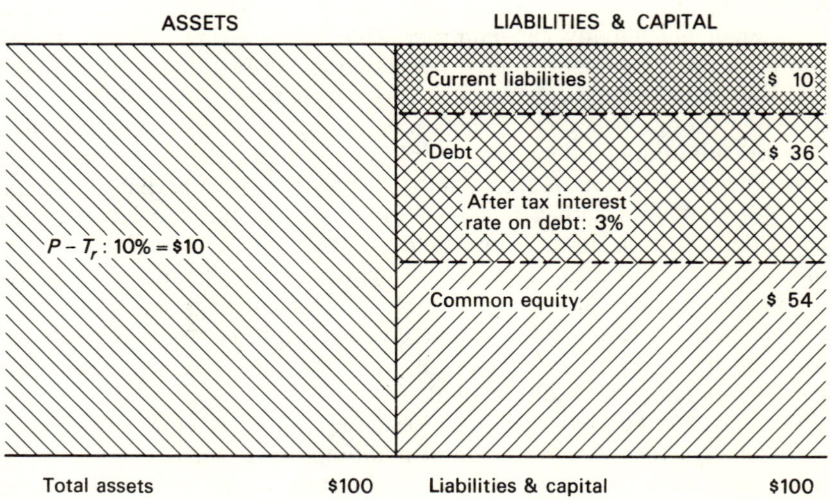

FIGURE 14–2

Data for Calculating the Leverage Ratio

The Debt Ratio

The approach to estimating the future non-current debt ratio is to examine the historical size of this ratio. This series for several past years tells what the company's capitalization policy has been and indicates any change in policy. Then you consider the probable implications of the previously estimated asset turnover ratio and profitability ratio for the future financial requirements of the company and how they are likely to be met.

Long-term lease rentals and preferred stock must be included in our definition of debt and their cost is a part of the rate of cost of non-current debt. Lease rentals would be capitalized at a rate estimated to be about the rate the company would have to pay on well-secured non-current debt, and that amount would appear in the debt section of a concept such as Figure 14–2. Lease rentals would, of course, be taken on an after-tax basis. Preferred stock is not debt, but it provides leverage when the stipulated dividend is paid and would be included in the debt section for our present purpose. The dividend on preferred stock is not a tax-deductible item, so no tax adjustment is required.

Some companies have well-established capitalization policies that seem likely to continue in the future in the absence of some important development in the business that would probably bring about a change. The simplest policy is one of no debt. Many companies abstain from long-term borrowing, take pride in having no funded debt, and are not likely to change that policy in the future time period with which we are concerned. So, the estimate would be a continued zero debt ratio.

The opposite kind of policy often found in the historical record is one of using debt up to a company's full debt capacity. Full debt capacity is the amount of debt a company can contract without impairing the investment rating of its bonds. Presumably the current bond rating is satisfactory to management. But to increase the debt ratio very much would likely bring a reduction in the rating. This concept gets more complex when a company has secured debt, subordinated debt, convertible subordinated debt, and preferred stock, or some combination of these kinds of securities. But the basic concept remains that companies with a policy of using debt to full capacity tend to maintain a debt ratio at about a constant level.

Many utility companies exemplify the debt-ratio-at-full-capacity capitalization policy. They have a relatively stable rate of earnings and they have learned by experience about the size of their debt capacity. As they amortize debt they replace it with new borrowing, and they increase debt about in proportion to increases in equity capital.

There have to be some qualifications, of course. A company that is expected to have a relatively high rate of additional investment in assets may raise its concept of an appropriate debt ratio even at the risk of lowering the quality of its bonds, because debt capital on an after-tax basis is usually cheaper than equity capital provided by new stock issues. Or, if debt is at about the maximum amount considered acceptable, there may be further financing by issuing preferred stock. Sometimes a company that has raised its debt ratio to a relatively high level to provide funds for expansion subsequently moves to a policy of debt reduction. The implication is that management is uneasy about heavy debt and wants to lessen both the leverage and risk. And sometimes a company reduces debt during a period when the need for funds is small in order to have unused debt capacity when there is again a need for larger amounts of funds.

The problem of estimating a future debt ratio is most difficult for companies that have considerable latitude in debt capacity and no very clearly established capitalization policy. In this situation you can develop a rough estimate of the amount of funds likely to be required over the next several years by referring to the previously calculated profitability ratios. In that section of the analysis you have an estimate of sales and of total assets for several years in the future. The increase in assets is the total amount to be financed. Depreciation expense will do no more than replace existing assets and may not be sufficient even to do that.

Retained earnings will help finance expansion of assets. You can see from the historical record the extent to which retained earnings have been used to finance expansion in the past, and you may have some idea by this time whether this source of funds is likely to be larger or smaller in the future. Some amount of funds may be obtained by an increase in current liabilities. The difference between total additional funds required and estimated funds from increase in current liabilities plus internal sources is the amount that will have to be obtained by external financing. If these sources of funds appear to be much less than sufficient, then new debt financing is a likely source because it is the cheapest source. Uncertainty about future financing may very well require a frequency distribution of estimates of the future debt ratio with different magnitudes based on different assumptions about future financial policy.

The Average Cost of Debt

When a company has more than one debt instrument (or leverage-type instrument) with different contractual rates, the cost of debt must be a weighted average after-tax rate. You can adjust contractual rates to an after-tax basis by multiplying the contractual rates by 1 minus the effective income tax rate. You compute the effective tax rate from published financial statements by dividing the amount of income tax for which provision was made in a period by the amount of taxable income for the period.[1] It may be something different from the statutory rate of the corporate income tax. Suppose, for example, that the effective tax rate is found to be 40 per cent and the contractual interest rate is 6 per cent. Then the after-tax rate is 6 per cent times

[1]The amount of taxable income and amount of income tax in published income statements may not be the same as the amount of taxable income and amount of tax actually paid or accrued. Since corporate income tax reports to the Internal Revenue Service are not public documents, you have to work with the published data.

(1 − 0.40), which is 6 per cent times 0.60, or 3.60 per cent. The same kind of adjustment can be made for lease rentals. The annual rate of dividend on balance sheet amount of preferred stock is the after-tax rate. The weights are the principal amounts as they appear on the balance sheet and the capitalized amount of lease rentals.

A company with $10,000,000 of bonds with a 6 per cent contractual rate and an effective tax rate of 40 per cent, and $6,000,000 of 7 per cent preferred stock, would have a weighted after-tax cost of leverage-type securities of 4.875 per cent. The bonds have a weight of 10 and the preferred stock, a weight of 6.

The average annual weighted cost of debt for the next several years will be affected by the amount of new debt contracted, the interest cost of the new debt, and the reduction in previously outstanding debt contracted at rates different from the new debt. You can think of a company's debt issues as "turning over," just as the bond portfolio of an investor turns over with the redemption of some issues and the purchase of others. You can estimate the amount of outstanding debt to be retired annually by referring to sinking fund provisions or other arrangements for repayment, and you know the interest rates on outstanding issues. You estimate the amount of new debt from the preceding consideration of financial policy in capitalization. The hardest part is to estimate the average interest cost of new debt. Forecasts of average yields on high-grade corporate bonds extending several years in the future may be inaccurate. Perhaps the safest course is to adopt a rate that is about the median of the rates indicated by economists in their forecasts.

The presence of convertible securities in a company's capital structure may complicate the problem of estimating both the debt ratio and the average cost of debt to the point at which it cannot be solved with any worthwhile degree of confidence. Convertible securities may be converted to common stock at any time the market price of the stock makes conversion attractive[2] and thus may be eliminated from both the debt ratio and the average cost of capital. Callable bonds may be called for refunding, or simply redeemed out of available funds. The likelihood of converting convertible issues must be appraised with regard to the conversion price, the current market price for the common stock, and whatever expectation you may have for future change in its price. The likelihood of bond refunding has to be judged on the basis of estimates of the future course of interest rates.

The Equity Capital Ratio

The amount of equity capital is total assets minus non-current debt and its equivalent, and also minus current liabilities. The additional variable is the amount of current liabilities as a percentage of total assets. You can use balance sheets for past years to compute the ratio of current liabilities

[2]Companies often force conversion of convertible securities by calling them for redemption at a time when the market value of the stock that may be obtained by conversion is greater than the redemption price of the bonds.

to total assets and use that historical series as a basis for estimating future change.

In most lines of business the ratio of current liabilities to total assets fluctuates with little trend. There is some usual amount of accounts payable that is related to amounts of sales, and some usual amounts of accrued current liabilities that are related to sales or to taxable income. The ratio may fluctuate cyclically around a mean for the past several years, and this record may be sufficient basis for estimating that the historical mean will be the best estimate for the future.

There are possible changes, however, and one may be able to foresee them. Frequently, a major component of current liabilities is notes payable to banks or other institutional short-term lenders. Sometimes these current liabilities increase in amount over a period of several years when a business experiences considerable sales growth and a corresponding increase in amounts required for accounts receivables and inventories. Very often, the next development is a recognition by management of the need to provide larger amounts of capital from long-term sources by selling long-term debt or equity securities. The funds from such sources are used to reduce current liabilities.

The retention of earnings policy will of course influence the amount and proportion of equity capital. Current liabilities may be reduced by funds from this source, or an insufficiency may contribute to an increase in short-term obligations.

It would be fatuous to think that anyone can estimate all of these relationships that determine the leverage ratio for any very long period in the future with anything like precision. But when an analyst has worked with a company and gained a fairly definite impression of management's policies and of the direction in which a company is moving, he may very well be able to foresee a change in the size of the leverage ratio that will have a significant effect on the future growth of earnings per share.

THE RETAINED EARNINGS RATE

The third of the primary financial relationships is the one most closely correlated with change in EPS. Therefore, it deserves most careful consideration.

The approach to estimating the proportion of earnings likely to be retained in the next several years is again historical. Just as the debt ratio for a series of years past indicates policy in capitalization, so the retained earnings ratio indicates retained earnings policy. How that ratio is likely to change in the future depends very much on your previous estimates of the financial development of a company.

The most common policy among companies with well-defined earnings experience is one of retaining percentages of earnings that may vary from year to year as earnings fluctuate, but that tend to vary around a median figure. The median is likely to be within the range of 40 to 50 per cent of earnings. But there are very different patterns to be found in different companies. Utilities tend to have a lower rate of earnings retention than industrials, ranging around 30 per cent. Rapid growth companies often pay no dividends, or nominal amounts, because their need for funds for expansion is great and their stockholders are generally much more interested in capital gains than in dividend income. Table 14–1 illustrates different types of dividend policies.

A change in retained earnings policy may very well be anticipated when there has been an earlier estimate of a significant change in rate of asset

TABLE 14–1

Types of Dividend Policies

Years: 1967–71	*1*	*2*	*3*	*4*	*5*
Industrial companies					
Eastman Kodak					
Earnings per share	$2.18	2.27	2.48	2.50	2.60
Dividends per share	1.05	1.14	1.25	1.32	1.32
Retained earnings ratio	52%	50	50	48	49
General Electric					
Earnings per share	$1.98	1.95	1.54	1.81	2.60
Dividends per share	1.30	1.30	1.30	1.30	1.35
Retained earnings ratio	34%	34	14	28	48
Proctor and Gamble					
Earnings per share	$2.05	2.15	2.30	2.60	2.91
Dividends per share	1.05	1.15	1.25	1.33	1.45
Retained earnings ratio	49%	47	46	49	50
Electric utility companies					
Commonwealth Edison of Chicago					
Earnings per share	$2.97	2.99	3.00	2.95	2.86
Dividends per share	2.15	2.20	2.20	2.20	2.20
Retained earnings ratio	27%	27	27	25	23
Consolidated Edison of N.Y.					
Earnings per share	$2.57	2.57	2.68	2.30	2.35
Dividends per share	1.80	1.80	1.80	1.80	1.80
Retained earnings ratio	30%	30	24	19	23
Pacific Gas & Electric Co.					
Earnings per share	$2.49	2.55	2.58	2.47	2.75
Dividends per share	1.40	1.45	1.50	1.50	1.61
Retained earnings ratio	44%	43	42	38	41
Growth Companies					
Marion Laboratories					
Earnings per share	$0.25	0.37	0.52	0.65	0.78
Dividends per share	0.04	0.06	0.12	0.12	0.17
Retained earnings ratio	83%	84	76	81	78
Skyline Corporation					
Earnings per share	$0.20	0.40	0.77	0.99	1.28
Dividends per share	0.07	0.07	0.11	0.16	0.20
Retained earnings ratio	65%	82	86	84	84

Source: *Value Line Investment Survey.*

growth. A higher rate of growth implies a higher retained earnings rate, because earnings retention is generally regarded by management as an excellent way to finance expansion. However, capitalization policy and management's concept of the desirability of debt financing enter into the financing decision. Actually, the debt ratio and the retained earnings ratio are both products of the apparent need for funds and the subjective judgement of management about the desirability of the two sources of funds.

A prospect for slower rates of asset expansion and a lesser need for funds may be a basis for expecting a lower retained earnings rate than in the past, especially when the earnings outlook continues favorable. Sometimes companies go through several years of relatively rapid expansion of assets and then the rate of growth slackens until the capacity of new plant and equipment becomes more fully utilized. At this point management may make a shift in financial policy in the direction of using more debt, which seems justified by the established earnings record, and of paying out a larger proportion of earnings.

PUTTING IT ALL TOGETHER

When you think about probable future changes in each of the financial policy ratios separately, you see that changes in any one of them influence the others. To avoid circularity you have to estimate them in order, using the historical data as a base. First is the after-tax rate of profit on total assets, then the leverage ratio, and finally the retained earnings ratio.

You can use amounts as they appear in the accounting statements, but it is easier to do the arithmetic if you reduce the data to amounts per share of common stock. Estimates in terms of a share of stock lead directly to estimates of earnings and dividends per share.

Projecting Uses and Sources of Funds

The typical business enterprise increases in size as time passes, if it is at all successful, because the total economy grows, sales increase, and assets increase. To work out the primary financial ratios you must first estimate the rate of increase in total assets and project as well as possible how the increase in assets will be financed. The sources of funds used for expansion affect the primary financial relationships with which we are concerned. One could foresee a shrinkage in a company's total assets, and the problem of estimating changes in uses and sources of funds would be the same.

Table 14–2 illustrates the projection of assets and the expected sources of funds for Hypothetical Company. All the data are on a per share of stock basis. The amount of total assets per share at the end of the year immediately past was \$100.

Let us assume that your previous work on the profitability ratios caused you to project growth in assets at the rate of 10 per cent a year compounded

TABLE 14–2

Expected Financial Growth on a Per Share Basis

	END OF LAST YEAR $t = 0$		*END OF YEAR 1* $t = 1$		*END OF YEAR 2* $t = 2$		*END OF YEAR 3* $t = 3$	
	Amount	*Percentage*	*Amount*	*Percentage*	*Amount*	*Percentage*	*Amount*	*Percentage*
1. Total assets per share	$100.00	100.0%	$110.00	100.0%	$121.00	100.0%	$133.00	100.0%
2. Current liabilities per share	10.00	10.0	11.00	10.0	12.10	10.0	13.30	10.0
3. Non-current debt	36.00	36.0	40.70	37.0	46.00	38.0	51.87	39.0
4. Common equity per share	54.00	54.0	58.30	53.0	62.90	52.0	67.83	51.0
5. Total liabilities and equities per share	$100.00	100.0%	$110.00	100.0%	$121.00	100.0%	$133.00	100.0%

annually. So the first line of the table shows assets per share increasing at that rate.

The latest balance sheet shows that 10 per cent of total assets is represented by current liabilities. In this instance there is no reason to expect that further increase in current liabilities will be at a rate greater or lesser than the rate of increase in total assets, so current assets at the end of each of the 3 future years are estimated at 10 per cent of year-end total assets. This does increase the amount of current assets and provides some additional funds.

Hypothetical Company has had a fairly high debt ratio in the past and you think that management will continue to rely on debt (or leverage-type instruments) in the future. Your corporate profile shows that management is aggressive, confident of the future financial success of the company, and well informed about the use of leverage. In view of the relatively high rate of growth in assets, it seems reasonable to think that the debt ratio will increase moderately. The table of projections shows the debt ratio increasing from 36 per cent at the end of last year to 39 per cent at the end of the third future year. This will provide almost one-half of the additional assets required. You can hardly hope to anticipate the exact pattern of debt financing, but these figures indicate that a substantial part of the asset growth will be financed with leverage-type instruments.

For Hypothetical Company the remainder of the funds to provide additional assets after use of debt is expected to come from retained earnings. The amounts of retained earnings required are the year-to-year increases in total assets minus the additions to current liabilities and leverage-type instruments. In preparing the table we started with the amount of equity capital per share at the end of the last year and added to it in each future year the amounts required from retained earnings to supply the remainder of the funds for asset expansion. You might have to make some trial projections to test the assumption that the amount of earnings for the common equity will be sufficient for this purpose, but for Hypothetical Company the relatively high rate of profit on total assets indicates that earnings will be sufficient. In this example the absolute amount of equity capital increases as a result of earnings retention, but the proportion of total assets per share represented by equity capital decreases slightly.

Projecting the Primary Financial Relationships

Now we have the projections necessary to develop the primary financial ratios, as shown in Table 14–3. The amounts of assets, liabilities, and equity capital for each year are averages of beginning and end of year amounts. This avoids the distortion that would come from applying rates for a year to end of year amounts.

In the earlier work on Hypothetical Company you estimated that the rate of profit on total assets would increase about 1 percentage point each year from 9 per cent in the past year to 12 per cent in the third future year. When these percentages are applied to the average amount of assets per share, the product is the amount of earnings per share before interest on debt.

TABLE 14-3
The Primary Financial Relationships on a Per Share Basis

	YEAR 1		YEAR 2		YEAR 3	
	Amount	*Rate*	*Amount*	*Rate*	*Amount*	*Rate*
1. Average amount of assets*	$105.00	–	$115.50	100.0%	$127.00	100.0%
a. Estimated $P - T_r$	–	10.0%	–	11.0	–	12.0
b. Amount of profit	10.50	–	12.70	–	15.24	–
2. Average amount of debt	38.35	–	43.35	–	48.94	–
a. Estimate of average debt rate	–	3.3	–	3.5	–	3.7
b. Amount of debt cost	1.27	–	1.52	–	1.81	–
3. Average amount of equity capital	56.15	–	60.60	–	65.36	–
a. Estimated earnings per share	9.23	–	11.18	–	13.43	–
b. Estimated EC_r	–	16.4	–	18.4	–	20.5
4. Leverage ratio ($EC_r/P-T_r$)	–	164.0	–	167.0	–	170.8
5. Amount of retained earnings	4.30	–	4.60	–	4.93	–
a. Retained earnings rate (RE_r)	–	46.6	–	41.1	–	36.7
6. Available for dividends	4.93	–	6.58	–	8.50	–

*Averages are of amounts at end of last year (from Table 14-2), at end of Year 1, at end of Year 2, etc.

The amounts of earnings per share required for interest on debt will increase not only because the debt increases, but also because you expect some increase in interest rates in the next several years. Some debt contracted earlier at relatively low rates will be amortized and new debt will be incurred at higher rates. The weighted average cost of debt on an after-tax basis, therefore, is estimated at 3.3 per cent in the first year of the future period, 3.5 per cent in the second, and at 3.7 per cent in the third year. The product of the average amount of debt at the average interest rate is the after-tax amount per share for interest.

Subtracting cost of debt from the amount of profit on total assets per share leaves the estimated amount of earnings per share. The equity capital rate is, of course, the amount of earnings per share divided by the average amount of equity capital per share. You can see in the table that estimated earnings per share increase from $9.23 in the first year to $11.18 in the second and to $13.43 in the third, which is an increase at an annual rate of approximately 20 per cent. And the rate of profit on equity capital increases from 16.4 per cent in the first year to 20.5 per cent in the third.

This relatively high rate of growth in earnings can be readily explained by the size and trend of the primary financial relationships. The estimated rate of profit on total assets is relatively high and increasing. The debt ratio, too, is high and rising, which provides a high and rising leverage ratio. With a high rate of return on equity capital, the amount of retained earnings required results in a moderate retained earnings ratio in the first year and a relatively low ratio in the third year. The relatively low retained earnings rate suggests that even if earnings per share are not quite so high as estimated, or if the growth in assets were a little more, the expected expansion of assets can be financed.

Explicit Recognition of the Uncertainty of Estimates

When you work out a set of estimates as we have done in these last two tables and emerge with exact numbers in dollars and cents for earnings and dividends per share, there is a natural tendency to think of them as precise statements. They are not. They are the product of a series of earlier estimates, all of which will prove inaccurate to some extent, except by coincidence.

You will find it a strong antidote to over-confidence to make a three-point distribution of estimates for each of the primary financial ratios for the first year of the 3-year period and see how the amount of estimated earnings per share varies. The three numbers for each of the ratios would be the highest estimate with, say, a 20 per cent probability, a median with a 60 per cent probability, and a low estimate with a 20 per cent probability.

In the example below (Table 14–4), we have estimated $P - T_r$ at 9, 10, and 11 per cent. The median of 10 per cent is the same as in Table 14–3, and other data not affected by the profitability rate are the same as in that table.

The different profitability rates make very significant changes in some of the numbers that follow. EPS at the median is $9.23, at the high the amount is $10.28, and at the low it is only $7.18. You could extend these high and low estimates to the second and third years and get a wider range of per share earnings. You could also calculate earnings per share using each estimated profitability rate with each of several estimates of the leverage ratio. The retained earnings rate has been a residual in this illustration, but in practice it, too, could be made to vary. You could have a matrix wherein each profitability rate would be combined with each level of the other two primary financial ratios and the data for each combination of primary ratios extended for several years.

If there is potential dilution of earnings per share by conversion of con-

TABLE 14–4

The Effect of Different Estimates of the Profitability Rate*

	Median	*High*	*Low*
1. Average amount of assets	$105.00	105.00	105.00
2. Estimated profitability rate ($P - T_r$)	10%	11%	9%
3. Amount of profit	$ 10.50	11.55	9.45
4. Amount of debt cost	1.27	1.27	1.27
5. Amount of equity capital	$ 56.15	56.15	56.15
6. Estimated EPS	$ 9.23	10.28	7.18
7. Equity capital rate	16.4%	17.9	12.8
8. Amount of retained earnings	$ 4.30	4.30	4.30
9. Retained earnings rate	46.6	41.8	59.9
10. Available for dividends	$ 4.93	5.98	3.88

*Median data are those for Year 1 in Table 14–3; data are on a per share of stock basis.

vertible securities or by exercise of stock purchase rights, there is a further element of uncertainty. You don't know at this point in time whether dilution will occur, or to what extent. The prudent course is to calculate the percentage dilution of earnings that would be caused by full conversion and exercise of rights and recalculate estimates of earnings per share on a diluted basis.

Obviously, these calculations could become very complex. You could make distributions with five estimates and you could use different sets of weights. You might use asymmetrical distributions of both numbers and weights to show that you think the probability of improvement is greater than the probability of deterioration. This would mean a lot of pencil-and-paper work, but with a computer a variety of estimates could be worked out and carried through several years. Eventually, of course, there has to be a subjective judgement about which figures are more likely to prove more nearly right than others. Computers do not give answers.

Now, at this point you have a distribution of estimated earnings per share for several years in the future. The variation of the numbers in the distribution for each year from the mean for the year may be taken as a measure of the uncertainty of the estimates. You could compute the variation or standard deviation of each distribution from its mean and take that number as a quantitative statement of risk. It would be a subjective estimate just as your projections of earnings per share are subjective. You also have projections of future dividends per share made by applying estimated retained earnings rates to estimated per share earnings.

These estimates of earnings and dividends and of the uncertainty of those estimates provide the inputs for the final step in appraising a stock, that is, the estimate of the rate of return it would provide if purchased at present price and held for a defined period of time.

THE EXPECTED RATE OF RETURN

The basic theory for valuing a stock, or calculating a rate of return, is that a stock is worth the sum of all future cash receipts to its owner discounted at a rate of return appropriate to the level of risk. One can take the market price as given, and the rate that discounts all future cash receipts to price is the rate of return on the stock.[3]

Projections to Infinity

If you are willing to project dividends increasing at a constant rate to infinity, you can use the formula $k = \frac{d}{p} + G_r$, in which k is rate of re-

[3]John B. Williams, *The Theory of Investment Value*, Cambridge, Mass., 1938, Harvard University Press. Reprinted by North-Holland Printing Co., Amsterdam, 1964, p. 55.

turn, d is dividends, p is price, and G_r is average compound rate of increase in dividends to infinity. Thus, if the amount of dividend at zero point in time is $1.00, the price at present is $20, and the expected growth rate of dividends is 5 per cent per annum, the rate of return is 10 per cent per annum. This assumes that price will continue to be 20 times the annual dividend. ($1 / $20 = 5% + 5% = 10%) The trouble with this concept is that hardly anyone is willing to project a rate of increase in dividends to infinity. An alternative is to project a rate for a limited period of years and to assume that the amount of dividend will remain constant from then to infinity.

Several scholars have developed tables that show the present value of future dividends increasing at a number of different rates for a number of different periods of years, then remaining constant from the end of the period to infinity, and discounted at a number of different rates. Tables are constructed on the basis of $1.00 of dividend per share per year in the year immediately ended. You can use these tables to find the statistical measurements that most nearly fit your expectations for rate of increase in dividends for duration of the period of increase, and for rate of discount. You read from the tables the rate that reduces the expected dividends to the current market price of the stock per dollar of current dividend.

The most elaborate of these tables are those prepared by Soldofsky and Murphy. Some of their tables show values for two different rates of increase in dividends—one rate for a period of years, a second rate for another period of years—and then zero rate to infinity. The table below shows present values at a 5 per cent rate of growth for different periods of years and different rates of discount.

Projections for Short Time Periods

For practicing financial analysts infinity is too long. Even 3 years is a long time, but it is a fairly common practice to estimate an average annual rate of increase in dividends for 3 to 5 years and a price at the end of that period. A simple method is to estimate the amounts of dividends for several years in the future, to estimate the market price at the end of that period of years on the basis of projected earnings or dividends per share, and then

TABLE 14–5

Present Values of Common Stocks per $1.00 of Dividend

Periods of years	*Discount rates*					
	5%	*6%*	*7%*	*8%*	*9%*	*10%*
5	$24.81	20.69	17.69	15.45	13.69	12.28
10	29.75	24.57	20.83	18.02	15.83	14.09
15	34.68	28.26	23.68	20.24	17.61	15.53
20	39.60	31.78	26.26	22.18	19.07	16.66

Note: The rate of increase in dividends is constant at 5 per cent annually for the indicated period of years and thereafter the amount of dividends is constant. Discount rates are at the head of each column.

Source: Robert M. Soldofsky and James T. Murphy, Growth Yields on Common stock—Theory and Tables, Iowa City, 19363, Bureau of Business and Economic Research, State University of Iowa, pp. 70–71.

to discount those future sums at an appropriate rate. The rate that produces a present value approximately the same as current market price is the expected rate of return. The present value formula for this purpose is:

$$MP_{1t=0} = \sum_{t=1}^{T} \frac{D_t}{(1+k)^t} + \frac{P_T}{(1+k)^T}$$

This method requires an estimate of market price at the end of the period of years. The notation on the left side of the equation means market price at the beginning of the first time period. In the notation to the right, *D* stands for dividends and *P* for price; *t* is time periods in which dividends are received and *T* is the entire period for which the estimates are made. In words, the market value at present time is the sum of dividends expected to be received in a series of future periods and the market value at the end of the periods discounted at a rate that reduces the sum of these present values to market price. The common practice is to estimate price relative to estimated earnings per share in the last year of the period for which rate of return is to be estimated. This is more a product of a traditional way of thinking than it is of modern valuation theory, but it is entirely practicable. However, it requires an estimate of the size of the price-earnings ratio for a stock at the end of the time horizon for which rate of return is to be estimated.[4]

The appropriate price-earnings ratio for a stock is determined by the expected rate of growth in per share earnings and the uncertainty of the projected growth of earnings. Stocks with high growth rates generally command high price-earnings ratios, and the greater the confidence of investors in the expected high growth rates the higher is the price-earnings multiple. Conversely, stocks with a record of slow growth in earnings or erratic fluctuation in earnings from year to year generally sell in the market at low multiples of their current earnings per share.

As a practical matter, you begin your thinking about what multiple the market is likely to apply to projected earnings per share for the stock you are studying by looking backward at its price-earnings ratios of recent years. You can divide the price at the end of each past quarter by amount of reported earnings for that quarter converted to an annual basis and develop a series of quarterly price-earnings ratios extending back over a number of quarters. This series shows the past pattern of market valuation relative to per share earnings. It reflects not only changes in the financial ability of the particular company, but also the broad swings in average market prices relative to earnings. It is likely to show higher ratios for periods when earnings were increasing and when market prices generally were rising, and lower ratios when the reverse is true.

[4]Price at end of period could also be estimated relative to the expected amount of dividend in the last year of the future period by capitalizing the dividend at whatever is considered an appropriate rate. This method is less commonly used because dividend yields on many stocks are small and the greater part of the rate of return is expected to be derived from price appreciation, which in turn is derived from increase in earnings, rather than from short-run amounts of dividends.

The base for estimating the most likely price-earnings ratio for the stock at the end of 3 years is an array of its quarterly price-earnings ratios for the past 10 quarters, or some other number of quarters that seems suitable for a particular purpose. This shows the median, or central tendency, of the distribution as well as the range from high to low. It is well to eliminate from the array extremely high or low ratios resulting from past erratic fluctuations in earnings or price. Then the question is whether this distribution of past multiples is likely to be valid for the future period with which we are now concerned. If not, how should it be changed? At this point you have to make subjective judgements, but you have a basis for them in your estimate of the trend and uncertainty of future earnings per share.

If the growth rate of earnings in the past period has been modest and if you expect an increase in the rate in the future, say from 4 per cent historically to 6 per cent, you would shift the whole array of past multiples upward. If the growth rate in the past has been 6 per cent and you conclude that it will continue to be about the same in the future but that earnings will be more stable and the growth rate less uncertain, you would also shift the array upward to reflect the lesser financial risk. You might conclude that a company is in a "turn around situation" in which earnings have recently declined severely, but are considered likely to improve markedly and become more stable in the next several years. Then you would estimate ratios at about the level that prevailed before the recent slump in earnings.

Obviously, a great deal of subjective judgement is required to make a distribution of probable future price-earnings ratios, but there are empirical historical data as a basis for judgement. You have the history of the particular stock. You may also have studies of past price-earnings ratios for large numbers of stocks grouped by growth rates of earnings per share and perhaps further divided into categories by estimated levels of risk.[5]

Calculation of an Expected Rate of Return

Perhaps the best way to bring this discussion to a conclusion is to estimate a future rate of return on a stock for a relatively short time horizon using hypothetical data. Your analysis of a company leads you to the conclusion that its earnings per share will increase at an average annual rate of 10 per cent for the next 3 years, and that the retained earnings ratio will be about 50 per cent. The earnings and dividends expected are shown in Table 14–6.

This stock has usually sold at price-earnings ratios of 15 to 16 times annual earnings, but its rate of increase in earnings in the past 5 years has been only about 7 per cent. If your estimate of a growth rate of 10 per cent for the next 3 years is justified, the price-earnings ratio at the end of that period will be significantly higher. You estimate it at a median figure of 18

[5]There is a vast literature on valuation of common stocks. The bibliography at the end of this book contains references to some of this work.

TABLE 14–6
Projections of Earnings and Dividends

	Last Year	*Year + 1*	*Year + 2*	*Year + 3*
E/S increasing at 10%	$2.00	2.20	2.42	2.66
D/S at 50% of earnings	$1.00	1.10	1.21	1.33

times per share earnings of $2.66 in the third year, which provides a liquidating value of $47.88 per share.

The current market price of the stock (at beginning of year +1) is $37.50 per share. By several trial-and-error calculations, you find that at this price the expected rate of return is between 11 and 12 per cent. The calculations might be set up as in Table 14–7.

By interpolation, the rate of return at $37.50 per share is approximately 11½ per cent.

A Distribution of Expected Rates of Return

We have illustrated the formulation of a one point estimate, but you know by this time that the realized rate of return at the end of the period may be quite different from the 11½ per cent rate you have estimated. It may be greater; it may be less. You would express your appraisal of the stock more completely by making a distribution of estimated rates of return.

You have tentatively projected the average annual rate of growth in EPS at 10 per cent. But it might be 9 per cent, or 11 per cent, or some other rate. If you use other rates, you get different numbers for earnings and dividends per share. You would use those several estimates as a basis for estimating rates of return. There would be smaller or larger amounts of dividends to be discounted. There would be smaller or larger amounts of earnings per share in the third year to be used as a basis for estimating market price at end of period. Finally, you would use different estimates of the price-earnings ratio to be applied to EPS in the third year. A P-E of 18

TABLE 14–7
Calculation of an Expected Rate of Return

Year	*Estimated dividend*	*Estimated liquidating value*	*Sum of cash flows*	*Present values at 11*	*at 12%*
+1	$1.10	–	$1.10	$ 0.99	$ 0.98
+2	1.21	–	1.21	0.98	0.96
+3	1.33	$47.88	49.21	35.97	36.98
Sum of present values				$37.94	$36.98

to 1 may be the most likely, but it could be 20 to 1 if developments are favorable, or 16 to 1 if they are not. The range could be even greater.

When you use different estimates of dividend amounts and of amounts of EPS to be capitalized at different P-E ratios, you emerge with a distribution of estimated rates of return. You would naturally apply probability weights to the different rates and conclude with a weighted probability distribution. The value of this distribution is the expected rate of return, and the variance or standard deviation of the numbers in the distribution is a measure of your uncertainty about your estimates. It is by definition a measure of your estimate of the risk level of the stock.

HOW GOOD ARE THESE NUMBERS?

When you have worked through a long process of statistical analysis and projection of prospects for a company, you have an estimate of the most likely *rate of return* and a *measure of risk.* Although these estimates are subjective, they can be compared with subjective estimates for other stocks developed in the same manner. They provide a basis for selecting individual stocks relative to other stocks, and serve as the input data for combining stocks in a portfolio to obtain maximum portfolio rate of return relative to portfolio risk.

But how good are these numbers? Do they have any predictive value? Are they useful?

It is easy to be cynical in answering those questions. You started with accounting data that are admittedly imperfect. You looked for patterns of change affecting profitability and estimated how these changes will develop in the future. Those projections were subjective judgements based on present knowledge. Even if a past pattern is distinct, you don't know that it will continue into the future or, if it does, how far. Future events that are completely unpredictable may change the course of earnings. In financial analysis, as in the physical sciences, there are unknown unknowns. It is much better to recognize the limitations of one's own work than to be deluded by numbers and statistical processes into thinking that you have exact answers.

When the limitations are clearly recognized, we can go on and say that estimates do not have to be exactly right every time in order to be useful. A professional financial analyst makes estimates not for one stock only, but for a number of stocks. His ability is properly measured by the outcomes of his entire set of estimates. Some conclusions may prove to be quite wrong and be more than compensated for by those that proved to be particularly right. It is the over-all results that count, and an analyst may achieve good results despite occasional gross errors.

If estimates for a stock indicate a favorable change that has not been anticipated by the market, either in level of risk or rate of return, they are useful. They enable an investor to buy a stock and realize a higher rate of return at a given level of risk than that generally afforded by the market. In terms of the market opportunity curve, he is enabled to achieve a rate of return better than that which marks the usual relationship of risk and rate of return provided by the market. The rate may be only a little higher, or it may be a lot higher. Or, if the expected change is a decrease in the level of risk, an estimate that proves only approximately right would enable an investor to realize a given rate of return at a somewhat lower level of risk than usually afforded by the market. Similarly, an estimate of change in the direction of a lower rate of return or a higher level of risk than expected by the market generally would enable one to shift funds to better investment opportunities.

Perhaps the greatest value of this kind of analysis is not in the accuracy of relatively long-term estimates at the time they are made, but in the framework they provide for observing and evaluating additional information as it becomes available. Your analysis is a statistical model setting forth your expectations. Each component is an estimate that you believed justified at the time you made it. Now, as time passes and further information comes into view, you may see that the justification for one of your estimates becomes weaker, or becomes stronger. You have the opportunity to revise it, and to revise other components of the model accordingly. If you can perceive the significance of new information either sooner or more accurately than others, you gain an important advantage.

QUESTIONS FOR DISCUSSION

1. A company has a relatively large debt ratio and its average rate of cost of debt is relatively high. The industry in which it operates is cyclically depressed, but there are now clear indications of recovery. Given the expected recovery, in what direction would you expect the company's leverage ratio to change? Would the change over the next 2 or 3 years be large or small? (Assume that the company's profitability rate will increase by at least several percentage points during these years).

2. After several years of increasing earnings during a period of cyclical expansion in the economy, the management of the company described in Question 1 has decided as a matter of policy to reduce its debt ratio by accelerating debt amortization. The objective is to repay one-half of the amount of debt over the next several years from internally generated funds. Assuming that this policy is carried out, what is the implication for the size of EPS in the future? What is the implication for the stability of EPS in the future?

3. Here is another company that operates in a stable industry and that has a record of comparative stability in its EPS. The company is in a strong cash position and it has no non-current debt. Management finds a lack of opportunity to employ the cash in the business at favorable rates of return. So the directors decide to pay out as dividends each year approximately the amount of EPS. Assuming that the company will continue to realize about the same profitability rate as in the past, what will be the trend in EPS?

4. A transportation company has financed its equipment chiefly by means of equipment trust certificates that mature serially year by year. Usually these issues are paid off over a period of 15 years. The company continues to buy new equipment and to finance in this manner. Interest rates have increased in the past year and economists predict a rising trend of market rates of interest for the next several years. If all else is equal, how would you expect the company's future EPS to be affected?

5. Should electric utility companies retain a larger portion of their earnings and finance their expansion to a greater extent by earnings retention? Your viewpoint of course is that of an investor in utility common stocks.
6. Amalgamated Manufacturing Company is a holding company that owns some twenty subsidiary companies engaged in manufacturing many different lines of products. The company's consolidated financial statements for the past 5 years show a steady increase in sales in current dollars at an average annual rate of 10 per cent. There have been no acquisitions of other companies during these years and none are expected in the future. With a summary of the consolidated financial statements before you, how would you go about estimating the total amounts of assets at the end of each of the next 3 years?
7. In the case of Hypothetical Company, we estimated an increase in the profitability rate from 10, to 11 and to 12 per cent. Now assume that the rate remains at 10 per cent in each of the 3 years. Use the other data given in Table 14–3 for amount and cost of debt and calculate the amount of earnings per share for the second and third years. Let the amount of retained earnings be the residual amount required to finance the expected growth in total assets.
8. You have been studying a nice, stable, uncomplicated merchandising company. Its record shows a growth in both sales and dividends at an average annual rate of about 5 per cent. You have made projections of earnings and dividends per share for the next 3 years and you have considerable confidence that these figures will prove to be about right. But you also observe that the price-earnings ratio for this stock has varied from as low as 9 to 1, to as high as 18 to 1. How can you take this variable into your estimate of risk and rate of return for this stock over the next 3 years?
9. What are the uses and limitations of the "growth yields" on common stocks developed by Soldofsky and Murphy (Table 14–5)?
10. Why do common stocks generally have a high level of financial risk?

IV

Investment Constraints

15

The System of Investment Constraints

I. The nature and function of investment constraints
    A. Limits lie in many directions
    B. The scope of analysis must be broad
    C. The use of negative thinking
    D. The areas where constraints exist
    E. A two-dimensional view of constraints

II. The investment income constraint in current dollars
    A. The range is from slight to severe
    B. An overall view of the problem
    C. To estimate the minimum expense budget
    D. Income from other sources
    E. The minimum investment income requirement

III. The minimum investment value requirement
    A. Principal values to provide income
    B. Principal values to support debt and contingent liabilities
    C. Plans for disposing of wealth

People are always eager to get on with the business of deciding what stocks to buy and watching what happens to them, especially after some exercise in financial analysis. But it is too soon to do that. You really don't know yet whether you should buy stocks; maybe bonds would better serve your purpose. If you are to buy stocks, what kind of stocks? Or, if bonds, what kind of bonds? Maybe you should own stocks and bonds in some proportions. If so, in what proportions?

If you are to perform the task of investment management rationally, you must have answers to these questions and to a great many more. The answers are investment policies, that is, predetermined decisions about the structure of the portfolio by kinds of securities and levels of risk. Success in investment management is highly dependent on the wisdom of policies and their faithful execution.

Investment policies in turn are based on a set of investment constraints. Constraints are conditions that limit assumption of risk. Thus, a prerequisite to determining policies is a study of all the financial circumstances and subjective judgements of the one whose funds are to be invested. Then policies are designed to fit the constraints.

THE NATURE AND FUNCTION OF INVESTMENT CONSTRAINTS

In our initial discussion of the basic problem of investment management, we said that the objective is to realize the highest possible rate of return from a securities portfolio at the highest acceptable level of risk. Constraints specify the maximum levels of risk in the securities portfolio. They are limits on risk, and also on the acceptability of the lower grades of securities in each of the desirability of ownership qualities. You might visualize a set of constraints as boundary lines around a field in which the investment operation is to be conducted. You can go so far in one direction in the effort to maximize returns, but no farther. And so far in another direction, but no farther. To go beyond the limits would expose an investor to the chance of greater loss than he can afford to accept, or to greater disadvantages in the desirability of ownership qualities than he can tolerate.

Limits Lie in Many Directions

Constraints are imposed by amounts of assets and liabilities and by amounts of income needed to provide for expenses. Initially you might think of an individual investor's financial circumstances as represented by a balance sheet and income statement. The balance sheet shows what assets he owns and what kind they are. It shows what liabilities they must support and sometimes be used to pay. Sometimes liabilities include contingent liabilities. The income statement for an individual indicates the amounts of funds available and the amounts required for expenses. For an individual, expenses are generally living expenses for himself or herself and for dependents, but in some instances the concept may be broader. In general terms, the difference between assets and liabilities is a margin for variation in the value of assets, and the relationship of amounts of income relative to expenses is a margin for variation in amounts of income.

More is involved, however, than the numbers from personal financial statements. People feel, they hope, they fear, they have aspirations and they get satisfactions in different ways. People are the center of the problem. You have to take account of subjective evaluations, and sometimes of emotional reactions.

Obviously, constraints are different for different individuals because their financial circumstances and their subjective judgements are different. There is sometimes, however, a tendency to skip over such differences and to try to assign people to general categories. A well-to-do business executive is said to be able to take "a businessman's risk," which seems to imply that he can assume high levels of risk. You may look more closely and see that the exact opposite is true because he is burdened with debt and has huge living expenses. A widow is supposed to be able to assume little risk; she should keep to conservative investments of the kind commonly recommended for widows and orphans. In fact, she may be so well endowed with funds from the estate of her late husband that she can afford to take a great deal of risk.

The Scope of Analysis Must Be Broad

The approach to analyzing investment requirements must be so broad that it brings into consideration everything that is relevant to risk and return in the securities portfolio. Generally, an investor has several kinds of assets other than securities. We are concerned with all of them, from his bank account to the building he owns. Each represents some level of risk and has some advantage or disadvantage in desirability of investment qualities. Risk in the securities portfolio is a component of risk in the entire set of assets. The riskiness of other kinds of assets affects the levels of risk that may be assumed in the securities portfolio. The marketability and taxability of assets other than securities has a bearing on the need in the securities portfolio for the higher grades of securities with these qualities.

It is important to understand that the risk level of a securities portfolio may raise or lower the average risk of the entire set of assets. A major question of policy is whether the average risk level should be raised, or lowered, and by how much. Similarly, the marketability or liquidity of the total structure of personal assets may be altered by the qualities of securities that go into the securities portfolio.

It is also important to see that the existence of debt, or even of contingent liabilities, adds to the risk of ownership of assets and may add to the size of total income, much as the use of borrowed money by a business firm provides financial leverage. Another major question is whether the risk level should be raised or lowered by increasing or reducing liabilities.

Any systematic review of an individual's personal assets and liabilities is likely to lead to a conclusion that the existing financial structure is not the best possible set of arrangements for the investor. More often than not, assets have been acquired by a series of disconnected decisions and whatever liabilities exist have been improvisations to meet immediate needs. Frequently, no provision is made for certain contingencies and for ultimate disposition of wealth. Such inadequacies and omissions should be remedied before you come to conclusions about investment constraints, because remedial action may change the conditions affecting constraints.

One national investment counseling firm, in a memorandum prepared for use within the organization, states:

> . . . the starting point in account management is an analysis of the client's overall investment position. In the case of individuals, consideration is given to their insurance programs, future retirement benefits, outside business interests, income requirements, tax situation and financial objectives. In addition to making investment recommendations, account managers work on estate planning, gift programs, creation of trusts and insurance programs and, in many cases, work closely with clients' lawyers, accountants and insurance agents.[1]

The Use of Negative Thinking

At this point we must think negatively, that is, we must be concerned with the probabilities that risks assumed will work out poorly for the investor. If we think of the several possible rates of return from a portfolio of securities as a probability distribution of rates, with some rates above the average of the distribution and some below, then our concern is with the below-average rates that have sufficient probability of realization to be significant. What are the possible consequences for the investor of realizing the lower rates in the distribution? Keep in mind that in the lower range of a distribution there may be negative rates.

As a beginning we can generalize that the limit of risk taking is the lowest rate of return that an investor can accept without serious financial or emotional injury. The terms in that statement must be subjectively determined. The lowest rate is whatever you estimate it to be. What constitutes serious injury in either financial or emotional terms is also an estimate. But you must have estimates and you must draw the line of investment constraints somewhere. You have to say that if the rate of return is no lower than such-and-such a rate, the investor can accept it; a lower rate cannot be risked.

If investments in securities were the only asset and if income from securities were the only income, the analysis of risk capacity would be fairly simple. You would have only to estimate the risk level of the securities portfolio. But for most investors the problem is complicated by ownership of other assets that provide returns and entail risk, and by income from sources not represented by tangible assets. The uncertainty of returns from other sources than the securities portfolio must also be subject to negative thinking. Mini-

[1]From a memorandum of Stein, Roe and Farnham. Quoted with permission.

mum rates or amounts from these sources enter into consideration of acceptable risk from securities.

We have been using the concept of total rate of return, which counts periodic income plus capital gains and losses as total return. However, investors generally make a sharp differentiation between income and changes in value of principal. They regard investment income as spendable, but usually consider that principal values must be reckoned separately. Therefore, in considering ability to accept risk we should differentiate between minimum rates of income and minimum values of principal.

We should also differentiate between returns in current dollars and returns in constant dollars, as we did in the study of investment risks. Both changes in interest rates and changes associated with the financial abilities of issuers affect the size and uncertainty of returns in current dollars, both of income and of principal. In this analysis it is not necessary to distinguish between the two causes of variation in current dollars. It is the size of returns in current dollars at the lower rates that concern us. And then there is the possible effect of inflation on returns in constant dollars and on investors' requirements both for income and for asset values in constant dollars.

The Areas Where Constraints Exist

There are several distinct areas, then, in which constraints exist, and there are also considerations that affect the need of investors for the desirability of ownership qualities of securities.

One area, clearly, is the need for some minimum amounts of *investment income in current dollars*, and a second is need for *minimum values of securities* at market prices. Sometimes one of these areas imposes the more severe constraint and sometimes the other.

These same areas influence purchasing-power risk. Historical experience indicates that some degree of price inflation must be expected in the future. So you convert amounts and values in current dollars to constant dollars at whatever rate of inflation seems likely, and consider such constraints as there may be in terms of *income and principal values in constant dollars*.

Risk as we usually think of it is a result of uncertainties external to the individual investor, that is, to variations in the total economy, in the profitability of different industries, and in the financial abilities of companies. But there are some conditions peculiar to individual investors that affect the level of risks that are acceptable.

One such condition may be termed *strength of tenure*. Tenure means ability to hold securities under the varying conditions of the future. Strong tenure means strong ability to retain ownership, and weak tenure means that there are discernible contingencies that would require liquidation of securities. An investor with weak tenure is at the mercy of the security markets; one with strong tenure is to some extent insulated from the fluctuations of market prices. Thus an investor with weak tenure is more likely to realize loss by being obliged to liquidate at some uncertain date than an investor who can sell any time he chooses.

Still another area in which conditions peculiar to individual investors may affect the acceptable level of risk is ability to select securities and to supervise a securities portfolio. We call this *quality of management*. If many selections of securities are made at random and if purchases and sales are made on randomly selected dates, some distribution of rates of return would result. It is generally presumed that investors with considerable expertise would obtain a better distribution by selecting securities on the basis of risk-return estimates and timing purchases and sales. Conversely, those with less ability would realize less favorable distributions, and the probability of obtaining rates in the lower end of the distributions would be greater. Poor quality of investment management must be considered a constraint on acceptance of risk.

There is a further condition peculiar to individuals that affects both ability and willingness to assume risk. It may be termed, for brevity, *the temperament of the investor*. It encompasses a variety of emotional and psychological reactions and subjective judgements that affect willingness to accept risk.

Finally, we must consider limits on ability to tolerate the lower grades of securities in *desirability of ownership qualities*. We have seen that securities of the lower grades, in such qualities as marketability, taxability, redeemability, and so forth, have disadvantages to their owners. Some investors can tolerate these disadvantages to a considerable extent, and by choosing issues of the poorer grades they may realize higher returns than on issues of the better grades. For other investors, however, the disadvantages of the lower grades imply greater costs than they can afford to pay for the opportunity to maximize returns. The specific questions, then, are: How much marketability does an investor need; How much advantage in taxability of returns; and so on, through the other desirability of ownership qualities.

A Two-Dimensional View of Constraints

One might visualize the problem of establishing constraints on the ability of an investor to strive for the larger returns on investments as a figure created by drawing arcs between radii extending from a central point, as in Figure 15–1. Each of the segments of the circle marked off by the radii represents an area of limitation. Thus, one segment represents ability to risk adverse variation in income in current dollars; another segment refers to ability to risk depreciation of principal in current dollars; another refers to quality of management, and so on. The arcs are boundary lines; they show about how far an investor's circumstances will permit him to go in the direction of lower-grade securities. The farther the arc from the center of the circle, the less restrictive is the constraint. When an arc is near the center, it indicates that the constraint is severe.

This kind of geometric figure not only helps to describe the general concept of a number of limitations that must be taken into account in formulating investment policies, but it may also be used to summarize the major conclusions drawn from the entire analysis and to put them in perspective.

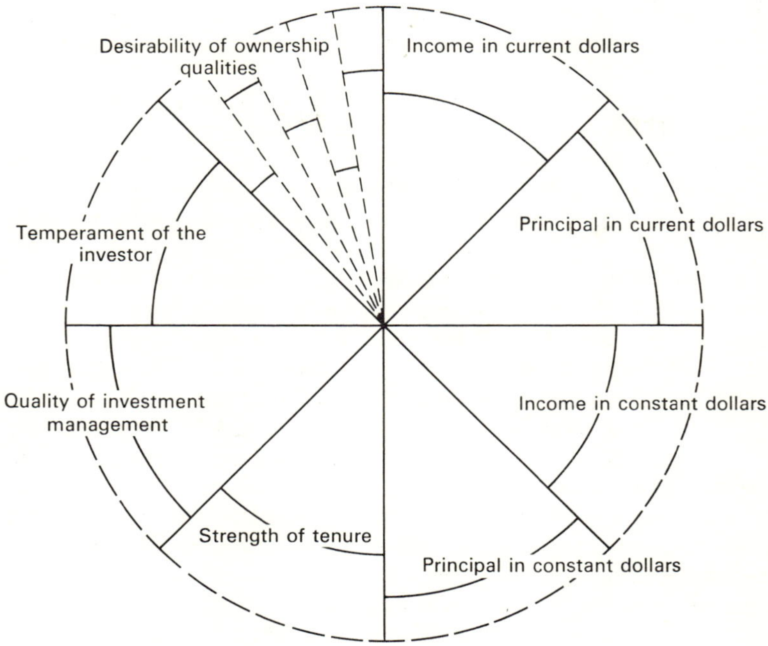

FIGURE 15–1

The System of Constraints

It is important that investment policies be formulated with all the constraints in mind. Sometimes one is more restrictive than another and sometimes a policy consistent with one limitation is inconsistent with another. There may have to be compromises between conflicting considerations in developing a complete program of investment policies.

THE INVESTMENT INCOME CONSTRAINT IN CURRENT DOLLARS

Among individual investors financial circumstances affecting the investment income constraint vary so widely that almost any generalization is open to question and any system of analysis broad enough to bring into consideration all that bears on the severity of the constraint may become too involved. A saving condition is that once the general approach to the problem becomes familiar, the chief limiting circumstances can be readily identified.

The Range is From Slight to Severe

The most common situation of individual investors is one of little or no constraint in the form of need for investment income. Most individuals earn their living by their employment, or derive it from earnings of another member of the household. Income from investment is usually accumulated and added to the principal amount invested.

The Census of Share-ownership published by the New York Stock Exchange shows that the median annual household income of owners of stocks was $13,500 in 1970. These data also show that almost one-half of all individual shareowners are adult females,[2] which means either that they have become financially liberated, or that they have been treated kindly by male chauvinists.

Data compiled by the Investment Company Institute show that almost 30 per cent of shareholder accounts of mutual fund companies have provision for automatic re-investment of dividends. The fact that these investors elect not to receive dividends, but rather to re-invest them, is evidence that they do not currently need investment income. The mutual fund data also show that about 40 per cent of shareholder accounts are owned by investors who regularly add to their purchases. Funds for additional investment must be derived from income in excess of their current requirements.[3]

There are, however, many people who rely on investments for all or part of their income. Most numerous in this category are retired people who have saved and invested during their working lives and in their later years have investment income as a supplement to social security benefits and often as addition to retirement income from an employer's pension fund. There are also the widows and orphans, the sick and the disabled. Sometimes they are beneficiaries of security investments owned directly, or held for their benefit in trust funds or guardianship accounts. For all of these people the investment income constraint may vary from slight to severe.

An Overall View of the Problem

The general problem is to invest in securities in such manner that the amount of investment income, together with whatever income there may be from sources other than the securities portfolio, will be sufficient under the least favorable circumstances that can be visualized to equal the minimum amounts required for living expenses and any other expenditures that may be required. Or, minimum investment income plus minimum income from other sources must equal minimum expenses.

If income from security investments is the sole source of income and ordinary living expenses is the sole use of income, the problem appears in its simplest form. The minimum amount of expenses is the minimum amount of investment income required. The rate of income on the principal amount invested that will provide the required amount of income is the lowest acceptable rate of income return on the securities portfolio.

For example, an elderly couple living in retirement has no income other

[2]*The 1971 Fact Book*, New York, 1971, The New York Stock Exchange, p. 47.

[3]*The Mutual Fund Fact Book, 1971*, Washington, D.C., 1971, Investment Company Institute, p. 26.

than that from security investments and their income requirement is their day-by-day living expenses. Their minimum expense budget is $10,000 a year and they have an investment fund with a principal value of $200,000. They require a minimum income return from securities at the rate of 5 per cent yearly. When you think of the dividend and interest yields that have been obtainable in the security markets in recent years, you realize that the 5 per cent minimum requirement is a severe constraint. If their investment fund was twice as great, the minimum rate of income return would be half as great and the constraint would be very much reduced.

Of course, the financial affairs of individual investors are not usually so simple. The minimum expense budget, or MEB, may change as time passes. Outlays of funds may be required for purposes other than regular living expenses. On the opposite side, there may be income from sources other than the securities portfolio. Income from these other sources may be applied to expenditures and reduce the dependence on investment income. But amounts of income from other sources may also vary and variations must be taken into account insofar as they can be estimated. There are two variables, then, total income and total expense. And on each side there are components that vary. The problem is to invest in securities in such a way that under least favorable conditions affecting income, amounts of income will cover expenses at a minimum level.

To Estimate the MEB

There is no objective scale or yardstick by which a minimum expense budget can be calculated. It is mainly a question of the standard of living to which the investor is accustomed. But the emphasis here is on a minimum amount, the amount that would be considered a "bare bones" living. It is also a question of the extent to which an investor is willing to establish a minimum that would substantially reduce his current living standard. One man may be capable of accepting a concept of a minimum expense budget much lower than his current level of spending. Another may be psychologically incapable of conceiving a lower standard. Thus you start with the present expense budget and estimate how much it could be reduced without real hardship to the investor financially and emotionally.

Frequently you can estimate with some confidence future changes in the minimum expense budget, and future changes should be taken into account insofar as possible. Change in the price level will of course affect the size of expenses, but at this point we will assume a constant price level and consider requirements in constant dollars as a separate constraint.

For families there is a pattern of change in living expenses that is much the same for all of them in the lower- to upper-middle income categories. For a young family the MEB constantly increases, and most young families consider their present standard of living a "bare bones" living. There is almost always the mortgage loan on the house with its requirement of periodic payment of interest and principal plus property taxes and insurance. There may be installment payments on various kinds of consumer goods. Life insurance premiums absorb some part of the family income, and there may also be contributions to an employer's pension fund. Sometimes there are elderly parents to be provided for, at least in part. The typical middle-class family expects to send its children to college, and when they go away to school the family budget swells. A minister with great sensitivity to the troubles of his people once prayed, "God help the middle-aged, for they must support both the young and the old."[4]

Fortunately, as the MEB grows, the earned income usually grows. The young husband moves up the establishment ladder and sometimes the young wife also earns an income. In the young family, whatever security investments there may be are usually a result of gift or inheritance. Income from securities may serve only to supplement earned income, or to provide for educational expenses, or to cover unusual medical expenses. For the individual investor or investment advisor the task is to establish clearly the extent of dependence on investment income. This task requires careful examination of family financial circumstances, consideration of plans for the future, and evaluation of subjective attitudes toward personal financial matters.

The pattern of change in the family budget continues as parents become middle-aged and elderly. Children grow up and leave home. Expenses attributable to them are eliminated from family living expenses. There is a milestone in family finance when the mortgage on the house is finally paid off. Older people become less active socially and expenses related to this area diminish.

When the husband retires from his business or profession, there is a considerable readjustment in both the income and expense sides of the family budget. If there is a working wife, she usually retires at about the same time. Earned income is replaced by social security benefits, retirement income, and by investment income. Even the people who were not able to save while their children were dependent on them generally accumulate investments of some kind and size during their later income-earning years.

Living expenses for a retired couple are usually much less than they were before retirement. Sometimes people move to a smaller house or to an apartment. One car may become sufficient rather than two. The cost of clothing and transportation diminishes when people no longer go to the office, or place of employment. By this time life insurance is likely to be paid up, so that there are no further premiums. A lower level of income and larger personal exemptions means lower income tax payments. Medical expenses may increase as people get older, but there are medical expense insurance programs offered by the federal government and by private insurance companies.

So it is entirely possible to arrive at a minimum expense budget for a family at the present time and to project it at least a few years into the future. An individual doing it for himself knows his own circumstances, or at least can find out about them with reasonable effort. An outsider serving as an advisor would have to probe rather deeply into financial affairs generally con-

[4]From an unpublished sermon by Dr. W. Douglas Rae, at the time Minister at the First Baptist Church, Bloomington, Indiana.

sidered private and he would have to learn the financial expectations of the family he advises. But it can be done with some approximations, and projections can of course be revised from time to time.

Income from Other Sources

We have mentioned several possible sources of income other than investment income, but now it is time to examine systematically income from sources other than the securities portfolio. The size of this income is important because it affects the size of investment income required, and the stability of other income affects the need for stability of investment income. For brevity and with some irregularity of grammar, let's call this other income IFOS (income from other sources).

The amount of IFOS at the present time can easily be ascertained. There is earned income, there may be income from proprietary investments, and after a time there is retirement income. In our earlier example we had an elderly couple with a MEB of $10,000. If retirement income and social security provide, say, $5,000, then the minimum amount of investment income required is $5,000. And it is this amount that sets the constraint on investment income.

Earned income tends to vary over relatively long periods with the age and seniority of individuals. A young person starts near the bottom of the salary schedule and gradually moves up to whatever level his or her abilities permit. Some people reach this level early and further increases in earned income result chiefly from upward revision of the pay scale. Others advance much further and earned income advances substantially through middle age and even up to the point of retirement.

There are many variations in the earned income pattern. Professional athletes and most people in the theatrical arts rise to their maximum earnings level relatively early in life and the decline from the peak may be both sudden and severe. Frequently, people who have enjoyed early success in one kind of employment find a second career that provides a smaller but more stable income. Employed women often interrupt their employment to have children and later return to their careers.

The earnings of some people fluctuate with the business cycle, and this is important because it is the minimum level of this kind of income that is important for the investment income requirement. Salesmen who are compensated largely or entirely on the basis of sales volume are an obvious example of earned income instability. But in a period of severe business recession it is not uncommon for salaries to be reduced at the management level and for people to be reassigned to positions at lower salary levels.

There may be little uncertainty in job tenure, or there may be considerable. Civil service employees, for example, are rarely discharged, but employees of state and local governments who owe their appointments to political patronage may find themselves unemployed after the next election. In private business job tenure is affected by the cyclical stability of the company that provides employment. Companies in some industries have pronounced swings in their level of activity as business expands and contracts. Usually they are obliged to reduce the number of their employees when business is poor. In any very severe or prolonged recession termination of employment may reach well up into the echelons of management. And sometimes older employees at the top management level are obliged to retire earlier than they expected.

One uncertainty is that of life itself. When life ceases, earned income ceases. No one knows the time of his exit from this world, but there are mortality statistics that indicate the probabilities. A man at age 60 is 15 to 20 times as likely to die within the next year as a man aged 30.[5] The general health of an individual of course affects his longevity, and some occupations are more hazardous than others. A long illness or prolonged disability are hazards to earned income.

For many people *income from proprietary-type investments* is an important source of income. A proprietary investment is any kind of asset owned entirely or in part by an individual and managed by the owner either singly or with others. All over the country there are literally millions of small business enterprises owned by one individual or one family. They may or may not be incorporated; when incorporated the ownership is represented by unmarketable securities. For the man who owns and runs his own business, the income from the business may be both salary and return on investment, and the difference between the two may be somewhat arbitrary.

Another common type of proprietary investment is real estate. Many individuals own commercial buildings, apartment houses, residential properties, and even undeveloped land. Some people own farms, motels, marinas, and fishing camps.

The uncertainty of future amounts of income from proprietary-type investments is part of the problem. Little can be offered by way of valid generalization. It might be said that direct ownership of such assets is roughly equivalent in uncertainty to returns from common stock, but that leaves a broad range of uncertainty. Much depends on the nature of the asset. Income from commercial property leased for a long term to financially responsible tenants may be no more uncertain than income from a bond. Income from a small business in a cyclical industry may be even more uncertain than income from a speculative stock. Farms owned by absentee owners often provide widely varying amounts of income and sometimes they are operated at a loss. Undeveloped land may be a source of expense rather than income, and future returns may be both remote and uncertain in amount. The riskiness of assets in this category is also affected by the amount of debt used to finance them. A very large mortgage loan or term loan to finance a proprietary enterprise or the ownership of real estate may magnify the risk several times. Risk is also affected by the management ability of the owner, which may vary widely.

You have to appraise the uncertainty of income from each proprietary

[5]*Life Insurance Fact Book*, New York, 1971, The Institute of Life Insurance, pp. 106–107.

investment separately, much as you would analyze stocks and bonds for risk. But the focus must be on minimum amounts that are likely to be realized over a considerable period of future time. The minimum amount of income from these investments, together with the minimum amount of earned income, affect the minimum amount of income required from security investments.

When *retirement income* is something for the future, its size and uncertainty come into consideration. Most major private and public employers now have pension plans for their employees, and most employed persons look forward to some amount of retirement income. There is often a disposition to think that future retirement income is something very well assured. This may not be true. At least the question of uncertainty of retirement income should be considered.

It is possible that right to future retirement income may be lost and, even if it is not, amounts to be received in the future may be uncertain. Retirement income often is based on salary or wages in the last several years of employment. Since the base is not known, the amount of pension is unknown and has to be estimated on the basis of probable future salary levels. Some plans require a number of years of employment before an employee is eligible to participate. All too often an employee leaves one employer for another and finds that he leaves behind all rights to income and to assets from the pension fund in which he had participated for years. He has to start over again with the new employer. The expectation of a pension when retirement comes should not be built into an individual's personal financial planning without examining some of these uncertainties.

Almost everyone is now covered by the *federal social security program*, but future amounts are uncertain. A principal variable is the average amount of earnings on which the social security tax has been paid over a long period of years. Other variables are age of retirement and existence of a spouse or dependent children when benefits are received. Amounts of benefits are now related to change in the price level with adjustments made whenever the price index increases 3 per cent from one year to another.

When you have examined all possible sources of other income for an investor, you have estimates of minimum amounts that can reasonably be relied on even under the most adverse circumstances that may be expected in the next several years. The minimum amount of IFOS is deducted from the minimum expense budget to arrive at the minimum investment income requirement for the securities portfolio. The securities in a securities portfolio should represent an average level of risk that is not likely to result in amounts of investment income less than the difference between the MEB and total IFOS.

The Minimum Investment Income Requirement

It is the size of this minimum investment income requirement (MIIR) relative to the principal amount invested in securities (PRIN), that determines the severity of the investment income constraint. If MEB minus IFOS is zero, there is no MIIR and therefore no constraint in this area; the investor has no need for investment income.

If MIIR is a small percentage of PRIN, the way is open for investment in more risky securities at expected rates of income well above that small percentage. The difference between expected rates and MIIR as a percentage of PRIN is the margin for shrinkage in investment income under adverse conditions. For example, if MIIR is 2 per cent of PRIN, you might invest in a well-diversified portfolio of stocks of well-established companies with a record of continuous dividend payments to yield, say, 3½ or 4 per cent. You have a margin for such reduction in dividend payments as might be experienced during a future period of business recession. But need for a larger percentage rate of income would impose a stricter constraint. If MIIR equals 5 per cent of PRIN, you could obtain that rate of yield from bonds but you could not afford the risk of common stocks even if current dividend yields were at 5 per cent or even a little higher.

This kind of analysis sometimes leads to the conclusion that the principal amount invested, or to be invested, in securities is not large enough to provide the required amount of investment income. If the minimum amount of investment income required is $5,000 and the total amount for securities investment is $50,000, you have a minimum rate of 10 per cent. There is no way to invest that will provide a minimum amount of income in the form of interest or dividends at that rate at a low level of uncertainty. Sometimes in such circumstances there is a disposition to buy risky securities in the hope that income plus capital gains will provide the required rate. That hope may not be fulfilled and there is a chance of disastrous loss.

THE MINIMUM INVESTMENT VALUE REQUIREMENT

Most individuals who invest in securities are sensitive to changes in market prices. Many open their morning newspapers first to the financial pages to see how their stocks are doing, and the plus or minus numbers they find start the day off well or poorly. Whatever the pleasure–pain reaction, these day-by-day changes in market prices are of no great significance for investment returns or investment constraints.

There are, however, valid limits on the ability of investors to risk depreciation in market prices of their securities, just as there are limits on the minimum amount of income needed from the securities portfolio. The limits on decline in market values are imposed by the use or uses the values must serve. You have to learn what the uses are and how they affect the minimum investment value requirement.

There are many investors who look to their security investments only for income and have a minimum investment value requirement only as principal is required to provide income. But in some instances the market value of securities serves to support personal debts or contingent liabilities for future cash outlays, and some individuals have plans for eventually disposing of their wealth that affect the value requirement.

Principal Values to Provide Income

When the investment income requirement is the governing constraint, investors can be largely indifferent to the usual cyclical fluctuations in average prices for general categories of securities, provided their portfolios are well diversified as to risk and provided there is little chance that they will be forced to liquidate securities under adverse market conditions. This does not imply that investors should be unaware of such price changes or oblivious to opportunities they provide for improving the total rate of return.

Even income-oriented investors must be concerned with changes in market prices of the issues they own. Sometimes a decline in prices for individual issues relative to average market prices signifies deterioration in the financial abilities of companies to make the usual payments of income. Sometimes entire industries experience declining earnings because of conditions peculiar to those industries. Sometimes companies report declining earnings as a result of their own particular misfortunes. These financial adversities may not be remedied by the next upward movement of the business cycle. They cause market values to depreciate and eventually income payments to decline.

When the purpose to be served by principal amounts is the production of income, the minimum investment value requirement is the amount of principal that will provide the necessary investment income. If principal is lost by price depreciation and there is no recovery, then a source of income is lost. The severity of the market value constraint, then, is a function of the income constraint. If there is presently a large margin of investment income over the minimum amount of investment income required, there is also a large margin of principal value over the minimum value requirement. Similarly, a small margin of income means a small margin for risking principal values.

Principal Values to Support Debt and Contingent Liabilities

Most individual investors who are affluent enough to own even a modest portfolio of securities do not have debt that is significant for the minimum investment value constraint. There may be a mortgage on the family residence that is supported by the value of the house and paid from earned income. There may be installment debt to be paid off from wages or salary. There are exceptions, however, and the exceptions are important. Some investors do have substantial amounts of personal debt, or contingent liabilities, that depend to some extent on the values of securities owned. Such liabilities affect the minimum investment value requirement.

Sizable personal debts arise most frequently from personal borrowing to finance proprietary-type investments. Investment in real estate is commonly financed to a large extent by borrowing. The value of the property may support the debt, but the willingness of a lender to lend on favorable terms may be influenced by the size of a borrower's net worth represented in some part by the value of his securities.

It is not at all uncommon for the owner of a small business to borrow money on his own personal credit to provide funds needed by the business. An alternative arrangement is a loan to such a proprietary-type business endorsed by owner and spouse. An endorsement is a personal guarantee of debt. If there are several principal owners of a business, all of them and their spouses may endorse a loan to the business. The result is a contingent liability that becomes an actual liability only if the business firm fails to pay, but it should be taken into account in the system of investment constraints because the value of such guarantees depends on personal wealth and because sometimes guarantees have to be made good by payment of debt.

The contraction of debt and assumption of contingent liabilities associated with proprietary-type investments are alternatives to the sale of securities. The investor chooses the borrowing alternative because he doesn't want to disturb his securities portfolio. The cost of borrowed money may be less than the rate of return he expects from his security investments, or he may want to postpone the realization of capital gains that would be taxed, or he considers that the securities portfolio also serves other purposes that are important to him.

There is another kind of contingent liability that exists for everyone who has even a moderate amount of wealth. That is the contingent liability for payment of estate and inheritance taxes and expenses of estate settlement after death. The amounts that will have to be applied to these taxes and expenses at some time in the future is uncertain, especially for individuals who are relatively wealthy. If such amounts seem likely to be large, estimates can be made by lawyers and tax accountants after the task of estate planning has been completed.

You can evaluate the significance of debt and contingent liabilities for investment constraints by putting them into a personal balance sheet. On the one side are all personal assets, and on the other is debt. Contingent liabilities, even if they may be only roughly estimated, should be treated as actual liabilities. The greater the difference in total amounts, the less is the influence of debt on the minimum investment value constraint. When debt is small relative to total wealth, it may be supported entirely by assets other than securities, so that there is no minimum investment value requirement for the securities portfolio. But when debts and contingent liabilities are large relative to assets, the opposite is true; some market value in securities may be necessary to support debt. That value would be the minimum investment value requirement.

In this kind of analysis the uncertainty of values that may be realized from proprietary investments is an important consideration. The greater the uncertainty of those values, the greater the need for stability in market values of securities. Typically, proprietary investments are not readily marketable and the values at which they are saleable can only be estimated. It is one thing to say that a piece of real estate is worth so much, or that ownership of a retail store has such and such a value on the basis of its record of assets and earnings, but it is often quite a different thing to realize those values when assets are offered for sale. The conclusion of course is that proprietary-type investments should be valued conservatively in estimating a minimum value requirement for the securities portfolio.

Plans for Disposing of Wealth

The old adage, "You can't take it with you," states a condition that affects investment requirements for many investors, particularly those of considerable wealth but even for many of moderate means. This topic leads directly into estate planning, which is a large and complex subject and is treated in general terms in a subsequent chapter. It is sufficient to say at this point that the intentions of investors to use their wealth at some time in the future for the benefit of individuals or for institutions of an educational or charitable nature should be taken into account in the analysis of investment constraints.

Investors may provide for members of their immediate family by gifts or by creation of personal trusts while they live, or they may defer the transfer of property for this purpose until after their death. Trusts established while the trustor is living may be revocable, or irrevocable. There may be important differences in the taxation of both income and principal resulting from the time and method of making provision for dependents.

It has become a fairly common practice in modern society for people to give some part of their wealth to what are sometimes called "do good" organizations. Some very wealthy citizens and some who are only moderately wealthy create their own charitable foundations to receive their gifts, to invest principal, and to apply the income (sometimes the principal, too) for the purposes prescribed by the founder. It is not necessary, of course, to have a personal foundation. Most eleemosynary institutions have ready-made arrangements for receiving gifts and bequests by will. Colleges and universities have their own foundations; churches and hospitals often have general trust funds to which contributions may be made.

Perhaps the point to be stressed in concluding this discussion is that you may have to look in several different directions to discern conditions or circumstances that affect the minimum investment value requirement. Not all conditions appear in a personal financial statement. An apparent lack of need for market values to support debt may become a considerable need for stability of principal when income requirements and plans for disposing of principal are fully examined.

QUESTIONS FOR DISCUSSION

1. It is sometimes said that individuals should invest a sizable percentage of their investment funds in bonds of good investment quality and the remainder in diversified common stocks. The bonds are said to serve as a "backlog" and the diversification takes most of the risk out of owning common stocks. Comment critically on this concept of investment policy.

2. George Huntington is a self-made man. He invested a very small amount in a grocery store when a young man. By hard work, good sense, and some fortunate decisions he retired at 65 owning stock of a chain grocery company with a market value of $10 million. Recently, he created trust funds for his seven grandchildren, all under the age of 18 at the present time. He wrote into the trust instruments a provision that the trust funds shall be invested only in common stocks. What do you think of that?
3. James Jordan owns and manages a small machine shop that manufactures several small but very specialized components for computer main-frames. Three companies buy his entire output. He makes a good living from this business but the business is his only asset except his house. However, his wife recently inherited from her father a portfolio of high-grade corporate bonds with a market value of $200,000. If you were investment adviser to the Jordans, would you leave that money in bonds?
4. The Mr. Huntington mentioned above has made a will in which he leaves everything except the $1,400,000 he has already put in trust for the grandchildren to his wife, if she survives him, and to his three children equally if she does not. His estate consists almost entirely of the stock of his chain grocery company. With your very elementary knowledge of investments and investment constraints, what do you see wrong with Mr. Huntington's arrangement for disposal of his estate?
5. You are an imaginative youth, you are about to finish school and enter business, and you have a fair measure of confidence that you will be successful. Estimate the amount of your annual income in current dollars at age 25, at age 35, at 45, and 55. At about what point in your life cycle will you begin to save some of your income and invest in securities? What may go wrong with your estimates?
6. To do a good job of planning investment policies, you have to be something of a pessimist. Is that a valid statement?
7. Mr. Cherbuski makes his living by operating an insurance and real estate brokerage business, and it is a pretty good living. He also invests in real estate whenever he finds a property that seems to be a particularly good bargain, and he has put some of his profits from sales of real estate into securities. As you go about studying his investment constraints with a view to advising him about his security investments, you find that his annual earnings from the real estate and insurance business have varied in the past 5 years from $12,000 to $24,000 a year. He owns a store and office building near the center of town that is valued at $100,000, but mortgaged for $60,000. Interest, debt amortization, property insurance, and taxes require just about all the rental income from this building. He also owns 100 acres of land just beyond the outskirts of town, which he intends to develop into building lots as soon as water and sewer facilities become available. Taxes on the land amount to $2,500 a year. He owns his home, which is valued at $50,000 and is mortgaged for $30,000. He has made no provision for retirement income. What does this sketch of a man's personal financial circumstances imply about the level of risk he should assume in his securities investments?
8. How can you determine about what annual amount may reasonably be considered a minimum expense budget for the executive vice-president of a county-seat bank?

16

Constraints of Money and of the Mind

I. The purchasing power of investment returns
  A. The minimum expense budget in depreciated dollars
  B. Income from other sources in depreciated dollars
  C. MIIR in depreciated dollars
  D. The minimum investment value requirement in depreciated dollars

II. Tenure of ownership

III. The quality of investment management
  A. Appraising your own management ability
  B. Professional investment managers
  C. Alternatives for small investors

IV. The temperament of the investor
  A. Your own risk aversion
  B. The risk aversion of someone else
  C. Non-pecuniary returns and irrationalities

V. The desirability of ownership constraints
  A. The need for the more highly marketable issues
  B. Constraints on use of taxable securities
  C. Constraints affecting other desirability of ownership qualities

We have been thinking about constraints in terms of investment returns in current dollars at an unchanging price level, but we cannot escape the specter of inflation and its consequences for the purchasing power of the dollar. For most investors you must examine constraints not only in terms of an unchanging price level, but also on the basis of some estimated average annual rate of increase in the price level. Rising prices may change conclusions about investment policies in construction of a portfolio.

THE PURCHASING POWER OF INVESTMENT RETURNS

When you start thinking about returns in the purchasing power of amounts of money, you have to decide at the outset what rate of inflation you think is likely for some period in the future. At any particular time peoples' fears of price inflation vary widely. In the early 1960's many economists forecast a very modest rise in the price level and attributed most of the rise to imperfections in statistical methods used in constructing the Consumer Price Index. In the early 1970's the rate of inflation was so high as to be a major political issue and there was fear that the rate would increase further. Thus conditions change and you have to make your estimate of a future rate of price inflation on the basis of conditions as they appear from time to time. But there should be an explicit estimate of an annual rate with some recognition that the actual rate will prove to be somewhat more or somewhat less than the most likely rate.

The size of the estimated rate of inflation makes a great deal of difference when such a rate is projected over relatively long periods of years. Table 16–1 shows a price index with 100 as the present level and the increase at several compound annual rates over periods of widely varying duration. Future dollar amounts estimated on the basis of a constant price level can be multiplied by such index numbers to express the number of depreciated dollars necessary to maintain the purchasing power of dollar amounts.

The Minimum Expense Budget in Depreciated Dollars

The obvious place to begin to think about constraints in depreciated dollars is with the earlier estimates of a minimum expense budget in current dollars. You could do no more than multiply the previous year-by-year MEB estimates in current dollars by the index numbers. However, when the problem of purchasing power of investment returns seems sufficiently important, you may consider more particularly how inflation would affect an investor's living expenses. The Consumer Price Index is constructed for the expenses of a defined category of people and it may not be a good measure of change in living costs for people in quite different circumstances.

There are some expenses that do not vary as the general price level changes. Interest and amortization of a mortgage loan on one's home could be expected to continue unchanged. Rental payments for living quarters may change very little for several years, when the investor is a good tenant. When an investor owns his own home, property taxes may tend upward and so would the cost of maintenance, but changes would not necessarily cor-

TABLE 16–1

Increase in Price Level at Various Rates of Increase

Annual Compound Rate	*Present* time	*Years* +3	+5	+10	+15	+25
1/2 of 1%	100.0	101.5	102.5	105.1	107.8	113.3
1%	100.0	103.0	105.1	110.5	116.1	128.2
1-1/2%	100.0	104.6	107.7	116.1	125.0	145.1
2%	100.0	106.1	110.4	121.9	134.6	164.1
3%	100.0	109.3	115.9	134.4	155.8	209.4
4%	100.0	112.5	121.7	148.0	180.1	266.6
5%	100.0	115.8	127.6	162.9	207.9	338.6

Source: Financial Compound Interest and Annuity Tables, 2d ed., (Boston: Financial Publishing Company, 1960).

respond closely to changes in the Consumers Price Index. Life insurance premiums would remain the same, although a rising price level might indicate a need for additional life insurance.

On the other hand, the cost of medical treatment and hospital care has been rising at a much higher rate than other major items of living expenses. Insurance may solve this problem but only at the cost of rising premium payments for such insurance. The cost of utilities has generally increased less than the rise in the CPI, but the wages of people who may be employed for housework and lawn care has increased at a greater rate. So you have to look at the components of the minimum expense budget and make projections with regard to probable differences in rate of increase in prices for different categories of expenditures and for their relative size in the minimum expense budget.

Income from Other Sources in Depreciated Dollars

Income from sources other than investments may also vary in a manner quite different from the rise in the price level. Earned income, which is a large element in the financial circumstances of most individual investors, tends to increase as the price level rises. For many years the average annual earnings of employed persons in the United States in current dollars have increased at an average annual rate of four to five per cent. When earnings increasing at this rate are reduced to constant dollars, the rate of increase is from zero to two to three per cent. It may be truly said that a good job is the best inflation hedge. Of course, the earnings of a particular individual may not correspond to the average. The bright young man or woman is likely to experience greater gains in earnings by individual achievement, whereas the earnings of an older man or woman may lag behind the general increase in earnings.

The probable increase or even decrease in income from proprietary investments under conditions of price inflation poses another estimating problem, and a particularly difficult one, because the estimates in current dollars are often quite uncertain. Generally, income from small businesses owned and managed by an investor fares well in an era of price inflation and growth in the national economy. Returns from investments in real estate are usually expected to increase by at least as much as the rise in the price level. However, all such generalizations are subject to significant exceptions. Whenever income from a proprietary investment is large relative to an investor's total income, it is well to examine it individually and make an estimate for the future based on the particular characteristics of that investment. A privately owned business enterprise may experience a decline in earnings; real estate that has produced little income may be converted to property that provides much more income.

When individual investors are old enough to be thinking of retirement, the manner in which retirement income will vary, or not vary, with changes in the price level becomes important. Social security incomes for retired people have now been tied to the Consumers Price Index; a year-to-year increase of 3 per cent or more results in increased benefits. This arrangement does much to solve the inflation problem for the elderly. However, most retirement plans of private and public employers provide fixed dollar amounts of income. When you retire you get so many dollars a month and that's it. But, again, the persistence of inflation has caused some change in employers' plans in the direction of making retirement incomes vary more or less with variation in the price level. We will describe such plans in the next chapter.

MIIR in Depreciated Dollars

The conclusion is a series of estimated amounts of MEB in depreciated dollars, the amounts of IFOS in dollars of the purchasing power they may have at the time received, and the MIIR in depreciated dollars. Then investment income is estimated in dollars at the projected price level. If it is sufficient to cover estimated MEB, the purchasing power constraint is slight; to the extent it falls short the constraint becomes more severe.

Table 16–2 shows how estimates might work out for a man and wife who have just retired. They own their home, there is no mortgage on it, their children are financially independent, and there are no more insurance premiums to be paid. These old people are content to live quietly, but they want to be comfortable. In the table the MEB increases at 3 per cent a year, which assumes a fairly high rate of price inflation. Amounts of IFOS increase at an average annual rate of only 1 per cent. Most of it is a pension from a private employer, which is a fixed amount per month; the remainder is social security income, which is assumed to increase at 3 per cent a year. The principal amount invested in securities is $100,000 at current market prices. The entire amount is in bonds that now provide income at the rate of 5½ per cent a year. These are long-term corporate bonds and it is assumed that there will be no change in amount of income in the foreseeable future.

TABLE 16–2
The Effect of Inflation Upon the Minimum Investment Income Requirement

	Present year	*Plus 1 year*	*Plus 3 years*	*Plus 5 years*	*Plus 10 years*
MEB	$10,000	10,300	10,920	11,590	13,439
IFOS	$ 5,000	5,050	5,150	5,255	5,525
MIIR	$ 5,000	5,250	5,770	6,335	7,914
Investment income	$ 5,500	5,500	5,500	5,500	5,500
Margin above MEB	$ 500	250	—	—	—
Margin below MEB	$ —	—	270	835	2,414

You can see that at the present time the amount of investment income provides adequately for the needs of these good people. But as the price level rises, investment income fails to cover the estimated MEB, and if they should live for another 10 years they will suffer economic hardship. This presents a serious problem of investment policy.

The Minimum Investment Value Requirement in Depreciated Dollars

We have said that for a large category of investors, income rather than principal is important. It follows that preservation of values in depreciated dollars is important for these investors chiefly as a source of income. A severe constraint in terms of depreciated dollars of income is also a severe constraint in depreciated dollar amounts of principal. An unrecovered loss of principal reduces amounts of income, other things being equal. An important variable, of course, is the rate of interest or dividend income from a given principal amount. An increase in rate of income in current dollars greater than the rate of increase in the price level would provide larger constant dollar income, and conversely. In fact, the problem of constraints in terms of purchasing power is not essentially different from the problem in terms of current dollars. Current dollar amounts of both principal and income are depreicated dollar amounts after adjustment for change in the price level.

There are many instances, however, in which it appears that principal will have to be liquidated from time to time to provide funds for living expenses. An example easy for college students to understand is an investment fund accumulated over a period of years to provide for the education of children. The period of accumulation and investment may extend over a number of years as children are growing to college age, and the period of liquidation and expenditure may also cover a number of years as first one child and then another enters college. In the meantime, the cost of education increases with the cost of living. Assuming that funds available for this purpose are minimal, the constraint in terms of principal in depreciated dollars is severe.

At the other end of the life cycle is the all too familiar situation of an elderly couple living on a meager fixed pension and obliged to draw on their savings to meet living expenses even at a minimum standard. The market values they can liquidate in terms of depreciated dollars have much to do with their material well-being.

When market values of a portfolio of securities are important to support liabilities in fixed dollar amounts, uncertainty about the price level is not a problem. Dollars of debt and interest on debt are payable in current dollars. However, current dollar amounts of debt may vary. In the case of personal borrowing to finance a proprietary enterprise, a persistant rise in the price level may increase the dollar amounts required to be borrowed. This would imply some constraint in current dollars and in depreciated dollars. Much the same may be said of contingent liabilities that are likely to vary in amount with the price level.

Plans for disposing of wealth by gift, or by will at death, may also require consideration of the need for minimum values in purchasing power. When principal amounts of gifts or inheritances are intended to provide livelihood for dependents, the constraints in depreciated dollars would have to be examined as though the dependent were the investor.

In this area of constraint assets other than securities may be a major element of the problem. Real estate tends to increase in depreciated dollar value and may provide an effective inflation hedge. Shares in a family corporation may be publicly distributed and the market price may appreciate. Almost any kind of asset that is owned and has market value may become worth more over a period of time. It is not uncommon for the prospect of improvement in values of proprietary assets to reduce or eliminate any appreciable constraint on the need to be concerned about the purchasing power of principal amounts of securities.

TENURE OF OWNERSHIP

The problem is to identify conditions that may at some time in the future require sales of securities with little or no regard for market conditions at the time to provide funds for use by an investor. A forced sale in a depressed market may mean a realized loss that might well be avoided if securities could be retained until market prices were more favorable. A forced sale is usually a result of some financial exigency, but it may be a deliberate choice when not to do so is a less desirable alternative in the value system of the investor.

We have mentioned sales of securities to provide funds for personal consumption. There are other purposes that are less urgent but may be considered highly desirable. A young family may want very much to have a second home for week-ends and vacations. Older people often want to relocate geographically at time of retirement even if some expenditure of principal is required.

The existence of personal debts and contingent liabilities that affect the need for stability of market values also affect strength of tenure. Generally, short-term debt is more of a hazard than long-term debt because principal amounts must be repaid sooner. And contingent liabilities may be more or less important depending on whether or not they will become actual liabilities, on their amount if they do, and on the future remoteness when such uncertainties are likely to be resolved.

For some investors, it is necessary to take into account the likelihood that securities will be sold to provide funds for proprietary-type investments. Some people are natural entrepreneurs. They are attracted by business opportunities and they like to manage business enterprises. It may be prudent to regard some part of a securities portfolio as a sort of reserve to be liquidated whenever the owner sees an opportunity of this kind.

The severity of the tenure of ownership constraint cannot be fully appraised without considering the possibility that funds may be obtained from other sources for all of these purposes. Proprietary-type investments may be sold rather than purchased, life insurance may be sufficient to pay estate taxes and expenses, and there are many types of insurance to cover medical expenses, casualty losses, and liabilities for damages to others. Savings accounts are often used to accumulate funds for planned personal expenditures. Often the easiest way to meet a financial emergency is to borrow from a lending institution. An investor with a portfolio of securities has collateral to satisfy even an exacting lender. But borrowing may not be the best way unless a future flow of funds sufficient to provide for payment of interest and principal is clearly visible.

There are many uncertainties affecting tenure of ownership and often contingencies cannot be foreseen. But a thoughtful review of the financial and personal circumstances of an investor should provide a basis for estimating the likelihood of forced liquidation of securities, the probable amount that would be involved, and the time period within which events may happen. This estimate is an important consideration in formulating investment policy.

THE QUALITY OF INVESTMENT MANAGEMENT

The ability of the individual or organization that manages a securities portfolio has a great deal to do with the suitability of the different kinds of investment policies for that portfolio. As a general rule, the poorer the quality of investment management, the more restrictive are all the other constraints on efforts to maximize returns by investing in securities of the poorer grades. Conversely, an investor of unusual ability may be justified in adopting more aggressive policies. In the system of investment constraints you sometimes find that lack of good management is one of the more severe limitations on the level of risk that may properly be assumed.

For individual investors there is, first, the crucial decision whether to manage their own securities portfolios or to shift this function to someone else.

Appraising Your Own Management Ability

When you consider whether you should manage the job yourself, you should at least ask yourself some searching questions and be as objective as possible in your answers.

Men are known by the records they make, so an obvious point to begin is with the question, How well have you done? How well have you done over a relatively long period of time that extends through both bull and bear markets? Some of the financial and personal tragedies that come to investors result from an illusion created by strong bull markets that they are really geniuses at this business. When virtually every stock goes up, you can hardly lose. There are times when the more speculative the stock, the greater is the price appreciation, at least for the period of the bubble. There are times when any "system" for playing the stock market works. The story is still told of a man who was at least slightly demented yet made a fortune by purchasing only stocks of companies whose presidents were bearded. There was once an investment service sold to many individual investors that based its forecasts on certain happenings in a comic strip. Some subscribers testified in court that the system worked well for them. It is easy to kid yourself about your ability as an investment manager if you consider only experience during periods of strongly rising stock prices.

The opposite kind of illusion is sometimes experienced. An individual whose only experience is during a bear market may come to the conclusion that everything he touches turns to dross. There are times when perfectly well-conceived and well-executed investment policies provide very poor returns.

The test of experience is admittedly a difficult test to apply to oneself because it is difficult to be objective. It is also difficult to compare one's experience with that of others. Other people may tell you of their especially gratifying successes or their particularly horrible mistakes, but it would be very unusual for one person to tell another the total annual rates of return he has realized over some period of time. It would be unusual, if for no other reason, because individual investors seldom make such calculations or even know how to make them.

There are some conditions that affect the quality of management that can be observed and evaluated. One is simply the amount of time that an individual can devote to this function. Some very able people are just too busy with other affairs to perform the management function properly. Poor investment experiences may stem from neglect as well as inexpertness. Still another consideration is the probable ability of an individual to continue to perform the investment management function over a period of time. Clearly, the quality of management is doubtful when illness, infirmity, or adverse developments of one kind or another are likely to prevent adequate attention to the task. The advance of years and deterioration of health are among the strongest and most common reasons for turning the task of investment management over to professional counsel.

Professional Investment Managers

Almost anyone whose investments in securities have a value written in six figures or more would do well to consider employing professional investment counsel. It is just as reasonable to employ professional aid in managing investments as it is to employ a lawyer or an architect. As the variety of choices in the security markets has become greater and the complexity of the task has increased, more and more individual investors have turned to professionals for help in managing their investments. Large business corporations with huge sums in their employee pension funds usually employ professional investment counsel firms. Colleges and universities often do the same, and there is now an arrangement whereby they can participate jointly in The Common Fund for Nonprofit Organizations which provides professional management at moderate cost.

There are thousands of professional investment counsel organizations all over the country that offer investment advisory service on a professional basis. Most of these firms are not in the securities business but derive their income from fees charged their clients. Some are one-man operations; others consist of a group of partners or senior officers with staffs of specialists in various phases of investment. A number of banks offer investment counsel service on a fee basis and so do some broker-dealer firms. Investment advisers (other than banks) who have a number of clients are required to be registered with the Securities Exchange Commission and are subject to a certain degree of supervision by that agency under the Investment Advisors Act of 1940.

There are two principal types of arrangements between professional investment advisors and their clients. In one the advisor advises and the client makes the decisions. Clients do not have to follow the advice they receive, but frequent failure to do so would likely cause the advisory arrangement to be discontinued. The second type has become more common in recent years. This is an arrangement in which investors give investment advisors discretion in handling their accounts. Usually there is an understanding about investment constraints and about investment policies that are appropriate to a particular account, but once the ground rules are laid the investment counseling organization has discretion in management. Professional investment advisory firms generally believe that they obtain better returns when they can make changes in a securities portfolio at their own discretion rather than having to go to the client, explain the reasons, experience some delay in decision-making, and sometimes fail to obtain approval.

The fee schedule for either kind of service generally begins at about ½ of 1 per cent of market value of principal annually and graduates downward as amounts increase to about ¼ of 1 per cent. Unfortunately for small investors, the investment counsel firms generally will not accept accounts with less than a prescribed minimum amount of principal. The minimum varies, but for practical purposes you would have to have somewhat more than $100,000 to employ one of these firms.

The task of selecting a professional investment counsel firm should be taken seriously. Just as an individual would consider his own record as an investment manager in appraising his own ability, so also would he check carefully the past record of a professional investment management organization. Sometimes these firms will provide data indicative of results achieved with funds they manage. Sometimes a prospective client must rely largely on the firm's reputation in financial circles. Commercial banks and broker-dealer firms may be good sources of information on this point. There should be opportunity for discussion between prospective client and professional counsel about policies the counselor would consider appropriate for his portfolio, which provides some basis for an individual to make a judgement. And there is also some opportunity in personal conversations for an investor seeking counsel to estimate how well he will get along with the particular people who would be assigned to his account.

Alternatives for Small Investors

There are alternatives for small investors. Broker-dealer firms generally provide some advice to their customers incidental to their functions as intermediaries in the security markets. Their only compensation is broker's commissions and dealer's mark-up. However, a broker compensated only by what he earns as a market middleman cannot afford to devote the time and effort to a customer's account that an investment advisory organization can give it in return for a fee. There are also some very strict rules of the SEC and self-regulatory organizations about broker-dealer firms' behavior relative to their customers.

Another way to deal with the problem of investment management is to shift it completely to a financial institution. This can be done by creating a personal trust with a bank as trustee, the securities portfolio as the trust property, and the investor as beneficiary of the trust. Then the trustee assumes full responsibility for managing investments and is accountable at law for properly performing his fiduciary function. We will examine the trust arrangement more fully in chapter 25.

A second alternative is to invest in shares of mutual funds instead of directly in stocks and bonds of corporate and governmental issuers. Shares of these companies provide participation in a portfolio of securities under professional management and usually well diversified as to risk. Investment companies, too, are the subject of chapter 23.

THE TEMPERAMENT OF THE INVESTOR

Very often the most severe constraint on risk taking resides not in an individual's financial circumstances but in the temperament of the investor.

This is a very broad term that encompasses risk aversion, utility curves, nonpecuniary returns, emotional reactions, and even subjective judgements that may not seem entirely rational to someone else. At this elementary level of discussion it may be well to make risk aversion a principal basis for appraising the temperament of the investor.[1]

You can readily visualize risk aversion increasing as the level of risk increases. People generally do not like uncertainty, and the more uncertainty there is the less they like it. At some point they refuse to move to a higher level of risk no matter what the potential rate of return may be. But risk-aversion curves for different people are different. For some people the curve rises steeply and the level of risk they are willing to assume is reached at a relatively low point on the scale. Others have a greater tolerance for risk, their curve rises more slowly, and they are willing to risk more when the promise of reward is enticing. If you invest for yourself, you should try to estimate the shape of your aversion curve at least approximately, and if you are advising someone else you have to estimate his curve. There are no objective data for this purpose. You have to estimate by trial and observation.

Your Own Risk Aversion

Imagine that you have some considerable amount of money for investment but that none is yet invested. Think about investing it in high-grade, long-term corporate bonds. There is little uncertainty about the financial ability of the issuers to pay, but there is the risk of gains or losses caused by changes in interest rates and there may be considerable uncertainty about the size of returns in constant dollars. How do you feel about owning a portfolio with this level of risk? If you are young and venturesome, you are likely to respond with a vigorous, "No." Both the level of risk and the size of returns are too low. You are not sufficiently far out on your scale of risk or far enough up on your scale of expected returns. You want to accept more risk for the marginal utility of greater returns.

Consider another portfolio composed of common stocks of large companies with long records of relatively stable earnings and dividends. Imagine about twenty issues well diversified in terms of individual risks. The portfolio risk is greater and the returns that may reasonably be expected are higher. You know that even these "blue chip" stocks may experience sizable declines in market prices in a period of recession, but that does not disturb you very much. The prospect of significantly larger returns is important to you. Then this kind of portfolio represents about the right balance of risk and return for you.

[1]An adequate discussion of utility theory would require more detail, more math, and more space than seems appropriate in an elementary textbook. An excellent source for those who want to go further is Baumol, *op. cit.*

You could go a step further and think about a portfolio composed of a relatively small number of speculative growth stocks. The issuers of these stocks are smaller companies with narrower product lines and greater uncertainty of future returns than that of the blue chip stocks. You could make a lot of money with these stocks, or you could lose a lot. Does uncertainty about the size of returns frighten you? Then you are too far out on the risk dimension. If you can accept the risk with equanimity and the chance of large returns excites you, this may be the right position for you on the risk-return relationship.

The Risk Aversion of Someone Else

When you have to apply this trial and observation procedure to someone else it is harder to estimate the approximate shape of his or her risk aversion curve, but professional investment advisors do so in the regular course of their work. You can present to a client tentative proposals for different kinds of portfolios representing different risk levels and watch the reaction. When a middle-aged widow hesitates over a portfolio proposal, you have passed the risk level acceptable to her. When the young man who has inherited some money becomes impatient with your talk of bonds and blue chips, you haven't gone far enough.

A problem with this method of estimating a utility curve is that most people have rather vague notions of how much risk is associated with the several risk categories of securities, or combinations thereof, and sometimes they are unrealistic about the size of potential returns for taking risks. An elderly man may have a vivid memory of what happened to common stocks in the 1930's and may think that he is risking everything by investing in them. On the other hand, a young man who has enjoyed remarkable success in his common-stock speculations during a recent period of prolonged rise in average stock prices may be influenced almost entirely by his hopes for large capital gains.

Another cause of difficulty in estimating the utility curve is that we don't know how much other people would be disturbed by low rates or negative future rates of return. You, the financial advisor, may talk to a client about the possibility of a 25 per cent decline in average stock prices and he may seem unperturbed. But when prices do dip that much the emotional reaction may be very strong. Or, you may put an obviously timid client into a list of A-rated bonds and subsequently find that client very much upset by a decline in bond prices attributable to a rise in interest rates.

Although we have pointed to difficulties and approximations, a good investment advisor can judge pretty well about how far a client should go in assuming risk. He knows the signs of timidity and the indications that a rising scale of prospective returns bring greater satisfaction. And he should have the benefit of experience with his clients as he goes along. He learns that the man who wanted to speculate for large returns turns pale with fright when the stock market declines, and he may learn that the timid widow is not so timid as he thought.

Non-Pecuniary Returns and Irrationalities

Adam Smith's economic man was a mechanical creature who obtained economic satisfactions from increments of wealth, but he was not a real-life man. Real people obtain non-pecuniary returns from investments. These returns are satisfactions derived from the experience of investing that are additional to returns in money. A familiar example is the office worker who enjoys talking to his associates about the stocks he owns and about his successes in picking the right stocks. He can lord it over the people who have no stocks to talk about.

There are so many different kinds of non-pecuniary returns that it would take enormous psychological research to catalogue them. There is the sense of security that government bonds provide to the timid, which may be worth more in satisfaction than whatever increment in dollars might be realized by investment in more risky securities. There is the thrill of speculation, especially when it is successful. There is satisfaction in the social status that wealth provides and even in the emotional attachment to stocks of "my companies."

One discerning observer and clever writer tells more about the psychology of investors in a series of sketches of people (probably apocryphal) than either investment experts or psychologists have been able to put in print. He tells of a man who enjoys his investment mistakes, of a pretty girl who owned a few shares of Communications Satellite and has an emotional commitment to that stock. "I just love Comsat," she said, "and I'll never sell it. I don't care if it goes down."

One of the best stories is about a stock broker who had a grandmother who was a widow and had lots of money from the estate of her deceased husband. The broker specialized in finding growth stocks and in selling them to his customers. The wealthy old lady persuaded her grandson to tell her about some of those growth stocks. She, in turn, told two of her elderly friends, also widows who had been well endowed by their deceased husbands. The three old ladies bought the stocks the grandson mentioned with such enthusiasm and such an abundance of financial resources that they pushed prices of the stocks up sharply before the young man could get very many of his customers into them. When he protested to his grandmother she pleaded, "Don't take my stocks away. This is the most fun I've had in years." Neither risk nor return meant anything to the grandmother.

Mr. Goodman sums up some of his thinking about non-pecuniary returns in this passage:

> "The very bright people," says one of my Wall Street philosopher friends, "know how to worm their way around the Street, and they do very well. And the ones who just buy the stock and put it away probably do all right.

But the investors who really follow the market, the one's who call up all the time, ninety percent of them really don't care whether they make money or not."[2]

THE DESIRABILITY OF OWNERSHIP CONSTRAINTS

There are constraints not only on risk, but also on the abilities of investors to include in their portfolios securities that rank low in desirability of ownership qualities. These constraints are important because they affect the effort to maximize portfolio rate of return. We have seen that there are differentials in expected rates between poorer-grade and better-grade securities in these qualities. Some investors can take advantage of these differentials by selecting issues of the poorer grades. But first there may be a need for the advantages offered by the better grades. We have to define the boundary lines for investment policy for these needs just as we do for risk.

The Need for the More Highly Marketable Issues

The constraint on use of poorly marketable issues is the cost of poor marketability in terms of dealers' spreads annualized relative to expected rates of return on issues that are otherwise about equal in risk. It is essentially a matter of which issue provides the higher "after dealers' charge" rate of return.

Consider, for example, two corporate bond issues that are equal except for differences in market rates of yield at which they may be purchased and differences in size of spreads between dealers' bid and asked prices. The poorly marketable issue is offered at a price to yield, say, 7.10 per cent and the spread is 3 points. The more highly marketable issue is offered to yield 6.90 per cent and the spread is 2 points. It is expected that whichever bond is bought will be held for 10 years and sold at the bid price at the time. On an annualized basis the dealers' spread for the highly marketable issue is 0.20 per cent and for the poorly marketable issue is 0.30 per cent. Thus:

	Yield at purchase price	*Dealers' spread*	*Yield minus spread*
Highly marketable bond	6.90%	0.20	6.70
Poorly marketable bond	7.10%	0.30	6.80

Although the difference is small, the poorly marketable issue would provide the higher rate of yield minus annualized spread.

As a practical matter, the marketability constraint is determined not so much by market rates and annualized spreads as it is by rate of portfolio turnover.[3] When portfolio turnover is high, the cost of dealers' spread is high

[2]Adam Smith (George J. W. Goodman), *The Money Game*, New York, 1967, Random House, pp. 59–75.

[3]The annual rate of turnover is the sum of all purchases and sales for a year divided by 2 and that quotient divided by the average value of the portfolio for the year.

relative to expected rates of return. With some exaggeration to make the point, change the example above so that the holding period is 1 year instead of 10. Then:

	Yield at purchase price	*Dealers' spread*	*Yield minus spread*
Highly marketable bond	6.90%	2.0	4.90
Poorly marketable bond	7.10	3.0	4.10

In these circumstances the investor clearly needs the highly marketable issue. His constraint in this area is severe.

Investors do not usually buy and sell long-term bonds after a year's holding, but they often turn over stock portfolios at a high rate. Consider, for example, an individual who regularly buys stocks, holds them for 6 months plus 1 day, and sells them for a long-term capital gain or loss. If he buys stocks that are usually quoted with a spread of 2 per cent of the asked price, his dealers' cost is 4 per cent a year of amount invested. If he buys stocks with a usual spread of 0.5 per cent, his dealers' cost is 1 per cent a year. People who play the stock market need highly marketable issues. For long-term investors the need is much less severe a constraint.

It is sometimes said that an advantage of highly marketable issues is that you can sell them quickly. This is fallacious; you can sell any security quickly at the price bid by a dealer. Neither are highly marketable issues more "liquid" than poorly marketable issues. Whichever kind you sell, you get your money within 5 days if you sell on the regular settlement basis.

Constraints on Use of Taxable Securities

The need for securities of the higher grades in taxability is a function of the federal income tax rates applicable to investors and of the yields obtainable on fully taxable issues relative to those having some tax advantage—and thus being higher grade in taxability. We will consider this kind of constraint only as far as the federal income tax is concerned, but in some instances it may be desirable to take account of taxes on securities imposed by state or local governments.

You can make the same kind of analysis of the need for tax exemption that we made of the need for high marketability. A tax-exempt municipal bond may be bought to yield 5 per cent, and a taxable corporate bond is offered on a 7.30 per cent yield basis. These issues are otherwise equal. If your personal income tax rate applicable to bond interest is 20 per cent, you will maximize your return by purchasing the corporate issue. If your rate is 50 per cent, you gain much more from the municipal issue. Here is the calculation.

	Yield at purchase price	*Tax rate*	*After-tax rate*
Municipal bond	5.00%	zero	5.00
Corporate bond	7.30	20%	5.84
Corporate bond	7.30	50	3.65

The more common approach to determining the need for securities with tax advantage is to convert expected rates of return on these tax-exempt securities to a tax-equivalent rate. The tax-equivalent rate is the rate the investor would have to obtain on a fully taxable issue to pay the tax and emerge with an amount after tax equal to the rate on the securities with tax advantage. If the tax-equivalent rate for the securities with tax advantage is higher than the expected rate on securities without tax advantage and all else is equal, you obtain the better rate of return on the securities with tax advantage.

The tax-equivalent yield on a municipal bond is the yield divided by 1 minus the applicable tax rate. Using the data in the example above, the tax-equivalent rate on the 5 per cent municipal bond is $5 / (1 - 0.20) = 5 / 0.80 = 6.25$ per cent. Since you can get an equivalent rate on the corporate bond of 7.30 per cent, you don't need tax exemption. But at a tax rate of 50 per cent, the tax-equivalent rate for the municipal is 10 per cent, which is considerably better than the yield on the taxable corporate issue.

The problem becomes more difficult when there is partial tax exemption or a preferential tax rate. Consider a problem involving the tax-equivalent rate for investment in common stocks. An investor contemplates purchasing stocks with the expectation of return solely in the form of long-term capital gains; the stocks he intends to buy pay no dividends. He expects an average annual rate of return from these stocks of 10 per cent. His maximum personal income tax rate is 50 per cent and that rate would apply to the capital gains. But only one-half of long-term capital gains constitute taxable income, so the effective tax rate is 25 per cent. The 10 per cent expected rate is equivalent to a rate of 13.3 per cent on a fully taxable return. Short-term capital gains are, of course, fully taxable. If the rate of return on common stocks includes dividends, you have to figure the tax-equivalent yield for both dividends and capital gains, taking into account the dividend exclusion.

The need for securities with tax advantage may vary from time to time for an individual investor. The highest income tax rate that would apply to income if it were taxable may change as the amount of taxable income changes. There are also differences from one time to another in the differential in market rates of yield between tax-exempt and fully taxable issues. Thus this constraint should be re-examined from time to time.

Constraints Affecting Other Desirability of Ownership Qualities

The need for the higher grades of securities in the other qualities by which securities are graded—such as convertibility, redeemability, and deepness of discount—may not be readily apparent from examining an investor's financial circumstances. Questions about these needs usually arise in the process of formulating investment policies relative to the principal investment risks.

The question of owning high-grade convertible securities, for example, appears only after a decision has been made that bonds or preferred stocks will be included in the portfolio. An individual thinking about allocating his funds between bonds and stocks might decide on a percentage of the total in corporate bonds, but with the additional provision that some or all be high-grade convertible bonds. A need for convertibility would arise from a desire to raise both the risk level and the expected rate of return from the portfolio by including bonds that provide an opportunity for conversion into common stock. Or, convertible bonds may be needed to reduce the purchasing-power risk in bond investments.

The need for bonds with strong protection against redemption before maturity would arise only if the bonds are to be held to maturity. And it would become a matter of some importance only in a period of relatively high interest rates with prospect of lower rates in the future.

Generally, the same circumstances that create a need for high-grade securities in redeemability also make deep discount bonds desirable. However, the purchase of deep discount bonds also provides an opportunity for capital appreciation in the event of a decline in interest rates. Thus they would be appropriate to a policy of trying to realize profits from cyclical fluctuations in bond prices.

QUESTIONS FOR DISCUSSION

1. With a given change in the Consumer Price Index over a period of years, the minimum expense budget for one investor may change more than it does for another investor. How can that be?

2. Your analysis shows that the minimum expense budget of an investor is likely to rise at a significant rate over the next several years. Does this mean that there is a severe constraint in terms of investment income in constant dollars? What are the other elements of the problem?

3. What particular circumstances would indicate a real need to try to preserve the principal value of a securities portfolio in constant dollars?

4. What difference does it make if an investor is likely to be obliged to liquidate a considerable part of his portfolio at some indeterminable time in the future?

5. Investors are not able to estimate the quality of their own investment management ability accurately, or even that of professional investment managers. Argue the affirmative or the negative.

6. Assume that you have somehow acquired $100,000 to invest in securities. Estimate the level of your own risk aversion.

7. If you had that portfolio of securities worth $100,000, what non-pecuniary returns would you expect to realize? How important would they be to you?

8. Your broker advises you to invest only in stocks listed on the New York Stock Exchange. Is this good advice for you?

9. The annual report of your university or college shows that 30 per cent of the total endowment fund is invested in municipal bonds. What do you think of that?

10. If you were managing a portfolio consisting largely of long-term corporate bonds, would you accept an appreciably lower yield on bonds with strong call protection relative to equivalent bonds with weak call protection? Consider the present level of interest rates and the probable direction of change in rates during the next several years.

17

Personal Financial Planning

I. The personal financial statement
  A. Deposit-type assets
  B. Proprietary-type assets
  C. Personal debts

II. The federal social security program

III. Employers' retirement income plans
  A. Pension plans of private employers
  B. Pension plans of public employers
  C. The variable annuity concept
  D. Income tax encouragement for pension funds
  E. Evaluating retirement income in terms of risk

IV. Life insurance in the portfolio of personal assets
  A. The kinds of life insurance contracts
  B. Settlement options
  C. Insurance in personal financial planning
  D. Life insurance in terms of investment risk

V. Estate Planning
  A. Distribution by the living hand
  B. Distribution by mortmain
  C. Taxation of distribution of wealth

We have seen that the financial circumstances of individual investors largely govern their investment limitations. What they own and what they owe, what they earn and what they spend, how their financial fortunes ebb and flow—all these things constitute a financial structure for each individual into which a securities portfolio must be fitted to his best possible advantage.

It is not unusual for investors and investment advisers to assume that an individual's existing financial circumstances must be accepted as given, and that investment policies should be adapted to whatever the situation may be. This assumption is at best a doubtful one and at worst it may be a tragic mistake. The financial facts of life may be wrong.

In fact, few people have all their financial affairs in good order, with the several parts neatly integrated and organized. The current state of financial affairs for most people is a product of disconnected responses to problems as they have developed, and of lack of responses to problems that have not been anticipated. To construct an investment program on the basis of financial circumstances that fail to serve properly the needs of the investor is to build a house on sand.

What we propose to do in this chapter is a "flashback." We want to turn back the calendar to a point in time just before the analysis of investment constraints and examine all the financial circumstances of the individual whose money is invested. The essential question is how well they serve the uses he wants to make of his material wealth, what level of risk he can afford to assume, how much liquidity he needs for the several kinds of financial contingencies, and how his securities portfolio can best be fitted into his personal financial plan. This leads into the whole broad field of financial and estate planning, which is by itself one in which several different kinds of experts specialize. We shall do no more than to indicate the directions in which solutions may be found.

Chronologically, financial and estate planning should be done before consideration is given to investment requirements, because the changes in an individual's financial affairs that may result would change the investment constraints. But for the purpose of pedagogy it seems best to establish the concept of constraints and then go back to the more technical problems that should precede.

Some of the elements of the total problem are already familiar. We have considered earned income and income from sources other than investments, and have taken account of the existence of both actual and contingent liabilities. But there are some kinds of assets that have not been considered and some uses of funds that have not been planned. We need to examine assets and liabilities of the kind that would ordinarily appear on a personal financial statement, consider the very considerable variety of arrangements for retirement income, take account of the use of life insurance to provide both income and liquidity, and, finally, give some attention to estate planning.

In this review we will estimate at least approximately the riskiness of assets other than securities, identify the principal elements of uncertainty, grade assets in marketability and taxability, and in general treat them in the same way that we do securities. When all kinds of assets can be compared in terms of all of those qualities that are important to an individual, the securities portfolio can be properly fitted into the whole personal financial program.

THE PERSONAL FINANCIAL STATEMENT

The way to begin is to draw up a personal financial statement listing assets and liabilities. The qualities of the usual kinds of assets can be readily appraised, but there may be difficulties with proprietary-type investments. The cash value, or non-forfeiture value, of life insurance policies may be listed among personal assets but we will go beyond that value to consider the uses of life insurance. On the opposite side are personal debts.

Deposit-Type Assets

If you are conditioned by conventional accounting practice, you would begin by listing the more liquid assets first in a statement of assets. For individuals this would usually mean deposit-type assets. Almost everyone who owns securities has a demand deposit at a bank—a checking account—in which he deposits income and from which he pays expenses. The usual question about this kind of asset is what the amount should be.

The function of a checking account, besides its use as a means of settling transactions, is to compensate for interim differences between inflows and outflows of cash in the ordinary course of affairs. The more regular the flows in and out, the smaller is the balance required relative to cash flows. For a man whose cash receipts consist of a monthly salary plus some small amount of interest or dividends from securities and who spends most of his income for regularly recurring living expenses, the balance at the beginning of the month need be little more than the monthly income plus a minimum balance sufficient to avoid bank service charges.

For some people, however, cash flows are not entirely regular by the week or month. Investment income may tend to be concentrated around quarterly or semi-annual dates, and some expenditures may be made less frequently than monthly. Insofar as the personal income tax liability is not covered by withholding from earnings, payments are required to be made quarterly. Local property taxes are usually paid semi-annually and there may be other irregularities in both inflows and outflows that require deposits at times equal to several times average monthly income.

From the standpoint of good personal financial planning, the purpose should be to have no more money in the checking account than necessary. Banks pay no interest on demand deposits. In financial terms money in a checking account has an opportunity cost, which is the rate of return that could be obtained by investing it in another kind of asset. Some people leave more funds on demand deposit than they really need, either because they have not examined their need, because they don't know what else to do with the money, or because they derive satisfaction from having a large bank balance.

Savings deposit-type assets are used by many people as a reserve fund, or as an investment, or both. These assets include time deposits at commercial banks, savings accounts at mutual savings banks, share accounts at savings and loan associations, and deposits with credit unions. They also include U. S. Savings Bonds and certificates of deposit with commercial banks.

As reserve funds these kinds of assets are excellent. There is little or no risk of the financial abilities of issuers to pay principal and income. Indeed, deposits in banks and savings and loan associations are insured by agencies of the federal government up to certain maximum amounts, and the Savings Bonds of course are debts of the federal government. There is no uncertainty about market prices; principal amounts are payable in designated dollar amounts. Income may vary as institutions change the rates they pay on deposits, but deposit rates are more stable than market rates. There is the uncertainty of future amounts in constant dollars because there is no provision in these instruments for values to change with changes in the price level.

One quality of savings-type assets that is particularly important in many personal financial programs is liquidity. Liquidity is a counterpart of marketability, but it is better than marketability in that you get the full principal amount invested and there are no transactions costs. There is, however, no advantage in taxability; interest is fully taxable.

The sacrifice you make for these advantages is relatively low rates of return. At a time when Treasury securities due in 3 to 5 years could be bought in the market to yield about 6 per cent and long-term, high-grade corporates were selling at yields of 7½ to 8 per cent, rates on several kinds of savings-type assets were in the range of 4 to 5 per cent.

The practical question, then, is what amount of savings-type assets is appropriate to the circumstances of an individual. These assets may, of course, be used to reduce the level of investment risk in the total set of assets. They may also be used to provide liquidity. From an investment viewpoint the question is related to the riskiness of other kinds of assets and the several kinds of conditions that require provision for liquidity, and the answer can be determined only when a personal financial review has gone far enough to establish these risks and conditions.

For most people the question is not that complicated. They own savings-type assets as a means of accumulating funds for planned expenditures or as a reserve for unknown contingencies. The idea of a "rainy day" fund, generally attributed to Benjamin Franklin, has not yet gone out of style. Amounts people need for such purposes are subjective judgements. A young couple saving for the down payment on a house needs whatever amount they think is sufficient for a down payment. Some people scorn the concept of an emergency reserve entirely; others are not comfortable without a few thousand dollars in a savings account. You have to know yourself or the person you are advising.

Proprietary-Type Assets

The category of assets we have termed proprietary investments represent the greater part of the wealth of literally millions of individuals all over the country. Wall Street financiers may have reason to be surprised at the amount of wealth in this form owned by people along Main Street who appear to be quite ordinary citizens. Because there is a great diversity of assets under this one heading, it is impossible to describe with very much accuracy their risk characteristics. In a particular situation, you have to examine the assets and make a specific estimate of risk. We can, however, make some generalization that may be helpful.

Ownership of one's own business—usually a small business—may have about the same level of financial risk as marketable common stocks. Or, the risk may be higher because the small business lacks diversification of products and markets, and because it often depends on the ability of one individual. But a well-established and well-managed small business is often a source of relatively stable income. Undeveloped land bought with the expectation of a large increase in its value falls into about the same category as speculative growth stocks. A well-located retail store building leased to a good tenant, however, may be characterized by low financial risk and so may loans secured by liens on real property. You would usually put these kinds of assets in the same financial risk category as corporate bonds bearing the higher ratings.

Interest-rate risk is not usually an important consideration. Rates of return on mortgage loans and leases tend to rise and fall with the general level of interest rates, but the correlation is relatively weak. Returns from equity-type investments generally would be affected by pronounced changes in market rates of interest in about the same way that common stocks are affected.

In terms of purchasing-power risk, ownership of a local business enterprise may be about as good an inflation hedge as you can find. There are no market values of the ownership interest to fluctuate as people anticipate favorable or unfavorable developments, and usually there is adequate opportunity to raise selling prices as the Consumer Price Index advances. Debt-type proprietary investments and real estate leased for a long term have about the same level of purchasing-power risk as marketable bonds.

The great disadvantage of proprietary investments is that they are not marketable. They are saleable, but it may take a long time to find a buyer and prospective buyers' notions of a fair price may differ greatly from that of prospective sellers. This disadvantage often becomes a matter of considerable importance when the owner of a small business begins to plan for retirement and when he comes to estate planning.

There are no explicit tax advantages in this area because both income from proprietary investments and whatever capital gain may be realized from them are taxable as personal income. There may be opportunities, however, to minimize taxable income by accelerated depreciation of physical assets and by taking capital losses as offsets to gains.

In personal financial planning for a person with a substantial part of his wealth in proprietary-type investments there are several important questions. One is whether the amount committed to this type of asset should be increased. A prospering and expanding small business generally requires additional ownership capital. If there is personal wealth in the form of marketable securities, there may be justification for shifting funds from one kind of asset to another. The problem is that of risk and return. Can you increase returns by doing so, can you afford whatever increase in risk may be involved, and is the loss of marketability important? For a vigorous and ambitious man the answer may well be affirmative.

Sometimes there are clear indications that proprietary investments should be reduced and funds shifted to securities. A business interest may be too risky when all of the personal financial circumstances of the owner are considered. Or, the size of returns may not justify the risk involved. The marketability of securities becomes a more important consideration when an individual turns to the serious business of estate planning. Management of proprietary assets may be a problem. An assortment of real estate, for example, may be entirely suitable for a man who bought it, but too much of a problem for his widow.

Finally, the need for tax exemption may require special consideration. When the applicable tax rates on ordinary income are high, municipal bonds may provide a larger return than the after-tax income from proprietary investments and at a much lower level of risk.

Personal Debts

Personal debts are not usually a problem for individuals who have accumulated any very sizable amount of investment in securities, but there are exceptions and the exceptions may present difficult problems of financial planning. Debt increases the riskiness of a set of assets, whatever may be the risk level of the assets themselves. Interest has to be paid and in most instances there are periodic payments to amortize debt. The question of ultimately liquidating principal amounts may have to be taken into consideration.

The most common type of personal debt is a mortgage loan to finance home ownership. When the amount is moderate and existing sources of income are both adequate and stable, you would ordinarily do nothing about it. Income, however, may not be adequate nor stable or may not exist or may cease to exist. Unemployment or disability may reduce earned income, and retirement may substitute a pension much smaller in amount than the former salary. When earned income is the principal source of income and the wage earner dies, the problem may become acute.

Credit insurance is sometimes used to provide funds for payment of principal amount of debt on the death of the insured. Usually the amount of insurance decreases as the principal amount of a home mortgage loan is reduced, and the cost of such insurance is sometimes included in periodic payments to service the debt. Credit insurance is simply a specialized form of life insurance, and any kind of life insurance may be used that provides an amount of cash settlement at death equal at least to the amount of debt.

In some conditions, however, consideration should be given to reducing mortgage debt even at the cost of liquidating assets. A couple entering on retirement is likely to feel more comfortable without the mortgage loan when income is reduced, and a widow who has to adjust to considerably more modest financial circumstances may need relief from mortgage loan payments. Here, again, the emotional reactions of the people concerned may affect the decision.

Personal debts or debt guarantees associated with borrowing to finance proprietary enterprises often present difficult problems. The businessman who owns and operates his own business may feel that he has no alternative to this type of liability. The business is his livelihood and he needs the money. Life insurance payable to the lender in event of death of the borrower is one obvious way of reducing this element of risk, and often that is about all one can do. But there are possible alternatives. One is to reduce the size of operations of the business enterprise so that less debt is required. Another is to raise additional equity capital by selling an interest in the business to someone else in the form of a partnership or ownership of a block of stock.

THE FEDERAL SOCIAL SECURITY PROGRAM

The foundation of almost everyone's personal financial program is the system of rights to income provided by the Social Security Administration in accordance with federal legislation. For a great many the foundation is the entire structure, but for many others it is a foundation on which other financial arrangements may be based. Unfortunately, a great many people have only vague ideas of amounts of income to which they will become entitled under the social security system.

Almost every category of employed persons is covered by social security, including ministers, members of the military services of the United States on active duty, employees of state and local governments, and farmers and household workers. The benefits are financed by taxes based on workers' earnings. One-half of the tax is deducted from employees' earnings and the other half is paid by employers. The tax is on all earned income up to a fixed maximum per year. Taxes are paid to federal trust funds. They are used to pay benefits and administrative expenses, and funds not so required are invested in interest-bearing U.S. government securities.

The members of Congress change the provisions of the Social Security Act from time to time and they do so frequently enough that any description of particular details soon becomes out of date. Generally changes have been in the direction of liberalization, that is, increasing amounts of benefits and relaxing restrictions on eligibility or qualification. A major change enacted in 1972 provides that in a year when the Consumer Price Index increases by 3 per cent, the amount of benefits shall increase in the same proportion.[1]

The most important of the social security benefits for most people is the retirement income (old-age and survivors benefits) it provides for workers when they retire. The usual retirement age is 65, but one may retire at an earlier age with somewhat reduced benefits. The amount of retirement income is based on the average amount of earnings on which the social security tax was paid during a past period of employment with the 5 years of lowest amounts deleted. The amount on which tax has been paid may not be the full amount of earnings, because the tax is paid only on amounts up to a maximum

[1]Pamphlets describing the social security program may be obtained without charge from offices of the Social Security Administration.

provided by law. Amounts of benefits are not affected by income from sources other than earnings. Both rich and poor receive social security checks.

In addition to old-age payments to retired workers, the program includes benefits to dependents of retired persons. The wife of a retired worker receives benefits based on the amounts paid her husband. A widow who is caring for a dependent child is entitled to benefits regardless of her age as long as there is a dependent child. Since both men and women workers are covered by social security, the law provides for payments on account of a retired wife to her dependent husband. The amounts of retirement income are moderate relative to amounts of earnings on which social security tax has been paid. Generally a worker who retires at 65 would receive an income equal to about thirty-five to forty per cent of the average income on which tax was paid. The spouse, if 65 or older, would receive an amount equal to about one-half of the retired worker's income. There are benefits of different amounts for widows or for widowers of deceased workers. Sex makes no difference; the requirement for a widow's or widower's allowance is dependency on a deceased worker. Survivors benefits may also be paid to dependent parents and to a divorced wife who has been dependent on a deceased worker for support.

When a person covered by the social security program becomes fully disabled before the age of 65, he and certain members of his family receive benefits in the same amounts as though he had retired at 65. A disabled person is one who is unable to engage in any substantial gainful activity.

In 1965, Congress greatly enlarged the social security system by enacting the Medicare bill, which provides a broad program of financial aid to pay medical expenses for persons 65 or older. A major part of this program is compulsory for all persons whose employment is covered by the federal social security legislation, and everyone participating is entitled to the benefits regardless of financial need. This part is financed by the social security tax on workers' earnings. Another part of the medical care program is voluntary, and a third part increases the federal contribution to state-administered medical assistance programs.

The compulsory part of the medical care program provides for hospitalization for a maximum period in one spell of sickness, with patients paying an initial amount of hospital expense and the social security administration paying the remainder. A further provision allows for payment of the full cost of post-hospital extended care in a skilled nursing home for a limited time period. The voluntary part of Medicare—eligible persons may participate or not as they please—provides funds for payment of doctors' fees and certain other medical expenses not provided for under the compulsory part of the program. Participants pay a fixed amount monthly.

Sometimes people who have provided reasonably well for their own economic welfare pay little attention to the benefits they are entitled to receive under the federal government's social welfare legislation. But from a strictly financial point of view, the benefits are important. A rather large amount of capital accumulated and invested in securities would be required to provide income equal to amounts of benefits to which individuals are entitled under this legislation. In personal financial planning, one does well to start with the several kinds of benefits under the social security laws and add income available, or expected to be available, from other sources in the retirement period.

The social security system does much to reduce the over-all level of risk in the personal financial circumstances of many investors. Amounts to which people are entitled are fixed by law and there is no more uncertainty about financial ability to make these payments than there is about payments on U. S. Treasury obligations. There is no uncertainty attributable to interest-rate risk because there are no market values to fluctuate and amounts of income are fixed by law rather than by market rates of interest. The provision tying current dollar amounts of benefits to the price index, eliminates much of the uncertainty about amounts in constant dollars. There is no marketability, because rights cannot be sold; but benefits are not subject to the personal income tax, which puts this income in the highest grade in terms of taxability.

EMPLOYERS' RETIREMENT INCOME PLANS

It used to be that young people seeking employment were often counseled not to inquire about employers' retirement plans, because such inquiry was supposed to suggest that they were more interested in what they would get at age 65 rather than in the employment opportunity for the next 40 or 45 years. If that was ever good counsel, it isn't anymore. The contributions that employers make to employee pension funds and the payments they make for other employee benefits are a part of employees' compensation and they are legitimately of as much interest as salary. They are very much a part of an individual's personal financial program and, indeed, may be most of it for many years to come.

Pension Plans of Private Employers

There has been a great growth in pension plans of private business enterprises for their employees. Several decades ago pensions for corporate employees were the exception rather than the rule; presently the opposite is true. After World War II the major labor unions launched a strong drive for including pensions in collective bargaining contracts and subsequently this right was judicially validated. It has also become common practice for state and local governments and their agencies to provide pensions for their employees. Currently the number of employees covered by pension plans of private and public employers is somewhat more than 41 million, and the number is growing at the rate of about 1 million persons a year.[2]

One principal kind of retirement income arrangement is generally termed an *insured pension plan*, because the pension liabilities are insured by a life insurance company. These plans generally are group plans under which premium payments are made to an insurance company by an employer on

[2]*The Talley*, March, 1972, The Institute of Life Insurance.

behalf of employees, and the insurance company assumes responsibility for payment of retirement income to employees in accordance with terms of the pension contract. In some plans the employer makes the entire contribution, and in others employer and employees share the contribution.

In recent years legislation has been enacted in a number of states authorizing insurance companies to provide separate account pension funds. The distinguishing feature of this arrangement is that contributions to such funds in the hands of insurance companies are held in separate accounts (from life insurance assets) and invested by the companies with much greater latitude in choice of securities. Separate pension accounts usually are invested to some extent in common stocks. Annuities are purchased for employees at retirement from the separate account.

Annuities purchased under the several kinds of insured pension plans are contracts whereby an insurance company, in consideration of sums of money paid to it, agrees to pay certain amounts periodically to a designated person (annuitant) for life. The amount of periodic annuity payments, usually paid monthly rather than annually, is governed by the amount paid to an insurance company for a contract, by the expected length of life of annuitants according to actuarial tables, and by the assumed rate of return on investment of the annuity reserve.

Usually, life companies offer as an alternative to a single life annuity a joint-and-survivor annuity, which provides for payments to an annuitant and to a designated second person as long as either lives. Usually, the second person is the wife of the annuitant and the purpose of the joint-and-survivor arrangement is to provide annuity income for the wife if she survives her husband.

Noninsured pension plans are distinguished from insured plans by the fact that they do not make use of an insurance company. They are sometimes called self-administered plans. Retirement income is paid to employees from a pension fund or from current contributions by the employer. The amounts of retirement income to which employees are entitled are determined by the provisions of each plan; they are usually based on length of service, level of compensation, or some combination of these two ways of measuring service to employers.

When funds are accumulated from contributions by employer or employees, or both, plans are said to be funded. A plan is fully funded when the amount of funds accumulated and invested is sufficient, under the actuarial assumptions adopted, to pay all pension liabilities existing at the time without further contributions. When the accumulated assets are less than sufficient to discharge existing pension liabilities, a plan is said to be partially funded.

Funded noninsured pension plans are termed *trusteed plans* when contributions are paid into a trust, usually with a bank as trustee. The trustee invests the funds in trust and pays benefits to employees in accordance with the terms of the plan. Many noninsured funds of large companies are administered by the company themselves without a trustee. They commonly employ banks and private investment counsel firms to manage their pension fund investments. In some instances labor union representatives participate in administration of company pension plans.

Still another kind of retirement income arrangement is the deferred profit-sharing plan. This arrangement, as its name suggests, is characterized by contributions by employers from profits. Thus the amount of contributions varies from time to time. Shares in accumulated assets are apportioned to employees, and benefits at retirement depend on accumulations to the accounts of individual employees. Frequently, profit-sharing arrangements supplement either insured or noninsured pension funds.

Pension Plans of Public Employers

A large portion of all employees of the federal, state, and local governments, and of their agencies and instrumentalities, participate in public pension plans. The federal government has long provided pensions for civilian employees and there are separate systems for most governmental agencies. Currently, most career employees of states and local governments participate in public plans. They include particularly teachers, policemen, and firemen.

There is wide variety in public pension fund arrangements and provisions. The public employers have much the same options as private employers. Some use plans insured by insurance companies and some place funds with a trustee, but the larger plans are generally self-administered by a board appointed by state officials with some representation of participants. It has become fairly common practice for such boards to employ professional investment counsel to perform the investment function. Some public plans are only partially funded and some are fully funded. Public plans, like those of private employers, generally require several years of employment as a condition of eligibility and amounts of retirement incomes are defined in terms of average salary in a period of time as well as length of service.

The Variable Annuity Concept

There is another kind of retirement income arrangement that has recently become of public interest and is being used by both private and public employers. It is called a variable annuity because the amounts of annuity income in current dollars vary. The theory is that payments to a variable annuity fund are invested chiefly in common stocks, and that the returns from common stocks over long time periods in current dollar amounts will increase more or less as the price level increases. The amounts of annuity payments vary from period to period with changes in the market value of the securities owned by the variable annuity fund. If market values of such security portfolios do increase in some relatively high correlation with the price level, amounts of retirement income are likely to be more stable in constant dollars than income in constant dollars from a conventional fixed annuity.

Participants in variable annuity funds are credited with "accumulation" units in funds' assets as contributions are made by them, by employers on their behalf, or by both. *Accumulation units* are shares in the ownership of a fund's portfolio of securities; they are comparable to shares in mutual funds.

The market value of a portfolio is computed periodically, small liabilities incurred in the ordinary course of business are deducted, and the net value is divided by the number of accumulation units outstanding to arrive at the value of accumulation units on a particular date. Each participant is credited periodically with the number of accumulation units his periodic contributions will buy at the value per units on the dates contributions are received.

When a participant retires, the total number of his accumulation units at the values they have at that date are converted to *annuity units*. Annuity units are shares in a variable annuity fund. This is done by dividing the total value of the accumulation in thousands of dollars by the periodic amount of fixed annuity income that may be purchased with $1,000, as provided by the annuity tables of the issuer, for the kind of annuity option selected and according to the age and sex of the annuitant. Assumptions about future operating expenses and a future rate of return on invested funds are taken into account in the annuity tables. Thus a participant at retirement has a given number of annuity units to his credit. Subsequently his monthly income varies according to variations in rates of return per period from the securities portfolio.

The variable annuity was devised and is privately offered to faculty members of participating colleges and universities by Teachers Insurance and Annuity Association, a life insurance company chartered by the State of New York but also qualified as a corporation organized and operated exclusively for charitable and educational purposes. TIAA itself offers a fixed dollar amount type of annuity and most of its assets are invested in bonds and mortgages. But it has an affiliate called the College Retirement Equities Fund, CREF for short, created by special act of the legislature of the State of New York, and it is this affiliate that offers the variable annuity to academic employees of educational institutions. Participants may allocate contributions on their behalf between the two types of annuity funds in whatever proportions they choose—from zero to one and 100 per cent to the other, or the opposite.

Life insurance companies selling annuity contracts to the public soon became interested in offering variable annuities, but they encountered serious legal difficulties that required many years of effort to overcome. The United States Supreme Court ruled that variable annuities are not annuities, because issuers do not assume the investment risk, but that they are securities within the definition of securities in the Securities Act of 1933. There was a long period of negotiation between the life companies and the SEC plus some amendment of the Securities Act and the Investment Companies Act that finally resulted in statutes and SEC regulations that the life companies could live with.

By the late 1960's the way was clear for large-scale entry of life insurance companies into the public offering of variable annuities and they went about it with considerable enthusiasm. Most principal life companies now offer variable annuity contracts of one kind or another and some offer several kinds. At the end of 1970 the asset values of publicly offered variable annuity funds of insurance companies totaled $274 million. Unless historical trends in stock prices and in the price level change considerably in the future, variable annuities may prove to be the most innovative financial instrument of the twentieth century.

Income Tax Encouragement for Pension Funds

Public concern with the welfare of retired persons has influenced the enactment of amendments to the Internal Revenue Code that provide tax incentives for several kinds of pension arrangements. Many years ago the law was changed to permit business corporations to treat as tax-deductible expense their contributions to qualified employee pension plans and to exempt from the income tax the returns on investment of these pension funds. Corporate plans are required to meet certain conditions to qualify and thus to gain such tax advantages.

Still another provision of the Internal Revenue Code permits "self employed individuals and owner-employees" to make contributions to pension plans that are deductible from their taxable personal income. These plans, sometimes called Keogh Plans for the congressman who chiefly sponsored the legislation, must be qualified with the Treasury and must meet certain conditions as to provisions of plans and equality of benefits. The amounts that may be contributed annually are limited to a maximum amount, or a maximum percentage of earned income.

An incentive for establishing retirement funds by tax-exempt organizations has been provided by another portion of the federal law permitting a percentage of salary contributed to a qualified pension fund for employees to be exempt from employees' personal income tax.[3]

Evaluating Retirement Income in Terms of Risk

The risk involved in the retirement income portion of an individual investor's total financial situation has an important bearing on the risk level of his total financial program, and it may influence strongly the level of risk he is able to assume in his securities portfolio. For an individual who is presently receiving retirement income, the risks are not difficult to estimate. For one whose retirement income is somewhere in the future, there may be uncertainties about amounts to which he will become entitled.

Annuity income from an insured pension fund is very low in financial risk. The obligation is that of an insurance company and ability of insurers to pay is rarely subject to question. But this kind of income is fully exposed to erosion in the purchasing power of the dollar. Interest-rate risk does not affect the amount of annuity income, except as there may be variation in amount of dividends (extra payments from earnings on insurance company assets in excess of the assumed rate). Annuity incomes are payable only to annuitants; therefore, they are not marketable or even saleable.

[3]Principal provisions of the Internal Revenue Code affecting pension funds are Sections 401 thru 404, and Section 501.

The income from annuities, both insured and uninsured, is taxable as ordinary income when contributions have been made by employers. However, there is usually a tax advantage in that total amount of personal income is lower after retirement and therefore the maximum income tax rate is smaller. However, annuity income derived from contributions by an annuitant (rather than an employer) is tax exempt. The legal assumption is that the personal income tax has already been paid on the premiums.

Financial risk in retirement income (immediate annuities) from noninsured pension funds is negligible when the plans are fully funded. Pension fund reserves are presumed to be actuarily adequate to discharge all future income payments. But if such plans are not fully funded, further contributions must be made by employers to provide for future payments. A business corporation with well-established earnings should be able to make such future contributions, and the same is true of public employers with broad power to levy and collect taxes. However, the possibility of exception exists. What we have said about other elements of risk and the desirability of ownership qualities for insured funds also applies to noninsured funds.

Variable annuity income represents about the same level of financial risk as common stocks, and to the extent that stock prices are affected by changes in market rates of interest they are affected by interest rate risk. If total rates of return on common stocks vary over long periods of time in such manner as to compensate approximately for changes in the general price level, variable annuity income is low in purchasing-power risk.

When retirement income is in the future (deferred annuities), there are important uncertainties about future amounts. Benefits, as we have observed, vary according to length of service, or average earnings in a period of employment, or both. At any given time an employee does not know what his earnings base will be; it depends on his future earnings. When length of service is a component in determining retirement income, it may be calculated from date of entrance into the pension fund to date of compulsory retirement, but sometimes there are options about date of retirement on the part of employees, employers, or both. It is possible to estimate both future earnings and length of employment, but they are approximations.

Another element of uncertainty about the amount of a deferred annuity is the uncertainty of continued employment and participation in the employer's pension plan. An employee may quit his job, or he may be fired. In such events, the value of past contributions on his account depends on the vesting provisions of the pension plan. An employee has a vested interest in pension fund accumulations when he has the right to some or all of the amount to his account on termination of his employment. Some noninsured plans provide no vested interest. An employee who leaves his employment loses everything. If he has several long periods of employment with participation in nonvested pension funds, he may wind up at retirement age with very little retirement income.[4]

[4]Ralph Nader calls the present private pension system a lottery because of eligibility requirements and lack of vesting. He says, "At least one-half of all persons participating . . . will not receive pension benefits when they retire. More than one-half

It has become more common in recent years for both private and public pension plans to contain some provision for vesting. Thus, an employee may gain a vested interest in some percentage of the pension fund accumulation to his credit after a defined period of employment, and that percentage may increase after another period of employment has passed. After some total period his right may be fully vested. When an employee with a vested right leaves his employment, he is entitled to be paid the vested amount. Or, it is sometimes provided that he may leave it in the pension fund until he retires and then receive retirement income provided by the vested interest. Most uninsured pension plans have no provision for portability, that is, for transfer of an employee's vested interest in the fund of one employer to the fund of another.

It is apparent that amounts of retirement income for an individual participating in an uninsured pension fund or a variable annuity, but with some years to go before retirement, may be subject to a wide range of uncertainty. How does that affect the level of risk he may reasonably assume in his securities portfolio?

LIFE INSURANCE IN THE PORTFOLIO OF PERSONAL ASSETS

Life insurance salesmen and securities salesmen often find themselves in competition for a prospective customer's dollars. Competition is a good thing, but in planning an investor's personal financial program it is important to arrange life insurance and security investments so that the two kinds of assets complement and support each other. Some minimum amount of life insurance is needed by almost every investor. Beyond that minimum, investment constraints are affected by amounts, kinds, and terms of settlement of life insurance contracts. The life insurance part of an individual's personal financial program may relax constraints on investment policy, or it may make them more severe. In any event, it is important to review the life insurance program and to consider what changes may be desirable to improve the total financial framework for investment in securities.

The Kinds of Life Insurance Contracts

One begins, obviously, by examining the life insurance contracts a man owns and their terms. But one must know something about life insurance contracts and the several kinds of arrangements that can be made for payment of proceeds. Life insurance is a complex subject, but one can seek the counsel of experts in this field as well as in other areas of personal financial planning.

---

of all persons who receive private pension benefits receive less than $1,000 a year." He charges that, "In terms of dollar impact, the private pension system represents one of the most comprehensive consumer frauds that many Americans will encounter in their lifetime." (From "Remarks by Ralph Nader before the Sixth Annual Conference on Employee Benefits," New York City, May 24, 1972.)

The first distinction to be made is between group life insurance and individual life insurance. A group life contract provides for insurance of all people in a group. The group usually consists of employees of a company or an institution, and a person covered by group life insurance loses it when he leaves the group. The principal amount of insurance on each employee is determined by the employer and is defined in the group insurance contract. Amounts may vary according to salary levels or levels of responsibility. The right of a group member is simply to have the amount of his insurance paid to his beneficiary at his death, according to whatever settlement option has been chosen. Group insurance has no cash surrender value, or any other kind of realizable value, to insured persons. Group insurance is attractive because it is relatively inexpensive. Frequently, it provides substantial amounts of insurance that would not be owned if it had to be obtained with individual policies.

Individual insurance takes the form of a contract between an insurance company and an individual policyholder. Although insurance companies often devise special language to describe their policies in an effort to improve their sales appeal, there are only a few basic types of individual life insurance contracts. Policies with names intended to have favorable connotations are usually combinations in one way or another of the principal types.

The three basic kinds of individual life insurance are whole life, term, and endowment. Whole life policies are contracts for the entire life of an insured person, and proceeds are paid at death. There are two principal variations of whole life insurance that are distinguished by a difference in the time period in which premiums are paid. An ordinary life insurance policy requires payment of premiums for as long as the insured lives or, to be more precise, up to the age when he becomes "actuarially dead." Insurance actuaries assume that insured persons will not live longer than some maximum number of years, such as 100, and if an insured person actually lives beyond that age he may not only stop paying premiums but also collect the face amount of insurance just as though he had died.

Many people dislike the idea of continuing to pay premiums on life insurance after they have reached the age of retirement, because they expect to have a reduced amount of income after that time. Therefore, the life companies offer a variation of whole life insurance called limited payment life. It differs from ordinary life in that insurance premiums are required to be paid only for a maximum period of time, such as 20 or 30 years, or to attainment of a specified age by the insured. At the end of the period, with the insured still living, the policy becomes paid up. This kind of policy requires larger periodic premium payments than an ordinary life policy for any given individual.

Term insurance differs from whole life insurance in that it is written for a specified term of years and not for the whole life of an insured person. The usual term is 5 or 10 years, but some companies offer this type of contract for as long as 15 years. If the insured person dies during the term of the policy, the face amount is paid to his beneficiary. If he lives through the period, the contract expires and no one gets anything.

An endowment policy is a combination of term insurance and a savings account. Like term insurance, it is written for a specified time period—usually 10, 15, or 20 years. If the insured dies within the period, the face amount is paid to his beneficiary. But if he lives to the end of the period, he is paid the face amount. This kind of life insurance is the only one that an insured person can collect by living for the term of the contract. The distinguishing feature of endowment insurance is that a portion of each premium paid is used to pay the cost of term insurance, and the remainder is invested and accumulated by the insurer. This is the savings account part. The schedule of premiums is so arranged that the portion invested and accumulated will equal the face amount of the policy at maturity.

The combinations of these basic types of insurance are limited only by the imagination of people who sell insurance and the abilities of insurance actuaries to compute the premiums required. A kind of insurance designed especially for young men in the early years of their business careers when earnings are low provides for relatively low premium payments during an initial period of 5 or 10 years and for much larger premium payments thereafter. This is a combination of term insurance for the initial period and of whole life thereafter.

Settlement Options

Life insurance companies offer policyholders their choice of several different arrangements for payment of death benefits. It may be as important for achievement of the purposes of an investor to choose the most suitable settlement option as it is to choose the most suitable kind of life insurance.

By far the most common method of paying insurance proceeds is the lump-sum cash payment on proof of death of an insured person. But under this arrangement there are several further choices. Payment may be made to a named beneficiary, to the estate of the insured, or to a trust created by the will of an insured.

A much less common but often desirable method is to use proceeds to buy an annuity from the insurer for a named beneficiary. Several different kinds of annuity or installment income arrangements are possible. One is simply a life annuity. Proceeds are applied by a company to purchase of an annuity, and a beneficiary receives an amount of monthly income for life.

However, a life annuity ends at death of the annuitant. To hedge the contingency of death soon after annuity payments begin, the companies generally offer to make payments for a specified time period even if an annuitant dies during the period. This arrangement is termed an annuity for a period certain. The period may be 10, 15, or 20 years. If an annuitant dies before the end of the period, the insurer pays to the annuitant's estate, or to a named secondary beneficiary, the cash equivalent of the amount of payments for the period that remain unpaid. Besides the annuity arrangement, life companies offer several arrangements for payment of proceeds of insurance on an installment basis.

Insurance in Personal Financial Planning

Life insurance may be used for one or more of several different purposes in an investor's personal financial program. The questions of how much insurance, what types of policies, and what methods of settlement must be approached much as we have the problem of investment management, that is, with the objective of fulfilling the needs of the individual so far as possible.

The most elementary concept of the use of life insurance is that proceeds at death serve to pay funeral expenses. This use of insurance is still an important one for many people at the lowest income levels. A concept only a little more advanced is that insurance provides an emergency fund to be used to aid a wife and children following death of a husband and wage earner.

A more sophisticated use of funds from the cash settlement of life insurance is to pay estate and inheritance taxes and expenses of estate settlement. This may be a very important use when the size of an estate is sufficiently large that these taxes and expenses are relatively large. Again, however, liquidity for estate purposes may be provided by security investments. It is important that a choice be made and that estate liquidity be provided in one way or another.

When life insurance proceeds are to be used to provide income in addition to emergency expenses and estate settlement expenses, arrangements for the payment of insurance must be designed for the purpose. Any of the income options may be used, that is, a life annuity or installment payment of income for a limited time period. The amount of income required must be determined by reference to estimated living expenses and other sources of income. All sorts of combinations are possible—income from insurance proceeds with social security income, with income from a pension fund, with income from proprietary investments, and income from marketable securities. It is no small task in some circumstances to work out a plan to provide income that will make the best use of available resources and meet the need adequately. Even when a good plan is devised, it may have to be changed after a lapse of time to adapt it to an evolving pattern of family needs.

One way to use insurance proceeds to provide income is to make it payable to a trust fund created by an insured's will. A will may direct only the proceeds of life insurance to a trust, or it may provide that insurance and other property be placed in trust. In either case, a principal amount is placed in the hands of a trustee upon death of the maker of the will with whatever instructions the will provides concerning investment of trust assets and use of income and principal for one or more beneficiaries.

When an investor's life insurance arrangements are examined along with his investments and with the needs to be served by insurance well in mind, the suitability of an existing insurance program can be appraised. Sometimes insurance has been bought without particular reference to all the financial circumstances of an investor and there are opportunities for improvement in amount, type of insurance, and arrangements for payment of proceeds in the course of systematic personal financial planning.

Review of a man's insurance arrangements may show that he has more insurance than he really needs. The need for insurance to provide income for dependents tends to decrease with the passage of years. Children grow up and become financially independent. The amounts of retirement income to which an employee is entitled usually become larger as the number of years of service increases. Thrifty people accumulate savings and sometimes inheritance adds to their financial well-being. Such favorable developments may permit the face amount of an investor's insurance to be reduced, or existing policy contracts to be converted into paid-up insurance. Conversion to paid-up insurance involves the use of accumulated policy reserves to pay a single premium.

A review of the suitability of an insurance program must include consideration of the designation of beneficiaries and choice of methods of payment. Arrangements that serve the purpose very well at one time may become unsuitable at another time, as the purpose for which insurance is to be used changes. When insurance is intended primarily to provide income for a wife and children, the designation of the wife as beneficiary and the selection of an option may be quite appropriate. But after some years have passed and some wealth has been accumulated, it may be better to make insurance payable to the insured's estate or to a trust created by his will. The idea to be emphasized particularly is that the uses for insurance change and that arrangements for payment should be re-examined from time to time.

Life Insurance in Terms of Investment Risk

Life insurance is safe as far as the ability of life companies to pay is concerned. They are strictly regulated by the states and managed with full regard for the sanctity of their financial obligations. Changes in interest rates affect the cost of life insurance rather than amounts of contractual payments. Larger earnings on invested assets generally result in larger dividends, which are essentially a return of premiums paid. The high level of purchasing-power risk in long-term contracts for payments of fixed dollar amounts is obvious. Presently the life insurance companies are endeavoring to adjust to an economic climate of continual inflation by developing life insurance contracts with variable benefits.

The proceeds of life insurance contracts are not taxable as income under the federal personal income tax because premiums are presumed to have been paid from income of insured persons that has already been taxed. However, insurance proceeds are a part of the taxable estate under the federal estate tax.

There is no marketability, because life contracts are not saleable, but this type of asset may be an important source of liquidity. Principal amounts may of course be taken in cash at termination of a contract, but the reserve value of individual policies may also serve as a source of cash. Life companies are required by state laws to loan a policyowner any amount up to the non-forfeiture value, which is essentially the amount of reserve accumulated by the company for a policy, at a rate of interest specified in the life insurance contract. The non-forfeiture value is security for the loan. If it is not repaid, the principal amount of the loan together with any accrued interest is deducted at the time proceeds are paid. Banks and other institutional lenders also consider the non-forfeiture value good collateral for loans. As a last resort a life insurance policy can be cancelled and the non-forfeiture value taken in cash.

When you know the amounts and terms of life insurance owned by an investor, you can add it into the total structure of assets with a level of risk and with one particular advantage in desirability of ownership qualities. Generally the effect of life insurance is to lower the average risk level of the set of personal assets as far as uncertainty of future dollar amounts is concerned, to increase the risk level in terms of constant dollars, and to improve the liquidity of the personal estate.

ESTATE PLANNING

For some people the term "estate planning" brings to mind a man who counts his wealth in millions and is sometimes beset by relatives courting his favor. The question of who fed the old man the arsenic has been the basic plot of countless murder mysteries. This is, of course, a wholly unrealistic concept of estate planning. A person does not have to have a million dollars to have a problem of estate planning. Whatever he owns is his estate and somebody will get it when he dies. Frequently, it is to his advantage for somebody to get it before he dies.

The manner in which a person in possession of some considerable amount of wealth plans the distribution of his estate has a very considerable bearing on his investment constraints. An estate plan may greatly reduce the amount an investor retains for investment in securities, it may increase or decrease the need for liquidity in his estate, and it will certainly affect the amounts that have to be paid in taxes during life and at death.

Anyone who has even a modest amount of wealth needs some expert advice on how to dispose of it, and a person with considerable wealth may need a whole corps of attorneys, tax experts, and investment counselors. Perhaps the most important single thing that can be said in this brief discussion is: get good expert advice.

There are several principal questions involved in estate planning. One is whether to give away some wealth while the owner is living and the other is how to dispose of what is owned at time of death.

Distribution by the Living Hand

People of considerable wealth often give away part of their wealth while they live. Our system of federal income and estate taxation favors living distribution and there is reason to think that people like to see the benefits of their gifts to members of their families, to close associates, and to eleemosynary institutions. At the very least, living persons can give some direction to how wealth they have given away is used and, by observing the results of their benefactions can decide how further distributions will be made.

Some of the reasons for distributing property while the owner lives come readily to mind. One is to provide for dependents. By the living hand one can make arrangements that provide a maximum of economic security for people who cannot obtain it in any other way, thus giving them the sense of financial independence that is so important to peace of mind. Such arrangements can be made sufficiently flexible to permit adjustment to changes in economic needs within the terms of the initial arrangement or by subsequent action of the donor of property.

A common purpose of living distribution is to accomplish a charitable objective. Very wealthy people sometimes establish charitable foundations with such huge sums of money and such a broad range of activities that their names become very well known. But it is not necessary to have great wealth to establish a charitable foundation. Many people who consider themselves "just ordinary millionaires" have used a personal or family foundation as an instrument for administering the funds they allocate for charitable objects.

Another way to use money for charitable purposes is to give it to colleges, churches, hospitals, or other kinds of eleemosynary institutions. Frequently such gifts are used to construct physical facilities that bear the name of the donor; many a family name has been memorialized in this manner.

The simplest method of distributing property is to make an outright gift. Gifts to eleemosynary institutions are usually made outright. But where individuals are concerned an outright gift may not be the best arrangement either for the donor or the donee. A gift to one person becomes the property of that one person. He can sell it, or give it away, lose it by speculating or spend it in riotous living. Thus it may not serve the purpose intended by the donor.

There is, however, a legal arrangement that serves well for making gifts to individuals a person wants to provide for while he is living. It is the personal trust. The principle is simple, but the legal details are complex. In modern law and legal practice the trust arrangement is very flexible. One trust may benefit a number of persons, it may benefit them in different ways, and it may last a long time.

The basic concept of a personal trust is that one person, or more than one person acting jointly, may transfer property to a second party to keep in trust and to use for the benefit of a third party, or parties. The one who creates a trust is the trustor, or creator; the one to whom the property is given in trust is the trustee; and the person or persons to receive the benefits are the beneficiaries. Usually banks are named as trustees because they have trust departments staffed by persons trained and experienced in administering trusts, but any legally competent individual may be named by a trustor as a trustee.

The duties of trustees are defined by law and trustees are held strictly accountable for performing their duties. They must administer a trust with care, skill, and prudence; they must make the trust property productive of returns for beneficiaries; they must provide accurate accounts of their administration.

Personal trusts may not continue in existence forever. At some point in time, they must be terminated and the property in trust must be liquidated. This rule against perpetuities does not seriously limit the use of personal trusts for the benefit of several generations of people. A person who has children and grandchildren could create a trust that would continue until the death of the last of two living grandchildren.

Trustors may further increase the flexibility of trust provisions by giving a power of appointment to a beneficiary of a trust. The power of appointment is a power to designate who will succeed the named beneficiary as the next beneficiary. Thus a man may create a trust with his wife as beneficiary and give her the right to appoint whom she chooses to succeed her. She could appoint one or more children, one or more grandchildren, or anyone else she wants to benefit from the trust.

One use of a trust is for the benefit of the trustor himself. He can name himself as beneficiary, or man and wife may jointly create a trust for their joint benefit. This kind of arrangement may be particularly advantageous when the owners of property have little ability or inclination to devote their time to its management.

One major impact of living distribution on the financial circumstances of an individual, and therefore on his investment constraints, is to reduce his wealth. Any kind of property may be given away, but more often than not the kind that can be disposed of most conveniently is marketable securities. When wealth is reduced, income may be reduced correspondingly, and the entire set of investment constraints may be changed.

A second effect may be to reduce or even eliminate entirely the problem of managing personal investments. Securities given away no longer have to be managed, and securities placed in personal trusts are managed by trustees.

Still another effect is on taxation. A reduction in wealth very likely means a reduction in size of personal income tax rates applicable to an investor, and his constraint in terms of taxability may be changed. Reduction in wealth also affects the size of the federal estate tax and expenses of estate settlement.

Distribution by Mortmain

Lawyers like to use the term "mortmain" because it sounds better than "dead hand," although it means the same thing. When the owner of property dies, its ownership must be transferred to someone. This may be done by will, but in the absence of a will it is done according to the law of the state having jurisdiction. Distribution by will is testate distribution; distribution without a will is intestate distribution.

In order to distribute property by will, you must leave a legally valid will. The chief requirement for making a valid will is to obtain the services of an attorney with more than a little skill in drafting wills. The drafting of a will that actually accomplishes the purposes of the maker requires fine legal draftsmanship.

One of the advantages of using a will to dispose of property as opposed to intestate distribution is that the owner of property can indicate in his will the person or institution he wishes to serve as executor of his estate. A testator may also name a person or institution to serve as guardian of his minor children if both parents should be deceased. Frequently, a bank is appointed guardian of the property of minors and a relative or close friend is appointed guardian of their persons. The attorney for an estate may be named in a will, and it may be important to designate an attorney familiar with the affairs of the testator.

One of the first steps to be taken in the legal process of distributing an estate under will is to probate the will. To probate is to prove to a court that the will presented is the last will of the testator and that it is legally valid. When that is done, the court admits the will to probate and appoints the executor of the estate. Then it is the duty of the executor to assemble the property of the testator, to safeguard it and manage it while the estate is being settled, to pay debts, taxes, and expenses, and to effect distribution according to the terms of the will.

Property may be disposed of by will in several different ways. One way is to grant legacies, which are gifts of personal property. The property may be cash, a specified quantity of any kind of personal property, or a particular item of personal property. A son, rather than a daughter, may be given as a legacy stock representing a controlling interest in a closed corporation. Gifts of real property are called devises. Thus a testator can devise a specified number of acres of land from a larger number owned by him, or devise a particular lot in a city. He may devise the family home to a daughter rather than to a son. The balance of a testator's property after all such legacies and devises is known as the residuary estate. The residuary estate may represent the greater part of the property owned and usually it is from the residuary estate that a testator makes provision for members of his family.

One form of testate distribution is to put property in trust for beneficiaries. A trust created by will is termed a testamentary trust. Such trusts, like those created while the creator is living, permit considerable flexibility in distributing property and they may have the additional advantage that the property left in trust will be managed professionally by a trust institution.

When a person dies without a will, a court appoints an administrator of his estate. The function of the administrator is to make an inventory of the property owned by the deceased, to take custody and management of it, to pay debts and taxes, and to make distribution of the residue according to the laws of the state governing descent of property. Thus it is often said that if you do not make a will, the state makes one for you in the sense that state law determines how your property will be distributed.

Most states recognize the common-law right of a widow to a dower, that is, to a share in the property of her deceased husband. In many states the dower right is to one-third of the estate, but the proportion may be different in different states and under different circumstances. A widower may have a right of curtesy in the estate of his deceased wife, which is a right to a life estate in real property of his wife or a right to some stipulated share of the estate.

After the share of a surviving spouse, if any, property generally descends next to children of the deceased person. State laws frequently provide that a surviving spouse shall receive one-third of such an estate and all children of the couple shall share equally in the remaining two-thirds. But the statutes provide for all sorts of situations. If a child who would be entitled to a share if he were living is deceased, his children may be entitled to his share. Sometimes living parents of a person who dies intestate are entitled to a share along with the children of the deceased. If you think you don't need a will, read the law of your state governing intestate distribution of property.

Taxation of Distribution of Wealth

You not only can't take it with you; you must pay a tax when you give it away—with some exceptions. For this reason one of the important considerations in estate planning is minimizing of taxes. It should not, however, obscure the main objective, which is to give it to the people or the institutions you really want to have it.

There are two kinds of federal taxes on the distribution of property. One is the gift tax, which is a tax on gifts of property during life, and the other is the estate tax, which applies to the disposition of property at death. In addition, most states impose inheritance taxes.

The federal gift tax is levied on all gifts of property to donees (those who receive gifts) other than charitable institutions above certain exempted amounts. However, the provisions of the gift tax law encourage living distribution of property by providing certain exemptions and applying lower rates to taxable gifts than to property subject to the federal estate tax.

There are two kinds of exemptions. The *annual exemption* permits an individual to give annually up to $3,000 a year to each of as many donees as he pleases without gift tax. A man and wife jointly may give up to $6,000 a year to any number of donees without tax. The *lifetime exemption* permits a person to give away $30,000 during his lifetime, in addition to the annual exemption, without a gift tax. A man and wife have a lifetime exemption of $60,000. Gifts made from time to time in excess of the annual exemptions count against the lifetime exemption, and only when both exemptions have been used up do gifts become taxable under the gift tax law.

The federal estate tax is levied on the transfer of property from the estate of a deceased person; it is payable from the estate. There may be three kinds of deductions from the adjusted gross estate, that is, the amount remaining after debts and expenses. First, and very important, is the marital deduction. This is the amount of the estate left by a man to his wife, or by wife to husband, up to 50 per cent of the adjusted gross estate. Whatever amount up to 50 per cent goes to a surviving spouse is deductible, but the deduction may be no more than 50 per cent even if a larger proportion is left to wife or husband. Obviously there can be no such deduction from the estate of one who dies without a surviving spouse. The second kind of deduction is all property left to charity, and there is no limit on this amount. The third is the standard exemption of $60,000 that applies to all estates. Thus estates with no more than this amount remaining after previous deductions escape the tax entirely, and if the remainder is small, the effective tax rate is low. Whatever remains is termed the taxable estate and it is taxed at the rates shown in Table 17–1. Rates of the gift tax are also shown.

It requires only a little reflection to realize that the ability of a well-to-do investor to assume risk may be very considerably affected by the provisions of his estate plan. Gifts may reduce the size of the estate. Provisions for transfer of property by will may affect the nature of the property that may be held most advantageously for this purpose. Specific devises may significantly reduce the size of the residual estate intended to go to family members. And a good estate plan serves to delineate the need for higher grades of securities in the desirability of ownership qualities. It may be clear, for example, that some securities will have to be sold in the process of estate settlement to pay taxes and expenses. Or, alternatively, it may be that the estate plan will provide life insurance in amounts sufficient for these purposes and that the securities portfolio may be freed of that constraint. The need for tax-exempt securities may be changed by reduction in size of income subject to the personal income tax.

TABLE 17–1

Federal Estate and Gift Tax Rates

Federal estate tax			*Federal gift tax*	
Tax on amount in center column	*Bracket rate on excess over amount center column*	*Taxable estate or taxable gift*	*Tax on amount in center column*	*Bracket rate on excess over amount in center column*
$ 0	3%	$ 0	$ 0	2-1/4%
150	7	5,000	112.50	5-1/4
500	11	10,000	375	8-1/4
1,600	14	20,000	1,200	10-1/2
3,000	18	30,000	2,250	13-1/2
4,800	22	40,000	3,600	16-1/2
7,000	25	50,000	5,250	18-3/4
9,500	28	60,000	7,125	21
20,700	30	100,000	15,525	22-1/2
65,700	32	250,000	49,275	24
145,700	35	500,000	109,275	26-1/4
233,200	37	750,000	174,000	27-3/4
325,700	39	1,000,000	244,275	29-1/4
423,200	42	1,250,000	317,400	31-1/2
528,200	45	1,500,000	396,150	33-3/4
753,200	49	2,000,000	564,900	36-3/4
998,200	53	2,500,000	748,650	39-3/4
1,263,200	56	3,000,000	947,400	42
1,543,200	59	3,500,000	1,157,400	44-1/4
1,838,200	63	4,000,000	1,378,650	47-1/4
2,468,200	67	5,000,000	1,851,150	50-1/4
3,138,200	70	6,000,000	2,353,650	52-1/2
3,838,200	73	7,000,000	2,878,650	54-3/4
4,568,200	76	8,000,000	3,426,150	57
6,088,200	77	10,000,000	4,566,150	57-3/4

Source: *Tax Service, Estate and Gift Taxes,* Englewood Cliffs, N.J., Prentice-Hall, Inc.

We said at the outset that this discussion of personal financial planning is a flashback. It should be done first before you even begin to think about investment constraints, because it may change greatly the situation you have to deal with.

QUESTIONS FOR DISCUSSION

1. The personal assets of a retired individual include a modest home, a certificate of deposit issued by a local bank in the amount of $20,000, and an automobile. The certificate of deposit pays 5 per cent interest a year and matures at the end of 2 years. Without further information, but with whatever inferences you feel justified in drawing, discuss the desirability of owning the certificate of deposit.
2. Some years ago a man and his wife bought a home just outside a small city. The house is located on eight acres of land, which the man used to pasture a couple of cows. Then the man died and title to the property went to his wife, who assumed the mortgage loan in the amount of $10,000. The widow lives on $3,000 of social security income plus about $5,000 annually in interest from bonds. Now she is offered $10,000 for seven acres of the land; this would leave the house and one acre. The price is considered a fair one. Should she sell?
3. Sarah Spinster has been a public school teacher all of her life and she is looking forward to retirement after 10 more years with a pension from the state public employees retirement fund. This state retirement fund is only partially funded and a considerable amount of the money to pay future retirement income to state employees must come from future appropriations by the state legislature. How does this situation affect Sarah's personal financial planning from this point in time forward?
4. Is it a good thing for the Internal Revenue Code to provide tax incentives for the creation and operation of employee retirement systems for private and public employers?
5. Ask your professor whether he participates in the retirement plan of Teachers Insurance and Annuity Association. If he does, ask him to evaluate the manner in which his participation affects his personal financial planning. If he does not, ask the same question about the retirement income plan in which he does participate.
6. Joseph Jordan just bought a life insurance policy on his own life in the amount of $100,000. Everybody knows that Jordan is the richest man in town. Why should he buy all that insurance?
7. This same Mr. Jordan, together with his wife, have created separate personal trust funds for each of their four children. They put $15,000 in each of the trusts and they plan to add $6,000 a year to each of them for at least the next 10 years. Does this make good sense for such a man as Jordan?
8. Your grandfather owns a large farm with a considerable amount of livestock and farm equipment. He has made no will and when you suggest that perhaps he ought to make one he says that he doesn't need a will because at his death everything he owns goes to his wife and children. Do you still think he needs a will?
9. Problem for special study: Do a financial profile of a real individual who has some money invested in securities, owns some proprietary-type assets,

has some personal debt, owns some life insurance, has some earned income, and has such other financial circumstances as have been described in this chapter. This individual may be middle-aged or elderly (these are the people who have the money) and it should be someone who will give you the essential facts in confidence. It might be your parent, grandparent, or rich uncle. When you get the information, write recommendations for improvement in this individual's financial affairs and show how they would change his investment constraints.

V

Investment Policies

18

Policies for Constructing the Securities Portfolio

We now come to the problems toward which all of our study has been directed—problems of policy in managing a securities portfolio. These are the really important problems in investment management, and this is where the decisions are made that so largely influence the size of investment returns. It has sometimes been said of the management of business enterprises that when major policy decisions are good, a company is well managed. This proposition is equally valid for managing the securities portfolio.

FORMULATING INVESTMENT POLICIES

In this chapter and the several following we are going to examine a variety of investment policies, to appraise the implications of these policies for gain and loss, and to develop a process of reasoning from particular investment constraints to conclusions about suitable investment policies. First, however, we must establish a foundation of general concepts.

Such terms as *portfolio* and *investment policies* may sound grandiose to an individual who has only a few security issues, but they imply no more than some commitment in securities and some action to be taken affecting security investments. A portfolio may be no more than a few shares of stock and some cash available for investment from time to time. Or, a portfolio may consist of a hundred issues of bonds and stocks of widely varying kinds and grades. An investment policy is a conclusion about a course of action to be taken; it may be no more than a decision to buy more of the same stock as funds become available, or to invest additional funds in a short-term bond.

There are two broad and distinct areas of investment policy decisions. In one area are all the decisions about what kinds and grades of securities should be included in a securities portfolio at a particular time. In the other are decisions about changes to be made from time to time in the securities owned, either as the circumstances of the investor change or as prices and yields in the market change. These two kinds of decisions are of course closely related. If you decide to sell stocks because prices are too high, you change the structure of the portfolio. Then, if you decide to buy bonds because yields are high, you make a further change. Nevertheless, it is an aid to orderly thinking to start with the general problem of constructing a securities portfolio of various grades of securities, and then to consider how the portfolio might be changed from time to time.

It is also helpful to have some general terms to apply to broad categories of investment policies. The term *defensive* has long been used to refer to policies designed to minimize risk of loss. Defensive policies are conservative policies; they are intended to preserve the value of principal and to provide stability of income. *Aggressive* policies are just the opposite. They are intended to produce larger returns in some manner; they are policies for taking larger risk. Accordingly, they are associated with instability of principal and income.

There are semantic difficulties in using these general terms. There are different degrees of defensiveness and aggressiveness and there is no clear dividing line between the two kinds of policies. Differences are relative. Nevertheless, they are useful terms for indicating the general character of some kinds of investment policies.

Left to act according to our own inclinations, most of us would not develop our concepts of investment policy very far. It is easy to say, "I buy common stocks for long-term investment," or "My policy is to sell stocks at the top of the business cycle and reinvest in bonds," and to think that such brief statements are sufficient description of policy. They are not. They leave many questions of policy unanswered and imply that the questions are not even recognized.

Ideally, investment policy should encompass every kind of question that is likely to develop in managing a securities portfolio. The man who buys stocks for long-term investment needs to say what grades of stocks he buys, how and to what extent he diversifies, whether he concentrates his purchases when he thinks stock prices are low or buys regularly without regard to estimates of the level of prices, and under what circumstances he would sell, if at all. The investor who buys bonds needs to describe the kinds of bonds he buys not only according to the total risk, but according to the principal causes of uncertainty and according to the several desirability of ownership qualities.

Why should investors develop clear and complete statements of investment policy? Probably the best reason is that to do so requires explicit consideration of the whole array of problems involved in managing a securities portfolio. If we force ourselves to study a problem, we are likely to find that it is much more complex than we thought at first, that we need more information about it in order to come to reasoned conclusions and, frequently, that it has more than one plausible solution. Throughout the process we must be conscious of the need to justify conclusions by a process of reasoning. This disciplined thinking is likely to result in better policy decisions than a more casual approach.

Clear definition of policy is the best safeguard against gradual and often unrecognized shifts in policy. The circumstances of investors change and conditions in the security markets change. In day-to-day operations the response to change may be small shifts in policy that ultimately amount to significant change without explicit consideration of the desirability of change. It is not uncommon for individuals to start out as long-term investors and to end up as speculators trying to profit by swings in stock prices. Sometimes this kind of metamorphosis is unconscious and nonrational. Investment policies do have to be changed from time to time, but change should be a product of explicit consideration of the question.

Well-defined policies are also a protection against impulsive action and decisions based on short-run considerations. One experienced investment manager advocates a "more formalized process" for making policy decisions to reduce the influence on management thinking of isolated events or emotional reactions, which "in their immediacy can take on more importance than is warranted in the stream of history."[1]

The thinking of people actively engaged in investment management has been influenced in recent years by contributions from academicians. Econo-

[1]Shelby M. C. Davis, "Elements of Perspective and Policy," *The Financial Analysts Journal*, Vol. 21, No. 3 (May–June, 1965), pp. 98–100.

mists and mathematicians, who long restricted their efforts to more esoteric topics, have become concerned with such workaday problems as how to value a common stock, whether future changes in stock prices can be predicted by study of past changes, and how to construct an "efficient" portfolio of securities. Psychologists have been investigating such questions as whether people generally pay more than they ought to pay on the basis of probable outcomes for the opportunity to win at long odds, and they have become involved with such behavioral problems as the true motivations of people who invest in securities. Further development in these directions is as certain as anything that can be said about investment in securities.

RISK IN CONSTRUCTING THE PORTFOLIO

The easiest way to begin thinking about policies in the construction of a securities portfolio is to assume that you have a considerable sum of money in cash that is to be invested in securities. The question is: What kind of securities should you buy? In what proportions should you buy the different kinds? In practice, an investment manager would seldom be confronted with the problem in these terms; a portfolio is usually already in existence. But he is continually confronted with essentially the same question: At this point in time how should it be constructed?

The problem must, of course, be in terms of risk and return. The problem is to select individual securities by their risk qualities and to combine them in a securities portfolio so that the risk level of the portfolio will be the highest risk that can be assumed by the investor within the constraints that have been established. Such a portfolio would provide the highest expected rate of return.

Risk means total risk. But it is entirely reasonable in theory and a virtual necessity in practice to think of the riskiness of security issues in terms of the chief causes of uncertainty. When we consider risk in common stocks, we have to think chiefly of the uncertainty of the future financial abilities of their issuers. When we think of bonds of government, municipal, and corporate issuers, we think of risk as mainly a function of changes in interest rates. So, it is convenient to use such terms as "financial risk" and "interest-rate risk" as causes of uncertainty.

Traditional Concepts of Portfolio Construction

We can think about constructing a portfolio, at least initially, in a mechanistic fashion. Securities are differentiated by grade of financial risk, and a portfolio is made up of securities of one grade, or of more than one grade in whatever proportions may be deemed appropriate. A portfolio consisting entirely of government obligations would have zero financial risk. But a portfolio might consist of corporate bonds, preferred stocks, and common stocks representing a number of different financial-risk grades of securities.

TABLE 18–1
Constructing a Portfolio with Securities of Different Grades of Financial Risk

Corporate bonds: 30%	Triple A:	10%
	Double A:	10%
	Single A:	10%
Common stocks: 70%	High-grade common stocks:	50%
	Low-grade common stocks:	20%

Table 18–1 shows a portfolio composed of five grades of securities ranging from high- to low-grade. Portfolio construction policies are usually defined in terms of proportions or percentages of total portfolio, rather than in dollar amounts.

Designing Policies to Meet Investment Constraints

To begin thinking about policies in assuming financial risk, we should return to our earlier conclusions about ability to risk loss of income and principal in current dollars. Constructing a portfolio in terms of the grades of securities and the distribution of risks represented by individual issues must be so designed that maximum losses under the most adverse conditions that may be experienced in a period of several years are unlikely to exceed the established loss limits. The approach is negative. At this point we are concerned with potential losses rather than with gains.

We usually think of instability in market values and investment incomes for security portfolios in terms of fluctuations associated with the business cycle, because these fluctuations are most important to the design of investment policies. Sometimes lesser fluctuations over shorter time periods are also important and should be taken into account. In other circumstances, it may be necessary to consider future developments over time periods longer than the usual business cycle. When a portfolio includes a relatively large number of issues of a particular risk grade, well dispersed as to possible causes of loss or gain, we may assume that experience with these issues will not vary greatly from the general experience of investors with securities of this grade. However, when a securities portfolio, or a portion of it, consists of only a few issues of a risk grade, experience with the sum of those few issues may vary widely from the experience of investors generally with securities of that grade.

The development of a systematic line of thought about construction of a portfolio requires careful organization. There are the several kinds of investment constraints, and there are different risk levels of securities in terms of the principal causes of uncertainty. The focus is first on the risk of loss of principal as a limitation on assumption of financial risk. Then we will consider the risk of loss of income and other limiting conditions. Initially, loss of principal will be taken to mean any depreciation in market value of securities below their cost.

FINANCIAL RISK IN PORTFOLIO CONSTRUCTION

In considering the risk of price depreciation, we shall first assume that the securities portfolio will include securities of only one grade and that the number of issues is sufficient that price depreciation for the portfolio may be expected to correspond approximately to price depreciation for all securities of that grade outstanding in the market. This presents the problem in its simplest form. We will also assume that the principal concern of the investor is with depreciation of market values during a period of general decline in prices associated with the business cycle.

Cyclical Price Fluctuations for Grades of Securities

With some knowledge of the history of cyclical price movements of the several grades of securities, you can estimate approximately the maximum price depreciation that may be suffered in a future cyclical decline. You may conclude that for a certain grade of securities the maximum decline in average prices from top to bottom of a cycle will be, for example, 15 per cent. Then you must consider whether the investment constraints affecting this portfolio will permit that much depreciation in the total portfolio without seriously adverse consequences to the investor. If they will, this grade of securities fits within the investment limitations.

To be specific, consider first the size of changes in market prices that may be expected for high-grade, long-term bonds during a business cycle. In our earlier study we observed that in the downward phase of the business cycle, market prices for securities of this grade of financial risk are influenced very little by investors' appraisals of issuers' financial abilities to pay the sums required by bond contracts. Thus, as far as financial risk is concerned, a recession would have little adverse influence on market prices for high-grade securities. A decline in interest rates would have a pronounced effect on prices, but we will consider separately problems of policy presented by interest-rate risk.

How would you estimate the cyclical price depreciation for medium-grade bonds—those rated about double B—and preferred stocks of about the same grade? Financial risk in these issues is sufficiently high that some depreciation of average prices may be expected in any severe and extended cyclical decline in business activity. The financial position of issuers of these securities is not strong, as evidenced by relatively low ratings, and they are likely to be weakened by economic recession. Moreover, investors' confidence in issuers of securities of this grade tends to be unstable. Toward the peak of an expansion phase of the cycle, it is not difficult for investors to project further improvement in the financial position of relatively weak companies. Toward the bottom of a cyclical trough it is easy to project further serious financial deterioration. Thus, variation in financial abilities and in investors' confidence with the business cycle causes price fluctuations of considerable amplitude for securities of this grade.

If you are thinking about a portfolio consisting of a large number of issues of common stocks representing a rough cross-section of all issues actively traded in the market, you can base your estimate of cyclical price depreciation on past experience with some broad index of stock prices. However, there are different grades of common stocks, and stocks of some industries are more affected by cyclical fluctuations than those of others. A portfolio consisting largely of blue chip stocks may be expected to fluctuate in market value less than one composed of stocks of poorer grade, and one composed of stocks of companies in cyclically stable industries may vary in price less than those representing cyclically unstable industries.

Correlation of Cyclical Price Fluctuations for Grades of Securities

A portfolio may be constructed entirely of securities of one grade of financial risk, but investors generally use two or more grades in their effort to obtain the largest returns consistent with their ability to assume risk. If there is more than one grade, the amplitude of cyclical price fluctuation in portfolio value from peak to trough is the weighted average of price changes for the several grades with the proportions of the grades used as weights. We continue to assume that changes in average market value of the securities of a particular grade in the portfolio correspond approximately to changes in average value for all securities of that grade in the hands of all investors.

As a hypothetical example, consider a portfolio composed of securities of three financial risk grades in the proportions of 30, 20, and 50 per cent. It is estimated that the maximum cyclical price depreciation for Grade *A* is 10 per cent, for Grade *B* is 15 per cent, and for Grade *C* is 25 per cent. The estimated price depreciation for the entire portfolio is 18.5 per cent. The arithmetic is in Table 18–2.

TABLE 18–2

Weighted Price Depreciation for a Portfolio

Grade	*Proportion*	*Cyclical price depreciation*	*Proportion times depreciation*
A	0.30%	–0.10%	–0.030
B	0.20	–0.15	–0.030
C	0.50	–0.25	–0.125
	1.00%		–0.185

You can see that it would be possible to combine these three grades in such proportions as to produce a wide range of estimated maximum cyclical price depreciation for a portfolio. If most of the portfolio consisted of Grade *A* securities, the size of portfolio depreciation would be much smaller than 18.5 per cent. If most of it consisted of Grade *C* securities, the estimated depreciation would be larger. Thus, the larger the proportion of securities high-grade in financial risk, the less is the potential price depreciation.

We have been thinking about depreciation in market prices of securities in a period of business recession, but we know that prices of money-rate type securities generally rise as business recedes and interest rates decline. This contracyclical price movement for high-grade bonds can be used to compensate in whole or in some part for the cyclical price movements of lower-grade securities. Thus, if long-term, high-grade bonds comprise one-half of a portfolio, and the average price of these issues is expected to increase 10 per cent from the peak to the trough of the business cycle, and if lower-grade securities in financial risk make up the other half and the average price of these issues is expected to decline as much as 10 per cent from peak to trough, then the two price movements would approximately compensate and there would be but little change in market value of the portfolio. One can hardly expect estimates of price movements to be realized perfectly; nor will negative correlation in price changes between securities of two grades over a time period be perfect, but the general idea of price appreciation in some grades of securities offsetting price depreciation in other grades of securities is a useful one.

Price Correlation Among Issues of the Same Grade

You need only a few issues of high-grade securities in a portfolio to obtain about average price experience for issues of that grade. If you have ten issues of triple A rated long-term corporate bonds in a portfolio, the average value of these bonds will change in close correlation with change in average value of all such bonds in the market. If you double the number to twenty issues, you will not significantly increase the correlation between changes in average value of triple A bonds in the portfolio and changes in average value of all triple A corporate bonds in the market.

The lower the grade of securities in financial risk, the weaker is the tendency for prices of individual issues to rise or decline together. These issues are by definition subject to great uncertainties in terms of the financial abilities of their issuers. Differences in the prosperity of industries and in the quality of corporate managements are more important influences on financial abilities than in the area of very high-grade issues. In a period of booming business some companies may prosper to a great extent, some to about an average extent, and some may not prosper at all. In fact, some companies deteriorate financially even when general business conditions are excellent.

In addition, the emotions of investors are more volatile where these lower-grade securities are concerned. If a company reports good increases in earnings per share for its common stock for several years in succession during the expansion phase of the business cycle, investors' optimism about the future of its stock grows, and the percentage increase in its market price may be much greater than the percentage increase in earnings per share. Conversely, a company that reports lower earnings in periods of general expansion in business looks increasingly bad to investors. Their disappointment and pessimism may depress the market price of that company's stock disproportionately to the decline in earnings per share.

The implication is that you need a larger number of issues of low-grade securities in a portfolio than you do of high-grade issues if you want changes in average value of those issues to correspond closely with changes in average value of all issues of that grade in the market. If you have only a half-dozen common stocks, changes in average value of the stocks in the portfolio may correspond poorly with changes in value of all actively traded stocks in the market. But if you increase the number to thirty, there will be marked improvement in the correlation of portfolio average value and market average value.

Or, you can turn this idea around. If you want change in value of stocks in your portfolio to be different from changes in a broad index of stock prices, you should hold relatively few stocks. Then, if you have made very good selections, or are lucky, the average value of your few stocks will increase much more than the increase in the stock price indexes. Or, if the market declines, your stocks will decline less. If you have made poor selections, the average value of your stocks will not rise as much as the average of the market, or will decline more. In fact, the value of your stocks might move in an opposite direction to change in average market value.

This concept is very important for designing a portfolio consistent with constraints on the ability of an investor to risk price depreciation. An investor who can hold thirty or more industrial common stocks of diverse companies and industries in his portfolio can estimate potential price depreciation for his stocks by estimating potential price depreciation for Standard & Poor's 425 industrial stocks. But an investor able to own only one common stock can rely very little on the movement of average market prices in estimating the outcome of his one-stock investment. The value of his one stock may soar far above market averages, or it may sink far below them.

This discussion of price changes for securities differentiated by grade in financial risk now provides the basis for considering diversification and concentration as investment policies.

Diversification—a Policy for Minimizing Portfolio Risk

Diversification is undoubtedly the best known and most widely used of all investment policies. Unfortunately, misunderstandings often occur about what it is and what it may be expected to accomplish. As the term is often used, diversification is simply a policy of distributing investment funds over many issues. It is sometimes called the policy of not putting all your eggs in one basket, but rather in a number of baskets. The "eggs in baskets" version says nothing about how the baskets will be selected. The purpose, however, is clearly implied. If you put all your eggs in one basket, that basket may be upset and all the eggs broken. But if you put your eggs in a number of baskets and scatter them around, not more than one or two is likely to be upset, and you don't lose all your eggs. The object of diversification, therefore, is to minimize losses. It is a defensive policy. There are two kinds of diversification —random and selective.

To *diversify randomly* is to select a number of securities of a risk grade from all issues of that grade in the market in such manner that each issue has as much chance of being selected as any other. You could obtain a randomly selected list of thirty or forty common stocks by numbering all the common stocks listed on the New York Stock Exchange in order and selecting those issues whose numbers appear in a table of random numbers. Some of these issues will work out well and some poorly over a period of time. Those that work out well will compensate more or less for those that work out poorly, and the average return will be similar to the average return on all listed stocks.

Institutional investors often have funds distributed over 100 or more leading common stocks. It is no coincidence that appreciation and depreciation in value of their common stock portfolios more or less parallels the rise and fall of the broadly based indexes of stock prices. This is not to imply that the institutional investors have selected their issues by the random number method, but it is evidence of the operation of the law of averages applied to large numbers of similar securities.

Another way to diversify is to *diversify selectively* by selecting those securities not likely to be depressed in value by the same kinds of adverse developments affecting the financial abilities of their issuers. If you do this successfully, you will have a portfolio more stable in value than one composed of securities of the same grade selected at random. To accomplish this purpose, analysts look for issues differently affected by the varying fortunes of industries, geographical areas, and companies.

Manufacturers of office equipment have in recent years experienced an unusual growth in demand for their products and a parallel growth in earnings for their common stocks, mainly as a result of remarkable technological improvements in some of the products of the industry. But if you invested all your money in the stocks of three or four companies in this industry, you would assume the risk of unusual depreciation in market value in the event that the favorable development of this industry comes to an end. Market prices have heavily discounted future growth of earnings for these stocks, and if the prospect of growth dims or disappears, prices would almost certainly decline much more than average prices.

If you want to reduce the risk of such poor price experience, you can invest part of your money in stocks of companies in industries that have no important relationship to office equipment as far as earnings are concerned. You might buy stocks of companies engaged in making motion pictures for theatres and television. Their earnings depend chiefly on their ability to produce pictures that people like to see, an accomplishment that has nothing to do with the rate of technological development of office equipment. However, if both these industries should happen to fall on hard times, the total value of your portfolio would depreciate relative to the average of all stocks. So you might use some of your money to buy stocks of companies in the ethical drug industry. The future earnings of these companies will be influenced strongly by their ability to develop improved drug products with broad markets. Their success in product development has no direct relationship to the success of the motion picture companies in producing entertaining movies, or with the success of the office equipment manufacturers in further improving their products.

If you diversify in this manner, the future value of your common stock portfolio depends on the fortunes of three industries and these fortunes are largely unrelated as far as principal specific influences on earnings for common stocks are concerned. They are related, of course, in that market for products of all three industries are affected by general business conditions, change in the political climate, and so forth. You cannot select risks that are entirely uncorrelated, but you can diversify even more broadly by industries.

It may be desirable to include stocks of more than one company in an industry to improve diversification. Within an industry, different companies often concentrate their operations in products that comprise only one segment of the total product line of the industry. A company with a specialized line of products might do very well when other companies in the same industry, but with other lines of products, are doing poorly. Sometimes companies in the same industry use different methods of marketing their products and the company that has the more effective merchandising system may prosper at the same time others with the same products but different ways of selling them find their sales lagging.

This kind of reasoning about diversification can be applied to companies differentiated on the basis of the geographical area they serve, wherever they are limited to such areas, and wherever differences in the economic development of areas is important. Thus, if you wanted stocks of two food store chains in your portfolio, you might well select one that operates principally in the eastern part of the United States and one engaged principally in the western part. If several stocks of electric utility operating companies are to be included, the companies might well be selected for geographical diversification.

As the world becomes smaller, geographical diversification has become a less important basis for diversification. Within the United States, differences in the economic development of geographical areas has decreased as an important influence on the financial success of companies whose operations are restricted to particular geographical areas. Moreover, most larger companies operate on a national scale, and many consider the entire world to be their market. The stocks of some leading industrial companies represent rather broad international geographical diversification.

Concentration—a Policy for Assuming Larger Portfolio Risk

Just as diversification serves to minimize portfolio risk, so concentration is a policy for assuming larger portfolio risk. Concentration means selecting one or a very few security issues and investing all your money in those issues. It means putting all your eggs in one basket. If that basket is a particularly good one, you profit greatly. If it is a poor one, your loss is likely to be large.

We have said that prices for securities of the same grade tend to move together, but we have also recognized that prices for some issues, particularly in the lower grades, may vary widely from an average of prices. The objective of a policy of concentration is to select the one issue (or the few issues) from among all issues of a grade in the market that will have the most favorable variation in price from an average of prices. An investor who succeeds in doing so realizes much better than average returns.

The lower the grade of securities, the greater the tendency for prices of particular issues to vary from the average for all issues of the grade. Therefore, the greatest opportunities for maximizing returns by concentration are found among lower-grade securities. It is in this area that you may find a stock that doubles in price while average prices change very little, or that quadruples in price while the average price doubles.

Just as diversification applies the principle of averaging, so concentration applies the principle of not averaging. If you buy only one issue and it appreciates greatly in price, you have a high return, which is not diluted by the lower returns that you probably would have obtained if you had distributed your money over a large number of issues.

Concentration is relative. The individual who commits all his money to one highly speculative common stock is about as aggressive in assuming financial risk as he can be. But if he puts all his money in one triple A corporate bond, he is relatively unaggressive. The price of the bond might rise a point or two more than the average price for such bonds, but that is about the extent of potential gain relative to average price. Thus, aggressiveness varies with the grade of securities in which one concentrates.

It also varies with the extent of concentration. The greatest extreme is to invest in one issue, but of course you can spread your money over two, or three, or even a slightly larger number of issues. The more issues, the greater the averaging effect. And as you increase the number of issues, you move from concentration toward diversification.

A policy of concentration to any marked degree in lower-grade financial risk securities affords the opportunity for large returns, but there is inherent in such a policy the risk of large loss. It is a suitable policy only for investors who can afford the possible loss. The size of possible loss should not be underestimated, as it often is by people who let their enthusiasm for an attractive speculation overpower their judgment of risk. An individual who buys one or two speculative stocks risks losing a large part of his money. He can try to limit his loss by selling quickly whenever he concludes that the speculation is not working out well, but there is many a possible slip between buying a stock and selling it. As a generalization, money used for a strongly aggressive policy of concentration should be money that an investor can afford to lose.

Now, having pointed to the large risk of loss, it may be well to say something in support of concentration. Concentration in speculative investments is one of the few ways you can get rich if you are not the heir of a rich relative. If you have only a little money to start with and you want to be rich so much that you are willing to take the chance of becoming much poorer, you should concentrate. And you should concentrate where the risk is high, because that is where the big money is.

QUANTITATIVE-THEORETICAL CONCEPTS OF PORTFOLIO STRUCTURE

About the time that the principal political rival of the United States startled both politicians and scientists in this country by shooting a rocket completely outside the earth's field of gravity, the application of mathematics to almost every academic discipline began to advance at an exponential rate. In the area of security investments the mathematicians found a fascinating set of problems suitable for mathematical analysis, a vast supply of numbers that could be used as inputs, and greatly increased availability of computers for making complex calculations. The result has been a whole new theory of portfolio construction based on quantitative measurements of the risk characteristics of individual security issues and combinations of securities with different risk characteristics in portfolios. Most of the theory and the math is beyond the scope of this elementary textbook and the students for whom it is intended, but we can at least examine the basic concepts and provide a basis for further study for those who want to do so.[2]

The Use of Expected Values of Distributions

At the very beginning of portfolio theory you encounter the concept that estimates of risk and return can be expressed as distributions of estimated outcomes of investment in individual security issues. Probability weights can be attached and you can compute the value of a distribution of estimated rates of return as described in Chapter 1 and used in the description of financial analysis.

When you express an estimate of risk and return for a security in this manner, you can calculate with mathematical precision the value of the distribution that is the expected rate of return and is often expressed as E(r). The mathematics are precise; the estimates are assumed to be about right, but may not be. The general formula is

$$\bar{x} = \sum_{i=1}^{n} x_i/n = \Sigma\, x_i\, f(x_i).$$

Table 18–3 illustrates the calculation.

You can see at once that the expected rate for each of the stocks is the sum of each rate in its distribution multiplied by its frequency. When the distribution of rates and frequencies is symmetrical, the expected rate is the median rate in the distribution of estimated rates. But these distributions may not be symmetrical and then you have to calculate the value of the distribution.

The usefulness of E(r) in portfolio construction is that you can average

[2]For further study see William J. Baumol's *Portfolio Theory: The Selection of Asset Combinations*, New York, 1970, The McCaleb-Seiler Publishing Company.

TABLE 18–3

The Expected Value of Estimated Rates of Return from a Pair of Stocks

Stock A			Stock B		
x_a	f	fx_a	x_b	f	fx_b
18%	0.1	1.8	12%	0.1	1.2
14	0.2	2.8	10	0.2	2.0
10	0.4	4.0	8	0.4	3.2
6	0.2	1.2	6	0.2	1.2
2	0.1	0.2	4	0.1	0.4
$\Sigma\ (x_{ar})$		10.0	$\Sigma\ (x_{br})$		8.0

x_a is the distribution of rates for Stock *A*
f is the frequency or probability for Stock *A*
fx_a is rate times frequency for Stock *A*
x_b is the distribution of rates for Stock *B*
f is frequency for Stock *B*
fx_b is rate times frequency for Stock *B*

the expected values for each of as many stocks as you select for your portfolio, using the proportions of each stock's value to the total value of the portfolio as weights, and arrive at a weighted average expected rate of return on the portfolio. If you have only the two stocks in the table above and each is 50 per cent of the total portfolio, the average E(r) for the portfolio is (1/2) (10) + (1/2) (8) = 9 per cent. If the proportions are 25 per cent of Stock *A* and 75 per cent of Stock *B*, the weighted average E(r) is 8.5 per cent. Given a number of stocks for which E(r) has been calculated and the ability to own each in whatever proportions you choose, you can devise a portfolio with whatever average rate of return you please within the limits of the rates for the several stocks.

The Use of Risk Measurements

Risk is measured by the average deviation of the estimated rates in a distribution from its mean. This measurement may be the variance, or standard deviation, or any of several other measures of deviation. We have previously used some of these methods. You may have noticed from the distributions of *x* and *y* in Table 18–3, that Stock *A* is more risky than Stock *B*, because the range of rates for *A* is from 18 to 2 per cent, whereas that for *B* is from 12 to 4 per cent. The usefulness of the standard deviation is that it provides an exact measurement of the difference in riskiness. From Table 18–4, the standard deviation of *A* is twice as great as that of *B*.

Covariance Among Stocks

At first glance it might seem that you could measure the riskiness of a portfolio by averaging the standard deviations of the stocks with each weighted according to its percentage of the total portfolio. But this would require that rates estimated for each stock be in the same range, such as 4 to

TABLE 18–4

The Variance and Standard Deviation of Estimated Rates of Return for a Pair of Stocks

	Stock A				*Stock B*
x_a	$x_a - \bar{x}_a$	$(x_a - \bar{x}_a)^2$	x_b	$x_b - \bar{x}_b$	$(x_b - \bar{x}_b)^2$
18	+8	64	12	+4	16
14	+4	16	10	+2	4
10	0	0	8	0	0
6	−4	16	6	−2	4
2	−8	64	4	−4	16
$\bar{x}_a = 10$		160/5	$\bar{x}_b$		40/5
		$s^2 = 32$			$s^2 = 8$
		$s = 5.7$			$s = 2.8$

12 per cent, and that all stocks fare equally well in each period for which rates are estimated. However, ranges are different and not all stocks fare equally well in a given period. Therefore, we need a calculation for the riskiness of a portfolio that will take these imperfections in covariance of returns into account.

You take the deviation of the highest rate in the distribution for a stock, multiply it by the deviation of the highest rate in the distribution for a second stock, and you have the product of those deviations. Do the same for the next higher rate for each of the two stocks, and so forth, until all the rates have been multiplied across. The sum of the products divided by the number of rates in the distributions is the covariance. The notation is:

$$cov_{xy} = \Sigma\,(x_i - \bar{x})\,(y_i - \bar{y})/n.$$

Table 18–5 illustrates the calculation.

That example tells only a small part of the story of how portfolio risk may be reduced by combining stocks with imperfect covariance. Let's swing to an opposite extreme and assume that Stock *A* provides its highest rates under conditions of business boom and that Stock *B* provides its highest rates under conditions of deep recession. Stock *B* may be that of a financially strong public utility company with a long record of stability of earnings and dividends around a moderately rising trend line. This stock would rise in price during recession because interest rates would greatly decline and it would be priced on the basis of a lower discount rate applied to future returns. Now we can

TABLE 18–5

The Covariance of a Pair of Stocks with Positive Covariation

Stock A $(x_a - \bar{x}_a)$	*Stock B* $(x_b - \bar{x}_b)$		*Covariance* $(x_a - \bar{x}_a)\ (x_b - \bar{x}_b)$
+8	+4		32
+4	+2		8
0	0		0
−4	−2		8
−8	−4		32
		Covariance	80/5 = +16

TABLE 18–6

Covariance of a Pair of Stocks with Negative Covariation

Stock A $x_a - \bar{x}_a$	*Stock B* $x_b - \bar{x}_b$		*Covariance* $(x_a - \bar{x}_a)(x_b - \bar{x}_b)$
+8	−4		−32
+4	−2		− 8
0	0		0
−4	+2		− 8
−8	+4		−32
		Covariance	−80/5 = −16

reverse the order of rates for Stock *B* and calculate the covariance with Stock *A*. Table 18–6 shows the calculation.

Calculating Portfolio Risk

With the calculations we have made for each of a number of stocks to be included in a portfolio, it is possible to calculate the riskiness of the portfolio in terms of variance and standard deviation. This calculation is a little more complicated, but it is not difficult to do manually for a two-asset portfolio. When there are many stocks to be considered and many pairs of stocks to be compared, you need a computer.

Here is the step-by-step arithmetic:

1. Square the proportion of *a* and multiply by the variance of Stock *A*. Using data from preceding tables: ½² times 32 = ¼ (32) = 8
2. Add: two times the proportion of Stock *A* times the proportion of Stock *B* and multiply by the covariance of *A* and *B*. Using the data: 2 (½ times ½ times + 16) = 2 (¼ times 16) = 2 times 4 = 8
3. Add: the proportion of Stock *B* squared times the variance of Stock *B*. Using the data: ¼ times 8 = 2

Portfolio variance 18

Standard deviation 4.2

Using lower-case *a* and *b* to represent stocks *A* and *B*, the math notation is:

$$\sigma^2 = \alpha_a \ \sigma_a^2 + 2\alpha_a\alpha_b \ \text{cov}_{ab} + \alpha_b\sigma^2{}_b.$$

If there is negative covariance between the two stocks as in Table 18–6, the portfolio variance is reduced to 2. Just substitute − 16 for + 16 in the second step above. Negative covariance does a great deal to reduce portfolio risk.

Calculating Optimum Portfolio

The optimum portfolio for any investor is the highest average portfolio rate of return at whatever level of portfolio risk he chooses to assume, or the lowest risk at any portfolio rate of return he seeks. The inputs required are:

1. the value of the distribution for each stock;
2. the proportion of each stock to the total value of the portfolio;
3. the covariance of each stock with each other stock in the group of stocks from which the portfolio is to be selected.

By a system of quadratic computer programming it is possible to select from a number of stocks the combination that provides the highest portfolio rate at any level of portfolio risk. This, in most general terms, is the Markowitz portfolio selection concept.[3]

Figure 18–1 shows what this model may accomplish for portfolio construction. A few minutes study of the figure will tell you more about the concept than several thousand words. Risk is on the vertical axis and expected returns on the horizontal axis. The straight diagonal line identified as x to x_i represents a number of individual stocks arranged in order of estimated risk and expected rate of return; they form a perfect linear progression from the least risky and least expected return to the most risky with the highest expected rate of return. The upward-curving concave line represents a series of portfolios that could be constructed from stocks on the straight diagonal line. The curved line between the two points x and x_i is below the diagonal line in risk.

If you want a rate of return at the point on the horizontal axis indicated by $E(r)_1$, you can get it by investing in the single stock on the diagonal line that has a value of its rate of return distribution equal to $E(r)_1$; it is marked i_1. But that stock has a level of risk represented by V_2 on the risk axis. But why

[3]Harry Markowitz, Portfolio Selection, New York, 1959, John Wiley & Sons, Inc.

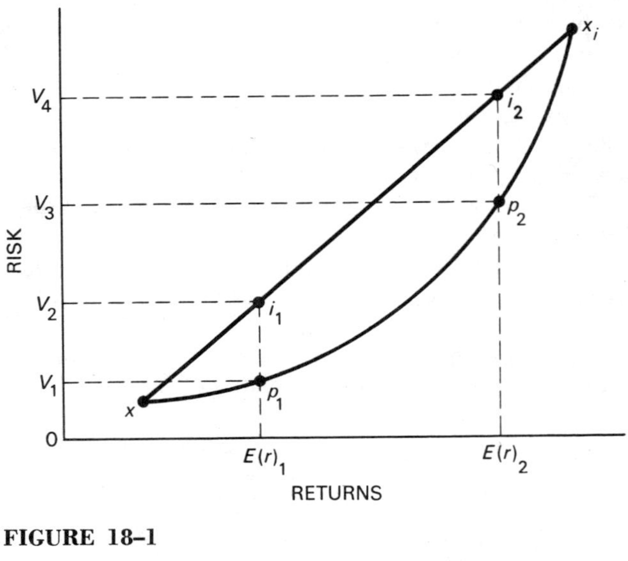

FIGURE 18–1

Risk-Return Relationships in Portfolio Construction

do that? If you use the Markowitz computer program, you can select a combination of stocks from the array on the diagonal line that will constitute portfolio p_1, and provide the same $E(r)_1$, but at a much lower level of risk indicated by V_1. The lower level of risk is achieved by combining stocks with the best combinations of expected values, variance of estimated rates, and covariance of rates. If you want to try for a higher rate of return, you would do better with portfolio p_2 than with the single stock i_2. Both provide the same expected rate of return, but the portfolio is much less risky.

For Further Study

Since Professor Markowitz published his pioneering study on the theory and mathematics of portfolio construction, the literature of portfolio construction has grown at a rapid rate. William F. Sharpe is generally regarded as another pioneer in this area. Several other leading contributors are listed in the biography at the end of this book. A great many variations of portfolio models have been developed. The list of doctoral dissertations in which bright young scholars have endeavored to examine some particular aspect of portfolio theory is a long one. Some are mentioned in the two books by Richard A. Brealey, who has done a remarkable job of digesting and presenting in a very literate manner a vast amount of research and publication.

There are clearly some limitations to this kind of effort to construct "efficient" portfolios, that is, portfolios with the highest expected rate of return at a given level of risk. They require statistical inputs. Given the inputs, the rest is a problem in logic and mathematics. If the inputs are right, the logic is valid, and the mathematical methods are properly applied, the output is indisputable. The important element is the accuracy of the inputs.

If the random walk theorists are literally right, the future rate of return on a stock for a given period of time cannot be predicted. If future rates are completely unpredictable, there are no valid inputs and portfolio construction is no more than an exercise in math and logic.

Financial analysts believe that they can predict future rates of return within some range of rates. The range of a frequency distribution of expected rates for a stock is a sort of "ball park," estimate. But is this sufficient for such data to be valid inputs for portfolio construction? You can say that the range of the distribution is from one number to another number, assign probability weights, compute the mean, and then the standard deviation. But these numbers are subjective. They have to be subjective because they are estimates of the future. And they are subject to such large margins of error that one may at least question their usefulness for the series of calculations that produce a most efficient portfolio.

There are unpredictable events that cause sizable changes in realized rates of return from stocks in any such time period as 1 year. Sometimes management mistakes come to light, companies that have been highly profitable and are generally regarded as having very bright futures sometimes have to absorb huge write-offs, and the series of annual earnings per share figures that have been steadily increasing for a number of years suddenly decline below zero with a corresponding decline in market price that makes all earlier estimated rates look fanciful. Sometimes an industry that has long been regarded as a sure growth industry ceases to grow, demand slackens, product prices sag, and earnings of leading companies decline. Sometimes the entire stock market is affected by unpredictable economic and political events. Sometimes the most carefully designed frequency distributions of expected rates of return are not even in the ball park.

This agnostic conclusion is not intended to deny that there is value in the new math-theory of portfolio construction. The theorists have made important contributions, but until ability to predict the future improves their mathematical answers are less than completely satisfactory.

QUESTIONS FOR DISCUSSION

1. Why should an individual or an institutional investor adopt a clearly defined statement of investment policy in constructing a securities portfolio?

2. Suppose that an analysis of investment constraints for an individual investor shows a severe constraint on ability to assume risk of decline in purchasing power of income in constant dollars and at the same time a severe constraint on ability to risk depreciation in market prices in current dollars. In terms of principal categories of securities, how would you construct a portfolio to meet these constraints?

3. You think that the next 12 months will be a year of severe business recession and declining interest rates. How could you construct a securities portfolio that would provide relatively high stability of market value of the total portfolio under those conditions? If the forecast of recession proved to be wrong and indeed the year turned out to be one of moderate expansion in business activity, would the portfolio you designed provide good, bad, or indifferent stability of total market values?

4. A bank owns forty different issues of municipal bonds rated either triple A or double A. Assuming that investment in this category of securities is right for the bank, criticize the portfolio.

5. If you are to own thirty common stocks with about the same level of risk and you want to obtain good diversification, are you likely to get better diversification by random selection from among all the common stock issues at that level of risk, or by selective diversification?

6. Is a policy of concentrating a portfolio in two or three carefully selected stocks ever justified? Under what circumstances?

7. You own the two stocks designated *A* and *B* in Table 18–3. Is it possible to reduce the riskiness of this portfolio by adding a third stock that is distinctly more speculative than *A* and *B*?

8. In Figure 18–1 the portfolio designated P_1 has a lower portfolio risk than the sum of the stocks on the x–x_i line. Apparently the sum is less than the total of the several parts. Explain.

9. In the last section of this chapter the author expresses a view that may well be a minority view among experts in investments. What do you think about about it? Reach your own conclusion without regard to the author or to your instructor.

19

Other Elements of Risk in Portfolio Construction

I. Interest-rate risk in portfolio construction
   A. Investment in terms of stability of principal
   B. Investment in terms of stability of income
II. The purchasing power of investment returns
   A. The ambiguity of answers
   B. Common stocks for long-term holding
   C. Aggressive policy for large current dollar returns
   D. Some other media for defensive policy
III. The desirability of ownership qualities
   A. Grades of securities in marketability
   B. Grades of securities in taxability
   C. Other desirability of ownership qualities
IV. Designing the portfolio to the terms of the market

An investor who has carefully worked out his policies for assuming risk with particular regard for the financial abilities of issuers has done an important part of the task of formulating policies for constructing his securities portfolio. But much remains to be done, and it is this remaining part that is so often neglected even by professional investors. There are those categories of securities whose risk is affected chiefly by changes in the level of interest rates in the market, and the portfolio must be planned from the standpoint of the level of interest-rate risk to be assumed. Then there is the troublesome problem of thinking about risk in the total portfolio in terms of uncertainty of returns in constant dollars. Finally, we must take some account of the need for securities of the higher grades in marketability, taxability, and other desirability of ownership qualities.

Our general concept, of course, is that all the elements affecting uncertainty comprise total risk. We will continue to refer to that element of total risk attributable to changes in market rates of interest as interest-rate risk and to the element associated with uncertainty of returns in constant dollars as purchasing power risk.

INTEREST-RATE RISK IN PORTFOLIO CONSTRUCTION

If an investor's requirements for stability of principal or income in current dollars are sufficiently restrictive to require investment entirely or partially in securities with a low level of financial risk, then he is at once confronted with the policy problem: How much interest-rate risk may he assume?

We will discuss problems of policy in terms of bonds that have a very low level of financial risk, but the discussion also applies to preferred stocks whose prices change in relatively high correlation with changes in prices of high-grade bonds, and it applies to some extent to very high-grade common stocks purchased chiefly for income.

There are really two policy problems to be considered under this heading. Changes in market rates of yield cause market prices to fluctuate. How much price depreciation stemming from this cause can an investor tolerate? Changes in portfolio rates of yield also change as market rates change and funds are invested or re-invested. How much shrinkage in income can an investor risk?

Investment in Terms of Stability of Principal

When you think about portfolio construction in terms of stability of market prices for high-grade bonds, the key concept is that the longer the maturity the greater is the fluctuation in bond prices with changes in interest rates. You can invest in short-term obligations and minimize the risk of loss of principal in the event that securities have to be sold after a rise in interest rates. You can invest in long-term issues and assume the full risk of price changes as interest rates change, or you can space maturities over a long period of time.

The policy of investing in obligations of short maturity is sometimes called *maintaining a secondary reserve*. The term implies its purpose; a secondary reserve consists of securities that are deliberately held in reserve against the contingency that they will have to be converted into cash by sale in the market, because the owner urgently needs cash for some other purpose than investment in securities. It also suggests that this reserve in securities is secondary to a primary reserve in the form of cash.

A secondary reserve should be designed with care. First, the amount should be large enough to equal the largest amount of cash likely to be required from the securities portfolio in the near future; otherwise, it will not completely serve its purpose. Estimates may have to be revised from time to time and the size of the secondary reserve changed accordingly. When the reserve is partially depleted by sale of securities, it may have to be replenished. Second, securities must be selected with particular regard for their expected price stability.

The price stability requirement means that secondary reserve securities must have little financial risk and little interest rate risk. Some investors avoid financial risk entirely by including only U.S. Treasury obligations. Others accept the very small financial risk in government agency issues and corporate and municipal bonds of the highest ratings. To minimize interest-rate risk, maturities of from a few weeks to one or two years are commonly used. With some increase in the size of potential price depreciation, maturities of 3-to-5 years may be included.

When the yield curve for interest-rate risk issues is upsloping, the purchase of obligations of short maturity involves a sacrifice of yield relative to yields obtainable on long maturities. This sacrifice is the price paid for liquidity. Sometimes, however, yields on obligations due in periods up to 3 years are the highest in the entire range of maturities and there is no cost for liquidity.

Many investors try to space maturities of secondary reserve securities more or less evenly over a period of several years. Thus, a portfolio may consist of one issue due within a few months, another in 6 months, a third in 1 year, and so on. Then funds are rotated through this maturity schedule. When an issue matures, the proceeds are used to buy an issue at the long end of the secondary reserve schedule, and when the next one matures the funds are again invested in the longest maturity considered suitable for the secondary reserve.

The regular rotation of funds through a schedule of secondary reserve securities can be maintained only when the reserve is not used as a source of cash, or is used only to a limited extent. If part of the securities must be liquidated, the schedule can be restored by purchasing issues of about the same maturity as those sold when funds again become available. If the entire reserve must be converted to cash, a new schedule of maturities must be created when there are funds for that purpose.

Usually, a secondary reserve should consist only of highly marketable issues. The turnover of this section of a securities portfolio tends to be relatively high and transactions costs must be amortized over relatively short time periods.

Investment in short maturities is sometimes called a defensive policy because it minimizes potential price depreciation. In the same kind of terminology, *investment in long maturities* is aggressive. The definition of long maturities varies considerably. Some investors consider any issue due in more than 10 years to be a long maturity. Others generally think of bonds due in 20 to 30 years as long maturities. But a precise definition within this rather wide range is not a matter of great importance because there is little difference in the size of price fluctuations for obligations of different maturities beyond about 15 years. In practice, investors usually distribute maturities over a considerable time range and classify all those due beyond some specified number of years as long-term issues.

In this long-term segment of the securities portfolio the standards for marketability may be less strict than for the secondary reserve. Since long-term issues are generally intended to be held to maturity, it is not important that they be highly marketable.

The motive for an aggressive policy in this respect, as in others, is to maximize investment returns. When the yield curve is upsloping, the average yield on long maturities is much larger than the yield on short maturities. However, as we observed in our study of the nature of interest-rate risk, the yield curve is sometimes relatively flat and there is little or no yield advantage in long maturities relative to the shorter-term issues, except that the yield on long maturities is likely to be realized for a longer period.

A bond investor is not limited to one or the other of these policies—defensive or aggressive—as we have defined them. In practice, bond investors use an arrangement of maturities that has the effect of combining the two and realizing some benefits from each. We will call it a policy of *broad distribution of maturities*, that is, of owning bonds with maturities ranging from very short term to long term with a more or less uniform distribution of amounts over the whole range of maturities.

If you construct a portfolio of high-grade bonds so that 5 per cent of the total amount is invested in an issue due in 1 year, 5 per cent in an issue due in 2 years, and so on, with 5 per cent in an issue due each year for a period of 20 years, you have a broad distribution of maturities. If you hold all issues to maturity, 5 per cent of the total portfolio will be redeemed each year and you can use the proceeds to buy other issues due in 20 years.

Bond maturities are seldom so symmetrical as in this example because all sorts of conditions cause variations from the pattern of a uniform amount each year over a fixed time period. Some issues are called and redeemed before maturity, leaving holes in the maturity schedule that may or may not be filled. Some issues are sold voluntarily because price has appreciated and it is pleasant to take a profit. Often no issues are available in the market of the particular maturity desired to fill a gap in the maturity schedule. Sometimes the yield curve provides higher yields at some point other than at the long end of the schedule, so that yield is maximized by re-investing in a short or intermediate maturity. But even with such irregularities it is not difficult to follow a policy of broad distribution of maturities with sufficient fidelity to obtain some distinct advantages.

First, there is usually the advantage of a relatively high average yield on the entire portfolio obtained by buying bonds regularly at about the highest point on the yield curve. When the yield curve rises from short to long maturities, average yield on the bond portfolio is significantly greater than it would be if it were limited to short or intermediate maturities.

A second major advantage is that this arrangement of maturities provides a secondary reserve almost automatically. As bonds are held and time passes, they become shorter in maturity. After 17 years an obligation bought as a 20-year maturity becomes a 3-year maturity; in another year it is only 2 years to maturity, and so on. In a portfolio with 5 per cent of the total amount maturing each year over a period of 20 years, 15 per cent would mature within 3 years. If these short-term maturity issues are high grade in financial risk and in marketability, they constitute a secondary reserve. There is no sacrifice of yield because these issues were bought as long maturities at the higher yields usually obtainable on long maturities, rather than at the lower yields usually prevailing in the market for short maturities.

The spacing of bond maturities over a relatively long period is aggressive in that a large part of the portfolio consists of long maturities subject to relatively large price depreciation when interest rates rise. This aggressiveness can be reduced, if need be, by reducing the length of the maturity schedule. If maturities are distributed uniformly over only 10 years, instead of 20, only one-half of the portfolio matures in more than 5 years and the secondary reserve portion is relatively larger.

Investment policy in this matter of length of maturities must be determined by the *investor's investment constraints*. The strictly defensive policy of investment in short maturities is required only to the extent that an investor has very limited ability to tolerate depreciation in market value and weak tenure of ownership. Its purpose is to reduce the size of potential price depreciation from the 15 to 25 per cent range associated with long maturities to the 1 to 3 per cent decline characteristic of short maturities. When tenure of ownership is weak, the need for a strictly defensive policy is greatly increased because sale of securities means converting whatever price depreciation there may be into realized loss. Even though an investor is able to absorb realized losses on the longer maturities, it is a poor policy to buy them when he does not know how long he can hold them and may have to sell at an inopportune time.

The policy of broad distribution of maturities falls within the investment limitations of most investors who find themselves restricted entirely or partially to high-grade bonds. It provides a secondary reserve sufficient to meet most contingencies and, at the same time, affords a portfolio yield that is an average of yields on long-term issues purchased from time to time over a period of years.

An investor seldom deliberately concentrates in long maturities if the investment fund is sizable. An individual who has only enough money to buy one or two bond issues might select 20- or 25-year maturities and hold them to maturity, provided they are not called or liquidated under future circumstances that cannot be anticipated. Usually, individual and institutional investors add long-term issues to their portfolios as funds become available to effect a broad distribution of maturities.

The investor's temperament may be a constraint even in this area of low financial risk. For an individual who thinks he has obtained safety of principal by investing in a government bond, a decline of 5 or 10 per cent in market price may be more of a shock than the effect on an intelligent speculator of a 25 per cent decline in the price of a common stock.

Investment in Terms of Stability of Income

For many investors the controlling constraint on the bond portfolio, or bond portion of the portfolio, is need for stability of investment income. Individual investors may need a stable income for living expenses; institutions may need it for operating expenses. Again, the analysis of investment constraints continues to be the controlling influence on investment policy.

The basic *defensive policy*, that is, the policy that provides the smaller fluctuations in amounts of income over considerable periods of time, is that of distributing maturities over a relatively long time period, holding to maturity, and re-investing at the long end of the maturity schedule. This policy is sometimes called "rotating maturities."

Yields on long maturities fluctuate less than those on short maturities, so there are smaller changes in average portfolio yield on reinvestment of portions of a fund periodically. If bonds are held to maturity, only a small portion is re-invested from year to year. When a portfolio is constructed in this manner, the average yield at any point in time is the average of the yields at which each of the issues was purchased, weighted by the amount of each. Average yield changes from time to time only to the extent that issues are redeemed and new issues purchased at yields different from those realized on the redeemed bonds.

The policy of rotating funds over considerable periods of years causes an averaging of the effects of both cyclical and secular changes in interest rates on portfolio rate of return. Figure 19–1 shows graphically how the averaging operates. It depicts a bond portfolio with 5 per cent of the total maturing each year and the proceeds immediately re-invested at market rates of yield.

Rotating funds smooths out cyclical variations in market rates on portfolio returns. Panel A of the figure shows that if cyclical fluctuations were perfectly symmetrical in the size and duration, the rate of return on the entire portfolio would be constant after one complete cycle of the interest rate. Securities have been purchased in some years at cyclically high rates and in others at cyclically low rates.

The rotation of funds retards the effect of trends in interest rates on portfolio rates of return. The effect when the trend is downward is illustrated in Panel B of Figure 19–1. Here the same assumptions have been made about constructing the portfolio as in Panel A, that is, 5 per cent of the portfolio matures each year and is re-invested at market rates of yield. Portfolio yield declines, with some intermediate increases and decreases owing to cyclical fluctuations. If the trend of interest rates is upward rather than downward, the effect of rotating funds retards the increase in portfolio rate of return.

When the secular trend changes from upward to downward (or conversely) during the time period over which maturities are distributed, the spaced maturity policy provides some averaging of the effect of secular change. In Panel B, if the downward trend were reversed after 10 years, and yields were to move upward in about the same pattern as the preceding downward

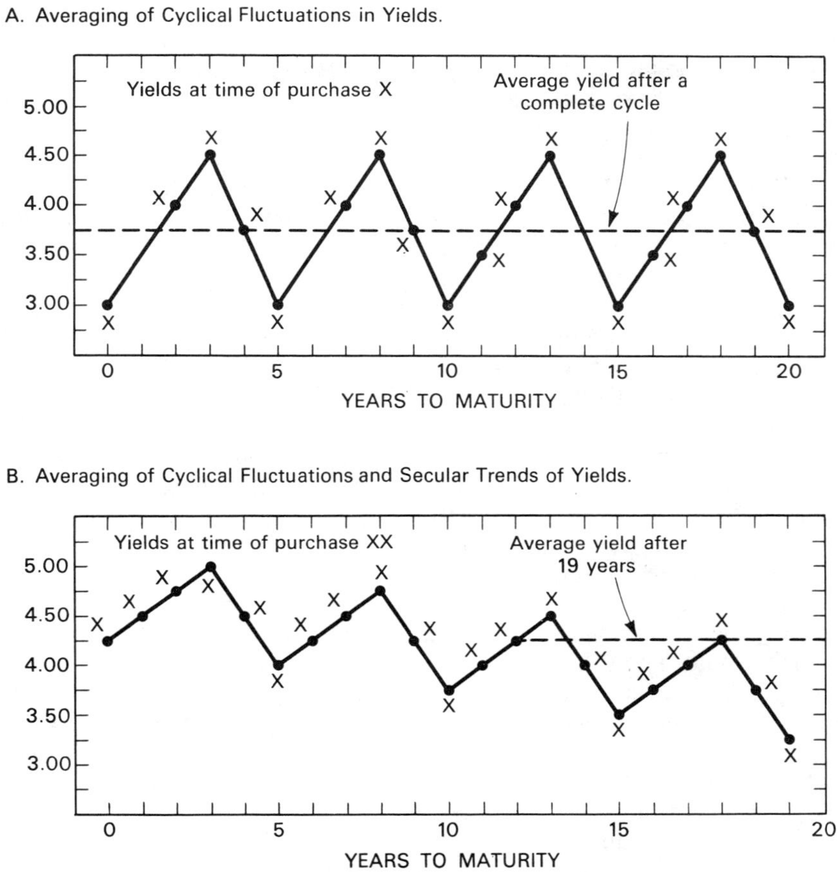

FIGURE 19–1

The Averaging Effect of Rotating Maturities

movement, at the end of the nineteenth year the average yield on the portfolio would be at the midpoint of the range of yields during the 20 years.

Needless to say, the assumptions used in this figure greatly simplify the problem of stabilizing portfolio yield. In practice, yields on long maturities do not fluctuate in such a regular fashion; the range of cyclical fluctuation is irregular; the amounts re-invested from one year to another may not be uniform; maturities are not always 20 years; and sometimes bonds are sold before maturity. The simplifying assumption that the principal amount of a bond portfolio remains unchanged over any very considerable period of time is seldom valid in practice. Sometimes additional funds become available for investment and the principal amount of the portfolio is increased; in other instances, principal may be liquidated, and the amount is reduced. However, the general idea of stabilizing income by rotating funds through a system of spaced maturities may be applied even when funds are added to, or withdrawn from, the bond portfolio.

When new money is added to a portfolio, the most literal application of the rotation of maturities policy is to buy bonds of about the same maturities as those presently in the portfolio and in about the same proportions. Thus, if a portfolio is so arranged that about 5 per cent of the total amount matures each year over the next 20 years, 5 per cent of additional funds would be used to buy obligations maturing in each of the 20 years. This would keep the pattern of distribution the same as it was before the new money was invested, and it would maintain the same system of averaging the yields obtained on re-investing funds from matured obligations.

An alternative is to add the new money at the long end of the maturity schedule by purchasing obligations of longer maturities than those presently owned. This lengthens the maturity schedule. Thus, if maturities are evenly spaced over 20 years, new money could be applied to purchase of obligations due in 21 years in about the same amount as maturities in each of the preceding 20 years. If the amount of new money is larger than the amount of annual maturities, the excess would be invested in a 22-year maturity, and so on. Thus the system of regular rotation of funds would be maintained.

Bond investors may, however, be influenced in their choice of maturities for investment of additional funds by the shape of the yield curve at time of investment. If yields are higher for obligations due in 2 or 3 years, or in 6 or 8 years, they may apply additional funds to purchase bonds due in those periods. This practice has the immediate effect of maximizing portfolio yield, but it also causes some concentration of funds in obligations that will mature within a relatively short time period. The danger is that a relatively large portion of the portfolio will mature and have to be re-invested at a time when the level of yields in the market is relatively low. Then, upon re-investment, portfolio yield would be reduced.

When funds have to be withdrawn from a bond account by liquidating securities, the system of spaced maturities can be maintained by selling a sufficient amount of obligations of each maturity to provide the total amount required. Portfolio managers are often influenced, however, by the relationship of current prices for securities owned to their cost (or amortized cost). Often they prefer to sell those maturities that can be sold at a profit rather than those that could be sold only at a loss. When prices generally are lower than cost, the decision may be to sell the shortest maturities, because generally they will result in the least amount of realized loss. Again, the effect of choosing securities for sale on the basis of resulting profits or losses is to disturb the even spacing of maturities and to impair the averaging effect on portfolio yield of regularly rotating funds through a maturity schedule. Sometimes withdrawals of funds are only temporary, and distortions of the maturity schedule caused by sale can be remedied by repurchasing desired maturities when funds are returned for investment.

An *aggressive policy toward income* is designed to obtain an increase in income rather than to stabilize it. Short-term interest rates fluctuate much more than long-term rates, and a portfolio of short maturities turns over faster than a portfolio of long maturities. Therefore, the shorter the maturities, the more unstable is the yield from a portfolio of interest-rate risk securities.

One kind of aggressive policy is to buy short-term issues in anticipation of a rise in short-term rates, and then to re-invest the proceeds at maturity in obligations of short maturity. If short-term rates should double in a year, as they have done at times in the past, the yield on a portfolio of short-term issues would double.

However, investors usually are not interested in increasing income from short-term issues by this kind of aggressive policy. Generally, they buy these securities for stability of principal rather than for income and take the variations in yields as they come. But there is a kind of aggressive policy sometimes used by portfolio managers, which involves investing in short maturities in anticipation of a rise in long-term yields. Then, when the improvement in long-term yields develops they liquidate short-term issues and buy the long terms at the higher yields. When this kind of policy is executed successfully, it results in obtaining significantly higher-yields on long-term investments than could have been obtained on these issues at the time of initial purchase of the short maturities.

THE PURCHASING POWER OF INVESTMENT RETURNS

A securities portfolio planned to keep the elements of financial risk and interest-rate risk at the highest levels consistent with the investor's ability to assume risk in current dollars leaves out of account the manner in which these returns are likely to be affected by changes in the price level. There remains the problem of considering the level of risk in constant dollars as the general price level changes.

Our thinking on this subject goes back again to the system of investment constraints. In some situations this constraint is not severe and it may be quite overshadowed by considerations of financial risk and interest-rate risk. The conclusion may be that a portfolio planned to fit the constraints in terms of current dollars is satisfactory in terms of constant dollars.

The Ambiguity of Answers

However, when there is a clear need to try to preserve the purchasing power of income or principal, or both, the construction of the portfolio must be reviewed in terms of levels of risk and returns in constant dollars. The problem is a difficult one because of inability to estimate exactly how the size of investment returns in current dollars will vary with changes in the price level.

Diversified common stocks is the usual answer to the question of how to preserve the purchasing power of investment returns. But we have seen that over relatively short periods of years there has been poor correlation between changes in the price level and changes in returns in current dollars from diversified common stocks. We have also seen that there is a tendency for current dollar amounts of income from bond portfolios to increase more or less as the price level rises. It may very well be that a portfolio of bonds with maturities spaced over about 10 years would provide greater stability of income in constant dollars than would a portfolio of common stocks. With a complete portfolio turnover in 10 years, the interest income from the total portfolio would move positively with a rise in interest rates.

We have to admit that on the basis of historical experience there is no category of securities that can be relied on to provide investment returns in current dollars that are likely to vary in high positive correlation with the price level. The answer for an investor may be that he can only go along with whatever category of securities seems appropriate and try to achieve returns at a sufficiently high rate in current dollars to compensate as nearly as possible for price inflation. If he can obtain sufficiently high returns, it makes no difference from what category of securities he obtains them. Indeed this problem may well be dealt with not as a problem in portfolio construction but as one of portfolio management under changing conditions in the economy and in the market.

Common Stocks for Long-Term Holding

There is, however, one fact that may well be the basis for building some protection from inflation into a securities portfolio. That is the historical record, which shows that over relatively long time periods diversified portfolios of common stocks have provided average annual rates of return in current dollars that have translated into relatively good average annual rates of return in constant dollars. We cannot be sure that this kind of experience will obtain in the future, but whenever the time horizon for portfolio management is a long one, the inclusion of common stocks may provide average rates of return in constant dollars greater than those obtainable from other general categories of securities. Indeed, the constraints that governed portfolio construction in terms of interest-rate risk and financial risk may provide a portfolio that is about as good as any other portfolio from the standpoint of risk and returns in constant dollars.

Aggressive Policy for Large Current Dollar Returns

When constraints in terms of current dollars permit, the best defense against inflation may be an aggressive policy in assuming risk in current dollars. In other words, you can try to beat the average returns from common stocks by selecting issues that provide better than average returns. Actual experience with individual common stocks varies widely. You can buy risky stocks and try to achieve a high rate of return by capital appreciation. Some stocks rise even in declining markets, and in rising markets some stocks appreciate much more than others. This kind of effort is of course speculative in terms of both current and constant dollars. It requires good management and strong tenure of ownership.

You can also be aggressive in the bond market by investing in the lower-grade issues that sometimes sell on a yield basis almost as high as the rate of return usually expected from common stocks. You can seek out undervalued bonds, buy them cheaply, and sell at a higher price. You can make money by arbitrage in bonds, that is, by purchasing issues that seem priced a little too low and selling equivalent bonds at a higher price. You can buy high coupon bonds with borrowed money at a lower interest rate and benefit by the leverage effect. But some of these policies may be too risky or require too much expertness in the market to be feasible for the individual investor.

Some Other Media for Defensive Policy

Although our concern is with investment in marketable securities, it may be worthwhile to note in passing that other media may be used in an effort to protect purchasing power of invested funds in a time of rising prices. We have mentioned that ownership of real estate and equity interests in proprietary business enterprises have much the same qualities as common stocks in terms of purchasing power risk. But the range of alternatives is much broader.

At times when the price level is rising steeply or is expected to do so, investment in staple commodities and precious metals has been a popular inflation hedge. Through the facilities of the commodity markets, one may purchase contracts for the future delivery of wheat, corn, oats, butter, coffee, and even pork bellies. At time of delivery on such contracts, commodities may be sold for immediate delivery and, if the price has increased, the amount recovered in current dollars is larger than the amount invested. The operation can be repeated by purchasing new future contracts. The theory is that prices for staple commodities will rise as much as the rise in the general price level, or more. In practice, such price changes are a matter of some uncertainty. A disadvantage of this kind of inflation hedging is that it provides no income, except as profits may be realized and treated as income. It might be mentioned, too, that most people are unfamiliar with the procedures for trading in commodities and that, for the small investor, the minimum unit of trading may be too large for his pocketbook.

In countries that have experienced extremes of price inflation, the most popular inflation hedges have been gold, silver, platinum, and other precious metals. Gold cannot be purchased in the United States and it may not be owned legally, except for use in industry and the arts and for export. Silver and some other precious metals can be bought in the market in the United States and a number of other countries. It is said that platinum has been purchased by some inflation-fearing investors and put away in safe-deposit boxes.

An enterprising distillery in Scotland has offered an opportunity for investing in Scotch whiskey. You may buy casks of whiskey soon after distillation and hold them for a period of years until matured for blending, and then sell them at a price that may provide a good rate of return on your investment. The distillery keeps the casks for you, insures them, and eventually sells them for you. It has been pointed out that the demand for this product is almost universal and that the quantity demanded shows a strong upward trend. If you can't sell the whiskey at a good price, there is something else you can do with it.

Paintings, sculpture, and other objects of art, as well as rare coins and stamps, have been used as an inflation hedge. Assets of these kinds, it is believed, have a value relative to the average cost of goods and services that is likely to continue or increase under conditions of pronounced inflation. In addition, they have the advantage of being small in size and weight relative to value, and thus may be readily concealed or moved. However, like staple commodities they provide no income, are expensive to buy and keep safely, and their market value is difficult to judge.

Sometimes investors fear that their country's currency is to be devalued relative to currencies of other countries. A possible defense against this hazard is the purchase of currency of another country that is not likely to be devalued. Currency devaluation is not the same as price inflation, but it is usually accompanied by a rise in the price level of the country whose currency has been devalued. In recent international monetary crises there have been large sales of currencies considered weak for other currencies considered strong. Several countries have actually revalued their currencies upward in relation to gold and to other currencies.

In some countries bonds have been issued with amounts of income and sometimes amounts of principal variable with changes in the price level. In one country mortgage-lending institutions sell bonds with amounts of payments linked to the price of gold or to a foreign currency. If changes in the prices to which they are linked increase, the amounts of payments on the bonds are increased correspondingly. The mortgage-lending institutions then increase the charges on their outstanding loans to borrowers.

THE DESIRABILITY OF OWNERSHIP QUALITIES

Policy decisions about the grades of securities in the desirability of ownership qualities are an integral part of the general problem of designing the structure of a portfolio. Logically, these questions of policy should receive full consideration in investment planning, but in practice they are often neglected. Perhaps the reason for neglect is that rates of return usually are not so much affected by policy decisions in this area as they are in structuring a portfolio in terms of investment risk. Even so, the objective of maximizing returns may be materially aided by paying attention to this phase of portfolio policy.

Grades of Securities in Marketability

The earlier analysis of need for the higher grades of securities in marketability has indicated about how far an investor can go in endeavoring to maximize investment returns by selecting securities of the poorer grades. The remaining problem is merely to specify the grade, or grades, in terms of marketability, that are to be included in the portfolio and, if there is to be more than one grade, the proportions of each.

To specify grades of securities in marketability requires more than some general statement that a portfolio will include "only listed securities" or "only actively traded issues." We have seen that there is great variation in the marketability of listed stocks and in activity of trading. It is much more meaningful to define grades of marketability by some readily ascertainable measure. If the policy decision is to include only highly marketable stocks, the highly marketable grade might be defined as stocks usually quoted with a spread between bid and asked prices equal to not more than one-half of 1 per cent of the bid price. This definition would include over-the-counter stocks that have narrow spreads as well as those listed on organized exchanges, but it would exclude listed stocks that do not have such close quotations. Average daily volume of trading over a period of time might also be used as a basis for differentiating grade.

When there is a distinct need for highly marketable securities, it is usually recognized by investors and their counselors. But when an investor can accept the disadvantage of poor marketability for the sake of maximizing investment returns, he is often reluctant to decide to invest in poorly marketable issues. The term "poorly marketable" has an unfavorable connotation, just as the term "broadly diversified" has a favorable connotation. People generally do not like to say that they invest in poorly marketable issues, and investment advisors generally do not like to recommend investment in poorly marketable issues. They know that it is generally much easier for them to deal with the more highly marketable issues. These are the issues with which they are most familiar and that can be bought and sold most readily in the market. Thus a person who wants to invest in securities of low grade in marketability may have to overcome some resistance.

The successful operation of a policy of selecting poorly marketable issues requires no little sophistication in security analysis. The object is to realize a differential rate of return attributable to poorness of marketability. It is necessary to be able to discern differences in rate of return attributable to differences in marketability among securities that are of about the same grade in other investment qualities. One may compare long-term, high-grade bond issues and find small differences in yield that reflect differences in marketability. It is more difficult to see differences in expected returns from common stocks owing to differences in marketability grade because the size of returns is so uncertain. The aggressive policy of investing in issues with a low grade of marketability is likely, therefore, to be profitable only when the quality of investment management is high.

Grades of Securities in Taxability

The investor's tax rate largely determines his need for securities of the higher grades in terms of taxability. However, the differences in yields, or expected rates of return, from securities of different grades in taxability influence the investment decision. These differentials change and they may make tax advantage more or less important from time to time.

In its simplest form the problem of policy in constructing a securities portfolio can be examined by assuming (1) that taxable investment income would be taxed at the highest tax rate applicable to the investor, and (2) that the choice is among securities of the same grade in all other investment qualities except taxability. Then you compute the tax-equivalent rate for an issue having a tax advantage and compare it with the other issue that has no tax advantage. Computing the tax-equivalent rate is a problem in arithmetic, but people who work regularly with such comparisons use tax-equivalent tables. Table 19–1 is a tax-equivalent table for taxable and tax-exempt bonds.

Investors generally consider that income from securities is the top layer of their income and so they assume that this income is subject to the highest tax rate applicable to them. This is reasonable because they have the choice of taxable or tax-exempt income. In some instances the amount of income that may be taxable or tax-exempt may be so large that several rates of the income tax may have to be considered.

The problem of investment policy becomes more complex when the choice is between securities of different grades not only in taxability but also in other investment qualities. You can look at the yields on tax-exempt securities and compute tax-equivalent yields just as we have done, but in addition you have to allow for differences in grade of financial risk, interest-rate risk, and possibly in other qualities.

To visualize this kind of policy problem in rather extreme terms, consider an individual investor who has concluded that his choice lies between high-grade, long-term municipal bonds and speculative common stocks. Let us say that municipals can be purchased to yield 5 per cent. The common stocks he is considering pay no cash dividends; his return, if any, will be in the form of long-term capital gains. This investor's tax rate on long-term capital gains is 25 per cent. You can see at once that capital gains at an average annual rate of 6.67 per cent would provide the same after-tax returns as the 5 per cent yield from municipal bonds. But can one rely on capital gains at an aver-

TABLE 19–1

Tax-Equivalent Bond Yields

	Marginal tax rates					
	16%	*28%*	*42%*	*53%*	*62%*	*70%*
Tax-exempt yields	*Equivalent taxable yields*					
2.00%	2.38%	2.78%	3.45%	4.26%	5.26%	6.67%
2.50	2.98	3.47	4.31	5.32	6.58	8.33
3.00	3.57	4.17	5.17	6.38	7.89	10.00
3.50	4.17	4.86	6.03	7.45	9.21	11.67
4.00	4.76	5.56	6.90	8.51	10.53	13.33
4.50	5.35	6.25	7.76	9.57	11.84	15.00

Source: *Federal Taxes*, Vol. 1, Englewood Cliffs, N.J., 1972, Prentice-Hall, Inc.

age annual rate of 6.67 per cent? Obviously, the uncertainty of such returns is greater than the uncertainty of the yield on municipal bonds. When you make allowance for the difference in risk, the expected rate of return on common stocks would have to be much greater than the tax-equivalent yield on municipal bonds for the stocks to be an attractive alternative.

When common stocks must be considered as alternatives to other kinds of securities for individual investors, the dividend exclusion provided for individuals in the federal personal income tax law should be taken into account because it gives dividend income from stocks a degree of tax exemption. In fact, it makes common stocks fully tax-exempt (on income) up to an amount providing dividends of as much as $100 per person filing a single return and as much as $200 of dividends on a joint return. Thus, if a married couple filing a joint return owns common stocks having a market value of $6,600 and receives a dividend return on market value at 3 per cent, their dividend income ($198) is entirely tax-exempt. At an applicable tax rate of 42 per cent, the tax-equivalent dividend yield is 5.17 per cent.

Even if dividend income considerably exceeds the amount of dividend exclusion, the exclusion lowers the applicable tax rate on dividend income. If a couple filing a joint return has $1,000 a year of dividend income, they pay tax on only 80 per cent of it ($1,000 minus $200 equals $800), and the applicable tax rate is 80 per cent of the rate that would apply to fully taxable income. With a tax rate on ordinary income of 42 per cent, the applicable tax rate on their dividend income would be 33.6 per cent. You can figure the applicable rate to dividend income in any situation by multiplying 1.00 minus the percentage of dividends excluded times the tax rate that would apply to dividend income.

Although we have devoted considerable attention to the advantages of some kinds of securities relative to others under the tax laws, tax advantage is only one consideration in choosing securities for a portfolio. The grades of securities in other investment qualities and the need of the investor for the higher grades of securities in these other qualities must be taken into account.

Other Desirability of Ownership Qualities

Questions about the structure of a portfolio in grades of securities differentiated on the basis of convertibility, redeemability, legality for investment, and deepness of discount bring the investment manager down to some of the finer points of policy. The disadvantages of the poorer grades of securities in these qualities are usually small, and the differences in expected returns between grades are also small. For this reason investment managers, even professionals, may give too little attention to these finer points, but they are nevertheless worth attention. The questions of policy apply chiefly to portfolios of bonds and preferred stocks, wherein yields are relatively low and a few basis points in portfolio yield make the difference between a fair job of management and an excellent job.

Some matters of policy are decided for institutional investors by laws or regulations affecting their security investments. Commercial banks may not buy convertible bonds when the purchase price includes an appreciable consideration for the conversion right. Life insurance companies domiciled or doing business in the state of New York may invest only in common stocks of companies that have earned and paid cash dividends in each of the preceding 10 years. Beyond these restrictions, questions of policy about grades of securities in desirability of ownership qualities have to be decided on the basis of the need of the investor for issues of the higher grades and the size of yields.

Attitudes toward financial risk and purchasing-power risk determine the need for convertible bonds and preferred stocks in the portfolio. If an investor is limited to bonds and preferred stocks, he may want to modify his defensive risk policy to some extent in the direction of aggressiveness by using convertible issues. They would provide opportunity for returns larger than those obtainable on straight bonds and preferred stocks. The investor must also be able to assume the somewhat larger degree of financial risk added by the conversion right, that is, the risk of price depreciation owing to lower market evaluation of conversion rights.

Consideration of the purchasing-power risk affects the question of convertibles in the same way. If the need for a high degree of stability of income and principal in current dollars has forced an investor into assuming the level of purchasing-power risk in bonds and preferred stocks, he can escape from that position to some extent by the use of convertible issues. However, the opportunity to realize a larger return by conversion is accompanied by lower yield and greater instability of market price. If the market price of a convertible is influenced strongly by the prospect of profitable conversion, it tends to fluctuate with the market price of the stock into which it is convertible. Thus, both the sacrifice in yield and the potential price depreciation must be acceptable in terms of other considerations of investment policy.

Whether a portfolio should include securities of the higher grades in redeemability and deepness of discount is a matter of differences in expected rates of return of securities graded in these qualities. Strong call protection may cost money in terms of yield differentials relative to issues with weak call protection, and so may call protection in the form of deep discount bonds versus those selling at little discount from par. Do you want to pay the price? The answer is usually a subjective one; it hinges on your estimate of future changes in interest rates. If you are clearly of the opinion that interest rates will decline and you want the protection provided, you will pay for it. Otherwise you will not.

DESIGNING THE PORTFOLIO TO THE TERMS OF THE MARKET

In this discussion we have taken investment constraints as the principal variable on which investment policies depend. However, we have also recognized at times that there is another variable affecting policy decisions about the structure of the portfolio. That variable is the size of the differential between yields, or expected rates of return, at which the better grades of securities (in many of the investment qualities) may be purchased in the market relative to yields at which the poorer grades may be purchased. The size of this differential varies from time to time. Sometimes it provides liberal compensation for the greater risk, or other disadvantages, but at other times provides little compensation. It is only reasonable, then, that the willingness of investors to purchase the poorer grades of securities should be influenced by the size of the yield differentials existing in the market. Sometimes the size of the prospective reward for higher risk or poorness of grade is not worthwhile.

It is helpful to think of the yield on securities relative to the degree of risk attached to them. The concept of a yield/risk ratio is illustrated in Table 19–2, which uses entirely hypothetical quantitative data. The yield figures express the idea of yields increasing with increasing degrees of risk or other kind of disadvantage. Index numbers are used to express subjective judgments of differences in risk. The degree of risk in securities of the highest grade is assigned the index number 1.0; the degree of risk in securities of the second grade is indicated by the number 1.1, and so forth. The figures in this model have been selected so that they provide a yield/risk ratio that rises as risk increases. When something like this pattern of a rising yield/risk relationship is provided by the terms at which securities can be bought in the market, the terms are relatively favorable for assuming the greater risk or disadvantage. When terms are less favorable, the policy decisions may be to limit investments to the higher grades.

The historical record of yields and yield spreads between averages for different categories of securities provides abundant evidence that the yield/risk ratio does vary significantly from time to time. Sometimes the yield spread between average yields on triple A rated corporate bonds and triple B rated bonds is large and sometimes it is small. At times the differential in yield between long-term and short-term Treasury obligations is large and sometimes it is zero. Sometimes the yield differential between corporate bonds and municipal bonds is large and sometimes small. Shrewd investment managers give considerable attention to these differentials and invest in the categories of securities that provide the best yield/risk ratio.[1]

[1]Salomon Brothers, a New York broker-dealer firm, publishes privately for its customers an historical record of average yields on different categories of securities under the title *An Analytical Record of Yields and Yield Spreads.*

TABLE 19–2

The Concept of a Yield/Risk Ratio

	First grade	*Second grade*	*Third grade*	*Fourth grade*
Yield	4.00%	4.50%	5.00%	6.00%
Risk index	1.00	1.10	1.20	1.30
Yield/risk ratio	4.00	4.10	4.18	4.62

Note: These figures are hypothetical and do not represent a pattern of yield/risk ratios existing in the market.

QUESTIONS FOR DISCUSSION

1. Julliette Jones is a difficult customer. She wants safety and a stable rate of income. You don't even mention common stocks in your discussion with her. Municipal bonds are out because her income is small. You suggest some triple A rated corporate bonds due in 20 to 25 years. She snorted at that, saying, "I won't be here that long." So you proposed triple A corporate bonds due at the end of 5 years from the present date. Mrs. Jones liked that and you bought the bonds for her. What is wrong with the solution to the investment problem that the lady forced on you?
2. How can you obtain a secondary reserve in a bond portfolio without buying short-term securities?
3. How does the strength of tenure of an investor affect his policies in constructing a portfolio?
4. How would you construct the bond portion of a securities portfolio to obtain maximum stability of interest income from the bonds?
5. How would you construct the bond portion of a securities portfolio to obtain an increase in income in current dollars during a coming period of greater price inflation and higher interest rates?
6. You are the investment officer of a life insurance company and you have a net cash inflow of funds for investment in the amount of $1 million a day. You are permitted to invest only a very small percentage of this money in stocks. You are quite confident that market rates of yield on long-term corporate bonds will rise by at least 1 percentage point during the next 12 months. What will you do with the million dollars a day?
7. An insurance company offers your instructor a fixed annuity, a variable annuity, or any combination of the two. He has to participate because his educational institution offers only this kind of a retirement plan. What should he do?
8. What do you think of the idea of linking the amounts of interest and principal payments in current dollars on U. S. government bonds to the Consumer Price Index in much the same manner that amounts of social security payments are now linked?
9. Jim MacDonald retired from his position as chief executive officer of a large company and he now lives on a retirement income from the company's pension fund of $40,000 a year. He files a joint federal income tax return with his wife, he has no other dependents, and uses the standard deduction instead of itemized deductions. His retirement income is fully taxable. Now he asks you whether he should keep his municipal bonds. He owns these bonds with a current market value of about $100,000 and the income therefrom is $4,500 a year. He has no other investments in securities.
10. "The way to hedge inflation at a low level of risk is to invest in convertible bonds," says Mr. Bunk. Either support or deny this statement.

20

Defensive Policies toward Price Changes

In the days of your grandfather, Mr. J. P. Morgan was the greatest name in finance. He was head of J. P. Morgan & Co., and the House of Morgan was one of the highest pinnacles of the financial world. His opinions on financial matters were highly respected and widely sought after. On one occasion when he returned to this country after a grouse-shooting vacation in Scotland, he was met at the dock in New York by the usual group of newspaper reporters. One of them asked the inevitable question: "What is the outlook for the stock market, Mr. Morgan?" The financier assumed his most dignified manner and replied, "Young man, I expect that stock prices will continue to fluctuate."

This story is a bit worn from many tellings, but it serves to introduce the second phase of investment planning, that is, the formulation of policies for dealing with the phenomenon of constantly changing market prices. Estimates of future changes in prices are common currency in the financial community. Hardly anyone in Wall Street does not have an opinion about which way stock prices will move and, with the spread of common stock ownership, a great many people on Main Street also have opinions. High-grade bonds are seldom regarded as a medium for speculation, but at almost every meeting of men engaged in the management of bond investments the outlook for interest rates and bond prices is one of the most popular topics for discussion.

Estimates of future price changes confront investors almost everywhere, and they present the very vital question, "What to do?" Shall one buy, or sell, or ignore these estimates?

THE BROAD PROBLEM OF POLICY

There is almost always some latitude for buying or selling in managing a securities portfolio. We have been concerned with the structure of a portfolio in terms of risk levels of securities, but even when these policies have been determined the structure is not necessarily fixed and rigid. There is usually room for some variation in grades of securities and in the proportions of different grades within established investment limitations. And there is frequently the option of converting securities into cash, or cash into securities. Thus the question of what response to make to estimates of future changes in security prices is a very ubiquitous one.

It is important that policies be defined clearly before the question of buying or selling arises, for at such a time emotional pressures are almost always present. If you think that the market is going to decline, you are motivated by fear of loss and, possibly, even by concern about damage to your ego from holding stocks in a declining market. If you are engaged in some investment advisory capacity, you are concerned about the reactions of others. If you think that stocks are going to rise and you have the means to buy, your thinking is affected by visions of profits to be made and of the satisfaction that comes from being knowledgeable. You can hardly avoid having your judgment influenced by emotions. Naturally, these considerations affect bond investors as well as those chiefly interested in stocks.

The time to make policy decisions is when you can do it in the abstract, that is, without reference to any particular estimate or any immediate course of action. Then you have a good chance to think rationally. When the question is not immediate, you can consider how well a particular policy is likely to work in the long run when followed consistently; how large are the gains that may be realized and also how uncertain; how large are the possible losses and how probable. You can assess the probabilities of gains and losses judiciously with the benefit of experience and with the perception provided by historical perspective. You can consider alternative courses of action and compare their merits. And you can take into account explicitly the investment limitations that have molded policies in construction of the portfolio.

Concepts of Defensive and Aggressive Policies

We have used the terms *defensive* and *aggressive* to describe policies in construction of a portfolio, and we can continue to use them with much the same meanings to describe policies toward estimated price changes.

Thus an *aggressive* policy is one intended to obtain benefits for an investor by successfully estimating future changes in prices within some fairly well-defined time period and by selling or buying accordingly. Aggressive action assumes a risk of loss that would not be assumed if the action was not taken. Although this kind of policy is usually concerned with market prices, it may have as its principal objective benefits in the form of larger income returns on securities.

A *defensive* policy involves buying and selling from time to time with no particular regard for estimates of how prices are likely to change in the future. Some one has termed this a "know-nothing" policy, because those who pursue it profess to know nothing about future changes in prices. A common version of defensive policy is to arrange purchases and sales so that they are distributed more or less evenly over time so as to average prices paid or received as prices fluctuate. We will call this strategy a defensive policy based on time diversification.

Kinds of Changes in Market Prices

For these concepts of policy to be clearly delineated, we must specify what kinds of price changes we are talking about. First, we mean changes in average prices for a particular category, or risk level, of securities. When you examine a chart showing the record of fluctuations in average stock prices over a considerable period, you see three distinct types of changes distinguished on the basis of time duration. They are generally termed intermediate, cyclical, and secular.

There are *cyclical* movements in average stock prices that stand out clearly in the charts of stock price indexes. They are associated with the business cycle, but are not exactly coincident with it. Historically, stock prices have tended to turn up before a general upswing in business has become evident. For this reason stock price indexes are classified among the leading indicators of business cycles. Usually the cyclical upward movement of stock prices continues for some short period of time after the business cycle has turned downward.

The magnitudes of changes in stock prices, however, are different for different risk levels of stocks. Generally the low-risk, blue chip stocks lead other risk categories in the upswing, but their cyclical variation is less than that of higher risk stocks. High-risk stocks lag in the early phase of a bull market and gain upward momentum as investors' confidence increases both in the business recovery and in the prospects for weaker companies. Their variation is greater. So when you speak of cyclical movements in stock prices it is well to be fairly specific about what kinds of stocks you are talking about.

Within the broad cyclical pattern of bull and bear markets for stocks there are *intermediate price fluctuations*. In a bull market prices often spurt ahead vigorously for a few weeks or a few months and then decline briefly. Their duration is relatively short.

Bond prices also fluctuate cyclically. In our earlier study of interest rates we found that they generally decline in a period of business recession with an accompanying rise in bond prices. In the period of recovery, interest rates rise and bond prices decline. These changes tend to lag behind changes in the broad indicators of the movement of business cycles. Again, there are differences in the magnitude of bond-price fluctuations for the different risk grades of bonds. Prices for short-term obligations fluctuate much more than prices of long-term issues. Prices for bonds representing the higher levels of uncertainty of future financial ability of issuers do not respond so precisely to changes in interest rates as prices for those issues governed almost entirely by movements of interest rates. Indeed, lower-grade bond prices have at times moved contrary to prices for high-grade issues during severe business recessions.

Third, there are *secular trends* in security prices, that is, trends that extend over two or more business cycles. Average stock prices, we have previously seen, may establish a trend extending over a decade or more. Bond prices, too, are characterized by such long-term movements. As stock prices rose for about 2 decades beginning at mid-century, so did bond prices decline.

DEFENSIVE POLICIES OF TIME DIVERSIFICATION

A policy of arranging purchases and sales so that they are distributed more or less evenly over time is defensive because gain is not sought by attempting to select the time when prices are low for buying and high for selling, and loss is not risked when estimates of future price movements prove wrong. It is a policy of taking prices as they come and being content with realizing an average of prices on purchases from time to time as well as an average of prices on sales from time to time.

You can grasp the full implications of defensive policy by contrasting it with aggressive policy to see the risk that the defensive policy seeks to avoid. Suppose that you have been studying steel stocks and you have decided that you want to add some of these stocks to your portfolio. But you think that market prices will soon decline and that you can buy at lower prices if you wait awhile. This is a policy of speculating on future change in market prices. If steel stocks decline in price and you buy after the decline, your speculation worked out well. If prices rise, either you buy at higher prices or you do not buy and this "loss" is the amount you might have gained by buying at lower prices.

The same sort of speculation is involved in trying to choose the right time to sell. You own some chemical stocks, you think that prospects for the industry have deteriorated, and you have decided to sell them. But you think that current market prices are too low and you defer the sale in expectation of higher prices. If the price does rise, you have gained relative to the price at the time the decision to sell was made; if the price goes down, the result is a loss relative to the earlier price.

When you decide that purchase of a particular kind of securities is desirable, the simplest version of defensive policy is to buy at once. Thus you avoid the risk that prices for securities to be bought will rise and forego the opportunity to buy at lower prices in the event that prices decline. When you decide to sell, you sell at that time and forego the chance of higher prices.

It is striking evidence of the need of human beings to rationalize their behavior that people who try to time purchases and sales of securities to obtain better prices than those currently prevailing in the market often use such words as "cautious," "prudent," or "shrewd" to describe their actions. When they have decided to buy certain securities but to defer actual purchase in expectation of lower prices, many people rationalize the decision by using one of the adjectives that has a favorable connotation; they fail to recognize that the decision was to speculate on which way prices will move. If the speculation works out well, then it was prudent or shrewd.

One Wall Street saying that has lured many people to loss is: "You never get poor by taking a profit." When the current market price of a stock is higher than the price you paid, you can certainly realize a profit by selling. You also pay an income tax on the profit as a capital gain. Now, if the price of this good stock continues to rise and you buy it back eventually at a higher price, the trip out and back will have been costly. By taking the profit you are poorer than you would have been if you had not taken it. If you do not buy it back, you have lost the opportunity for further price appreciation.

This discourse is intended to differentiate between defensive and aggressive policies toward estimates of cyclical changes in prices, but not to advocate generally one policy or the other. If we have pointed particularly to the possible adverse outcome of aggressive policy, it is to make clear the nature of such a policy. The glamour and challenge of aggressive policy will be apparent when we discuss some of the ways of trying to make money in the stock market in the next chapter.

Theory of Time Diversification

The practice of spacing purchases and sales of securities over time is called *time diversification*. The principle is the same as that of random diversification of financial risk in a portfolio of securities. The investor who diversifies financial risk by spreading his commitments randomly over a number of companies in different industries and geographical areas says, in effect, "I don't know which of all these issues will work out well and which poorly, so I'll buy all of them and settle for the average." The investor who spreads his purchases and sales of securities over a period of time says, in effect, "I don't know which unit of time (day, week, or month) in the next year or so will provide the lower prices and which will require the higher prices, so I'll buy in all time periods and settle for the average."

One professional investment counselor calls time diversification the fourth principle of diversification, and quotes Shakespeare to show that the principle has long been recognized.[1] In "The Merchant of Venice" Antonio says:

> I thank my Fortune for it, my ventures are not in one bottom trusted, not to one place; nor is my whole estate upon the Fortune of the present year. Therefore my merchandise makes me not sad.

In practice, time diversification usually means buying or selling at more or less regular time intervals, which is unlike random selection of time periods but does not involve trying to select favorable periods. Of course, time periods could be selected randomly.

There is a peculiar ambivalence in the thinking of many financial analysts about time diversification and diversification by issues. They not only accept but advocate strongly the principle of diversification by issues. The ability of investing institutions with large aggregations of funds to diversify broadly by issues is one of the important reasons why they are thought to do a better job of investment management than individuals with such small amounts that they cannot diversify broadly. At the same time, however, many of them reject the principle of time diversification. They will settle for average results one way, but not the other.

Aversion to time diversification may be a sort of occupational psychological complex induced in those who are engaged professionally in investment management or in investment advising by the expectations of those they serve. People want to make money by investing in securities. They can always look backward and see how easily money could have been made by buying at one time and selling at another. Customers, clients, beneficiaries, and shareholders seem to infer, implicitly or explicitly, that one who knows the business should be able to make money by knowing when to buy and when to sell. People are willing to pay—and pay handsomely—for the services of those who are supposed to have this knowledge. It is not surprising, then, that some people in the investment business endeavor to make their living by trying to provide the kind of knowhow that is so much sought after. In addition, Wall Street is a highly competitive place in which people not only have to be smart to get ahead, but also have to convince others that they are. Modesty on the part of ambitious men about ability to forecast market prices might be inconsistent with the impressions they wish to create.

Time Diversification by Dollar Averaging

The best known and probably the most widely practiced application of the principle of time diversification is *dollar averaging*. This is the term applied to a policy of investing equal dollar amounts of money periodically in

[1]Bruce A. Valentine, "Shakespeare Revisited," *Financial Analysts Journal*, Vol. 21, No. 3 (May–June, 1965), pp. 91–97.

securities, usually in common stocks. The provision that equal amounts be applied to purchases is important. The effect of equal amounts and regular times for purchase is that one buys more shares when prices are low and fewer shares when prices are high. When prices fluctuate up and down in more or less symmetrical cycles, the investor who follows this policy acquires securities at an average price per share (or per bond) that is less than the average of prices paid. The effect is illustrated in Table 20–1.

However, prices do not necessarily fluctuate as this illustration assumes. For any single stock, the price pattern over a time period may take almost any conceivable form. If the price movement is steadily upward with no appreciable downward fluctuation, the effect of dollar averaging is simply to buy stocks periodically at constantly advancing prices. If the movement is steadily downward, the opposite is true.

As the term is generally used, dollar averaging refers to the purchase of securities. It may just as well be applied to a policy of selling securities at regular intervals. To realize an average price per share (or per bond) greater than the average of prices at which sales are executed, it would be necessary to increase the number of shares sold as market price rises and to reduce the number as prices decline.

There is considerable evidence that dollar averaging is widely used by individual investors in accumulating common stocks. Some years ago New York Stock Exchange member firms began to offer to the public the Monthly Investment Plan. This arrangement facilitates the regular application of uniform amounts of money to the purchase of one or more stocks. An investor who wishes to use the MIP enters into an agreement with a member firm to invest a stipulated dollar amount periodically. The feature of the arrangement that makes it particularly useful to people with such amounts to invest on a regular schedule is that they can buy both full and fractional shares. For example, if the amount to be applied to a monthly purchase is $100 and if the price of the stock at the moment is $40 (including the odd-lot differential) the

TABLE 20–1

The Arithmetic of Dollar Averaging

Date	*Amount Invested*	*Market Price Paid*	*Number of Shares Purchased*
First date	$100	$10	10
Second date	100	12-1/2	8
Third date	100	20	5
Fourth date	100	12-1/2	8
Fifth date	100	10	10
	$500		41

Total amount invested	$500.00
Average market price	13.00
Number of shares purchased	41
Average cost per share ($500 ÷ 41 shares)	$ 12.20

$100 buys 2½ shares of stock and the investor is credited with that number of whole shares and the fraction. Fractions are carried out to thousandths of a share.

People who use this plan pay regular brokerage commissions, the odd-lot price differential, and transfer taxes. In the example above, commissions and taxes have been disregarded for the sake of simplicity. No special charges are levied for beginning or terminating an agreement. An agreement can be canceled by a customer at any time without penalty. Recently, about 343,000 MIP accounts were in force. Open-end investment companies, or mutual funds, offer similar arrangements for the regular purchase of their shares.

The dollar-averaging principle is especially suitable for investors who have more or less uniform amounts of funds for buying stocks at fairly regular intervals, whose general policy is to buy and hold securities, and who have no disposition to try to forecast stock prices. It is usually used for the purchase of stocks, but could also be applied to bonds. Thus it is generally used by individuals who are able to save regularly from income and to apply their savings, or some part, to investment in securities. However, people whose funds for investment come from annual bonuses, seasonally high earnings, or other irregular income can use dollar averaging by spreading such amounts over equal monthly or quarterly purchases.

Formula-Timing Plans

In the disillusion and frustration of common-stock investors with stock price forecasting the very simple idea of dollar averaging evolved into a more complex concept for determining when to buy, and when to sell, by a more or less mechanical method for determining when transactions are likely to be advantageous. It may have been that someone using the dollar-averaging principle said to himself, "This works much better when I buy at times prices are low. Therefore, what I should do is to limit my buying to periods of low prices and not buy when prices are high." But unwillingness to try to forecast stock prices was carried over into the new concept. The problem of buying when prices are low and still not explicitly forecasting prices from time to time was attempted to be solved by adopting a formula for determining when stocks should be bought and sold. The essence of the formula is that stock prices are low after they have declined and high after they have risen. By defining "high" and "low," the developers of formula timing endeavored to eliminate forecasting.

The management of a securities portfolio by a formula-timing plan is generally termed a defensive policy because it is not supposed to be based on estimates of which way stock prices will move in a particular future time period, even though it does seek to profit by such price fluctuations. There is room for argument about this, but the purpose of formula-timing plans is to avoid recurring questions about which way stock prices are going to move.

All variations of the formula-timing idea provide for dividing the investment portfolio into two parts. One part consists of securities having high price stability, such as high grade short term bonds. This is called the "defensive" portion. Price fluctuations in this portion are not expected to be significant. The other part consists of a diversified list of common stocks, the prices for which are expected to fluctuate with the general movement of stock prices. The stocks are selected in advance but may be changed from time to time. This is the "aggressive" portion—the portion to be used to obtain profits.

The initial division of the total portfolio between the two parts may be in any proportions considered appropriate for the investor, such as 30 per cent stock and 70 per cent bonds, or 40–60, or 50–50 per cent. In a specific situation, a decision on the proportion of common stocks would be influenced by the need of the investor for stability of principal and income, and by the current level of stock prices relative to a long-term price average or trend. The more rigid the limitations on the ability of an investor to own common stocks, the smaller the stock portion; and the higher the current level of market prices, the smaller the stock portion.

A second common characteristic of all plans is a provision for "automatic" sales and purchases. As stock prices rise, parts of the aggressive portion are sold. They are sold at certain points previously established in terms of (1) the market value of the aggressive portion, or (2) the ratio of stock value to total value of the portfolio, or (3) the level of a stock price average. The amount or proportion of stocks to be sold at each point is also fixed by the provisions of the plan. The proceeds from sales are transferred to the defensive portion. Similarly, as stock prices decline, bonds are sold and stocks are purchased to increase the aggressive portion at predetermined points. As far as the individual security issues in a portfolio are concerned, purchases and sales are "across the board," that is, about the same proportion of each issue in terms of market value is bought or sold. Thus, no judgment is required on the part of the fund manager on when to buy or sell, or how much to buy or sell.

The principle of formula timing is illustrated in Figure 20–1. Here a certain amount of stock is purchased whenever a stock price index declines 10 points, and the same amount is sold whenever the index rises 10 points.

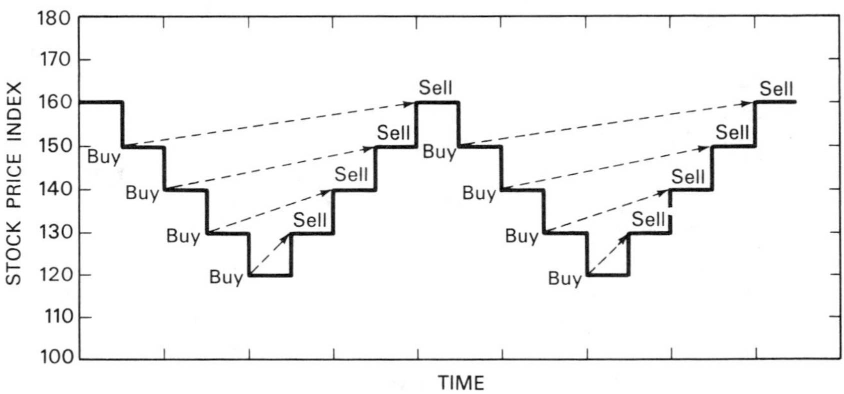

FIGURE 20–1

The Principle of Formula-Timing Plans

The chart shows how in a declining market additional stock would be bought at several successively lower levels of prices and then sold on the cyclical upward movement. A complete and uniform price cycle would produce a profit because each lot of stock would be sold at a level of the market 10 points higher than the level at which it was bought. For simplicity of illustration, this figure presents symmetrical cyclical price movement in a horizontal plane. We have previously seen that market prices do not really fluctuate in such precise geometric patterns.

Almost everyone who sets out to devise a formula plan suitable to his investment requirements and predispositions emerges with a plan different from those of other investors. If you wanted to make up such a plan you would have to decide, first, whether you want the proportion of common stocks at market values to remain relatively constant or to change from time to time; second, how buying and selling action will be determined; and, finally, what amount or proportion of stocks will be bought or sold when action is taken.

The principal distinction among plans is usually made on the basis of whether the ratio of stock to total market value of the portfolio changes as stock prices fluctuate. Some plans prescribe that a given percentage of the total fund shall be in stocks. Then, if market values fluctuate in such a way as to change this ratio to a significant extent, stocks are bought or sold to restore the prescribed ratio. These are called *constant ratio plans.* Other plans provide that the ratio of stocks will be changed deliberately as stock prices fluctuate; these are *variable ratio plans.*

In *constant ratio plans*, buying and selling action may be determined by a change in the proportion of common stock at current market values, by a change of a given magnitude in a specified stock price index, or simply by lapse of a given period of time.

If you decide, for example, that you want 50 per cent of your investment fund to consist of common stocks, you might specify that stocks would be sold whenever their current market value rises to 55 per cent of the total fund. The amount to be sold would be the amount that, when transferred to bonds, would restore the 50 per cent ratio. The plan would work in the opposite manner when stock prices decline. If the value of stock declines to 45 per cent of the value of the total portfolio, you would sell bonds and buy stocks to restore the 50 per cent constant ratio.

The simpler kinds of *variable ratio plans* provide for changes in the ratio of stocks to the total portfolio at current market values as stock prices rise or fall. The purpose is to reduce the proportion of stocks in a rising market and to increase the proportion in a declining market. If such a plan works well, the investment fund will contain the smallest percentage of stocks at the peak of a stock market cycle and the largest percentage at the bottom of the cycle. Action may be determined by fluctuations in one of the well-known stock price indexes. When such an index rises a given number of points, or a given percentage, the proportion of stock in the portfolio at current market values is reduced by so many percentage points.

A different version of the same idea is to maintain the market value of the stock portion at a constant amount, making adjustments at regular time intervals. Suppose that you start with $50,000 in stocks and $50,000 in bonds. After 3 months (or some other predetermined time period) you find that your stocks are worth $60,000. So you sell $10,000 of stocks in order to reduce the value of your stocks to $50,000 and use the proceeds to increase the bond portion of the fund (which rises to $60,000). Stock prices continue to rise, and after another period you again sell stocks to bring the stock portion back to $50,000 and add the proceeds to the bond portion. The sale of stock in a rising market and the purchase of bonds reduces the ratio of stocks to bonds.

When formula-timing plans first came into use their designers seemed tacitly to assume that stock prices fluctuated cyclically in a horizontal plane, and there was little in the record of the stock price averages through the thirties and forties to suggest anything different. But the long bull market of the fifties and sixties ran away from plans that assumed some cyclical ceiling, and investors who adhered to them were left in their minimum stock position.

Formula-plan designers were quick to notice the secular trend in stock prices, and they set about revamping their plans to take account of it. The simplest thing to do was to project the trend of prices upward at some average annual rate of increase believed to be justified by past experience and the present outlook. Then the assumption was made that prices would fluctuate cyclically around the trend line. Plans with such a built-in trend assumption are called *norm type plans* because they assume that the rising trend is normal.

Figure 20–2 illustrates a kind of norm-type plan. It is based on the assumption that stock prices, as measured by a broad index, increase at an average annual rate of 10 per cent. The lines above the trend line represent

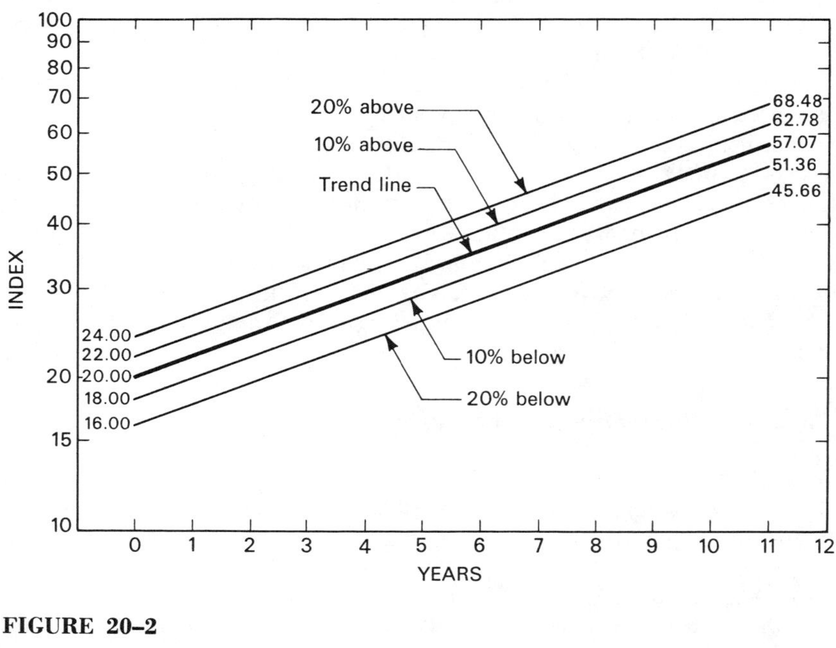

FIGURE 20–2
Norm-Type Formula-Timing Plan Using Projected Stock Price Trend

numbers 10 per cent greater and 20 per cent greater than the trend value projected for each year. Similarly, the lines below the trend line indicate quantities 10 per cent less and 20 per cent less than trend values. The trend rate may be whatever percentage is considered appropriate.

A plan using this concept of the future movement of prices might provide for 50 per cent of a fund in stocks when the price index is near the trend line, for reduction of the stock proportion to 40 per cent when the price index crosses 10 per cent above-trend line, and for reduction to 30 per cent when the index crosses 20 per cent above-trend line. Buying would be governed in the same manner by the movement of the price index relative to the trend line. When it declines beyond 10 per cent below-trend line, stock would be bought in amounts sufficient to increase the stock portion to 60 per cent, and a decline under 20 per cent below-trend line would cause the stock portion to be increased to 70 per cent of the portfolio. Of course, one could design a plan with more lines and more "zones" for buying and selling.

The trouble with formula-timing plans is that they require investors to do what they purport to avoid doing, that is, to forecast future change in stock prices. A forecast has to be made to construct a plan. Even the simplest kind requires an estimate of the amplitude of cyclical fluctuations in stock prices so that the portfolio will achieve its maximum desired proportion of stocks when prices are at the cyclical bottom and so that the minimum proportion will be held when prices are at the top of the cycle. The non-norm type plans assume that there is no secular trend in stock prices, which is itself an implicit forecast. The norm-type plans try explicitly to forecast the price trend as well as the amplitude of cyclical fluctuation in prices around the trend line.

We have included formula-timing plans under the heading of defensive policy because in the operation of such plans no forecast of change in stock prices is required. But it is clear that the basis for formula timing is a long-range forecast of prices, which may be more difficult than the shorter-range forecasts used in pursuing aggressive policies.

Nevertheless, the concept of formula timing remains an intriguing one. If forecasts of stock prices could be revised periodically on the basis of historical experience and current prospects, and if plans could be readjusted accordingly, they may be very useful. Revision would require repeated forecasting, and formula plans would become a mechanical aid to aggressive policy toward cyclical price movements. Maybe that is the way they should be regarded, and the idea of adhering rigidly to fixed formula plans should be abandoned.[2]

Time Diversification in Purchasing Bonds

When you space purchases of bond issues more or less evenly over a period of time, you achieve time diversification of the markets' terms for reinvestment. In chapter 19 the system of spacing maturities and rotating funds

[2]See: Alan E. Grunewald and Robert C. Klemkosky, "If you Believe Growth is Dead, Try the Formula Timing Plan," *MSU Business Topics*, Summer, 1972, pp. 57–65.

was described as a means of stabilizing income. In this chapter, it is a means of applying defensive policy toward price fluctuations. When you space maturities and re-invest as funds become available, you disregard estimates of how prices will change in the future and pay the market price at time of investment.

Defensive policy may be applied to several kinds of situations that frequently arise in managing a bond portfolio. In a period of declining interest rates, a common problem is the redemption of portfolio issues before their maturity. The effect is to add to the amount of funds regularly available for re-investment and to disrupt the schedule of bond maturities that is depended on to provide regularity in the flow of funds for re-investment. The defensive way to deal with the problem is to re-invest funds from early redemptions at the time the funds become available in obligations of about the same maturity as those redeemed.

This policy restores the maturity schedule and does all that can be done to provide a steady flow of funds in the future from redemptions at maturity. It has the disadvantage, from the defensive viewpoint, of resulting in an above-average proportion of the total portfolio being re-invested in a period when before-maturity redemptions are heavy. However, even heavy redemptions are usually spread over a period of several years, so that re-investment over such a time span provides a degree of time diversification. In addition, the yields obtained on re-investing funds in unusually large amounts are averaged with yields on the remainder of the portfolio so that change in average portfolio yield is small.

Another kind of situation requiring a decision about how purchases will be influenced by price estimates is the addition of a substantial amount of new money to a bond fund. If the spaced maturity policy is being followed in constructing the portfolio, the defensive policy involves buying bonds of about the same maturities as those in the portfolio and in amounts proportionate to amounts already owned. There is also the question of when the new money shall be invested. The defensive policy would be to spread purchases over some period of time in order to average prices paid. You might decide how much is to be purchased of each maturity, divide those amounts by 12, and invest one-twelfth of the new money each month in the desired maturities. Thus one would obtain a degree of time diversification of the terms of purchase in the market.

Adapting Defensive Policies to Changes in the Market

The adoption of defensive policies does not mean that securities are never sold or bought. You don't just buy a portfolio of securities and put them away in a safe-deposit box. A defensive posture requires continual supervision in order to achieve the avowed objective of maximizing return at a given level of risk. Time passes and there is change.

The market changes. Expected rates of returns for categories of securities characterized by different levels of risk change, and the differentials between categories change. When the differential in yields between securities of the poorer and better grades increases and thus provides greater compensation for poorness of grade, there may be a shift of funds to issues of lower grade. Or, conversely, the lack of sufficiently larger returns on lower grades of securities may justify reducing or eliminating securities of these grades. When such changes are made in the structure of a portfolio they are defensive. They represent a response to past change rather than an anticipation of change. This is an application of the risk/yield ratio concept.

Security issues change. As time passes some issues deteriorate in grade of financial risk and have to be sold. A corporate bond, for example, that was bought as a single A rated issue to fulfill a policy of investing some portion of a portfolio in bonds of this grade may change into a triple B rated bond. If policy permits, it might simply be regrouped with the triple B bonds in the portfolio, but if not, it should be sold. Change in grade may be in the opposite direction. The single A rated bond may change to a double A rated bond. If policy permits, it would be retained as a double A rated bond; if not it would be sold. There is, incidentally, no objection to taking a profit on sale of securities that improve in grade. Such profits help to compensate for losses on securities that are sold after they have deteriorated.

Securities may move up or down the scale of grade in other qualities besides financial risk. A long-term, high-grade bond automatically becomes higher in grade of interest-rate risk as time passes and the maturity becomes shorter. An investor who buys obligations due in 20 years may sell them as they become 2- or 3-year maturities simply because he does not need bonds of that maturity. At times when the yield curve is upsloping, he is likely to realize a profit on obligations that were bought as long-term issues and sold as short-term issues. Relatively high coupon bonds due within 1 or 2 years sell at prices two or three points above par when they are priced at a low yield. To take a profit in this way is by no means inconsistent with defensive policy, because it is not based on estimating future price changes.

Similarly, a security may change in marketability grade to an extent that justifies selling. A stock, for example, may have had an active market at the time it was bought, and then its marketability may deteriorate as the number of shares available for buying and selling in the market declines for one reason or another. Even the tax advantage of some kinds of securities may change. For example, dividends on a stock that have been partially or entirely income tax-exempt by reason of payment from capital rather than earnings may cease to be tax-exempt.

Finally, the investment of new money, or the re-investment of funds from securities redeemed or liquidated, provides an opportunity to adapt the portfolio to the changing terms of the market. If the yield differential between high-grade and medium-grade corporate bonds has increased, it may be consistent with portfolio-construction policy to invest the cash inflow in medium-grade issues. If the yield curve provides the highest yields on Treasury issues in some particular segment of the yield curve, new purchases may be concentrated in this area. The yields on tax-exempt obligations relative to taxable issues may change in such a way as to make the tax-exempts more or less attractive for investment. Directing the flow of cash into securities that provide the largest returns relative to risk, within the established investment constraints, is one of the most important functions of investment management.

POLICIES FOR PROFIT FROM SECULAR PRICE TRENDS

The opportunity for relatively large returns from common stocks has fostered the development of a wide variety of ideas about how to maximize returns from common stocks by anticipating correctly future changes in prices. Most ways of seeking profits from price changes are aggressive policies, but there are two kinds of policies that are designed to profit from longer-term changes in prices. They are based not so much on forecasts as on the assumption of a secular rise in stock prices. With some room for argument, they may be described as defensive policies.

Common Stocks as Long-Term Investments

One of the earliest and most widely publicized concepts of a policy for investment in common stocks is the "theory" of common stocks as long-term investments. The theory is simply that a well-diversified list of common stocks of leading companies in major industries purchased at prevailing prices will over a period of years provide an average rate of return on investment larger than the rate obtainable from investment in bonds of good quality.[3] When this idea was first publicized in the 1920's, it was regarded as a theory, and by many people as a rather radical theory. In the intervening decades, the statistical evidence of larger returns on stocks than on bonds has become so impressive that the theory of common stocks as long-term investments may now be regarded as a descriptive statement rather than a theory.

It is worthwhile, however, to examine some of the language used in describing the policy of buying common stocks for long-term investment. In the first place, the policy involves assuming a considerable degree of risk, since the investment medium is common stocks. According to the definitions of policy we have used, it is an aggressive policy in constructing the portfolio. But its aggressiveness is modified by the usual stipulation that the stocks will be those of leading companies in major industries. Thus they must be relatively high grade in financial risk among all common stocks. The policy of assuming risk is further modified by the prescription that the portfolio of stocks be well diversified.

It is reasonable to characterize this policy as defensive toward price fluctuations, because there is nothing in it about explicitly estimating future price movements. The proviso that stocks be purchased at prevailing prices

[3]Edgar Lawrence Smith, *Common Stocks as Long-Term Investments*, New York, 1924, The Macmillan Company; Kenneth S. Van Strum, *Investing in Purchasing Power*, New York, 1926, Barrons Publishing Company.

suggests the distribution of purchases over time, which is a policy of time diversification. The usual description of the policy makes no reference to selling securities, but there is an implication that stocks be held indefinitely. It would be a logical extension of the idea of buying at average prices to say that sales should be at prevailing prices.

Neither is there anything about selecting and managing issues to maximize returns. In fact, the early studies from which this concept of investment policy developed used stocks selected more or less randomly and held for arbitrarily defined periods. Thus the policy assumes only average returns for securities of a grade. If an investor is able to select issues with the better prospects, he would, of course, improve his returns.

The policy of diversified investment in the better grade of common stocks for long-term holding has considerable appeal to individual investors. It requires no great skill in selecting issues or concern about stock-price forecasting.

Investment in Growth Stocks

Not long after common stocks became a respectable kind of investment for ordinary people, the idea of investment in growth stocks developed and the term "growth stocks" became a part of the lexicon of Wall Street. However, there is no standard description of an investment-in-growth-stock policy comparable to the common-stocks-for-long-term-holding policy, and there is not even a generally accepted definition of a growth stock. The main idea is to try to select issues that are expected to provide unusually large rates of return in the form of price appreciation and increases in dividend payments over a period of years, and to hold them over a period of years with little regard for cyclical price fluctuations.

A good working definition of a growth stock is one that provides a rate of return to investors over a period of more than one complete business cycle at least twice as great as the average return on a broadly diversified group of stocks. It is important to specify a sizable difference in rates of return between growth stocks and average stocks, because most stocks have a record of growth at some rate during a complete business cycle. What distinguishes growth stocks is a higher rate of growth.

We classify investment in growth stocks under defensive policies toward estimated price changes because the success of the policy does not depend on specific estimates of average price changes for common stocks. It depends rather on expected unusual improvements in earnings and the financial strength of particular issuers. When there is unusual improvement in financial ability of an issuer, unusual appreciation in price of its stock follows.

The definition of growth stocks has no clear implication about the grade of these stocks in financial risk. Any stock that has a record of unusual price appreciation over a period of years is a growth stock. Any stock that is believed likely to experience unusual price appreciation over a period of years, regardless of its past record, may be termed a growth stock. Some stocks that are growth stocks by their records are generally regarded as high grade because of the consistency of their upward trend in price and dividends per share. The growth stocks of the past, however, are not always the growth stocks of the future. The future financial ability of an issuer is always uncertain; the greater the uncertainty, the lower the grade of a stock.

The largest returns from a policy of investment in growth stocks are often obtained by purchasing stocks with little in their records to identify them as growth stocks, but with exceptionally good prospects. The advantage is that at such an early stage of development they are more moderately priced relative to current amounts of earnings and dividends per share. When their good prospects actually materialize in the form of rapidly increasing earnings and dividends, price appreciation is the greater by reason of rising price-earnings and price-dividend ratios. A stock at the stage before unusual improvement in financial ability, however, often appears to be relatively low grade. The disadvantage of investing in stocks generally identified as growth stocks is that they are currently high priced relative to earnings and dividends and are subject to severe price depreciation in the event that growth ceases, or even diminishes materially.

Investing in growth stocks generally means assuming a somewhat higher level of risk in constructing the portfolio than the common-stocks-as-long-term-investments policy insofar as stocks selected for growth are lower in grade than stocks of leading companies in major industries. It is also more aggressive in assuming financial risk because there is no provision that investments be well diversified. Nothing prevents an investor from diversifying over a long list of stocks believed to be of the growth variety, but generally the idea of investing in growth stocks carries the implication of buying only a few issues that promise the most growth. Neither is there a provision that purchases of growth stocks should be diversified over time. Rather, the idea is that you buy a growth stock whenever you recognize it. Purchases could be highly concentrated in a time period, which would prove later to be either a good or a poor time to buy.

This policy is suitable for investors who are strongly motivated to maximize returns, who can afford to risk losses, and whose chances for success are favored by ability to foresee unusually favorable developments in the earnings of companies.

QUESTIONS FOR DISCUSSION

1. Why is an aggressive policy toward price fluctuations more risky than a defensive policy?
2. To say that bond prices fluctuate in a contra-cyclical pattern is an easy generalization. How should it be qualified or made more explicit?
3. Shakespeare seemed to know a good bit about diversification. What are the three conditions of his ventures that make Antonio not sad?
4. What possible difficulties do you see in carrying out a policy of time diversification by dollar averaging?
5. How would you construct a norm-type formula-timing plan using a projected

stock price trend as of today? What will be the trend of average stock prices on an average annual rate of change basis? What will be the amplitude of cyclical price fluctuations around your projected trend line for average stock prices?

6. You are the beneficiary of a trust fund in which there are about $100,000 of high-grade corporate bonds. There are ten issues and one matures each year over the next 10 years. What are the advantages, or disadvantages, of this arrangement from your standpoint as beneficiary of the trust? (Assume that investment in high-grade corporate bonds is entirely appropriate for this fund.)
7. Why not just buy some good common stocks and put them away for a few years?
8. What evidence is there that the policy of investing in common stocks for long-term holding is a good one? You will find some evidence in earlier presentations of results of research on experience with common stocks.
9. If growth stocks have a high level of risk, how can you justify the proposition that this policy is defensive in terms of future price changes?

21

Aggressive Policies toward Price Changes

- I. The concept of aggressive policies
  - A. Aggressive policy increases risk and the size of possible returns
  - B. Investment constraints affect an aggressive policy
- II. The problem of estimating changes in average stock prices
  - A. Are stock prices predictable?
  - B. Forecasting stock prices by the business outlook
  - C. Forecasting by the use of monetary statistics
  - D. Forecasting by the use of market statistics
  - E. The Dow Theory
  - F. The advance-decline series
  - G. Some other market statistics
  - H. Theory of contra opinion
  - I. The St. Louis stock-price model
- III. Policies for aggressive action in the stock market
- IV. The problem of forecasting bond prices
  - A. The business cycle and bond prices
  - B. Federal Reserve policy and bond prices
- V. Policies for aggressive action in the bond market

A popular periodical once published a story about a brokerage house that acquired a huge computer and tried to solve the problem of making money in the stock market by using the machine. Data about earnings, dividends, prices, historical tops and bottoms, support levels, sunspots, and the migrations of lemmings were put into the computer. Everyone stood around while the program ran and watched the printout. It was very short: Buy low and sell high.

The machine's answer tells what people try to do when they adopt aggressive policies toward future price changes. They try to estimate change. If they think that prices will rise, they buy; if they think that prices will decline, they sell. Action is based on a forecast of security prices.

THE CONCEPT OF AGGRESSIVE POLICIES

Aggressive policies are usually defined in terms of expected changes in average prices for categories of securities defined according to level of risk, or according to the principal causes of uncertainty. In the broadest terms, they may be conceived as policies for buying or selling common stocks, or of policies for buying or selling bonds. But of course, these two very broad classes can be subdivided. An investor may adopt an aggressive policy in managing the more speculative stocks in his portfolio, or the more cyclical stocks. He may pursue a strictly defensive policy of maintaining a secondary reserve of short-term bonds with regularly spaced maturities, but endeavor to buy and sell long-term bonds according to his estimates of probable changes in market prices for these issues.

This concept of aggressive policy does not apply to decisions concerning individual security issues. These decisions are based primarily on financial analysis of the individual issues and their apparent attractiveness at a point in time according to the estimated relationship of risk and return. However, decisions about individual issues may be influenced by a policy of trying to profit by estimates of changes in prices for categories of securities. Thus the decision might be to buy no more common stocks at this time because prices generally are too high. This would preclude purchasing an individual issue no matter how attractive it might appear relative to other stocks at the time. There is of course the principle of the exception, and a particularly attractive stock might be purchased; or it might be placed high on the list of stocks to be bought whenever the general policy is to go back into the stock market.

In this discussion we will be concerned chiefly with cyclical changes in average prices for securities. There are many investors so aggressive that they seek to profit from the intermediate price movements within the cyclical pattern of price changes, but they do so on the basis of "feel for the market," intuition, statistical systems, and subjective judgments that cannot be described adequately in an elementary text.

Aggressive Policy Increases Risk and the Size of Possible Returns

When you try to buy and sell on the basis of estimates of future price changes, you increase the uncertainty of returns from a category of securities.

If an aggressive policy is successful, it increases the size of returns relative to the size of returns that would be obtained by following the defensive policy of investing in the same category of securities for the same time period. If the policy is unsuccessful, the relative size of returns is reduced. Aggressiveness widens the variation of returns and may bring much higher or much lower rates of return than the opposite kind of policy.

Suppose, for example, that you buy several issues of long-term, high-grade corporate bonds because you think that interest rates will soon decline and you will be able to sell them in a year or two at a higher price. The average price you pay for the bonds is approximately 100 (for simplicity of illustration) and the interest per annum is $5 per $100 of principal invested. After a year you sell, and the average price realized per bond is 105 per cent of par. The $5 of interest income plus the $5 of capital gain make a return of $10 realized in 1 year on $100 invested. That is about twice the rate you would have obtained if you had followed the defensive policy of simply buying and holding the bonds.

Prices could go the other way, of course, and that is why we say that aggressive policy increases uncertainty of returns. Using the example above, suppose that your estimate is completely wrong and after 1 year the average price of those bonds is $95. You admit the error of your estimate and liquidate them. Your capital loss of $5 per $100 approximately offsets your interest of $5, and your rate of return is zero. By aggressive policy you changed a return of 5 per cent with little uncertainty to a return that might vary from zero to 10 per cent. Actually, variations in market prices might be much greater or much less than in this illustration, and time periods might be much longer or shorter.

Investment Constraints Affect an Aggressive Policy

The simple fact that an aggressive policy increases risk is reason for reviewing the investment constraints that have been previously estimated. Do they permit taking the greater level of risk relative to the level that would be associated with a defensive policy?

Many investors cannot afford to increase the uncertainty of returns by pursuing aggressive policies. In purely financial terms, they may not be able to tolerate a drop in investment income that may result for a period of time even if there is a subsequent increase in size of income. In the markets of recent years a shift from corporate bonds to common stocks might well result in cutting the size of dividend returns by one-half. A change from long-term to short-term governments might bring an even greater reduction in income.

However, the ability to risk loss of principal amounts by selling securities at much less than the prices paid is usually the more severe constraint in financial terms. It isn't hard to lose 10 per cent of your principal by making an erroneous estimate of future price changes and failing to correct the error until a significant decline in prices has taken place. And if you are using the more volatile common stocks as the medium for an aggressive policy, the proportion of principal that may be lost can be considerably larger.

In psychological terms the temperament of the investor may virtually compel an aggressive policy, or rule it out completely. Some people like to speculate; they are temperamentally incapable of just sitting with a portfolio of securities. These people, whether individuals or institutional investment managers, may start off with the idea that their policy will be basically defensive and then shift gradually toward an aggressive policy. Other people do not like to make the decisions that aggressive policies require, and they may be greatly disturbed by having to realize losses—even if losses have been offset by realized gains. Perhaps there should be some sort of a psychological test that a person would have to pass in order to qualify as an aggressive investor.

Strong tenure of ownership is a requisite to an aggressive policy. One who endeavors to profit by the fluctuations of security prices must be free to buy at the time he thinks securities should be bought and to sell when he thinks they should be sold. A sale forced on an investor by his financial circumstances may cause a negative outcome when a positive outcome might otherwise result.

Tax considerations may affect the policy decision. Since the federal income tax rate on long-term capital gains is generally much less than on ordinary income, the tax advantage of capital gains over ordinary income may be a consideration supporting an aggressive policy. And an aggressive policy generally requires investment in the more highly marketable securities to minimize transactions costs.

THE PROBLEM OF ESTIMATING CHANGES IN AVERAGE STOCK PRICES

If you are going to use aggressive policies in managing a securities portfolio, you have to estimate future changes in prices for categories of securities and time your purchases and sales so that you buy when prices are low and sell when they are high. The problem is the same for all categories of securities, but the methods used in estimating stock prices may be quite different than those used in estimating bond prices. Thus we will treat stock-price forecasting and bond-price forecasting separately.

Are Stock Prices Predictable?

If you deliberately adopt an aggressive policy, you say implicitly or explicitly that you can forecast stock prices with sufficient accuracy to realize profits from your transactions. The random walk theorists say you are wrong. There is no way to forecast prices for individual stocks or average stock prices on the basis of public information at any point in time. At best you have a 50—50 chance of winning, which is the same as the odds you would have if you made security price forecasts on a random basis. And when transaction costs and taxes are taken into account, the odds are against you.

There is, of course, vigorous disagreement on this question of predictability of prices. By casual observation it appears that a majority of the professionals in the business of managing investment funds believe that they can estimate future price changes with sufficient accuracy to increase their portfolio rates of return. There are any number of stock-price forecasting services that anyone can obtain on a subscription basis, and the people who sell them insist that their forecasts have been right more often than wrong. Some professional investment counsel firms manage portfolios for their clients on the basis of a fee schedule that provides for larger fees when portfolio rates of return exceed the rates that would be obtained by investing in one of the broad stock price averages and smaller fees when they fail to achieve rates as high as those provided by the price averages. Obviously, they believe that they can do a better job of selecting issues and estimating prices than the data taken as representative of the market.

If you do not believe in the randomness of stock-price fluctuations, it may be well to examine some of the methods used to forecast stock prices. There are many variations in the methods the forecasters use, but they can be classified generally under three headings. One method uses forecasts of cyclical variations in business activity, another relies chiefly on changes in monetary conditions, and the third uses the historical statistics of the market as a basis for forecasting.

Forecasting Stock Prices by the Business Outlook

The method of forecasting stock prices by the business cycle relies on a positive correlation between the stock-price cycle and the cycle of business activity. When business activity is depressed, stock prices are also depressed. When business expands cyclically, stock prices rise; when recession appears, stock prices decline. It is reasonable to expect a positive correlation because general business conditions affect corporate sales and earnings, and because the confidence of investors in the future financial ability of companies tends to vary with the business cycle. After several years of business expansion, investor optimism is high and prices surge upward; after some period of recession, gloom prevails and depresses market prices.

However, the correlation of stock prices and such broad measures of business activity as Gross National Product, the Index of Industrial Production, and the leading indicators of business activity is by no means perfect. Historically, stock prices have tended to lead the business indicators and, in fact, the stock-price indexes are considered a leading indicator. Thus, if you wait for a clear indication of an upturn in business after a period of recession, you would likely miss the first few months of increasing average stock prices. Moreover, the lead-lag relationship is not constant. There may be no lead time, that is, the turning points may be virtually coincident. Or the lead may be as long as 6 months. Finally, there have sometimes been major changes in average stock prices that cannot be explained by changes in general business conditions.

Given the imperfections, one way to estimate the future course of stock prices is to read the business outlook estimates of economists, business observers, and government officials who write for publication. Then you can adopt whatever estimate seems best. There is usually considerable agreement among the business forecasters. At many times in recent years, forecasts have been so nearly unanimous that journalists have sometimes referred to "the standard forecast." At any rate, it is not difficult to discover the consensus of published estimates and the variations therefrom.

Forecasts of stock prices on the basis of estimates of change in business conditions simply shifts the forecasting problem. It requires estimates of the business cycle, and the accuracy of stock-price forecasts depends on the accuracy of the economists who make the estimates. Business forecasting is about as hazardous as any other kind of forecasting. Frequently, economists who speak or write for publication are all too vague about what they foresee both in the timing and in the magnitude of change in business conditions. It is easy to say, "The recession has about run its course," or that, "An upturn in business will occur within the next year." With variations in the length of the lead-lag time between stock prices and business activity, forecasts in these terms are not very helpful.

It is hardly to be expected that business forecasts will prove to be exactly right, even for the short term, and sometimes the error is considerable. One careful study of a number of "sets" of forecasts from a variety of sources shows that the average error in annual forecasts of Gross National Product was about 2 per cent. This seems small, but it is not much smaller than the error "which would have resulted had the forecasters simply assumed that GNP would advance next year by the average amount it had advanced in preceding years." This study also led to the conclusion that economists commonly underestimate the size of year-to-year changes in GNP and that the record can be interpreted ". . . as implying an effective forecasting range of no more than two quarters."[1]

Although these findings have been regarded in some quarters as uncomplimentary to the business forecasters, they are not at all inconsistent with the idea of using published forecasts as a basis for estimating cyclical movements in stock prices. Estimates do not have to be right very far in advance—a good forecast for the next two quarters is sufficient for the purpose of investment policy. And estimates are subject to constant revision. Almost anyone endeavoring to profit by cyclical movements in stock prices should review his estimate of business conditions and of stock prices at least once a month. The GNP estimates are published quarterly and business economists frequently publish revisions of their own estimates.

Many economists formulate their forecasts by estimating developments within the framework of the national income and product accounts published quarterly by the Department of Commerce. They examine each of the principal "sectors" of the economy and try to estimate how each will develop in the next several quarters or in the next year. Thus they are very much concerned with government purchases of goods and services, and they find some

[1]Victor Zarnowitz, "On the Accuracy and Properties of Short-Term Economic Forecasts," in *The Task of Economics, Forty-fifth Annual Report of the National Bureau of Economic Research, Inc.* (June, 1965), pp. 16–25.

basis for estimating changes in this sector by studying the federal budget estimates and the fiscal policies of the federal government. They scrutinize prospective changes in gross private domestic investment, particularly new construction, business outlays for plant and equipment, and changes in business inventories—which are the more volatile sectors. Personal consumption expenditures have been relatively stable cyclically with a secularly rising trend.

Another way to estimate cyclical developments in the economy, particularly the turning points of the business cycle, is to observe changes in the economic indicators developed by the National Bureau of Economic Research as an aid to business forecasting. These economic indicators are statistical series that measure changes in various kinds of business and financial activity. After long study, the Bureau classified some of them as "leading indicators" because they have almost always turned down in advance of a general recession in business and have turned up before cyclical recovery began. In addition to stock prices, the leading indicators include such series as the layoff rate in manufacturing, new orders in durable goods industries, commercial and industrial construction contracts, change in business inventories, and industrial material prices.[2] When most of these leading indicators are rising, the business outlook is favorable. A downward movement in most of the series signals a recession. And an increase in the indexes after a period of recession indicates business recovery.

If all the leading indicators changed uniformly in advance of the swings in the business cycle, forecasting business would be merely a matter of looking at some lines on a chart and drawing the obvious conclusion. Unfortunately, all the statistical series do not move in the same direction at the same time. At times some of the leading indicators move upward while others decline and still others move horizontally. So there remains a problem of interpretation—of deciding when the changes in the business indicators are sufficiently strong and consistent to justify a forecast of expansion or contraction in business activity in the next several months.

Forecasting by the Use of Monetary Statistics

Some students of the stock market bypass the whole idea that cyclical movements in stock prices may be inferred from forecasts of the business cycle. Their thesis is that both the cycle of stock prices and of general business activity are related causally to changes in the liquidity of the national monetary system. Thus they go directly to statistical data measuring changes in liquidity. Any marked decrease in liquidity presages a decline in both stock prices and business activity; a marked increase in liquidity indicates that improvement in stock prices and in business will soon follow.

The term "liquidity" refers to assets in the form of cash and assets readily convertible into cash in the hands of business enterprises and individuals

[2]These and other series are published monthly in U.S. Department of Commerce, *Business Cycle Developments*, Washington, D.C., U.S. Government Printing Office.

relative to the volume of business being carried on. The reasoning is that when people (including business managers) think their liquidity is inadequate, they attempt to convert nonliquid assets into liquid form. Thus they tend to sell stocks, to reduce business inventories, to reduce spending relative to income, and to reduce debts. This kind of economic behavior causes stock prices to decline and economic activity to recede. Conversely, at certain times people think their liquidity is greater than it needs to be. Then they spend money for less liquid assets, such as stocks, as well as for various kinds of personal and business assets. Spending money in this fashion raises stock prices and stimulates business activity.

Interest in the use of monetary statistics for forecasting stock prices has been revived in recent years by the writing of Beryl W. Sprinkel, who vigorously advocates the merit of the monetary theory and has developed methods of applying it.[3] Dr. Sprinkel takes as the measure of liquidity the rate of growth in money supply. Money supply is defined as private demand deposits (excluding deposits of domestic commercial banks, the U.S. government, and certain other liabilities) plus currency in the hands of the public. The best measure of change in liquidity for the purpose of forecasting, he says, is a 6-months' moving average of the monthly rate of change in total money supply. The Board of Governors of the Federal Reserve System publishes data showing monthly averages of daily amounts of money supply adjusted for seasonal variation. Thus it is very simple to compute the rate of change month by month and to take the average of the last 6 months. The usual practice is to annualize the monthly rates of change by multiplying them by 12. Sprinkel concedes that this method of stock-price forecasting does not work when changes in stock prices are dominated by strong emotional reactions among investors. Sometimes lack of confidence or overconfidence affects stock prices for a time in such manner as to overcome changes in liquidity.

Forecasting by the Use of Market Statistics

The methods of stock-price forecasting reviewed to this point attempt to relate movements in prices to statistical series measuring developments in the economy. But another important method of forecasting uses only the statistics of the market itself. The basic idea is that the data of the market show certain characteristic changes as the peaks and troughs of price cycles approach, or as they pass, and that probable future price movements can be inferred from these characteristic changes.

The statistics of the market include, of course, data on changes in the general level of stock prices. They also include a number of series such as the number of issues that have advanced and declined each day on the New York Stock Exchange, the number of shares bought and sold daily in odd lots, the short sale statistics, and the amount of customers' net debit balances with New York Stock Exchange member firms.

[3]Beryl W. Sprinkel, *Money and Markets: A Monetarist View*, Homewood, Illinois, 1971, Dow Jones-Irwin.

The earliest and still the most widely used statistics of the stock market are those that depict changes in average prices. At about the turn of the twentieth century, a newspaperman sensed the need of the public for data to show changes in average prices for stocks. He was Charles H. Dow, an early editor of the *Wall Street Journal.* Dow devised the price average that has come to be known as the Dow-Jones average, with its three subdivisions—the industrials average, the transportation average, and the utilities average. Initially, the price averages were literally average prices for lists of stocks, that is, the sum of the prices divided by the number of stocks. Subsequently it became necessary to make the divisor a lesser number than the number of issues to keep the average from being reduced by stock splits and stock dividends.

The Dow-Jones averages are crude statistically, the stocks included are not a good sample of the several thousand issues traded regularly, there is no weighting of the component stocks, and they have proved to be less satisfactory as measures of changes in the general level of stock prices than some other indexes and averages. Even so, they continue to be the most widely used.

The broadest averages are the average price data computed by the New York Stock Exchange and by the American Stock Exchange. They are calculated daily and show change in average price per share for all listed issues on the respective exchanges on the basis of the day's trading. The National Quotations Bureau publishes daily an index of change in average prices in over-the-counter stocks based on a sample of issues traded in that market.

We have frequently used Standard & Poor's Index of five hundred stocks in the tables and figures of this book. The five-hundred-Stock Index is much broader than the Dow-Jones averages, and prices of the individual stocks are weighted in computing the index according to the market value of the outstanding shares of each issue. Standard & Poor's have spliced this index to an index developed by the Cowles Commission for the period 1871 to 1937 in such a way to provide comparable figures over a period of about 100 years. This index is broken down by industry categories of stocks so that indexes of stock prices by industries can be compared with the total index and with one another. Moody's Investors Service has its index of stock prices. There are 200 stocks in the total index, and subdivisions for industrial, rail, public utility, and some other categories by industry.

The Dow Theory

The best-known system for forecasting cyclical movements in the general level of stock prices is the Dow theory. It began with published observations on the behavior of stock prices by Charles H. Dow and was further developed by William P. Hamilton, a subsequent editor of the *Wall Street Journal.* Many others have contributed to the evolution of the Dow theory, and some have evolved their own particular versions of the theory.

In simplest terms, the Dow theory is a statement that the general level of market prices rises and falls more or less with the business cycle and that inferences may be drawn about the future cyclical movement of prices by observing the past pattern of cyclical change. In his early writing, Dow used an analogy between the price cycle and the tides of the ocean to explain his idea. He wrote, ". . . a person watching the tide coming in . . . sets a stick in the sand at the points reached by the incoming waves until the stick reaches a position where the waves do not come up to it, and finally recede to show that the tide has turned."[4] Thus, the price averages serve as sticks to measure the cyclical rise and fall of the market. Whenever a peak has been reached, you know it soon afterward because the following wavelike price fluctuations do not come up to the high point previously established.

The main premise of the Dow theory is the truism that a cyclical price movement, once begun, will continue in the same direction until it changes. When the direction is upward, each wavelike intermediate price rise of a few weeks' or a few months' duration is followed by an intermediate reaction. But in a cyclically rising market, the price reaction stops short of the low point reached by the immediately preceding reaction, and each succeeding intermediate price rise attains a higher level than the peak of the preceding movement. Thus in a bull market the chart of stock prices shows a sort of zigzag upward movement.

Eventually the cyclical price rise reaches a peak and prices turn downward. A prime objective of those who use this system is to read the signals that indicate the turning point as soon as possible. The first sign that a cyclical peak may have been reached is an intermediate price rise that fails to exceed the high point of the preceding intermediate rise. However, the wavelike movements of stock prices are irregular, so that one instance of an intermediate rise failing to exceed the top of the preceding rise is not conclusive. But when a second intermediate price rise fails to exceed the preceding peak, the evidence of a cyclical turning point becomes stronger. In the declining phase of the stock-price cycle, the chart of stock prices forms a zigzag downward movement. The turn from a bear market to a bull market is indicated similarly by an intermediate rise that goes higher than the preceding intermediate rise and is followed by a decline that does not fall as low as the preceding low point. Thus, the zigzag movement starts upward.

One difficulty in applying the Dow theory is that the price averages do not always make clear-cut formations on the charts. Sometimes the waves are small and do not seem to follow one another in any definite progression; erratic fluctuations occur that disturb the cyclical pattern. Then it is hard to tell whether the tide is ebbing or flowing. Dow theorists have all sorts of rules for interpreting these irregular movements. One of the most common is that a movement in the industrials average must be "confirmed," that is, accompanied by a similar movement in the transportation average, in order to be significant. Another is that "dullness" in a bull market, that is, relatively small volume of trading, indicates an accumulation of strength and lays the foundation for a further advance in prices. In a bear market dullness is evidence of further weakness. A sideways movement of prices so that the charts show a horizontal line with only small irregularities is an indication of weak-

[4] *Wall Street Journal*, January 31, 1901.

ness when it occurs after a long cyclical rise in price, and an indication of strength when it comes after a long decline. These are some of the simpler rules; it takes an expert to make full application of the Dow theory as it has been developed by Dow's successors.

Of course, a great deal of controversy exists about whether the Dow theory really works. The answer depends very much on one's concept of what it is supposed to do. It may be regarded merely as a convenient way to describe past developments in the market and as a basis for very general inferences about probable future cyclical movement. In this view the Dow theory is not a theory and is not predictive. There is nothing theoretical about a statistical description of past changes in stock prices and inferences are not predictions.

Some Dow theory advocates, however, take a much different view of what it is supposed to do. They say the purpose is to predict not only the primary cyclical movements, but also the intermediate fluctuations. These people regard their charts of stock prices—with "head and shoulders" formations, "triple tops," and all sorts of configurations—as mechanistic devices for prediction. They think that when they see a particular formation on their charts, a certain pattern of change in prices will follow. The theory is that patterns of price change are repetitive.

When the Dow theory is construed in this manner, there is nothing to be said for it. There is no basis in fact or theory for the notion that some past movement of prices must necessarily be followed by a particular future movement. It is completely denied by the random walk thesis. The prices at which people will buy and sell stocks tomorrow, next week, or next month, will be determined by their evaluations of stocks at that particular point in time and not by some past series of evaluations. From one day to another, events occur that affect the prices at which people are willing to buy or sell. You cannot tell today what happening tomorrow or next week will radically change people's attitudes toward stock prices.

The Advance-Decline Series

Each day that stocks are traded on the New York Stock Exchange, prices of some issues advance and prices of others decline. The number of issues in each category is counted, and the data are published. Thus, one can observe the day-to-day record of the number that advanced and the number that declined. These data may be used to construct indexes or other statistical series that are used as a basis for forecasting fluctuations in stock prices. One way is simply to express the number of issues that advance each day as a percentage of the number that decline. Then a percentage greater than 100 indicates a rising market, and a percentage less than 100 shows a declining market.

The first premise of forecasting with advance-decline data is the same as that of the Dow theory, namely, that there are major cycles in the general level of stock prices and that a cyclical price movement, once begun, will continue. However, users of advance-decline data believe that they signal turning points in prices before the turning point in prices actually appears in the stock price indexes. The second premise is that in the late stage of a cyclical price rise the number of issues rising begins to decrease relative to the number declining, and, in the last stage of a bear market, the number of issues advancing begins to exceed the number declining.

The explanation given for this phenomenon is that the blue chip stocks continue to advance in the final phase of a bull market, while the less well-known and less popular issues begin to decline. Since the blue chip stocks are used in the Dow-Jones averages and are heavily weighted in other indexes, these measures of price change may show that the market is still rising when it has begun to decline and that it is still declining when it has begun to rise.

Some Other Market Statistics

Technical analysts of the market use a variety of other statistical series that measure different aspects of developments in the stock market. One author describes more than fifty series that he finds useful.[5] We cannot go so far in this volume, but it may be worthwhile to mention several other series commonly used in forecasting.

For 1 day each month the New York Stock Exchange reports the total number of shares of listed stocks sold short (and not covered by purchases) by its member firms for account of their customers and for their own account. These figures measure the "short position." The number of shares sold short may be related to the total number of shares listed and stated as a percentage, or it may be stated as a percentage of the average daily number of shares traded in the month preceding the date for which the short position is reported.

This historical record shows that the relative size of the short position increases to a peak at or near the bottom of a bear market and declines to a low point near the peak of a stock-price cycle. It is said that short sales are made chiefly by professional traders and that they follow the movement of market prices. When the price movement is distinctly downward, they increase their short position. When prices turn upward, they cover their short sales. Of course, there is always some amount of stock sold short because there are always some traders who anticipate a decline in stock prices in general, or in prices for particular stocks.

Two statistical series that some people think are useful in market forecasting are the number of shares bought and sold in odd lots. (Odd lots are lots of less than 100 shares for most issues.) These data are provided daily for NYSE listed issues. The two series may be related by dividing sales by purchases. The hypothesis used in interpreting these data is that the odd-lot buyers and sellers in the aggregate are usually wrong about the future movement of stock prices. They are the "little people," or the outsiders, as opposed to the professionals. Thus they come into the market with large purchases

[5]Joseph E. Granville, *A Strategy of Daily Stock Market Timing for Maximum Profit*, Englewood Cliffs, N.J., 1960, Prentice-Hall, Inc.

relative to sales in the latter phase of a bull market. Therefore, a marked increase in odd-lot purchases relative to odd-lot sales is said to indicate that the price cycle is approaching a peak. Similarly, it is said that the "odd-lotters" tend to sell when prices are near a low point in the cycle, and a rise in sales relative to purchases is interpreted to mean that the trough of the cycle is approaching.

Whenever there is great enthusiasm for speculation in common stock, margin trading increases and there is an expansion in the use of credit to finance the purchase and carrying of securities. Credit used for this purpose tends to reach a peak at about the time stock prices reach a peak and to decrease as stock prices decline. Thus, some students of the statistics of market use the data on stock market credit in forecasting the stock-price cycle.

Several kinds of statistical series measure the use of credit to finance the purchase and carrying of securities, but the one that best indicates the behavior of the public in the stock market is the total of customers' net debit balances with New York Stock Exchange firms secured by collateral other than U.S. government obligations. Net debit balances are amounts loaned by brokerage firms to their customers to finance margin trading, minus credit balances in customers' accounts. The amount of these debit balances has been affected by changes in the margin requirements set by the Board of Governors of the Federal Reserve System and in recent years by the relatively high rates of interest charged on debit balances. However, distinct cyclical fluctuations in debit balances correspond to the major peaks and troughs in average prices for common stocks. The implication is that when the amount of debit balances has been increasing markedly for a period of time, along with a rise in stock prices, a cyclical peak is approaching. And when these balances have been sharply reduced during a period of declining prices, a trough is approaching.

One researcher tested statistically several hypotheses formulated in terms that denied predictive value to several of the market statistics series. In some instances he found greater probability of higher stock prices subsequent to a high level in a series, such as a high short-interest ratio, than of lower prices. Tests of some hypotheses were inconclusive, but generally the high and low points of a series coincided more or less with the turning points of the business cycle and the stock price cycle.[6]

Theory of Contra Opinion

The simplest and most cynical of all systems for forecasting cyclical movements in average stock prices is the theory of contra opinion. This theory holds that whenever investors' generally are highly optimistic, when they have bid up prices for several years and when price-earnings ratios have increased to relatively high levels, a marked decline in average prices will follow. And the opposite is that when everyone is depressed, stock prices have declined

[6]Lambert, William R., Evidences of Risk Aversion in the Stock Market, unpublished doctoral dissertation, Indiana University, 1970.

and the business outlook is particularly poor, a cyclical upturn in average prices will soon come about. Thus, you buy stocks when everyone says to stay out of the stock market. You sell stocks when they are all saying that prices will continue to rise strongly for some indefinite time period.

There is a great deal of support for this concept in the history of the stock market. In 1929 we had the greatest bull market in history and even the ribbon clerks were buying stocks with borrowed money. Investors' state of mind was euphoric. Then came the crash and the steepest decline in stock prices in history. At the bottom of that bear market few investors had the courage to increase their holdings of stocks. Subsequent cycles in investors' attitudes have been less pronounced, but there was a great deal of cheerfulness in Wall Street when the market averages reached a new all-time peak in 1968. About 18 months later you could buy stocks at an average price equal to about 65 per cent of peak prices, and gloom hung over Wall Street like a dark cloud.

Anyone who sells securities or manages accounts for customers knows that the easiest time to persuade people to buy more stocks is near the peak of a stock-price cycle and the time when you waste your time recommending stocks is near the trough of a stock-price cycle.

The St. Louis Stock-Price Model

A great deal of the writing and talking about how to forecast stock prices is pseudo-scientific, or without pretense of being scientific. Recently, however, a well-developed quantitative study was made of influences on the general level of stock prices as measured by the quarterly average of Standard & Poor's 500 Stock Index.[7] The method of the study is too technical to describe adequately here, but it may be said that the standard method of valuing stocks by discounting future dividends and prices to present values was used to determine the present value of expected corporate earnings over some future time horizon.

The conclusions of the study, stated briefly, are that the general level of stock prices is influenced mainly by expected corporate earnings and expectations of inflation. The summary states that "Expectations of increasing inflation were found to lower the level of stock prices and not to raise it as is commonly argued." This finding is consistent with our earlier generalization that a positive correlation between stock prices and the general price level may not be assumed for any relatively short time period, but it introduces an entirely new concept in stock-price forecasting. None of the forecasting methods we have discussed refers to changes in the price level as an influence upon stock prices. The author of the study comments that changes in inflation expectations exert a much greater influence on the rate of discount of expected future earnings than on amounts of expected corporate earnings.

The earnings expectations of investors are the second major influence

[7]Michael W. Keran, "Expectations, Money, and the Stock Market," *Review*, Federal Reserve Bank of St. Louis, Vol. 53, No. 1 (January 1971), pp. 16–31.

on stock prices. This is not a new concept; it is included in the idea of forecasting by the business outlook and by the theory of contra opinion. Dr. Keran says that, "Corporate earnings expectations are formed on the basis of actual earnings over the preceding five years." This lends support to the idea expressed in our discussion of financial analysis that investors' concepts of both risk and return for stocks are very largely a product of past experience and not of any very well-developed powers of prediction.

There is considerable support for the use of monetary statistics to forecast stock prices. The St. Louis study states that monetary actions, measured by changes in the monetary stock, exercise an important influence on GNP, the price level, and real output. However, the study goes on to say, "The major influence of changes in money on the level of prices was found to be indirect—operating through induced changes in expectations."

POLICIES FOR AGGRESSIVE ACTION IN THE STOCK MARKET

When you have an estimate of how stock prices will change cyclically, the next problem is what to do as a matter of policy to profit by the estimate. Policies for action range from very weak to very strong, and the size of the gain they seek to realize varies correspondingly from small to large. Similarly, the risk assumed by following aggressive policies depends not merely on the possible inaccuracy of price forecasts, but also on the kind of policy adopted. You can risk very little on your forecast of stock prices, or a great deal.

The weakest kind of reaction to a forecast of a cyclical change in direction of stock prices is to alter the amount of funds being used periodically to buy stocks. This implies a more or less regular inflow of funds for investment in securities. If you think that prices are approaching a peak and that a cyclical decline will follow, you might stop buying stocks and use the funds that become available for investment to buy bonds or investment media with a high degree of liquidity. If your forecast is right and a cyclical decline develops, you resume purchases of stocks when prices are at lower levels. Funds withheld from stock investment when prices were too high may be switched from bonds or liquid assets to stocks after prices have declined.

Although we have labeled this kind of action a weak policy, it will bring about a considerable change in the proportion of stocks in a portfolio when the flow of funds for investment is large relative to the amount of the portfolio, and when the policy of deferring, or of accelerating, stock purchases is continued over a year or two. When it is used successfully over several cycles, it results in purchase of stock at the lower levels of prices during the cycle rather than at average or higher levels and in obtaining higher dividend yields. In the long run, larger yields contribute materially to maximization of investment returns. Purchase at lower prices also tends to increase the size of realized gains, or to reduce the size of losses, when stocks are sold in the ordinary course of portfolio management.

The penalties for mistakes in estimates of the price cycle when this policy is followed are the reverse of the rewards. If you defer further purchases of stocks because you think prices are in the upper stages of the price cycle, and then prices continue to rise for a considerable period, you have missed the opportunity to buy at prices that would have been advantageous in the light of subsequent developments. Then, if the ensuing cyclical decline is small, there may be only a short time in which to purchase stocks with funds that have been accumulating. In fact, you may miss the opportunity altogether if you estimate a much more severe decline in prices than actually occurs, and therefore wait too long to start buying.

At the opposite end of the investment spectrum is the strong policy of outright cyclical trading. When you think stock prices are at a cyclical peak, you sell all your stocks and put the money in the bank or invest it for the time being in short-term, high-grade bonds. Then, when stocks decline cyclically and reach what you think is the trough of the cycle, you liquidate the temporary investments and buy stocks. After the cyclical rise has almost run its course, you sell again and take your profit.

When you do this successfully, it maximizes investment returns tremendously. When you fail, losses may be large. The danger lies in selling too soon, or too late, and also in buying back too soon or too late. When you sell too soon in the bull market, you miss part of the cyclical rise. If you buy back too soon in the ensuing bear market, the prices you pay are too high. If you buy back too late after a new bull market has begun, the prices you pay are too high. If you sell too late after the cyclical peak, you miss part of the profit. The costs of buying and selling must also be considered, and the income taxes on capital gains must be deducted from profits that may be realized. If funds are held in cash, income is lost during the period when you are out of the stock market. A loss of income also occurs if you invest in liquid assets to the extent that the yield on such assets is less than the yield that would have been obtained by continuing to hold stocks.

The intermediate policy between what we have termed weak and strong policies is to liquidate only a portion of the stocks owned when you think stock prices are approaching a cyclical peak, and re-invest in bonds. Then you reverse the position near the bottom of the price cycle. The larger the portion of stocks sold in anticipation of the cyclical decline, and the larger the amount bought back, in expectation of a rise, the more aggressive is the policy.

This policy can be made less aggressive by spacing sales and purchases over some period of time, as contrasted with selling the entire amounts to be switched at one time and buying back all at one time. For example, you might decide that the cyclical peak will be reached within the next 12 months, divide the entire amount of stock to be liquidated into 12 equal parts, and sell one part each month for the next 12 months. Price averaging in this manner minimizes the potential profit and also the potential loss.

THE PROBLEM OF FORECASTING BOND PRICES

The idea of maximizing returns by buying and selling bonds at a profit is much less familiar to the general public than that of trading in stocks, but it works on basically the same concept and it is practiced in much the same way. The practice is confined mostly to institutional investors, but anyone with funds to invest can try to make money in the bond market. The problem, of course, is to forecast the cyclical movements in bond prices and to buy and sell at the low and high points in the price cycle.

The size of potential gains in the bond market is smaller than in the stock market, because the amplitude of cyclical price changes for bonds is smaller than for stocks. For investors who are limited to relatively low-yielding bonds, however, the improvement in total returns that may be realized by an aggressive policy is very sizable. In our study of interest-rate risk, we observed that prices for long-term, high-grade bonds may rise or fall as much as 15 to 20 percentage points in the interest-rate cycle. A capital gain of these proportions in the course of a year or two would be much more than the income yield during such a period of time, and it would be in addition to income. Even if capital gains are not realized by sale, as when bonds are held to maturity, yield is maximized by concentrating purchases in the part of the interest-rate cycle when prices are low.

The Business Cycle and Bond Prices

The problem of forecasting cyclical changes in bond prices (or in interest rates) is the same kind of problem as that of forecasting stock prices. It starts with the general proposition that bond prices fluctuate inversely to the business cycle. However, bond prices generally lag behind the statistical indexes of business activity. In the first stage of business recovery, interest rates are low and bond prices are high. But as expansion continues, interest rates begin to move upward, and bond prices decline. Toward the peak of the business cycle there is a pronounced rise in interest rates and a corresponding decline in bond prices. After the peak of the cycle has passed and interest rates decline, bond prices begin to rise and continue upward to about the trough of the recession.

The expectations of investors also affect the bond-price cycle, because bond investors—like stock investors—are constantly trying to foresee the course of market prices. When they observe developments that cause them to expect a rise in prices, an increase in buying interest gives impetus to an upward movement in prices. Prices may also be sharply depressed by the opposite kind of development.

An important element in the problem of forecasting bond prices is the credit policy of the Federal Reserve System. The Board of Governors and the Federal Reserve banks have great power to influence the movement of interest rates. The manner in which this power is used affects the course of interest rates and bond prices relative to the business cycle.

To forecast the cyclical movements of prices for high-grade bonds, therefore, you begin with an estimate of the further development of the business cycle, try to anticipate how the Federal Reserve authorities will use their influence, and then estimate how investors are likely to behave. What we have said earlier about forecasting the business cycle will also serve for the present problem, so we will go on to the subject of Federal Reserve policy.

Federal Reserve Policy and Bond Prices

The avowed objectives of the Board of Governors of the Federal Reserve System are to enable the commercial banks to provide adequate credit for sustained growth in the national economy, to prevent misuse of credit for speculative purposes, and to maintain a stable price level. Some economists say these objectives are inconsistent in that adequate credit for vigorous economic growth cannot be provided without applying upward pressure on the price level. Nevertheless, the general pattern of Federal Reserve credit policy in the business cycle is well established.

In the recession phase of the business cycle, the influence of the Federal Reserve System, or "the Fed," is exercised to provide the commercial banks with ample funds for loans and investments. Its purpose is to make it as easy as possible for banks to meet the loan needs of their customers. As borrowers spend borrowed money, they contribute to checking the recession. After the trough of the cycle has passed and business again expands, the "easy money" policy continues. It is not until the expansion phase is well developed that the Fed begins to exercise restraint. Toward the peak of the cycle, when speculative excesses appear, the Fed's policy changes to one of active restraint. This policy is designed to slow the continued expansion of credit by the commercial banks, to make credit more expensive to borrowers, and to discourage banks from making loans for speculative purposes.

The Federal Reserve authorities have several means of influencing the lending and investing policies of the commercial banks. One is variation in the discount rate; a second is open-market operations in Treasury securities; a third is change in member bank reserve requirements; and a fourth is something called "moral suasion." By observing how these means (or instruments) are being used, a careful student can not only determine Fed policy at any particular time, but also possibly anticipate the next development in credit policy.

The discount rate charged member banks for discounting obligations of the banks' customers was intended by the designers of the Federal Reserve System to be the principal means of tightening or loosening bank credit. But the evolution of our banking system in the past several decades has been such that banks seldom discount their customers' paper. The modern practice is to borrow from the Federal Reserve banks using government securities as collateral, and the discount rate is now significant as the interest rate charged by the Federal Reserve banks on these advances.

The original idea was that the Federal Reserve banks could restrain lending by the commercial banks whenever they had expanded loans to such an extent that they needed to borrow from the central institutions by raising the discount rate and thus increasing the cost of borrowed money to the banks. This idea has not worked very well. Relatively small changes in the cost of Federal Reserve advances seem to have little effect on the lending policies of banks, except to cause them to raise their loan rates. Today the discount rate is important chiefly as a barometer of Federal Reserve credit policy. An increase in the discount rate means that the monetary authorities think there should be increased restraint on bank lending, but they use other means to apply restraint. A decrease in the rate after it has been at a relatively high level indicates a shift in Federal Reserve policy, although the change may already have become manifest in other ways.

The major instrument of Federal Reserve policy is the purchase and sale of Treasury obligations in the open market; thus, it is termed "open-market operations." To understand how open-market operations affect lending and investment by commercial banks, you must first understand the system of reserve requirements for member banks. Briefly, each member bank of the Federal Reserve System is required to maintain a legal reserve equal to a specified percentage of demand deposits and a different specified percentage of time deposits. Legal reserves consist of member banks' deposits with the Federal Reserve banks, plus currency in banks' vaults.

Open-market operations of the Federal Reserve System affect the amount of legal reserves owned by the member banks. When the Federal Open-Market Committee[8] buys Treasury securities in the market, it pays for them by checks drawn on a Federal Reserve bank. These checks are cleared through the commercial banks in such a manner that they end up as credits to member banks' deposits with the Federal Reserve banks. Since these deposits serve as legal reserves, additional deposits created by such credits (in the absence of offsetting decreases) enable banks to expand their deposits by increasing their loans and investments. The sale of Treasury securities in the market by the System has the opposite effect on legal reserves and on the base for member banks' deposits.

There are a number of other influences on amounts of member bank reserves besides open-market operations. More often than not open-market operations are designed chiefly to offset these other influences, such as changes in the amount of currency in circulation, an inflow or outflow of gold, changes in Treasury cash holdings, and fluctuations in Treasury currency outstanding. The full story of factors supplying reserve funds and factors absorbing reserve funds is too long for this book, but it can be found in standard texts on money and banking.

The Board of Governors also has authority to change the percentage of member bank deposits required to be held in the form of legal reserves against demand and time deposits of member banks. Change in reserve requirements is a powerful weapon. Merely by increasing percentages the Board can reduce excess reserves or cause a deficiency in reserves. The power to change reserve requirements has been used infrequently in recent years.

The use of moral suasion can be observed merely by reading the newspapers. Moral suasion is the effort by Federal Reserve authorities to influence member bank lending by public statements. Near the peak of a business cycle it is usual for some member of the Board of Governors of the Federal Reserve System, or the president of one of the Federal Reserve banks, to make a statement warning of the danger of excessive expansion of bank credit. In

[8]Open-market operations are conducted by the Federal Open-Market Committee for account of all twelve Federal Reserve banks.

the recession phase of the cycle, such public statements are designed to encourage bank lending. Some amateur humorist, with the phrase "open-market policy" in mind, has termed moral suasion the "open-mouth policy," and the name has stuck. The effectiveness of the open-mouth policy seems to vary with the times and with the identity of the speaker, but the views of individuals highly respected in the business and financial community generally carry considerable weight.

Changes in Federal Reserve credit policy can be observed most readily by the week-to-week changes in an amount designated as "free reserves." Free reserves consist of total excess reserves of member banks minus their total borrowings from the Federal Reserve banks. Excess reserves are the difference between total reserves held by all member banks and the total amount they are required to hold. When some banks have excess reserves, others have to borrow from the Fed. The borrowings are subtracted from the excess reserves and the remainder is free reserves. This nomenclature developed during a period when it was usual for the member banks to have excess reserves greater than their borrowings, leaving a "free" balance. When borrowings are greater than excess reserves, the minus balance is termed "negative free reserves."

POLICIES FOR AGGRESSIVE ACTION IN THE BOND MARKET

Policies for profiting by estimating correctly cyclical fluctuations in prices of high-grade bonds are parallel to those for attempting to realize gains from fluctuations in the general level of stock prices. We have only to substitute long-term high-grade bonds for common stocks as the media for speculation and continue to use cash or highly liquid securities as a repository for funds not invested in bonds. We can also characterize aggressive policies in management of a bond portfolio as varying from weak to strong.

The weakest response to an estimate that bond prices are about to decline, or have begun a cyclical decline, is simply to stop buying bonds while the downward movement is in progress. Money from matured or called issues and new funds for investment would be invested temporarily in liquid assets. Then, when the price cycle seems to have turned upward, or is expected to do so, investment in bonds of longer maturities is resumed. Funds becoming currently available as well as accumulated liquid assets would be used for bond purchases while prices are low.

If an investment manager is successful in executing such a policy, he buys long-term issues at the lower levels of the price cycle and gains by obtaining a higher average portfolio yield than he would obtain if he bought at the upper levels of the price cycle, or if he made purchases at all levels of prices through a price cycle. Such gains are not spectacular. An investor whose timing is good might well realize an average yield on a high-grade bond account over a period of years at a rate 25 to 50 basis points higher than the yield that would be obtained by diversifying purchases over time with no attempt to buy when prices are cyclically low or to avoid buying when they are high. Nevertheless, this gain is very worthwhile in the area of high-grade bond investments. If bonds have to be sold before maturity, there is less chance of realizing loss when they have been bought at relatively low levels and more chance of a gain.

The hazard in pursuing this policy of timing purchases is that, on the one hand, you may buy too soon in anticipation of a rise in bond prices and, on the other, you may buy too late. If you buy too soon and prices continue to decline, you may have bought in the upper rather than the lower phase of the cycle. If you buy too late in a cyclically rising market, you have made your purchases in the upper phase of the cycle. The penalty for error is a lower average portfolio yield than would have been obtained by a policy of regular diversification of purchases over time. Moreover, there is a greater chance that sales before maturity will be made at a loss.

Whether or not timing is good, an opportunity cost is usually incurred in holding funds in liquid assets until the shift to long-term bonds. The cost is the difference between the yield that could have been obtained had funds been invested in long-term issues, and the return actually realized on cash or very short-term issues. When the yield curve is steeply upsloping, this cost is sufficiently large that you have to be at least moderately successful in timing purchases of long-term bonds to recover it. When the yield curve is only slightly upsloping the opportunity cost is small. In those unusual periods when the yield curve is downsloping, there is no such cost; rather the yield differential is in favor of short-term issues.

The most aggressive policy in managing bond investments relative to the price cycle is to sell all bond holdings when prices are believed to be near the peak of the cycle, to hold the proceeds in highly liquid assets, and to buy

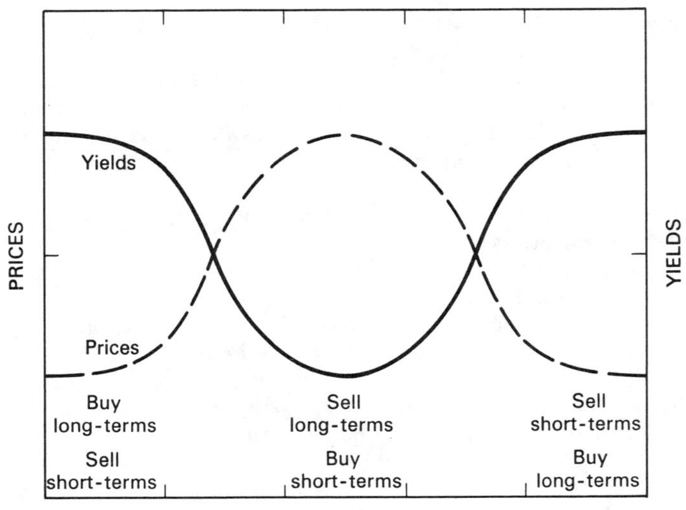

FIGURE 21–1

Aggressive Policies in the Bond Market

long-term bonds when prices are believed to be near a cyclically low level. If this policy works as expected, you hold long-term obligations while prices rise cyclically and get the maximum appreciation available in this field of security investment. Then you sell at the top and take the profit. Figure 21–1 is a conventionalized graphic depiction of how this policy is intended to work. The more nearly you can concentrate purchases at the bottom of the price cycle and sales at the top, the greater the gain.

What we said earlier by way of evaluating aggressive policies in the stock market applies generally to aggressive policies in the bond market. In the bond market, price fluctuations are smaller in amplitude and the size of potential losses is also smaller, not only because of the lesser price movements but also because high-grade bonds are payable ultimately at par. The forecasting problem is much the same, although some hold that bond prices are more difficult to forecast because of the influence of Federal Reserve policy. Federal Reserve policy is sometimes regarded as less predictable than the business cycle.

QUESTIONS FOR DISCUSSION

1. How would the shape of the utility curve of an investor who pursues distinctly aggressive policies in managing a securities portfolio differ from that of an investor who follows a defensive policy?
2. Describe, at least in general terms, the investment constraints that would reasonably qualify an individual to adopt an aggressive policy in managing a portfolio of common stocks.
3. How can you reconcile the general belief among academic theorists that prices fluctuate in the manner of a random walk with the general acceptance among professional investment managers that they can "beat the averages"?
4. Ascertain the standard economic forecast at the present time (by reading the business and financial press), and make your forecast of the direction and amplitude of change in average stock prices for the next 6 months.
5. What is the rationale for the proposition that changes in amount of money supply govern both changes in business conditions and changes in stock prices?
6. What is the Dow theory? Can it be used successfully to predict future changes in average stock prices?
7. What is the basic assumption that is said to impart validity to the advance-decline series as a basis for forecasting stock prices?
8. If you really believe your forecast of the next major change in either stock or bond prices, why use a "weak" aggressive policy? Why not go all the way?
9. Does Federal Reserve policy have much effect on changes in market rates of interest? Or are these changes caused mainly by the business cycle?
10. If you are managing a portfolio limited to bonds, both long-term and short-term, how would your portfolio rate of return be affected by estimating with approximate accuracy the bond-price cycle and using an aggressive policy?

VI

Investment Policies of Institutional Investors

22

Investment Policies of Commercial Banks

I. Constraints on investment policies of commercial banks
   A. The need for stability of investment income in current dollars
   B. The need for stability of market value of the portfolio
   C. Tenure of ownership
   D. Quality of management and the temperament of bankers
   E. The need for stability of returns in constant dollars
   F. Other investment requirements

II. Investment policies of commercial banks
   A. The uncertainty of financial abilities in constructing the portfolio
   B. The uncertainty of interest rates in constructing the portfolio
   C. The system of secondary reserves
   D. The tertiary reserve
   E. Instability of investment income
   F. The desirability of ownership qualities
   G. Policies toward price fluctuations

III. Bank portfolios demonstrate constraints and adaptation

We have pursued a long and at times somewhat tedious study of security portfolio management. Most of the discussion has necessarily been somewhat abstract. We have had to study risk in general and the general relationship of risk and return. Investment constraints have been considered mostly from the standpoint of individuals and individuals are heterogeneous; almost anything you say about them is too general. Investment policies both in constructing security portfolios and in managing them under the changing conditions of the security markets have lacked the reality of who the investor is and what is peculiar to him.

In this last part of the book, however, we have an opportunity to examine the investment policies of principal types of institutional investors. These types of investors are much more homogeneous than individuals. Each commercial bank and each insurance company is different from every other bank and insurance company, but the restrictions imposed on management of their security investments both by the conditions of their business and by the regulatory authorities enable us to be a great deal more specific about investment constraints and how security portfolios are affected by them. In these last chapters we have the opportunity to look at the real world of investment in securities and to bring to a sharper focus the entire line of thought about investment management.

CONSTRAINTS ON INVESTMENT POLICIES OF COMMERCIAL BANKS

Commercial banks are engaged principally in accepting deposits from large numbers of depositors and lending money to a wide variety of borrowers, but investment in securities is an important part of their operation. Among all the principal types of investing institutions, they rank first in amount of securities owned—about $170 billion at the end of 1971.[1] The manner in which they invest in securities is strongly conditioned by the structure of their assets and liabilities, by the relative size of their sources of income, by the provisions of federal and state laws, and by supervision by bank regulatory authorities.

Need for Stability of Investment Income in Current Dollars

We can examine the need of commercial banks for stability of investment income using the approach described in Chapter 15. The total amount of current operating expenses may be taken as the minimum expense budget. Certainly a bank has to earn enough to cover these expenses to stay in business. Income from other than security investments is interest on loans, service charges, and other current income. The difference between income from these sources and total operating expenses is the minimum investment income requirement.

Table 22–1 shows that in 1971 all insured commercial banks in the

[1] *Assets and Liabilities—Commercial and Mutual Savings Banks—December 31, 1971*, Washington D.C., 1972, Federal Deposit Insurance Corporation, Board of Governors of the Federal Reserve System, Office of the Comptroller of the Currency, p. 3.

TABLE 22–1

Income and Expenses of all Insured Commercial Banks in 1971

	Amounts (millions)
Operating expenses	
Salaries, wages, and other employee benefits	$ 8,395
Interest on deposits	12,218
Other operating expenses	9,038
Total operating expenses	29,651
Operating income (excluding investment income)	
Interest and fees on loans	23,069
Trust department income	1,258
Service charges on deposit accounts	1,231
Other operating income (excluding investment income)	3,129
Total operating income (excluding investment income)	28,687
Minimum investment income requirement	964
Investment income	7,677
Total operating income	36,364
Income before income taxes and securities gains or losses	6,713
Net income after taxes and extraordinary items	5,237
Dividends on capital	2,231
Retained earnings	$ 3,006

Source: *Assets and Liabilities—Commercial and Mutual Savings Banks—December 31, 1971, op. cit.,* p. 114.

United States earned almost enough (in the aggregate) from sources other than investment income to pay regular operating expenses. The difference between the minimum expense budget (total operating expenses) and income from other sources (all operating income except investment income) was only $964 million. The total amount of investment income was $7,677 million, which is about 8 times the minimum investment income requirement. This might lead to the conclusion that banks have little need for stability of income from their investments in securities.

There are, however, several other elements of the problem. First, the principal item of operating income—interest and fees on loans—varies considerably from year to year with changes in amounts of loans and changes in rates charged for loans. The principal item of operating expense—interest on deposits—is also capable of considerable variation from year to year. So there are variations in both operating income and operating expense that may change the item we have termed "total operating income (excluding investment income)" very considerably from year to year, with corresponding fluctuations in the minimum investment income requirement.

Second, operating income isn't the entire story. Commercial bankers have some extraordinary charges for losses on both loans and securities as well as credits for recoveries on loans and gains on securities. These amounts vary from year to year. Sometimes the net of extraordinary gains and losses is a gain and sometimes a loss. Banks must also pay income taxes. Thus, net income after extraordinary items and after taxes is usually less than operating income.

Banks like to pay dividends to their stockholders. In fact, the tradition is to maintain a highly stable dividend rate with occasional increases whenever the upward trend in earnings seems to assure that the higher dividend can be maintained. The last thing that a bank wants to do is to reduce its dividend. A dividend reduction might be regarded as an indication of financial weakness, and at the very least would arouse the ire of stockholders who have long been accustomed to regular and sometimes rising amounts of dividends. It is not remarkable, then, that bank officers think of the current amount of dividend per common share as something approaching a fixed charge.

Finally, banks need retained earnings. Bank liabilities have increased at a relatively high rate in recent years and larger amounts of capital are needed to support the risk involved in owing this money to depositors and investing it for the most part in loans to banks' customers. Indeed, many banks have run up against such a relative shortage of capital that they have issued their own bonds, notes, and preferred stocks to the public. These securities are subordinate to deposit liabilities.

If you ask your friendly banker whether he needs stability of income from the bank's bond account, you are likely to get a definite affirmative answer.

The Need for Stability of Market Value of the Portfolio

What makes commercial banks so different from other institutional investors is that they have heavy liabilities relative to their capital and that most of the liabilities are payable on demand or short notice. This means that banks are highly leveraged in terms of borrowed money and that their liabilities are unstable.

The assets, liabilities, and capital accounts of all insured commercial banks at the end of 1971 are shown in Table 22–2.

It is evident at once that banks need a high degree of stability of principal in their investment portfolios. In the language of our system of investment constraints, they have a high minimum investment value requirement. The value of their assets cannot depreciate very much without jeopardizing their solvency, because the amount of capital available to absorb losses is small. For the aggregate of all insured banks in the United States, total capital accounts represented only 7.4 per cent of total assets at the end of 1971. There are also valuation reserves for losses on loans and securities equal to 1.0 per cent of total assets, which serve as a cushion for loan losses. Thus the total cushion is about 8½ per cent of assets for the aggregate of all insured commercial banks. Of course individual banks may have stronger or weaker capital positions.

The need for stability of principal in the securities portfolio is even greater than you might infer from the balance sheet because not all the capital may be used to absorb losses on bank assets. Some substantial amount of

TABLE 22–2

Assets and Liabilities of All Insured Commercial Banks (in billions of dollars; end of 1971)

	Amounts	*Percentage of total*
Assets		
Cash, due from banks and collection items	$ 99.8	15.6%
Securities	169.6	26.5
Loans and discounts	327.7	51.1
Other assets	43.8	6.8
Totals	$640.9	100.0
Liabilities, reserves and capital accounts		
Business and personal deposits	$438.5	68.4
Government deposits (U.S. Government, states and subdivisions)	58.7	9.2
Domestic interbank deposits	32.1	5.0
Foreign government and bank deposits	9.3	1.4
Total deposits	538.6	84.0
Of which:		
Demand deposits	262.7	41.0
Time deposits	275.9	43.0
Miscellaneous liabilities	48.7	7.6
Total liabilities	587.3	91.7
Reserves on loans and securities	6.4	1.0
Capital accounts:		
Capital notes and debentures	3.0	0.5
Equity capital		
Preferred stocks	0.1	*
Common stocks	11.9	1.9
Surplus	19.9	3.1
Undivided profits and reserves for contingencies	12.3	1.9
Total capital accounts	42.7	7.4
Totals	$640.9	100.0%

*Less than 0.1 per cent

Source: *Assets and Liabilities—Commercial and Mutual Savings Banks—December 31, 1971, op. cit.*, p. 2.

capital must remain after charge-off of whatever losses may be incurred on loans and investments in order for a bank to remain open. The effective cushions for losses are total operating income, valuation reserves, and undivided profits.

Bankers pay a great deal of attention to the adequacy of their capital to support the risks they assume in their loans and investments. Differences in capital adequacy often influence their conclusions about their ability to assume risk of loss of principal invested in securities. A bank officer responsible for managing his institution's bond account would examine carefully the riskiness of loans and discounts in the process of formulating investment policies.

Bankers and bank supervisors have developed several statistical measurements of capital adequacy. It used to be a rule of thumb that a bank should have capital funds equal to 10 per cent of total deposit liabilities, but this measurement was largely discarded during the 1940's when expansion of bank deposits greatly exceeded expansion of bank capital and few banks were able to maintain such a relationship. It also came to be recognized that the amount of deposits is not a measure of the risk of loss and that the amount of capital is more logically related to the amount of assets subject to risk. Thus a "risk-asset ratio" was substituted. The ratio is usually defined as the amount of capital divided by total assets minus cash, due from other banks, and U.S. Treasury securities. A general rule of thumb is that a 20 per cent ratio indicates adequate capital.

The continued concern of bankers with the question of capital adequacy led to further efforts to develop better measures. The next step was to take account of differences in degree of risk among the several principal categories of loans and investments. Capital adequacy formulas were developed for classifying assets and allocating amounts of bank capital to each category by applying percentages to the amounts of assets. The allocations of capital are designed to be of sufficient amounts to absorb such losses (after losses charged to current earnings) as might have to be charged to the capital accounts and still leave enough capital for a bank to continue in operation.

A capital adequacy formula developed by the Federal Reserve Bank of New York provided for dividing assets into six classifications and for allocating an amount of bank capital equal to specified percentages of amounts of assets. The percentages are designed to provide the minimum amounts of capital. This formula is described in the schedule on the following page.[2]

The use of this capital adequacy formula, or some similar method of allocating capital to support assets, may show a banker that his capital cushion is relatively thin. If so, he has a particularly severe limit on his ability to assume risk in the bank's bond account. A weak capital position is a compelling reason for drastically limiting financial and interest-rate risk in the securities portfolio. An unusually strong capital position, of course, would indicate a less severe limitation.

Although the ability of commercial banks to risk loss of principal is severely limited by the financial framework in which they operate, they are aided in one respect by the rules of the bank supervisory authorities. Some years ago the three federal agencies that examine banks[3] agreed on a uniform regulation governing bank investments, and most state supervisory authorities have subsequently adopted similar regulations. The uniform regulation provides, among other things, that all bonds of "investment quality" shall be valued at amortized cost. Bonds of investment quality are, for practical purposes, those that are rated in one of the first four quality classifications by

[2]Howard D. Crosse and George Hempel, *Management Policies for Commercial Banks*, Englewood Cliffs, N. J., 1973, Prentice-Hall, Inc., p. 77.

[3]They are the Office of the Comptroller of the Currency, for national banks; the Board of Governors of the Federal Reserve System, for state member banks; and the Federal Deposit Insurance Corporation, for state nonmember banks.

Classification	*Description*	*Percentage required*
No-risk assets	Cash and due from banks, Treasury obligations due within 5 years, and similar high-grade, short-term instruments.	0
Minimum risk	Government and government guaranteed obligations due in more than 5 years and loans secured by excellent collateral.	5
Portfolio assets	Assets representing the usual banking risks; the remainder of the loan portfolio not adversely classified by examiners and remainder of securities portfolio not classified as substandard.	12
Substandard assets	Loans and securities classified as more risky than usual banking risks.	20
Work-out assets	Stocks, defaulted bonds, real estate, and all other assets required by examiners to be disposed of promptly.	50
Banking house, furniture, and equipment	Real property and physical assets used in conducting the banking business.	100

two of the regular bond-rating services. A bank that holds nonrated bonds has the responsibility of proving that they are of at least as good quality as bonds in the triple B rating class. Amortized cost is the price paid for a security less any premium above par that has been written off. The significance of this provision is that banks are permitted to value their bonds of good quality on their books without regard to prevailing market prices. The effect is to reduce somewhat the significance of market-price fluctuations. As long as a bond remains of good investment quality and as long as a bank does not have to sell it, it has a stable value for accounting purposes. Bonds that do not meet the quality standard of the uniform bank regulation on investments must be valued on the basis of market values.

Tenure of Ownership

Although the system of valuating securities does much to insulate banks from the effects of fluctuations in market prices, the terms on which banks hold the funds they invest makes their tenure of ownership relatively weak. All liabilities are payable on demand or short notice. A very large part of liabilities are demand deposits. Time deposits include savings deposits, which, for practical purposes, are payable whenever depositors want their money. Other time deposits, generally known as certificates of deposit, have fixed maturity dates, usually from 90 days to 2 years, and are payable at maturity.

If the owners of any very large proportion of a bank's liabilities were to demand their money at once, or on short notice, the bank would have to liquidate a large proportion of its assets; fortunately, this rarely happens. In practice the withdrawals of some depositors are more or less offset by the additional deposits of others. There have been times in the past, particularly in the early 1930's, when concerted demands for money by bank depositors forced banks into large-scale liquidation of assets and in more than a few instances caused bank failures. Since the establishment of the Federal Deposit Insurance System, which guarantees deposits up to a maximum amount per account, such "runs" on banks have been virtually eliminated.

Even in the ordinary course of business, however, bankers must expect periods in which there are sizable net outflows of funds that require liquidation of securities. Many banks experience a distinct seasonal pattern of fluctuation in loans and deposits caused by seasonal variation in the economy of the area. Farmers, for example, make large outlays for seed, fertilizer, and equipment in the early part of the year, and a bank serving them experiences a seasonal increase in loans and decrease in deposits. The sale of crops in the fall provides an inflow of funds; farmers reduce their loans and increase deposits. The operation of manufacturers whose sales and current assets are much larger at one time of year than at another causes similar changes in loans and deposits. Often the deposits of states and political subdivisions fluctuate around tax collection dates, with the peak shortly after a date when property tax payments are due and the trough just before the next tax collection date. Sometimes local governments borrow from banks to tide them over a period between tax collection dates.

Cyclical fluctuations of business also affect banks' tenure of ownership of securities. Typically, the demand for loans increases during the expansion phase of the business cycle and banks liquidate securities to some extent to obtain funds to meet the demand. A need for funds to make loans generally overrides strictly investment considerations and leads bankers to sell securities even at a loss in order to make loans to customers. In the recession phase of the business cycle there is usually a reduction in bank loans and re-investment in securities.

There are many other possible causes of variation in the flow of funds affecting individual banks. A community may experience unusually rapid growth over a period of years and its bank may have to liquidate virtually its entire holdings of securities to meet loan demand. Or, there may be the opposite kind of economic development, with declining loans and increasing amounts for investment in securities. And there may be erratic movements in loans and deposits resulting from changes in business operations of one or more large business firms, such as a shift of production facilities to or from a city.

We are therefore led to the conclusion that for a large part of their securities portfolios the tenure of ownership by commercial banks is relatively weak. Some part of bank security portfolios is subject to liquidation as the need may arise to provide funds for depositors or for loans to customers. This condition, combined with the very limited ability to suffer realized loss of principal, creates an unusually high requirement for stability of principal in the securities portfolio.

Quality of Management and the Temperament of Bankers

The quality of management is seldom an important constraint on bank investment policy. Within the area of interest-rate risk securities, to which banks are confined by law and by other kinds of constraints, the officers who manage bank investments are generally competent. The larger banks, of course, are well staffed with officers who are specialists in the kinds of securities banks generally own and are thoroughly familiar with the operation of the money and capital markets. In the smaller country banks, management of the investment portfolio may be in the hands of less technically qualified people; sometimes the bond account is something that the chief executive officer attends to in his spare time. However, banks with limited time and talent for this function frequently use the services of outside experts.

One important source of investment advice available to all country bankers is their correspondent banks in the larger cities. All banks have correspondent banks with which they maintain deposits for the purpose of clearing checks and to compensate them for several kinds of services. Most big-city banks have a correspondent bank division in which there are officers who devote themselves particularly to advising their country bank customers on investment matters. They make no direct charge for this service, but the banks that use it are expected to maintain deposits of appropriate size with the banks that furnish it.

The other important source of outside help in managing bank investments is the professional investment counsel firms. Some banks employ such counsel on a fee basis. They are visited periodically by a representative of the firm for thorough review of the securities portfolio and discussion of whatever problems of policy there may be. Client banks may also obtain advice on specific questions from time to time by mail or telephone. Several investment counsel organizations have been particularly successful in developing a clientele among banks.

Bankers have the reputation of being conservative. They have to be because they operate to such a great extent with borrowed money and are so greatly affected by the public interest. They borrow money on their promise not only to pay dollar for dollar but to repay on demand or short notice. Because the public has such a vital interest in the solvency of banks, bankers do business with bank examiners practically looking over their shoulders. They cannot afford to make very many mistakes and no very big ones. The conservatism of bank management, then, is a restrictive influence on investment policy.

The Need for Stability of Returns in Constant Dollars

The fact that the funds invested in securities by commercial banks consist almost entirely of the deposits of their customers is the significant condition affecting the need for stability of purchasing power of principal. Deposits are payable simply in dollars, without any condition or obligation whatever about the purchasing power of the dollars. Consequently, as long as principal values in current dollars are relatively stable, a shrinkage in the purchasing power of the dollars does no harm to a bank. Any loss of purchasing power is transmitted through the bank to its depositors, who realize the loss when they withdraw deposits and use their dollars to buy goods and services.

From the point of view of income, banks may seem to be somewhat vulnerable to inflation because bank operating expenses increase when the price level rises. If there were no compensating increase in income, the dollar amount of earnings would decline. However, inflation usually increases bank income. A period of rising prices is generally one of expanding loans and higher interest rates. It may also bring about an increase in amount of security investments and larger investment income. In fact, the net income of commercial banks as a percentage of equity capital has been relatively stable during recent years of price inflation at abnormally high rates.

Thus, we come to the conclusion that the inflation risk can be eliminated for all practical purposes in considering investment policies for commercial banks. Unless bonds prove to be a good inflation hedge, there is little banks can do about it because their investments are restricted to bonds.

Other Investment Requirements

There are two other important limitations on bank investment policy. One is the need for highly marketable issues. The weak tenure of ownership that makes banks so vulnerable to the risk of loss of principal tends to cause a relatively high rate of portfolio turnover and thus requires investment for the most part in the more highly marketable bonds. This requirement has been incorporated in the uniform federal regulation of bank investments to the extent that banks are permitted to invest only in marketable securities, but unfortunately the term *marketable* is not defined in such a way as to emphasize the need for high marketability.

The other need is for tax-exempt securities. Commercial banks are subject to the federal corporate income tax just as are other business corporations. At the tax rates that have prevailed in recent years they have been able to retain as income only about one-half of the interest collected on fully taxable securities after operating expenses. Usually, high-grade tax-exempt securities are available in the market at tax-equivalent yields much higher than the yields obtainable on taxable issues of similar grade and maturity.

INVESTMENT POLICIES OF COMMERCIAL BANKS

The well-defined and relatively severe constraints on investment policies of commercial banks have resulted in similarly well-defined and conservative policies in the construction and management of bank security portfolios. Risk minimization policies are imposed on banks by conditions under which they operate, by banking laws, and by bank supervisory authorities.

The Uncertainty of Financial Abilities in Constructing the Portfolio

Inability and unwillingness to assume any very high level of risk in terms of the financial abilities of issuers to pay causes commercial banks to limit their investments almost entirely to high-grade bonds. The regulation of the Comptroller of the Currency, which applies to national banks and to state-chartered banks that are members of the Federal Reserve System, provides that banks may buy investment securities. It defines an investment security as a corporate bond, note,, or debenture that is not predominately speculative in nature. Banks may also invest in public securities, which are defined as U.S. government obligations and obligations of the states, cities, and political subdivisions. The regulation says that banks may invest in public securities subject only in the exercise of prudent banking judgment.[4] Nonrated obligations are eligible provided a bank owning them satisfies bank examiners that they are not predominately speculative and have been acquired as the result of prudent banking judgment. State laws and regulations affecting nonmember state banks are similar to those of the Comptroller of the Currency, although there are variations.

Generally, commercial banks are not permitted to buy stocks other than stock of Federal Reserve Banks and of bank subsidiary companies authorized by law. However, they may acquire stock that has been pledged as collateral for loans and taken in satisfaction of unpaid debt. Stock taken in satisfaction of debt by federally supervised banks must be liquidated within a reasonable time period. Several states permit banks they have chartered to purchase and own stocks, subject to certain restrictions.

In practice most banks are more conservative than banking regulations require. They have long invested heavily in U.S. government obligations in preference to corporate bonds that provide higher yields with small financial risk. Recently about one-half of all securities owned by insured commercial banks have been Treasury issues and those of government agencies. Until recent years most banks have had relatively small commitments in municipal bonds, but the inflow of time deposits in response to increases in interest rates paid on liabilities of this type has resulted in a marked increase both in the amount and proportion of state and local government obligations in their portfolios. Yields on high-grade municipals in the range of 5 to 6 per cent provide tax-equivalent yields of about twice that much. Presently almost one-half of aggregate bank investments are municipals. Bank holdings of corporate bonds are relatively small and most of the obligations of this kind in their portfolios bear the first three ratings (the A ratings). There has been little disposition by banks to assume financial risk to the extent of investing in triple B rated corporate bonds.

Table 22–3 shows the amounts and proportions of the four principal classes of securities held by all insured commercial banks. It should be kept

[4] *Federal Reserve Bulletin*, Washington, D.C., November, 1963, Board of Governors of the Federal Reserve System, pp. 1505–1508.

TABLE 22-3

Principal Categories of Securities Owned by All Insured Commercial Banks (in billions of dollars; end of 1971)

Category	*Amounts*	*Percentage of total*
U. S. Treasury securities	$ 64.9	38.2%
Securities of other U. S. Government agencies and corporations	17.9	10.6
Obligations of states and subdivisions	82.4	48.6
Other securities	4.4	2.6
Totals	$169.6	100.0%

Source: *Assets and Liabilities—Commercial and Mutual Savings Banks—December 31, 1971, op. cit.*, p. 2.

in mind that these are aggregate data and that the distributions for individual banks vary considerably.

To the extent that they assume risk affected to any considerable extent by the financial ability of issuers to pay, banks generally diversify broadly. This kind of risk is important chiefly in municipal bonds somewhat below the top ratings, and the usual practice is to diversify such municipals geographically.

The Uncertainty of Interest Rates in Constructing the Portfolio

Because banks limit themselves so largely to the kinds of securities in which the level of risk is chiefly a function of change in interest rates, interest-rate risk is their most important concern in constructing their bond portfolios. The same constraints that require a defensive policy toward financial risk also require a defensive policy toward fluctuations in market prices of bonds caused by changes in interest rates. The effort of banks generally to minimize interest-rate risk in their securities portfolios is evidenced by data on the maturity distribution of government bonds owned by a large number of banks, shown in Table 22–4.

The concentration of holdings of Treasury obligations in the shorter maturities evidences the defensive policy of banks toward fluctuations in market prices of securities and their own need for liquidity. For commercial banks generally, the proportion of all government securities maturing within 1 year varies between about one-third and one-fourth. In addition, banks use short-term issues of government agencies and corporations to reinforce their liquidity positions. It is significant that more than one-half of all government issues owned by banks mature in 1 to 5 years and that less than 2 per cent have maturities of more than 10 years. Generally, the larger banks in metropolitan centers are particularly conservative in arranging their government bond maturities because their inflows and outflows of funds are more volatile than those of banks in the smaller cities and towns.

There are no published data on maturity distributions of municipal

TABLE 22–4

Maturity Distribution of U. S. Government Marketable Securities Owned by Commercial Banks* (millions of dollars; December 31, 1971)

Maturity	*Amount*	*Percentage of total*
Due within 1 year:		
Treasury bills	$ 8,287	16.1%
Other	6,633	12.9
Total within 1 year	14,920	29.0
Due in 1 to 5 years	28,823	56.1
Due in 5 to 10 years	6,847	13.3
Due in 10 to 20 years	555	1.1
Due in over 20 years	217	0.5
Totals	$51,363	100.0%

*Data based on Treasury survey data for about 90% of all commercial banks.

Source: *Federal Reserve Bulletin*, May, 1972, Board of Governors of the Federal Reserve System, A 45.

bonds and of the small proportion of corporate issues, but it is the general practice of banks to space maturities of obligations of these categories over relatively short time periods. Many banks will not buy municipal issues with maturities of more than 10 years and generally they try to space maturities more or less evenly over their maximum time horizon.

The System of Secondary Reserves

The structure of banks' bond accounts by length of maturity of bonds, particularly government obligations, is very much influenced by their use of securities as secondary reserves. At some times securities have to be liquidated to meet the need for funds for other bank purposes, and at other times inflows of funds must be invested in securities for short or indeterminate periods. Bankers recognize these variations as normal conditions of carrying on the banking business and design their investment policies accordingly.

To provide the liquidity required for conducting their business, banks maintain both primary and secondary reserves. Primary reserves consist of cash; that is, cash in vault, balances with Federal Reserve banks, deposits with correspondent banks, and cash items in process of collection. Day-to-day inflows and outflows of funds may usually be taken care of by increases or decreases in primary reserves, although at times it may be necessary for a bank to make adjustments in its reserve balances at Federal Reserve banks by purchasing or selling "federal funds," or by advances from Federal Reserve banks or repayment of advances. Federal funds are balances of member banks on deposit at Federal Reserve banks. A bank with a larger balance than required to meet its legal reserve requirement may sell (literally, loan) a portion of its balance to a bank that is deficient in legal reserves under an agreement that the funds will be returned, usually on the next business day, with interest at a stipulated rate. There is an active market in federal funds in New York City and other financial centers.

Primary reserves, however, provide little more than day-to-day liquidity. They are seldom maintained in amounts much larger than necessary for routine operations. To hold larger amounts of cash and balances with other banks is unprofitable because these funds earn no interest. Therefore, banks rely heavily on secondary reserves to provide liquidity.

Secondary reserve securities are short-term, low risk, highly marketable obligations that can be converted into cash quickly when the need arises with little or no loss of principal. The essential requirement is price stability and only securities of the highest grade in interest-rate risk, financial risk, and marketability have the requisite price stability. There is no generally agreed on definition of secondary reserve securities in terms of financial risk and interest-rate risk. Some bankers include only government bonds due within 1 year; others count as secondary reserves obligations with maturities as long as 5 years and include short-term corporate and municipal bonds with the highest ratings. In practice, they rely most heavily on Treasury obligations with the shorter maturities and expect to use issues of longer maturities and less than triple A ratings only to meet the more remote contingencies.

Managing Secondary Reserves. The segment of bank assets classified as a secondary reserve is highly variable in amount. At times it may be reduced sharply to provide for a decrease in deposit liabilities or to provide funds for additional loans. At other times it may increase considerably as funds not required for other purposes become available for temporary investment in securities. The problem is to invest funds in secondary reserve assets in such manner as to obtain the best possible yield and the required liquidity.

A very important part of secondary reserve management is estimation of future fund flows that will increase or decrease the amount of the secondary reserve. The principal variables are changes in amounts of loans and in amounts of deposits. Other things being equal, an increase in deposits provides funds that may be added to the secondary reserve or used to acquire other banking assets; a decrease in deposits has the opposite effect. An increase in loans may require liquidating secondary reserve securities and a decrease provides funds for adding to the reserve.

However, other things are never equal. In any particular time period, changes in one of these variables may offset changes in another, or add to the effect of changes in another. Even so, there are some general patterns of change in loans and deposits that bankers are familiar with and that aid them in estimating their liquidity needs.

We observed earlier that most banks experience seasonal variations in loans and deposits of some magnitude. Bankers familiar with the pattern invest the seasonal inflow of funds in secondary reserve securities with the full expectation of liquidating them to provide for the seasonal outflow of funds. The business cycle also affects banks' liquidity needs. An individual bank that increases its loans at a greater rate than that of the banking system is likely to experience a net outflow of funds as loan proceeds are used to make payments outside the area. Thus there may be a drain on the secondary reserve. Conversely, a bank with a less than average loan expansion may experience a cyclical inflow of funds.

The better a bank officer can estimate the effect of seasonal and cyclical changes in business on the liquidity position of his bank, the more efficiently he can manage the secondary reserve. If, for example, loan demand is slack in the bank's market area even after a cyclical expansion in the general economy is well under way along with a steady upward trend in deposits, he may conclude that funds becoming available for investment may be used to buy obligations in the 5- to 10-year maturity range. Thus he would obtain larger yields, to the extent that the yield curve is upsloping, than he could get from short maturities.

In the opposite situation, when strong cyclical expansion has caused some outflow of funds from the bank and further outflow is expected, the investment officer would move to strengthen the secondary reserve. If bonds mature and the proceeds are not immediately required to meet cash outflow, he would re-invest in very short-term issues. If longer-term obligations can be sold in the market at little or no loss, he might very well liquidate some of these issues and reinvest in shorter maturities. This would be better than waiting until further expansion in business has caused an increase in interest rates and a decrease in bond prices, so that significant losses would be realized on subsequent sale of these longer maturities.

There are, of course, other influences on the liquidity requirements of commercial banks that do not follow a seasonal or cyclical pattern and that have to be appraised as they appear. For example, banks generally have had a considerable increase in time deposits in recent years as a result of raising the interest rate they pay on these deposits. The funds inflow has helped them to meet the steadily increasing demand for bank loans and in many instances to increase their security investments. Any reversal of this trend in time deposits would, of course, place a strain on the liquidity position of banks. The credit policy of the Federal Reserve Board also has a direct bearing on banks' liquidity position. By selling securities in the open market, or by increasing required legal reserve ratios, the Fed can apply strong pressure on banks to check loan expansion, or to liquidate securities, or both. It can also operate in the opposite direction to ease the liquidity position of banks and thus aid them to meet increasing loan demand.

Managing secondary reserve assets to obtain maximum income and also to provide adequate liquidity is a difficult task. The officer responsible must deal constantly with estimates of future changes in the bank's position and make subjective judgments about how much is enough. Past experience is his guide, but the future is never like the past. Some bankers have tried to simplify the problem by adopting standard ratios for the relationship of primary and secondary reserves to deposits, or to different categories of deposits. However, the system of standard ratios is very likely to operate in such a way that longer-term rather than shorter-term issues vary with inflows and outflows of funds.

For example, a bank decides to maintain a secondary reserve in the form of government securities due within 3 years equal to, say 20 per cent of demand deposits when deposits are at about their usual level. Then as deposits increase, the amount of the secondary reserve is increased, and as deposits decline, the secondary reserve is reduced. Consider how this policy would operate in a period of seasonal decline in deposits. Let the amount of deposits at the usual level equal 100; the amount of the secondary reserve is an amount equal to 20 to provide a 20 per cent ratio. Now deposits decline to a seasonal low of 90. With no other significant changes in the bank's position, secondary reserve securities would have to be sold in an amount equal to 10. One-half of the secondary reserve would be used up.

Some bankers, however, become disturbed by the seasonal shrinkage in secondary reserve securities. When the secondary reserve declines seasonally, they become concerned that the low ratio is not enough. So they move to increase it by reducing loans or securities of longer maturity. When this is done, the effect is not to use the secondary reserve (except in part) for the purpose for which it has been provided, but instead to use securities of longer maturity. Very often, unnecessary losses result.

The Tertiary Reserve

The portion of a bank's securities portfolio not classified as a secondary reserve is often termed the *tertiary reserve*. The term is appropriate because the remainder may properly be considered a third reserve after the primary and secondary reserves. It serves as a reserve for the more remote contingencies and longer-term developments affecting banks' need for liquidity. Sometimes this part of a bank's security portfolio is termed an *investment reserve* and sometimes it is called the *bond account*.

When bonds in the tertiary reserve are high grade in financial risk and in marketability they become secondary reserve securities with the lapse of time. And when maturities of these bonds are well spaced they regularly replenish, or add to, the secondary reserve. The general concept of how the tertiary reserve may be related to the secondary reserve is shown in Table 22–5.

In practice, bond maturities are not arranged as neatly as we have depicted in this schedule, but the general pattern illustrates how a bank can buy bonds with relatively long maturities at the somewhat higher yields usu-

TABLE 22–5
Maturity Distribution of Secondary and Tertiary Reserves

	Secondary			*Tertiary*							*Total*
Years to maturity	*1*	*2*	*3*	*4*	*5*	*6*	*7*	*8*	*9*	*10*	
Line 1	$10	$10	$10	$10	$10	$10	$10	$10	$10	$10	$100
Line 2	10	10	10								30
Line 3	10	10									20
Line 4	10										10
Total	$40	$30	$20	$10	$10	$10	$10	$10	$10	$10	160

ally obtainable on the longer maturities and have them move into the secondary reserve category as time passes and maturities become shorter. The total amount of securities in the distribution depicted is $160 (plus as many zeroes as you care to add); of which $100 (the amounts on the first line of the schedule) were bought initially as 10-year maturities at the rate of $10 a year and held as time passed and their maturities became shorter. Those bought 9, 8 and 7 years ago are now due in 1, 2 and 3 years. Similarly, $30 on the second line were bought as 3-year maturities, $20 on the third line as 2-year maturities and only $10 as 1-year maturities. About 56 per cent of the total securities portfolio is in the secondary reserve, if this portion is limited to issues due within 3 years, and a larger proportion if it is defined to include maturities within 5 years.

With this kind of arrangement of maturities, there is a substantial cash inflow from the securities portfolio from the maturing of obligations, and sales to meet cash outflows may be avoided or at least minimized.

Instability of Investment Income

Because banks must adopt such a strongly defensive policy toward interest-rate risk affecting principal, they inevitably assume considerable interest-rate risk affecting income from security investments. In practice, the flows of funds into and out of the secondary reserve are sufficiently irregular that banks buy Treasury bills and other short-term government obligations in large amounts and, to the extent that they are not required to be liquidated, roll over these issues into new short-term instruments. Thus changes in short-term interest rates have a considerable impact on income from the total portfolio. The effect can be minimized to some extent by purchasing the longest maturities consistent with liquidity requirements and spacing maturities, but it cannot be eliminated.

In recent years the general upward movement of interest rates has benefited bank yields from securities. When yields on Treasury bills were in the area of 7 per cent, the total rate of return on bank portfolios considerably improved and the availability of 3- to 5-year maturities in the range of 5 to 6 per cent raised portfolio yields. A return to lower interest rates and a steeply upsloping yield curve would bring a considerable reduction in portfolio yields. Bankers don't like this instability of investment income, but it is less undesirable than instability of principal amounts.

The Desirability of Ownership Qualities

The need of banks for securities that are high grade both in marketability and taxability has a strong influence on the construction of their portfolios. They have a choice between fully taxable issues—governments and corporates—and between highly marketable issues—governments—and the less highly marketable corporates and municipals. The result, as shown in Table 22–3, is a kind of compromise. For the most part the banks have used Treasury issues for high marketability despite the fact that interest from them is fully taxable, and they have used tax-exempt municipals to minimize the income tax.

This compromise is an interesting example of the concept of tailoring the securities portfolio to the conditions of the market. Some years ago when yields on municipal bonds were lower relative to yields on Treasury issues of comparable maturity than they have been more recently, the banks placed a smaller proportion of their total security investments in municipals. But as municipal yields rose relative to yields on comparable maturities of Treasury issues, banks increased their proportionate holdings of the tax-exempt issues.

In sharp contrast to the need of banks for securities of high grade in the several investment qualities we have been discussing, the commercial banks have virtually no interest in convertible bonds. The Board of Governors of the Federal Reserve System has a regulation prohibiting the purchase of convertible bonds by banks subject to its jurisdiction (state-chartered member banks) whenever the purchase price includes any significant amount of consideration for the conversion right. The Comptroller of the Currency's regulation applying to national banks permits purchase of convertible issues, but requires that book value be written down at once to investment value independent of the conversion feature.

Similarly, commercial bankers have little interest in securities considered high grade in deepness of discount. The reason is that bonds considered high grade in this respect are of relatively long maturities and bankers generally consider long maturities to have too much interest-rate risk for bank investment. There are exceptions to this general statement, and in periods when demand for loans is small the exceptions become more numerous.

Policies Toward Price Fluctuations

Commercial banks generally take a defensive attitude toward fluctuations in market prices of securities. They buy bonds of the maturities they need and hold them to maturity, or sell them when the exigencies of the business require. They depend on distributing purchases over time to average out the effect of fluctuations in market prices on what they pay for securities and, when they have to sell, on prices they receive.

This policy reflects the generally conservative attitude of bankers toward risk and the disapproval by bank supervisory authorities of speculative transactions even in high-grade bonds. But it is basically a product of the severe constraints on assumption for risk that limit banks so rigidly in structuring their portfolios. To seek profits from high-grade bonds by forecasting changes in interest rates requires switching from short to long maturities and back again. The need for secondary reserves and for structuring the tertiary reserve so that it will serve as a reserve for more remote contingencies and also supply securities to the secondary reserve leaves little room for radical changes in the arrangement of maturities.

This is not to say, however, that bank investment officers never try to make a little profit by acting according to their estimates of future changes in bond prices. Bankers are like other people in that they prefer larger rather than smaller returns and some have a very natural disposition to think that they can forecast market prices for high-grade bonds. And there is usually some room, although not a great deal, within the investment constraints to permit some shifting of maturities with a view to realizing a profit from anticipated price changes.

Banks are somewhat disadvantaged by the effect that the business cycle has on expansion and contraction of the securities portfolio. The disadvantage is that at the peak of the business cycle when long maturities are cheapest in price their secondary reserves are likely to be so depleted that they cannot sell short-term issues and buy long-term issues without jeopardizing liquidity. At this point in the cycle bankers generally are continuing to project loan demand upward and are reluctant to take action that would be disadvantageous if the demand for loans continues to increase. Then, in the recession phase of the cycle, after bond prices have risen, the disposition is to invest in long-term issues because they provide higher yields than short maturities. These long-term issues are then vulnerable to price depreciation during the next expansion phase of the cycle.

BANK PORTFOLIOS DEMONSTRATE CONSTRAINTS AND ADAPTATION

The commercial banks are a particularly good example of severe constraints on ability to assume investment risks and to tolerate the lower grades of securities in important desirability of ownership qualities. They can afford little risk of loss of principal because their capital cushions are thin and because they can afford losses equal to only a small part of their capital. They are further limited by their obligation to pay liabilities on demand or short notice, which results in the weakest tenure of ownership of any of the major types of investing institutions. They require for the most part highly marketable securities and also find securities of high grade in taxability very desirable.

Our examination of bank security portfolios shows how their investment policies have been designed to meet these constraints. Risk attributable to uncertainties of the ability of issuers to pay are held to a minimum by investment almost entirely in U.S. government obligations and in high-grade municipal bonds. Interest-rate risk affecting principal is minimized by heavy concentration in short-term issues and by spacing maturities. The need for securities of high grade in marketability is an important reason for concentrating a large portion of investment funds in Treasury issues. The need for securities of high grade in taxability is the reason for relatively large commitments in municipal issues. The conflict between the need for high marketability and the need for tax exemption is resolved by using Treasury securities chiefly for the secondary reserve and municipal bonds chiefly for the tertiary reserve.

The most common policy for dealing with fluctuations in market prices of securities is to take prices as they come and to depend on the system of spacing maturities to average, more or less, the effect of price fluctuations on the prices they pay for securities and the prices they receive when they are obliged to sell. Their ability to assume risk does not permit aggressive policies of buying and selling securities in an effort to enlarge returns.

QUESTIONS FOR DISCUSSION

1. In a period of business recession it is likely that a commercial bank will experience a decline in its operating income owing to a decline in amount of loans and in rates of interest on both loans and securities. Other things being equal, this would increase the minimum investment income requirement. But at the same time there should be some compensating change, or changes, in the expense section of a bank's income statement. What are they? (Use Table 22–1 in thinking about this question).
2. If banks can value their bonds at amortized cost, why should they be concerned with fluctuations in market prices of their investments?
3. Who takes the risk of variation in the size of returns in constant dollars from the loans and investments of banks?
4. How would you use the capital adequacy formula to determine about how much capital remains available as a margin for losses on securities?
5. Are there any distinct seasonal factors that influence the demand for loans and the size of deposits in your community, or in any community with which you are familiar?
6. Why don't banks buy more corporate bonds at the relatively high rates of yield that have been obtainable on these issues in recent years?
7. Why don't banks buy convertible corporate bonds and thus increase greatly the range of potential rates of return from the bond account?
8. If you were managing a bank's security investments would you be satisfied to use a system of maturity distribution of government securities something like that shown in Table 22–4?
9. By some odd circumstances you found your way into the office of the president of a local bank and talked to him about investment policies of the bank. You learned that he bought no securities of any kind with a maturity of more than 5 years, that the portfolio was about evenly divided between government and municipal securities, and that maturities in both categories were very evenly spaced. You remarked that this is a very conservative portfolio. The banker replied, "Young man (or woman), when I take risk I take it in the loan account." Is that the right attitude for a banker?

23

Investment Policies of Life Insurance Companies

I. The business of life insurance companies

II. Constraints on investment policies of life insurance companies
   A. Need for stability of investment income
   B. Tenure of ownership
   C. Need for stability of market value of portfolio
   D. The quality of management and temperament of investment officers
   E. The need for stability of returns in constant dollars
   F. Constraints on the desirability of ownership qualities

III. Investment policies of life insurance companies
   A. The financial abilities risk in constructing the portfolio
   B. The uncertainty of interest rates in constructing the portfolio
   C. The desirability of ownership qualities
   D. Policies toward price fluctuations
   E. Adapting policies to the terms of the market
   F. Life insurance portfolios demonstrate the effect of investment constraints

The life insurance companies of the United States rank second only to the commercial banks in the total amount of their investments in securities, but they rank first in amount of holdings of corporate securities. Whereas banks invest chiefly in public securities, that is, government and municipal obligations, life insurance companies invest about 45 per cent of their total assets in bonds and stocks of business corporations.

There are several kinds of institutions and organizations that provide life insurance and life annuities, including savings banks in several states, a variety of fraternal organizations, and the United States Government, which provides life insurance to veterans of military service. We are concerned here only with legal reserve life insurance companies, that is, private organizations operating under state laws that require maintenance of prescribed reserves for life and annuity contracts. The legal reserve companies have about 94½ per cent of the assets of all organizations providing life insurance, excluding the Veterans Administration, which administers National Service Life Insurance for the federal government.

The greater part of the assets of all legal reserve companies is owned by mutual companies, that is, by companies that have no stock and are owned by their policyholders. There are, however, a number of large insurance companies that have capital stock and operate for the benefit both of policyholders and stockholders. There is little difference in the insurance operations and in the investment policies of mutual and stock life companies.

THE BUSINESS OF LIFE INSURANCE COMPANIES

The business of life insurance companies is somewhat more complex than that of commercial banks in that they issue a number of different kinds of contracts that have different implications for investment policy. They are also required by law to maintain liability reserves and certain valuation reserves for these contracts, and they are subject to government regulation only by the states and not by the federal government.

These companies not only sell life insurance, but also annuities and health insurance. They are required by state laws to provide liability reserves, usually termed policy reserves, on an actuarial basis. They must hold assets to fund reserves. Two-thirds of their policy reserves are for life insurance contracts, 30 per cent are for annuity contracts, and the remainder is for health insurance and for supplementary contracts to make periodic payments to beneficiaries of life insurance contracts.

The structure of the industry has changed considerably in recent years as the companies have increased their efforts to compete with other institutions for group and individual annuities. About $7.5 billion of assets is now held by the companies in separate accounts. A separate account is held separate from all other assets of a company, and by the laws of the several states separate accounts may be invested without regard to the usual investment restrictions on life company assets. Some of the separate accounts are for variable annuities and some are for fixed annuities. The most recent innovation is variable life insurance, which will further increase the assets of separate accounts.

In addition to policy reserves, the life companies have amounts representing accumulated policy dividends left with them at interest, and there is another small amount on the liability side representing provision for policy dividends (return of premiums) to be paid in the following year. Another item is called simply "Other obligations" and represents the sum of incurred expenses, mandatory reserves for fluctuations in security values, and insurance premiums paid in advance.

The difference between total assets and total obligations represents the surplus and the capital of stock companies, and the surplus of mutual companies. Special surplus funds are provided for particular contingencies, unassigned surplus is the difference between total assets and total obligations, and capital is the capital stock of stock companies.

Table 23–1 is a condensed statement of assets, obligations, and surplus funds of all U.S. life insurance companies.

CONSTRAINTS ON INVESTMENT POLICIES OF LIFE INSURANCE COMPANIES

The investment policies of life insurance companies, like those of banks, are conditioned by the terms on which they hold the money they invest as well as by the laws and regulations under which they operate. At first glance, it might seem that these conditions are similar. Both types of institutions mainly invest money for which they are liable and both have a relatively small

TABLE 23–1

Assets, Obligations, and Surplus Funds of U. S. Life Insurance Companies (in billions; end of 1971)

	Amounts	*Percentage of total*
Assets		
Securities	$110.8	49.9%
Mortgage loans	75.5	34.0
Real estate	6.9	3.1
Policy loans	17.1	7.7
Miscellaneous assets	11.8	5.3
Total assets	222.1	100.0%
Obligations and surplus funds		
Policy reserves	179.3	80.7
Policy dividend accumulations	6.5	2.9
Funds set aside for policy dividends	3.7	1.7
Other obligations	14.8	6.7
Total obligations	204.3	92.0
Special surplus funds	3.8	1.5
Unassigned surplus	12.7	5.7
Capital (of stock companies)	1.7	0.8
Total surplus funds	17.8	8.0
Total obligations and surplus funds	$222.1	100.0

Source: *Life Insurance Fact Book*, New York, 1972, The Institute of Life Insurance.

amount of capital cushion in the form of capital and surplus. It will soon become apparent, however, that there are some significant differences in the terms on which they hold money, which lead to important differences in their investment policies.

Need for Stability of Investment Income

It is the practice of American life insurance companies to accrue interest on policy reserves at a stipulated rate of interest and to pay or accrue interest at such a rate on policy proceeds left with companies for future disbursement. This rate, commonly termed the *assumed rate*, is established for each contract at the time it is made and continues for as long as the contract remains in effect. In recent years most companies have been using assumed rates of 3 to 4 per cent. The assumed rate on new contracts may be changed from time to time, but the average rate required to be earned on all contracts changes only slightly from year to year.

The amount of income required to be earned on policy reserves and other liabilities to which assumed rates apply is the minimum investment income requirement for life insurance companies. Operating expenses must be paid, of course, but a portion of premium income is allocated to cover these expenses. It is essential to the financial health of a life insurance company that its return on investments at least equals the weighted average of assumed rates on its outstanding obligations.

Failure to earn the assumed rate would result in a greater increase in liabilities (by accrual of interest) than the increase in assets and, therefore, a decrease in surplus or surplus reserves (other things being equal). The life companies have endeavored to minimize the chance of failing to earn assumed rates by using rates well below the average rate currently being earned and by reducing assumed rates on new contracts when the trend of average yields on their investments has been persistently downward.

Investment earnings in excess of the amounts required to maintain policy reserves and to make additions to surplus are returned to policyholders by mutual companies. These insurance dividends are a return of premiums paid in excess of amounts required for the insurance operation, and are not to be confused with dividends on stock of corporations. Some stock companies issue participating life insurance contracts that provide for policyholders to participate to some extent in the excess of premiums over amounts required for insurance, and some do not. Dividends on stock of stock companies are the same as dividends on stock of other companies having capital stock.

The life insurance companies compete vigorously to maximize returns on investments within their framework of constraints. The higher the rate of return on investments, the less the cost of insurance to policyholders of mutual companies and to owners of participating policies in stock companies.

The steady upward movement of market rates of interest in recent years has brought increasing average annual rates of return on investments of life insurance companies, as shown in Table 23–2. These data are net rates after

TABLE 23–2

Net Rates of Interest Earned on Invested Funds of All U.S. life insurance companies

Year	*Rate*	*Year*	*Rate*
1965	4.61%	1969	5.15
1966	4.73	1970	5.34
1967	4.83	1971	5.52
1968	4.97		

Source: *Life Insurance Fact Book, 1972, op. cit.*, p. 61.

investment expenses, but before federal income taxes. They do not include earnings of assets held in separate accounts.

These rates are for all admitted assets (admitted to the balance sheet) and not for the securities portfolio alone. However, most of the other part of insurance assets are mortgage loans, and it appears that average rates on these assets are usually at about the same level as the average rate on security investments. Rates on policy loans are lower than average rates on other kinds of assets.

There are no data on amounts required to maintain policy reserves and to pay rates on other liabilities, which are the minimum expense budget for life companies. When you consider that assumed rates have varied from about 3 to 4 per cent, with 2½ per cent on older contracts, it appears that the current net rates of return are well in excess of the minimum required. It has not always been so. In 1948, at the end of a long period of declining interest rates, the average net rate of return for life insurance companies was only 2.88 per cent. The conclusion, then, is that life companies have a moderate constraint in the area of stability of investment income.

Tenure of Ownership

We must turn next to the area of constraint termed tenure of ownership, because it is the relative lack of limitation in this area that enables the life insurance companies to assume a considerably higher level of risk than the commercial banks.

The greater part of the funds invested by the life companies represent policy reserves. By law these reserves are subject to withdrawal by policyholders on short notice either by cancelling their policies or by demanding loans equal to the value of their policy reserves. In fact, the cancellation of insurance policies is much more than offset by the sale of new policies. The total amount of life insurance in force in the United States has increased steadily throughout the twentieth century.

Policy loans, however, are a somewhat different matter. During recent years of relatively high interest rates, many policyholders became aware that they could borrow from their life insurance companies up to the amounts of their policy reserves at loan rates of interest specified in their policies and that these rates were considerably less than the rates at which they could borrow from banks or other lending institutions. As a result, policy loans increased in amount about 2½ times in a 7-year period ending in 1971, and the proportion of total assets represented by policy loans increased in the same period from 4.8 to 7.7 per cent of total assets.[1]

This unusual expansion of policy loans, however, did not create acute liquidity problems for the life companies. The steady inflow of insurance premiums more than compensated for the outflow of funds for policy loans and there was also a steady inflow of funds from maturity or amortization of bonds and mortgages. The effect was some reduction in the net inflow of funds available for investment.

The conclusion, then, is that tenure of ownership of securities by life insurance companies is unusually strong. What they buy they can ordinarily hold to maturity or to such time as they may choose to sell.

Need for Stability of Market Value of Portfolio

If you compare the aggregate financial statement of life insurance companies with that of the commercial banks, it appears that the life companies have a minimum investment value requirement almost as high as that of the commercial banks. We found that about 92 per cent of the total assets of banks consist of liabilities (Table 22–2), and for the life companies total obligations are the same percentage (Table 23–1). Both types of institutions have relatively thin margins for absorbing losses on securities and other assets.

There is also a similarity between banks and life insurance companies in the system of valuating assets. As a general rule, most of the assets of both kinds of institutions are valued on an amortized cost basis. By general agreement of state insurance regulatory authorities, the valuation of life insurance assets is governed by the rules of the National Association of Insurance Commissioners, known usually by the acronym NAIC. The full set of rules on valuation of assets is complex, but in general they permit bonds to be valued at amortized cost unless in default, preferred stocks to be valued on the same basis provided they meet a minimum standard of earnings to dividends, and mortgage loans not in default to be carried at cost. However, common stocks must be valued at market prices in year-end statements.

The laws of the several states define the kinds of assets eligible for investment by life insurance companies subject to their jurisdiction, usually by reference to the record of earnings of issuers relative to amounts required for interest or dividends, or to the ratio of debt to value of assets of a borrower, or both. Most of them provide a "leeway clause" that permits the companies to hold some proportion of their total assets in securities that do not meet the statutory requirements. They also limit the relative amounts that may be invested in common stocks. Companies organized in New York State, or doing business in that state, are permitted to invest the lesser of 10 per cent of assets or 100 per cent of surplus funds in common stocks. Since most companies qualify to do business in New York, this rule has broad applicability.

[1]*Life Insurance Fact Book, op. cit.*, p. 68.

To a considerable extent, however, the policies of life companies involving assumption of financial risk are affected by the NAIC rules concerning valuation of securities. The rates of annual contribution to the mandatory security valuation reserve (MSVR) and the maximum amount of the several components of this reserve are determined by certain "tests" established by the NAIC. The rate of annual contribution for bonds of good investment quality is 0.1 per cent of cost until the reserve equals 2 per cent of the amount of bonds to which it applies. Bonds of lower grade are subject to the requirement of 1 per cent annual contribution to the reserve until it equals 20 per cent of the amount of these obligations. Preferred stocks in good standing require annual credits to the reserve equal to 0.25 per cent until the reserve equals 10 per cent, and those preferred stocks not in good standing (not meeting certain prescribed tests) require a 1 per cent annual contribution and a maximum reserve of 20 per cent. For common stocks, 1 per cent of the amount owned must be credited each year to the valuation reserve until it equals one-third of the value of these securities on the books. Net realized capital gains are credited to the reserve as long as it is below the maximum, and net realized capital losses are charged to the reserve. The mandatory security valuation requirements discourage investment in the poorer grades of securities because of the larger credits required to be deducted from income.

The effect, though, of valuing most assets at amortized cost plus the strong tenure of ownership causes the constraint in terms of the effect of fluctuation in market prices to be much less severe than it is for commercial banks.

The Quality of Management and Temperament of Investment Officers

The investment management function in life insurance companies is typically performed by a staff of officers under the general supervision of a finance committee. However, there is a wide range in number of personnel engaged in managing security investments. In small companies the investment department may consist of one officer and a clerk-secretary. In larger companies there are usually several officers supported by a staff of specialists. Virtually all companies use external service agencies, such as investment information organizations, and depend to some extent on information from other financial institutions. Some of the smaller companies employ investment counsel.

The principal seat of authority over investments in life insurance companies is the finance committee. These committees establish policies and pass on recommendations from officers for the purchase or sale of securities. They are generally composed of directors who are not officers and senior insurance company officers. Many outside directors serving on finance committees are investment and commercial bankers, attorneys, and executives of business firms.

Life insurance investment officers are almost always men of considerable experience and ability in investment management. Most have come up through the ranks of the investment department, or have gained experience with another kind of investment or securities marketing organization. Some have earned the designation Chartered Financial Analyst, and many go back to school for two weeks each year as participants in an investment seminar conducted by an association of life insurance companies.

However, one academic student of the investment function of life insurance companies found much to criticize. In summarizing the results of extensive study of investment departments of a number of companies, he concluded that staff shortages led to neglect of some worthwhile investment opportunities and to a preference for easy-to-evaluate investment proposals. He reported instances of inadequate skills and inexperience and concluded that inadequate incentives for investment officers produced mediocre performance. He thought that there was too much reluctance on the part of investment officers to deviate from common patterns of investment behavior and that finance committees often narrowed the scope of investment opportunities.[2]

Practical men might reply that all organizations fall short of perfection, that ideal conditions are never obtained, and that the shortcomings of the investment function in life insurance companies are also to be found in other investment management organizations. Even so, some life investment officers readily agree that there is need for more and better personnel in investment departments and for better incentives to investment management. Some say privately that they are deterred to some extent in efforts to exercise initiative and imagination by the conservatism of finance committees. But when all this is said, it seems a reasonable conclusion that life companies are not seriously limited by the quality and temperament of management in formulating investment policies consistent with other constraints on investment.

The Need for Stability of Returns in Constant Dollars

Life insurance companies, like commercial banks, deal in current dollars. They receive dollars at whatever their purchasing power may be when received and they pay dollars at whatever their purchasing power may be when they are paid. Thus the purchasing power of the currency unit is not an important consideration in the investment of their funds.

This generalization requires some qualification. Life companies endeavor to maximize returns in current dollars and insofar as they succeed they maximize returns in constant dollars. There is a relationship between the size of investment returns and the size of payments to policy and annuity holders in that premiums received in excess of amounts required to maintain all reserves are returned to policyholders as dividends. Accordingly, the larger the rate of return in current dollars, the larger the dividends in current and in constant dollars. Since dividends are considered to reduce the cost of life insurance, larger earnings rates reduce the cost of insurance in constant dollars.

The life companies, however, are very much aware that in a climate of inflation their insurance and annuity contracts providing for payment of fixed amounts in current dollars over long periods of time suffer in sales appeal.

[2]James E. Walter, *The Investment Process*, Boston, 1962, Division of Research, Graduate School of Business Administration, Harvard University, pp. 14–19.

They have moved in the direction of selling instruments that may provide better returns in constant dollars. For several years most of the larger companies have offered to the public participations in separate accounts used to fund group and individual pension contracts. Separate account laws of the several states provide that assets in separate accounts (from insurance assets) may be invested without regard to the usual investment restrictions on life company assets. All income and all gains and losses of a separate account belong to the accounts that participate. There are no minimum guarantees for these accounts. The major part of all separate account assets are in the form of common stocks.

Some life insurance companies are developing variable life insurance contracts that are funded by separate account assets. The assets for variable annuity contracts are also included in separate accounts.[3]

Constraints in the Desirability of Ownership Qualities

The life insurance companies are in a rather unusual position in that they have little need for highly marketable securities and they derive little benefit from tax-exempt issues. On the other hand, they are very much interested in securities rated high in such desirability of investment qualities as redeemability and deepness of discount.

Highly marketable securities are required only for that very small portion of security investments held as a secondary reserve to be drawn on when cash outflows temporarily exceed cash inflows. Because inflows normally exceed outflows by substantial margins, these investors are able to buy securities, after providing a small secondary reserve, with full confidence of being able to hold them to maturity. We shall see presently how the life companies have been able to use their ability to tolerate poorly marketable securities to maximize investment returns.

Tax-exempt securities have less interest for life companies generally than for some other types of investors because of provisions of the federal corporate income tax statutes that permit them only a part of the benefit of tax-exempt income. Insurance companies are taxed according to provisions of a special law enacted in 1959. The provisions of this law are complex and the extent to which companies benefit from investment income that is normally tax exempt varies from company to company and, for any one company, may vary from year to year.

Any brief description of the Life Insurance Income Tax Act of 1959 is necessarily incomplete as to details, but the general rule is that the portion of investment income in excess of the amount required to maintain policy reserves belongs to the company. Thus, if the total amount of investment income from all kinds of investments is $1 million and the amount required to maintain policy reserves is $800,000, the amount of investment income

[3] Life Insurance Fact Book, *op. cit.*, p. 86.

subject to the income tax is $200,000. However, if some of the investment income is of the kind that would be tax exempt to other corporate investors, this "tax-exempt" income is divided between that part of total investment income allocated to maintain legal policyholders' reserves and the part that is considered to be investment income to the life insurance company. The division of tax-exempt income is in the ratio of the amounts of these parts to the amount of total investment income. The portion that is allocated to the company is tax exempt to the company, but the portion allocated to policy reserves is no different than any other kind of investment income. Thus a company gets no benefit from the portion of tax-exempt income allocated to policy reserves. For example, if total investment income is $1 million and the division of income is in the proportion of 80 per cent for policy reserves and 20 per cent to the company and if tax-exempt income is $100,000, then $20,000 is tax-exempt income in computing the company's tax liability. There is no tax benefit to the company for the other 80 per cent.

Effective tax rates on total income from investments and from insurance underwriting are affected by several other conditions and some companies have much higher effective rates of the federal income tax than others. In any particular instance it is necessary to know a company's effective rate in order to determine the need for securities with tax exemption. But the general effect of the system of taxation of life companies is to reduce the attractiveness of tax-exempt securities. In the language of our system of constraints, this constraint is slight.

Because life insurance companies are long-term investors, they have a particularly pronounced need for securities with strong call protection or deep discount from par during periods of relatively high interest rates. When these institutions are able to buy corporate bonds yielding high rates, they want to be able to hold these bonds to maturity and not have them called in the next period of low interest rates when funds could be re-invested only at much lower rates.

INVESTMENT POLICIES OF LIFE INSURANCE COMPANIES

After studying the investment constraints on life insurance companies and reflecting on the kinds of policies necessary to comply with those restraints and still obtain the best possible return on investment funds, you could almost write a general description of life insurance investment policies with no information at all about the policies they actually follow in managing their security portfolios. You would conclude logically that most of their investments would consist of fixed-income obligations, that they would be acquired initially as long-term issues, that they would not be highly marketable securities, that most investments would be fully taxable under the federal income tax law and that investments generally would be held to maturity or to redemption. And thus you would have inferred in broad outline the investment policies these companies would follow.

TABLE 23–3

The Security Portfolios of U.S. Life Insurance Companies (in millions; end of 1971)

Kind	*Amounts*	*Percentage of total*
Bonds		
U. S. government and federal agencies	$ 4,455	4.0%
Foreign government and international agency	3,182	2.9
U. S. state and local	3,363	3.0
Corporate notes and bonds	79,198	71.5
Total bonds	90,198	81.4
Stocks		
Common	16,779	15.1
Preferred	3,828	3.5
Total stocks	20,607	18.6
Total securities	110,805	100.0

Source: *Life Insurance Fact Book, 1972, op. cit.*

The distribution of the securities investments of all U.S. legal reserve life companies among the several principal categories of securities is shown in Table 23–3.

The Financial Abilities Risk in Constructing the Portfolio

The level of financial risk assumed by the life insurance companies is relatively low in that more than 80 per cent of their security holdings are debt obligations. There are no data on the proportions of bonds bearing the several different ratings provided by the rating organizations, but it is a reasonable inference from the rules governing eligibility of securities for investment and from the valuation rules that a large part of their bond investments are in grades equal to triple A to triple B, with some smaller portion having financial risk equal to lower ratings.

By far the most important category of security investments is corporate bonds. The life companies supply a large part of the long-term funds required by business firms and their aggregate holdings of corporate obligations are much larger than the total for any other kind of investing institution. Corporate bonds have constituted about three-fourths of total security investments in recent years. Within the general category of corporate bonds, investments in obligations of industrial companies are the largest segment. The relatively large proportion of industrial bonds reflects to some extent the vigorous efforts of some of the companies in the area of private placements. In recent years a large percentage of the corporate bonds purchased by life companies have come through the private placement route. Many of these issues are obligations of smaller companies that might experience some disadvantage in financing by public offering, and frequently the life companies obtain some form of equity participation with private placements. It is not uncommon for the insurance companies to purchase bonds convertible into common stocks of the issuers on favorable terms, or to obtain rights to purchase shares of the common stocks of the issuers at specified prices that afford an opportunity for a higher rate of return.

There is a distinct trend in the portfolios of most life companies in the direction of investing a larger portion of their funds in common and preferred stocks. This trend has followed liberalization of state laws limiting ownership of stocks and the relatively favorable experience of investors generally with common stocks. At the end of 1971, stock (of both classes) owned by the insurance companies represented 9.3 per cent of total assets as compared with approximately 5 per cent at the end of 1961. Common stocks now represent about 15 per cent of the total securities portfolios of the life companies.

Holdings of low-financial-risk obligations of the U.S. government and federal agencies are small and municipal issues make up only 3 per cent of the total.

Risk is broadly distributed among security issues of life insurance companies. For the most part they have no alternative; they must own hundreds of issues in order to invest the large amounts of funds they manage. The larger companies have at times bought entire bond issues in amounts of $100 million or more, but even these amounts represent but a small fraction of 1 per cent of their total assets. Investment managers generally avoid placing any very significant percentage of their resources in any one issue or group of closely related issues.

The Uncertainty of Interest Rates in Constructing the Portfolio

The life insurance companies with their strong tenure of ownership and system of securities valuation are not overly concerned about fluctuations in market prices of bonds. They are defensive in that they own obligations with a wide range of maturities. This system of maturity distribution, however, is more a product of regularly buying long-maturity issues and holding them until redeemed than it is to a deliberate spacing of maturities. Because the size of their portfolios has grown steadily, their maturity distributions tend to be more heavily weighted with the longer maturities; they buy larger amounts of bonds each year.

This system of buying long-term obligations and holding them provides an average annual rate of return on bonds that is an average of the rates at which purchases were made weighted by the amounts purchased. The effect has been a steady increase in the average rate in recent years as the trend of interest rates has been upward.

The life insurance companies have no need for large primary and secondary reserves such as those maintained by banks. Their strong cash inflow relative to outflow virtually eliminates the possibility of forced sale to obtain cash. Generally, their cash holdings are no larger than the amount required for operating balances and usually represent less than 1 per cent of total assets. Investments in U.S. Treasury issues and federal agency issues due within 1 year also amount to less than 1 per cent of total assets and less than 2 per cent of total securities.

The Desirability of Ownership Qualities

We have observed that the life companies have little need for the more highly marketable securities in constructing their portfolios. It is this lack of constraint that makes it possible for them to engage in the practice of buying securities by direct placement. These directly placed issues are not marketable at all in the usual sense of that term, but they can be sold to other institutional investors by private transactions. This is a striking example of investors taking advantage of a lack of constraint to maximize returns. Of course, the corporate bonds the companies buy from public offerings are marketable and the marketability grade of the larger public issues is relatively high.

Tax-exempt securities play a small role in life company investments because the tax law affords them so little benefit from the tax exemption of municipal bonds. Some companies buy these issues when the expected rate of return compares favorably with those obtainable in the market on corporate issues.

Life companies are more concerned with the qualities of *redeemability* and *deepness of discount* than any other major category of investors. This concern stems from their policy of investing in long-term bonds, of holding to maturity, and of seeking to maximize investment income. Accordingly, the life companies have generally directed their funds into issues that are high grade in redeemability or in deepness of discount. In arranging private placements they have insisted on strong call protection by making bonds non-callable for a period of years, or callable only at high premiums. In the case of issues maturing serially, they have sometimes used low coupon rates on the longer maturities and priced these maturities at large discounts from principal amounts to be repaid. The deep discounts make it very expensive for issuers to redeem these bonds before maturity.

Policies Toward Price Fluctuations

In managing their portfolios, life insurance companies are highly defensive. More than any other major type of institutional investor they buy regularly at the prices obtaining in the market and hold to maturity, or over long time periods. In fact, the conditions under which they operate make it impractical to do anything else to any great extent.

One condition is the steady inflow of premium payments on which they must accrue interest for policy reserves. Accruals start when funds are received. If funds are not invested, they earn nothing and liabilities increase more than assets. The same is true of the continuous inflow of funds from amortization and repayment of obligations in which policy reserves have been invested. The money must be quickly re-invested and made to earn interest because interest continues to accrue. Thus it is that the life companies are buyers of bonds almost every day; they cannot afford to wait very long for lower prices or higher yields. By force of circumstances they practice time diversification in buying and settle for the average of yields prevailing in the market from time to time.

There are, of course exceptions to the defensive policy rule. Life investment officers are men of diverse views who endeavor in all sorts of ways to earn a little higher rate of net return on assets. In a period of low interest rates funds becoming available for investment are sometimes invested to some extent in short maturities, because investment officers believe that interest rates will soon rise. They speculate on the rise in rates by accepting the lower yields obtainable during such a period on short-term obligations with the object of realizing higher rates on long-term issues when these temporary investments mature and the funds are permanently invested. However, the constraints we have previously observed prevent use of any very large amounts of funds for such a policy.

In managing their common-stock investments the life companies struggle with the same problems of determining when stocks are cheap and should be bought, and when stocks are dear and should be sold. But in this area, too, they are generally defensive. They buy common stocks for long-term investment and hold them for as long as prospects appear satisfactory. Some life companies use formula-timing plans in an effort to realize gains from cyclical fluctuations in stock prices, but such plans have often been abandoned when they required sale of stock at times when management did not believe that stocks should be sold. Some companies apply the dollar-averaging principle by using some fixed amount of money per period of time for purchases of stock; some use a periodic amount that varies inversely with the level of stock prices.

Adapting Policies to the Terms of the Market

The aggregate data for all life insurance companies show a distinct tendency to adapt security portfolios and, indeed, their total asset portfolios, to the terms of the market. Over a period of years they have steadily reduced their holdings of government securities both in absolute amount and in percentage of total assets because higher yields were obtainable from other investment media. Since enactment of the special federal income tax provisions for taxation of insurance companies, they have also reduced their holdings of municipal obligations in amount and in percentage, because other kinds of investments have provided higher yields than the tax-equivalent yields on municipals.

Although the proportion of corporate obligations has fluctuated in a relatively narrow range, larger amounts of these issues have been purchased by the direct placement method because interest rates and equity participations have provided larger expected rates of return. Finally, they have moved increasingly into common-stock investments in an effort to realize larger rates of return from dividends and price appreciation.

Life Insurance Portfolios Demonstrate the Effect of Investment Constraints

The survey of life insurance investments illustrates again how investment policies of institutional investors are influenced by their ability to assume risk and to accept lower grades of securities in the desirability of ownership qualities. Sometimes differences in the terms on which they hold funds for investment that might not seem very important to a casual observer have a strong influence on investment policies.

If you look at the balance sheets of life insurance companies and compare them with the statements of commercial banks, you might conclude that there is little difference between the two in ability to assume financial risk. The chief differences in investment policies are a result of the extreme difference in tenure of ownership of securities. The commercial banks must be prepared continuously to repay a substantial part of their liabilities; this is not so for the life companies. Thus, the life companies can invest almost all of their funds in long-term obligations with a high degree of confidence that they can hold them to maturity, whereas the banks must maintain large liquid asset reserves. Ability to assume financial risk and interest-rate risk is strengthened by the system of valuing most life company assets at cost. This basis of valuation is more important to the insurance companies than to the banks because there is so little chance that securities will have to be sold and market values realized. However, the need for stability of investment income is greater for life companies than for banks because of the system of accruing interest at an assumed rate on policy and annuity reserves.

It is not surprising, then, that the securities portfolios of life insurance companies have a vastly different appearance from portfolios of commercial banks. Whereas the banks are constrained to commit a large part of their funds for security investment to government obligations—and most of it to short maturities—the life insurance companies own chiefly corporate obligations purchased as long maturities. In contrast to banks, the life companies have little need for highly marketable securities. We also found that differences in the system of federal income taxation result in a vast difference in the role that municipals play in the structure of their portfolios.

Aggressiveness on the part of the insurance companies takes the form of seeking out investment opportunities with favorable yield/risk ratios rather than trying to realize capital gains by purchases and sales of securities in the market. In fact the conditions under which they invest strongly deter aggressiveness in the market and almost compel a defensive policy of investing their money as it comes in on a day-by-day basis and holding securities to redemption or maturity.

QUESTIONS FOR DISCUSSION

1. Are those large amounts that appear in the financial statements of life insurance companies with the designation "policy reserves" actually liabilities?
2. What is there in the income statements of life insurance companies that corresponds to "interest on deposits" in the income statements of commercial banks?
3. Why are the liabilities of life insurance companies so stable around a rising trend?
4. Is the treatment of interest on municipal bonds owned by life insurance companies consistent with the general principle that such interest is tax exempt under the Internal Revenue Code?
5. If life insurance companies should realize unusually high rates of return on their invested assets during a period of price inflation, would owners of life insurance policies and annuities receive any benefit in constant dollars?
6. Life insurance companies don't have to worry about cyclical fluctuations in interest rates. Either affirm or deny this statement.
7. Why do life companies engage in the rather difficult and time-consuming process of negotiating private placements of securities?
8. How does the system of valuing securities owned by life companies serve to deter investment in securities at the higher levels of financial risk?
9. The text doesn't say much about the mortgage loans that comprise a large segment of life insurance company assets, but what can you infer about the financial risk and interest-rate risk in this type of asset that is relevant to the companies' policies in constructing their securities portfolios.
10. Life companies are major buyers of corporate bonds publicly offered by investment bankers, and these are securities of good grade in marketability. Why should they buy these bonds when they can buy bonds by direct placement?

24

Investment Companies and Their Investment Policies

I. The nature of investment companies

II. Open-end investment companies
   A. The issuance and redemption of shares
   B. Shareholders' services
   C. Management and costs of operation
   D. The mutual fund principle as a financial innovation

III. Closed-end investment companies

IV. The regulation of investment companies
   A. The Investment Companies Act
   B. Tax legislation

V. The investment policies of investment companies
   A. The principal investment constraints
   B. The financial incentives of management
   C. Investment policies of open-end companies
   D. Investment policies of closed-end companies

VI. Investment company securities for the small investor
   A. Whether to choose investment company shares
   B. Which investment company to choose?

Investment companies are firms engaged solely in the business of investing in securities; investing is their only activity and reason for being. In this primary and exclusive concern with investment these companies differ sharply from the other kinds of institutions we have studied. Banks are operated primarily to make loans and to provide a variety of banking services; investment in securities is distinctly secondary. The main business of the insurance companies is to underwrite risks; they invest only the funds that come into their hands in the conduct of the insurance business. The business of investment companies is not only restricted to investment but principally to securities of the kind that are regularly bought and sold in the security markets.

THE NATURE OF INVESTMENT COMPANIES

The typical investment company is simply a business corporation without a special charter or special powers such as those of banks and insurance companies. It sells its own securities to the investing public and re-invests the proceeds in a portfolio of securities. A share of common stock in an investment company is a fractional interest, after liabilities and whatever prior claims there may be, in the securities owned by the company.

Investment companies used to be called *investment trusts*, and that term is still sometimes used. The reason for the older name is that many of the early investment companies were organized as business trusts under a Massachusetts statute. However, it soon became clear that the purposes of such an enterprise could be accomplished just as well under the regular business corporation statutes, and therefore the corporate form of organization has come to be widely used. The term *companies* is actually preferable to *trusts* because the latter has the implication of an arrangement such as the personal trust, which may mislead people into thinking that these companies operate under laws governing personal trusts. Even companies organized under declarations of trust are not fiduciary arrangements according to the law of personal trusts, and their trustees have only the duties and responsibilities of corporate directors generally.

The history of investment companies begins with companies organized in the early nineteenth century in Europe for the purpose of investing in securities. They began to be established and promoted on a significant scale in the United States during the 1920's. Since then American ingenuity has devised and developed several versions of the original concept and several kinds have become particularly American institutions.

The early investment companies were of a kind now known as *managed closed-end companies*. In general, they are organized and operated much like business corporations—that is, they sell their securities to the investing public and invest the proceeds in a portfolio of securities. They are called *managed* because they manage their portfolios—buying and selling securities from time to time according to their judgment of which securities are most advantageous to own. They are described as *closed-end* because they do not continuously offer their own securities for sale. They raise their capital by an offering of their own stock in the same manner as business corporations generally.

The American innovation in investment companies is a kind known as *managed open-end companies*, or *mutual funds*. They, too, manage their portfolios like any other investor. What distinguishes them from the closed-end companies is that they continuously offer their shares for sale to the public and continuously redeem their own shares on demand by shareholders. Under federal law they are not permitted to issue securities other than common stock.

A third kind of investment company is known as a *fixed trust*, or *unit investment trust*. Its distinguishing characteristic is that its portfolio of securities is selected at the time it is organized and is not subsequently changed, except as bonds may be redeemed and in certain other stipulated circumstances. Thus, it is unmanaged, or fixed. The fixed trusts were very popular in the 1930's and then fell into disfavor with investors. In recent years, however, this form of organization has been used for tax-exempt bond funds. Municipal securities are deposited with a bank as trustee and the sponsor (usually an investment banking firm) sells to investors units representing fractional undivided interests in the portfolio. This type of organization also continues to be used for trusts that invest in securities of other investment companies.

A fourth variation of the investment company is known as *face amount certificate* companies. Their distinguishing feature is the sale of periodic payment plan certificates for certain face amounts of money. Buyers contract to make payments over a specified period of years. Funds raised in this manner are invested in securities and face amounts of certificates are paid from income and principal derived from the portfolio.

A more recent innovation is a kind of investment company that issues two classes of shares. One class is entitled to receive all income from the portfolio after expenses and the other class receives the capital gains. These are called *dual purpose investment companies*.

As students of investments we are interested in investment companies because they have security portfolios to be managed, they are important customers of broker-dealer firms, and they generally play an important role in the security markets. We are also interested in them as institutional intermediaries for investment in securities. The instruments they issue, that is, their shares, have become important investment media for individual investors and even for some institutional investors.

OPEN-END INVESTMENT COMPANIES

We will examine the open-end investment companies first because they have a much larger amount of assets than do the other types of investment companies and their shares are of greater interest to most investors. The first open-end companies were organized in 1924, but they failed to gain much favor with investors during the 1920's and suffered along with other kinds of investment companies during the depressed security markets of the 1930's. Their growth began in about 1940 with the passage of the Investment Companies Act in that year and with enactment of legislation exempting them from the corporate income tax provided certain conditions of the tax law were met by the companies.

For a period of about 25 years up until 1968 these companies experienced a remarkable growth in the aggregate value of their assets. They were aided by an increasingly prosperous society, a steadily rising trend of stock prices, and a large corps of salesmen. From a value of only a little more than $1 billion in the mid-forties, their aggregate assets increased to a peak of $55 billion in 1968. The bear market that began toward the end of 1968 reduced asset values considerably and increased the sales resistance of investors. At the end of 1972 total assets had increased again to a new high level of about $60 billion.[1]

The Issuance and Redemption of Shares

The shares of open-end companies are sold to the public at their net asset value per share plus, in most instances, a selling, or "loading," charge. Net asset value per share is the market value of total assets minus liabilities divided by the number of shares outstanding. The selling charge covers the cost of distribution. Most companies compute the net asset value of their shares daily on the basis of market prices. If an investor wants to buy shares he has to pay an amount equal to the net asset value per share at the time plus the selling charge.

Most open-end companies have an affiliated organization that sells their shares. It is known as a *distributor*, or *principal underwriter*. The investment company sells its shares to the underwriter at net asset value. Most underwriters offer shares to investors through independent broker-dealer firms all around the country. The greater part of the selling charge goes to the retailer and the underwriter retains the smaller part for his services. However, some underwriters have their own retail organizations and sell directly to investors.

The selling charge varies somewhat from one fund to another, but usually it is in the range of 7½ to 8½ per cent of the total amount paid, including the charge. This means that if you invest $1,000 in mutual fund shares, $75 to $85 is deducted for the selling charge and the balance is applied to purchase of shares at their net asset value. An 8½ per cent selling charge is equal to one-twelfth of the total outlay for shares. A 1970 amendment to the Investment Company Act authorized the Securities and Exchange Commission to make rules regulating the size of the sales load so that it not be excessive, but it delegates this regulation to the National Association of Securities Dealers. The sales charge covers the cost to the investor not only of purchasing but also of redemption. At the usual rate of sale charge, the transactions cost is about the same as that for investing a moderate amount of principal directly in a diversified list of stocks.

[1]Data are for companies that are members of the Investment Company Institute. The Institute publishes a monthly statistical report showing total net assets at month-end as well as sales and redemptions of shares.

There are, however, a number of open-end companies that sell their shares with no charge, or only a nominal charge. They are commonly known as "no load" funds. They are sponsored usually by investment counsel firms that perform the management function for them. Investors buy their shares by sending orders by mail to the sponsoring firms. In recent years there has been a considerable increase in the proportion of total mutual fund assets owned by no-load companies, and some companies that previously made a sales charge have converted to no-load funds.

A second distinctive feature of mutual funds is that they stand ready to redeem their shares at net asset value on request by shareholders. You have only to send in your shares for redemption in order to get your money. Federal law requires that when shares are ready to be transferred back to the company, payment must be made within 7 days. Some funds also have the right to make a small charge for redemption, but actually make no charge.

Shareholders' Services

In the competition for investors' dollars, the mutual funds have developed several services designed to make their shares attractive to investors and to encourage further investment by people who own their shares. One widely used arrangement is termed an *accumulation plan*. The voluntary accumulation plan, which is most common, is an informal arrangement whereby anyone who has made an initial investment may undertake to invest additional sums at more or less regular intervals. The normal sales charge is made on shares sold in this way, except, of course, that there is no charge by the no-load funds. Although investors who use voluntary accumulation plans fill out a form indicating their intention, there is no obligation to continue to buy shares. The amount invested periodically may be changed, and an accumulation plan can be discontinued at any time. Apparently, though, the adoption of a voluntary plan provides some psychological stimulus to continued purchase of shares, because about 40 per cent of total shareholder accounts are of the accumulation type.[2]

Mutual funds also encourage their shareholders to invest their dividends in additional shares and most offer some kind of re-investment arrangement whereby their dividends are automatically applied to the purchase of additional shares. Some funds require a minimum holding of shares for automatic re-investment and some do not. Some invest dividends at the regular offering price for shares, and some invest at net asset value per share.

Most mutual funds offer regular withdrawal plans. These plans permit investors to receive their dividend income in regular monthly amounts, or to receive larger amounts periodically by gradually liquiding shares, or to receive periodic payments in fluctuating amounts based on the current value of the account. Some funds limit the withdrawal service to investors who own shares worth not less than $10,000 and they usually require that the minimum periodic withdrawal be not less than $50.

[2]1971 Mutual Fund Fact Book, Investment Company Institute, Washington, D. C., p. 26.

The voluntary accumulation plans described above should not be confused with contractual plans for face amount certificates offered by some funds. An investor who buys a contractual plan undertakes to invest a specified amount of money periodically, usually monthly, for a period of 5, 10, or 15 years. The sales charge is based on the total amount required to be invested under a contract. The Investment Companies Act limits the sales load to 9 per cent of the total amount of the contract, and not more than 20 per cent of the load may be deducted from payments made during the first year, or more than 16 per cent during the first 4 years. There is an alternative arrangement that permits as much as 50 per cent of the load to be deducted during the first year, but investors have a right to refund all of their money within 45 days after sale or at any time within the next 18 months with a sales charge of 16 per cent.

Management and Costs of Operation

Open-end companies are managed by their directors, or by trustees in the case of companies organized under a declaration of trust. However, it is common practice in the industry for companies to employ as an adviser another firm that performs the function of investment management and takes care of some administrative tasks. Some adviser firms are engaged in the general business of advising mutual fund companies and serve as advisers to more than one mutual fund. The management of open-end companies is highly concentrated in several large adviser firms.

Thus, the mutual fund industry is characterized by a three-part structure. First there is the fund, with its directors or trustees, which owns the portfolio of securities. Next there is the adviser, which manages the portfolio under contract with the fund. Third is the distributor organization, which has a contract with the fund for distributing its shares. Generally all three parts are under the control of a person or small group of persons who exercise control by ownership, or by proxies from shareholders, or both. Frequently the functions of adviser and distributor are combined in one company, which is known as a *mutual fund management company*. Contracts for advisory service and for the distribution service must be renewed each year.

The fee paid by mutual funds to their investment advisers used to be ½ of 1 per cent per annum of total assets at market value. However, there was considerable critical comment to the effect that this percentage was too high and some mutual fund management companies reduced their fees to ½ of 1 per cent on a specified amount of market value, to ⅜ths of 1 per cent on an amount in excess of the amount to which the first rate applies, and to ¼th of 1 per cent on additional amounts.

The 1970 amendment to the Investment Company Act endeavored to solve the problem of what management fee is justified by providing that the management of a fund has a fiduciary responsibility to its shareholders with respect to the management fee it pays. This means, in effect, that the directors are trustees for the shareholders and must safeguard their interests in a fiduciary capacity. It is also provided that the terms of an advisory contract must be approved by vote of a majority of directors who are not parties to the contract or interested persons of any party. A shareholder who feels that a fund has been paying too much for management services can sue the manager in court or the Securities and Exchange Commission may sue on behalf of shareholders.

The total expense of operation, which includes some expenses other than the investment management fee, is generally measured by annual total expenses as a percentage of average market value of the portfolio. For many funds this ratio is about ½ of 1 per cent, but it is higher for some and lower for others.

The Mutual Fund Principle as a Financial Innovation

It may not be an exaggeration to say that the development of the principle of the mutual fund is one of the great financial innovations of the twentieth century. It has provided an entirely new kind of financial instrument for investors, and one that seems particularly appropriate to a private enterprise economy characterized by widespread ownership of securities, considerable government management of the economy, and a rising price level. We have observed how the principle has been adapted to the variable annuity and is currently being adapted to variable life insurance policies. We will subsequently see how it is applied in the common trust funds of commercial banks.

For a long period of history there have been financial institutions that receive funds from buyers of their instruments and invest the proceeds in one way or another. Their instruments are bank deposits, insurance policies, savings and loan accounts, and similar obligations payable in fixed dollar amounts. Holders of such instruments for the most part are not affected by the investment experience of the issuers—they get their money back dollar for dollar. As an important exception, the rate of interest or dividend received by holders of some kinds of instruments has varied with the rate of return earned by the institutions that held their funds. None, however, provided an opportunity for investors to participate directly in ownership of diversified portfolios of securities. These portfolios, when composed largely or entirely of common stocks, have provided larger returns over long periods —in both current and constant dollars—than fixed dollar amount obligations of financial institutions.

CLOSED-END INVESTMENT COMPANIES

The closed-end investment company is the European version that was imported to the United States in the 1920's. This kind of organization enjoyed great popularity in the several years preceding the stock market crash of 1929 and then was threatened with extinction by the subsequent steep decline in common-stock prices. Generally, the closed-end companies fared worse than the open-end companies because most of them had issued senior securities—that is, bonds or preferred stock, or both. These senior securities were issued to provide financial leverage for their common stockholders in expectation of more or less continuously rising prices for the stocks in their investment portfolios. When market prices turned sharply downward, the value of portfolios often became less than the amount of their senior securities outstanding. Many companies were liquidated, some were merged with others, and some survived without merger. Those that came through this period of distress have generally fared very well. Most of them have eliminated their bond and preferred stock issues and financial leverage is no longer one of their general characteristics.

Two relatively new kinds of closed-end investment companies with specialized functions have recently appeared: small-business investment companies organized to provide funds for direct purchase of the securities of small companies, and real estate investment trusts for the purpose of investing in the ownership of real estate or obligations based on real estate. Both of these types of investment companies are governed by special legislation authorizing their organization. The rest of the discussion of closed-end companies refers only to the older kinds of companies.

The closed-end companies have had a much slower rate of growth than the open-end companies and their combined assets are but a small fraction of the huge amounts accumulated by the mutual funds. The slower growth of the closed-end companies relative to mutual funds is largely attributed to the fact that their shares are not sold as aggressively. After initial public distribution, closed-end company shares are bought and sold among investors in the same manner as other marketable stocks. Some are listed on the exchanges and a broker who executes an order in a listed issue gets the same commission he would on any other order for a listed stock for an equivalent amount of money. In the over-the-counter market these stocks are traded in the same manner as other kinds of securities.

The structure of closed-end companies is simpler than that of most mutual funds. Some are managed by their directors and officers with no external adviser and of course no distributor. Others are managed by advisers in much the same manner as open-end funds. Expense ratios vary widely from a small fraction of 1 per cent to more than 1 per cent of total portfolio values, but most fall within the range of ½ to 1 per cent.

Since closed-end companies do not continuously issue and redeem their shares, they cannot offer accumulation and withdrawal plans in the same manner as the mutual funds; however, shares of closed-end companies listed on the New York Stock Exchange can be purchased by regular periodic payments under the Exchange's Monthly Investment Plan. Plans for automatic re-investment of dividends are offered by several of the companies, with shareholders' payments used to purchase the companies' shares in the market.

The absence of an arrangement for continuous issue and redemption of shares means that they do not sell on the basis of net asset value, but at whatever prices people are willing to pay and receive in the market. The market price may be more, or less, than net asset value. The shares of most closed-end companies have more often sold at a discount from net asset value than at a premium. The principal reason for the discount is that capitalization of per share earnings at the going rate in the market for the risk represented by the company's securities portfolio provides an amount less than net asset value per share. What makes the difference is the deduction of the company's operating expenses from gross income to arrive at net earnings applicable to the stock. The capitalization rate for per share earnings ought to be about the same as the rate that the market applies to securities representing the same level of risk as the closed-end company's portfolio. This rate, however, is not applied to the total portfolio return but to total return minus operating expenses. The effect is a lower market value for the closed-end company shares than the net asset value per share at current market prices. Another explanation is that investors prefer the certainty of redemption of open-end company shares at net asset value to the uncertainty of market prices for the closed-end company shares.

There are, of course, many variations from the generalization that closed-end company shares sell at a discount from their net asset value. When investors are optimistic about future returns on an investment company's portfolio, they may capitalize a larger amount of per share earnings than the amount currently reported, or they may apply a lower capitalization rate to current per share earnings. Thus market price may equal or exceed net asset value per share. Conversely, when investors are especially pessimistic the discount becomes larger.

THE REGULATION OF INVESTMENT COMPANIES

We have previously made brief reference to certain provisions of the Investment Companies Act, but a proper understanding of the development of this type of institution requires a more complete description of the statute. Prior to 1940, when the Law was enacted, the investment companies had a relatively poor record, and there was evidence of abuses affecting the public interest. The new Law and the supervision by the Securities and Exchange Commission that it provided gave the investment companies a new lease on life and helped establish the base for subsequent growth.

At about the same time, legislation was enacted granting investment companies exemption from the federal corporate income tax, on compliance with conditions provided by law. Tax exemption was a great boon to the investment company industry and it also contributed to the regulatory framework under which the companies subsequently developed.

The Investment Companies Act

The Investment Companies Act of 1940 has three main purposes. One is to give the public access to all material information about each investment company. Following both the principle and the method of the Securities Act, this legislation requires each investment company that has more than 100 securityholders or that proposes a public offering of its securities in interstate commerce to file a registration statement with the SEC.

The statement must give complete and accurate information about the company, its officers and directors, and its business affiliations; this includes full details of any management contract with investment advisers, and any contract with a distributor of the company's securities. The business affiliations of the company's directors (or trustees) and officers must be revealed along with the exact amount of compensation each has received from the company in the last fiscal period. The registration statement includes a complete list of the securities owned by the company, with the amount or number of shares of each, and the usual financial statements prepared in accordance with SEC regulations. After a company is registered, it must keep this information up to date. The requirement of a prospectus was also applied to investment companies. Each buyer of newly issued shares must be given a current prospectus and prospectuses must be up-dated from time to time. A further requirement is that companies issue quarterly reports to their shareholders showing the securities they own and their market value. Issues bought or sold during a quarter must also be indicated. Full and frequent disclosure of information has done much to win investor confidence in mutual fund shares.

A second main purpose of the Investment Company Act is to prevent exploitation of the companies by persons in position of control or by parties particularly interested in their operation. No registered investment company may have a board of directors of which more than 60 per cent are interested parties. In opposite terms, at least 40 per cent of the directors must be outside directors. This requirement is modified for no-load companies and those that have a sales load of not more than 2 per cent. Provided certain conditions are met, these companies are required to have no more than one outside director.

One study of mutual funds expressed doubt about the effectiveness of the requirement concerning outside directors. It pointed out that the terms of the law do not bar from the category of outside directors persons who are friends, relatives, or business associates of interested parties and that the selection of outside directors is in the hands of the interested parties.[3]

There are, however, stringent provisions against "self-dealing" by directors and officers and against the holding by these persons of any positions that involve conflicts with their proper interest in the investment company. There is also the requirement that no investment company may offer its securities to the public unless it already has capital funds of at least $100,000. This rules out irresponsible promoters and "shoestring operators."

Finally, the Investment Company Act goes beyond the requirement of full publicity and the safeguards against improper management to impose some specific limitations on the policies of investment companies. One group of limitations applies to the companies' capital structures. Open-end companies are permitted to issue only one class of securities—common stock. Closed-end companies may issue bonds only if their assets have a value at

[3] *A Study of Mutual Funds Prepared for the Securities and Exchange Commission by the Wharton School of Finance and Commerce*, Report of the Committee on Interstate and Foreign Commerce, Washington, D. C., 1962, U. S. Government Printing Office, p. 8.

least three times as great as the amount of their bonds, and they may issue preferred stock only if it is covered at least twice by assets.

Other limitations apply to investment policy. Companies that register as "diversified investment companies," as most of them do, must diversify the investment of at least 75 per cent of their assets, with cash and government securities counting as diversified investments. In the diversified portion a company may invest not more than 5 per cent of its assets in securities of any one issuer and may not own more than 10 per cent of the voting securities of an issuer.

Tax Legislation

In 1936 the mutual funds were exempted from the corporate income tax under certain conditions and in 1943 the exemption was applied to closed-end companies. Presently the provisions exempting both types of companies are embodied in Subchapter M of the Internal Revenue Code. The basic philosophy of Subchapter M is that a company that is strictly an intermediary between investors and the ownership of securities shall not be liable to the federal corporation income tax. In order to limit the exemption of companies of this nature, the regulation establishes a number of conditions that a company must meet to qualify as a "regulated investment company" under the Internal Revenue Code. First, a company must be registered with the SEC under the Investment Company Act. Second, it must indicate to the Bureau of Internal Revenue that it elects to be a regulated investment company, and once this decision is made it is irrevocable. Almost all open-end companies and most closed-end companies have so elected. The provisions of Subchapter M also set up boundaries within which an investment company must operate in order to be qualified for tax exemption.

A regulated investment company for tax purposes must be engaged primarily in investment. Specifically, it must derive at least 90 per cent of its gross income from interest, dividends, and gains from securities. It must be mainly an investment company and not a holding company; not more than 25 per cent of total assets may be invested in securities of controlled companies. Investment policy is further affected by the condition that no more than 30 per cent of gross income for any year may consist of gains on sales of securities held for less than 3 months.

The other main requirement is that a regulated company pay out at least 90 per cent of its net income, exclusive of capital gains, each tax year. Any income retained within the 10 per cent limit is subject to the corporation income tax. Capital gains may be retained, or paid out. If retained, they are subject to the corporation income tax. If paid out, they are subject to taxation as capital gains in the hands of the investment company's shareholders. Regulated investment companies always indicate the amount of any dividend derived from capital gains so that shareholders may take such amounts into their personal income tax computations as capital gains rather than as regular income. An amendment to Subchapter M permits a procedure whereby an investment company may retain its capital gains and pay the corporate income tax thereon. Any shareholder of such a company who is subject to a lower tax rate on his share of the capital gains as personal income than is the investment company may then take credit on his personal income tax for the difference between the amount paid by the company on his pro rata share of the capital gains and the amount he has to pay as personal income tax on his share of the capital gains.

These provisions of the federal income tax law have had a pronounced influence on the evolution of investment companies, particularly on the open-end type, which began to conform with the tax regulation several years before the Investment Company Act was passed. In general they have tended to make the experience of investors in investment company shares more like the experience investors would have if they invested directly in the securities that comprise the investment company portfolios.

THE INVESTMENT POLICIES OF INVESTMENT COMPANIES

Our study of investment companies now provides a basis for examining the conditions and considerations that influence their investment policies. These conditions are similar for both open-end and closed-end companies. Where they are different, we will point out the differences as we go along.

The Principal Investment Constraints

The open-end companies and most of the closed-end companies are in the remarkable position, among financial institutions, of having no appreciable amount of liabilities. Their only debts are current liabilities incurred chiefly in the process of buying and selling securities, and they constitute a relatively small percentage of total assets. Thus, there is a very large margin of equity capital; almost the entire right-hand side of the balance sheet is represented by outstanding common stock. So far as the use of assets to support liabilities is concerned, these companies have very little need for stability of market value of principal in their security portfolios.

Some of the closed-end companies are in a different position in that they do have liabilities in the form of bonds, or senior securities in the form of preferred stock. In terms of the value of assets, they require a minimum investment value of portfolio at current market value equal to not less than the amount of debt or preferred stock. As a practical matter this constraint is not severe; most closed-end companies have retired their senior securities, or greatly reduced the amount of these issues.

The same kind of analysis shows very moderate need for stability of investment income as far as minimum expense requirements are concerned. The operating expenses of open-end investment companies, we have observed, usually amount to less than 1 per cent of the market value of their assets. With investment income usually at the rate of 3 to 5 per cent on their assets, the expense requirement is a relatively small portion—usually in the range of one-eighth to one-fourth of investment income. From the financial viewpoint this is not a serious constraint. Closed-end companies that have senior securities in their capitalization have the additional requirement of covering interest or dividends on such issues, but few of them have sufficient leverage for this condition to be seriously restrictive.

The tenure of ownership of portfolio securities by closed-end companies is stronger than that of open-end companies. All the funds of closed-end companies, except small current liabilities, represent permanent capital that is not subject to withdrawal at the desire of those who have supplied it or because of some contingency that may arise in the regular operation of the business. Those companies that have leverage may need to apply funds from time to time to repay bonds or retire preferred stock, but usually such payments are regularly scheduled and are not large relative to amounts of assets. Closed-end company managers are in the comfortable position, after their financing has been completed, of being able to manage a fund with a very small liquidity requirement.

The tenure of ownership of open-end companies is quite different, because they have the obligation to redeem their shares on request of shareholders. It is easy to imagine that in a period of business recession and declining stock prices, a mutual fund might have to redeem its shares in large amounts and, therefore, have to liquidate a sizable portion of its securities portfolio. This contingency is not, however, so bad as it might seem. For one thing, liquidation in this manner at depressed prices would not cause loss to an investment company as it would to a life insurance company or a bank. The amounts that would have to be paid to shareholders vary with changes in market value of portfolio—they are entitled only to net asset value at current market prices. If securities must be sold at a loss to meet demand for redemption of shares, it is the withdrawing shareholders who take the loss. The other mitigating condition is the continual sale of new shares by the mutual funds. As long as the cash inflow from shares sold exceeds the cash required for shares redeemed, there is no need for liquidating portfolio securities.

The quality of management of investment companies generally must be rated good to excellent. Both types of companies are managed by professional investment managers who work full-time at their task, employ specialized personnel for financial analysis, and have access to a wide range of investment information. This does not mean that they obtain equally good results. As a matter of fact, the performance of some funds has been conspicuously poor. For investment companies individually, investment results tend to vary from year to year—sometimes being a little better than average and sometimes falling below the average for similar investment companies. Generally, the quality of management should not constrain the use of whatever investment policies seem appropriate on the basis of other conditions, but in any specific instance the quality of management might well be a subject of inquiry.

Purchasing-power risk is not particularly important from the standpoint of the investment companies, although it may be quite important for their shareholders. The companies are engaged in investing current dollars, receiving returns in current dollars, and making payments to investors who own their stock in current dollars. Their operating expenses may increase with a rise in the general price level, but generally this is not a problem.

As regards marketability we find some difference in constraints between the two kinds of investment companies. Mutual funds clearly need a relatively high degree of marketability for most of the securities in their portfolios. This follows from the obligation to redeem their shares on request of shareholders and from the practice of computing net asset values daily. For the closed-end companies this constraint is slight because of the relative permanence of their capitalization and the fact that they need not frequently price their portfolios.

Subchapter M effectively eliminates a need for securities of high grade in taxability for both types of companies, provided they meet the requirements of this portion of the Internal Revenue Act. Most companies in which there is public interest qualify for tax exemption.

The Financial Incentives of Management

The picture we have drawn of constraints is one of liberal limitations on investment policies. With a few qualifications, it appears that investment companies are free to adopt whatever policies they consider appropriate. However, this is not quite the entire story. The managements of open-end investment companies must sell their merchandise—that is, their shares—in order to realize larger financial rewards for themselves. And they must avoid buying back their merchandise. The closed-end companies with their relatively fixed capitalizations are not in quite the same position, but even in this group the rewards of management are related to their success in realizing good investment returns.

The advisory firms for open-end companies, we have observed, are usually compensated on the basis of the average market value of assets during a given period. Obviously, this kind of arrangement provides a strong incentive toward expansion in value of assets. One way to expand is to obtain appreciation in the market value of securities; this suggests some emphasis in investment policy on capital gains rather than on income. However, another and more consistently practical way for this type of company to expand is to sell more and more shares. An advantage of the latter method for companies that have a sales load is that there is also compensation to be earned by performing the distributive function. In order to sell more shares, a company must look good to the investing public, by reason of both its past record and the present composition of its portfolio. This constitutes an important influence on the investment policies of open-end companies—their shares must appeal to investors.

There are various ways in which an open-end investment company's shares may be made to appear attractive to the investing public, but in general people like to see portfolios composed of securities of well-known companies. Prospectuses, annual reports, and quarterly reports give the full list of securities owned, and prospective investors scan these lists. They like company names they recognize and are doubtful about securities of the more obscure companies. This fact alone causes most open-end companies to restrict their investments largely to the more popular issues that are listed on the organized exchanges and are highly marketable.

Since investors also like to see their dollars grow, a record of appreciation in the value of an investment company's shares is a good selling point. However, many people who buy open-end shares also want regular dividends at a fairly good rate. A low dividend yield on an investment company's shares, or a decrease in amount of dividend from one date to another, makes them harder to sell. Unfortunately, the effort to obtain price appreciation and to provide both liberal and stable dividends involves investment company managements in some conflicting considerations of policy. Sometimes the best prospects for price appreciation are among stocks of companies paying low or highly unstable dividends, but any very large commitment in securities of this kind is likely to result in a low dividend yield or unstable dividend payments on the investment company's shares. Policies directed at appreciation, therefore, tend to be limited by the desire to establish a good dividend record.

The need to make portfolios look good to investors also restricts major changes from common stocks to bonds (or cash), or vice versa, in an effort to profit by estimates of future changes in market prices. If management expects a major decline in common-stock prices, for example, the aggressive policy would be to sell stocks and hold the proceeds in cash or short-term bonds. However, a portfolio with a high proportion of liquid assets is not attractive to the typical investor. A large cash and liquid assets position may also reduce income. A further deterrent is the fact that when a shift is made in anticipation of a major upward or downward movement in market prices for stocks and the movement fails to develop, regularly published reports make the error of judgment all too clearly apparent to an observing public.

Management incentives appear to influence investment policy decisions much more in open-end than in closed-end companies. In the latter there is motivation to do a good job, but still wide latitude for deciding how it shall be done. But in both types of companies there is considerable room for variation in policy, and actually there are many different kinds of investment policies among the open-end as well as the closed-end companies.

Investment Policies of Open-End Companies

The main difference in the policies pursued by investment companies is in the degree of financial risk represented by the securities in their portfolios. They cover the entire risk spectrum. At one end are the companies that invest almost entirely in common stocks of the more speculative variety; at the other are those holding only high-grade bonds. Some diversify broadly; some diversify only within an industry. There are also important differences in the policies of these companies toward price fluctuations. Some are entirely defensive and some endeavor to profit from cyclical price fluctuations by making changes in the composition of their portfolios. Prospectuses for mutual fund shares and for new issues of closed-end company shares always contain a summarized statement of investment policy.

The mutual funds are usually classified on the basis of the kinds of securities that predominate in their portfolio. A system of classification and nomenclature used by Arthur Wiesenberger & Company in its widely used *Investment Companies*, published annually, distinguishes seven kinds of mutual funds. This system also recognizes differences in policies toward price fluctuations.

The most important class on the basis of amount of assets is *diversified common stock funds*. Just as the term indicates, these funds invest almost entirely in common stocks and diversify broadly in this category of securities. They follow a defensive policy for the most part toward cyclical changes in average stock prices by investing net cash inflows as the money comes in and by keeping more or less fully invested all the time, except for small amounts of cash and short-term government securities to provide operating liquidity. Generally, these funds prefer the better known and higher-grade stocks of large companies, but most include some proportion of growth stocks, or stocks that they hope will become growth stocks. Some funds shift from the more cyclical to the less cyclical stocks, or in the opposite direction, according to their judgment of probable future changes in stock prices. Some liquidate a portion of their stocks and invest the proceeds in high-grade bonds in anticipation of a cyclical decline in average stock prices. But these changes are essentially temporary variations from a diversified-common-stocks-for-long-term-investment policy.

Some of the diversified common stock funds indicate in their published statements of investment policy that they place particular emphasis on capital appreciation, and are termed *growth funds*; others are more concerned with liberal income and are known as *income funds*.

A slightly different name is given to a kind of mutual fund that makes more substantial changes in proportions of common stocks and bonds from time to time—they are called *flexibility diversified funds*. These companies invest chiefly in common stocks, but make pronounced shifts to bonds in anticipation of a general decline in stock prices. If their estimate is correct, they avoid some price depreciation. When they are optimistic about stock prices, they sell bonds and buy stocks. Thus they are more aggressive toward price fluctuations than the straight diversified common-stock funds.

A third major category is designated as *balanced funds*. Their distinguishing characteristic is that they regularly hold a substantial part of their assets in the form of bonds and preferred stocks along with common stocks. Their object is to obtain a greater degree of stability of income and net asset value by reason of the bond and preferred stock holdings than would be possible with a straight common-stock portfolio. At the same time they seek long-term appreciation in market values and in size of income from the common stocks. In recent years the balanced funds have invested from 50 to 80 per cent of their assets in common stocks.

A rather heterogeneous group of funds is described by the general term *specialty funds*. The term means simply that their policy in constructing their portfolios is specialized in one way or another. One form of specialization is investment chiefly in common stocks of companies in a particular industry, as distinguished from broad diversification by industry. Some of these industry funds were formed to capitalize on the popularity with investors of certain industries, such as chemicals and electronics. Their specialization, however, is not so restrictive as their names might indicate. Generally, they define the industry of specialization in terms that permit some diversification over related industries.

Bond and preferred-stock funds are often classified as specialty funds. Their specialty is simply that they restrict their investments to either bonds or preferred stocks. The idea is to offer investors participation in whatever kind of portfolio suits them, or an opportunity to make up their own combination of investment company shares from the different specialty funds.

Still another variety of specialty fund is distinguished by a policy of investing in securities of companies domiciled in countries other than the United States. Thus several funds specialize in Canadian issues and some in stocks of European companies.

A kind of fund that does not fit particularly under any of the above terms is one known as a "*swap fund*," or tax-free exchange fund. It is formed by exchanging its shares for large blocks of stocks owned by wealthy individuals. Frequently people whose personal wealth is heavily concentrated in stock of one company want diversification. They can get it by swapping with one of these funds. Such an exchange of stock is free of capital gains tax. The swap funds generally hold mostly common stocks and in the course of a number of swaps achieve a fair degree of diversification.

Investment Policies of Closed-End Companies

In the other principal category of investment companies there is considerably less diversity in structure of portfolios. The typical closed-end company invests most of its total funds in a well-diversified list of common stocks of leading companies. Usually there are some holdings of bonds and preferred stocks, with the proportions varying from one company to another and from time to time in the individual companies.

With little need to keep their portfolios "dressed up" for sales appeal, the closed-end companies are better able to engage in bargain hunting for promising issues of the smaller and more obscure companies. With no responsibility to redeem their shares, they are not confined to the more highly marketable issues. Some companies have taken advantage of these circumstances to invest in securities of secondary companies and to place relatively large portions of their funds in one or two industries. However, the most interesting deviation from conventional policy is investment in "special situations."

The policy of investing in *special situations* involves committing a large part of total investment funds to one issue or a few issues that are believed to offer much better than average prospects for price appreciation. This is the aggressive policy of concentration of risk. Several closed-end companies have invested in special situations as a matter of policy, and their experience generally has been favorable. For regulated investment companies, the policy of concentration is limited by the diversification requirement, but there is some latitude for this kind of policy.

Closed-end companies generally are more aggressive in their attitudes toward market price fluctuations than are open-end companies, although there are many variations of policy. They are more inclined to change the proportions of different types of assets in an effort to profit by expected future changes in market prices. Some companies follow a policy of seeking undervalued stocks and selling them to realize price appreciation when they feel that appreciation potential has been almost exhausted. The primary purpose of the special situation policy, of course, is to realize profits from the sale of securities.

INVESTMENT COMPANY SECURITIES FOR THE SMALL INVESTOR

Investment companies provide another interesting study of investment policies and how they are adapted to the constraints of institutional investors. However, most students of investment companies are interested in them not as investing institutions, but as media for investing their own funds. They study investment company policies as a means of distinguishing and appraising the investment characteristics of investment company shares. They are interested in the question: How well do investment companies serve as intermediary investment institutions for the individual investor, particularly those with relatively small amounts to invest in securities? No single answer to this question applies to everyone, but we can apply the system of reasoning about investment constraints to the problem of deciding whether investment company shares in general are a desirable alternative to direct ownership of a portfolio of securities and even to the selection of particular investment company shares.

Whether to Choose Investment Company Shares

The desirability of investment company shares in general as an alternative to direct ownership of securities of the kinds bought and sold in the market depends very much on the conditions we have termed *quality of management* and *temperament of the investor*. A great many people with money to invest have very little ability to select individual security issues and to manage a portfolio of securities. These people ought not to undertake such a difficult and time-consuming task, where there is much to be gained and much to be lost by the decisions that have to be made. We have previously observed that there are several kinds of institutions that will invest other peoples' money, and that offer a variety of financial instruments. Now we add shares of investment companies to this list of ways to shift the investment management function to professional managers.

The prejudices, predilections, and emotional qualities of people certainly have a bearing on the choice of instruments and institutional arrangements. There are people who should not buy investment company shares or use any of the other means of shifting management of security investments to others. These are people who, first and foremost, consider themselves well qualified to appraise security issues, to estimate the risks, to forecast future price movements, and thus to maximize returns on their investments. Under the heading of temperament, their chief characteristic as far as security investments is concerned is self-confidence and aggressiveness. There are other people so timid or lacking in aggressiveness that they should invest only in instruments that pay income and principal in fixed dollar amounts.

Some of the other investment constraints have a bearing on selecting investment company shares from among the several alternatives. A need for extreme liquidity for much of the amount invested in securities cannot be met satisfactorily with investment company shares because their values are too unstable (except for bond funds) and because the middlemen's charges are too high (except for no-load funds). With the exception of fixed trusts for tax-exempt bonds, they do not meet the need for securities of high grade in taxability.

Which Investment Company to Choose?

If the decision is to use investment company shares rather than alternative media, the next question is, of course, which company or companies. And the answer again may be derived from analyzing the constraints affecting individual investors.

A major policy decision is what grade, or grades, of securities in terms of risk will be owned. There are investment companies whose portfolios represent almost every level of risk, from very high to very low. When an investor's requirements in terms of risk policy have been determined, it is a simple matter to select one or more investment company whose portfolios suit the requirements.

Finally, some consideration should be given to the cost of using investment company shares. We have observed that the sales charge may range from zero for no-load funds to 8½ per cent. Other things being equal, a low sales charge is better than a high one. Other things are not equal, of course, but when you pay a higher charge rather than a lower one, you should have a good reason for it. The kind and cost of investors' services offered by an investment company may enter into the problem of selection. Most companies offer accumulation plans and dividend re-investment plans, but the cost and minimum amounts required vary. For some investors the availability of a suitable withdrawal plan may well affect the choice of one company rather than another.

There has been a great deal of discussion, both in the investment company industry and in the literature of investments, about investment company performance. "Performance," in this sense, refers to the size of investment returns obtained by investment companies on their portfolios over past periods of time. It encompasses both dividends paid and change in net asset value per share from one time to another. A company that has realized relatively high returns has performed well and one with low returns has performed poorly.

A simple statistical procedure is to compute investment performance relatives for investment companies, using net asset values at beginning and end of period and dividends from income as well as dividends from capital gains during the period. The mean of IPR's for a series of periods is a measure of the size of total return, and the variation of the IPR's from their mean is a measure of risk. When there is a distinct trend over a time period, the coefficient of determination is a better measure of risk. Such computations for individual companies can be compared with the same kind of calculation for a broad index of stock prices by computing the Beta coefficient.

Many discussions of investment company performance seem to say that one ought to select shares of companies with the best performance records. This method of selection is quite contrary to our entire system of thought about investment policy because it ignores the question of what kinds of investment media are suitable for particular investors in their particular circumstances. An investment company with a fine performance record for a past period may be quite unsuitable for an investor who cannot accept a high degree of risk because its portfolio consists of speculative stocks. After a long period of business expansion, growing investor confidence and rising stock prices, the record of such an investment company is very likely to be much better than that of a company with a more conservative common-stock portfolio or one owning a combination of common stocks, preferred stocks, and bonds. But it is also very likely that in an ensuing period of business recession and falling stock prices the performance of the speculative stock fund will be much poorer than that of the more conservative funds. Choice of investment company shares certainly should take account of what happens on the down side as well as on the up side.

If performance records are used in selecting investment companies, only the records of companies with like portfolio structure and like policies toward security price fluctuations should be compared. Even then, performance records should be extrapolated into the future only with full realization that such an extrapolation may prove to be quite inaccurate. In the business of selecting securities, particularly common stocks, the results obtained are attributable to some combination of good judgment and good luck—and it is hard to tell one from the other.

QUESTIONS FOR DISCUSSION

1. Why have open-end investment companies (mutual funds) been much more popular with investors than closed-end companies?
2. If you were buying shares in a dual purpose mutual fund that invests almost entirely in common stocks of leading companies in principal industries, would you choose the class of shares entitled to income or the class entitled to capital gains? Assume that the price of the two classes of stock is the same.
3. You buy 100 shares of a mutual fund at $10 per share and 100 shares of another mutual fund at the same price. The first has a sales load of 8½ per cent. The second is a no-load fund. Over a period of 3 years you receive

exactly the same amounts of returns from the two stocks. Which one afforded you the higher rate of total return on investment?

4. At your present age and financial condition, which of these services interests you more: the opportunity to re-invest dividends on your mutual fund shares without paying a sales load on the shares purchased by re-investment, or the opportunity to withdraw from your mutual fund share account a fixed amount of money per month?
5. Do you think that the provision of the Investment Companies Act that places on fund management a fiduciary responsibility to its shareholders with respect to the management fee it pays its investment advisor provides reasonable assurance that the fee will be fair and reasonable for the service provided?
6. If you were a professional investment manager, would you rather work for an open-end company or a closed-end company?
7. Does the public have access to adequate information about registered investment companies?
8. Why is it that there are so many different mutual funds and that they have adopted such widely different investment policies?
9. It is sometimes said that in a generally declining stock market the operations of mutual funds tend to depress stock prices. Do you think this is true?
10. Your teacher of, say, history, is a man of moderate income and only a few thousand dollars of savings. Should he invest these savings in mutual fund shares?

25

Investment Policies of Fiduciaries

I. The growth of pension fund assets

II. Investments of private noninsured pension funds
   A. Constraints on investment policy
   B. Investment policies of private pension funds

III. Investments of state and local government pension funds
   A. Constraints on investment policy
   B. Investment policies of public pension funds

IV. Banks' investments as fiduciaries
   A. Banks in their fiduciary capacity
   B. Legal constraints on investment of trust funds
   C. Investment constraints issuing from the financial circumstances of beneficiaries
   D. Investment policies of trustees
   E. Common trust funds of banks

V. Investments of educational and charitable organizations
   A. Investment constraints
   B. Investment policies

A very important part of all the money invested in securities in the United States is in the hands of fiduciaries, or those who invest in a fiduciary capacity. Fiduciaries, broadly defined, are people and institutions that hold property in a position of trust for the benefit of others. Besides the federal government, which manages social security funds and certain other pension funds for government employees, there are three principal types of institutional investors that manage funds as fiduciaries. They are pension funds, personal trust funds, and endowment funds of educational and charitable organizations.

In terms of total amounts of assets, the pension funds have become a major element in the investment markets, with total assets at the end of 1971 of about $288 billion, including funds administered by the federal government. The value of funds in personal trusts and estates is placed at $137 billion at the end of 1970. Total investment funds of charitable and educational institutions are probably about $35 billion. Thus, the total amount of such fiduciary-type assets is in the neighborhood of $460 billion.

GROWTH OF PENSION FUND ASSETS

The great growth of pension funds of all kinds has been one of the important financial phenomena of our times. It was only a few generations ago in the rural small-town society that included most of the population that the elderly relied on whatever they had been able to save during their working lives for their livelihood when they could no longer work, and if savings were not sufficient, on whatever was provided by their children. Presently, most people can look forward to some kind of pension or retirement income when they reach the conventional retirement age.

Pension funds are generally classified as public or private, according to whether they are administered in the public or private sector of the economy. Private-sector funds recently had an estimated book value of more than $150 billion and a somewhat larger amount at market values. Public funds consist of those administered by the state and local governments, and those handled by the federal government. Here the total is about $135 billion at book value. These funds are not trust funds in the strict sense, but they are generally considered to be held and managed in a fiduciary capacity for the persons benefited or to be benefited.

Table 25–1 shows the assets of all public and private pension funds at the end of 1971, and the growth in dollar amounts of these assets during the 5 years ending with 1971. It is interesting that the percentage increase in all four major categories of pension funds during the 5-year period (at book value) was about the same. The increase of 16 to 17 per cent in 5 years is an average annual rate of increase of about 3.25 per cent.

The federally administered pension funds are invested for the most part in special issues of U.S. government obligations. The insured pension fund reserves are held by life insurance companies and have been included in their reserves already discussed. This leaves the private noninsured pension funds and the pension funds of state and local government for our further consideration.

TABLE 25–1

Assets of All Private and Public Pension Funds (book value, end of year; in billions of dollars)

	1966		*1971*		*Change in 5 years*	
	Amount	*Percentage of total*	*Amount*	*Percentage of total*	*Amount*	*Percentage increase*
Private						
Insured pension fund reserves	$ 29.4	16.7%	46.4	16.1	17.0	+15.8%
Noninsured pension funds	66.2	37.6	106.4	36.9	40.2	+16.1
Total private	95.6	54.3	152.8	53.0	57.2	+16.0
Public						
State and local funds	36.9	21.0	64.8	22.5	27.9	+17.6
All federally administered funds	43.3	24.6	70.8	24.5	27.5	+16.4
Total public	80.2	45.6	135.6	47.0	55.4	+16.9
Total pension funds	$175.9	100.0%	288.3	100.0	112.4	+16.3

Source: *Statistical Bulletin*, June, 1972, Securities and Exchange Commission, p. 29.

INVESTMENTS OF PRIVATE NONINSURED PENSION FUNDS

The distribution of investments of private noninsured pension funds among the several principal types of assets is shown in Table 25–2.

If you compare asset totals on the basis of market values you will find that the increase in value of private noninsured pension funds in a recent 5-year period was 60 per cent, as compared with 16 per cent when assets are taken at book value. The difference, of course, is a result of appreciation in market prices of assets.

Constraints on Investment Policy

These private pension funds provide a particularly clear-cut example of investors whose primary objective is to maximize long-run investment returns. The larger the return on investments, the less the cost to a company of providing retirement income at the levels provided by a pension plan. It is long-run returns that are important because current contributions on behalf of present employees are for the most part invested for relatively long periods.

In general, the constraints on investment policies of pension funds are not severe. If we go through the usual process of analysis, we come first to the need for stability of investment income. As far as financial requirements are concerned, noninsured pension funds can tolerate wide fluctuations in income; they have no minimum investment income requirement such as life insurance companies have for life and annuity contracts. It is true that actuaries estimate the sufficiency of pension fund assets to meet retirement income obligations and in the process assume some conventional rate of return on

TABLE 25–2

Assets of Private Noninsured Pension Funds (market value, end of year; in billions of dollars)

	1966		*1971*	
Kind of asset	*Amount*	*Percentage of total*	*Amount*	*Percentage of total*
Cash and deposits	$ 0.9	1.2%	$ 1.6	1.3%
U. S. Government securities	2.7	3.7	2.8	2.2
Corporate and other bonds	22.5	30.9	26.1	20.9
Preferred stock	0.8	1.1	2.0	1.6
Common stock	38.7	53.1	84.8	67.8
Mortgages	3.8	5.2	3.2	2.6
Other assets	3.5	4.8	4.5	3.6
Total assets (market)	$72.8	100.0%	$125.0	100.0%
Total assets (book)	$66.2	–	$106.4	–

Source: *Statistical Bulletin*, Securities and Exchange Commission, *op. cit.*, pp. 27–28.

the assets. If actuarial calculations are to be valid, the assumed rate would have to be earned on the average over a period of years, but interim fluctuations would have no adverse consequences for the purpose of a pension fund. One possible limitation in this area is an aversion to instability of investment income on the part of those responsible for managing a fund and perhaps on the part of employees. Any marked decline in investment income from one year to another might be a cause for alarm and for renewed emphasis on the fiduciary responsibility of pension fund managers to employees.

Neither is there any marked need for stability of market value of pension fund assets. Again, actuaries may compute the present value of future pension fund obligations and may relate the market value of assets to such an amount, but it is not necessary that market value of assets plus income at an assumed rate always equal the estimate of obligations; if they do, a pension plan is fully funded, but many are not fully funded and are not intended ever to be so funded. A fully funded plan might become less than fully funded on the basis of market values of assets during a period of cyclical decline in security prices. But, assuming cyclical recovery in prices, such instability would have no adverse consequences for the purpose of the fund. The practical limit, of course, is the ability of those concerned to stand the strain of declines in market values.

Pension funds have strong tenure of ownership. Ordinarily, current inflows of funds in the form of new contributions and investment income greatly exceed current outflows for pension payments and expenses of operation. Generally, the labor force covered by company pension systems is increasing and the level of wages and salaries is rising, so that current contributions for present employees' future retirement are much more than amounts required for presently retired employees. It is possible, of course, that in any particular instance the reverse could be true—or could become true. Even in the event of an excess of cash payments over cash inflow, liquidation of securities could be accomplished gradually and in an orderly manner. In fact the total receipts of private pension funds have exceeded total disbursements by $7 to 10 billion a year in recent years.[1]

It seems reasonable to conclude that the pension funds generally are competently managed by conventional standards, since they are usually managed by banks under investment agency agreements or by professional investment counsel firms.

Pension funds have no very restrictive need for securities that are high grade in either marketability or taxability. Usually they do not trade actively in the security markets. Since investment returns of pension funds are ordinarily tax exempt, they have no need for issues with tax exemption.

The conclusion, then, is that pension fund managers have wide latitude to pursue their general objective of maximizing long-run investment returns.

Investment Policies of Private Pension Funds

The investment policies of pension funds vary according to the particular views of their managers concerning what policies are appropriate, but we can draw some general conclusions from the aggregate data for all noninsured funds. One important conclusion is that common stocks comprise a large portion of these funds. At the end of 1971 common stocks represented about two-thirds of total assets at market value. The pension funds have, of course, been favored by the steady rise in stock prices during the 1960's and their common-stock holdings at market value at the end of 1971 were more than twice as great as 5 years earlier. A large part of net receipts in recent years has been invested in common stocks. The next largest category of assets is corporate bonds, which represent about one-fifth of total assets. Government bonds are a small 2 per cent of the total and municipal bonds do not appear as a separate category of assets. Preferred stocks and mortgages represent relatively small portions of total assets.

Like the life insurance companies, some of the pension funds purchase securities by private negotiation with issuers. When they buy securities in the market, pension fund managers prefer issues that are sufficiently marketable to be bought and sold in relatively large amounts without significantly affecting market price so that they can make changes in their portfolio holdings in the ordinary course of management with no particular difficulty.

Pension funds generally follow a defensive policy toward price fluctuations. They buy securities when funds become available for investment, hold bonds and mortgages to maturity, and retain common stocks until individual issues no longer appear attractive for holding. There is no evidence in the aggregate data that they reduce stock holdings in anticipation of cyclical declines in stock prices or of buying in expectation of cyclical price increases. However, there are considerable changes in common-stock portfolios from time to time. In one recent year, for example, the private pension funds purchased $11 billion of common stocks and sold $2.1 billion.

[1]All of the data in this discussion of private and public non-insured pension funds are from the *Statistical Bulletin*, June, 1972, Securities and Exchange Commission, Washington, D. C.

INVESTMENTS OF STATE AND LOCAL GOVERNMENT PENSION FUNDS

The pension funds of state and local governments for public employees have a slightly higher rate of growth in total assets at book value (market values not available) than any of the other major segments of the pension fund area during the past few years. This change may reflect some lag in the development and funding of such pension plans in earlier years and some catching up in later years. There are, however, considerable disparities among the different states in the extent of coverage of public employees and in the extent of funding of pension plans. The trend is clearly in the direction of wider coverage and more complete funding.

The distribution of the assets of total state and local government pension funds among the principal categories of assets is shown in Table 25–3.

Constraints on Investment Policy

There are a number of differences in the way public pension funds and private pension funds are operated. Most important from the investment point of view is the restriction of investments by statutes, ordinances, and regulations. Most of the public funds were created by statutes that spell out the provisions of retirement plans, including the kinds of securities in which funds may be invested. Some statutes limit pension fund investments to securities that are legal investments for savings banks or insurance companies; others specify in some detail the types of securities that may be owned. Some permit investment in relatively small portions of common stocks with long records of earnings and dividend payments. Legislative restrictions are in-

TABLE 25–3

Assets of State and Local Government Retirement Funds (book value, end of year; in billions of dollars)

	1966		*1971*	
Kind of asset	*Amount*	*Percentage of total*	*Amount*	*Percentage of total*
Cash and deposits	$ 0.4	1.0%	$ 0.5	0.8%
U. S. government securities	7.9	21.4	6.0	9.3
State and local government securities	2.5	6.8	1.9	2.9
Corporate and other bonds	18.9	51.1	36.2	55.9
Common and preferred stock	2.1	5.7	11.2	17.2
Mortgages	4.5	12.1	7.1	10.9
Other assets	.7	1.9	2.0	3.0
Total assets	$36.9	100.0	$64.8	100.0%

Source: *Statistical Bulletin*, Securities and Exchange Commission, *op. cit.*, p. 24.

tended to prevent speculation with pension funds, to preserve safely the dollars contributed to them, and to provide safeguards against political corruption.

The administration of public pension funds is generally entrusted to boards, councils, or commissions created by state and local governments. Some such bodies employ professional investment counsel, but the practice of placing pension fund assets in trust with banks as trustees and relying on banks for management is not usually followed. State laws usually provide for public reporting of pension fund operations and for some degree of state supervision. Pension fund managers are usually required to file annual reports with appropriate state or local bodies and several states have a pension examinations division in the state insurance department.[2]

From a strictly financial point of view the investment constraints on public pension funds are much the same as those for private funds. The primary objective is maximization of investment returns in the long run; in fact, the realization of this objective may be more important for public than for private funds because public funds generally are only partially funded and provide less than liberal retirement incomes. To obtain larger rather than smaller returns would do much to strengthen their position. However, the legal constraints imposed have limited the opportunity for maximization of returns.

Investment Policies of Public Pension Funds

The pension funds of state and local governments have generally accepted a lower level of financial risk in constructing their portfolios and a higher level of interest-rate risk. Bonds and mortgages represent about four-fifths of their total assets, whereas these categories of assets comprise only about one-third of the portfolios of the private noninsured pension funds. Both proportions are computed on the basis of book values. There are no data to indicate the financial risk grade of the bonds and mortgages, but casual observation suggests that the public pension funds limit themselves largely to obligations of good investment quality. The investment of such relatively large amounts in obligations with fixed interest and principal payments indicates acceptance of considerable uncertainty caused by fluctuations in interest rates.

Corporate bonds alone comprise somewhat more than one-half of the public pension fund assets; both the absolute amount of these securities and the ratio to total assets have increased in recent years. U.S. government securities, usually the lowest-yielding of taxable obligations, comprise almost 10 per cent of the total, but this ratio has declined sharply in recent years. It is surprising to find that these funds invest a small proportion of their assets in municipal securities. Since they are tax-exempt funds, they derive no benefit from the exemption of interest on these issues from the federal income tax. However, this percentage, too, has declined in recent years.

Common and preferred stocks (the two classes are not reported sepa-

[2]This description of state and local pension funds is based largely on the study entitled "State and Local Government Pension Funds" published by the New York Stock Exchange in 1965.

rately) at book values, constitute about 17 per cent of total assets. At market values the proportion probably would be larger. However this category has increased greatly in amount in recent years and as a per cent of total on a book value basis, indicating increased interest in common stocks. In general, it appears that the reduction in government and municipal bond holdings and the increase in common- and preferred-stock investments represent an effort to improve total rates of return.

BANKS' INVESTMENTS AS FIDUCIARIES

Commercial banks and trust companies invest funds as trustees for personal trusts, as executors of estates, and as professional investment managers for clients. They manage a substantial part of the assets of the noninsured private pension plans and some of the investment funds of individuals and of educational and charitable organizations. When they act as trustees for personal trusts and in other strictly fiduciary capacities, they operate under trust law. As professional investment managers they serve as agents for their clients by the terms of agency agreements.

A recent study shows that banks administer, either as trustee or agent, funds valued toward the end of 1970 at $292 billion. About 47 per cent of this total consisted of personal trusts and estates, another 32 per cent was in employee benefit trusts, about 18 per cent was personal agency accounts and the remainder was employee benefit agency accounts.[3]

Banks in Their Fiduciary Capacity

Any person who is legally competent may act as trustee for a personal trust or as executor or guardian, and some fiduciaries are individuals. Banks, however, have specialized in this kind of activity and it is believed that most trust assets are held by banks. Banks have trust powers only when such powers are conferred on them by statute or by action of bank regulatory authorities. Most banks now have trust powers.

Banks, as corporations, have certain advantages over individual persons for performing the functions of trustee. A corporation cannot die, be incapacitated by illness, or become mentally incompetent. Most trust institutions have perpetual or long-term charters. They also have personnel specially trained and experienced in the administration of trust estates; the staff of a large trust company collectively possesses far more technical competence than could any single individual. Trust institutions ordinarily have very substantial resources to which an injured person may look for reparation if a trust is not faithfully and prudently executed. Some people think that the impersonality of a trust institution may be a disadvantage, however, and it is not uncommon for people creating trusts to name a friend or relative to act as co-trustee. In such a

[3]Edna E. Ehrlich, "The Functions and Investment Policies of Personal Trust Departments," *Monthly Review*, Federal Reserve Bank of New York, October, 1972, pp. 255–270.

case the trust institution does the actual administration but must secure approval of the co-trustee on important decisions.

Trustees receive fees for their services. The fees are usually based on the amount of income from the trust estate, or the principal amount of the estate, or both. In some states a schedule of trustees' fees is fixed by statute, and usually the amount of such charges is subject to approval by the court having jurisdiction over a trust. The laws of the State of New York allow annual fees to trustees of personal trusts at the rate of ½ of 1 per cent of the first $50,000 of principal, ¼ of 1 per cent on the next $450,000, and 1/5 of 1 per cent on all amounts over $500,000.

Legal Constraints on Investment of Trust Funds

When a trust investment officer begins to think about policies to be pursued in investing funds of a particular trust, he begins with the terms of the instrument creating a trust—the trust agreement—for instructions about how trust assets will be invested. Frequently the instruction is merely that investment shall be governed by provisions of state law concerning investment of trust funds and in that case the statute applies. Sometimes trust instruments fail to say anything about how money will be invested. In the absence of express direction, the courts have consistently ruled that trust assets must be invested in accordance with the state statute. Thus, a great many trusts are "legal" trusts, that is, subject to state law in the matter of investments. We will examine the state laws affecting legal trusts first, since they are very important, and then return to the trust instrument to examine several other kinds of directions to trustees about how trust funds will be invested.

Almost every state has a statute or a well-established judicial rule directing and limiting trustees in the investment of legal trusts. The prudent-man rule has been widely adopted in recent years and is now in effect in 45 states. In 3 states there are no trust investment regulations and in 2 the law limits trust investments to fixed-income securities.[4]

The prudent-man principle was established by judicial rule (by court decision) in Massachusetts many years ago and several other states have long followed that precedent. However, poor experience with other legal rules in periods of business depression caused great dissatisfaction and sentiment in favor of the prudent-man rule became much stronger. A Model Prudent-Man Investment Statute was drafted by a group of lawyers and this statute, or variations of it, has since been enacted by most states.

The statement of the prudent-man rule in the model statute is as follows:

> In acquiring, investing . . . and managing property for the benefit of another, a fiduciary shall exercise the judgment and care under the circumstances then prevailing, which men of prudence, discretion, and intelligence exercise in the management of their own affairs, not in regard to speculation but in regard to the permanent disposition of their funds, considering the probable income as well as the probable safety of their capital.

[4]Edna E. Ehrlich, *op. cit.*, p. 259.

The trust officer who examines the terms of a trust instrument may find some entirely different statements than one providing for investment in accordance with state law. Actually, the creator of a trust may give whatever directions he pleases about how a trust fund will be invested and the express provisions of trust instruments govern trustees regardless of state statutes, except when they are determined by a court to defeat the purpose of a trust and are judicially set aside. Trusts to which the state law is not applicable by reason of provisions of the trust instruments are generally known as *nonlegal* trusts.

It is very common practice for a trustor to state clearly in the trust instrument that his trustee will not be limited to legal investments but will have authority to invest in all kinds of securities at his full discretion. A trust with this provision is known as a *discretionary* trust. This kind of authorization might seem to permit a trustee to do anything he pleases; it does, provided that he acts prudently. This requirement of prudence is the most basic rule governing trust investment. What is prudent in any particular case is for a court to decide. Generally, the criteria are as set forth in the prudent-man rule. Thus, discretionary trusts have been used in some states to escape restrictive provisions of state law governing trust investments and, in effect, to create trusts subject to the prudent-man rule.

Sometimes there are specific instructions in trust instruments directing or restricting investment of trust funds. These trusts are sometimes termed *stipulated* trusts. A trustor could write out a complete investment program for his trustee to follow and his trustee would be obliged to do so. More commonly the investment provisions of a trust stipulate authorizations rather than directions; when this is the case a trustee must decide to what extent his authority will be exercised. Sometimes particular kinds of investments are prohibited by the terms of a trust and sometimes there are instructions to hold designated investments put in trust by the trustor, or to sell such particular investments only when certain conditions are met. Whatever specific instructions there may be in a trust instrument, they must be followed by the trustee unless relieved from the duty to do so by action of a court.

This brief survey of legal constraints on investment of trust funds indicates clearly the emphasis on prudence in the management of trust funds, and prudence usually means investment in assets with a low level of financial risk. The law pays little attention to interest-rate risk, but generally seems to assume that securities with a low level of financial risk are prudent investments without considering the uncertainty of amounts of income and market values caused by changes in market rates of interest. Neither is there explicit concern in the statutes with changes in the purchasing power of currency as a cause of risk. Of course the creator of a trust could write into a trust instrument whatever directions he wishes to give his trustee about assuming risk from the several causes of uncertainty of future returns.

Trust statutes and court decisions say little about the duty of trustees to earn a rate of return for beneficiaries of a trust. The prudent-man rule seems to say that trustees shall be prudent and accept whatever return may result. There is no recognition of the concept of maximizing rate of return at an acceptable level of risk. The literature of trust investments says that investments shall be "fruitful", but doesn't say how fruitful.[5] On the other side there is the influence of competition between trust institutions. Trustees that fail to earn rates of return at a reasonable level of expectations on the part of trustors and beneficiaries, may lose business.

Investment Constraints Issuing from the Financial Circumstances of Beneficiaries

When a trustee has determined what is legally required and permitted he turns, or should turn, to a study of the financial and personal circumstances of the beneficiary(ies). He is, in fact, required by generally recognized rules of law to consider the particular conditions affecting each trust. In selecting securities he must take account particularly of (1) requirements as to amounts of income, (2) the aggregate value of the trust estate and the nature of other investments, (3) the other assets of the beneficiary or beneficiaries, including earning capacity, and (4) the effect of any investment on increasing or diminishing taxes. The duration of a trust is also specified as a condition affecting investment policy.[6]

At this point a trustee's problem is often complicated by the existence of more than one beneficiary and sometimes by two or more beneficiaries with conflicting interests in the trust estate. Frequently, a beneficiary, known as the *life tenant*, is named to receive the income from a trust for as long as he lives. A trust instrument may further provide that, on the death of the life tenant, the trust will be terminated and the property divided among one or more named persons. Those to receive the trust estate at termination are known as *remaindermen*. In this kind of situation, the life tenant may be interested in obtaining a maximum amount of income from the trust and have little interest in appreciation of capital that would go to a remainderman. Conversely, the remainderman may want a trust managed in such manner that he will receive the maximum amount of principal on termination of the trust. Such differences in interest among beneficiaries often make life difficult for trustees and sometimes result in litigation. Trust instruments often provide for a succession of beneficiaries with one generation succeeding another. Thus the prospective needs of children and grandchildren may have to be taken into account insofar as it is possible to do so.

The main idea is that investment constraints of beneficiaries should affect the determination of what is prudent for a particular trust under the rule of prudence. For example, the prudent-man rule allows trustees considerable latitude in buying common stocks. But if there is only about $100,000 in a trust and the beneficiary is a widow with no other income than social security benefits, the beneficiary needs highly stable investment income. A careful trustee might well conclude that this limitation precludes investment of any large portion of the trust estate in common stocks. On the other hand,

[5]See: "The Regulation of Risky Investments," *Harvard Law Review*, January, 1970, pp. 603–625.

[6]*Restatement of the Law of Trusts*, Vol. I, Sec. 227, St. Paul, Minnesota, 1935, American Law Institute.

if a trust estate is large and the beneficiary is well able to tolerate considerable instability of income and market values of principal, a trustee would be much more disposed to invest the whole estate in equity securities. Similarly, the greater the need for stability of investment income, the greater the need for diversification of financial risk.

Provisions for invasion of the principal of a trust estate and for liquidation at a fixed or determinable time may have an important influence on investment policy. A trustee required to sell securities at regular intervals and to pay proceeds to a beneficiary would be likely to hold some trust property in the form of high-grade bonds of relatively short maturity. He might arrange bond maturities so that appropriate amounts come due at about the dates he expects to make payments from principal to a beneficiary. A provision that trust property is to be converted into cash at termination of a trust and cash distributed to a beneficiary would influence a trustee to limit bond maturities to a period not longer than the expected termination date.

Although not explicitly required by law to take account of the purchasing power risk, many trustees use discretion granted them under the prudent-man rule, or investment provisions of a trust instrument, to invest in equities with the thought that over relatively long time spans increases in dividends and prices in current dollars will compensate to some extent for an expected increase in the price level.

Generally, trust accounts have little need for highly marketable securities. They are supposed to be invested with regard to the permanent disposition of their funds and not to be used for short-term trading. Thus the turnover of trust portfolios is low and there is little need to minimize transactions costs by seeking out the highly marketable issues.

The need for tax advantage must certainly be taken into account. Sometimes beneficiaries have small incomes and pay low income taxes. In this case there is little benefit to be derived from tax exemption and better yields may be obtainable on fully taxable issues. On the opposite side is the wealthy widow whose husband left her several million dollars in trust. It may be that the trustee for such a trust can maximize returns by investing largely or entirely in tax-exempt municipal bonds.

Investment Policies of Trustees

Because information about individual personal trusts is held in confidence by trustees, there are no available data about investment policies used in investing funds of individual trusts. It may be reasonably inferred from differences in trust laws, in the provisions of trust instruments, and in the investment concepts of trustees that there are wide variations in the kinds and proportions of securities held in individual trust accounts. It is likely that some accounts consist entirely of bonds, some entirely of common stocks, and that most consist of some combination of the several kinds of bonds plus preferred and common stocks.

Ehrlich's study provides a breakdown of aggregate investments of all personal trusts administered by banks as of 1970. The common stock portion represented two-thirds of the total, but the data indicate a larger proportion of equities in the funds of larger banks and a small percentage in funds of smaller banks. Municipal bonds comprised about 9 per cent of total personal trust assets of all banks, corporate bonds about 7 per cent, U. S. government and agency obligations about 6 per cent, and the remainder consisted of real estate, real estate mortgages and unspecified other assets.[7]

Common Trust Funds of Banks

One of the greatest practical difficulties encountered by trust institutions is the administration of small trusts. There is a popular inclination to think that trust funds are created only by extremely wealthy people and that they typically represent large sums in securities and other assets. Actually, many trusts are relatively small in size.

Small trusts present two particular problems. One is the familiar problem of obtaining adequate diversification for a small investment fund. The other is the relatively large expense of individually administering such small funds. It may take almost as much of a trust officer's time to supervise properly a fund of modest size as to look after a fund with assets running into seven figures. Thus, administrative expense per dollar of trust assets tends to be high for small funds.

Some years ago the concept was developed that the problems of administration of small trust funds could be solved by pooling them for investment purposes. Although they could retain their individual identities as trust accounts, their assets could be co-mingled and managed as one fund. This idea may have come from observing the operation of mutual funds.

The co-mingling of trust funds was, however, contrary to law and a great deal of legislation had to be enacted to permit the use of common trust funds on a large scale. But both the legislation and the regulations of bank supervisory authorities came about in the course of time, and the Internal Revenue Code was amended to exempt from the corporate income tax the investment returns of common trust funds. Investment returns are taxed to the individual trusts that participate in a common fund.

The common trust fund uses the trust form of organization, with a bank as trustee and with the various participating individual trusts in the position of beneficiaries. Beneficial interest in the common trust is divided into shares, or units, in which the funds of the participating trusts are invested. Only the trusts for which the bank is trustee may purchase shares in the common fund (and then only if the provisions of their trust instruments permit). Shares are purchased at their net asset value, determined in much the same manner as for shares of open-end investment companies, but there is no selling charge, since no selling function is performed except incidentally. Usually, shares in a common trust fund may be purchased for individual trust funds only on certain dates, usually quarterly, when the market value of the assets of the common fund is determined. Similarly, the shares held by any individual fund

[7]Ehrlich, *op. cit.*, pp. 260–261.

may be redeemed on any evaluation date at their net asset value. The income from the common trust is distributed to the individual trusts periodically according to the number of shares each individual fund holds. It is not necessary that all the assets of any individual fund be invested in shares of the common fund; sometimes a part is invested directly in securities or other assets and only a part is transferred to the common fund.

Most relatively large banks now have common trust funds and some have several kinds of common funds. Some banks have one common trust fund that has a portfolio much like that of trust funds generally, that is, with a large proportion of common stock and a smaller portion of corporate bonds and preferred stocks. Thus one fund might serve as a general purpose fund for small trust accounts. However, as the use of common trust funds developed some banks created common trust funds that invested largely or entirely in common stocks, largely or entirely in bonds, and in some instances entirely in municipal bonds. This arrangement permitted one portion of a small trust account to be invested in one particular type of fund and another portion in another type.

Total common trust fund assets at the end of 1970 amounted to about $10 billion, equal to 9.3 per cent of all personal trust account assets. There were 412,000 trusts participating in the common trust funds.[8]

INVESTMENTS OF EDUCATIONAL AND CHARITABLE ORGANIZATIONS

There are thousands of investment funds held in a fiduciary capacity by educational and charitable organizations. They range in size from more than a billion dollars in the endowment fund of Harvard University to the very small funds of many liberal arts colleges, and from the several billions of dollars in a few huge charitable foundations to several hundred thousand dollars in foundations created to administer the benefactions of individuals and companies. Again, data on the total size of these funds is lacking. About a decade ago a study by the New York Stock Exchange placed the total at about $22 billion.[9] By rough extrapolation, that amount may be about $35 billion in 1972.

Investment Constraints

The uses of endowment funds and the purposes of charitable foundations differ so much that only the broadest generalizations may be made about their investment requirements. However, the method of analyzing investment constraints that we developed in earlier chapters can be applied to any particular fund and used to define the principal limitations affecting its investment policy.

[8]Ehrlich, *op. cit.*, pp. 263–264.

[9]*Institutional Shareownership*, New York, 1964, The New York Stock Exchange, p. 13.

Ordinarily there are no legal requirements to be observed by managers of endowment and charitable funds beyond the general rule of prudence, diligence, and care, except that endowment funds of public institutions may be affected by state statutes. Donors may of course restrict the manner in which their donations may be invested and the creators of charitable foundations may give some general direction about how funds should be invested in articles of incorporation. Sometimes donors stipulate that the securities they give may not be sold, or may be sold only under specified conditions. Contrarywise, those who establish charitable foundations by gift of a large amount of a single security (stock in a company) may direct liquidation and re-investment in a diversified list of issues.

The function of endowment funds for educational institutions, hospitals, and similar eleemosynary organizations has long been regarded as that of providing income to pay some part of the operating expenses of such institutions. Accordingly, these funds have generally felt a severe constraint in terms of stability of investment income and a principal consideration has been maximization of income over relatively long periods of time. And it has generally been considered that principal must be preserved and not used up to pay expenses.

This concept of a sharp distinction between income and principal was vigorously challenged in one legal study, that concluded that there is no legal reason why realized capital gains may not be treated as income[10] unless the terms of a gift or other governing instrument provided expressly for the contrary. This authoritative study has caused a shift from the "lore" that investment returns for endowment funds were income alone to the "law" that investment returns are total returns. This concept reduces the need of institutions for stability of investment income and opens the way for them to seek larger returns by appreciation in principal amounts. A number of leading colleges have adopted the rule that realized capital gains may be used as income for operating expenses to some defined extent. One further consequence is the modification in 1970 of the Not-for-Profit Corporation Law of the State of New York to authorize directors of a charitable corporation to allocate a prudent portion of realized gains to income. A recent study urges the importance of establishing maximum long-term total return as the primary objective of endowment management.[11]

The purchasing-power risk is properly a matter of concern to those who manage endowment funds. Expenses for which income is used tend to increase as the price level rises, and if there is no compensating increase in amounts of returns in current dollars the purchasing power of endowment returns decreases.

Since endowment funds are usually in perpetuity, they have strong tenure of ownership. As a general rule endowment funds are very unlikely to be forced to sell securities at a time other than that of their own choosing.

[10] William L. Cary and Craig B. Bright, *The Law and the Lore of Endowment Funds,* New York, 1970, Ford Foundation.

[11] Managing Educational Endowments, Advisory Committee on Endowment Management, 2nd ed., New York, 1972, Ford Foundation, p. ix.

There may be exceptions where principal amounts donated to such a fund are intended to be expended for capital improvements or to be used up in payment of operating expenses.

Inexpert investment management may limit the use of any very aggressive policies in assuming risk. Frequently, boards of trustees are composed of very sincere people who serve with great devotion, but who have little competence in the field of investments. Sometimes the management of endowment funds is delegated largely to an administrative officer who performs the function in his spare time with little comprehension of basic problems of investment policy. The trustees of many educational institutions have recognized the limitations of their own facilities for investment management and employ professional investment counsel.

Substantial aid in the management of investments is now provided by the Common Fund for Non-Profit Organizations created by Teachers Insurance and Annuity Association with financial support from the Ford Foundation. This institution is organized much like the common trust funds of commercial banks. In effect, it accepts such contributions from the endowment funds of educational institutions as they wish to have invested in common stocks (with certain limitations regarding amount) and pools them for the purpose of investment. Investment returns from the pooled fund are tax exempt under the Internal Revenue Code and are distributed to participating institutions. The pooled fund is managed by several professional investment counsel firms and supervised by a board of trustees composed of individuals from institutions of higher education.

There is little need in endowment fund investment for the higher grades of securities in marketability because of their strong tenure of ownership and relatively low portfolio turnover. However, some other considerations such as the desire to own sizable proportions of common stocks of well-known companies usually result in the selection of the more marketable issues.

Tax-exempt securities have no attraction for endowment funds because they are exempt from the federal income tax.

Investment Policies

In spite of constraints that tend to reduce their willingness to accept any very high level of risk, the leading endowment funds have moved steadily in the direction of acquiring a larger proportion of common stocks for their portfolios. To some extent this is a result of rising stock prices, but there appears to be a tendency to direct a substantial part of new funds for investment into stocks. One compilation of the aggregate endowment funds of a relatively large sample of colleges and universities shows that at market values the proportion of common stocks varies from about 60 to 70 per cent.[12]

Corporate bonds are the second largest category at about one-fifth of asset totals and there is a small amount of convertible securities. Most of the

[12] *The Study of College and University Endowments*, 1969, Boston, Massachusetts, 1969, Boston Fund.

remainder consists of income-producing real estate, mortgage loans, cash, and short-term obligations for temporary investment. One college owns and operates a race track, and others own proprietary enterprises that have been given to them.

Although no comprehensive data are available to show the investment policies of charitable foundations, it appears that a large proportion of their assets consists of common stocks. This might be expected because most of them were created through donations of large blocks of stocks. However, some of them are endeavoring to divest themselves of the large blocks initially contributed and to re-invest in more broadly diversified portfolios, with common stocks predominating.

QUESTIONS FOR DISCUSSION

1. What is the implication, if any, of the growth of pension funds for the long-term trend of common-stock prices?
2. Why is it that the noninsured pension funds have greater latitude for assuming higher levels of risk in their portfolios than do life insurance companies?
3. If you were the chairman of the board of directors of a large industrial company with a large noninsured pension plan, how would you arrange for the fund to be managed? Why?
4. Is there any very serious constraint on investments of state and local government pension plans that does not apply to investments of private pension plans?
5. Can you think of any valid reason why a state employees' pension fund should invest in bonds of cities and other political subdivisions within the state?
6. Do you approve the principle of the prudent-man rule applied to trust investments?
7. Why don't trust investment officers make a greater effort to maximize returns from trust funds to which the prudent-man rule applies?
8. If you were able to create a small trust fund for your children, would you authorize investment of some part or all of the trust in the bank's common trust fund? Why?
9. Does it make sense to you that realized capital gains of non-profit organizations should be treated as income and expended for current expenses? Will this practice jeopardize principal amounts of college endowment funds?
10. Why should a charitable foundation created by the gift of a large block of stock of a successful company sell large amounts of that stock and put the money into other common stocks?

Bibliography

BOOKS

BAUMOL, WILLIAM J., *Portfolio Theory: The Selection of Asset Combinations.* New York: The McCaleb-Seiler Publishing Company, 1970.

BREALEY, RICHARD A., *An Introduction to Risk and Return from Common Stocks.* Cambridge, Mass.: The M.I.T. Press, 1969.

BREALEY, RICHARD A., *Security Prices in A Competitive Market.* Cambridge, Mass.: The M.I.T. Press, 1971.

BROOKS, JOHN, *Once in Golconda.* New York: Harper & Row, 1969.

CARY, WILLIAM L., and BRIGHT, CRAIG B., *The Law and The Lore of Endowment Funds.* New York: Ford Foundation, 1970.

COOTNER, PAUL, ed., *The Random Character of Stock Market Prices.* Cambridge, Mass.: The M.I.T. Press, 1964.

CROSSE, HOWARD D., and HEMPEL, GEORGE, *Management Policies for Commercial Banks.* Englewood Cliffs, N.J.: Prentice-Hall, 1973.

D'AMBROSIO, CHARLES A., *A Guide to Successful Investing.* Englewood Cliffs, N.J.: Prentice-Hall, 1970.

EDWARDS, R. D., and MAGEE, JOHN, JR., *Technical Analysis of Stock Trends,* 4th ed. Springfield, Mass.: John Magee, 1958.

EITEMAN, WILFORD J., DICE, CHARLES A., and EITEMAN, DAVID K., *The Stock Market,* 4th ed. New York: McGraw-Hill Book Co., 1966.

ELTON, EDWIN J., and GRUBER, MARTIN J., *Security Evaluation and Portfolio Analysis.* Englewood Cliffs, N.J.: Prentice-Hall, 1972.

ENGEL, LOUIS, *How to Buy Stocks,* 5th ed. Boston: Little, Brown and Company, 1971.

FERBER, ROBERT, ed., *Determinants of Investment Behavior.* New York: National Bureau of Economic Research, Columbia University Press, 1967.

FRANCIS, JACK CLARK, *Investments: Analysis and Management.* New York: McGraw-Hill Book Co., 1972.

FRANCIS, JACK CLARK, and ARCHER, S. H., *Portfolio Analysis*. Englewood Cliffs, N.J.: Prentice-Hall, 1971.

GORDON, M. J., *The Investment, Financing and Valuation of the Corporation*. Homewood, Ill.: Richard D. Irwin, 1962.

GRANGER, CLIVE W. J., and MORGANSTERN, OSCAR, *Predictability of Stock Prices*. Lexington, Mass.: D. C. Heath & Co., 1970.

HESTER, DONALD H., and TOBIN, JAMES, eds., *Risk Aversion and Portfolio Choice*. New York: John Wiley & Sons, 1967.

HICKMAN, BRADDOCK, *Statistical Measures of Corporate Bond Financing Since 1900*. Princeton, N.J.: National Bureau of Economic Research, 1960.

HOMER, SIDNEY, *A History of Interest Rates*. New Brunswick, N.J.: Rutgers University Press, 1963.

Investment Company Portfolio Management, C.F.A. Research Foundation. Homewood, Ill.: Richard D. Irwin, 1970.

LATANÉ, HENRY A., and TUTTLE, DONALD L., *Security Analysis and Portfolio Management*. New York: The Ronald Press Co., 1970.

LEVY, R. A., *The Relative Strength Concept of Common Stock Forecasting*. Larchmont, N.Y.: Investors Intelligence, 1968.

LINDOW, WESLEY, *Inside the Money Market*. New York: Random House, 1972.

MALKIEL, BURTON C., *The Term Structure of Interest Rates: Theory, Empirical Evidence, and Applications*. New York: The McCaleb-Seiler Publishing Co., 1970.

MARKOWITZ, HARRY M., *Portfolio Selection*. New York: John Wiley & Sons, 1959.

PECORA, FERDINAND, *Wall Street Under Oath*. New York: Simon and Schuster, 1939.

Pension Fund Investment Management, C. F. A. Monograph Series No. 3. Homewood, Ill.: Richard D. Irwin, 1969.

Personal Trust Investment Management, C. F. A. Monograph Series No. 2. Homewood, Ill.: Richard D. Irwin, 1968.

SHADE, PHILIP A., *Common Stocks: A Plan for Intelligent Investing*. Homewood, Ill.: Richard D. Irwin, 1971.

SHARPE, WILLIAM F., *Portfolio Theory and Capital Markets*. New York: McGraw-Hill Book Co., 1970.

SIMON, JOHN G., POWERS, CHARLES W., and GUNNEMAN, JON P., *The Ethical Investor*. New Haven, Conn.: Yale University Press, 1972.

SMITH, ADAM (GEORGE J. W. GOODMAN), *The Money Game*. New York: Random House, 1968.

SMITH, ADAM (GEORGE J. W. GOODMAN), *Supermoney*. New York: Random House, 1972.

SOLDOFSKY, ROBERT M., and MURPHY, JAMES T., *Growth Yields on Common Stocks—Theory and Tables*. Iowa City, Iowa: Bureau of Business and Economic Research, State University of Iowa, 1961.

SPRINKEL, BERYL W., *Money & Markets: A Monetarist View*. Homewood, Ill.: Richard D. Irwin, 1971.

STEPHENSON, GILBERT T., *Estates and Trusts*, 4th ed. New York: Appleton-Century-Crofts, 1960.

VALENTINE, JEROME L., and MENNIS, EDMUND A., *Quantitative Techniques for Financial Analysis*. Charlottesville, Va.: C. F. A. Research Foundation, 1970.

VAN HORNE, JAMES C., *Function and Analysis of Capital Market Rates*. Englewood Cliffs, N.J.: Prentice-Hall, 1970.

WALTER, JAMES E., *The Investment Process*. Boston: Division of Research, Graduate School of Business, Harvard University, 1962.

WIESENBERGER, ARTHUR, *Services, Investment Companies* (annual editions), New York.

WOODWORTH, G. WALTER, *The Management of Cyclical Liquidity of Commercial Banks*. Boston: The Bankers Publishing Co., 1967.

ARTICLES

GILBERT BURCK, "That Ever Expanding Pension Balloon," *Fortune*, October, 1971, pp. 100–103, 130–133.

ALBERT E. BURGER, LIONAL KALISH III, and CHRISTOPHER T. BABB, "Money Stock Control and Its Implications for Monetary Policy," *Review*, Federal Reserve Bank of St. Louis, October, 1971, pp. 6–19.

EUGENE FAMA, "The Behavior of Stock Prices," *Journal of Business*, January, 1965, pp. 39–105.

LAWRENCE FISHER, "Outcomes for 'Random' Investments in Common Stocks Listed on the New York Stock Exchange," *Journal of Business*, April, 1965, pp. 149–161.

LAWRENCE FISHER and JAMES H. LORIE, "Rates of Return on Investments in Common Stocks," *Journal of Business*, January, 1964, pp. 3–7.

FORD FOUNDATION, *Managing Educational Endowments*, 2nd ed., Report to the Ford Foundation, Advisory Committee on Endowment Management, New York, 1972.

ALAN E. GRUNEWALD and ROBERT C. KLEMKOSY, "If You Believe Growth Is Dead, Try the Formula Timing Plan," *MSU Business Topics*, Summer, 1972, Graduate School of Business Administration, Michigan State University, pp. 59–65.

MICHAEL W. KERAN, "Expectations, Money, and the Stock Market," *Review*, Federal Reserve Bank of St. Louis, January, 1971, pp. 16–31.

R. A. LEVY, "Random Walks: Reality or Myth," *Financial Analysts Journal*, November–December, 1967, pp. 69–76.

JOHN LINTNER, "Security Prices, Risk, and Maximal Gains from Diversification," *Journal of Finance*, December, 1965, pp. 587–615.

GEORGE E. PINCHES, "The Random Walk Hypothesis and Technical Analysis," *Financial Analysts Journal*, March–April, 1970, pp. 104–109.

EDWARD F. and VERNON D. RENSHAW, "Simulating the Dow Jones Industrial Average: A Further Test of the Random Walk Hypothesis," *Financial Analysts Journal*, September–October, 1970, pp. 51–59.

ALEXANDER ROBICHEK, "Risk and the Value of Securities," *Journal of Financial and Quantitative Analysis*, December, 1969, pp. 51–59.

HARRY C. SAUVAIN, "The Revolution in the Securities Markets, *Business Horizons*, August, 1970, pp. 5–18.

DANIEL SELIGMAN, "A Bad New Era for Common Stocks," *Fortune*, October, 1971, pp. 73, 168.

WILLIAM F. SHARPE, "Mutual Fund Performance," *Journal of Business*, January, 1966. (Supplement: Security Prices, pp. 119–138.)

WILLIAM F. SHARPE, "Risk Aversion in the Stock Market: Some Empirical Evidence," *Journal of Finance*, September, 1965, pp. 416–422.

WILLIAM F. SHARPE, "Risk, Market Sensitivity and Diversification," *Financial Analysts Journal*, January–February, 1972, pp. 74–79.

Index

A

B

D

E

F

N

Q

R

S

T

U

V

W

Y

Z